Music of Our Time

The Catalogue

SCHOTT

Mainz · London · Madrid · New York · Paris · Tokyo · Toronto

BN 326-30 · ISBN 3-7957-0326-3
© 1996 Schott Musik International · Mainz

Copy date: 1st April 1996

Foreword

This catalogue brings together for the first time the 20th Century works published by Schott Music International in Mainz, London, Paris, Tokyo, Madrid, Toronto, as well as their American associates European American Music Distribution Corporation.

In it, you will find a comprehensive listing of the music of all our composers. They reflect the broadest spectrum of the music of our time, from early Schönberg and Stravinsky to the newest generation, who are reaching out to an ever wider public.

It is music not only for the theatre and the concert hall but for music-making in the broadest context, embracing every kind of musical style and tradition.

Much of this music has helped to form our contemporary culture and includes some of the most famous modern classics. But, we hope this catalogue will also stimulate you to explore less familiar territory.

We will continue to develop our repertoire of contemporary music into the 21st century, thus this catalogue will grow continuously. You will find regular updates on our Internet Site http://www.schott-music.com.

Dr. Peter Hanser-Strecker
Chairman, Schott Musik International

Notes for the user

This catalogue contains the 20th century works published by Schott Musik International, Schott & Co. Ltd., Schott Japan Co. Ltd., European American Music Corporation and Helicon Music Corporation up to 1 April 1996. It also lists various co-productions with other publishers.

All titles with edition numbers are available on sale and can be ordered from any good music shop. All other materials are available on hire from the Schott offices and their agencies listed below.

Some works listed in this catalogue are subject to restrictions on distribution. For further information, please contact your local Schott representative.

Edition numbers without any further specification generally refer to playing scores or scores including a set of parts.

Edition numbers marked with an added „*" or „X" indicate that these are archive titles, which can be made available as photocopies on request.

Key to edition codes and abbreviations (sale material):

ED 1000 (four-digit Numbers)	Schott Mainz Edition
ED 10000 (five-digit Numbers)	Schott London Edition (territory: Europe)
AS	Arnold Schönberg Complete Edition (distribution rights for the whole world except Austria, Brit. Commonwealth of Nations, Ireland, Southafrica)
AVV	Ars Viva Edition Mainz
B	Bausteine
BAT	Percussion Series
BLK	Wind Ensembles Series
BN	Text Books (with ISBN codes)
BSS	Schott Musik International Domestic Series
C	Choral Series
CB	Cello Library
CHBL	Choral Series
CON	Concertino Series
COR	Horn Series
CRZ	Cranz Edition Mainz
EAM-Helicon/EA	European American Music Corporation - Helicon Edition (represented by Schott in Germany)
ETP/Eu	Eulenburg Edition
FAG	Bassoon Series
FG	Schott Band Series
FTR	Flute Series
GA	Guitar Archive
KIN	International Series Kompositor (Distribution: Worldwide except Russia)
KLB	Clarinet Library
OBB	Oboe Library
OFB	Recorder Series
PHA	Paul Hindemith Complete Edition
SHS	Schott Band Series
SJ	Schott Japan
SKR	Schott Chamber Choir Series
SL	Schott London Edition
SM	Schott Mainz Edition
SMC	"Music for Children" Series (Orff Schulwerk)
TMR	The Modern Recorder Series
TR	Trumpet Series
VAB	Viola Library
VLB	Violin Library
WKS	"Workshop" Series

Key to edition codes and abbreviations (hire material):

AVV	Ars Viva Edition Mainz
CRZ	Cranz Edition Mainz
EAM-Helicon/EA	European American Music Corporation - Helicon Edition
SJ	Schott Japan
SL	Schott London Edition
SM	Schott Mainz Edition

Countries:

AL	Albania
A	Austria
B	Belgium
BCW	British Commonwealth, Israel
CDN	Canada
C	Cuba
CZ	Czech Republic
FEB	Countries of the former Eastern block
F	France
D	Federal Republic of Germany
H	Hungary
J	Japan
LAT AM	Central America, South America
MEX	Mexico
NKOR	Northern Korea
VN	Vietnam
PL	Poland
SK	Slovak Republic
CH	Switzerland
UK	United Kingdom
USA	United States of America

The catalogue is in three parts:

I Alphabetical listing of composers and their works
II Index by category
III List of birthdays and anniversaries

Copy deadline of the catalogue was the 1st April 1996.

Instrumentation is given in full except for the operas and ballets, which are listed with title and duration only. For full information on these works please refer to our Stage Works catalogue, available on request.

Unauthorized reproduction (photocopying of copyrighted works with the exception of the special cases stated in §53 and §54 of the Copyright Act) is prohibited by law (including for teaching purposes).

List of agents for hire material

Australia
BOOSEY & HAWKES PTY. LTD.
P.O. Box 188, Unit 12/6 Campbell Street,
AUS-Artarmon, NSW 2064
Tel: (+61) 2 - 439 4144
Fax: (+61) 2 - 439 2912

Austria
(incl.Hungary,
Romania, Bulgaria)
UNIVERSAL EDITION AG
Bösendorferstr. 12, A-1015 Wien
Tel: (+43) 1 - 505 8695
Fax: (+43) 1 - 505 2720

Belgium
SCHOTT FRERES (Small Rights)
Rue Saint Jean 30, B-1000 Bruxelles
Tel: (+32) 2 - 512 3980
Fax: (+32) 2 - 514 2845

AUTEURSBUREAU ALMO BVBA (Grand Rights)
Frankrijklei 132, B-2000 Antwerpen
Tel: (+32) 3 - 233 2605
Fax: (+32) 3 - 226 1654

Brazil
MUSAS - Editora & Distribuidora Musical Ltda.
Rua Augusto Stresser, 861 (Juvevê),
Caixa Postal 6040
BR-80011-970 Curitiba / Pr.
Tel: (+55) 41 - 263 1001
Fax: (+55) 41 - 262 2223

Canada
SCHOTT MUSIC PUBLISHERS (Canada) LTD.
Mr. Jan van Matejcek
28 Tarlton Road
CDN - Toronto, Ontario M5P 2M4
Tel: (+1) 416 - 489 4155
Fax: (+1) 416 - 489 8474

Croatia
ZAMP
Ulica baruna Trenka 5, POB 959,
HR-41001 Zagreb, Croatia
Tel: (+385) 41 - 42 9818; 42 9406
Fax: (+385) 41 - 42 9818

Czech Republic
DIVERTIMENTO S.R.O. (Small Rights)
Pařížská 13, CZ-11000 Praha 1 - Staré Město
Tel: (+42) 2 - 2481 1258
Fax: (+42) 2 - 2481 0614

DILIA (Grand Rights)
Krátkého 1, CZ-19003 Praha 9 - Vysočany
Tel: (+42) 2 - 254 520
Fax: (+42) 2 - 824 009

Denmark
WARNER CHAPPELL MUSIC SCANDINAVIA AB
NORDISKA MUSIKFÖRLAGET
P.O. Box 533, Vendevägen 85B, S-18215 Danderyd
Tel: (+46) 8 - 755 1210
Fax: (+46) 8 - 755 1596

Finland
WARNER CHAPPELL MUSIC SCANDINAVIA AB
NORDISKA MUSIKFÖRLAGET
P.O. Box 533, Vendevägen 85B, S-18215 Danderyd
Tel: (+46) 8 - 755 1210
Fax: (+46) 8 - 755 1596

France
(incl. Algeria,
Marocco, Tunisia,
Luxembourg)
EDITIONS SALABERT
22, rue Chauchat, F-75009 Paris
Tel: (+33) 1 - 4824 5560
Fax: (+33) 1 - 4247 1756

Germany
SCHOTT MUSIK INTERNATIONAL
Postfach 3640, D-55026 Mainz
Weihergarten 5, D-55116 Mainz
Tel: (+49) 6131 - 246 883/888
Fax: (+49) 6131 - 246 252

Greece
SOPE
51, Samou Street, GR-15125 Amarousio
Tel: (+30) 1 - 685 7481
Fax: (+30) 1 - 685 3174

Israel
ISRAELI MUSIC PUBLICATIONS LTD.
25 Keren Hayesod St., P.O.B. 7681,
IL-94188 Jerusalem
Tel: (+972) 2 - 241 377
Fax: (+972) 2 - 241 378

Italy
EDIZIONI SUVINI ZERBONI
Via Quintiliano, 40, I-20138 Milano
Tel: (+39) 2 - 508 41
Fax: (+39) 2 - 508 4261

for Hans Werner Henze works:
G. RICORDI & C.
Via Salomone, 77, I-20138 Milano
Tel: (+39) 2 - 8881 4216, 4220, 4213
Fax: (+39) 2 - 8881 4258

Japan
SCHOTT JAPAN COMPANY LTD.
Kasuga Bldg., 2-9-3 Iidabashi, Chiyoda-ku,
J-Tokyo 102
Tel: (+81) 3 - 3263 6530
Fax: (+81) 3 - 3263 6672

Mexico
EUROPEAN AMERICAN MUSIC
2480 Industrial Boulevard, Paoli, PA 19301, USA
Tel: (+1) 610 - 648 0506
Fax: (+1) 610 - 889 0242

Netherlands
MUZIEKHANDEL ALBERSEN & CO.
(Small Rights)
Groot Hertoginnelaan 182, NL-2517 EV Den Haag
Tel: (+31) 70 - 345 6000
Fax: (+31) 70 - 361 4528

AUTEURSBUREAU ALMO BVBA (Grand Rights)
Frankrijklei 132, B-2000 Antwerpen
Tel: (+32) 3 - 233 2605
Fax: (+32) 3 - 226 1654

New Zealand
BOOSEY & HAWKES PTY. LTD.
P.O. Box 188, Unit 12/6 Campbell Street,
AUS-Artarmon, NSW 2064
Tel: (+61) 2 - 439 4144
Fax: (+61) 2 - 439 2912

Norway
NORVEGEMUS
Hegdehangsveien 31, N-0352 Oslo
Tel: (+47) 22 - 602 831
Fax: (+47) 22 - 698 579

Poland
POLSKIE WYDAWNICTWO MUZYCZNE
Ul. Fredry 8, PL-00097 Warszawa
Tel: (+48) 22 - 269 780
Fax: (+48) 22 - 269 780

Portugal
EDEMS S.L.
Alcalá 70, E-28009 Madrid
Tel: (+34) 1 - 577 0751
Fax: (+34) 1 - 575 7645

Slovak Republic	**SLOVENSKY HUDEBNY FOND** (Small Rights) Medená 29, SK-81102 Bratislava 1 Tel: (+42) 7 - 5332 645 Fax: (+42) 7 - 5332 645
	SLOVENSKA LITERARNA AGENTURA LITA (Grand Rights) Partizánska 21, SK-81530 Bratislava Tel: (+42) 7 - 313 645 Fax: (+42) 7 - 313 645
Slovene Republic	**EDICIJE DRUSTVA SLOVENSKIH SKLADA-TELJEV** Trg Francoske revolucije 6/I, SLO-61000 Ljubljana Tel: (+38) 61 - 1251 310 Fax: (+38) 61 - 213 487
South Africa	**ACCENT MUSIC CC** P.O. Box 30634, Braamfontein 1027 11th Floor, Devonshire House, 49 Jorissen Street, Braamfontein, ZA-2001 Johannesburg Tel: (+27) 11 - 339 1431 Fax: (+27) 11 - 339 7365
South America (except Brazil)	**RICORDI AMERICANA** (Small Rights) Tte. Gral. Juan D. Peron 1558 RA-1037 Buenos Aires Tel: (+54) 1 - 409 841 Fax: (+54) 1 - 476 3459
	SGAE (Grand Rights) Calle Uruguay No. 775-30A, RA-1015 Buenos Aires Tel: (+54) 1 - 476 2851 Fax: (+54) 1 - 476 2603

Spain	**EDEMS S.L.** Alcalá 70, E-28009 Madrid Tel: (+34) 1 - 577 0751 Fax: (+34) 1 - 575 7645
Sweden	**GEHRMANS MUSIKFÖRLAG** Box 6005, Odengatan 84, S-10231 Stockholm Tel: (+46) 8 - 610 0620, 610 0609 Fax: (+46) 8 - 610 0627
Switzerland	**ATLANTIS MUSIKBUCH VERLAG AG** Tramstr. 71, CH-8050 Zürich Tel: (+41) 1 - 311 6667 Fax: (+41) 1 - 311 6667
United Kingdom (and British Commonwealth)	**SCHOTT & CO. LTD.** 48, Great Marlborough Street, GB-London W1V 2BN Tel: (+44) 171 - 437 1246 Fax: (+44) 171 - 437 0263 Hire Library: Music Distribution Services 38, Eldon Way, GB-Paddock Wood, Kent TN12 6BE Tel: (+44) 892 - 838 083 Fax: (+44) 892 - 836 038
USA	**EUROPEAN AMERICAN MUSIC** 2480 Industrial Boulevard, Paoli, USA PA 19301, Tel: (+1) 610 - 648 0506 Fax: (+1) 610 - 889 0242

List of agents for sale material

Austria	**HOFMEISTER-FIGARO VERLAG** Brucknerstr. 6, A-1040 Wien, Austria Tel: (+43) 1 - 505 7651-0 Fax: (+43) 1 - 505 9185	Italy	**BMG RICORDI S.P.A.** Via Salomone 77, I-20138 Milano Tel: (+39) 2 - 5082 Fax: (+39) 2 - 5082 280

Austria **HOFMEISTER-FIGARO VERLAG**
Brucknerstr. 6,
A-1040 Wien, Austria
Tel: (+43) 1 - 505 7651-0
Fax: (+43) 1 - 505 9185

Belgium **SCHOTT FRERES**
30, Rue Saint Jean, B-1000 Bruxelles
Tel: (+32) 2 - 512 3980
Fax: (+32) 2 - 514 2845

Brazil **MUSAS - EDITORA & DISTRIBUIDORA MUSICAL LTDA.**
Rua Augusto Stresser, 861 (Juvevê)
Caixa Postal 6040, BR-80011-970 Curitiba - PR,
Tel: (+55) 41 - 263 1001
Fax: (+55) 41 - 262 2223

Canada **SCHOTT & CO. LTD.**
Brunswick Road, GB-Ashford, Kent TN23 1DX,
Tel: (+44) 1233 628987
Fax: (+44) 1233 610232

E.A.M.D.C. (EUROPEAN AMERICAN MUSIC DISTRIBUTORS CORPORATION)
P.O. Box 850, Valley Forge, PA 19482-850, USA
Tel: (+1) 610 - 648 0506
Fax: (+1) 610 - 889 0242

France **SCHOTT PARIS S.A.R.L.**
40 rue Blomet, F-75015 Paris
Tel: (+33) 1 - 4566 8366
Fax: (+33) 1 - 4567 7591

Italy **BMG RICORDI S.P.A.**
Via Salomone 77, I-20138 Milano
Tel: (+39) 2 - 5082
Fax: (+39) 2 - 5082 280

Japan **SCHOTT JAPAN COMPANY LTD.**
Kasuga Bldg., 2-9-3 Iidabashi, Chiyoda-ku,
J-Tokyo 102
Tel: (+81) 3 - 3263 6530
Fax: (+81) 3 - 3263 6672

Spain **EDEMS S.L.**
Alcalá 70, E-28009 Madrid
Tel: (+34) 1 - 577 0751; 577 0752
Fax: (+34) 1 - 575 7645

United Kingdom (and British Commonwealth) **SCHOTT & CO. LTD.**
Brunswick Road, GB-Ashford, Kent TN23 1DX
Tel: (+44) 1233 628987
Fax: (+44) 1233 610232

USA **E.A.M.D.C. (EUROPEAN AMERICAN MUSIC DISTRIBUTORS CORPORATION)**
P.O. Box 850, Valley Forge, PA 19482-850, USA
Tel: (+1) 610 - 648 0506
Fax: (+1) 610 - 889 0242

Agents for works in co-production

Austria **UNIVERSAL EDITION AG**
Bösendorferstr. 12, A-1015 Wien
Tel: (+43) 1 - 505 8695
Fax: (+43) 1 - 505 2720

Germany **SIKORSKI MUSIKVERLAG**
Johnsallee 23, D-20148 Hamburg
Tel: (+40) 41 41 00-0
Fax: (+40) 41 41 00-41

Poland **POLSKIE WYDAWNICTWO MUZYCZNE**
Ul. Fredry 8, PL-00097 Warszawa
Tel: (+48) 22 - 269 780
Fax: (+48) 22 - 269 780

POLSKIE WYDAWNICTWO MUZYCZNE
Ul. Krasinskiego 11a, 31 111 Krakow, Poland
Tel: (+48) 22 - 7328; 0174
Fax: (+48) 22 - 7328; 0174

Key to Scoring

Orchestral and ensemble scorings appear under the title of the work by instrumental families in score order as follows:

woodwind/brass/timpani & percussion/other percussion instruments (if separate player is necessary)/keyboards, harp and other plucked instruments/strings(with numbers of players)/tape and other electronic equipment

Within the woodwind, brass and string groups, the usual instruments are indicated by numbers unless an abbreviation is clearer.

Example: *2.2.3.2-4.3.3.1-str(2.2.2.2.1)* which indicates: 2 flutes, 2 oboes, 3 clarinets, 2 bassoons - 4 horns, 3 trumpets, 3 trombones, 1 tuba - strings (2 first violins, 2 second violins, 2 violas, 2 cellos, 1 doublebass)

Other situations are indicated as follows:

Doubling instruments:

1(pic)	One flute doubling piccolo
4(2pic,2afl)	Two flutes doubling piccolo **and** two flutes doubling alto flute

Optional instruments:

3(3pic).[afl]	Three flutes (all doubling piccolo) **and** one optional alto flute

Alternative instruments:

pno/org	One piano **or** one organ
pno([cel])/org	One piano doubling **ad libitum** celesta **or** (only) One organ

Below is an example of a complicated scoring and its meaning:

(Hans Werner Henze: „Das Floß der Medusa")

*4(2pic, 2afl).1.ob d'am.ca.heck.Ebcl.1.
acl/bsthn.bcl.asax.tsax.2.cbn-4.Dtpt.2btpt.atbn.ttbn.btbn.
aoficl/bomb/tuba in F.wagnertuba.btuba.cbtuba-
timp.5perc-pno.eorg.2hp.egtr.begtr-str(12.0.8.6.4)*

4 flutes (2 doubling piccolo, two doubling alto flute)
1 oboe
1 oboe d'amore
1 cor anglais
1 heckelphon
1 piccolo clarinet in Eb
1 clarinet
1 alto clarinet or 1 bassethorn
1 bass clarinet
1 alto saxophone
1 tenor saxophone
2 bassoons
1 contra bassoon

4 horns
1 piccolo trumpet in D
2 bass trumpets
1 alto trombone
1 tenor trombone
1 bass trombone
1 alto oficleide or bombardino or tuba in F
1 wagner tuba
1 bass tuba
1 contrabass tuba

timpani
percussion (5 players)

1 piano
1 electric organ

2 harps
1 electric guitar
1 electric bass guitar

12 first violins
(0 second violins)
8 violas
6 cellos
4 double basses

List of Abbreviations

Woodwind instruments:

ocar	Ocarina
pic	Piccolo
fl	Flute
bengalfl	Bengalian flute
bamboofl	Bamboo flute
afl	Alto flute
Gfl	Alto flute in G
bfl	Bass flute
inkafl	Inkaflute
rec	Recorder
soprec	Sopranino recorder
srec	Soprano recorder
arec	Alto recorder
trec	Tenor recorder
brec	Bass recorder
ob	Oboe
ob d'am	Oboe d'amour
ob da caccia	Oboe da caccia
aob	Alto oboe
bob	Bass oboe
ca	Cor anglais
cl	Clarinet
acl	Alto clarinet
Acl	clarinet in A
Dcl	clarinet in D
Ebcl	clarinet in Eb
bcl	Bass clarinet
cbcl	Contrabass clarinet
cacl	Contra alto clarinet
jazzcl	Jazzclarinet
bsthn	Basset horn
sax	Saxophone
sopsax	Sopranino saxophone
ssax	Soprano saxophone
asax	Alto saxophone
tsax	Tenor saxophone
barsax	Baritone saxophone
bsax	Bass saxophone
crumhorn	Krummhorn
tcrumhorn	Tenor Krummhorn
bcrumhorn	Bass Krummhorn
bn	Bassoon
cbn	Contra bassoon
Ebcnt	Soprancornett in Eb

Brass instruments:

hn	Horn
ahn	Alto horn
Ebhn	E flat Horn
thn	Tenor horn
nathn	Natural horn
flhn	Flugal horn
aflhn	Alto flugal horn
tflhn	Tenor flugal horn
bflhn	Bass flugal horn
cnt	Cornet
tpt	Trumpet

btpt	Bass trumpet
Bbtpt	B flat trumpet
Bachtpt	Bach-trumpet
Ctpt	Trumpet in C
Dtpt	Trumpet in D
Ebtpt	E flat trumpet
Ftpt	Trumpet in F
Atpt	Trumpet in A
Bbtpt	Trumpet in Bb
jazztpt	Jazz trumpet
pictpt	Piccolo trumpet
tbn	Trombone
atbn	Alto trombone
jazztbn	Jazz trombone
ttbn	Tenor trombone
bartbn	Baritone trombone
tbtbn	Tenor-bass trombone
btbn	Bass trombone
cbtbn	Contrabass trombone
aoficl	Altoficleide
boficl	Bassoficleide
euph	Euphonium
sous	Sousaphone
bomb	Bombardino
tuba	Tuba
btuba	Bass tuba
ttuba	Tenor tuba
cbtuba	Contrabass tuba

Percussion instruments:

perc	Percussion (number before indicates number of players)
aglsp	Alto glockenspiel
ametph	Alto metallophone
axyl	Alto xylophone
bmetph	Bass metallophone
bxyl	Bass xylophone
cymb	Cymbal
glasshp	Glassharp
glsp	Glockenspiel
lotosfl	Lotosflute
marac	Maracas
marimb	Marimba
sglsp	Soprano Glockenspiel
sxyl	Soprano xylophone
tâbla	Tabla
tamb	Tambourin
timp	Timpani (number before indicates number of players)
trgl	Triangle
vib	Vibraphone
xyl	Xylophone

Keyboard Abstruments:

cel	Celesta
ehpd	Electric harpsichord
ekeybd	Electric keyboard
eorg	Electric organ

epno	Electric piano
hpd	Harpsichord
keybd	Keyboard
org	Organ
orgportative	Portable organ
pianino	Pianino
picorg	Small organ
pno	Piano
regal	Small organ

Plucked instruments:

mand	Mandoline
gtr	Guitar
egtr	Electric guitar
begtr	Bass electric guitar
sitar	Sitar
hp	Harp
vibrahp	Vibraharp
lyre	Lyre
sistr	Sistrum
banjo	Banjo
tbanjo	Tenor banjo

String instruments:

str	Strings (number in parenthesis indicates players)
vn	Violin
va	Viola
va d'am	Viola d'amour
va da gamba	Viola da gamba
vc	Violoncello
ecello	Electric violoncello
db	Doublebass

Other instruments:

char	Charango
acc	Accordion

Traditional Japanese instruments

biwa
futozao
gagaku
hichiriki
hitsu
hitsu-kin
jushichigen
kokyu
koto
kugo
nijugen
noh
noh-kan
noh-kit
reigaku

ryuteki
sangen
shakuhachi
shamisen
shinobue
shô
shômyô

Vocals

S	Soprano
MS	Mezzo-soprano
A	Alto
C	Contralto
CT	Counter-tenor
T	Tenor
Bar	Baritone
B	Bass

General

alt.	Alternative
Arr	Arrangement
amp	Amplified
conc	Concertante
ens	Ensemble
hnd	Hand(s)
grp	Group
oct	Octet
orch	Orchestra/Orchestration
prt	Parted
prep	Prepared
qnt	Quintet
qrt	Quartet
rev	Revised
spt	Septet
sxt	Sextet

A

Abe, Keiko
b.1937

Chamber & Instrumental Works

Ancient Vase (1986) 5'
marimba solo
SJ 50

Little Windows (1986) 4'
marimba solo
SJ 50

Memories of the Seashore
(1986) 5'
marimba solo
SJ 50

Variations on Japanese Children's Songs 7'
marimba solo
SJ 50

Wind in the Bamboo Grove
(1986) 6'
marimba solo
SJ 50

Ahrens, Joseph
b.1904

Chamber & Instrumental Works

Cantiones Gregorianae pro organo (1957)
Vol. I
organ solo
ED 4787

Cantiones Gregorianae pro organo (1957)
Vol. II
organ solo
ED 4788

Cantiones Gregorianae pro organo (1957)
Vol. III
organ solo
ED 4789

Choralpartita (1947)
on "Verleih uns Frieden gnädiglich"
organ solo
ED 3814

Choralpartita "Lobe den Herrn" (1947)
organ solo
ED 3813

Christus ist erstanden (1935)
organ solo
ED 2552

Orgelmesse (1945)
organ solo
ED 3841

Toccata eroica and Fugue
(1934)
organ solo
ED 2427

Triptychon über Bach
organ solo
ED 4194

Veni Creator Spiritus (1947)
Hymn
organ solo
ED 3815

Verwandlungen I (1963)
organ solo
ED 5397

Verwandlungen II (1964)
organ solo
ED 5435

Verwandlungen III (1965)
organ solo
ED 5768

Choral Works

Ave Maria 2'
Chorus: mixed
org
C 38003

Missa choralis (1945)
Chorus: mixed (S, A, male voice)
org
C 37465

Missa Dorica (1946)
Chorus: mixed
org
C 37464

3 weihnachtliche Liedsätze 9'
Chorus: mixed
org
C 38004

Albert, Eugen d'
1864-1932

Stage Works

Liebesketten (1912)   full evening
Opera in 3 Acts
Text: Rudolf Lothar
Material on hire
SM

Tragaldabas (1907)   full evening
Comic Opera in 4 Acts
Text: Rudolf Lothar
Material on hire
SM

Andreae, Helmut

Orchestral Works

Suite for Orchestra
after Felix Mendelssohn-Bartholdy
2.2.2.2-2.2.2.0-timp.perc-hp-str
Material on hire
SM

Andreae, Volkmar
1879-1962

Stage Works

Abenteuer des Casanova, Op. 34 (1924)   full evening
4 Operatic Scenes
Text: Ferdinand Lion
Material on hire
SM

Chamber & Instrumental Works

Trio, Op. 1
vn.vc-pno
Parts **ED 3101**

Andriessen, Louis
b.1939

Chamber & Instrumental Works

Melodie (1972-74)
Arranger: Frans Brüggen
arec-pno
TMR 5

Sweet (1964)   10'
alto recorder solo
TMR 2

Antheil, George
1900-1959

Stage Works

Transatlantic - The People's Choice (1930)   full evening
Opera in 3 Acts
Text: George Antheil
Material on hire
EAM

ApIvor, Denis
b.1916

Concertos

Concertino, Op. 26 (1954)   22'
Soloist: guitar
2.1.2.2-2.2.0.0-timp.3perc-cel.hp-str
Material on hire
Piano reduction **GA 203**

Arlan, Dennis
1945-1979

Stage Works

The Ballad of the Bremen Band (1977)   45'
Opera for Children
Text: James Billings
Material on hire
Vocal score **EA 427**

Antheil, George

b.Trenton, NJ 8.7.1900, d. New York 12.2.1959

A gifted and intuitive modernist whose innovations and lifestyle won him the self-styled title of "bad boy" of music, Antheil and his works personify the dizzy experiment of the period between the two world wars. Admired by Pound, he championed jazz and technology as forces for progress. Their influence can be heard in his iconoclastic opera "Transatlantic" (1930), a send-up of an American presidential campaign that follows in the traditions of Křenek's popular jazz-opera "Jonny spielt auf".

Arnell, Richard
b.1917

Concertos

Piano Concerto, Op. 44
(1946)   27'
Soloist: piano
3.2.2.3-4.3.3.1-timp.perc-str
Material on hire
Piano reduction **ED 10135***

Violin Concerto, Op. 9
(1940)   22'
Soloist: violin
3.2.2.2 4.3.3.1-timp-str
Material on hire
Piano reduction **ED 10182***

Chamber & Instrumental Works

Allegro, Op. 58/2 (1952)   3'

tpt-pno
ED 10236

Andante and Allegro, Op. 58/1 (1950)   3'

fl-pno
ED 10535*

Recitative and Aria, Op. 53

(1948)   6'

pno
ED 10133*

Sonatina, Op. 61 (1950)   5'

pno (4hnd)
ED 10134*

Violin Sonata No. 2, Op. 55

(1948)   14'

vn-pno
ED 10214

Atterberg, Kurt Magnus

1887-1974

Orchestral Works

Ballad and Passacaglia, Op. 38 (1935)   9'

on a Swedish Folk Theme
2.2.2.2-4.2.3.1-timp.perc-hp-str
Material on hire
Eu

Auric, Georges

1899-1983

Orchestral Works

Symphonic Suite from "Chemin de Lumière"

(1951)   35'

3(pic).2.ca.2.bcl.2.cbn-4.3.3.1-timp.perc-cel.pno.hp-str
Material on hire
SM

Badings, Henk

1907-1987

Stage Works

Orpheus und Eurydike

(1941)   90'

Dance Drama
Text: J.W.F. Werumeus Buning
Material on hire
Piano reduction **ED 3988**

Orchestral Works

Symphony No.2 (1932)   30'

pic.2.2.ca.2.bcl.2.cbn-4.3.3.1-2perc-str
Material on hire
SM

Symphony No.5 (1949)   30'

3(pic).2.ca.2.bcl.2.cbn-4.3.3.1-timp.perc-cel.hp-str
Material on hire
SM

Chamber & Instrumental Works

Arcadia - Vol.1 (1945)   4'

pno
ED 4176

Arcadia - Vol.2 (1945)   5'

pno
ED 4177

Arcadia - Vol.3 (1945)   4'

pno
ED 4178

Arcadia - Vol.4 (1945)   8'

pno (4hnd)
ED 4179

Arcadia - Vol.5 (1945)   8'

pno (4hnd)
ED 4180

Capriccio (1936)   4'

vn-pno
ED 3688

Cello Sonata (1941)   10'

cello solo
ED 3786

Piano Sonata No.1 (1934)

ED 2339

Badings, Henk

b. Bandoeng 17.1.1907, d. Maarheze
26.6.1987

Badings studied until 1932 engineering in
Delft where he worked as a teacher of pala-
eonthology. After various jobs as a teacher
of composition in Rotterdam, Amsterdam,
The Hague and Stuttgart he worked as a
free-lance composer. In 1950 he became an
associate member of the Académie Royale
de Belgique. From 1951 he concentrated on
the 31-note scale. From 1961 he was teacher
of acoustics at the Utrecht Rijksuniversiteit
and from 1962 professor of composition at
the Stuttgart Conservatory.

Piano Sonata No.2 (1941) 20'

ED 2833

Piano Trio (1934) 21'

vn.vc-pno
Parts ED 3169

Reihe kleiner Klavierstücke

(1939) 3'

pno
ED 2897

Sonata for Flute and Guitar

(1983) 14'

fl-gtr
FTR 135

Sonatina (1936) 6'

pno
ED 2576

String Quartet No.2 (1935) 18'

Score **ED 3520** / Parts **ED 3177**

Trio Cosmos (Nos.1-16)

3vn (solo/orch)
VLB 53 (-72)

Violin Sonata No.2 (1940) 12'

vn-pno
ED 3650

Violin Sonata No.3 (1951) 13'

violin solo
ED 4912

Bamert, Matthias

b.1942

Orchestral Works

Keepsake (1979) 13'

*4(pic,afl).4(ca).3(Ebcl,bcl).barsax.4(cbn)-
4.4.3.1-timp.4perc-cel/pno.hp-str*
Material on hire
EAM

Mantrajana (1971) 8'

*3(pic).3(ca).3(bcl).3(cbn)-4.4.3.1-perc-
pno.hp-2solo vn.str*
Material on hire
EAM

Ol-Okun (1976) 13'

str
Material on hire
EAM

Once Upon an Orchestra

(1975) 30'

Overture and Ballet Music
*3(pic).3(ca).3(bcl).3(cbn)-4.4.3.1-
timp.3perc-hp-str*
Material on hire
EAM

Septuria Lunaris (1970) 18'

*2(pic).2(ca).2(bcl).2(cbn)-2.2.2.1-3perc-
hpd.hp-str*
Material on hire
EAM

Concertos

Concertino (1966) 14'

Soloist: cor anglais
str-pno
Material on hire
EAM

Rheology (1970) 8'

Soloist: harpsichord
str
Material on hire
EAM

Bamert, Matthias

b. Ersingen/Switzerland 5.7.1942

Bamert brings to his music his extensive
experience both as an orchestral oboist and
as a conductor of rare distinction whose
gifts are internationally recognised. Built on
a vast bedrock of quiet technical assurance,
works such as "Circus Parade" and "Once
Upon an Orchestra" exhibit a highly personal quality of verbal and musical humour.

Chamber & Instrumental Works

Actions (1977) 22'

3vc
Parts EA 388

Trio

2cl.bcl
EA 504

Solo Voice(s) and Instrument(s)/ Orchestra

Circus Parade (1979) 12'

Soloist: speaker
2(2pic).2.2(bcl).2-4.2.2.0-perc-pno.hp-str
Material on hire
Study score EA 436

Once Upon an Orchestra

(1975)   50'

for Narrator, 12 Dancers and Orchestra
*3(pic).3(ca).3(bcl).3(cbn)-4.4.3.1-
timp.3perc-hp-str*
Material on hire
Study score **EA 444**

Banks, Don
1923-1980

Orchestral Works

Assemblies (1966)   14'

*2.2.2.2-4.2.2.[1]-timp.3perc-pno.hp-
str(min:12.10.8.6.4)*
Material on hire
SL

Divisions (1964-65)   16'

*3(pic).3(ca).3(bcl).3(cbn)-4.3.3.1-
timp.3perc-pno/cel.hp-str*
Material on hire
SL

**Dramatic Music for Young
Orchestra** (1969)   7'

*2.2.2.2-4.3.3.1-2timp.2perc-
str(min:8.8.6.4.2)*
Material on hire
SL

Elizabethan Miniatures

(1962)   6'

fl-lute/gtr/hp-va da gamba/vc-str
Material on hire
SL

Episode (1958)   3'

*1.1.1(bcl).0-1.1.1.1-perc-cel/pno.hp-
str(1.1.1.1.1)*
Material on hire
SL

Equation III (1972)   8'

*cl(bcl)-hn-vc-eorg-perc-pno-jazz qrt(fl/cl-
egtr.begtr/db-drums)-electronics*
Material on hire
SL

**Fanfare and National
Anthem** (1970)   3'

God Save the Queen
2.2.2.2-4.4.3.1-timp.2perc-hp-str(7.6.5.4.4)
Material on hire
SL

Intersections (1969)   7'

*2.2.2.2-4.2.3.1-timp.2perc-hp-
str(12.10.8.6.4)-tape*
Material on hire
SL

Banks, Don

**b. South Melbourne 25.10.1923, d. Sydney
5.9.1980**

**One of the first Australian composers
thoroughly to absorb the serial method,
Banks made his home in England, but
maintained strong Antipodean links in his
music. The son of a jazz musician, he wrote
with equal facility for voices and instruments, amateurs and professionals, and
composed prolifically for the cinema.**

Meeting Place (1970)   27'

*2.1.2.1-1.3.1.0-2timp.perc-str(2.0.1.1.1)
jazz group: asax.tsax.barsax-tpt.tbn-jazzkit-
gtr-db*
Material on hire
SL

Music for Wind Band

(1971)   11'

4.6.12.3-4.6.3.1-timp.perc
Material on hire
SL

Nexus (1971)   20'

*2(2pic).2(ca).2(bcl).2(cbn)-4.2.3.1-
timp.2perc-pno-str
jazz qnt: asax(fl)-tpt/flhn-drums-pno-db*
Material on hire
SL

4 Pieces (1953)   14'

*2.2(ca).3(bcl).3(cbn)-4.2.3.1-2perc-cel.hp-
str*
Material on hire
SL

Prospects (1974)   9'

*3(pic).3.3(bcl).3(cbn)-4.3.3.1-timp.2perc-
hp-str(12.12.10.8.6)*
Material on hire
SL

Concertos

Horn Concerto (1965)   18'

Soloist: horn
*3(2pic).3(ca).3(bcl).3(cbn)-3.3.3.1-
timp.3perc-pno(cel).hp-str*
Material on hire
Study score **ED 10985***

Violin Concerto (1968)   25'

Soloist: violin
*3(3pic,afl).3.3(bcl).3(cbn)-4.3.3.1-
timp.3perc-cel/pno.hp-str(12.12.10.8.6)*
Material on hire
Study score **ED 11090**

Chamber & Instrumental Works

Commentary (1971)   10'

pno-tape
Material on sale
SL

3 Episodes (1964)   10'

fl-pno
ED 10942

Equation I and II (1969)   13'

*chamber group: vn.va.vc.hp-perc
jazz group: tsax.tpt-2perc-gtr-db*
Material on hire
SL

Horn Trio (1962)   15'

vn-hn-pno
Study score **ED 10928***

Pezzo Dramatico (1956)   7'

pno
Manuscript score on sale
SL

4 Pieces for String Quartet

(1971)   14'

Material on sale
SL

**Prologue, Night Pieces and
Blues for Two** (1968)   5'

cl-pno
ED 11092

Sequence (1967)   18'

cello solo
ED 11074

Sonata da Camera (1961)   15'

fl.cl.bcl-perc-pno-vn.va.vc
Material on hire
SL

3 Studies (1955)   7'

vc-pno
ED 10421*

Take Eight (1973)   10'

str qrt-cl/ssax-egtr-str bass/begtr-jazzkit
Material on hire
SL

Trio (1976)

bcl-pno-synth
Material on sale
SL

Violin Sonata (1953)   15'

In one Movement
vn-pno
ED 10259

Solo Voice(s)/Voice(s) and Piano/Guitar

3 North Country Folk Songs

(1955)   6'

soprano-pno
Manuscript score on sale
SL

5 North Country Folk Songs

(1953)   9'

soprano-pno
ED 10165*

Solo Voice(s) and Instrument(s)/ Orchestra

Aria from "Limbo" (1972)   5'

Soloist: mezzo-soprano
cl(bcl)-hn-vc-egtr.pno-vib-[tape]
Material on hire
SL

Limbo (1971)   30'

Soloists: soprano, tenor, bass-baritone
fl.cl-hn-pno-vn.va.vc.db-tape
Material on hire
SL

5 North Country Folk Songs

(1954)   9'

Soloist: soprano
str
Material on hire
Vocal score **ED 10165***

Settings from Roget (1966)   12'

Soloist: female jazz singer
asax-perc-pno-db
Material on hire
SL

---

3 Short Songs (1971)   8'

Text: Samuel Daniel/anonymous
Soloist: female jazz singer
asax.pno.egtr.db.jazzkit
Material on hire
SL

Tirade (1968)   16'

Text: Peter Porter
Soloist: mezzo-soprano
pno.hp-3perc
Material on hire or sale
Study score **ED 11073***

Walkabout (1972)   6'

Text: Don Banks
Soloists: children's voices
3fl/3rec-2gtr-2vc-perc-pno
Material on hire
SL

Choral Works

Benedictus (1976)   20'

voices-jazz qrt-synth.epno-tape
Material on hire
SL

Bantock, Granville

1868-1946

Orchestral Works

The Frogs - Comedy Overture (1936)   7'

after Aristophanes
3.1.2.3-4.2.0.0-timp.perc-str
Material on hire
Eu

Barraud, Henry

b.1900

Orchestral Works

Poème (1933)   9'

3.3.3.3-4.3.3.1-timp.perc-hp-str
Material on hire
Eu

Basi, Daniel, R.

b.1933

Solo Voice(s) and Instrument(s)/ Orchestra

Dos Alusiones   9'

Cantata
Text: Daniel Borges
Soloist: tenor
0.0.1.0-0.2.0.0-perc-gtr-str
Material on hire
AVV

Bate, Stanley

1911-1959

Perseus (1938)   full evening

Ballet in 7 Scenes
Material on hire
Piano reduction **ED 10047***

Concertos

Viola Concerto, Op. 46

(1946)   23'

Soloist: viola
2.2.2.2-4.3.2.1-timp-str
Material on hire
Study score **ED 10203 (min.)***

Chamber & Instrumental Works

7 Piano Pieces

pno
ED 10012*

Sonatina (1960)   8'

arec-pno
ED 10040*

Sonatina (1960)   8'

fl/arec-pno
Manuscript score on sale
SL

Bausznern, Waldemar von
1866-1931

Solo Voice(s) and Instrument(s)/ Orchestra

8 Kammergesänge 26'
Soloist: high voice
str qrt-fl.cl
Material on hire
SM

Beaser, Robert
b.1954

Orchestral Works

Double Chorus (1990) 11'
*3(pic).3(ca).3(bcl).3(cbn)-4.4.3.1-
timp.4perc-pno-str*
Material on hire
EAM-Helicon

Concertos

Piano Concerto (1988) 32'
Soloist: piano
3.3.3.2-4.3.3.1-timp.4perc-hp-str
Material on hire
EAM-Helicon

Song of the Bells (1987) 13'
Soloist: flute
*1(pic).2(ca).2.2-3.1.0.0-timp.3perc-pno.hp-
str*
Material on hire
EAM-Helicon

Chamber & Instrumental Works

Canti Notturni (1974) 17'
guitar solo
EA 507X

Il est né, le Divin Enfant
(1982) 4'
fl-gtr
EA 575

Beaser, Robert

b. Boston 1954

A highly regarded name amongst composers committed to the ideal of "new tonality", Beaser has been described by the New York Times as possessing „a lyric gift comparable to that of the late Samuel Barber". In its balance, melodic sweep and architectural clarity his music is indebted both to European tradition and American Vernacular. Since 1977, when he became the youngest American composer to win the Prix de Rome, he has been the recipient of many distinguished awards, while his music has been performed and commissioned by many of America's leading orchestras and ensembles.

Landscape with Bells (1986) 3'
pno
EA 591

Minimal Waltz (1986) 1'
fl-pno
Material on sale
EAM-Helicon

Mountain Songs (1985) 28'
fl-gtr
EA 576

Notes on a Southern Sky
(1980) 13'
guitar solo
EA 509

Shadow and Light (1978-80) 18'
fl.ob.cl.bn-hn
Material on hire
EAM-Helicon

String Quartet (1975-76) 28'
Material on sale
EAM-Helicon

Variations (1981-82) 22'
fl-pno
EA 506

Solo Voice(s)/Voice(s) and Piano/Guitar

The Old Men admiring themselves in the Water
(1986) 4'
Text: William Butler Yeats
voice-pno
Material on sale
EAM-Helicon

Quicksilver (1978) 3'
Text: Daniel Mark Epstein
tenor-pno
Material on sale
EAM-Helicon

The Seven Deadly Sins
(1979) 16'
Text: Anthony Hecht
tenor/baritone-pno
EA 510X

Solo Voice(s) and Instrument(s)/ Orchestra

The Seven Deadly Sins
(1984) 24'
Text: Anthony Hecht
Soloist: tenor/baritone
*2(2pic).2.2(asax).2-4.2.3.1-timp.3perc-
pno.hp-str*
Material on hire
Vocal score **EA 510X**

Silently Spring (1973) 10'
Text: E.E. Cummings
Soloist: soprano
fl.asax.bn-tpt-pno-perc-va
Material on hire
EAM-Helicon

Songs from "The Occasions"
(1985) 24'
Text: Eugenio Montale
Soloist: tenor
fl.cl-hn-pno-vn.va.vc
Study score **EA 573X**

Infoline · e-Mail
Schott Musik International
Mainz: Schott.Musik.com@T-Online.de
London: 101627.166@compuserve.com

Symphony (1967-77)   30'

Text: E.E. Cummings, William Butler
Yeats, John Fowles
Soloist: soprano
3(pic,afl).3(ca).2(Ebcl,bcl).2-4.2.3.1-
timp.perc-pno.hp-str
Material on hire
EAM-Helicon

Choral Works

Psalm 119 (1983)   13'

Soloists: soprano, alto, tenor, bass
Chorus: mixed [a cappella]
[brass qnt]
Material on hire
EAM-Helicon

Beck, Conrad
1901-1989

Stage Works

Der große Bär (1935-36)   55'

Ballet in 5 Scenes by Leopold Chauveau
Material on hire
SM

Orchestral Works

Aeneas Silvius Symphonie
(1957)   28'

2.2.ca.2.bcl.2-4.3.3.1-timp.2perc-str
Material on hire
Study score **ED 4596**

Chamber Concerto (1971)   20'

2(pic).2.2.2-2.2.0.0-timp.perc-str
Material on hire
SM

Concertato (1964)   12'

2.2.ca.2.bcl.2-4.3.3.1-timp.2perc-str
Material on hire
SM

Concerto for Orchestra
(1928)   20'

Symphony No 4
2.2.ca.2.bcl.2-4.3.2.btuba-timp.perc-str
Material on hire
SM

Fantasie (1969)   23'

2.2.2.bcl.2-4.3.3.1-timp.perc-vib.cel.hp-str
Material on hire
SM

Hommages (1965)   12'

2.3.3.2-4.3.3.1-timp.perc-str
Material on hire
Study score **ED 5511**

Beck, Conrad

**b. Lohn, Canton Schaffhausen 16.6.1901,
d. Basel 31.10.1989**

**A composer of great economy of means and
formal concision, Beck acquired his early
training in Paris. Closely associated with
the school of Roussel and Honegger, he
developed their neo-baroque manners in a
direction of his own that reconciled
Teutonic and Latin spirit in a sequence of
string quartets and orchestral works. In his
postwar period Beck deliberately simplified
his style even further, occasionally admit-
ting folksong elements into his music.**

Hymn   11'

2.2.ca.2.bcl.2-4.4.3.1-timp.perc-hp-str
Material on hire
SM

Innominata (1931)   10'

*2.2.ca.2.bcl.2.cbn-4.3.3.btuba-timp.2perc-
str*
Material on hire
SM

Lichter und Schatten (1982)   17'

2hn.2perc-str
Material on hire
SM

Little Suite (1930)   15'

str
Material on hire
SM

Nachklänge (1984)   16'

Tripartita for orchestra
2.2.2.2-4.2.0.0-timp.2perc-str
Material on hire
SM

Ostinato (1936)   12'

2([pic]).2.ca.2.2.cbn-4.3.3.1-timp.perc-str
Material on hire
SM

Sonatina (1958)   10'

2.2.2.2-2.2.0.0-timp.perc-str
Material on hire
Study score **ED 5022**

Suite (1947)   20'

pic.2.2.ca.2.bcl.2-4.2.2.0-timp.perc-str
Material on hire
SM

Suite Concertante (1961)   19'

pic.2.2.ca.2.bcl.2-4.3.3.1-timp.perc-cel-db
Material on hire
SM

Symphony No.3 (1927)   25'

str
Material on hire
SM

Symphony No.5 (1930)   18'

2(pic).2.ca.2.bcl.asax.2-2.2.0.0-timp-str
Material on hire
SM

Symphony No.6 (1950)   32'

2.3.3.3-4.3.3.1-timp.perc-str
Material on hire
SM

Concertos

Chamber Concerto (1949)   28'

Soloist: violin
1.0.1.1-2.1.0.0-str
Material on hire
Piano reduction **ED 4190**

Clarinet Concerto (1967-68)   16'

Soloist: clarinet
2.2.2.2-2.2.0.0-timp.perc-str
Material on hire
Piano reduction **KLB 1**

Concert Music for Oboe
(1932)   20'

Soloist: oboe
str
Material on hire
SM

Concertino for Clarinet and
Bassoon (1954)   20'

Soloists: clarinet, bassoon
2.2.0.0-3.2.0.0-str
Material on hire
SM

Concertino for Oboe (1962)   17'

Soloist: oboe
2.0.2.bcl.2-3.2.0.0-str
Material on hire
Piano reduction **OBB 3**

Concertino for Piano

(1927-28)   20'

Soloist: piano
2.2.2.bcl.2-2.2.0.0-timp-str
Material on hire
Piano reduction **ED 2068**

Concerto for String Quartet and Orchestra (1929)   25'

Soloists: string qrt
2.2.ca.2.bcl.2-4.2.0.0-timp.perc-str
Material on hire
SM

Concerto for Wind Quintet and Orchestra (1976)   19'

Soloists: wind qnt
2.2.2.2-4.2.0.0-timp.perc-str
Material on hire
SM

Piano Concerto (1933)   33'

Soloist: piano
2.2.ca.2.bcl.2.cbn-4.2.1.1-timp(perc)-str
Material on hire
SM

Serenade (1935)   17'

Soloists: flute, clarinet
str
Study score **ED 3307**

Viola Concerto (1949)   23'

Soloist: viola
2.1.2.2-2.2.0.0-timp-hp-str
Material on hire
Piano reduction **VAB 3**

Chamber & Instrumental Works

Alternances (1980)   12'

cl-vc-pno
ED 7007

Chorale Sonata (1948)   18'

organ solo
ED 4149

Duo (1934-35)   17'

vn.va
ED 2447

Duo (1960)   13'

2vn
ED 5199

3 Epigramme   5'

cello solo
ED 6683

Facetten (1975)   5'

3 Impromptus
tpt-pno
TR 11

Piano Pieces Vol.1 (1929)   16'

pno
ED 2109

Piano Pieces Vol.2 (1930)   14'

pno
ED 2145

2 Preludes (1932)   22'

organ solo
ED 2244

Sonata No.2 (1954)   17'

vc-pno
ED 5062

Sonatina (1927)   12'

organ solo
ED 2132

Sonatina (1928)   24'

vn-pno
ED 2067

Sonatina (1928)   16'

pno
ED 2072

Sonatina (1955)   10'

2pno (4hnd)
ED 4909

Sonatina (1968)   12'

2fl
FTR 8

Sonatina (1959-60)   14'

fl-pno
FTR 100

Sonatina (1941/53)   10'

ob-pno
OBB 4

Sonatina (1977)   12'

va-pno
VAB 50

Sonatina No.2 (1941)   8'

pno
ED 4042

String Quartet No.3 (1926)   16'

Material on sale
Parts **ED 3113**

String Quartet No.4 (1934)   25'

Parts **ED 3166**

String Quartet No.5 (1963)   21'

Study score **ED 5508** / Parts **ED 5751**

String Trio No.1 (1928)   16'

vn.va.vc
Study score **ED 10200**

String Trio No.2 (1946)   18'

vn.va.vc
Score and parts **ED 10253**

Trio (1983)   16'

fl.ob-pno
ED 7090

Solo Voice(s)/Voice(s) and Piano/Guitar

3 Herbstgesänge (1930)   5'

Text: Rainer Maria Rilke
high voice-pno/org
ED 2131

Solo Voice(s) and Instrument(s)/ Orchestra

Bicinien

20 zweistimmige Phantasien aus der Zeit um 1600
Soloist: high voice
2fl
ED 2208

Elegie (1972)   21'

Solo-Cantata after the fragment "Die Musse"
Text: Friedrich Hölderlin
Soloist: soprano
2.2.2.bcl.2-4.3.0.0-timp.2perc-hp-str
Material on hire
SM

Herbstfeuer (1956)   18'

Text: Ricarda Huch
Soloist: alto
2.0.2.0-2.2.0.0-cel.pno.hp-str
Material on hire
Vocal score **ED 4774**

Kammer-Kantate (1937)   25'

Text: Louïze Labé
Soloists: soprano, flute, piano
str
Material on hire
Vocal score **ED 5399**

Die Sonnenfinsternis (1967)   15'

Cantata
Text: Adalbert Stifter
Soloist: alto
fl.cl-hpd-str
alt. version: S-fl.cl-hpd-str qnt
Material on hire
Vocal score **ED 6102**

Infoline · e-Mail
Schott Musik International
Mainz: Schott.Musik.com@T-Online.de
London: 101627.166@compuserve.com

Choral Works

Lyrische Kantate (1934)   25'

Text: Rainer Maria Rilke (Sonets to Orpheus)
Soloists: soprano, alto
Chorus: female (min. 20 voices)
1.1.ca.1.bcl.2-1.1.0.0-cel.pno-trgl-str
Material on hire
SM

Der Tod des Oedipus (1928)   20'

Cantata
Text: René Morax
Soloists: soprano, tenor, baritone
Chorus: mixed
2tpt.2tbn-[timp]-2org
Material on hire
SM

Der Tod zu Basel (1952)   65'

Ein großes Miserere
Soloists: soprano, bass, 3 speakers
Chorus: mixed
pic.2.2.ca.2.bcl.2-4.4.3.1-timp.2perc-cel.pno.hp-str
Material on hire
Vocal score **ED 5058**

Beckerath, Alfred von
1901-1989

Orchestral Works

Symphony for Wind Orchestra   22'

2fl.2ob.Ebcl.2cl-2flhn.2nathn.2thn.2tpt.2tbn.euph.2tuba-timp.perc
Material on hire
SM

Bender, Wilhelm
1911-1944

Chamber & Instrumental Works

Sonate (1948)

arec-pno
OFB 2

Benguerel, Xavier
b.1931

Orchestral Works

Dialogue orchestrale (1969)   11'

pic.2.2.ca.2.bcl.2.cbn-4.3.3.1-perc-vib(marimb).cel.pno.hp-str
Material on hire
AVV

Musica Riservata (1969)   10'

str(3.3.2.2.1)
Material on hire
AVV

Concertos

Organ Concerto (1970)   17'

Soloist: organ
pic.2.2.ca.2.bcl.2.cbn-4.3.3.1-perc-xyl(glsp).vib(marimb).cel-str(14.12.10.8.6)
Material on hire
AVV

Bentzon, Niels Viggo
b.1919

Concertos

Brillantes Concertino   3'

No. 5 from the "Divertimento für Mozart"
Soloist: piano
2.2.2.2-2.2.0.0-timp-str
SM (CO-prod: Hansen/Kopenhagen)

Bergmann, Walter
1902-1988

Chamber & Instrumental Works

Sonata (1965)

srec-pno
ED 10934

Sonata (1973)

arec-pno
ED 11240

Solo Voice(s) and Instrument(s)/ Orchestra

Pastorale (1947)

Text: Norman Cameron
Soloist: alto
srec
ED 10377

Berio, Luciano
b.1925

Concertos

Variazioni (1956)   3'

No. 2 from the "Divertimento für Mozart"
2bsthn-str
Material on hire
SM (Co-prod: UE)
Copyright USA: EAM/Italy: Ed. Suvini Zerboni

Berkeley, Lennox
1903-1989

Concertos

Sonatina (1940)   10'

Arranger: Rodney Newton
fl-str
Material on hire
SL

Chamber & Instrumental Works

4 Concert Studies, Op. 14/1
(1940)   12'
pno
ED 10014*

Sonatina, Op. 13 (1940)   10'
arec-pno
OFB 1040

Bialas, Günter
1907-1995

Orchestral Works

Concerto (1947)　　28'

doubled str-timp
Material on hire
SM

Biersack, Anton
1907-1982

Orchestral Works

Bagatelles　　17'

2(pic).2.2.2-0.1.0.0-timp.perc-str
Material on hire
SM

Fantasia fugata (1943)　　20'

Symphonic Music 2
3(pic).2.2.2.cbn-4.3.3.1-timp.perc-str
Material on hire
SM

Skizzen　　11'

str
Material on hire
SM

Symphonic Music (1937)　　32'

pic.2.2.2.2.cbn-4.3.3.1-timp.perc-str
Material on hire
SM

Choral Works

Passions-Kantate (1946)　　25'

Soloists: soprano, bass
Chorus: mixed
1.1.2.2-4.0.0.0-timp-str(0.0.1.1.1)
Material on hire
SM

Bittner, Julius
1874-1939

Stage Works

Der Musikant (1910)　　full evening

Opera in 2 Acts
Text: Julius Bittner
Material on hire
SM

Die rote Gred (1907)　　full evening

Opera in 3 Acts
Text: Julius Bittner
Material on hire
SM

Blake, David
b.1936

Choral Works

Lumina (1968-69)　　60'

Text: Ezra Pound
Soloists: soprano, baritone
Chorus: mixed
3(2pic,afl).3(ca).3(Ebcl,bcl).asax.3(cbn)-4.3.4.1-timp.4perc-cel.mand.hp-str
Material on hire
Vocal score **AVV 202**

Blech, Leo
1871-1958

Orchestral Works

Waldwanderung, Op. 8
(1901)　　15'

Symphonic Poem
3(pic).2(aob).3(bcl).2.cbn-4.3.3.2-timp-hp-str
Material on hire
SM

Bloch, Augustyn
b.1929

Orchestral Works

Dialoghi (1964)　　21'

0.0.1.1-0.1.3.0-perc-egtr-str
Material on hire
Study score **ED 5924 (Co-prod: PWM)**
Copyright not for: AL, C, NKOR, VN, CHINA, FEB

Enfiando (1970)　　11'

3.3.3.3-4.3.3.1-4timp.perc-org(pno)-str
Material on hire
Study score **ED 6325 (Co-prod: PWM)**
Copyright not for: AL, C, NKOR, VN, CHINA, FEB

Solo Voice(s) and Instrument(s)/ Orchestra

Salmo Gioioso (1970)　　12'

Soloist: soprano
fl.Ebcl.ob.hn.bn
Study score **ED 6059-01** / Score and parts **ED 6059 (Co-prod: PWM)**
Copyright not for: AL, C, NKOR, VN, CHINA, FEB

Choral Works

Gilgamesh (1968)　　20'

Ballet-Suite
Chorus: baritone-chorus
3.0.6.asax.1-0.4.4.0-2timp.perc-str(0.0.8.8.6-8)
Material on hire
SM (Co-prod: PWM)
Copyright not for: AL, C, NKOR, VN, CHINA, FEB

Blomdahl, Karl-Birger
1916-1968

Stage Works

Aniara (1957-59)　　180'

Opera in 2 Acts
Text: Erik Lindegren after Harry Martinson
Material on hire
Vocal score **ED 10690*** /
Libretto **ED 10690-11/-12**

Blomdahl, Karl-Birger

b. Växjö 19.10.1916, d. Kungsängen,
nr. Stockholm 14.6.1968

Famous for his "space opera", "Aniara",
Blomdahl was an immensely gifted composer and a powerful influence on the direction and vitality of 20th-century Swedish
music. A founder member of the "Monday"
group of radical young musicians that flou-
rished in the 1930's and 40's, he later occu-
pied important roles in the ISCM and
Swedish Radio. Starting as a disciple of
Hindemith's New Objectivity, he encompassed serialism and jazz in the 1950's, ventu-
ring into the realm of electronic music in
the last decade of his life.

Herr von Hancken

(1962-63)   full evening

Comic Opera in 3 Acts
Text: Erik Lindegren after Hjalmar
Bergman
Material on hire
Vocal score **ED 10783***

Minotauros (1957)   25'

Dance Suite
Material on hire
SL

Sisyphos (1954)   21'

Dance Suite
Material on hire
Study score **ED 10890**

Orchestral Works

Fioriture (1960)   20'

3(pic).2.3(2Acl,bcl).3(cbn)-4.4.3.1-
timp.3perc-str
Material on hire
Study score **ED 10763***

Forma Ferritonans (1961)   11'

3(pic).3.2.2cbcl(bcl).2.2cbn-4.4.4(btbn).0-
timp.perc-pno-str
Material on hire
Study score **ED 11017**

Minotauros (1957)   25'

Dance Suite
2(pic).2.2(bcl).2(cbn)-4.3.3.1-timp.4perc-
hp-str
Material on hire
SL

Sisyphos (1954)   20'

Dance Suite
3(pic).3(ca).3(bcl).2.cbn-4.3.3.1-
timp.5perc-xyl(vib/marimb).pno.hp-str
Material on hire
Study score **ED 10890**

Spiel für Acht (1962)   25'

Dance Suite
1(pic).1(ca).1(asax,bcl).1(cbn)-1.1.1.1-
timp.4perc-cel(xyl.vib.glsp).pno(4hnd)-
str(2.0.2.2.2)
Material on hire
Study score **ED 11018**

Symphony No.3 - "Facetter"

(1950)   25'

3(pic).3(ca).3(bcl).3(cbn)-4.4.3.1-
timp.perc-str
Material on hire
Study score **ED 10605***/ED 10485 (min.)

Concertos

Chamber Concerto (1953)   16'

Soloist: piano
pic.2.2.ca.2.bcl.2.cbn-0.0.0.0-timp.3perc
Material on hire
Piano reduction **ED 10278**

Chamber & Instrumental Works

Trio in B Flat (1955)   19'

cl-vc-pno
ED 10508*

Solo Voice(s)/Voice(s) and Piano/Guitar

5 Canzone (1954)   7'

Text: Quasimodo/Arcangioli
male voice-pno
ED 10822

Solo Voice(s) and Instrument(s)/ Orchestra

Resan i denna nat (Le Voyage cette Nuit) (1966)   14'

Text: Erik Lindegren
Soloist: soprano
3.3.3.0-4.3.0.0-timp-pno.hp-str
Material on hire
SL

Choral Works

Anabase (1956)   60'

Text: Saint-John Perse
Soloists: speaker, baritone
Chorus: mixed
2(pic).2(ca).2(bcl).2(cbn)-3.2.1.0-
timp.4perc-xyl(vib).pno.hp-str
Material on hire
Vocal score **ED 10644***

In the Hall of Mirrors

(1951-52)   35'

Text: Erik Lindegren
Soloists: S.A.T.Bar(speaker).B
Chorus: mixed
3(pic).3(ca).3(bcl).ssax.3(cbn)-4.4.3.1-
timp.perc-cel.pno.hp-str
Material on hire
Study score **ED 10297-01*** / Vocal score **ED 10297***

Borck, Edmund von

1906-1944

Orchestral Works

5 Orchestral Pieces, Op. 8

(1933)   15'

pic.1(pic).1.1(asax).bcl.1.cbn-2.3.2.1-
4perc-str
Material on hire
SM

Präludium und Fuge, Op. 10

(1934)   10'

pic.1.2.2.1.cbn-2.2.2.1-perc-str
Material on hire
SM

Concertos

Concertino, Op. 15b (1936) 11'

Soloist: flute
str
Material on hire
SM

Piano Concerto, Op. 20

(1920)   25'

Soloist: piano
pic.2.2.2.cbn-4.3.3.cbtuba-timp.perc-str
Material on hire
SM

Saxophone Concerto, Op. 6

(1932)   15'

Soloist: alto saxophone
pic.1(pic).1.0.1.cbn-1.2.2.1-perc-str(12.0.4.4.3)
Material on hire
SM

Borsheim, David J.

Chamber & Instrumental Works

Sonata   10'

after the 2nd Organ sonata (Paul Hindemith 1937)
hn.2tpt.tbn.tuba
Study score **ED 6880** / Parts **ED 6881**

von Bose, Hans-Jürgen

b.1953

Stage Works

Blutbund (1974)   55'

Opera in 1 Act
Text: Ramón del Valle-Inclán
Material on hire
AVV

von Bose, Hans-Jürgen

b. Munich 24.12.1953

Firmly established as one of the leading figures of the rising middle-generation of German composers, von Bose's output includes challenging instrumental pieces frequently based in literary or poetic sources. One of his most successful works, the "kinetic action" "Die Nacht aus Blei", dervies from a novel by Hans Henny Jahnn. Von Bose's "Sappho-Gesänge", premièred at Donaueschingen in 1983, are an important contribution to contemporary vocal repertoire.

Chimäre (1986)   30'

Musical Scene
Text: Federico García Lorca
Material on hire
AVV

Das Diplom (1975)   45'

Comic Opera in 1 Act
Text: Luigi Pirandello
Material on hire
AVV

63: Dream Palace

(1989)   full evening

Opera
Text: Hans-Jürgen von Bose after James Purdy
Material on hire
AVV / Libretto **BN 3111-90**

Die Leiden des jungen Werthers (1983-84)   full evening

Lyric Scenes in 2 Acts and Intermezzo
Text: Filippo Sanjust/Hans-Jürgen von Bose
Material on hire
AVV / Libretto **BN 3110-00**

Die Nacht aus Blei (1981/88) 70'

Ballet. Kinetic action in 6 Scenes
Text: Hans Henny Jahnn
Material on hire
Study score **AVV 316**

Werther-Szenen (1988) full evening

Ballet in 2 Parts
Material on hire
AVV

Orchestral Works

Concertino per il H.W.H.

(1991)   3'

1.1.1.1-1.1.1.0-timp-synth(pno)-str(1.1.1.1.1)
Material on hire
AVV

Idyllen (1982-83)   17'

3(2pic,afl).3.3(Acl,Ebcl,bcl).3(cbn)-4.3.3.1-timp.3perc-pno(cel).hp-str(12.10.8.6.6)
Material on hire
Study score **AVV 122**

Labyrinth I (1987)   30'

4(2pic).4.4(2bcl).4(2cbn)-6.4.4(cbtbn).1-2timp.3perc-eorg(pno).2hp-str(14.12.10.8.7)
Material on hire
AVV

Morphogenesis (1975)   16'

3(pic).3.3(Ebcl).bcl.3(cbn)-5.4(Dtpt).3.1-2timp.3perc-pno(cel).hp-str(16.14.12.10.6/8)
Material on hire
AVV

Musik für ein Haus voll Zeit

(1978)   14'

2(pic,afl).1(ob d´am).2(Ebcl,Acl).bcl.1(cbn)-1.1.1.0-timp(perc).2perc-cel(hpd.pno.eorg).2hp(amp)-str(4.0.3.3.1)
Material on hire
AVV

Prozess (1987-88)   12'

1(pic,afl).1(ca).1.bcl.0.cbn-1.1.1.0-timp(perc).2perc-pno-str(1.1.1.1.1)
Material on hire
AVV

Scene (1991)   23'

1(pic,afl).1.1(Ebcl,bcl).ssax(barsax,bcl).1(cbn)-1.1(Dtpt)1.1-2perc-2synth(pno).hp-str(1.1.2.2.2)
Material on hire
Study score **AVV 323**

Suite (1988)

from the Ballet "Werther-Szenen"
2(2pic,afl).2(ca).2(Ebcl,bcl).2(cbn)-2.2.2.0-timp.2perc-pno.hpd-str(14.0.4.4.3)
Material on hire
AVV

Symphony No.1 (1976) 22'

2pic.2.4.4.3.cbn-5.4.3.1-timp.perc-eorg-
str(28.0.12.12.8)
Material on hire
AVV

**Travesties in a Sad
Landscape** (1978) 12'

1(pic,afl).1(ca).bcl(cl).cbn-1.1(Dtpt).1.0-
perc-cel.acc(hammondorg).pno-
str(2.0.1.1.1)
Material on hire
AVV

Two Studies (1989) 10'

4(2pic).4(ca).4(Acl,2bcl).4(2cbn)-4.4.3.1-
timp.2perc-str(12.12.10.8.6)
Material on hire
AVV

Variations (1980/90) 20'

str(12.10.8.6.5)
Material on hire
AVV

Concertos

**"...other echoes inhabit the
garden"** (1987) 23'

Soloist: oboe
3(pic,afl).2(ob d'am,ca).2(bsthn,bcl).
cbcl.2(cbn)-2.2(F high).2(btbn).1-
timp.3perc-2hp-str(0.0.8.6.6)
Material on hire
Parts AVV 139 (solo)

Symbolum (1985) 18'

Soloist: organ
4(2pic).4(ca).4(Ecl.2bcl).4(2cbn)-
6.4(Dtpt).3.cbtbn.1-2timp.3perc-eorg.2hp-
str(10.10.10.8.6)
Material on hire
AVV

Chamber &
Instrumental
Works

Befragung (1988) 15'

cl-2vn.va.vc.db
Score AVV 146 / Parts AVV 147

Edge (1989) 7'

violin solo
AVV 152

3 Epitaphs (1987) 13'

wind sxt
Score AVV 137 / Parts AVV 138

Labyrinth II (1987) 6'

pno
AVV 319

3 Little Piano Pieces (1982) 5'

in: "Neues Klavierbuch"
ED 7095

Die Menagerie von Sanssouci
(1987-88) 23'

fl.asax-vc-perc
AVV 148

Nonett (1988) 11'

fl.ob.cl.bn-hn-vn.va.vc.db
Score AVV 142 / Parts AVV 143

Origami (1991) 10'

pno (4hnd)
ED 7963

Parerga (1984) 15'

1.1.1.1-1.0.0.0-str(1.1.1.1.1)
Score AVV 317 / Parts AVV 318

Solo (1978-79) 20'

cello solo
AVV 155

String Quartet No.1 (1973) 16'

AVV 120

String Quartet No.2
(1976-77) 15'

AVV 109

String Quartet No.3
(1986-87) 30'

AVV 136

String Trio (1978) 21'

vn.va.vc
Score AVV 114 / Parts AVV 115

3 Studies (1986) 10'

vn-pno
Score and parts AVV 135

**Threnos-Hommage à Bernd
Alois Zimmermann** (1975) 16'

va.vc
AVV

Violin Sonata (1975) 11'

violin solo
AVV

....„vom Wege abkommen"
(1981-82) 10'

viola solo
AVV 127

# Solo
Voice(s)/Voice(s)
and Piano/Guitar

Omega (1986) 15'

Text: Federico García Lorca
mezzo-soprano-pno
AVV 150

Solo Voice(s) and
Instrument(s)/
Orchestra

Achalm (1989) 5'

Soloist: soprano
7 instruments
Score and parts AVV 151

Ein Brudermord (1990)

Text: Franz Kafka
Soloist: baritone
acc-vc
Material on hire
AVV

5 Gesänge (1986) 22'

Text: Federico García Lorca
Soloist: baritone
1.1.1(bcl).1-1.0.0.0-str(1.1.1.1.1)
Material on hire
AVV

Guarda el canto (1981-82) 6'

Text: Miguel Angel Bustos
Soloist: soprano
str qrt
AVV

In hora mortis (1991) 20'

Text: Thomas Bernhard
Soloist: speaker
str(6.5.4.3.2)
Material on hire
AVV

5 Kinderreime (1976) 17'

Soloist: alto
5rec-tpt-cl(Ebcl,bcl)-va.db
Score AVV 121

4 Lieder (1988) 12'

For Greenpeace
Text: Georg Britting/Hans Magnus
Enzensberger
Soloist: soprano
1(pic).1.1(bcl).1-1.0.0.0-str(1.1.1.1.1)
Material on hire
AVV

Love after Love (1990-91) 6'

Text: Derek Walcott
Soloist: soprano
4.3(ca).3(bcl).3(2cbn)-4.3.3.1-timp.2perc-
str(12.10.8.6.4)
Material on hire
AVV

Sappho-Gesänge (1983)   17'

Text: Joachim Schickel
Soloist: mezzo-soprano
*1(pic,afl).1.1(bcl).1(cbn)-1.1.0.0-
timp(perc).perc-pno(cel).hp-str(2.0.2.2.2)*
Material on hire
AVV 119

Sonet XLII (1985)   10'

Text: William Shakespeare
Soloist: baritone
str qrt
Score **AVV 129**

7 Textos de Miguel Angel Bustos (1991)   11'

Soloist: soprano
acc-vc
AVV 154

Three Songs (1977)   18'

Text: Drayton/Sidney/Anon
Soloist: tenor
*1(pic,afl).1(ca).1(Ebcl).bcl.1-0.0.atbn.0-
timp(perc).2perc-hpd(hammondorg).hp-
str(0.0.2.2.1)*
Material on hire
AVV

Choral Works

...im Wind gesprochen

(1984-85)   22'

Spiritual Music
Text: various
Soloists: organ, soprano, 2 speakers
Chorus: mixed
*1(pic).2.2(Ebcl,bcl)0-0.3.3.0-timp.3perc-
hp-str(0.0.4.3.3)*
Material on hire
AVV

Karfreitags-Sonett (1986)   8'

Text: Andreas Gryphius
Chorus: mixed a cappella
Score **SKR 20016**

4 Madrigals (1985)   10'

Chorus: mixed a cappella (5 prt)
Score **SKR 20015**

Symphonic Fragment

(1979-80)   17'

Text: Friedrich Hölderlin
Soloists: tenor, baritone, bass
Chorus: mixed
*3(pic,afl).3(ob d´am,ca).3(Ebcl,bcl).2.cbn-
4.4(Dtpt).3.1-timp.3perc-cel.hp-
str(12.10.8.6.5)*
Material on hire
AVV

Todesfuge (1972)   15'

Text: Paul Celan
Soloist: baritone
Chorus: mixed
org
Score **SKR 20022** / Parts **SKR 20022-11
(organ)**

Both, Heinz
b.1924

Chamber & Instrumental Works

Captain Morgan's March and six other Pieces

4cl
ED 10775

Dancing Clarinet

10 easy pieces
cl/tsax-pno
ED 8484

Dancing Flute

10 easy pieces
fl-pno
ED 8485

Dancing Saxophone

10 easy pieces
asax-pno
ED 8486

Let's play together

12 nette Duette für Klarinette
clarinet solo
ED 8001

Brandts-Buys, Jan
1868-1933

Stage Works

Der Mann im Mond

(1933)   full evening

Opera in 2 Acts
Text: Bruno Warden/J.M. Welleminsky
Material on hire
SM

Die Schneider von Schönau

(1916)   full evening

Comic Opera in 3 Acts
Text: Bruno Warden/J.M. Welleminsky
Material on hire
Vocal score **ED 3201**

Orchestral Works

Bilder aus dem Kinderleben

18'
2.2.Acl.2-4.3.3.1-timp.3perc-hp-str
Material on hire
SM

Brauel, Henning
b.1940

Stage Works

Die Kaiserin von Neufundland (1978)   75'

Pantomime in 3 Scenes
Text: Frank Wedekind
Material on hire
AVV

Orchestral Works

Les Fenêtres simultanées

(1975)   11'

1.1.1.1-2.1.1.0-str(7.0.3.2.1)
Material on hire
AVV

Notturno (1987)   15'

from "Lyric Pieces" (1987-89)
*2(pic).afl.1.3.bcl.1-3.1.1.0-timp.perc-
pno.2hp-str(9.0.6.6.5)*
Material on hire
AVV

Optophon   18'

*4.2.ca.2.2bcl(cl).2.cbn-4.4.2tbtbn.btbn.1-
str(12.10.6.6.4)*
Material on hire
AVV

4 Orchestral Pieces (1973)   16'

*3(pic).3(ca).3(Ebcl,bcl).3-4.3.3.1-
timp.3perc-hp-str(12.10.8.6.4)*
Material on hire
AVV

Symphonic Paraphrases

(1966)   20'

*3(2pic).2.ca.2.bcl.2.cbn-4.4.2tbtbn.
btbn.cbtbn.0-2timp.4perc-pno.hp-str*
Material on hire
AVV

Infoline · e-Mail
Schott Musik International
Mainz: Schott.Musik.com@T-Online.de
London: 101627.166@compuserve.com

Brauel, Henning

b. Hanover 1.7.1940

Brauel began to study music at the Hanover Conservatory in 1958, took his final exams in piano 1962 and composition lessons with Alfred Koerppen and Heinrich Sutermeister in 1962/63. In 1964, he went on to the Salzburg Mozarteum where he continued his composition studies with Hans Werner Henze until 1968. Today, Henning Brauel lives in Aalen, Germany, where he composes and teaches music at the local music school.

Concertos

Mercurio (1977)   22'

Rondo
Soloist: violin
str(5.0.3.2.1)
Material on hire
AVV

Notturno (1968)   13'

Soloist: bassoon
*1.1.1.0-1.0.0.0-hpd(pno).hp.gtr-
str(6.0.0.3.0)*
Material on hire
AVV

Chamber & Instrumental Works

String Quartet No.2 (1968)   16'

Score **AVV 40** / Parts **AVV 41**

Solo Voice(s) and Instrument(s)/ Orchestra

Ophelia (1972)   16'

Text: Arthur Rimbaud
Soloist: soprano
*3(2pic).3(ca).3(Ebcl,bcl).asx.2.cbn-
4.0.atbn/btpt.ttbn.tbtbn.btbn.0-timp.3perc-
pno(cel).hp.egtr-str(10.8.6.6.4)*
Material on hire
AVV

Brehme, Hans
1904-1957

Stage Works

Liebe ist teuer (1950)   full evening

Opera in 2 Acts
Text: K.E. Jaroscheck/Franz Clemens
Material on hire
SM

Der Uhrmacher von Straßburg, Op. 36

(1941)   full evening

Opera in 3 Acts
Text: Paul Ginthum
Material on hire
SM

Orchestral Works

Liebe ist teuer, Op. 39 (1950) 9'

Overture
2(pic).2(ca).2.2-3.2.1.0-timp.perc-hp-str
Material on hire
SM

Triptychon, Op. 33 (1937)   31'

*3(pic).2(ca).2(bcl).2.cbn-4.3.3.1-timp.perc-
[cel/pno]-str*
Material on hire
SM

Variationen über eine mittel-alterliche Weise, Op. 38

(1944)   34'

*3(pic).2.ca.2(Ebcl,Acl).bcl.2.cbn-4.3.3.1-
timp.perc-hp-str*
Material on hire
SM

Concertos

Piano Concerto, Op. 32

(1931-36)   27'

Soloist: piano
*2(pic)2.(ca)2(Dcl,asax).2.cbn-4.3.3.1-
3timp.2perc-str(12.10.6.6.4)*
Material on hire
SM

Chamber & Instrumental Works

Concert Suite, Op. 37 (1942)

pno
ED 3953

Bresgen, Cesar
1913-1988

Stage Works

Brüderlein Hund (1953)   60'

Opera for the Youth in 3 Scenes
Text: Ludwig Andersen
Material on hire
Vocal score **ED 4315**

Der Igel als Bräutigam

(1950)   full evening

Opera in 5 Scenes
Text: Ludwig Andersen/Cesar Bresgen
Material on hire
Vocal score **ED 4302/4302-01**

Der Mann im Mond

(1958)   full evening

Opera in 6 Scenes
Text: Ludwig Andersen/Cesar Bresgen
Material on hire
Vocal score **ED 4980**

Die schlaue Müllerin (1943) 30'

Dance-Song Play in 1 Act
Text: Cesar Bresgen
Material on hire
Vocal score **ED 2864**

Das Urteil des Paris

(1943)   full evening

Musical Comedy in 1 Act
Text: Otto Reuther
Material on hire
Vocal score **ED 2867**

Bresgen, Cesar

b. Florence 16.10.1913, d. Salzburg 7.4.1988

A much admired educationalist and composer of youth music, Bresgen studied composition in Munich from 1930 to 1936, and later attended composition seminars with Hindemith in 1947 and 1950. Long associated with the Mozarteum, Salzburg, he was a skilled improviser and fluent composer of "Gebrauchsmusik". Strongly influenced by folksong and folkdance, he used its strong, simple melodies to excellent effect in a number of successful stage works for young people and professional performers.

Orchestral Works

Tänze vom Schwarzen Meer

(1956)   25'

2(pic).2.2(bcl).2-2.2.2.0-timp.perc-pno-str
Material on hire
SM

Concertos

Cello Concerto in D   (1940)   26'

Venezianisches Konzert
Soloist: cello
2.0.2.2-0.0.0.0-str
Material on hire
SM

Chamber Concerto   (1965)   15'

Soloist: guitar
1.0.0.1-1.1.0.0-str
Material on hire
Piano reduction **GA 226**

Jagdkonzert   (1938)   16'

Soloist: violin
2.1.2.2-1.0.0.0-str(0.0.0.0.1)
Material on hire
Piano reduction **ED 3635**

Mayenkonzert   (1938)   16'

Soloist: piano
1.2.0.0-0.0.0.0-str
Material on hire
Piano reduction **ED 2876**

Piano Concerto   (1951)   20'

Soloist: piano
1.1.1.1-2.1.1.0-2timp.[perc]-str
Material on hire
SM

Chamber & Instrumental Works

Flute Sonata   (1944)   14'

fl-pno
FTR 18

Malinconia   9'

guitar solo
GA 238

Morgenmusik   (1963)   4'

soprec.3srec.3arec-timp-axyl.cymb/trgl
Score **B 144** / Parts **B 144-11 (-20)**

Sonatina   (1950)   7'

srec-pno
ED 4513

Sonatine über altdeutsche Liebeslieder   (1939)

2arec-pno
ED 4513

Solo Voice(s) and Instrument(s)/ Orchestra

Kleine Musik über zwei altdeutsche Volkslieder   9'

Soloist: soprano
2arec-pno
ED 2654

Choral Works

Als ich noch ein armer Knecht war

Chorus: male a cappella
C 42626

Die alte Lokomotive   (1951)   40'

Text: Ernst Gärtner
Chorus: female/children's
srec/arec-glsp.xyl.perc-pno
Score **ED 4884** / Parts **ED 4884-11 (-14)** /
Vocal score **ED 4884-01**

Armer kleiner Tanzbär

(1959)   50'

Text: E. Gärtner/C. Bresgen
Soloist: voice
Chorus: children's
pno-vn-rec-perc-xyl.glsp
Parts **ED 5173-11 (-15)** / Vocal score **ED 5173**

Arra alá, drunten in Baranya   (1984)   2'

from "Drei Balkanlieder"
Text: Cesar Bresgen
Chorus: mixed a cappella
C 45369

Bäckerlied   (1952)   3'

Text: A. Teuber
Chorus: male a cappella
C 38088

Die Bettlerhochzeit   (1947/62)   15'

Text: Cesar Bresgen
Chorus: children's
rec-perc-[glsp-pno]
B 104 / Score and parts **ED 5244**

Christkindl Kumedi   (1960)   75'

Sacred Comedy Play from Bavaria
Soloists: 6 speakers
Chorus: mixed.children's
bfl(sfl,afl).ob.timp.perc.gtr.str
Score **ED 5443-10** / Parts **ED 5443-11 (-28)** /
Vocal score **ED 5443**

Den Letzten beißt der Hund

(1952)   2'

Text: Cesar Bresgen
Chorus: male a cappella
C 38525

Das dreifache Gloria   (1967)   12'

Chorus: female/mixed
vn-org-[timp]
Material on sale
Vocal score **ED 5669**

Dreimal rief die Amsel

Chorus: male a cappella
Score **C 42629** / Parts **C 42631-01/-02 (chorus)**

Drunten in Baranya

Chorus: male a cappella
C 42624

Es brennt die grüne Linde

(1984)   2'

from "Drei Balkanlieder"
Text: Cesar Bresgen
Chorus: mixed a cappella
C 45368

Infoline · e-Mail
Schott Musik International
Mainz: Schott.Musik.com@T-Online.de
London: 101627.166@compuserve.com

Es ist ein Ros entsprungen

(1937) 15'

Chorus: mixed
fl-3vn.vc.[db]
Score and parts **ED 2920**

L' Europe curieuse (1968) 30'

Soloist: speaker
Chorus: children's
3srec.arec-gtr-glsp.perc-pno-[tpt/cl.Ctpt-xyl-vn.vc]
Score and parts **B 175**

European Folk and Children's Songs Vols. 1 & 2

(1972)

Soloist: baritone
Chorus: children's
rec-gtr-vn-cl-tpt-[vc]-glsp.perc
Material on sale
Score and parts **B 177 / B 178**

Finstre Nacht (1951)

from "Chöre nach deutschen Volksliedern"
Chorus: male a cappella
C 38159

Für fünfzehn Pfennig (1951)

from "Chöre nach deutschen Volksliedern"
Chorus: male a cappella
C 38158

Glockensprüche (1963)

Chorus: mixed, female
fl-pno-str
Material on hire
SM

Der Goldvogel (1957) 3'

Text: Cesar Bresgen
Chorus: female/children's
Orff-instruments
ED 4875

Hufeisen und Rosen

Chorus: male a cappella
C 42627

Hum fauler Lenz (1952) 2'

Chorus: mixed
CHBL 69

Kantate von der Unruhe des Menschen (1953) 27'

Text: Hiob, Georg Trakl, Cesar Bresgen
Soloists: soprano, tenor
Chorus: mixed
1.0.1.0-1.1.2.0-timp.perc-pno-str
Parts **ED 4519-01** / Vocal score **ED 4519**

Die Kummermühle

Chorus: male a cappella
C 42623

Lino, Leano (1984) 2'

from "Drei Balkanlieder"
Text: Cesar Bresgen
Chorus: mixed a cappella
C 45370

Nachtlied (1951)

from "Chöre nach deutschen Volksliedern"
Chorus: male a cappella
C 38160

Nulla vita sine musica (1954) 6'

Text: Latin
Chorus: mixed a cappella
C 38882

Das Riesenspiel (1941) 12'

Little Scenic Cantata
Chorus: children's
rec/vn-perc
B 119

Ruf und Mahnung 12'

Chorus: mixed/female
fl-pno-strings
ED 5292

Das Schlaraffenland (1955) 30'

Little Scenic Cantata
Chorus: children's (1-3 prt)
srec.arec-xyl.perc-vn-[other instr]
Score **B 130** / Parts **B 130-10 (-15)** / Choral score **B 130-01**

Sonne, Sonne, scheine (1953)

Chorus: children's [a cappella]
[Orff-instruments]
B 115

Der Struwwelpeter (1950) 30'

Chorus: female
rec-xyl.glsp-perc-pno
Score and parts **ED 4235**

Tiertanzburlesken (1979) 25'

Text: E. Rechlin
Chorus: children's (1-3 prt)
pno-[fl.cl-vn.vc]
Score **B 187** / Parts **B 187-11 (-14)** / Choral score **B 187-01**

Uns ist kommen ein liebe Zeit (1954) 20'

Soloist: soprano/tenor
Chorus: female.[mixed]
srec.arec-str trio(1.1.0.1 or 1.0.1.1)-glsp-perc-[pno]
B 127 / Parts **B 127-11 (-16)** / Choral score **B 127-01**

Von Mäusen, Autos und anderen Tieren (1972)

Chorus: children's
rec-glsp-gtr
B 179

Wanderschaft (1959) 2'

Text: Hermann Hesse
Chorus: female a cappella
CHBL 580

Weinschröter, schlag die Trommel (1951)

from "Chöre nach deutschen Volksliedern"
Chorus: male a cappella
C 38157

Der Weizen muß reifen

Chorus: male a cappella
C 42629

Wenn sich junge Herzen heben (1959) 4'

Text: H. Grahl
Chorus: male/mixed a cappella
CHBL 200/357

Wer zum Teufel wird sich sorgen

Chorus: male a cappella
C 42625

Brod, Max
1884-1968

Orchestral Works

2 Israelische Bauerntänze, Op. 30 9'

2.2.2.2-4.2.2.0-timp.perc-cel.hp-str
Material on hire
AVV

Brouwer, Leo
b.1939

Orchestral Works

Dos conceptos del tiempo

(1965) 11-12'

for Orchestra
1(pic).2.ca.2.bcl.0 0.0.0-cel.pno.org
Material on hire
AVV

Exaedros I (1969) 45'

soloists & orchestration flexible
Material on hire
AVV 48

Sonograma II (1964) 15'

3.0.0.0-0.0.0.0-8perc-cel(hpd).pno.hp.gtr-str
Material on hire
AVV

Concertos

Exaedros II (1970) 30'

Soloist: percussion
Group 1:6.0.0.0-3.3.0.0-6timp.perc-str(6.0.3.3.3)
Group 2:0.2.2.2-3.0.2.0-perc-str(6.0.3.3.3)
[two conductors]
Material on hire
AVV

Brouwer, Leo

b. Havana 1.3.1939

Though trained in the USA at the Julliard School and the Hartt College of Music, Brouwer is a revolutionary artist whose mature work dates from the advent of the new Cuban society of Fidel Castro. Always open to avant-garde influence, he has emulated the example of Nono, Henze and other left-wing composers who have visited his homeland. He has composed extensively for his own instrument, the guitar, on which he is an internationally acknowledged virtuoso.

Chamber & Instrumental Works

3 Apuntes   8'

guitar solo
GA 426

Canticum   (1968)   5'

guitar solo
GA 424

Danza Caracteristica para el "Quitate de la Acera"   (1957) 3'

guitar solo
GA 422

Elogio de la Danza para Guitarra   (1964)   6'

guitar solo
GA 425

La Espiral eterna para Guitarra   (1971)   7'

guitar solo
GA 423

Memorias de "El Cimarrón"

(1970)   13'

(Hans Werner Henze)
guitar solo
ED 6485

Sonata "piano e forte"

(1970)   var.

pno
AVV 99

Variantes   (1962)

solo perc
BAT 12

Choral Works

Cantigas del Tiempo Nuevo

(1969)   10-14'

Soloist: speaker
Chorus: mixed, children's
perc-pno.hp
alt. version (1971): pic.1.1.1.1-1.0.0.0-
3perc-pno.hpd.hp-str
Material on hire
AVV

Brugk, Hans Melchior

b.1909

Choral Works

Bläsermesse, Op. 30   16'

Chorus: mixed
2tpt.thn.euph(tbn).2tbn
Score ED 5469 / Parts ED 5469-10 / Vocal score ED 5469-01

German Te Deum, Op. 15   21'

Text: Psalms, Robert Erbertseder
Chorus: mixed
0.0.0.0-2.3.3.0-timp-org-str
alt. version: 2.2.2.2.cbn-2.3.3.0-timp-str
Material on hire
SM

Brüll, Ignaz
1846-1907

Orchestral Works

Serenade in E Major, Op. 36

(1864)   15'

3.2.2.2-3.2.0.0-timp-str
Material on hire
SM

Bryars, Gavin
b.1943

Stage Works

Medea   (1982/86/95)   150'

Opera in 5 Acts
Text: after Euripides
Material on hire
SL

Orchestral Works

Jesus' Blood Never Failed Me Yet   (1971)   Var.

digital tape-flexible ensemble, based on the following: 1.1+/glsp.1.bcl.1-4.2.1.1-
str qrt.dbI.dbII+/gtr-hp.org-vib+/cel
Score ED 12480 (+DAT)

The Sinking of the Titanic

(1969)   Var.

flexible - possible materials inlude digital tapes,str ens,perc,low brass,brass qrt, bcl,taped speech,keybd,music box
Material on hire
SL

Concertos

By the Vaar   (1987)   20'

Soloist: double bass
bcl-perc-str(3.3.3.2.1/5.5.5.5.3)
Material on hire
SL

Cello Concerto   (1995)   35'

Soloist: cello
2(pic).1.ca.2(bcl).2(cbn)-2.0.0.0-2perc-hp-
str
Material on hire
SL

The East Coast   (1994)   20'

Soloist: bass oboe
bn-2hn-hp-str(6.6.4.4.2)
Material on hire
SL

Bryars, Gavin

b. Goole, Yorkshire, 16.1.1943

Gavin Bryars has emerged as one of Britain's most distinctive and original composers. Over the last 20 years, his compositions have ranged widely from the legendary multi-media work "The Sinking of the Titanic" (1969) and the opera "Medea", directed by Robert Wilson at the Lyon and Paris Opera Houses in 1984, to commissions for leading performers, including the Arditti Quartet, the Balanescu Quartet, the Hilliard Ensemble, saxophonist John Harle, jazz guitarist Bill Frisell, bassist Charlie Haden and the BBC Symphony Orchestra. Among the choreographers who have used Gavin Bryars music are William Forsythe, Lucinda Childs, Maguy Marin, Graeme Murphy, Siobhan Davies and Laurie Booth. His numerous albums include "Three Viennese Dances", "After the Requiem", and "Jesus Blood Never Failed me Yet" which topped the classical music charts and was nominated for the 1993 Mercury Music Prize. The Gavin Bryars Band, led by the composer himself, regularly undertakes international tours.

The Green Ray (1991) 20'

Soloist: soprano saxophone
1(pic).1.ca.1(bcl).2(cbn)-2.flhn.1.0-perc-pno-str(6.5.4.4.2; N.B. 21 divisi essential)
Material on hire
Study score ED 12463

The North Shore (1994) 14'

Soloist: viola
hp/pno-perc-str
Material on hire
SL

The North Shore (1995) 14'

Soloist: cello
hp/pno-perc-str
Material on hire
SL

Chamber & Instrumental Works

After Handel's "Vesper"

(1995) 10'

hpd
Manuscript score on sale
SL

After the Requiem (1990) 16'

egtr-2va.vc
Material on sale
SL

Alaric I or II (1989) 15'

sax qrt
score and parts ED 12476

Allegrasco (1983) 20'

Soloist: clarinet/sopranino saxophone
vn-egtr-db-2perc-pno
Material on hire
SL

Allegrasco (1983) 20'

ssax/cl-pno
ED 12468

The Archangel Trip (1993) 15'

2pan-pipes.2asax.bcl-2 sampling keybd.octopads(with sampler)-5-string vn.5-string vc-egtr.ebass
Material on hire
SL

Aus den letzten Tagen

(1992) 15'

2vn.vc-cl(bcl)-2perc-keybd
Material on hire
SL

The Cross-Channel Ferry

(1979) 12'

cl.bcl-thn-vib/marimbI-marimbII.bmarimb/marimbIII-pno-steel drums and chocolo-va.db+/tuba
Material on hire
SL

3 Elegies for Nine Clarinets

(1993) 19'

4cl.2Ebcl.2bcl.cbcl
alt. version: cl(bcl)-digital tape
Material on hire
SL

4 Elements (1990) 30'

asax.bcl.flhn.hn.tbn-pno.keybd-db(amp)-taped voice/alto-2perc
Material on hire
Study score ED 12479

Les Fiançailles (1983) 20'

Soloist: piano
str qnt-2perc
Material on hire
SL

"In Nomine" (after Purcell)

(1995) 10'

viol consort
Material on hire
SL

Die letzten Tage (1992) 28'

2vn
ED 12472

My First Homage (1978) 15'

2pno
ED 12471

The North Shore (1993) 12'

va-pno
ED 12473

The Old Tower of Löbenicht

(1987) 15'

Soloist: violin/viola
bcl-thn/tbn-vc.db-2perc-pno.egtr
alt. version (Roger Heaton and Dave Smith): pno-bcl-vn
Material on hire
Study score ED 12474

One Last Bar Then Joe Can Sing (1994) 15'

A Homage to Deagan
5perc
Material on hire
SL

Out of Zaleski's Gazebo

(1977) 12'

2pno (6/8hnd)
ED 12469

The South Downs (1995) 12'

vc-pno
Manuscript score on sale
SL

The Squirrel and the Ricketty-Racketty Bridge

(1971) Var.

2gtr(1 player), or multiples of this
Material on sale
SL

String Quartet No.1 (1985) 23'

'Between the National and the Bristol'
Score ED 12464 / Parts ED 12464-01

String Quartet No.2 (1990) 25'

Score ED 12467 / Parts ED 12467-01

Sub Rosa (1986) 10'

cl.rec-vib-pno-vn.db
ED 12478

Suite from "Wonderlawn"

(1994)   25'

egtr-va.vc.db(amp)
Material on sale
SL

Viennese Dance No.1 (M.H.)

(1985)   18'

1/2hn-6perc-[str trio]
Material on hire
SL

Solo Voice(s)/Voice(s) and Piano/Guitar

The Black River   (1991)   15'

Text: Jules Verne
soprano-org
ED 12462

Glorious Hill   (1988)   15'

Text: Pico della Mirandola
4 male voices (male alto.2 tenors.baritone)
ED 12461

Solo Voice(s) and Instrument(s)/ Orchestra

The Adnan Songbook

(1992-96)   40'

Text: Etel Adnan
Soloist: soprano
cl.bcl-gtr.egtr-2va.vc.db
Material on hire
SL

Doctor Ox's Experiment (Epilogue)   (1988)   22'

Text: Blake Morrison after Jules Verne
Soloist: soprano
*bcl-2perc-pno-egtr-str(1.1.1.1.1/3.3.3.2.1
min. db amplified with effects pedals)*
Material on hire
SL

Effarene   (1984)   38'

Text: Curie/Adnan/Pope Leo XIII/Verne
Soloists: soprano, mezzo-soprano
2pno.6perc
Material on hire
SL

Incipit Vita Nova   (1989)   6'

Text: Dante/Pico della Mirandola
Soloist: alto
vn.va.vc
ED 12465

A Man in a Room, Gambling

(1992)   Var.

String Quartet No.4
Text: Juan Muñoz
str qrt-pre recorded tape
Material on hire
SL

Pico's Flight   (1986)   18'

Text: Pico della Mirandola/Francis Bacon
Soloist: soprano
*pic.2.2(ca).2.bcl.1.cbn-3.2.2.0-timp.3perc-
pno-str(min: 5.5.5.5.3)*
*Alt chamber version :
1(pic).1.ca(ob).1(bcl).2(cbn)-2.0.0.0-perc-
pno-str*
Material on hire
SL

The White Lodge   (1992)   17'

Text: Jules Verne
Soloist: low contralto
2vn.va.vc.2db-2perc-elec.keybd
Material on hire
SL

The White Lodge   (1991)   17'

Text: Jules Verne
Soloist: mezzo-soprano
electronics-digital tape
SL

Choral Works

Cadman Requiem   (1989)   25'

Text: various
Soloists: 4 male voices (male alto, 2 tenors,
baritone)
2va.vc.[db]
ED 12475

On Photography   (1983/95)   18'

Text: Pope Leo XIII
Chorus: mixed
harm.pno
SL

The War in Heaven   (1993)   45'

Text: Genesis A/Chaikin/Shepard
Soloists: soprano, male alto
Chorus: mixed, semi-chorus
*3(pic).2(ca).2.bcl.2(cbn)-4.2(flhn).3.1-
3perc-hp-str*
Material on hire
SL

Burkhard, Willy
1900-1955

Orchestral Works

Concerto, Op. 50   (1937)   20'

str
Material on hire
Study score **ED 6099**

Fantasy, Op. 40   (1934)   15'

str
Material on hire
SM

Kleine Serenade, Op. 42

(1935)   8'

str
Material on hire
Study score **ED 6098**

Chamber & Instrumental Works

Choralvariationen No.1, Op. 28/1   (1930)   18'

Aus tiefer Not (H.L. Haßler)
organ solo
ED 2241

Choralvariationen No.2, Op. 28/2   (1930)   15'

In dulci jubilo (H.L. Haßler)
organ solo
ED 2242

Fantasy, Op. 32   (1931)   12'

organ solo
ED 2243

Sonatina, Op. 45   (1936)   9'

vn-pno
ED 2621

Solo Voice(s) and Instrument(s)/ Orchestra

Das ewige Brausen, Op. 46

(1936)   25'

Text: Knut Hamsun
Soloist: bass
1.1.0.0-0.1.0.0-timp.perc-pno-str
Material on hire
Piano reduction **ED 2973**

Herbst, Op. 36   (1932)   13'

Text: Christian Morgenstern
Soloist: soprano
vn.vc-pno
Score and parts **ED 2975**

Choral Works

Psalm 93, Op. 49   (1937)   6'

Der Herr ist König
Chorus: mixed
org
Score **ED 2622** / Choral score **ED 2622-01**

Te Deum, Op. 33 (1931) 10'
Chorus: mixed
tpt.tbn.timp.org
Material on hire
SM

Burton, Stephen Douglas
b.1943

Solo Voice(s) and Instrument(s)/ Orchestra

Ode to a Nightingale (1963) 23'
Text: John Keats
Soloist: soprano
fl.hp-str
Material on hire
AVV

Busch, Adolf
1891 - 1952

Orchestral Works

Capriccio, Op. 46 14'
2.2.2.2-2.2.0.0-timp-str
Material on hire
Eu

Casanova, André
b.1919

Orchestral Works

Symphony No.2, Op. 7
(1952) 22'
1.1.ca.2(bcl).1-2.2.1.0-timp.perc-cel.pno.hp-str
Material on hire
AVV

Casken, John
b.1949

Stage Works

Golem (1986-88) 95'
Chamber Opera
Text: Pierre Audi/John Casken
Material on hire
Vocal score **ED 12379** / Libretto **ED 12379-01**

Orchestral Works

Darting the Skiff (1992-93) 17'
str
Material on hire
SL

Maharal Dreaming (1989) 12'
2(pic).2(ca).2.2-2.2.0.0-perc-str(8.6.4.3.2)
Material on hire
Study score **ED 12374**

Orion Over Farne (1984) 20'
3(pic).3.3(bcl).3-4.2.3.1-timp.3perc-cel.pno-str(16.14.12.10.8)
Material on hire
Study score **ED 12335**

Sortilège (1995-96) 20'
3(pic).2.ca.bob.2.bcl.ssax.2.cbn-4.2.flhn.3.1-timp.3perc-pno(cel).hp-str
Material on hire
SL

Tableaux des Trois Ages
(1976-77) 18'
3.3.3.3-4.3.3.1-timp.3perc-str
Material on hire
SL

Vaganza (1985) 27'
1(pic,afl).1(ca).1(Ebcl,bcl,ssax).1(cbn)-1.1.1.0-perc-hp.org-str(1.1.1.1.1)
Material on hire
Study score **ED 12326**

Casken, John

b. Barnsley, Yorkshire 15.7.1949

Combining a keen musical imagination with the sense and instincts of a painter, John Casken has fashioned a series of remarkable scores in which evocations of landscape and atmosphere combine to powerful effect. The harsh terrain of Northumbria in the North of England has inspired the orchestral tone poem "Orion over Farne" and "To Fields We Do Not Know" for unaccompanied chorus. In the scena "Firewhirl" and his first opera "Golem", legend and folk ritual form the basis of impressive dramatic structures that confront the issues of creation, life and death. Even Casken's chamber music, including string quartets and ensemble works, have a strong identity of place. He remains at all times an unashamed poet in sound.

Concertos

Cello Concerto (1990-91) 20'

Soloist: cello
2(2pic,afl).2(ca).2(ssax,bcl).0-2.2.0.0-timp-str(8.6.4.4.2)
Material on hire
Study score **ED 12394**

Erin (1982-83) 13'

Soloist: double bass
2ob-2hn-str(8.6.4.4.1)
Material on hire
SL

Masque (1982) 24'

Soloist: oboe
2hn-str(6.4.3.2.1)
Material on hire
Study score **ED 12156**

Violin Concerto (1994-95) 30'

Soloist: violin
3(pic,afl).2.ca.2.bcl.2.cbn-4.2.3.1-timp.2perc-hp-str
Material on hire
Study score **ED 12497**

Chamber & Instrumental Works

A Belle Pavine (1980) 12'

vn-tape
Material on sale
SL

Amarantos (1977-78) 16'

1(afl).1.1(bcl).0-1.1.0.0-perc-pno-va.vc
Material on hire
Study score **ED 11483**

Clarion Sea (1984-85) 13'

2tpt.hn.tbn.tuba
Material on sale
SL

Cor d'oeuvre (1993) 7'

Soloist: horn
pno.hp-6db
Material on sale
SL

Infanta Marina (1993-94) 16'

fl.ca.cl-hn-hp-va.db
Material on hire or sale
SL

Kagura (1972-73) 18'

2.2.2.asax.2-2.2.0.0
Material on hire
SL

Music for a Tawny-Gold Day

(1975-76) 10'

asax.bcl-va-pno
Score **ED 11401**

Music for the Crabbing Sun

(1974) 10'

fl.ob-vc-hpd
ED 11400

Piano Quartet (1989-90) 16'

vn.va.vc-pno
ED 12414

Salamandra (1986) 16'

2pno
ED 12375

A Spring Cadenza (1994) 7'

cello solo
ED 12490

String Quartet No.1

(1981-82) 15'

Study score **ED 12071** / Parts **ED 12071-01***

String Quartet No.2

(1993-94) 16'

Material on sale
SL

Thymehaze (1976) 10'

arec-pno
TMR 6

Solo Voice(s)/Voice(s) and Piano/Guitar

Ia Orana, Gauguin (1978) 16'

soprano-pno
ED 11460

Sharp Thorne (1991-92) 8'

4 solo voices
Manuscript score on sale
SL

Solo Voice(s) and Instrument(s)/ Orchestra

Firewhirl (1979-80) 16'

A setting of words by G. MacBeth
Soloist: soprano
1.0.1.1-1.0.0.0-str(1.0.1.1.0)
Material on hire
Study score **ED 11491**

Still Mine (1991-92) 25'

Text: various
Soloist: baritone
3(2pic).2.ca.2.bcl.3(cbn)-4.3.3.1-timp.perc-cel.hp-str
Material on hire
Study score **ED 12419**

Choral Works

A Gathering (1991) 5'

Chorus: mixed a cappella
ED 12421

The Land of Spices (1990) 5'

Chorus: mixed a cappella
ED 12421

Sunrising (1993) 7'

Text: Sylvia Townsend Warner
Chorus: mixed a cappella
ED 12421

To Fields We Do Not Know

(1983-84)   22'

Chorus: mixed a cappella
ED 12285

Castelnuovo-Tedesco, Mario

1895-1968

Concertos

Guitar Concerto No.1 in D Major, Op. 99 (1939)   15'

Soloist: guitar
1.1.2.1-1.0.0.0-timp-str(2.2.2.2.1)
Score **ED 153** / Parts **ED 153-10 (-15)** / Piano reduction **GA 166**

Guitar Concerto No.2 in C Major, Op. 160 (1953)   25'

Soloist: guitar
2(pic).1.2.1-2.1.0.0-timp.perc-hp-str
Score **ED 137** / Parts **ED 137-10 (-15)** / Piano reduction **GA 240**

Sérénade in D minor, Op. 118 (1943)   21'

Soloist: guitar
1.1.2.1-1.1.0.0-timp.perc-str
Material on hire
Piano reduction **GA 167**

Chamber & Instrumental Works

Fantasia, Op. 145 (1950)   10'

gtr-pno
GA 170

Guitar Sonata in D Major

(1934)   15'

guitar solo
GA 149

Quintet in F Major, Op. 143

(1950)   27'

gtr-str qrt
Study score **ED 4578** / Parts **GA 198**

Rondo in E minor, Op. 129

(1946)   10'

guitar solo
GA 168

Suite in D minor, Op. 133

(1947)   16'

guitar solo
GA 169

Castelnuovo-Tedesco, Mario

b. Florence 3.4.1895, d. Hollywood 16.3.1968

Castelnuovo-Tedesco, a native of Florence, was a romantic composer in the tradition of Respighi and Richard Strauss, and a prolific writer of orchestral and stage works - many inspired by Shakespeare. An important influence was the composer's Jewish heritage, witnessed in several choral works based on Old Testament texts and in a "Sacred Service" for the Sabbath Eve. His music is warm and graceful, often virtuosic, and direct in its appeal to performers and audience.

Tonadilla auf den Namen Andrés Segovia, Op. 170/5

(1954-67)   4'

guitar solo
GA 191

Variations à travers les Siècles (1932)   10'

guitar solo
GA 137

Castiglioni, Niccolò

b.1932

Stage Works

Sweet (1967)   full evening

Opera in 1 Act
Text: Niccolò Castiglioni
Material on hire
AVV

Orchestral Works

Caractères (1964)   15'

3(pic).3.3(Ebcl).3(cbn)-3.3.3.0-timp.4perc-pno-str
Material on hire
AVV

Concerto (1963)   6'

3.3.0.3-3.3.0.0-timp-str
(possibly:15.15.12.9.3)
Material on hire
AVV

Décors (1962)   11'

2pic.2.4.4.4-4.4.Bachtpt4.0-3perc-cel.pno-str(12.12.10.6.4)
Material on hire
AVV

Rondels (1960-61)   13'

4(2pic).4.4(bcl).0-4.4.4.0-5perc-cel.pno.2hp-12vn
Material on hire
AVV

Concertos

Le Chant du Signe (1967)   35'

Soloist: flute (piccolo)
0.2.2(bcl).0-2.2.2.0-timp.perc-vib.cel.pno.hp-str
Material on hire
AVV

Consonante (1962)   7'

Soloist: flute
1.0.2.0-0.1.0.0-perc-pno-str(1.1.1.0.0)
AVV 46 / Study score **AVV 72**

Ode (1966)   15'

Soloists: 2 pianos
3.3(ca).3.3-3.3.0.0-timp.perc-2pno
Material on hire
AVV

Castiglioni, Niccolò

b. Milan 17.7.1932

Studied in Milan at the conservatory with Giorgio Federico Ghedini and took master courses with Gulda, Zecchi and Blacher at the Salzburg Mozarteum. Apart from his compositional work, he has been known as a concert pianist since 1953. In 1966, he was invited to Buffalo by the Rockefeller Foundation. Until 1969, he was a visiting professor at various universities in the USA. Since then, he has been living in Italy.

Chamber & Instrumental Works

Alef (1965)

oboe solo
AVV 12

Masques (1966-67) 15'

A book of dances, chorales, symphonies and phantasies
12 instruments
Score **AVV 37** / Parts **AVV 37-10**

Sinfonie Guerriere et Amorose (1967) 30'

organ solo
AVV 33

Solo Voice(s) and Instrument(s)/ Orchestra

Canzoni (1966) 17'

Text: Ugo di Massa/Giacomo da Lentini
Soloist: soprano
2.0.0.0-2.2.0.0-perc-pno
alt. version: 2fl/fl.ob-perc-pno.harm
Material on hire
AVV

A Solemn Music I (1963) 10'

Text: John Milton
Soloist: soprano
2(pic).1.2(Ebcl).0-0.1.0.0-timp.2perc-pno.hp-str(4.0.3.2.1)
Material on hire
AVV

A Solemn Music II (1965) 14'

Text: John Milton
Soloist: soprano
1(pic).0.3(Ebcl).0-0.1.0.0-5perc-pno.hp-str(4.0.3.2.1)
Material on hire
Study score **AVV 77**

Sweet (1967)

Text: Niccolò Castiglioni
Soloist: bass
3.3.3.3-3.3.3.0-bells-pno
Material on hire
AVV

Choral Works

Anthem (1966) 25'

Chorus: mixed
3(pic).3(ca).3(Ebcl).3-3.3(Bachtpt).3.0-timp.perc-vib.cel.pno.[harm]-str
Material on hire
AVV

Aria (1968) 25'

From "Three miracle Plays"
Text: William Shakespeare
Soloists: soprano, tenor
Chorus: mixed
1.1.1.0-2.2.2.0-perc-pno.harm-vn
Material on hire
SM

Gyro (1963) 12'

Text: Latin
Soloists: mixed (32 prt)
4fl-4tpt-perc
Material on hire
AVV

3 Miracle Plays (1968) 60'

Text: William Shakespeare/various
Soloists: soprano, 2 tenors
Chorus: mixed
1.1.1.0-2.2.2.0-perc-pno.harm-vn
Material on hire
AVV

Symphony in C (1968-69)

Text: Bob Jonson, Dante, William Shakespeare
Chorus: mixed double
4.4.4.4-4.4.4.0-perc-cel.4pno(4hpd).hp-str
Material on hire
AVV (Co-prod: Ed. Suvini Zerboni)

Chisholm, Erik

1904-1965

Concertos

Piano Concerto No.2 (1951) 31'

On Hindustani Themes
Soloist: piano
3.2.2.2-4.2.3.0-timp.3perc-cel-str
Material on hire
SL

Ciry, Michel

b.1919

Orchestral Works

Pietà (1950) 11'

3.3.3.3-4.4.3.1-timp.perc-pno-str
alt. version: str
Material on hire
SL

Stèle pour un Héros, Op. 43

(1949) 8'

str
Material on hire
SL

Concertos

Piano Concerto (1948) 18'

Soloist: piano
2.2.2.2-2.2.3.1-timp.perc
Material on hire
SL

Chamber & Instrumental Works

Ballade No. 1, Op. 42 (1949) 6'

pno
ED 12069*

Capriccio, Op. 52

asax-pno
ED 10234*

Cooke, Arnold

b.1906

Concertos

Recorder Concerto (1957)   15'

Soloist: soprano recorder
str
Material on hire
Piano reduction **ED 10634**

Chamber & Instrumental Works

Qua (1964)

arec-vn.vc
SL

Rondo in B Major (1952)   4'

hn-pno
ED 10231

Serial Theme and Variations

alto recorder solo
ED 11666

Suite

arec-pno
SL

Cowie, Edward

b.1943

Stage Works

Commedia, Op. 12

(1976-78)   140'

Opera in 4 Acts
Text: David Starsmeare
Material on hire
SL

Orchestral Works

Atlas (1986)   35'

A practical guide through the Symphony
orchestra
*3(pic,afl).2.ca.2(Ebcl).bcl(asax).2.cbn-
4.3(flhn,Dtpt).3.1-timp.3perc-
pno(cel/hpd).hp-str*
Material on hire
SL

Cowie, Edward

b. Birmingham 17.8.1943

**Painter and composer Edward Cowie has
poured his love of nature, and in particular
the landscapes of Lancashire and the
Australian outback, into dark-hued, expres-
sionistic orchestral and choral works. A
noted ornithologist, he has also used bird-
song in his compositions, and is a much
sought-after teacher and educationist.**

Cathedral Music (1977)   25'

4hn.3tpt.3tbn.2tuba
Material on hire
SL

Concerto for Orchestra

(1982)   35'

*pic.1.afl.2.3.3-4.3.3.1-timp.3perc-
cel/hpd.pno.hp-str*
Material on hire
SL

Fifteen Minute Australia

(1984)   15'

*pic.2.2.ca.2.bcl.2-4.3.3.1-timp.2perc-
pno.hp-str*
Material on hire
SL

Leonardo, Op. 20 (1981-82)   25'

2(pic,afl).2(ca).2(Ebcl,bcl).2-2.0.0.0-str
Material on hire
SL

L' Or de la Trompette d'Été

(1977)   20'

str(8.8.8.8.4)
Material on hire
SL

Symphony (1983)   35'

"The American"
*3.2.3.ssax.tsax.3-4.3.3.1-timp.2perc-
pno(cel).hp-str*
Material on hire
SL

Concertos

Clarinet Concerto

(1972-73/75)   23'

Soloist: clarinet
*0.0.0.0-4.3.3.2-timp.3perc-pno(cel).hp-
str(14.14.10.6.4)*
Material on hire
SL

Piano Concerto (1976-77)   35'

Soloist: piano
2(pic,afl).2(ca).2.2-2.0.0.0-cel.hp-str
Material on hire
SL

La Prima Vera (1982-83)   35'

Soloist: harp
*1(pic,afl).2(ca).2(asax,bcl).2-2.0.0.0-
str(6.5.3.3.1)*
Material on hire
SL

Chamber & Instrumental Works

Cartoon Music (1985-86)   18'

pic.cl(asax)-2perc-pno-vn.vc
Material on hire
SL

Commedia Lazzia (1980)   17'

guitar solo
ED 12080*

The Falls of Clyde (1979)   25'

2pno
Manuscript score on sale
SL

Harlequin (1980)   10'

harp solo
ED 12079*

Kelly Passacaglia (1981)   10'

vn.va.vc.db
Material on sale
SL

Kelly Variations (1981)   14'

pno
ED 12129

Kelly-Nolan-Kelly (1981)   12'

clarinet solo
ED 12130

Piano Variations (1976)   30'

pno
Manuscript score on sale
SL

String Quartet No.2 (1977)   22'

Material on sale
SL

String Quartet No.3 (1983)   15'

Material on sale
SL

String Quartet No.4 (1983-84)

15'

Material on sale
SL

Voices of the Land (1987)   20'

vn-pno
Material on sale
SL

Solo Voice(s)/Voice(s) and Piano/Guitar

Ancient Voices (1983)   15'

counter tenor, 2 tenors, baritone
Material on sale
SL

Brighella's World (1979)   27'

baritone-pno
Manuscript score on sale
SL

Solo Voice(s) and Instrument(s)/ Orchestra

Columbine (1978)   30'

Soloist: coloratura-soprano
1.1.1.1-1.1.0.0-perc-pno.hp.gtr-str
Material on hire
SL

Kate Kelly's Road Show

(1983)   45'

Text: Edward Cowie
Soloist: mezzo-soprano
fl(pic/afl/srec).cl(Ebcl/bcl)-perc-pno-acc-vn/va.vc
Material on hire
SL

The Roof of Heaven

(1987-88)   15'

Cantata
Text: Edward Cowie
Soloist: tenor
2ob(ca)-2hn-str
Material on hire or sale
SL

Choral Works

Choral Symphony (1983)   45'

Text: J.W.M. Turner/T. Hook
Soloist: baritone
Chorus: mixed
2.2.2.3-4.2.3.1-timp.3perc-hp-str
Material on hire
SL

Elizabethan Madrigals Books 1, 2 & 3 (1980-81)

Chorus: mixed a cappella
Material on sale
SL

Gesangbuch (1975-76)   50'

Vols. 1-4
Chorus: mixed
fl.ca.cl-hn-perc-cel.hpd.pno.hp-vn.va.vc.db
alt. version: a cappella choir
Material on hire
Piano reduction **ED 11838 (-41)***

Kelly Choruses (1981)   20'

Chorus: mixed
pno/hp
Manuscript score on sale
SL

Missa Brevis (1983)   20'

Chorus: mixed
org
Material on sale
SL

Infoline · e-Mail
Schott Musik International
Mainz: Schott.Musik.com@T-Online.de
London: 101627.166@compuserve.com

D

Dahl, Ingolf
1912-1970

Orchestral Works

Hymn   5'
Arranger: Lawrence Morton
3.3.3.3-4.3.3.1-timp.5perc-pno(cel).hp-str
Material on hire
EAM

Concertos

Elegy Concerto (1963-70)   14'
Soloist: violin
2ob-2hn-str
Material on hire
Score **EA 145-01** / Parts **EA 145 (solo)**

Saxophone Concerto
(1949/53)   19'
Soloist: alto saxophone
*4(pic).3(ca).5(Ebcl,bcl).3(cbn)-4.4.3.2-
timp.3perc-4db*
Material on hire
Piano reduction **EA 442**

Symphony Concertante
(1952-70)   27'
Soloists: 2 clarinets
3(pic).2.0.2-2.2.2.1-2perc-hp-str
Material on hire
EAM

Chamber & Instrumental Works

Concerto a Tre (1947)   17'
cl-vn.vc
EA 138

5 Duets (1974)   14'
2cl
EA 136

Duo (1973)   17'
vc-pno
Material on sale
EAM

Fanfare on A and C (1970)   1'
3tpt.hn.euph.tuba
EA 143

2 Fugues by Anton Reicha
Arranger: Ingolf Dahl
pno
Manuscript score on sale
EAM

Hymn and Toccata (1943-47)
pno
Manuscript score on sale
EAM

I.M.C. Fanfare (1968)   1'
3tpt.3tbn
EA 137

Little Canonic Suite (1970)   5'
vn.va
EA 183

Notturno (1946)
vc-pno
Material on sale
EAM

Pastorale Montano (1936-43)
pno
Material on sale
EAM

Piano Quartet (1957)
vn.va.vc-pno
Material on sale
EAM

Preludio e Fuga Burlesca
pno
Manuscript score on sale
EAM

Reflections (1967)
pno
Manuscript score on sale
EAM

Variations on a French Folksong (1935)
fl-pno
EA 182

Variations on an Air by Couperin (1956)
fl-hpd
EA 140

Solo Voice(s)/Voice(s) and Piano/Guitar

A Cycle of Sonnets (1968)
Text: Petrarch
alto/baritone-pno
Material on sale
EAM

3 Songs (1933)
Text: Albert Ehrismann
soprano/tenor-pno
Manuscript score on sale
EAM

Dallapiccola, Luigi

b. Pisino, Istria 3.2.1904, d. Florence 19.2.1975

Dallapiccola was the leading Italian twentieth-century composer between Puccini and Berio, and one of the most original receivers and refiners of the twelve-note method. His music possesses a textural clarity and simplicity of line that owes as much to the tradition of bel canto as to the example of Berg and Webern. However sophisticated his harmonic and rhythmic invention, he never forgot that the origins of music lay in the voice.

Dallapiccola, Luigi

1904-1975

Orchestral Works

Piccola Musica Notturna

(1954)   7'

2.2.2.2-2.2.0.0-timp.perc-cel.hp-str
Material on hire
Study score **AVV 59**

Chamber & Instrumental Works

Piccola Musica Notturna

(1954/61)   7'

fl.ob.cl-cel.hp-vn.va.vc
Study score **AVV 85** / Parts **AVV 28**

Solo Voice(s) and Instrument(s)/ Orchestra

Tre poemi (1949)   13'

Text: various
Soloist: soprano
1.1.3.1-1.1.0.0-cel.pno.hp-str
Material on hire
Study score **AVV 62**

Dankworth, Johnny

b.1927

Orchestral Works

Improvisations (1959)   11'

In collaboration with Mátyás Seiber
2.2.2.2-4.3.3.1-timp.perc-hp-str   Jazzband: 2asax.2tsax.barsax.2bn-4tpt-perc-pno-db
Material on hire
Study score **ED 10728**

Degen, Helmut

1911-1995

Stage Works

Der flandrische Narr

(1939-41)   45'

Dance play in 4 Scenes
Text: Ellys Gregor/Bert Norbert
Material on hire
SM

Orchestral Works

Capriccio, Op. 90 (1938-39)   16'

2(pic).2.2.2-4.2.3.1-timp-str
Material on hire
SM

Degen, Helmut

b. Aglasterhausen (Baden) 14.1.1911, d. Trossingen 2.10.1995

Born into the family of a priest, Helmut Degen began in 1930 to study first composition with Wilhelm Maler at the Rheinische Musikschule of Cologne, then composition with Philipp Jarnach and conducting with Carl Ehrenberg at the Cologne Conservatory. These studies were followed by musicology studies in Bonn from 1933-37. At the same time, Degen was active as an organist and music teacher in Altenkirchen. In 1937 he became an emeritus professor, he was active as a professor of composition at the Trossingen Academy of Music.

Chamber Symphony (1947) 21'

Symphony No.2
2(pic).1.0.1-2.1.0.0-str
Material on hire
Study score **ED 3542**

Concerto for Strings (1946) 20'

In 2 Parts
str
Material on hire
SM

Concerto sinfonico (1947-48) 22'

Symphony No.3
pic.2.2.2.2.cbn-4.3.3.1-timp.perc-str
Material on hire
SM

Festliches Vorspiel (1935) 8'

Text: E.W. Möller
Chorus: [unison]
2.2.2.2-2.2.2.0-timp.[perc]-str
Material on hire
SM

Heitere Suite (1940-41) 12'

2.2.2.2-4.2.2.0-timp-str
Material on hire
SM

Hymnische Feiermusik
(1940) 12'

2.2.2.2-4.2.3.1-timp-str
Material on hire
SM

Serenade (1937) 15'

str
Material on hire
SM

Symphonic Concerto (1937) 27'

2(pic).2(ca).2.2(cbn)-4.2.3.1-timp.perc-str
Material on hire
SM

Variationen über ein Geusenlied (1936) 25'

2(pic).2.2.2.-4.2.3.0-timp.perc-str
Material on hire
SM

Concertos

Cello Concerto (1941-42) 20'

Soloist: cello
2([pic]).2.2.2-4.2.2.0-timp-str
Material on hire
SM

Concertino for 2 Pianos
(1942) 18'

Soloists: 2 pianos
2.2.2.2-4.2.0.0-timp-str
Material on hire
SM

Kleines Konzert No.1
(1942) 12'

Soloist: piano
str
Score **ED 80** / Parts **ED 80-01 (solo)/ED 80-11 (-15)**

Kleines Konzert No. 2
(1942) 15'

Soloist: violin
fl.ob-hn-vn.va.vc.db
Material on hire
Score **ED 80** / Piano reduction **ED 4542**

Kleines Konzert No. 3
(1943) 12'

Soloist: viola
2fl-str
Material on hire
SM

Kleines Konzert No. 4
(1943) 15'

Soloist: cello
2ob-timp-str
Material on hire
SM

Kleines Konzert No.6
(1944) 15'

Soloist: harpsichord
1.1.0.0-1.0.0.0-timp-str(0.0.1.1.0)
Material on hire
SM

Organ Concerto (1938) 18'

Soloist: organ
0.0.0.0-0.2.3.1-timp-str
Material on hire
Piano reduction **ED 3682**

Piano Concerto (1940) 27'

Soloist: piano
2(pic).2.2.2-4.2.3.1-timp-str
Material on hire
Piano reduction **ED 2884**

Chamber & Instrumental Works

Capriccio Scherzando (1938)

pno
ED 3713

30 Concert Studies (1948) 60'

In 3 Volumes
pno
ED 3955/3956/3957

Concerto in 2 Parts (1946) 20'

pno
ED 3679

Choral Works

Wenn der Bauer Hochzeit macht (1938-39) 35'

A gay Cantata
Soloists: soprano, alto, baritone, speaker
Chorus: mixed (4-5 prt)
fl.cl-str(1.1.0.1.1)
Material on hire
SM

Dessau, Paul
1894-1979

Stage Works

Die Verurteilung des Lukullus (1949/60) 90'

Opera in 12 Scenes
Text: Bertolt Brecht
Material on hire
AVV

Chamber & Instrumental Works

Concertino 22'

Soloist: violin
fl.cl-hn
Material on hire
AVV

Dianda, Hilda Fanny
b.1925

Orchestral Works

Impromptus (1970) 10'

str
Material on hire
AVV

Ludus-I (1968) 13'

pic.2.2.bcl.0.cbn3-4.3.3.1-timp.3perc-xyl(vib).pno.hp-str(16.14.11.10.6)
Material on hire
AVV

Concertos

Resonancias-III (1965) 21'

Soloist: cello
pic.2.0.2.bcl.0-4.3.3.1-timp.5perc-vib.cel(glsp).pno.hp-str(8.8.6.0.4)
Material on hire
AVV

Divertimento,

Divertimento für Mozart

12 aspects of the Aria "Ein Mädchen oder
Weibchen wünscht Papageno sich"
Collective Composition by:
Gottfried von Einem, Luciano Berio,
Heimo Erbse, Peter Racine Fricker, Niels
Viggo Bentzon, Roman Haubenstock-
Ramati, Giselher Klebe, Gerhard
Wimberger, Maurice le Roux, Jacques
Wildberger, Maurice Jarre, Hans Werner
Henze; s. detailed enumeration
Schott Mainz & Universal Edition

Dohnányi, Ernst von

1877-1960

Orchestral Works

Symphony in D minor, Op. 9

(1902)   58'

pic.3.2.ca.3(bcl).3.cbn-6.3.3.1-timp.perc-
hp-str(16.16.12.10.8)
Material on hire
SM

Chamber & Instrumental Works

Sonata, Op. 8

vc-pno
ED 1376

Dombrowski, Hansmaria

1897-1977

Orchestral Works

Böhmische Sinfonie   22'

2.2.2.2-4.2.3.1-timp.perc-str
Material on hire
SM

Donatoni, Franco

b.1927

Orchestral Works

Musica per orchestra da camera   (1955)   14'

2.1.1.1-2.1.1.0-timp-cel-str(10.0.8.6.3)
Material on hire
SL

Concertos

Concertino   (1953)   16'

Soloist. timpani
2hn.2tpt.2tbn.0-timp-str
Material on hire
SL

Divertimento   (1954)   21'

Soloist: violin
2.2.2.2-2.2.2.0-timp-str
Material on hire
Piano reduction **ED 10419***

Chamber & Instrumental Works

Composizione in quattro movimenti   (1955)   10'

pno
ED 10398*

3 Improvvisazioni   (1957)   18'

pno
ED 10657*

Duffy, John

b.1928

Orchestral Works

American Fantasy Overture   4'

2(pic).2.2.2-4.2.3.0-timp.2perc-pno.hp-str
Material on hire
EAM

David and Bathsheba   (1990)   5'

2(pic).2(ca).2.2-4.2.3.1-2perc-pno.hp-str
Material on hire
EAM

Donatoni, Franco

b. Verona 9.6.1927

Donatoni's questing reinterpretation of
avant-garde values places him in the vangu-
ard of composers of our time. A master
craftsman, he has never been content to rely
on past successes to determine future artistic directions. Instead, in a widely varied
and substantial output, he has reflected
upon the achievement of Webern, Cage and
Stockhausen, and channelled their discoveries into new forms of his own devising. With
Berio, he is the outstanding Italian composer of his generation and a gifted and inspi-
ring teacher.

Heritage Waltz   (1988)   4'

2.2.1.2-4.2.3.1-timp.2perc-pno(cel).hp-str
Material on hire
EAM

2 Jewish Dances   (1993)   8'

2(pic).2.2.2-4.2.3.1-timp.2perc-pno(cel).hp-
str
Material on hire
EAM

3 Jewish Portraits   (1993)   9'

2(pic).2.2.2-4.2.3.1-timp.2perc-pno(cel).hp-
str
Material on hire
EAM

Infoline · e-Mail
Schott Musik International
Mainz: Schott.Musik.com@T-Online.de
London: 101627.166@compuserve.com

Dunhill, Thomas Frederick
1877-1946

Stage Works

Gallimaufry, Op. 86 (1937) 21'
Ballet
Material on hire
SL

Orchestral Works

Gallimaufry, Op. 86 (1937) 21'
Divertissement after Andersen
2(pic).2.2.2-2/[4]3.2.0-timp.2perc-str
Material on hire
SL

van Durme, Jef
b.1907

Orchestral Works

Symphony No.5 (1950) 35'
2.2.2.2-4.2.3.1-timp.perc-str
Material on hire
AVV

Dutilleux, Henri
b.1916

Concertos

L' Arbre des songes

(1983-85) 25'

Soloist: violin
*3.3(ob d'am).4.3-3.3.3.1-timp.5perc-
pno(cel).hp-str*
Material on hire
Study score **ED 7627** / Piano reduction
ED 7434

Dutilleux, Henri

b. Angers, France 22.1.1916

In Henri Dutilleux's music time and memory operate in Proustian fashion weaving an entrancing magic through the subtlest nuance of harmony and timbre. In the Cello Concerto "Tout un monde lointain", written for Rostropovitch, Baudelaire's intoxicating world is a powerful stimulant. In the Violin Concerto "L'arbre des songes", commissioned for Isaac Stern, a fascination with natural processes parallels a technical mastery of variation and transformation. Two symphonies inject new life into a neglected French tradition. Here, as in "Timbres, Espace, Mouvement" and "Le Mystere de l'instant", his orchestral command is unrivalled. Dutilleux remains, in the words of critic Wilfred Mellers, a composer who is "unafraid to be beautiful".

E

Eben, Petr
b.1929

Chamber & Instrumental Works

Briefe an Milena (1990) 15'
Five Piano Pieces after letters by Franz Kafka
pno
ED 8125

Duetti per due Trombe
(1956) 10'
2tpt
TR 2

Fantasia vespertina (1967) 5'
tpt-pno
TR 3

Hommage à Dietrich Buxtehude (1987) 8'
Toccata Fugue
organ solo
ED 7543

Hommage à Henry Purcell
(1995)
organ solo
ED 8442

Tabulatora nova (1979) 11'
Rhapsodic variations on an old Bohemian love song
guitar solo
GA 501

Die Welt der Kleinen (1955) 10'
Twenty Short Pieces for Piano
pno
ED 7445

Choral Works

Eine Mozartgeschichte
(1990) 5'
Text: Jan Skácel
Chorus: female, children a cappella
C 48755

Heilige Zeichen (1993) 60'
Oratorio (Proprium)
Text: liturgic
Soloists: soprano, baritone
Chorus: mixed, children
1.3.0.3-0.2.2.0-perc-2org
Material on hire
Vocal score **ED 8581**

Eben, Petr

b. Zamberk 22.1.1929

"Symbiosis of lyric poetry and drama" is probably the most succint characterization of Eben's world of musical expression. It is the will to talk to others, not self-realization that is the origin of his subject, which are alwasy rooted in the humanistic spirit. As a composer whose peak creating period occured at a time of constant censorship though cultural bureaucracy, Eben has made allusions to the present (has actually made timeless, "eternally true" subjects a matter of topical interest) by using an expressive and freely tonal idiom. The musical structure, conceived as a second romantic level,counterpoints these texts often dating from the Renaissance and the Middle Ages which, due to their origin, appeared to be uninfluenced by ideology in the sense of a "socialist realism", this being protected from monopolization or abuse.

Medicamina sempiterna 2'
Text: Publius Ovidius Naso/Petr Eben
Chorus: female a cappella
C 47087

Prager Te Deum 1989 (1989) 8'
Chorus: mixed (SATB)
2tpt.2tbn-timp.perc-org
ED 7840 / Parts **ED 7840-11/-12** / Vocal score **ED 7840-01**

Verba Sapientiae - De circuitu aeterno (1990) 4'
Liber Ecclesiastes 3,1-8
Chorus: mixed a cappella
SKR 20026

Verba Sapientiae - De tempore (1990) 4'
Liber Ecclesiastes 3,1-8
Chorus: mixed a cappella
SKR 20025

Verba Sapientiae - Laus mulieris (1991) 5'
Liber Proverbiorum
Chorus: mixed a cappella
SKR 20027

Egk, Werner
1901-1983

Stage Works

Abraxas (1948) 75'
Ballet in 5 Scenes
Material on hire
Piano reduction **ED 3998** / Libretto **BN 50-70**

Casanova in London (1968) 70'
Ballet
Material on hire
Piano reduction **ED 6017**

Die chinesische Nachtigall
(1953) 40'
Ballet in 4 Scenes
Material on hire
SM

Columbus (1942/51) 100'
Opera in 3 Parts
Text: Werner Egk
Material on hire
Vocal score **ED 2870** / Libretto **BN 3190-90**

Danza (1960) 30'
Ballet. "Variationen über ein karibisches Thema"
Material on hire
Study score **ED 5013**

Französische Suite nach Rameau (1952) 18'
Ballet Version
Material on hire
Study score **ED 4074**

Der Fuchs und der Rabe
(1932) 30'
Song play for Children
Material on hire
SM

Die Historie vom Ritter Don Juan aus Barcelona (1932) 20'
Song play
Material on hire
SM

Egk, Werner

b. Auchsesheim 17.5.1901, d. Inning 10.7.1983

Egk was a distinguished composer who wrote in a colourful, conservative style owing much to the example of Richard Strauss. The folklore of his native Bavaria was an important inspiration, for example in the orchestral "Georgica", or "Peasant Pieces", his first success. In later years Egk served as President of the Association of German Composers.

Irische Legende

(1955/70)   full evening

Opera in 5 Scenes
Text: Werner Egk after William Butler Yeats
Material on hire
SM

Joan von Zarissa   (1940)   70'

Ballet in 4 Parts
Material on hire
Piano reduction ED 3191

Der Löwe und die Maus

(1931)   20'

Song play for Children
Material on hire
SM

Peer Gynt   (1938)   full evening

Opera in 3 Acts
Text: Werner Egk after Ibsen
Material on hire
Vocal score ED 3197 / Libretto BN 3192-50

Der Revisor   (1956)   full evening

Comic Opera in 5 Acts
Text: Werner Egk after Nikolai Gogol
Material on hire
Vocal score ED 4933 / Libretto BN 3193-30

Siebzehn Tage und vier Minuten (Circe)

(1966)   full evening

Opera Semibuffa in 3 Acts
Text: Werner Egk after Calderón
Material on hire
Vocal score ED 5540 / Libretto BN 3194-01

Ein Sommertag   (1950)   30'

Ballet after music by Clementi
Material on hire
SM

Die Verlobung in San Domingo   (1963)   full evening

Opera
Text: Werner Egk after Heinrich von Kleist
Material on hire
Vocal score ED 5270 / Libretto BN 3195-10

Die Zaubergeige

(1935/54)   full evening

Opera in 3 Acts
Text: Werner Egk/Ludwig Andersen after Franz von Pocci
Material on hire
Vocal score ED 3979 / Libretto BN 3196-80

Orchestral Works

Abraxas - Concert Suite

(1948)   28'

2(pic).2.2.2-4.3.3.1-timp.2perc-str
Material on hire
SM

Allegria   (1952)   25'

Godimento in 4 movements
3(pic).3.3.3-4.3.3.1-timp.3perc-str
Material on hire
Study score ED 4408

Divertissement   (1973-74)   10'

fl.2ob.2cl.2bn-2hn.tpt
Score ED 6465 / Parts ED 6465-10

"Englische Suite" from the ballet "Casanova in London"

(1968)   20'

pic.1.2.ca.2.bcl.2-2.2.2.0-timp.perc-pno.hp-str
Material on hire
SM

Französische Suite nach Rameau   (1949)   20'

3(pic).3.3.3(cbn)-4.3.3.1-timp.perc-hp-str
Material on hire
Study score ED 4074

Georgica   (1934)   15'

Three Farmer's Pieces
2(pic).2(ca).2.2-4.3.3.1-timp.2perc-str
Material on hire
SM

Joan von Zarissa - Triptychon   (1940)   10'

3.2.ca.2.bcl.2.cbn-4.3.3.1-timp.perc-cel.hp-str
Material on hire
SM

Little Symphony   (1926)   25'

2.3.2.3-2.2.1.0-timp.perc-pno-str
Material on hire
SM

Moira   (1972)   12'

Music in C
3(pic).3.3.asax.3-4.4.3.1-timp.4perc-pno.[eorg]-str
Material on hire
SM

Music for Small Orchestra

(1925-26)   22'

1.0.1.1-0.2.1.0-timp.perc-pno-str(1.0.1.1.1)
Material on hire
SM

Music for String Instruments - Passacaglia   (1923)   12'

str
Material on hire
SM

Nachtanz, Op. posth.   (1983)   4'

pic.2.3.(ca).3.3-4.3.3.0-timp.perc-hp-str
Material on hire
SM

Die Nachtigall   (1953)   14'

str orch/qrt
Score ED 7072 / Parts ED 7073

Overture   (1979-80)   12'

Music on a lost romance
3(pic).3.(ca)3.3-4.3.3.0-timp.perc-str
Material on hire
Study score ED 6982

Sonata for Orchestra   (1948)   20'

3(2pic).3(ca).3(bcl).2.cbn-4.3.3.1-timp.perc-str
Material on hire
SM

Sonata for Orchestra No.2

(1969)   23'

pic.2.2.ca.2.bcl.3-4.3.3.1-timp.perc-hp-str
Material on hire
Score ED 148

Spiegelzeit   (1979)   14'

2(2pic).2.2.2-4.3.3.0-timp.perc-hp-str
Material on hire
Study score ED 6919

Variationen über ein Karibisches Thema   (1959)   30'

2.2.2.2-4.3.3.0-timp.3perc-pno.hp-str
Material on hire
Study score ED 5013

Walzer für Orchester

pic.2.3.3.2.cbn-4.3.3.1-perc-str
Material on hire
SM

Die Zaubergeige - Overture

(1954)   7'

2(2pic).2(ca).2.2(cbn)-4.3.3.1-timp.perc-cel-str
Material on hire
SM

Die Zaubergeige - Overture

(1980)   7'

Arranger: Werner Egk
fl(pic).2ob(ca).2cl.2bn(cbn)-2hn.tpt
Material on hire
SM

Concertos

Canzone (1981)   8'

Arrangement of the 2nd movement of
"Geigenmusik"
Soloist: cello
2.2.2.2-4.0.0.0-timp-glsp-hp-str
Material on hire
SM

Geigenmusik (1936)   18'

Soloist: violin
2(pic).2(ca).2.2(cbn)-4.3.3.1-timp.3perc-cel.hp-str
Material on hire
Piano reduction **ED 2514**

Der Revisor - Concert Suite

(1980)   17'

Soloist: trumpet
1(pic).2.1.1-2.2.1.0-timp.3perc-pno.hp-str
Material on hire
SM

Chamber & Instrumental Works

Piano Sonata (1947)   12'

ED 1332

5 Pieces (1974)   16'

fl.ob.cl.bn-hn
Score and parts **ED 6345**

Polonaise, Adagio and Finale

(1975-76)   15'

ob(ca).cl.bn-hn-2vn.va.vc.db
Study score **ED 6611** / Parts **ED 6612**

Sinfonia concertante in Eb Major, Op. KV. 297b

(1982-83)   25'

(W.A. Mozart)
Arranger: Werner Egk
0.2.2.2-2.0.0.0-db
Score **ED 7525** / Parts **ED 7526**

La Tentation de Saint Antoine (1946)   28'

d'apres des airs et des vers du dix-huitième
siècle
alto-str qrt
Material on hire
Study score **ED 4559** / Vocal score **ED 4543**

Solo Voice(s) and Instrument(s)/ Orchestra

Chanson et Romance (1953)   15'

Text: Paul le Silentiaire/anonymous
Soloist: soprano
2(pic).2(ca)2.2-2.1.1.0-timp.perc-str
Material on hire
Vocal score **ED 4217**

Die Verlobung in San Domingo - 3 Pieces (1963)

Text: Werner Egk after Heinrich von Kleist
Soloists: mezzo-soprano, tenor
2(pic).2.2.2-4.3.3.0-timp.2perc-pno-str
Material on hire
SM

Joan von Zarissa - Suite

(1940)   30'

Soloists: 2 voices (male, female)
3(2pic).3(ca).3(bcl).3(cbn)-4.3.3.1-timp.perc-cel.[org].hp-str   backstage: 8tpt
Material on hire
SM

Nachgefühl (1975)   12'

Text: Klabund
Soloist: soprano
3(2pic).3(ca).3.3-4.3.3.0-timp.3perc-pno.hp-str
Material on hire
Vocal score **ED 6722**

Natur-Liebe-Tod (1937)   13'

Text: L.C.H. Hölty
Soloist: bass
2(pic).2.2.0-2.2.0.0-timp-str
Material on hire
SM

Peer Gynt - Tango, Zwischenspiel und Arie

(1938)   6'

Soloist: soprano
pic.2.2.ca.2.bcl.2.cbn-4.3.3.1-timp.perc-hp-str
Material on hire
SM

Quattro Canzoni (1932)   12'

Soloist: high voice
2(pic).2.2.2-4.3.3.0-timp.2perc-hp-str
Material on hire
Vocal score **ED 4923**

La Tentation de Saint Antoine (1946)   28'

d'apres des airs et des vers du dix-huitième
siècle
Soloist: alto
str qrt-str
Study score **ED 4559** / Parts **BSS 37096 (str qrt)** / Vocal score **ED 4543**

Variationen über ein altes Wiener Strophenlied (1937) 7'

Soloist: coloratura-soprano
2.2.2.2-2.2.0.0-pno.hp-str
Material on hire
Piano reduction **ED 3788**

Choral Works

Furchtlosigkeit und Wohlwollen (1930-31/59)   70'

Soloist: tenor
Chorus: mixed
pic.1.2.0.2-2.2.2.0-timp.perc-pno.hp-str
Material on hire
Study score **ED 5020** / Libretto **BN 3191-70**

Joan von Zarissa - 3 Choruses from the Ballet

(1968)   6'

Text: Fritz Schroeder
Chorus: mixed a cappella (SSAAATTBBB)
Score **ED 5846** / Vocal score **ED 5846-01/-02**

Mein Vaterland (1937)   2'

Text: Friedrich Gottlieb Klopstock
Chorus: male unison
2.2.2.2-4.3.3.1-timp-str
alt. version: org
Material on hire
SM

La Tentation de Saint Antoine (1978)   28'

d'apres des airs et des vers du dix-huitième
siècle
Chorus: mixed
pic.1.2.2.2-2.2.2.0-timp.2perc-hp-str
Material on hire
SM

Infoline · e-Mail
Schott Musik International
Mainz: Schott.Musik.com@T-Online.de
London: 101627.166@compuserve.com

Einem, Gottfried von

1918-1996

Stage Works

Glück, Tod und Traum, Op. 17 (1954)   32'

Dance Serenade
Text: Friedrich Rasche
Material on hire
Piano reduction **ED 4924 (Co-prod: UE)**

Pas de Cœur oder Tod und Auferstehung einer Ballerina, Op. 16 (1952)   30'

Ballet in 2 Parts
Material on hire
Piano reduction **ED 4030 (Co-prod: UE)**

Orchestral Works

Alpbacher Tanzserenade

(1952)   30'

ob.2cl.2bn-2hn.tpt
Material on hire
SM (Co-prod: UE)
Copyright USA: EAM/Italy: Ricordi

Introduktion: "Wandlungen", Op. 21   7'

No. 1 from the "Divertimento für Mozart"
Text: Hans Bethge
2.2.2.2-2.2.0.0-timp-str
Material on hire
SM (Co-prod: UE)
Copyright For separate performances: Bote & Bock, Berlin

Meditationen, Op. 18 (1954)   21'

2.2.2.2-4.2.2.0-timp-str
Material on hire
Study score **ED 4556 (Co-prod: UE)**
Copyright USA: EAM/Italy: Ricordi

Pas de Cœur - Orchestral Suite, Op. 16 (1954)   13'

2(pic).2.2.2-2.2.1.0-timp-pno-str
Material on hire
SM (Co-prod: UE)
Copyright USA: EAM/Italy: Ricordi

Solo Voice(s)/Voice(s) and Piano/Guitar

Japanische Blätter, Op. 15

(1951)   13'

Text: Hans Bethge
voice-pno
ED 4344

Eisenmann, Will

1906-1992

Stage Works

Bethsabé (1936)   75'

Scenic Oratorium
Text: André Gide
Material on hire
AVV

Der König der dunklen Kammer (1935)   full evening

Opera in 13 Scenes
Text: Rabindranath Tagore
Material on hire
AVV

Leonce und Lena

(1945)   full evening

Lyrical Comedy in 3 Acts
Text: Georg Büchner
Material on hire
AVV

Solo Voice(s) and Instrument(s)/ Orchestra

Orpheus, Eurydike, Hermes

(1947)   20'

Text: Rainer Maria Rilke
Soloist: speaker
1.1.ca.0.1-1.0.0.0-timp-pno-str(1.0.1.1.0)
Material on hire
AVV

Choral Works

Die Weise von Liebe und Tod des Cornetts Christoph Rilke

(1931)   30'

Soloist: narrator
Chorus: speaking
1.0.0.1-1.2.1.0-timp.perc-pno-str
Material on hire
AVV

Elgar, Edward William

1857-1934

Orchestral Works

Dream Children, Op. 43

(1902)   6'

2.2.ca.2.2-4.0.0.0-timp-hp-str
Material on hire
SL

Salut d'Amour, Op. 12

(1889)   4'

1.2.2.2-2.0.0.0-str
Material on hire
SL

Concertos

Sursum Corda, Op. 11

(1894)   8'

Soloist: organ
4.2.3.1-timp-str
Material on hire
SL

Sursum Corda, Op. 11

(1894)   8'

Arranger: Adolf Schmid
Soloist: organ/piano
2.2.2.2-4.2.3.1-timp-hp-str
Material on hire
SL

Chamber & Instrumental Works

Dream Children, Op. 43

(1902)   6'

Arranger: Herbert Withers
vc-pno
Material on hire
ED 11054*

Elgar, Sir Edward William

b. 2.6.1857 Broadheath nr. Worcester,
d. Worcester 23.2.1934

Elgar's abundant invention, largeness of vision and strength and singularity of musical character place him high among European romantic artists - and at the peak of British music of hs time. He drew inspiration from the culture and landscape of his own country, resourcefulness from the study of his continental colleagues; and he worked in all the major forms except opera, creating a significant body of symphonic literature, and in his popular music a style of direct appeal.

Salut d'Amour, Op. 12
(1888)   4'

pno (easy version; C-Major)
ED 11170-01

Salut d'Amour, Op. 12
(1888)   4'

organ solo
ED 11173

Salut d'Amour, Op. 12
(1888)   4'

(D Major)
vn-pno
ED 11174-02

Salut d'Amour, Op. 12
(1888)   4'

vc-pno
ED 11175

Salut d'Amour, Op. 12
(1888)   4'

2vn-pno
ED 11972*

Salut d'Amour, Op. 12
(1888)   4'

organ solo
SL

Salut d'Amour, Op. 12
(1888)   4'

pno (original version in E Major)
ED 11171

Salut d'Amour, Op. 12
(1888)   4'

pno (4hnd)
ED 11171

Salut d'Amour, Op. 12
(1888)   4'

vn-pno (E Major)
ED 11174-01

Enríquez, Manuel
b.1926

Orchestral Works

Ixamatl (1969)   11'
pic.2.2.ca.2.bcl.2.cbn-4.4.0.0-4perc-hp-str
Material on hire
AVV

Trayectorias (1967)   7'
pic.2.2.ca.2.bcl.2.cbn-4.4.3.1-timp.3perc-hp
Material on hire
AVV

Erbse, Heimo
b.1924

Orchestral Works

Allegro-Lento-Allegro   2'
No. 3 from the "Divertimento für Mozart"
2fl.2ob.2cl.2bsthn.2bn.cbn-2hn.2Ctpt-timp
Material on hire
SM (Co-prod: UE)
Copyright USA: EAM/Italy: Ed. Suvini Zerboni

Erding Swiridoff, Susanne
b.1955

Chamber & Instrumental Works

Chillam (1982)   2'
in: Frauen komponieren
pno
ED 7197

Maske und Kristall   6'
in: Frauen komponieren
pno
ED 8132

Evangelatos, Antiochos
b.1903

Orchestral Works

Variations and Fugue
(1946-47)   25'

On a Greek Folksong
3(pic).2.ca.2.bcl.3.cbn-4.3.3.1-timp.perc-cel.hp-str
Material on hire
SM

Infoline · e-Mail
Schott Musik International
Mainz: Schott.Musik.com@T-Online.de
London: 101627.166@compuserve.com

Fairchild, Blair
1877-1933

Concertos

Rhapsody (1924)　　　　10'
Soloist: violin
2.2.2.2-2.2.0.0-timp.perc-str
Material on hire
SM

Chamber & Instrumental Works

Mosquitos
Arranger: Dushkin
vn-pno
BSS 31811

Some (12) Indian Songs and Dances (1927)
pno
ED 1714

Ferrari, Luc
b.1929

Orchestral Works

Allo! Ici la Terre (1974)　　20-120'
Play Light and Time Show
4.4.4.4-4.3.3.2-perc-cel.pno.org-str(20.0.10.10.6)-tape.slides
Material on hire
AVV

Fetler, Paul
b.1920

Orchestral Works

Celebration (1977)　　　　24'
3(pic).3(ca).3(bcl).3(cbn)-4.3.3.1-timp.perc-cel-str
Material on hire
Study score **EA 429**

Concertos

3 Impressions (1981)　　　24'
Soloist: guitar
2(pic).2.0.2-2.0.0.0-perc-str
Material on hire
Piano reduction **EA 464**

Chamber & Instrumental Works

Cycles
perc-pno
Study score **BAT 14-01 (percussion)**

4 Movements
guitar solo
GA 428

5 Pieces
guitar solo
GA 99

Forsyth, Cecil
1870-1941

Concertos

Viola Concerto in G Minor　　　　25'
Arranger: John Ireland
Soloist: viola
2.2.2.2-4.2.3.1-timp.perc-str
Material on hire
Piano reduction **ED 1077**

Fortner, Wolfgang
1907-1987

Stage Works

Ballet blanc (1958)　　　　17'
Ballet
Material on hire
SM

Bluthochzeit (1956)　　full evening
Lyrical Tragedy in 2 Acts
Text: Federico García Lorca/Enrique Beck
Material on hire
Vocal score **ED 4934** / Libretto **BN 3230-01**

Carmen (Bizet-Collages)

(1970)   70'

Ballet by John Cranko
Arranger: Wilfried Steinbrenner/Wolfgang
Fortner
Material on hire
SM

Corinna (1958)   30'

Opera Buffa in 1 Act
Text: Heiner Schmidt after Gerard de
Nerval
Material on hire
SM

Creß ertrinkt (1930)   40'

School Play with Music in 3 Acts
Text: Andreas Zeitler
Material on hire
SM

Elisabeth Tudor

(1968-71)   full evening

Opera in 3 Acts
Text: Mattias Braun/Wolfgang Fortner
Material on hire
Vocal score **ED 6571**

In seinem Garten liebt Don Perlimplín Belisa (1961-63)   90'

4 Scenes of an erotic picture-sheet in a way
of a Chamber-Play
Text: Federico García Lorca/Enrique Beck
Material on hire
Vocal score **ED 5266** / Libretto **BN 3231-10**

Mouvements (1953)   22'

Ballet
Arranger: Krüger/Gsovsky
Material on hire
Study score **ED 4554**

That Time (1977)   43'

Opera in 1 Act
Text: Samuel Beckett
Material on hire
Study score **ED 6739**

Die Weiße Rose (1949)   45'

Ballet in 2 Parts after the Fairytale "The
birthday..."
Text: Oscar Wilde
Material on hire
Piano reduction **ED 4033**

Die Witwe von Ephesus

(1952)   20'

Ballet Pantomime
Text: Grete Weill after Petronius
Material on hire
SM

Fortner, Wolfgang

b. Leipzig 12.10.1907, d. Heidelberg
5.9.1987

Fortner's music represents the convergence
of many mainstream 20th-century aesthetic
trends: neo-classicism, serialism, and the
use of instrumental colour as both a structural and an impressionistic element.
Overtly dramatic, whether in balletic, operatic or concertante works, it nonetheless
shows a hardwon balance between head and
heart, a quality which also made Fortner
one of the outstanding teachers and admini-
strators in post-war Germany.

Orchestral Works

Bluthochzeit - Interludes

(1963)   20'

*3(pic).2.ca.2.bcl.tsax.2.cbn-0.3.3.1-
timp.3perc-cel.hp-str*
Material on hire
Study score **ED 5032**

Capriccio and Finale (1939)   15'

*3(pic).3(ca).3(bcl).3(cbn)-4.3.3.1-
timp.perc-str*
Material on hire
SM

La Cecchina (1954)   10'

Italian Overture after Nicola Piccini
2(2pic).2.2.2-2.2.1.0-timp-str
Material on hire
SM

Concertino (1934)

0.2.0.1-0.1.0.0-str
Material on hire
SM

Concerto for Strings (1933)   22'

str
Material on hire
SM

Immagini (1966-67)   15'

str(16.12.12.8.4)
Material on hire
Study score **ED 6307**

Impromptus (1957)   12'

*3(pic).2.ca.2.bcl.2.cbn-3.3.3.1-timp.perc-
hp-str*
Material on hire
Study score **ED 4584**

Lysistrata (1945)

Comedy by Aristophanes
2(2pic).0.2.bcl.1-0.3.1.1-2perc-pno.hp-db
Material on hire
SM

Marginalien (1969)   18'

In memory of a good dog
2.2.2.2-2.2.1.1-perc-cel-str
Material on hire
Study score **ED 6308**

Music for Wind Band (1957)   8'

2.2.ca.2.bcl.2.cbn-3.1.1.0
Material on hire
SM

Prolegomena (1973)   19'

To "Elisabeth Tudor"
*2(2pic).afl(pic).2.ca.Ebcl.2.bcl.asax.2.cbn-
0.3.btpt.3(btbn).1-timp.4perc-cel.eorg.hp-
str*
Material on hire
Study score **ED 6346**

Streichermusik II (1944)   24'

str(2.0.1.1.1)
Material on hire
SM

Suite for Orchestra (1930)   20'

After music of Jan Pieterszoon Sweelinck
(1562-1621)
2asax.tsax/2ca.2bn-2tpt-timp-str(0.0.1.1.1)
Material on hire
ED 3336

Symphony (1947)   30'

3(pic).2.2.bcl.2.cbn-5.3.3.1-timp.perc-str
Material on hire
Study score **ED 3539**

Triptychon (1977)   26'

3.3.4.3-6.3.3.2-str
Material on hire
Study score **ED 6826**

Variations (1979)   21'

*pno.hpd.marimb.hp.gtr-str(10.10.10.10.3
min:8.7.4.4.1)*
Material on hire
Study score **ED 6949**

Infoline · e-Mail

Schott Musik International
Mainz: Schott.Musik.com@T-Online.de
London: 101627.166@compuserve.com

Die Weiße Rose - Concert Suite (1949)   38'

2(pic).1.ca.2.bcl.2.cbn-3.3.3.1-timp.perc-cel.pno.hp-str
Material on hire
SM

Concertos

Aria (1951)   10'

From the drama "Mord im Dom"
Text: T.S. Eliot
Soloists: mezzo-soprano/alto, viola, flute
1.2.1.1-1.1.1.0-str
Material on hire
SM

Aulodie (1966)   25'

Soloist: oboe
0.0.0.0-3.3.3.1-timp.perc-cel.pno.hpd.hp.gtr-str
Material on hire
Study score **ED 6312** / Piano reduction **OBB 9**

Ballet blanc (1958)   17'

Soloists: 2 violins
str
Material on hire
SM

Cello Concerto (1951)   25'

Soloist: cello
3(pic).2.2.bcl.2.cbn-3.3.2.1-timp.2perc-cel.hp-str
Material on hire
Piano reduction **ED 4343**

Harpsichord Concerto
(1935)   19'

After the Organ Concerto (1932)
Soloist: harpsichord
str
Material on hire
SM

Klangvariation (1981)   12'

To the "Impromptus" (1957)
Soloists: 4 violas
3(pic).2.ca.2.bcl.2.cbn-3.3.3.1-timp.perc-hp-str(0.0.6.5.4)
Material on hire
SM

Mouvements (1953)   25'

Soloist: piano
2(pic).1.ca.1.bcl.asax.2-0.jazztpt.jazztbn.0-timp.3perc-xyl(vib).hp-str
Material on hire
Study score **ED 4554**

Organ Concerto (1932)   18'

Soloist: organ
str
Material on hire
SM

Phantasie über die Tonfolge b-a-c-h (1950)   18'

Soloists: 2 pianos
3.2.ob d' am(ca).2.bcl.2.cbn -3.3.3.1-timp.perc-hp
Material on hire
Study score **ED 4271**

Prismen (1974)   24'

Soloists: fl.ob.cl-hp-perc
3(pic).3.3.3.cbn-1.1.1.1-timp-str
Material on hire
Study score **ED 6654**

Triplum (1965-66)   25'

Soloists: 3 pianos
1(pic).1.ca.1.bcl.1.cbn-1.1.1.1-timp.4perc-str
Material on hire
Study score **ED 5513**

Violin Concerto (1946)   23'

Soloist: violin
1.1.2.2-2.1.0.0-timp.perc-str
Material on hire
Piano reduction **ED 4045**

Zyklus (1969)   15'

Soloist: cello
1.2.2.2-1.1.1.1-timp.perc-2hp
Material on hire
Study score **ED 6306**

Chamber & Instrumental Works

5 Bagatelles (1960)   15'

fl.ob.cl.bn-hn
Score **ED 5021** / Parts **ED 5177**

Caprices (1979)   13'

fl(pic).ob.bn
ED 6935

Cello Sonata (1948)   20'

vc-pno
ED 569

Duo (1983)   13'

7 Inventions
vn.vc
ED 7174

7 Elegies (1950)   16'

pno
ED 4191

Epigramme (1964)   16'

pno
ED 4810

Flute Sonata (1947)   17'

fl-pno
ED 1330

Intermezzi (1962)   18'

organ solo
ED 4718

9 Inventionen und ein Anhang (1976)   11'

2fl
ED 6675

Kammermusik (1944)   18'

pno
ED 2219

6 Late Pieces (1982)   18'

pno
ED 7121

Madrigal (1979)   9'

12vc
SM

6 Madrigals (1954)   16'

2vn.vc (solo or str orch)
Score and parts **CON 52**

New-Delhi-Musik (1959)   15'

Prelude, Variations and Epilogue to an own Theme
fl-vn.vc-hpd
ED 5064

Piano Sonatina (1935)   15'

ED 2345

Piano Trio (1978)   28'

vn.vc-pno
ED 6793

Praeambel and Fugue (1935)   16'

organ solo
ED 2269

4 Preludes for Organ (1980)   10'

organ solo
ED 6992

Serenade (1945)   25'

fl.ob.bn
Score **ED 3621** / Parts **ED 2276**

String Quartet No.1 (1929)   30'

Parts **ED 3152**

String Quartet No.2 (1938)   20'

Score **ED 3518** / Parts **ED 3176**

String Quartet No.3 (1948)   20'

Score **ED 4102** / Parts **ED 4120**

String Quartet No.4 (1975)   19'

ED 6663

String Trio No.1 (1952)   14'

vn.va.vc
Score **ED 4413** / Parts **ED 4479**

String Trio No.2 (1983)   6'

vn.va.vc
Score and parts **ED 7277**

Suite (1932)   15'

cello solo
ED 2255

Theme and Variations

(1975)   6'

cello solo
ED 6635

Toccata and Fugue (1930)   18'

organ solo
ED 2101

Violin Sonata (1945)   18'

vn-pno
ED 2275

Zyklus (1964)   15'

vc-pno
Piano reduction **ED 5436**

Solo Voice(s)/Voice(s) and Piano/Guitar

Shakespeare-Songs (1946)   36'

mezzo-soprano-pno
ED 1605

4 Songs (1933)   13'

Text: Friedrich Hölderlin
mezzo-soprano-pno
ED 3639

Terzinen (1965)   18'

Text: Hugo von Hofmannsthal
male voice-pno
ED 5834

Widmung (1981)   9'

Text: William Shakespeare
tenor-pno
ED 7026

Solo Voice(s) and Instrument(s)/ Orchestra

Berceuse royale (1958/75)   18'

From "Chant de Naissance"
Text: Saint John Perse
Soloists: soprano, violin
str
alt. version (1975): S-fl.cl-perc-vn.va.vc.db
Material on hire
Piano reduction **ED 4990**

The Creation (1954)   25'

Text: James Weldon Johnson
Soloist: medium voice
2.1.ca.1.bcl.0.cbn-0.2.2.0-timp.perc-vib.hpd.hp-str
Material on hire
Study score **ED 4572** / Piano reduction **ED 4612**

2 Exerzitien (1948)   11'

Text: Bertolt Brecht
Soloists: soprano, mezzo-soprano, alto
1.1.ca.1.bcl.1-0.3jazztpt.jazztbn.0-perc-cel.hp-str(1.1.0.0.1)
Material on hire
SM

Farewell (1981)   10'

Text: Pablo Neruda/Erich Arend
Soloists: 2 medium voices
2fl-vc-pno
Parts **ED 6883** / Vocal score **ED 6884**

Fragment Maria (1929)   20'

Chamber Cantata
Text: M. Raschke
Soloist: soprano
fl.ob.cl-2vn.va.vc-hpd/pno
Material on hire
SM

Immagini (1966-67)   15'

Text: Miroslav Krleza
Soloist: [soprano]
str(7.0.3.2.1)
Material on hire
Study score **ED 5941**

Isaaks Opferung (1952)   17'

Oratoric Scene
Text: Vulgata
Soloists: alto, tenor, bass
3.1.ca.1.bcl.2.cbn-0.jazztpt.jazztbn.0-timp.3perc-cel.hp-str(6.0.6.3.3)
Material on hire
Study score **ED 4416** / Piano reduction **ED 4310**

Machaut-Balladen (1973)   21-25'

Text: Guillaume de Machaut
Soloists: tenor/2 tenors
srec/fl.2arec/2fl.2fl.2fl(pic).afl.2ob.ca.2cl.bcl.2bn-2tpt.2tbn-timp.perc-hp-str
Material on hire
Study score **ED 6620**

Mitte des Lebens (1951)   14'

Cantata
Text: Friedrich Hölderlin
Soloist: soprano
fl.bcl-hn-hp-vn
Material on hire
Score and parts **ED 6594** / Vocal score **ED 6595**

Prelude and Elegy (1958-59)   10'

Appendices to the "Impromptus"
Text: Friedrich Hölderlin
Soloist: soprano
3(pic).2.ca.2.bcl.2.cbn-3.3.3.1-timp.2perc-cel.hp-str
Material on hire
SM

That Time (1977)   43'

Text: Samuel Beckett
silent actor.speaker.MS.Bar-pno.hpd.gtr-[live electronic]
Material on hire
Study score **ED 6739**

"Versuch eines Agon um...?"

(1973)   17'

Soloists: 7 singers
2.1.ca.2.2.cbn-1.1.1.0-timp.perc-xyl.marimb-str
Material on hire
Study score **ED 6340**

Choral Works

The 100th Psalm (1962)   4'

"Jauchzet dem Herrn alle Welt"
Text: Bible
Chorus: mixed (5 prt)
3hn.2tpt.2tbn
Score **C 40915** / Parts **C 40916-10**

The 46th Psalm

Text: Bible
Chorus: mixed
C 33572

Agnus Dei

Chorus: mixed a cappella
C 33571

An die Nachgeborenen

(1947)   20'

Cantata
Text: Bertolt Brecht
Soloists: speaker, tenor
Chorus: mixed (4 prt)
2.3.3.3-0.3.2.1-timp.perc-pno-str(0.0.1.1.1)
Material on hire
SM

Chant de Naissance (1958)   28'

Cantata
Text: Saint-John Perse
Soloists: soprano, violin
Chorus: mixed (5 prt)
2.3.3.3-2.2.2.1-timp.perc-hp-str
Material on hire
Study score **ED 4598**

Eine deutsche Liedmesse

(1934)   30'

Chorus: mixed a cappella
ED 2928

Die Entschlafenen (1931)

Text: Friedrich Hölderlin
Chorus: male a cappella
Score **C 33746** / Parts **C 33746-99**

Gladbacher Te Deum

(1973)   20'

Soloist: baritone
Chorus: mixed
2(pic).2.ca.2.bcl.2.cbn-3.2.2.1-timp.3perc-vib.marimb.cel.hp-str(18.0.8.6.4)-electronics
Material on hire
SM

Glaubenslied (1931)   3'

Text: Carl Zuckmayer
Chorus: male a cappella
Score C 33747

Grenzen der Menschheit

(1930)   16'

Cantata
Text: Johann Wolfgang von Goethe
Soloist: baritone
Chorus: mixed (5 prt)
2.2.0.2-1.2.1.0-timp-str
Material on hire
SM

Herr, bleibe bei uns (1945)   45'

Geistliche Abendmusik
Soloist: low voice
Chorus: mixed
[vn.vc.db]-org/hpd
ED 4219 / Score ED 4219 / Parts ED 4219-01
(chorus)/ED 4219-11 (-14)

Lied der Welt (1931)   2'

Text: Hugo von Hofmannsthal
Chorus: male a cappella
C 39780 / Parts C 39780-99

Nuptiae Catulli (1937)   25'

Soloist: tenor
Chorus: chamber
2.0.1.0-0.1.0.0-perc-hp-str
Material on hire
SM

4 Petrarca-Sonette (1979)   14'

Chorus: mixed a cappella
ED 6903

Die Pfingstgeschichte

(1962-63)   40'

After Luke
Soloist: tenor
Chorus: 6-part mixed
ob.ca.bn-tpt.tbn-perc-xyl(vib).org-
str(1.0.1.1.1)
Material on hire
Study score ED 5039

3 Sacred Songs (1932)   3'

Text: various
Chorus: mixed a cappella
C 33570/33571/33572

Foss, Lukas

b.1922

Orchestral Works

Baroque Variations (1966-67)

27'

3(pic).rec/ob.0.3(ssax/tpt/Ebcl).ssax/Ebcl/tp
t.1-3.3.1.1-4perc-cel.epno.eorg.hpd.egtr-str
Material on hire
Score BSS 42635 (SM; Co-prod: CF)

Foss, Lukas

b. Berlin 15.8.1922

Though Foss's extraordinary versatility
might be explained by his cosmopolitan
background - he was born in Germany and
trained in France before moving to America
in 1937 - the novel directions taken in the
course of his creative development are enti-
rely of his own devising. These include a
period exploring "controlled improvisation"
between 1957 and 1962, and a subsequent
phase of experimentation from which date
well-known works such as the "Concerto
for Cello and Orchestra" and the "Baroque
Variations".

For 24 Winds (1965-66)   12'

2.afl.2.ca.Ebcl.1.bcl.asax.tsax.barsax.2.cbn
-1.3/3cnt.3.1
Material on hire
Study score CF 5064 (SM; Co-prod: CF)

Phorion (1967)   10'

On a Bach Prelude
pic.2.2.3.ssax.1-3.3.ttbn.1-4perc-
epno.eorg.egtr-str(min: 3.3.3.3.3)
Material on hire
SM (Co-prod: CF)

Concertos

Cello Concerto (1966)   20'

Soloist: cello
0.0.0.0-2.1.2.0-3perc-pno.org.hp-str
Material on hire
Study score CF 5672 / Parts CF 5673 (solo)
(SM; Co-prod: CF)

Elytres (1964)   11'

Soloists: flute, 2 violins
3vn-perc-hp-pno
Material on sale
BSS 41720 (SM; Co-prod: CF)

Choral Works

The Fragments of Archilochos (1966)   10'

Text: Guy Davenport
Soloists: counter-tenor, male & female
speakers
Chorus: mixed
timp.3perc-mand.gtr
Material on hire
Study score CF 4914 (SM; Co-prod: CF)

Geod (1969)   28'

Chorus: mixed
1.afl.0.ca.2.bcl.3-4.2.3.0-4perc-
vib.marimb.hp-str(24.0.8.8.8)-11/12 folk
inst
Material on hire
CF 4894 (SM; Co-prod: CF)

Françaix, Jean

b.1912

Stage Works

Les Demoiselles de la Nuit

(1948)   45'

Ballet in 1 Act by Jean Anouilh
Material on hire
SM

Le Diable boiteux (1937)   20'

Comic Chamber Opera
Text: Jean Françaix after Alain René Le
Sage
Material on hire
Vocal score ED 4309

Le Jeu sentimental (1936)   20'

Ballet in 7 Movements
Material on hire
SM

Le Jugement d'un Fou

(1938)   17'

Ballet in 1 Act
Material on hire
SM

Die Kamelien (1950)   40'

Pantomime by Sonja Korty
Material on hire
SM

La Lutherie enchantée

(1936)   20'

Ballet in 1 Scene
Material on hire
SM

Les Malheurs de Sophie

(1935)   40'

Ballet in 3 Scenes
Material on hire
Piano reduction ED 3294

Françaix, Jean

b. Le Mans 23.5.1912

„It is a strange venture to make honest folk laugh," says Jean Françaix of his own music, quoting Molière. Yet with characteristic modesty he undervalues his own achievement. Adhering to the classical ideals of clarity and coherence - the virtues of his beloved Mozart - he has written music that delights in the play of stylistic manners, taking irony as an artistic virtue in itself rather than a source of expressive conflict. A case in point is "Mozart new-look", diverting, amusing, but never superficial - one of his many pieces for wind ensemble. The oratorio "L'Apocalypse selon Saint Jean" shows a more profoundly religious outlook. "L'Horloge de fleure" is perhaps his best known work, but all his music shares aspects of Gallic charm deriving in part from Poulenc and from the school of Boulanger, but mostly from that hidden ingredient which is distinctly Françaix.

Pierrot ou les Secrets de la Nuit (1980) 31'

Ballet
Text: Michel Tournier
Material on hire
SM

Le Roi nu - Des Kaisers neue Kleider (1935) 35'

Ballet in 1 Act
Material on hire
Piano reduction ED 3292

Scuola di Ballo (1966) 25'

Ballet in 1 Act on a Theme by Boccherini
Material on hire
Piano reduction ED 7255

Verreries de Venise (1938) 15'

Ballet
Material on hire
SM

Orchestral Works

85 Mesures et un Da capo

(1991) 3'

2.0.0.asax.tsax.1-0.2.1.0-perc-str(3vn.va.vc)
Material on hire
SM

Les Bosquets de Cythère

(1946) 17'

pic.2(ca).2.2.2-4.2.2.0-timp.perc-hp-str
Material on hire
SM

Cassazione (1975) 17'

For 3 orchestras
2.2.ca.2.bcl.1.cbn-2.2.2.1-timp-str
Material on hire
Score ED 6649

7 Dances (1971) 12'

from the Ballet "Les Malheurs de Sophie'
2.2.2.2-2.0.0.0
Score ED 6459 / Parts ED 6460

Danses exotiques (1981) 10'

2(pic).2.2.asax.1.cbn-2.0.0.0-2perc
Material on hire
SM

La douce France (1946) 13'

2(pic).2(ca).2.2-4.2.0.0-timp.perc-hp-str
Material on hire
SM

Elégie (1990) 5'

pour commémorer le Bicentenaire de la mort de W. A. Mozart
fl.afl.ob.ca.bassethn.bcl.bn.cbn-2hn
Material on hire
SM

L' Histoire de Babar (1962)

(Francis Poulenc)
Arranger: Jean Françaix
2(pic).2(ca).2(bcl).2(cbn)-2.2.1.1-timp.perc-hp-str
Material on hire
SM

Huit Pièces pittoresques

(1984) 26'

(Emanuel Chabrier)
Arranger: Jean Françaix
2(pic).1.ca.1.bcl.1.cbn-2.0.0.0
Material on hire
SM

3 Marches militaires (1987) 14'

(Franz Schubert)
Arranger: Jean Françaix
2(pic).2.2.2(cbn)-2.0.0.0
Score ED 7621 / Parts ED 7622

Ouverture anacréontique

(1978) 15'

pic.1.2.2.2-2.2.0.0-str
Material on hire
Study score ED 6846

Pavane pour un Génie vivant

(1987) 3'

2.1.ca.2.2-0.0.0.0-str(2.1.1.2.2)
Material on hire
SM

9 Pièces caractéristiques

(1973) 15'

2.2.2.2-2.0.0.0
Score ED 6471 / Parts ED 6472

6 Preludi (1963) 15'

str(3.3.2.2.1)
Material on hire
Study score ED 5504

Quasi Improvvisando (1978) 2'

2.2.2(bcl).2-2.1.0.0
Score ED 6762 / Parts ED 6763

Le Roi nu - Des Kaisers neue Kleider (1935) 35'

Ballet Suite
pic.2.2.2.2-4.2.2.0-timp.perc-2hp-str
Material on hire
SM

Scuola di Ballo (1950) 25'

Orchestral Suite on a Theme by Boccherini
2(pic).2.2.2-2.2.2.1-timp.perc-str
Material on hire
SM

Sérénade (1934) 10'

1.1.1.1-1.1.1.0-str
Material on hire
Study score ED 5010

Sérénade B E A (1955) 11'

str
Material on hire
SM

Symphonie d'Archets

(1948) 22'

str
Material on hire
Study score ED 4269

Symphonie en sol majeur

(1953) 17'

2(pic).1(ca,ob d' am).2(bcl).1.cbn-2.2.0.0-timp.perc-str
Material on hire
Study score ED 7708

Thème et Variations (1971) 17'

2(pic).2.2.2-2.2.0.0-timp.2perc-str
Material on hire
SM

La Ville mystérieuse (1973) 14'

Fantasy
pic.2.2.ca.2.bcl.2.cbn-4.3.3.1-timp.perc-glsp.cel.2hp-str
Material on hire
SM

Les Zigues de Mars (1950) 18'

Ballet for Orchestra
2(pic).2.2.2(2cbn)-3.2.2.1-timp.perc-hpd.hp-str
Material on hire
SM

Concertos

Bassoon Concerto (1979) 18'

Soloist: bassoon
pno/str(3.3.2.2.1)
Material on hire
Piano reduction **FAG 18**

Chaconne (1976) 10'

Soloist: harp
str(3.3.2.2.1)
Material on hire
Parts **ED 6723 (solo)** / Piano reduction
ED 6723

Concertino (1932) 12'

Soloist: piano
2.2.2.2-2.2.2.0-str
Material on hire
Piano reduction **ED 3288**

Concerto for 15 Soloists and Orchestra (1988) 24'

"Suivi d'une surprise"
Soloists: 1.1.1.1.cbn-1.1.1.1-hp-str qnt
(orchestral players)
2.1.ca.1.bcl.1-3.3.2.0-timp.perc-str
Material on hire
SM

Concerto for 2 Harps

(1978) 23'

Soloists: 2 harps
str(3.3.2.2.1)
Material on hire
Parts **ED 7160 (solo)** / Piano reduction **ED 7160**

Concerto for 2 Pianos

(1965) 25'

Soloists: 2 pianos
2(2pic).2(ca).2(bcl).2(cbn)-2.2.2.0-timp.2perc-str
Material on hire
Parts **ED 7507/7508 (soli)** / Piano reduction
ED 7525

Concerto Grosso (1976) 13'

Soloists: wind qnt-str qnt
2.2.2.1.cbn-2.2.2.1-timp.perc-str
Material on hire
SM

Concerto pour Accordéon et Orchestre (1993) 20'

Soloist: accordion
2(2pic).2.2.2(cbn)-2.2.0.0-str
Material on hire
Study score **ED 8582** / Piano reduction **ED 8225**

Divertimento (1974) 10'

Soloist: flute
0.1.1.1-1.0.0.0-str(4.4.2/3.2.1)
Material on hire
SM

Divertissement (1935) 23'

Soloists: violin, viola, cello
pic.2.2.2.2-4.2.2.1-perc-hp-3db
Material on hire
Piano reduction **ED 6263**

Divertissement (1942) 9'

Soloist: bassoon
str(5.5.3.3.2)
Score **CON 185** / Parts **CON 185-70/-71** / Piano reduction **FAG 17**

Double Bass Concerto

(1974) 15'

Soloist: double bass
2(2pic).2.2.2(cbn)-2.0.0.0-str
Material on hire
Piano reduction **ED 6653**

Double Concerto (1991) 16'

Soloists: flute (afl,pic), clarinet (Ebcl,bcl)
0.2.0.2(cbn)-2.0.0.0-str
Material on hire
Score **ED 8180** / Parts **ED 8078 (soli)** / Piano reduction **ED 8078**

Fantaisie (1955) 18'

Soloist: cello
2(pic).2.2.2-2.2.2.0-timp.2perc-str
Material on hire
Parts **ED 5055 (solo)** / Piano reduction **ED 5055**

Flute Concerto (1966) 25'

Soloist: flute
2(pic).2.2.2-2.2.1.0-timp.perc-str
Material on hire
Parts **ED 6238 (solo)** / Piano reduction **ED 6238**

Guitar Concerto (1982-83) 20'

Soloist: guitar
str(3.3.2.2.1)
Material on hire
Piano reduction **ED 7133**

Harpsichord Concerto

(1959) 17'

Soloist: harpsichord
fl-str(3.2.2.2.1)
Material on hire
Parts **ED 6246-01 (solo)** / Piano reduction **ED 6246**

L' Heure du Berger (1947) 9'

Soloist: piano
str(4.4.3.3.2)
Material on hire
SM

Impromptu (1983) 8'

Soloist: flute
str(3.3.2.2.1)
Material on hire
Parts **ED 7168 (solo)** / Piano reduction
ED 7168

Introduction et Polonaise brillante, Op.3 8'

(Frédéric Chopin)
Arranger: Jean Françaix
Soloist: cello
2.2.2.2-4.2.2.1-timp.perc-hp-str
Material on hire
Piano reduction **BSS 38620**

Jeu poétique en six Mouvements (1969) 20'

Soloist: harp
2(2pic).2.2.2-2.1.0.0-timp.perc-str
Material on hire
Parts **ED 6248-01 (solo)** / Piano reduction
ED 6248

Musique de Cour (1937) 19'

Soloists: flute, violin
1(pic).2.2.2-2.2.2ttbn.0-timp.perc-str
Material on hire
Piano reduction **ED 2797**

Piano Concerto (1936) 18'

Soloist: piano
2.2.2.2-4.2.2.0-str
Material on hire
Piano reduction **ED 3670**

Quadruple Concerto (1935) 11'

Soloists: flute, oboe, clarinet, bassoon
0.0.0.0-4.2.2.0-str
Material on hire
Parts **ED 7159 (soli)** / Piano reduction **ED 7252**

Rhapsodie (1946) 9'

Soloist: viola
2.2.2.2.cbn-2.2.0.0-timp.perc-hp
Material on hire
Piano reduction **ED 8116**

Suite (1934) 12'

Soloist: violin
2.2.2.2-2.2.2.0-perc-str
Material on hire
Piano reduction **ED 2452**

Trombone Concerto (1983) 18'

Soloist: trombone
2(pic).2.1.bcl.1.cbn-2.0.0.0
Material on hire
Piano reduction **ED 7253**

Variations de Concert

(1950) 15'

Soloist: cello
str
Material on hire
Piano reduction **ED 5656**

Violin Concerto No.1

(1968/70) 25'

Soloist: violin
2(pic).2.2.2-2.2.2.0-timp.2perc-str
Material on hire
Piano reduction **ED 6449**

Violin Concerto No.2 (1979) 19'

Soloist: violin
1.1.1.1-1.0.0.0-str(3.3.2.2.1)
Material on hire
Piano reduction **ED 6871**

Chamber & Instrumental Works

Aubade (1974) 14'

12vc
Score **ED 6710** / Parts **ED 6794**

8 Bagatelles (1980) 8'

2vn.va.vc-pno
Score and parts **ED 6979**

Bassoon Concerto (1979) 18'

arrangement for bn-pno
FAG 18

Berceuse (1953) 3'

Arranger: Maurice Gendron
vc-pno
BSS 38406

5 "Bis" (1965) 10'

pno
ED 5826

Le Colloque des deux Perruches (1989) 18'

fl-afl
ED 7764

Cortège burlesque (1989) 5'

(Emanuel Chabrier)
Arranger: Jean Françaix
pic.1.1.ca.1.bcl.1.cbn-2.0.0.0
Material on hire
SM

8 Danses exotiques (1957) 9'

2pno
ED 4984

5 Danses exotiques (1961) 6'

asax-pno
ED 4745

Divertimento (1953) 9'

fl-pno
FTR 96

Divertissement (1942) 9'

Soloist: bassoon
str qnt
Score **CON 185** / Parts **CON 185-70/-71** /
Piano reduction **FAG 17**

Divertissement (1947) 9'

ob.cl.bn
Score **ED 4268** / Parts **ED 4331**

Dixtuor (1986) 20'

1(pic).1.1.1-1.0.0.0-str(1.1.1.1.1)
Score **ED 7515** / Parts **ED 7516**

Duo baroque (1980) 15'

db-hp
ED 7030

Trois Ecossaises & Variations sur un Air populaire allemand (1989) 9'

(Frédéric Chopin)
Arranger: Jean Françaix
2(pic).2.2.2-2.0.0.0
Material on hire
SM

Éloge de la Danse (1947) 12'

pno
ED 4016

Le Gay Paris (1974) 11'

Soloist: trumpet
1.2.2.1.cbn-2.0.0.0
Score **ED 6242** / Parts **ED 6143/TR 10 (solo)** /
Piano reduction **TR 10**

Habañera (1985) 4'

(Emanuel Chabrier)
Arranger: Jean Françaix
vc-pno
CB 129

L' Heure du Berger (1947) 9'

fl.ob.cl.bn-hn-pno
Score **ED 6034** / Parts **ED 6035**

L' Heure du Berger (1972) 9'

Arranger: Friedrich K. Wanek
1.1.2.2-1.0.1.0-pno
Score **ED 6271** / Parts **ED 6272**

Hommage à l'Ami Papageno (1984) 10'

Soloist: piano
2(pic).1.ca.1.bcl.1.cbn-2.0.0.0
Score **ED 7513** / Parts **ED 7514**

7 Impromptus (1977) 17'

fl-bn
Parts **FTR 116**

L' Insectarium (1953) 11'

hpd
ED 4977

Messe de Mariage (1986) 14'

organ solo
ED 7694

Mouvement perpétuel (1944) 2'

Arranger: Maurice Gendron
vc-pno
BSS 37704

Mozart New-Look (1981) 3'

Soloist: double bass
2.2.2.2-2.0.0.0
Score **ED 7205** / Parts **ED 7206** / Piano reduction **ED 7207**

Nocturne (1951) 3'

Arranger: Maurice Gendron
vc-pno
BSS 37702

Nocturne (1994)

pno
ED 8471

„Noël Nouvelet" et „Il est né, le Divin Enfant" (1987) 5'

12vc
Score **ED 7557** / Parts **ED 7613**

Notturno

4hn
ED 7545

Notturno e Divertimento (1987-90) 6'

4hn
Score and parts **COR 13**

Octet (1972) 19'

cl.bn-hn-2vn.va.vc.db
Score **ED 6155** / Parts **ED 6156**

Petit Quatuor (1935) 8'

ssax.asax.tsax.barsax
Score **ED 7501** / Parts **ED 3182**

Petit Quatuor (1935/92) 8'

2cl.bsthn.bcl-pno
Score and parts **KLB 40**

Petite Valse européenne (1979) 8'

Soloist: tuba
2.2.2.1.cbn-2.0.0.0
Material on hire
Parts **ED 6934 (solo)** / Piano reduction **ED 6934**

Piano Sonata (1960) 8'

ED 5082

5 Piccoli Duetti (1975) 9'

fl-hp
ED 6128

2 Pièces (1977)

hpd
ED 8472

5 Portraits de jeunes Filles (1936) 13'

pno
ED 2483

Pour remercier l'Auditoire (1994) 7'

fl.cl.hn-vn.vc-pno
ED 8393

Infoline · e-Mail
Schott Musik International
Mainz: Schott.Musik.com@T-Online.de
London: 101627.166@compuserve.com

La Promenade d'un Musicologue éclectique
(1987)   18'

pno
ED 7629

Quartet (1970)   18'
ca-vn.va.vc
Study score **ED 6320** / Parts **ED 6518**

Quatuor (1994)   18'
cl.bsthn.bcl-pno
Score and parts **ED 8330**

Quintet (1934)   12'
fl-vn.va.vc-hp
Score **ED 5889** / Parts **ED 5206**

Quintet (1977)   22'
cl-2vn.va.vc
Score **ED 6737** / Parts **ED 6738**

Quintet (1988)   15'
rec/fl-2vn.vc-hpd
Score **ED 7644** / Parts **ED 7658**

Quintet No.2 (1989)   16'
fl-str trio-hp
Score **ED 7793** / Parts **ED 7794**

Rondino-Staccato (1953)   3'
vc-pno
BSS 37703

Scherzo (1932)   3'
pno
ED 2477

Schön Wetter angesagt
(1982)   0.20'
3hn.3tpt.tbn.tuba
ED 7203

Scuola di Ballo (1966)   25'
on a Theme by Boccherini
2pno
ED 7255

Scuola di Celli   40'
10vc
Score **ED 8034** / Parts **ED 7784**

Septet
fl.ob.bn-2vn.vc-pno
Material on hire
SM

Sérénade (1934)   2'
from the "Serenade for Orchestra'
Arranger: Maurice Gendron
vc-pno
BSS 37855

Serenata (1978)   14'
guitar solo
GA 495

Sixtuor (1992)   17'
1.1.1.bcl.1-1.0.0.0
Score **ED 8057** / Parts **ED 8058**

Sonata (1984)   13'
rec-gtr
OFB 164

Sonatina (1934)   16'
vn-pno
ED 2451

String Quartet (1938)   16'
Score **ED 3523** / Parts **ED 3173**

10 Stücke für Kinder zum Spielen und Träumen (1975)   9'
pno
ED 6665

Suite (1962)   12'
flute solo
ED 4821

Suite (1978)   20'
harp solo
ED 6780

Suite (1990)   17'
sax qrt
Score and parts **ED 8017**

Suite (1994)
from "L'Apocalypse selon St. Jean"
2tpt-org
Score and parts **ED 8452**

Suite profane (1984)   14'
organ solo
ED 7296

Tema con 8 Variazioni (1980)
11'
violin solo
ED 6980

Trio (1933)   12'
vn.va.vc
Score **ED 3163** / Parts **ED 3168**

Trio (1971)   19'
fl-hp-vc
Score and parts **ED 6499**

Trio (1986)   17'
vn.vc-pno
Material on sale
Score and parts **ED 7425**

Trio (1990)   18'
cl-va-pno
Score and parts **ED 7859**

Trio (1994)   16'
ob.bn-pno
Score and parts **ED 8417**

Trio (1995)   17'
fl-vc-pno
Score and parts **ED 8521**

11 Variations (1982)   10'
0.2.2.2-2.1.0.0-db
Material on hire
SM

8 Variations on the name Johannes Gutenberg (1982)   10'
pno
ED 7139

Variations sur un Thème plaisant (1976)   12'
Soloist: piano
2.2.2.2(cbn)-2.0.0.0
Material on hire
SM

Wind Quartet (1933)   11'
fl.ob.cl.bn
Score **ED 4424** / Parts **ED 4222**

Wind Quintet No.1 (1948)   18'
fl.ob.cl.bn-hn
Score **ED 4103** / Parts **ED 4121**

Wind Quintet No.2 (1987)   18'
fl.ob(ca).cl.bn-hn
Score **ED 7547** / Parts **ED 7548**

Solo Voice(s)/Voice(s) and Piano/Guitar

5 Poèmes de Charles d'Orléans (1946)   8'
voice-pno
ED 4112

Prière du Soir - Chanson
(1947)   4'
Text: Agrippa d'Aubigné/Clément Marot
voice-pno
ED 4189

Prière du Soir - Chanson
(1947)   4'
Text: Agrippa d'Aubigné/Clément Marot
voice-gtr
ED 4189

Solo Voice(s) and Instrument(s)/ Orchestra

La Cantate de Méphisto

(1952)   15'

Text: Paul Valéry
Soloist: bass
str
Material on hire
SM

Invocation à la Volupté

(1946)   7'

Text: Jean de la Fontaine
Soloist: baritone
2.0.2.0-2.0.0.0-hp-str(2.0.1.1.1)
Material on hire
SM

Triade de toujours   (1991)   20'

Text: various
Soloists: soprano, baritone
1.1.1.1-1.0.0.0-hp-str(1.1.1.1.1)
Material on hire
Vocal score **ED 7964**

Choral Works

L' Apocalypse selon St. Jean

(1939)   75'

Oratorio fantastique in 3 Parts for two
orchestras
Soloists: soprano, alto, tenor, bass
Chorus: mixed
orchestre céleste:
2.2.0.0-4.3.3.1-2timp.perc-2hp.org([eorg])-str
orchestre infernal:
pic.0.0.2.bcl.asax.tsax.barsax.2-sarrusophone.
cnt.tbn-2perc-harm.acc.mand.gtr-str(2.0.0.0.2)
Material on hire
Vocal score **ED 4035**

3 Poèmes de Paul Valéry

(1982)   8'

Chorus: mixed a cappella (4-8 prt)
SKR 20008

Fricker, Peter Racine
1920-1990

Orchestral Works

Fantasy   (1956)   3'
on a theme of Mozart
2.2.2.2-2.2.0.0-timp-str
Material on hire
SL (Co-prod: UE)
Copyright USA: EAM/Italy: Ed. Suvini
Zerboni

Fricker, Peter Racine

b. London 5.9.1920, d. Santa Barbara
1.2.1990

Fricker's substantial output of symphonies,
concertos and string quartets formed an
important contribution to the growth of a
more progressive, European outlook among
British composers in the immediate postwar
years. A contrapunctalist, he was influenced
by the examples of Bartok and Hindemtih,
though using serial methods as well. His
vocal and choral works were few in number,
though the oratorio "The Vision of
Judgement" remains highly regarded.

Comedy Overture, Op. 32

(1958)   5'

2.2.2.2-2.2.0.0-timp-str
Material on hire
SL

Dance Scene, Op. 22   (1954)   11'

2.2.2.2-4.2.3.1-timp.2perc-str
Material on hire
Study score **ED 10221 (min.)*** /
Piano reduction **ED 10183***

Litany, Op. 26   (1955)   16'

double str
Material on hire
Study score **ED 10561 (min.)**

Prelude, Elegy and Finale, Op. 10   (1949)   12'

str
Material on hire
Study score **ED 10205 (min.)**

Rondo Scherzoso   (1948)   12'

2.2.3.2-4.2.3.1-timp.2perc-str
Material on hire
SL

Symphony No.1, Op. 9

(1948-49)   32'

3.3.3.3-4.3.3.1-timp.perc-pno.hp-str
Material on hire
Study score **ED 10301***

Symphony No.2, Op. 14

(1950-51)   28'

3.3.3.3-4.3.3.1-timp.perc-str
Material on hire
Study score **ED 10303***

Symphony No.3, Op. 36

(1960)   29'

3.2.3.2-4.2.3.0-timp-str
Material on hire
Study score **ED 10748 (min.)**

Symphony No.4, Op. 43

(1964-66)   34'

3.3.3.3-4.3.3.1-timp.2perc-str
Material on hire
SL

Symphony No.5, Op. 74

(1976)   20'

pic(fl).2.3.3.3-4.3.3.1-timp.3perc-org-str
Material on hire
SL

Concertos

Concertante No.1, Op. 13

(1950)   8'

Soloist: cor anglais
str
Material on hire
Study score **ED 10090 (min.)*** / Piano reduction **ED 10408***

Concertante No.2, Op. 15

(1951)   15'

Soloists: 3 pianos
str-timp
Material on hire
Study score **ED 10215***

Piano Concerto, Op. 19

(1952-54)   21'

Soloist: piano
2.2.2.2-2.2.0.0-timp-str
Material on hire
Piano reduction **ED 10396**

Rhapsodia Concertante, Op. 21 (1953-54)   22'

Violin Concerto No.2
Soloist: violin
2(pic).2.2.bcl.2.cbn-4.2.3.1-timp.3perc-str
Material on hire
Piano reduction **ED 10262**

Toccata, Op. 33 (1958-59)   12'

Soloist: piano
2(pic).2.2.2-4.2.3.0-timp.2perc-str
Material on hire
Piano reduction **ED 10654**

Viola Concerto, Op. 18

(1951-53)   28'

Soloist: viola
2.2.2.2-4.2.3.0-timp.2perc-str
Material on hire
Piano reduction **ED 10270***

Violin Concerto, Op. 11

(1950/74)   22'

Soloist: violin
1(pic).1.2.1-2.0.0.0-hp-str
Material on hire
Piano reduction **ED 10183***

Chamber & Instrumental Works

Aubade (1951)   3'

asax-pno
ED 10235*

14 Aubades (1958)   8'

pno
ED 10805

Cello Sonata, Op. 28 (1956) 16'

vc-pno
ED 10036

Choral (1956)   9'

organ solo
ED 10564*

4 Fughettas, Op. 2 (1946)   5'

2pno
ED 10124*

Horn Sonata, Op. 24 (1955) 14'

hn-pno
ED 10473

4 Impromptus, Op. 17

(1950-52)   15'

pno
ED 10246*

Nocturne and Scherzo, Op. 23 (1954)   9'

pno (4hnd)
ED 10650*

Octet, Op. 30 (1957-58)   22'

1.0.1.1-1.0.0.0-str(1.0.1.1.1)
Study score **ED 10710 (min.)**

Pastorale (1959)   5'

organ solo
ED 10742*

Ricercare, Op. 40 (1965)   9'

organ solo
ED 10937

Serenade No.1, Op. 34

(1959)   10'

fl.cl.bcl-hp-va.vc
Material on sale
SL

Sonata for 2 Pianos, Op. 78

(1977)   22'

2pno
Manuscript score on sale
SL

4 Sonnets (1955)   5'

pno
ED 10547 ("Contemporary British Piano Music")

String Quartet in One Movement, Op. 8 (1948)   14'

Study score **ED 10118** / Parts **ED 10119**

String Quartet No.2, Op. 20

(1948)   20'

Study score **ED 10219-01 (min.)**

String Quartet No.3, Op. 73

(1974-76)   20'

Material on sale
SL

12 Studies, Op. 38 (1961)   25'

pno
ED 10804

Suite for Harpsichord

(1956)   10'

hpd
ED 10806*

Suite for Recorders (1956)   6'

2arec.trec
ED 11836*

Trio, Op. 35 (1959)   12'

Serenade No.2
fl.ob-pno
ED 10739*

Variations, Op. 31 (1957-58) 13'

pno
ED 10704*

Violin Sonata, Op. 12

(1950)   16'

vn-pno
ED 10128*

Wedding Processional (1960)   6'

organ solo
ED 10741*

Wind Quintet, Op. 5 (1947)   20'

fl.ob.cl.bn-hn
ED 10255 / Study score **ED 10216 (min.)**

Solo Voice(s)/Voice(s) and Piano/Guitar

O Mistress Mine (1961)   2'

Text: William Shakespeare
tenor-gtr
GA 210

Solo Voice(s) and Instrument(s)/ Orchestra

Cantata, Op. 37 (1961-62)   12'

Text: William Saroyan
Soloist: tenor
1.1.1.1-1.0.0.0-str(1.1.1.1.1)
Material on hire
SL

Elegy, Op. 25 (1955)   9'

The Tomb of St. Eulalia
Text: Prudentius
Soloist: counter tenor
va da gamba-hpd
ED 10483*

O longs Désirs, Op. 39

(1963)   21'

Text: Louïse Labé
Soloist: soprano
2.2.3.3-4.2.3.1-timp.2perc-str
Material on hire
Vocal score **ED 19776**

3 Sonnets of Cecco Angiolieri da Siena, Op. 7 (1947)   8'

Soloist: tenor
1.1.1.1-1.0.0.0-vc.db
Material on hire
SL

Choral Works

Musick's Empire, Op. 27

(1955)   13'

Text: Andrew Marvell
Chorus: mixed
1.1.1.1-1.1.1.0-timp-str
Material on hire
Vocal score **ED 10571***

Rollant et Oliver, Op. 6

(1949) 6'

Chorus: mixed a cappella
ED 10294

The Vision of Judgement, Op. 29 (1957-58) 50'

Text: Cynewulf (8th century)
Soloists: soprano, tenor
Chorus: mixed
3.3.3.3-4.4.3.1-2timp.3perc-2hp.org-str
additional: 2tpt.4tbn
Material on hire
Vocal score ED 10616*

Fromm-Michaels, Ilse

1888-1986

Chamber & Instrumental Works

Langsamer Walzer 4'

(in: Frauen komponieren)
pno
ED 7197

Frommel, Gerhard

1906-1984

Stage Works

Der Gott und die Bajadere, Op. 12 (1936) 40'

Ballet in 2 Scenes
Material on hire
SM

Orchestral Works

Concert-Suite (1936) 21'

from the ballet "Der Gott und die Bajadere"
2(pic).2(ca).2(bcl).2(cbn)-4.2.3.1-timp.2perc-hp-str
Material on hire
SM

Scherzo (1942) 11'

from the Symphony in E-Major
2(pic).2.2.2-4.3.3.1-timp.perc-str
Material on hire
SM

Sinfonisches Vorspiel, Op. 23

(1943) 17'

pic.2.2(ca).2.2.cbn-4.3.3.1-timp.perc-hp-str
Material on hire
SM

Suite, Op. 11 (1936) 12'

1(pic).1.1.1-1.1.1.0-timp.2perc-str(6-8.6.4.4.3)
Material on hire
SM

Symphony in E Major, Op. 13 (1943) 35'

2(pic).2.2.2-4.3.3.1-timp.perc-str
Material on hire
SM

Concertos

Concertino, Op. 24 (1943)

Soloists: tenor-horn, trombone
fl.ob.2cl.bn-hn
Material on hire
SM

Chamber & Instrumental Works

Caprichos, Op. 14 (1939)

pno
ED 2885

Choral Works

Begegnung in der Eisenbahn (1957)

Eine Szene aus dem Alltag
Text: Dieter Wyss
Soloists: soprano, tenor
Chorus: mixed chamber
1.1(ca).1.1-1.0.0.0-perc-pno-vc
Material on hire
SM

Furer, Arthur

b.1924

Choral Works

Portum Inveni (1960) 17'

Chorus: mixed
1.1.0.0-1.1.1.0-timp-pno-str
Material on hire
SM

G

Gál, Hans
1890-1987

Stage Works

"Die beiden Klaas", Op. 42
(1932-33)   full evening

Opera in 3 Acts
Text: K.M. v. Levetzow
Material on hire
SM

Orchestral Works

Burlesque, Op. 42b (1932-33) 7'
Overture to the 3 Act of "Die beiden Klaas"
2(pic).2.2.2-2.2.1.0-timp.perc-str
Material on hire
SM

Promenadenmusik für Blasorchester (1926)
concert band
Score **SHS 1007** / Parts **SHS 1007-70**

"Scaramuccio"- Ballet Suite, Op. 36 (1929) 25'
2.2.2.2-2.2.1.0-timp.perc-str
Material on hire
SM

Chamber & Instrumental Works

Divertimento, Op. 98 (1970) 10'
srec.arec.trec
Study score **OFB 120**

3 Intermezzi, Op. 103
(1974)   15'
arec/fl-hpd/pno
OFB 134

String Quartet No.2, A Minor , Op. 35 (1929) 27'
Score **ED 3496** / Parts **ED 3151**

Choral Works

4 British Folk Songs (1969)
Chorus: mixed a cappella
C 42310 (-13)

3 Portrait Studies, Op. 34
(1929)   7'

Text: Wilhelm Busch
Chorus: male a cappella
C 46936

Gál, Hans

b. Brunn, nr Vienna 5.8.1890, d. Edinburgh
3.10.1987

A prizewinning student of music and philosophy at Vienna University, Gál enjoyed a successful career as composer both in his homeland and in Britain, where he settled in 1938, becoming a lecturer at Edinburgh University in 1945. His musicianship was highly regarded by Sir Donald Tovey, and his choral works and chamber music are an important continuation of the central German tradition of Beethoven, Brahms and Schubert.

Gebhard, Hans
1897-1974

Choral Works

Es begab sich aber..., Op. 35 15'
Christmas Cantata
Chorus: mixed
recs.fl.ob-timp-xyl.glsp-str
ED 5767

Orchestral Works

Ländliche Suite, Op. 23 18'
1.1.1.0-0.2.1.0-timp.2perc-str
Material on hire
SM

Concertos

Piano Concerto, Op. 25   23'

Soloist: piano
1.1.1.1-2.2.1.0-timp.perc-str
Material on hire
SM

Choral Works

Auf einem Baum ein Kuckuck saß   2'

from "Ein ergötzlich Liedersingen"
Chorus: female, male
C 38539

Ein ergötzlich Liedersingen   4'

Chorus: male,children's/female a cappella
C 38538/38539

Es saß ein Käfer auf'm Bäumel (1953)   2'

Chorus: male a cappella
C 38540

Froh zu sein bedarf es wenig   1'

from "Ein ergötzlich Liedersingen"
Chorus: female, male
C 38538

Lustig, ihr Brüder   2'

from "Ein ergötzlich Liedersingen"
Chorus: female, male
C 38538

Missa gotica, Op. 20   15'

Chorus: mixed (3 prt)
org
C 33736

Wenn alle Brünnlein fließen, Op. 29   40'

Text: Hans Gebhard
Chorus: mixed
1.0.2.1-2.0.0.0-str
Material on hire
Study score **ED 3192**

Genzmer, Harald
b.1909

Orchestral Works

Divertimento di Danza

(1953)   16'

str
Score **CON 62** / Parts **CON 62-70**

Genzmer, Harald

b. Blumenthal nr Bremen 9.2.1909

A considerable figure in German musical life, Genzmer studied in Hindemith's composition class at the Berlin Hochschule für Musik, and continued his teacher's tradition of craftsmanly art generously applied to the enrichment of the entire range of instrumental and vocal repertoire. Highly regarded as a teacher, he experimented with electronic instruments in the 1940's, composing a pair of concertos for that rarely heard combination of trautonium and orchestra.

Festliches Vorspiel (1945)   8'

pic.2.2.2.bcl.2-4.3.3.1-timp.perc-str
Material on hire
SM

Kokua (1951)   17'

Dance Suite
2(pic).2(ca).2.2-3.2.2.1-timp.2perc-hp-str
Material on hire
SM

Konzert in C (1948)   16'

2(pic).1.ca.2.2-4.2.3.1-timp.perc-str
Material on hire
SM

Pachelbel Suite (1946)   16'

2(pic).1.0.2-2.2.0.0-timp.perc-str
Material on hire
SM

Sinfonietta (1955)   12'

str
Score **CON 60** / Parts **CON 60-70**

Sinfonietta Seconda   (1995)

str
Score **CON 246** / Parts **CON 246-70**

Symphony No.1 (1957/70)   24'

2(pic).2(ca).2(bcl).2-3.2.2.1-timp.perc-str
Material on hire
SM

Symphony No.2 (1958)   22'

str
Material on hire
SM

Concertos

Cello Concerto (1950)   30'

Soloist: cello
2(pic).2(ca).2.2-3.2.2.1-timp.perc-hp-str
Material on hire
SM

Chamber Concerto (1957)   13'

Soloist: oboe
str
Material on hire
Piano reduction **OBB 29**

Concertino No.1 (1946)   15'

Soloists: piano, flute/violin
str
Score **CON 58** / Parts **CON 58-01 (-03)/-70**

Divertimento Giocoso (1960)

13'
Soloists: 2fl/2arec/fl.ob
str
Score **CON 61** / Parts **CON 61-01/-02/-70**

Flute Concerto (1954)   19'

Soloist: flute
0.1.1.1-2.1.0.0-timp.perc-str
Material on hire
Study score **ED 4571** / Piano reduction
FTR 115

Piano Concerto (1948)   25'

Soloist: piano
2.1.ca.2.2-3.2.1.0-timp.perc-str
Material on hire
Piano reduction **ED 5278**

Trautonium Concerto

(1952)   27'
Soloist: mixture-trautonium
0.0.0.0-4.3.3.1-timp.perc-str
Material on hire
SM

Violin Concerto (1959)   17'

Soloist: violin
0.2.0.0-2.0.0.0-str
Material on hire
Piano reduction **ED 5162**

Infoline · e-Mail
Schott Musik International
Mainz: Schott.Musik.com@T-Online.de
London: 101627.166@compuserve.com

Chamber & Instrumental Works

Capriccio (1950) 7'
Piano Sonatina No.2
ED 4288

Cello Sonata No.1 (1954) 16'
vc-pno
ED 4603

11 Duets (1973) 8'
srec.arec
OFB 130

European Folksongs (1969-70)
trec.arec/2arec
OFB 23/24

8 Fantasien (1983) 13'
vibraphone solo
BAT 37

Flute Sonata in F Sharp minor (1956) 10'
2fl (or other melody-instruments)
FTR 92

Flute Sonata No.2 in E minor (1945) 8'
fl-pno
FTR 93

Kleines Klavierbuch (1945) 11'
pno
ED 1054

Konzertante Musik (1983) 18'
2tpt.2tbn-org
Score **ED 7054** / Parts **ED 7054**

Neuzeitliche Etüden - Vol.1 (1956) 2'
flute solo
FTR 87

Neuzeitliche Etüden - Vol.2 (1964) 2'
flute solo
FTR 88

Organ Sonata (1953) 12'
organ solo
ED 4489

Percussion Quartet (1982) 10'
(Gschwendtner)
Material on sale
BAT 33

Piano Sonata No.1 (1938) 12'
ED 2679

Piano Sonata No.2 (1942) 17'
ED 3951

Piano Sonatina No.1 (1940) 9'
ED 2886

Piano Sonatina No.3 (1950) 6'
ED 5067

Quartettino (1958) 5'
srec.arec.trec.brec
Score and parts **OFB 31**

Quintet (1995) 18'
cl-str qrt
Score and parts **ED 8379**

Recorder Sonata No.1 (1941) 10'
arec-pno
OFB 32

Recorder Sonata No.2 (1973) 11'
arec-pno
OFB 128

Septet (1944) 15'
hp-fl.cl-hn-vn.va.vc
Study score **ED 3623** / Parts **ED 1590**

Sonata (1954) 10'
2arec-pno
OFB 33/ED 4091

Sonata for 2 Pianos (1950) 14'
2pno
ED 4332

Sonatina for Mandoline and Piano (1985) 10'
mand-pno
ED 7241

Spielbuch (1941) 16'
3vn
ED 2753

Spielbuch No.1 (1942) 8'
pno (4hnd)
ED 2758

Spielbuch No.2 (1942) 5'
pno (4hnd)
ED 2759

String Quartet No.1 (1949) 26'
Score **ED 7834** / Parts **ED 4287**

Suite in C (1948) 13'
pno
ED 4023

Tanzstücke - Vol.1 (1961) 11'
2arec
OFB 34

Tanzstücke - Vol. 2 (1973) 10'
2arec
OFB 129

Trio (1948) 10'
srec.2arec (or other melody-instruments)
alt. version: srec.arec.trec
Score **OFB 35** / Parts **OFB 35**

Tripartita in F (1950) 8'
organ solo
ED 3842

Variationen 16'
über das hessische Volkslied "Ich kenne ein Land"
carillon solo
ED 8337

Violin Sonata No.1 (1943) 12'
vn-pno
ED 3663

Violin Sonata No.2 (1949) 13'
vn-pno
ED 4022

Violin Sonatina No. 1 (1953) 10'
vn-pno
ED 4482

Violin Sonatina No. 2 (1995) 12'
vn-pno
Material on sale
ED 8527

Violin Sonatina No. 3 (1995) 12'
vn-pno
ED 8529

Solo Voice(s)/Voice(s) and Piano/Guitar

Liederbuch (1941)
soprano-pno
ED 3797

Solo Voice(s) and Instrument(s)/ Orchestra

3 Songs (1942) 14'
Text: various
Soloist: soprano
2.2.2.2-2.2.0.0-timp-hp-str
Material on hire
SM

Choral Works

Ablösung (1956) 2'
from "8 Chorlieder" (Des Knaben Wunderhorn)
Chorus: female a cappella
C 39372

Adventsmotette (1980) 4'
Chorus: male
org
Score **C 44843** / Choral score **C 44844**

Am Abend (1989) 4'
from "7 Hölderlin-Chöre"
Text: Friedrich Hölderlin
Chorus: mixed a cappella
C 46570

An den Flamingo (1965) 2'
from "4 indische Lieder"
Chorus: male a cappella
C 41553

An die Zikade (1984) 5'
from "3 Anakreon-Chöre"
Text: Johann Wolfgang von Goethe
Chorus: female a cappella
C 45440

An ihren Genius (1989) 4'
from "7 Hölderlin-Chöre"
Text: Friedrich Hölderlin
Chorus: mixed a cappella
C 46571

3 antike Gesänge (1973) 10'
Chorus: mixed
brass(3tpt.2tbn)/pno (4hnd)
Material on sale
Score **ED 6570** / Parts **ED 6570-11 (-15)** /
Choral score **ED 6570-01/-02**

2 Chorsprüche (1984) 3'
Text: Friedrich Rückert
Chorus: female a cappella
C 45433

Christkindleins Wiegenlied
(1956) 3'
from "8 Chorlieder" (Des Knaben Wunderhorn)
Chorus: female a cappella
C 39376

Du bist min (1958) 1'
from "5 Chorlieder"
Text: Hesse von Rinach
Chorus: mixed a cappella
C 39666

Du sendest Schätze (1984) 1'
from "3 Goethe-Chöre"
Text: Johann Wolfgang von Goethe
Chorus: female a cappella
C 45442

Du tanzest leicht (1984) 1'
from "3 Goethe-Chöre"
Text: Johann Wolfgang von Goethe
Chorus: female a cappella
C 45442

Echo vom Himmel (1969) 2'
from "Englisch Horn"
Text: G. Herbert
Soloists: tenor, bass
Chorus: male a cappella (6 prt)
C 42486

Finnisches Lied (1964) 2'
from "Lieder der Welt"
Chorus: mixed a cappella (6 prt)
C 40991

Frau Nachtigall (1956) 2'
from "8 Chorlieder" (Des Knaben Wunderhorn)
Chorus: female a cappella (3 prt)
C 39372

Früh, wenn Tal, Gebirg und Garten (1984) 1'
from "3 Goethe-Chöre"
Text: Johann Wolfgang von Goethe
Chorus: female a cappella
C 45443

Frühling-Winter (1969) 2'
from "Englisch Horn"
Chorus: male a cappella
C 42492

Gebet für einen Unbelehrbaren (1989) 2'
from "7 Hölderlin-Chöre"
Text: Friedrich Hölderlin
Chorus: mixed a cappella
C 46566

4 Gedichte (1962) 10'
Text: Georg Britting/Carl Zuckmayer
Chorus: male
pno (4hnd)
Score **ED 5179** / Choral score **ED 5179-01**

2 geistliche Festsprüche
(1979) 3'
Text: Bible
Chorus: male
[org]
Score **C 44842**

5 Gesänge (1989) 9'
Text: various
Chorus: mixed a cappella
C 46634

Die Gewißheit (1958) 2'
from "Drei Chorlieder vom Wein"
Text: Gotthold Ephraim Lessing
Chorus: male a cappella
C 39972

Hälfte des Lebens (1989) 2'
from "7 Hölderlin-Chöre"
Text: Friedrich Hölderlin
Chorus: mixed a cappella
C 46567

Herz, wo warst du in der Nacht (1964) 2'
from "Lieder der Welt"
Text: Lope de Vega
Chorus: mixed a cappella (6 prt)

C 40993

Der Hoffnungslose (1964) 2'
from "Lieder der Welt"
Soloist: baritone
Chorus: mixed a cappella
C 40992

Hymn (1984) 3'
Chorus: male a cappella
C 45431

3 Hymns (1946) 48'
Text: Gertrud von le Fort
Soloists: soprano, alto, baritone
Chorus: mixed
2(pic).2(ca).0.2-2.2.0.0-timp-str
Material on hire
SM

Hyperions Schicksalslied
(1989) 2'
from "7 Hölderlin-Chöre"
Text: Friedrich Hölderlin
Chorus: mixed a cappella
C 46569

Ich will truren fahren lan
(1958) 1'
from "5 Chorlieder"
Text: Spervogel
Chorus: mixed a cappella
C 39665

In der Nacht gesungen
(1958) 3'
Chorus: male a cappella
CHBL 339

Käuzlein (1956) 2'
from "8 Chorlieder" (Des Knaben Wunderhorn)
Soloists: soprano, mezzo-soprano, alto
Chorus: female a cappella (3 prt)
C 39375

Kinderpredigt (1956) 2'
from "8 Chorlieder" (Des Knaben Wunderhorn)
Chorus: female a cappella
C 39373

Ein Klagegesang (1969) 2'
from "Englisch Horn"
Text: Percy Bysshe Shelley
Soloists: tenor, bass
Chorus: male a cappella (6 prt)
C 42487

Klageliche not (1958) 1'
from "5 Chorlieder"
Text: Hesse von Rinach
Chorus: mixed a cappella
C 39666

Knabe du (1984) 5'
from "3 Anakreon-Chöre"
Text: Eduard Mörike
Chorus: female a cappella
C 45440

Lebenslauf (1989)   2'

from "7 Hölderlin-Chöre"
Text: Friedrich Hölderlin
Chorus: mixed a cappella
C 46566

Lied des Vogelstellers (1979) 2'

from "Drei leichte Chorlieder"
Text: J. Prevert
Chorus: mixed a cappella (SATB)
C 44604

Lied des Vogelstellers (1958) 2'

from "5 Chöre"
Text: J. Prevert
Chorus: mixed double a cappella
C 41580

2 Lieder beim Wein (1972)   4'

Text: various
Chorus: male a cappella
C 43577

Mandalay (1964)   3'

from "Lieder der Welt"
Text: R. Kipling
Chorus: mixed a cappella (6 prt)
C 40994

Mass in E (1953)   45'

Soloists: soprano, alto, baritone
Chorus: mixed
2.1.ca.0.1-2.2.1.0-timp-str
Material on hire
SM

Mistral über den Gräbern

(1964)   2'

from "Lieder der Welt"
Text: A. Mac-Leish
Chorus: mixed a cappella (SATB)
C 40993

Mondaufgang (1965)   2'

from "4 indische Lieder"
Chorus: male a cappella
C 41552

Moosburger Graduale

(1971)   16'

Text: Latin
Chorus: mixed
[rec.fl.ob.bn]-str
Score **ED 6505** / Parts **ED 6505-01/-11 (-17)** /
Choral score **ED 6505-01**

Nachts   2'

Text: P. Bockelmann
Chorus: mixed a cappella
C 45373

Oft in der stillen Nacht

(1969)   2'

from "Englisch Horn"
Text: Th. Moore
Chorus: male a cappella
C 42485

Racine-Kantate (1949)   20'

Text: Jean-Baptiste Racine
Soloist: baritone
Chorus: mixed (4 prt)
2.1.ca.0.2-2.1.0.0-timp-str
Material on hire
SM

Rechenstunde (1979)   3'

from "Drei leichte Chorlieder"
Text: J. Prevert
Chorus: mixed a cappella (SATB)
C 44606

Rechenstunde (1958)   3'

from "5 Chöre"
Text: J. Prevert
Chorus: mixed a cappella (7 prt)
C 39971

Römische Weinsprüche

(1958)   2'

from "Drei Chorlieder vom Wein"
Chorus: male a cappella
Score **C 39974** / Parts **C 39975-01/-02**
(chorus)

Rondell (1969)   2'

from "Englisch Horn"
Text: G. Chaucer
Chorus: male a cappella
C 42488

Der schwarze Mond (1958)   2'

from "4 Südamerikanische Gesänge"
Text: V.G. Kemp
Chorus: mixed a cappella (5 prt)
C 39935

Seemannslied (1969)   2'

from "Englisch Horn"
Text: William Shakespeare
Chorus: male a cappella
C 42491

Sehnsucht (1965)   2'

from "4 indische Lieder"
Chorus: male a cappella
C 41551

Sensemayá (1958)   3'

from "4 Südamerikanische Gesänge"
Text: N. Guillen
Chorus: mixed double a cappella
C 39937

Singe, mein Herz (1974)   3'

Text: Hermann Hesse
Chorus: male a cappella
C 43937

Sonett (1969)   2'

from "Englisch Horn"
Text: William Shakespeare
Chorus: male a cappella
C 42490

Sonnenuntergang (1989)   2'

from "7 Hölderlin-Chöre"
Text: Friedrich Hölderlin
Chorus: mixed a cappella
C 46568

Stadturlaub (1979)   2'

from "Drei leichte Chorlieder"
Text: J. Prevert
Chorus: mixed a cappella (SATB)
C 44605

Stadturlaub (1958)   2'

from "5 Chöre"
Text: J. Prevert
Chorus: mixed a cappella (6 prt)
C 39970

Stürm, du Winterwind

(1969)   2'

from "Englisch Horn"
Text: William Shakespeare
Chorus: male a cappella
C 42489

Swel man ein guot wip hat

(1958)   1'

from "5 Chorlieder"
Text: Spervogel
Chorus: mixed a cappella
C 39667

Tagelied (1964)   2'

from "Lieder der Welt"
Chorus: mixed a cappella (7 prt)
C 40991

Tanzende (1964)   2'

from "Lieder der Welt"
Text: E. Pound
Chorus: mixed a cappella (6 prt)
C 40993

Tanzliedchen (1964)   2'

from "Lieder der Welt"
Chorus: mixed a cappella (5 prt)
C 40992

Das Täubchen (1984)   5'

from "3 Anakreon-Chöre"
Text: A. von Plathen
Chorus: female a cappella
C 45441

Tristissima Nox (1958)   3'

from "4 Südamerikanische Gesänge"
Text: M.G. Najera
Chorus: mixed a cappella (9 prt)
C 39936

Tropus ad Gloria (1984)   3'

Text: Latin
Chorus: mixed a cappella
C 45498

Über die Geburt Jesu (1995) 2'

Text: Andreas Gryphius
Chorus: mixed
C 46473

**Ungeheuer und rot erscheint
die Wintersonne** (1958)   2'

from "5 Chöre"
Text: J. Prevert
Chorus: mixed double a cappella
C 41579

Urlicht (1956) 2'

from "8 Chorlieder" (Des Knaben
Wunderhorn)
Chorus: female a cappella
C 39373

Der verschwundene Stern

(1956) 2'

from "8 Chorlieder" (Des Knaben
Wunderhorn)
Chorus: female a cappella (3 prt)
C 39374

Vom Abenteuer der Freude

(1960) 10'

Text: Stefan Andres
Chorus: mixed
0.0.0.0-4.3.3.1-timp.perc-str
Score ED 5168 / Parts ED 5168-10 / Choral
score ED 5168-01/-02

Wacht auf, ihr schönen Vögelein (1956) 2'

from "8 Chorlieder" (Des Knaben
Wunderhorn)
Chorus: female a cappella
C 39374

Warnung (1965) 2'

from "4 indische Lieder"
Chorus: male a cappella
C 41551

Der Weinschwelg (1958) 2'

from "Drei Chorlieder vom Wein"
Chorus: male a cappella
C 39973

Weiße Verlassenheit (1958) 4'

from "4 Südamerikanische Gesänge"
Text: L. Lugones
Chorus: mixed a cappella (7 prt)
C 39934

Wie man einen Vogel malt

(1958) 4'

from "5 Chöre"
Text: J. Prevert
Chorus: mixed a cappella (10 prt)
Score C 39670 / Parts C 39670-01/-02 (chorus)

Wurzel des Waldes (1958) 1'

from "5 Chorlieder"
Text: Spervogel
Chorus: mixed a cappella
C 39665

Gerster, Ottmar
1897-1969

Stage Works

Enoch Arden (1935-36) 120'

Opera in 4 Scenes
Text: Karl Michael von Levetzow
Material on hire
SM

Gerster, Ottmar

b. Braunfels, Hessen 29.6.1897, d. Leipzig
31.8.1969

**Gerster, like his fellow pupil Hindemith at
the Hoch Conservatory in Frankfurt am
Main, was an eminent violist who was much
involved in chamber and orchestral playing
before his involvement with workers' choirs
as a conductor in the 1920's and 30s. In 1947
he was appointed Professor of Composition
and Theory at the Weimar Musikhochschule,
which he directed from 1948 to 1952. His
output of operas, symphonies, concertos
and cantatas shows a refined understanding
of the great German tradition.**

Der ewige Kreis (1934) 35'

Ballet Pantomime in 4 Scenes
Material on hire
Piano reduction ED 3193

Die Hexe von Passau

(1939-41) full evening

Opera in 4 Scenes
Text: Richard Billinger
Material on hire
Vocal score ED 2875

Madame Liselotte (1932-33) 135'

Opera in 3 Acts
Text: Franz Clemens/Paul Ginthum
Material on hire
SM

Die Mondschein-Prinzessin

(1942) 90'

Opera
Text: Karl Stadler
Material on hire
Vocal score ED 2865

Das verzauberte Ich

(1943-48) full evening

Musical Drama in 4 Acts
Text: Paul Koch
Material on hire
Libretto BN 3270-00

Orchestral Works

Enoch Arden - Overture

(1936) 12'

2.2.2.2-4.3.3.1-timp.perc-str
Material on hire
SM

Ernste Musik (1938) 17'

*3(pic).2.ca.2.bcl.2.cbn-4.3.3.0-timp.3perc-
hp-str*
Material on hire
SM

Festliche Musik (1929/1936) 7'

2.2.2.2-4.2.2.0-timp.perc-str
Material on hire
SM

Festliche Tanzmusik from "Madame Liselotte" (1933) 15'

2.2.2.2-4.2.3.0-timp.perc-str
Material on hire
SM

Festliche Toccata (1941-42) 10'

pic.2.2.2.bcl.2.cbn-4.3.3.0-timp.perc-str
Material on hire
SM

Oberhessische Bauerntänze

(1938) 12'

1.1.2.1-2.2.1.0-timp.perc-str
Material on hire
SM

Oberhessische Bauerntänze

(1938) 12'

Arranger: Norbert Studnitzky (1991)
*2.[1].[Ebcl].3.2asax.tsax.[1]-
3.2flhn.3thn.3.3.euph.2- timp.2-3perc*
Score SHS 1002 / Parts SHS 1002-70

Symphony No. 1 (1933/34) 27'

Little Symphony
2.2.2.2-3.2.1.0-timp.perc-str
Material on hire
SM

Concertos

Capriccietto (1932) 7'

Soloist: timpani
str
Material on hire
SM

Concertino, Op. 16 (1928) 12'

Soloist: viola
ob-hn-timp-str(6.0.4.2.2)
Material on hire
SM

Chamber & Instrumental Works

Divertimento (1927/28)

pno
SM

Divertimento (1925)

vn.va
ED 1908

Introduktion und Perpetuum

(1945)

pno
SM

Kleine Musik zu festlichem Tag (1949) 5'

3vn
ED 4113

Solo Voice(s)/Voice(s) and Piano/Guitar

5 einfache Lieder

Text: Sappho Cäsar Flaischlen, Theodor Storm, Albert Geiger
medium voice-pno
SM

5 Lieder (1921-38) 15'

Text: Bierbaum
baritone-pno
ED 3195

5 Lönslieder (1918-19) 15'

voice-pno
ED 3794

Solo Voice(s) and Instrument(s)/ Orchestra

4 alte Lieder (1922) 18'

alto-va
ED 3796

Choral Works

An die Sonne (1937) 20'

Text: Ludwig Andersen
Soloist: soprano
Chorus: male, boy's
2.2.2.2-4.2.3.0-timp.perc-str
Material on hire
SM

Chor der Bergleute (1933) 4'

Chorus: male a cappella
SM

Festgesang (1932) 6'

from "Iphigenie in Aulis" by Ch.W.Gluck
Chorus: female a cappella
CHBL 544

5 Männerchöre (1938) 9'

Text: Albert Korn
Chorus: male
SM

Preis des Schöpfers (1933) 3'

Text: Albert Korn
Chorus: male a cappella
SM

4 Sinngedichte (1936) 6'

Chorus: female a cappella
SM

Soldatenlied (1930) 4'

Text: Johann Wolfgang von Goethe
Chorus: male
SM

Vini boni veritas (1940) 4'

Text: Albert Korn
Chorus: male
SM

Gervais, Terence White

b.1922

Concertos

Konzert

Soloist: piano
2.1.1.1-1.1.1.1-timp.perc-str
AVV

Gilbert, Anthony

b.1934

Stage Works

The Scene-Machine (Das Popgeheuer), Op. 18

(1970) 50'

Opera in 1 Act
Text: George MacBeth
Material on hire
Libretto **ED 11243**

Orchestral Works

Crow-Cry, Op. 27 (1976) 20'

1(pic).1.1(bcl).1-1.1.1(ttbn/btbn).0-perc-epno-str(1.0.1.1.1)
Material on hire
SL

Dream Carousels (1988) 12'

3(pic).2.2(bcl).2asax.2tsax.barsax.2-4.3.3.euph.1-2-3perc-db
Material on hire
SL

Ghost and Dream Dancing, Op. 25 (1974/81) 19'

3(pic).3(2ca).3(Ebcl,bcl).2.cbn-4.3(flhn).3(2ttbn,btbn).1-timp.3perc-cel.hp-str
Material on hire
SL

Mozart Sampler with Ground (1991) 10'

(After KV 550)
2(pic).2.1.bcl.2-2.0.0.0-str(1.1.1.1.1)
Material on hire
SL

Peal II, Op. 12 (1968) 9'

for Jazz or School Orchestra
2asax/2cl.2tsax/2fl.barsax/fl-4tpt.4tbn.btbn-[perc]-gtr-db
Material on hire
SL

Regions, Op. 6 (1966) 14'

2(2pic).2(2ca).2(bcl).2(2cbn)-4.2.2.1-timp.4perc-org.bgtr-str
Material on hire
SL

Sinfonia, Op. 5 (1965) 10'

1.2.1.1-2.1.0.0-hp-str
Material on hire
Study score **ED 10993**

Symphony, Op. 22 (1973/85) 39'

2(2pic).2(ca).3(Ebcl,bcl).2sax.2(2cbn)-4.2(flhn).2(ttbn,btbn).1-timp.5perc-org.egtr-str
Material on hire
SL

Gilbert, Anthony

b. London 26.7.1934

The whimsical, the mythical - anything, in fact, that casts an oblique view on Western music - are the province of Anthony Gilbert's music. Through the very different perspectives of Indian and Australian culture in particular, he has brought a novel outlook to bear on the commonplace and the familiar. His art is uncompromising in its singularity, but not without its sense of the tender, the lyrical, and the emphatically humorous as well.

Tree of Singing Names

(1989) 15'

1(pic).1(ca).1(bcl).1(cbn)-2.1.0.0-perc-str(6.0.6.4.2)
Material on hire
SL

Concertos

Igorochki (1991-92) 17'

Soloist: recorder
2perc-cimbalon-gtr-str
Material on hire
SL

Towards Asavari (1978) 20'

Soloist: piano
1(pic).0.1(Ebcl).1-1.1.0.0-perc-str(6.6.4.4.2)
Material on hire
Study score ED 12195

Chamber & Instrumental Works

Brighton Piece, Op. 9

(1967) 13'

cl-hn.tpt.tbn-2/3perc-vc
Material on hire
Study score ED 11257

Calls around Chungmori

(1980) 15'

fl.cl-va.vc-drums
Material on hire or sale
SL

Canticle I - „Rock Song"

(1973) 9'

2cl.bcl-2hn.2tpt.ttbn
Material on hire
SL

Crow Undersongs (1979/81) 11'

viola solo
ED 12099*

Dawnfaring (1981-84) 15'

va-pno
Manuscript score on sale
SL

The Incredible Flute Music

(1968) 11'

fl-pno
ED 11111

Moonfaring (1983/86) 19'

vc-perc
Manuscript score on sale
SL

Nine or Ten Osannas, Op. 10

(1967) 24'

cl-hn-vn.vc-pno
Material on hire
Study score ED 11066

O'Grady Music (1971) 24'

cl-vc-toy instruments
Manuscript score on sale
SL

Piano Sonata No.1 (1961-62) 14'

pno
ED 10824

Piano Sonata No.2, Op. 8/2

(1966-67) 25'

pno (4hnd)
ED 11019

Quartet of Beasts (1984) 12'

fl.ob.bn-pno
Score and parts ED 12334

Six of the Bestiary (1985) 12'

sax qrt
Material on sale
SL

Spell Respell, Op. 14 (1968) 12'

electric bstcl/Acl-pno
ED 11119

String Quartet No.2

(1986-87) 23'

Material on sale
SL

String Quartet No.3 (1987) 12'

Super Hoqueto „David" (Machaut)
Material on sale
SL

String Quartet with Piano Pieces, Op. 20 (1972) 24'

2vn.va.vc-pno
Material on sale
Study score ED 11249 / Parts ED 11250 (piano)

Treatment of Silence

(1970-73) 11'

vn-tape
ED 11416

Vasanta with Dancing

(1981) 17'

fl(afl).ob(ca)-perc-hp-vn.va-[voice]
Material on hire
SL

Ziggurat (1993-94) 18'

bcl-marimba
Material on sale
SL

Solo Voice(s)/Voice(s) and Piano/Guitar

Canticle II - „Anger" (1974) 6'

Text: William Blake
6 male solo voices
Material on hire
SL

Solo Voice(s) and Instrument(s)/ Orchestra

Beastly Jingles (1984) 10'

Text: Charles Leland/William MacGonagall/anonymous
Soloist: soprano
fl-perc-hp.mand.gtr-vn(va).db
Material on hire
SL

Certain Lights Reflecting

(1988-89)   19'

Text: Sarah Day
Soloist: soprano
2(2pic).2(ob d'am,ca).2(bcl).2(cbn)-
4.2.3.0-timp.3perc-cel.hp-str
Material on hire
SL

Inscapes, Op. 26   (1975/81)   30'

Text: Gerard Manley Hopkins
Soloists: soprano, speaker
2cl(ssax,2bcl)-timp.perc-harmonica
Material on hire
Study score **ED 11417**

Long White Moonlight

(1980)   15'

Text: Ancient Asian sources
soprano-db
Manuscript score on sale
SL

Love Poems   (1970/72)   10'

Text: Horovitz/Shang-Yin/Barron
Soloist: soprano
cl-vc-acc
alt. version (1972): cl-bcl-chamber
org/harm
Material on sale
SL

Upstream River Rewa

(1991)   29'

Text: various
Soloist: speaker
fl-keybd-vc-sitar-tabla
Material on hire
SL

Choral Works

Missa Brevis   (1964-65)   7'

Chorus: mixed a cappella
ED 10929

Girnatis, Walter
1894-1981

Orchestral Works

Festmusik der Schiffergilde 12'

2.1.2.1-2.2.0.0-timp.perc-str
Material on hire
SM

Gartenmusik   12'

2.1.2.1-2.2.1.0-timp-str
Material on hire
SM

Goehr,
Alexander
b.1932

Stage Works

Arden muss sterben - Arden Must Die, Op. 21   (1966)   90'

Opera in 2 Acts
Text: Erich Fried
Material on hire
Vocal score **ED 10908** / Libretto **ED 10908-10/-11**

Arianna, Op. 58   (1994-95)   120'

Lost Opera by Monteverdi
Text: Ottavio Rinuccini
Material on hire
Vocal score **ED 12457**

Behold the Sun - Die Wiedertäufer, Op. 44

(1981-84)   160'

Opera in 3 Acts
Text: John McGrath/Alexander Goehr
Material on hire
SL

La Belle Dame sans Merci

(1958)   25'

Ballet in 1 Act
Material on hire
SL

Naboth's Vineyard, Op. 25

(1968)   20'

Music Theatre Triptych No. 1
Text: Latin and English from I Kings XXI
Material on hire
Study score **ED 11108**

Shadowplay, Op. 30   (1970)   20'

Music Theatre Triptych No. 2
Text: Adapted by K. Cavander from Plato
Material on hire
Study score **ED 11164**

Sonata about Jerusalem, Op. 31   (1970)   20'

Music Theatre Triptych No. 3
Text: various
Material on hire
Study score **ED 11165**

Orchestral Works

...a musical offering (J.S.B. 1985)..., Op. 46

(1985)   25'

1.0.2(bcl).0-1.1.1.0-perc-pno-str(3.0.2.0.1)
Material on hire
Study score **ED 12257**

Goehr,
Alexander

b. Berlin 10.8.1932

As a symbol of the continuing intellectual and creative vitality of British music, Alexander Goehr is a unique figure. Son of the conductor and Schönberg pupil Walter Goehr, he himself has shown a lifelong aptitude for reconciling and extending the Schönbergian vision to aspects of today's culture. His operas tackle subjects of contemporary political importance. His orchestral works, trenchantly expressive, are the calculus of his compositional thought. Following classical tradition, Goehr is a skilled composer of chamber music. He enjoys an international reputation not only as a composer, but also as a lecturer and highly esteemed teacher.

Chaconne for Wind, Op. 34

(1974)   16'

2.2.ca.2(Ebcl).2.cbn-2.3.3.0
Material on hire
SL

Colossos or Panic, Op. 55

(1991-92)   25'

3(afl).2.ca.3(Ebcl).bcl.3-4.3.3.1-perc-pno.hp-str
Material on hire
Study score **ED 12444**

2 Etudes, Op. 43   (1980-81)   20'

3(2pic,afl).2.ca.3(Ebcl,bcl).2.cbn-4.2.3.1-timp.3perc-cel.hp-str
Material on hire
Study score **ED 11847**

Fantasia, Op. 4 (1954/59) 10'

3(pic).2.ca.3(Ebcl).bcl.2.cbn-4.3.3.1-4perc-
cel.hp-str
Material on hire
SL

Fugue on the Notes of the Fourth Psalm, Op. 38b

(1976) 16'

str
Material on hire
Study score **ED 11403**

Hecuba's Lament, Op. 12

(1959-61) 18'

3(pic).2.ca.3(Ebcl,bcl).asax.2.cbn-4.3.3.1-
timp.3perc-cel.hp-str
Material on hire
Study score **ED 10793**

Little Music for Strings, Op. 16 (1963) 11'

str
Material on hire
Study score **ED 10892***

Little Symphony, Op. 15

(1963) 29'

1(pic).2.2.0-2.0.0.1-str
Material on hire
Study score **ED 10885**

Metamorphosis / Dance, Op. 36 (1973-74) 19'

3(2pic).2.ca.2.bcl.2.cbn-4.3.3.1-3perc-hp-
str
Material on hire
Study score **ED 11300**

Pastorals, Op. 19 (1965) 18'

afl.0.1.0-4.4.4.1-timp.2perc-str
Material on hire
Study score **ED 10927**

3 Pieces from "Arden Must Die", Op. 21a (1967) 9'

2(pic).2.ca.3(Ebcl).bcl.2.cbn-4.3.3.1-
timp.3perc-hp
Material on hire
Study score **ED 11003**

Sinfonia, Op. 42 (1979) 23'

1(pic).2.0.2-2.0.0.0-str
Material on hire
Study score **ED 12076**

Still Lands (1988-90) 15'

2(afl).1.2(bcl).1-2.1.1.0-timp-str
Material on hire
SL

Symphony in One Movement, Op. 29 (1969/81) 29'

3(2pic).2.ca.2(Ebcl).bcl.2.cbn-4.3.3.1-
timp.5perc-cel.hp-str
Material on hire
Study score **ED 12101**

Symphony with Chaconne, Op. 48 (1985-86) 50'

3(pic,afl).2.ca.3(Ebcl,bcl).2-4.2.3.1-
timp.6perc-cel.hp-str
Material on hire
Study score **ED 12328**

Concertos

Cambridge Hocket, Op. 57

(1993) 8'

Soloists: 4 horns
3(pic).2.ca.3.3.0-0.2.3.0-2perc-pno-str
Material on hire
SL

Konzertstück, Op. 26

(1969) 12'

Soloist: piano
1(pic).2.0.2-2.0.0.0-str
Material on hire
Piano reduction **ED 11093**

Piano Concerto, Op. 33

(1972) 32'

Soloist: piano
2.2(ca).2(Ebcl,bcl).2(cbn)-0.3.0.1-timp-str
Material on hire
Study score **ED 12308**

Romanza, Op. 24 (1968) 24'

Soloist: cello
pic.afl.1.ca.3(Ebcl,bcl).0.cbn-2.1.1.0-
timp.2perc-hp-str
Material on hire
Study score **ED 11109**

Romanza on the Notes of the Fourth Psalm, Op. 38c

(1977) 20'

Soloists: 2 violin, 2 violas
str
Material on hire
Study score **ED 11109**

Violin Concerto, Op. 13

(1961-62) 25'

Soloist: violin
2(pic).2(ca).2(bcl).2.cbn-4.2.2.0-
timp.3perc-str
Material on hire
Study score **ED 10813***

Chamber & Instrumental Works

Capriccio, Op. 6 (1957) 6'

pno
ED 10674

Cello Sonata, Op. 45 (1984) 15'

vc-pno
ED 12256

Chaconne for Organ, Op. 34a (1979) 16'

organ solo
ED 11472

Concerto for Eleven, Op. 32

(1970) 17'

1.0.2(bcl).0-0.2.0.1-perc-str(1.1.1.0.1)
Material on hire
Study score **ED 12081**

Fantasias, Op. 3 (1954) 12'

cl-pno
ED 10509

...in real time , Op. 50

(1989-1992) 40'

pno
ED 12395

Lyric Pieces, Op. 35 (1974) 17'

1.1.1.1-1.1.1.0-db
Material on hire
Study score **ED 11279**

Nonomiya, Op. 27 (1969) 13'

pno
ED 11098

Paraphrase, Op. 28 (1969) 17'

on the Dramatic Madrigal "Il Clorinda"
Combattimento di Tancredi e Clorinda
(Monteverdi)
clarinet solo
ED 11118

Piano Sonata, Op. 2

(1951-52) 12'

ED 10417

Piano Trio, Op. 20 (1966) 20'

vn.vc-pno
ED 11004

3 Pieces, Op. 18 (1964) 10'

pno
ED 10910

Prelude and Fugue, Op. 39

(1978) 6'

3cl
ED 11438

String Quartet No.1, Op. 5

(1957/88) 25'

Material on sale
Study score **ED 12332**

String Quartet No.2, Op. 23

(1967) 25'

Material on sale
Study score **ED 11012**

String Quartet No.3, Op. 37

(1975-76) 25'

Material on sale
Study score **ED 12077**

String Quartet No.4, Op. 52

(1990) 11'

Material on sale
SL

Suite, Op. 11 (1961) 20'

fl.cl-hn-hp-vn/va.vc
Material on hire
Study score **ED 10794**

Variations, Op. 8 (1959) 10'

fl-pno
ED 10684

Variations on Bach's Sarabande (1990) 15'

from the English Suite in E minor
0.0.2.2asax.2-0.2.1.0-timp
Material on hire
SL

Solo Voice(s)/Voice(s) and Piano/Guitar

Das Gesetz der Quadrille - The Law of the Quadrille, Op. 41 (1979) 20'

Text: Franz Kafka
low voice-pno
ED 12078

In Theresienstadt (1962-64) 8'

voice-pno
Manuscript score on sale
SL

The Mouse metamorphosed into a Maid, Op. 54 (1991) 14'

Text: Marianne Moore
soprano solo
ED 12408

4 Songs from the Japanese, Op. 9 (1959) 9'

Text: Adapted from Lafcadio Hearn
voice-pno
ED 10725

Warngedichte, Op. 22

(1966-67) 10'

Text: Erich Fried
low voice-pno
Manuscript score on sale
SL

Solo Voice(s) and Instrument(s)/ Orchestra

Behold the Sun, Op. 44a

(1981) 15'

Concert Aria
Soloist: high soprano
1.1.1.1-1.1.1.0-vib.pno-str(1.1.1.0.1)
Material on hire
SL

The Deluge, Op. 7 (1957-58) 16'

Text: After Leonardo da Vinci
Soloists: soprano, contralto
1.0.0.0-1.1.0.0-hp-str(1.0.1.1.1)
Material on hire
Study score **ED 10703**

Eve Dreams in Paradise, Op. 49 (1987-88) 30'

Text: Milton
Soloists: mezzo-soprano, tenor
pic.2(afl).2.ca.2(Ebcl).bcl.2-4.2.2(btbn).1-timp.5perc-hp.org(cel)-str
Material on hire
Vocal score **ED 12381**

Sing, Ariel, Op. 51 (1989-90) 45'

Text: various
Soloists: principal mezzo-soprano, 2 sopranos
tsax(bcl)-tpt-pno-vn(va).db
Material on hire
SL

4 Songs from the Japanese, Op. 9 (1959) 9'

Soloist: voice
2.2.2.2-4.2.3.0-perc-cel.hp-str
Material on hire
Vocal score **ED 10725**

Choral Works

Babylon the Great is Fallen, Op. 40 (1979) 45'

Chorus: mixed
3(2pic).2.ca.3(Ebcl,bcl).2.cbn-4.3.3.0-timp.3perc-2pno-str
Material on hire
SL

Carol for St. Steven (1989) 4'

Chorus: mixed a cappella
Manuscript score on sale
SL

2 Choruses, Op. 14 (1962) 11'

Text: Milton/William Shakespeare
Chorus: mixed a cappella
ED 10888

The Death of Moses, Op. 53

(1991-92) 55'

Soloists: S.A.T.Bar.B
Chorus: mixed, children's
fl(pic).afl.2ssax-2ttbn.btbn-2perc-hp.2eorg/synth(cel).bgtr
Material on hire
Vocal score **ED 12427**

„I said, I will take Heed", Op. 56 (1992-93) 10'

Psalm 39
Chorus: mixed double
2ob-2bsthn-2tbn-2bn.cbn
Material on hire
SL

2 Imitations of Baudelaire, Op. 47 (1985) 12'

Text: Robert Lowell
Chorus: mixed a cappella
ED 12282*

5 Poems and an Epigram of William Blake, Op. 17

(1964) 12'

Chorus: mixed
tpt
ED 10891

Psalm 4, Op. 38a (1976) 17'

Soloists: soprano, alto, viola
Chorus: female
org
ED 11402

Sutter's Gold, Op. 10

(1959-60) 35'

Text: After S.M. Eisenstein
Soloist: bass
Chorus: mixed
3(pic,afl).3(ca).4(Ebcl,2bcl).ssax.3(cbn)-4.3.3(ttbn,btbn).2-8perc-hp-str
Material on hire
Vocal score **ED 10749***

Virtutes Nos. 1-9 (1963) 30'

A Cycle of Songs and Melodramas with texts compiled by Gordon Humpreys and based on a passage from St. Paul
Soloist: speaker
Chorus: mixed, female
[2cl]-timp.perc-2pno.org-[vc]
Parts **ED 10858 (-68)***

Goldmark, Karl
1830-1915

Orchestral Works

Im Frühling, Op. 36 (1888) 11'

Overture
2(pic).2.2.2-4.3.3.1-timp-str
Material on hire
SM

In Italien, Op. 49 (1904) 11'

Overture
2(pic).2.ca.2.bcl.2-4.3.3.1-timp.perc-hp-str
Material on hire
SM

Ländliche Hochzeit, Op. 26

(1876) 45'

Symphony
2.2.2.2-4.2.3.0-timp.perc-str
Material on hire
SM

Sakuntala, Op. 13 (1865)

Overture
2.2.ca.2.2-4.2.2.1-timp.perc-hp-str
Material on hire
SM

Goldschmidt, Berthold

b.1903

Orchestral Works

Komödie der Irrungen

(1925) 5'

Overture
pic.1.2.2.2-2.2.0.0-timp.perc-str
Material on hire
SM

Gotovac, Jakov

1895-1982

Orchestral Works

Guslar, Op. 22 (1940) 12'

Symphonic Portrait
3(pic).2.2.ca.3(bcl).2-4.3.3.1-timp.perc-hp-str
Material on hire
SM

Lied und Tanz aus dem Balkan, Op. 16 (1940) 11'

str
Material on hire
SM

Oraci (Die Pflüger), Op. 18

(1940) 15'

Symphonic Meditation
pic.2.2.ca.2.bcl.2.cbn-4.3.3.1-timp.perc-pianino.hp-str
Material on hire
SM

Symphonischer Kolo, Op. 12

(1927) 8'

pic.2.2.ca.3(bcl).2-4.3.3.1-timp.perc-hp-str
Material on hire
SM

Solo Voice(s) and Instrument(s)/ Orchestra

Lieder der Sehnsucht, Op. 21

(1940) 10'

Soloist: female voice
2(pic).1.2.1-2.1.0.0-timp.perc-hp-str
Material on hire
SM

Riswan Aga, Op. 19 (1940) 10'

Satirical Song
Soloist: baritone
2(pic).1.2.1-4.3.3.0-timp.perc-hp-str
Material on hire
SM

Choral Works

Am adriatischen Meer, Op. 71 (1950) 4'

from "3 Madrigals'
Text: R. Kataliniç-Jeretov
Chorus: male a cappella
C 37833

Das gestohlene Mäntelchen, Op. 15/3 (1950) 2'

Chorus: male a cappella
C 37835

Koleda, Op. 11 (1936) 15'

Text: Jakov Gotovac
Chorus: male
3cl.2bn-timp.tamb
SM

Gould, Glenn

1932-1982

Chamber & Instrumental Works

5 Little Pieces (1951) 4'

(in: "Piano Pieces")
pno
ED 8319

Gould, Glenn (Herbert)

b. Toronto 25.9.1932, d. Toronto 4.10.1982

The Canadian pianist Glenn Gould studied under Alberto Guerrero (piano) and Frederick Silvester (organ). When he was 14 he made his début with the Toronto Symphony Orchestra, in Beethoven's Fourth Concerto. Appearing throughout Canada in recitals and broadcasts, principally of the Classical repertory, he began a study of music of the modern Viennese school and later of such post-Romantics as Richard Strauss. These strongly influenced his early compositions - short pieces for piano alone and for bassoon and piano, and a long one-movement string quartet (composed 1953-5, later recorded and published).

2 Pieces (1951-52) 5'

in: "Piano Pieces"
pno
ED 8319

Sonata 10'

bn-pno
FAG 23

Infoline · e-Mail
Schott Musik International
Mainz: Schott.Musik.com@T-Online.de
London: 101627.166@compuserve.com

Graener, Paul

1872-1944

Orchestral Works

Comedietta, Op. 82   11'
3.3.3.2-4.1.1.0-timp.perc-hp.pno-str
Material on hire
Eu

Feierliche Stunde, Op. 106   8'
Prelude
3.3.3.3-4.3.3.1-timp.perc-hp-str
Material on hire
Eu

Die Flöte von Sanssouci, Op. 86   15'
Suite
2.2.0.2-2.2.0.0-timp.perc-cemb-str
Material on hire
Study score **ETP 872**

Prinz Eugen, der edle Ritter, Op. 108   17'
Variations
3.3.3.3-4.3.3.1-timp.perc-hp-str
Material on hire
Eu

Salzburger Serenaden, Op. 115   22'
3.2.2.2-3.1.2.0-timp.perc-hp-str
Material on hire
Eu

Sinfonia breve, Op. 96   20'
2.2.3.3-4.2.3.0-timp-str
Material on hire
Eu

Turmwächterlied, Op. 107   16'
Orchestral Variations
3.3.3.3-4.3.3.0-timp.perc-hp-str
Material on hire
Eu

Wiener Sinfonie, Op. 110   25'
2.2.2.2-4.2.3.0-timp.perc.glsp-str
Material on hire
Eu

Concertos

Violin Concert, Op. 104   25'
Soloist: violin
2.2.2.2-4.2.3.0-timp-str
Material on hire
SM

Grainger, Percy Aldridge

1882-1961

Distribution rights worldwide (except USA)

Orchestral Works

Blithe Bells (J.S.Bach)
(1930-31)   5'
2.1.2.1/2-1/asax.1/2.[1].0-perc-
[harm.vib.marimb.cel/pno].pno.[hp]-str
Material on hire
SL

Children's March: Over the Hills and Far Away   (1918)   7'
Arranger: A. Schmidt
pic.2.2.ca.2.[saxes].2-4.3.3.1-timp.perc-
[harm].hp/pno-str
Material on hire
SL

Colonial Song   (1911-14)   6'
[S.T.]-pic.2.2.2.2-4.3.3.1-timp.perc-
hp.[pno]-str
alt. version: theatre orchestra (elastic scoring)
Material on hire
SL

Country Gardens   (1949-50)   3'
(Stokowski version)
pic.2.2.ca.2.bcl.2.cbn-4.3.3.1-perc-
hp.pno/cel-str
Material on hire
SL

Country Gardens   (1908)   3'
Arranger: Artok
elastic scoring (max): 2.2.2.2-2.2.3.1-
timp.perc-harm.pno-str
Material on hire
SL

"The Duke of Marlborough" Fanfare   (1939)   3'
[asax.tsax.bsax.2bn]-
4hn.3/4tpt.3tbn.[euph].tuba-cym-[db]
Material on hire or sale
ED 12538*

Early one Morning   (1950)   4'
(Stokowski version)
2.1.2.bcl.2.[cbn]-2.1.1.euph.1-str
Material on hire
SL

Grainger, Percy Aldridge

**b. Brighton, Melbourne 8.7.1882,
d. White Plains, NY 20.2.1961**

Had Grainger never existed it would be necessary to invent him - but probably impossible. Truly a twentieth-century radical, he flaunted an originality that even today deserves greater recognition. Pupil of Busoni, friend of Grieg and Delius, he toured the world as a concert pianist before settling in the United States. His first love was folksong, yet his experiments in sonority, his attempts to devise a "free music" liberated from conventional restraints of rhythm and melody, and his interests in oriental and medieval music show a mind ranging further afield than the pleasures of "Country Gardens" and "Molly on the Shore" - "my fripperies" as he called them.

Eastern Intermezzo   (1899)   2'
from "Youthful Suite"
pic.2.2.2.2-4.1.3.1-timp.perc-
cel.pno.hp.org-str
Material on hire
SL

English Dance   (1899-1925)   12'
pic.2.2.ca.Ebcl.2.bcl.2.cbn-4.3.3.euph.1-
timp.perc-pno.org-str
Material on hire
SL

Green Bushes   (1905-1921)   9'
[pic].1.1.1.ssax.barsax.1.[cbn]-
2/2asax.1.0.0-timp.perc-harm(org).pno-
str(3.0.2.2.1)
alt. version: elastic scoring
Material on hire
SL

Handel in the Strand

(1911-12)   4'

vn.[va].vc-pno-str
Material on hire
SL

Handel in the Strand   (1949)   4'

(Stokowski version)
pic.1.1.2.2.cbn-4.3.3.1-timp.perc-hp.pno-str
Material on hire
SL

Handel in the Strand

(1911-49)   4'

Arranger: H. Wood
3.3.3.3-4.4.3.1-timp.perc-[org].1/2hp-str
Material on hire
SL

Harvest Hymn   (1932)   4'

Chorus: optional
*elastic scoring (max): 1.1.2.bcl.2-
1/asax.1/ssax.1.euph/tsax.0-org/harm.pno-
str*
Material on hire
SL

"In a Nutshell" Suite

(1915-16)   16'

*pic.2.2.ca.2.[bcl].2.[cbn]-4.3.3.1-timp.perc-
cel.pno.hp-str*
Material on hire
SL

Irish Tune from County Derry   (1913)   4'

[2hn]-str
Material on hire
Study score **ED 11998**

Irish Tune from County Derry   (1918)   4'

Arranger: Denis Wright
*Eb soprano cnt.5 Bb cnt.repiano
Bb/flhn.3Eb hn.2 Bb baritones.3tbn.Bb
euph.2 Eb basses-perc*
Material on sale
ED 12539

Irish Tune from County Derry   (1920)   6'

'County Derry Air'
*elastic scoring (max):
2.2.3.bcl.cbcl.ssax.asax.tsax.bsax.2.cbn-
4.4.3.euph.1.sarrusophone- harm/org-str*
Material on hire
SL

Irish Tune from County Derry   (1913-49)   4'

Arranger: Adolf Schmid
*2.2.2.[asax.tsax].2-4.2.[1].0-timp-harm-
str(1.1.1.1.1)*
Material on hire
SL

Irish Tune from County Derry   (1949)   4'

(Stokowski version)
2.1.2.2-2.1.3.euph.0-perc-str
Material on hire
SL

Jutish Medley   (1923-29)   8'

*elastic scoring (max):
pic.2.2.2.bcl.ssax.asax.tsax.bsax.2
-4.3.3.euph.1-timp.perc-
harm.2pno(8hnds).hp-str*
Material on hire
SL

Lincolnshire Posy   (1906)   16'

*pic.2.2.[ca].6sax.9.2.cbn-
4Ebhn.3.4.euph.1-perc-[2pno]-db*
Material on hire or sale
ED 11343-01 / Study score **ED 11343***

Lord Peter's Stable Boy

(1922-27)   3'

*elastic scoring (max):
cl.tpt/ssax.hn/asax.tbn/euph/tsax-timp.perc-
pno(2/4hnd).harm/org-str*
Material on hire
SL

Mock Morris   (1911)   4'

str
Material on hire
SL

Mock Morris   (1914)   4'

*elastic scoring (max): 2.1.2.1-2.2.1.0-
timp.perc-str(3.0.1.2.1)*
Material on hire
SL

Mock Morris   (1911-50)   4'

Arranger: Denis Wright
*Eb soprano cnt.5 Bb cnt.repiano
Bb/flhn.3Eb hn.2 Bb baritones.3tbn.Bb
euph.2 Eb basses-perc*
Material on sale
SL

Mock Morris   (1950)   4'

(Stokowski version)
pic.2.2.2.2.cbn-4.3.3.1-timp.perc-str
Material on hire
SL

Molly on the Shore   (1907)   4'

str
Material on hire
SL

Molly on the Shore   (1907-14)   4'

*elastic scoring (max): pic.2.2.2.2-4.2.3.1-
timp.perc-cel-str*
Material on hire
SL

Molly on the Shore   (1949)   4'

(Stokowski version)
pic.2.1.ca.2.2.cbn-4.2.3.1-timp.perc-str
Material on hire
SL

'The Nightingale' and "The Two Sisters'   (1923-30)   4'

*elastic scoring (max): pic.2.2.4.bcl.2.cbn-
sax quart-4.3.3.1-timp.perc-
org.harm.pno.2hp-str*
Material on hire
SL

The Power of Love   (1922-41)   4'

*elastic scoring (max): pic.2.2.2.bc.2.cbn-
4.3.3.1[saxes]-timp.perc-org.harm.pno.2hp-
str*
Material on hire
SL

Shepherd's Hey   (1908-09)   2'

fl.cl-[hn]-concertina-str(3.0.2.2.1)
Material on hire
SL

Shepherd's Hey   (1913)   2'

pic.2.2.2.2-4.3.3.1-timp.perc-pno.1/2hp-str
Material on hire
SL

Shepherd's Hey   (1908-49)   2'

Arranger: Denis Wright
*Eb soprano cnt.5 Bb cnt.repiano/flhn.3 Eb
hn.2 Bb baritones.3tbn.euph.2Eb bass.2Bb
bass-perc*
Material on sale
SL

Shepherd's Hey   (1949)   2'

(Stokowski version)
*pic.2.2.ca.2.bcl.0-4.3.3.1-timp.perc-pno.hp-
str*
Material on hire
SL

Spoon River   (1919-29)   4'

*elastic scoring (max): pic.1.1.1.tsax.1-
1/asax.1/ssax.3.1-timp.perc-
2pno.harm/org.hp-str*
Material on hire
SL

To a Nordic Princess

(1927-28)   14'

(Bridal Song)
*pic.2.2.ca.2.bcl.2-4.3.3.euph.1-timp.perc-
cel.harm.pno.[org].hp-str*
Material on hire
SL

The Warriors   (1913-16)   19'

*pic.2.2.ca.bob.2.bcl.2.cbn-6.4.3.1-
timp.perc-cel.3pno.2hp-str*
Material on hire
SL

Ye Banks and Braes O'Bonnie Doon   (1901-37)   3'

*elastic scoring (max):
pic.1.1.Ebcl.3.2bcl.saxes-2-2.2.2.1-
harm/org-str*
Material on hire
SL

Youthful Suite   (1899-1945)   26'

*pic.2.2.ca.2.bcl.2.cbn-4.3.3.1-timp.perc-
harm.pno.hp-str*
Material on hire
SL

Infoline · e-Mail

Schott Musik International
Mainz: Schott.Musik.com@T-Online.de
London: 101627.166@compuserve.com

Concertos

Youthful Rapture (1901/29) 6'

Soloist: cello
vn-harm/org.pno
alt vers: elastic scoring (max):
fl.cl/tpt/ssax.hn/asax-glsp-harm/org.pno-
hp-str
Material on hire
SL

Chamber & Instrumental Works

Après un Rêve (Fauré)

(1939) 3'

Arranger: Grainger
pno
Manuscript score on sale
ED 12543*

Arrival Platform Humlet

(1926) 3'

from "In a Nutshell Suite'
viola solo
Manuscript score on sale
ED 12558*

Blithe Bells (J.S.Bach)

(1931) 5'

pno (easy & concert versions)
Manuscript score on sale
ED 12545*

Blithe Bells (J.S.Bach)

(1932) 5'

2pno (4hnd)
Manuscript score on sale
ED 12544*

Children's March: Over the Hills and Far Away (1916) 7'

pno
ED 12578 (Solo Piano Album Vol. 4)

Children's March: Over the Hills and Far Away (1918) 7'

2pno (4hnd)
ED 12583 (2 Piano Album Vol. 5)

Colonial Song 6'

Arranger: Ross
organ solo
ED 12584 (Organ Album)

Colonial Song (1905/12) 6'

Soloists: [S.T.]
vn.vc-pno
ED 12524*

Colonial Song (1911-14) 6'

pno
ED 12575 (Solo Piano Album Vol. 1)

Colonial Song (1913) 6'

[2voices] - pno
ED 12525

Country Gardens 2'

Arranger: Bergmann
srec.arec-pno
ED 10876/10876-01

Country Gardens (1918) 2'

pno (simplified version)
ED 11005 (The Young Pianist's Grainger)

Country Gardens (1918) 2'

pno (very easy version)
ED 11179-03

Country Gardens (1918) 2'

pno (original version)
ED 12575 (Solo Piano Album Vol. 1)

Country Gardens (1932) 2'

2pno (4hnd)
SL

Country Gardens (1936) 2'

pno (4hnd)
ED 11198

Country Gardens (1936) 2'

2pno (8hnd)
ED 12058*

Cradle Song (Brahms)

(1923) 3'

Arranger: Percy Grainger
pno
ED 12546*

Eastern Intermezzo (1922) 2'

from "Youthful Suite"
pno/2pno (4hnd)
ED 12583 (2 Piano Album Vol. 5)

English Dance (1921) 12'

2pno (6hnds)
ED 12547*

English Waltz (1940) 3'

from "Youthful Suite"
2pno (4hnd)
ED 12583 (2 Piano Album Vol. 5)

Green Bushes (1919-21) 9'

2pno (6hnd)
Manuscript score on sale
ED 12549*

Handel in the Strand (1930) 4'

pno
ED 11180

Handel in the Strand (1947) 4'

2pno (4hnd)
ED 12579 (2 Piano Album Vol. 1)

Harvest Hymn (1932) 3'

vn-pno
Manuscript score on sale
SL

Harvest Hymn (1936) 3'

pno
ED 12576 (Solo Piano Album Vol. 2)

Hornpipe (Handel) (1923) 2'

from "Water Music"
Arranger: Grainger
pno
ED 12551*

The Hunter in his Career

(1928-29) 3'

pno
ED 12576 (solo Piano Album Vol. 2)

The Immovable Do (1940) 5'

organ solo
ED 12584 (Organ Album)

The Immovable Do (1940) 5'

pno
ED 12578 (Solo Piano Album Vol. 4)

In a Nutshell Suite (1916) 16'

pno
ED 12577 (Solo Piano Album Vol. 3)

Irish Tune from County Derry (1911) 4'

pno
ED 11181

Jutish Medley (1927) 8'

pno
ED 12578 (Solo Piano Album Vol. 4)

Knight and Shepherd's Daughter (1918) 3'

pno
ED 12575 (Solo Piano Album Vol. 1)

Lincolnshire Posy (1938) 16'

2pno (4hnd)
ED 12580 (2 Piano Album Vol. 2)

Lisbon (1937) 2'

fl.ob.cl.bn-hn
Score and parts **ED 11128**

Lullaby from "Tribute to Foster" (1915) 5'
pno
ED 12578 (Solo Piano Album Vol. 4)

The Merry King (1936-39) 4'
pno
ED 12576 (Solo Piano Album Vol. 2)

Mock Morris (1912) 4'
pno
ED 12576 (Solo Piano Album Vol. 2)

Mock Morris (1912) 4'
pno (concert version)
ED 11182-02*

Mock Morris (1912) 4'
vn-pno
ED 11200*

Molly on the Shore 4'
Arranger: Kreisler
vn-pno
BSS 31240

Molly on the Shore (1907) 4'
2vn.va.vc.[db]
Material on hire
SL

Molly on the Shore (1918) 4'
pno
ED 11183

Molly on the Shore (1947) 4'
2pno (4hnd)
ED 12579 (2 Piano Album Vol. 2)

My Robin is to the Greenwood Gone (1912) 6'
fl.ca-6str
Material on hire
SL

My Robin is to the Greenwood Gone (1912) 6'
vn.vc-pno
ED 12537*

My Robin is to the Greenwood Gone (1912) 6'
pno
ED 12578 (Solo Piano Album Vol. 4)

Now, o now, I needs must Part (John Dowland) (1937) 4'
Arranger: Percy Grainger
pno (easy and concert versions)
ED 12554*

One more Day my John (1915) 2'
pno
ED 12578 (Solo Piano Album Vol. 4)

Paraphrase on Tchaikovsky's "Flower Waltz" (1904) 7'
pno
ED 12555*

La Scandinavie - Scandinavian Suite (1902) 16'
vc-pno
ED 12563*

Scotch Strathspey and Reel (1937-39) 7'
pno
ED 12578 (Solo Piano Album Vol. 4)

Shepherd's Hey (1913/37) 2'
pno (simplified version)
ED 11184-02

Shepherd's Hey (1913/37) 2'
srec-pno
ED 10886-02

Shepherd's Hey (1913/37) 2'
trec-pno
ED 10886-03

Shepherd's Hey (1913/37) 2'
pno (original version)
SL

Shepherd's Hey (1947) 2'
2pno (4hnd)
ED 12579 (2 Piano Album Vol. 1)

Spoon River (1922) 4'
pno
ED 12576 (Solo Piano Album Vol. 2)

Spoon River (1922) 4'
2pno (4hnd)
ED 12583 (2 Piano Album Vol. 5)

The Sussex Mummers' Christmas Carol (1905-11) 4'
pno
ED 12576 (Solo Piano Album Vol. 2)

The Sussex Mummers' Christmas Carol (1905-15) 4'
vn/vc-pno
ED 12565*

To a Nordic Princess (1927-28) 7'
pno
ED 12578 (Solo Piano Album Vol. 4)

Two Musical Relics of my Mother (1905/12) 4'
2pno (4hnd)
ED 12583 (2 Piano Album Vol. 4)

Walking Tune (1911) 4'
pno
ED 11185

Walking Tune (1912/40) 4'
fl.ob.cl.bn-hn
Score and parts ED 11342*

The Warriors (1922) 19'
2pno (6hnd)
ED 12557*

Youthful Rapture (1901) 5'
vc-pno
ED 12566*

Zanzibar Boat Song (1902) 4'
pno(6hnd)
ED 11199

Solo Voice(s)/Voice(s) and Piano/Guitar

Bold William Taylor (1908) 4'
voice-pno
ED 12521*

British Waterside (The Jolly Sailor) (1920) 2'
voice(high or low)-pno
ED 12522*/12523*

David of the White Rock (1954) 2'
high voice-pno
ED 10809*

Dedication (1901) 2'
voice-pno
ED 12526*

Died for Love (1906-07) 1'
mezzo-soprano-pno
ED 12527*

Infoline · e-Mail
Schott Musik International
Mainz: Schott.Musik.com@T-Online.de
London: 101627.166@compuserve.com

The Love Song of Har Dyal

(1901) 3'

voice-pno
ED 12528*

The Men of the Sea (1899)

voice-pno
ED 12529*

The Pretty Maid Milkin' her Cow (1920) 2'

high/low voice-pno
ED 12530*

A Reiver's Neck Verse

(1908) 2'

voice-pno
ED 12531*

Shallow Brown (1910/25) 5'

solo voices-pno
ED 12342

Six Dukes went a-fishin'

(1905-12) 3'

high/low voice-pno
ED 12532*

A Song of Autumn (1899) 2'

voice-pno
ED 12562*

The Sprig of Thyme

(1907/20) 4'

high/low voice-pno
ED 12533*/12534***

The Twa Corbies (1903) 3'

tenor-pno
ED 12535*

Willow Willow (1902-11) 4'

voice-pno
ED 11340*

Solo Voice(s) and Instrument(s)/ Orchestra

Bold William Taylor (1908) 4'

Soloist: mezzo/baritone
1/2cl-harm-str(2.0.1.2.1)
Material on hire
SL

Died for Love (1906-07) 1'

Soloist: mezzo-soprano
fl/vn-cl/va-bn/vc
ED 12527*

The Twa Corbies (1903/09) 3'

Soloist: tenor
str(2.0.2.2.1)
Material on hire
SL

Willow Willow (1902-11) 4'

Soloist: voice
gtr/hp-str qrt
Material on hire
Vocal score **ED 11340***

Choral Works

Anchor Song (1921) 4'

Soloist: baritone
Chorus: male single voices or chorus (4 prt)
pno
ED 12511*

At Twilight (1900-09) 4'

Soloist: tenor
Chorus: mixed a cappella
ED 12512*

Australian Up-Country Song

(1905-28) 2'

Chorus: mixed a cappella
ED 11282

The Bride's Tragedy

(1908/14) 8'

Chorus: mixed
pic.2.2.2.bcl.[sax qrt].2.cbn-4.3.3.1-timp.perc-org/harm-str
Material on hire
SL

Brigg Fair (1906) 2'

Soloist: tenor
Chorus: mixed a cappella
ED 11190

Danny Deever (1903/22) 3'

Soloist: baritone
Chorus: male (5 prt)
pno
ED 12514*

Danny Deever (1924) 3'

Chorus: male double a cappella
pic.2.2.3.bcl.2.cbn-[saxes]-4.2.3.euph.1-3timp.perc-str
Material on hire
SL

Dollar and a Half Day

(1908-09) 4'

Chorus: male a cappella
ED 12115

Father and Daughter

(1908-09) 3'

Soloists: 5 solo male voices
Chorus: mixed double
4hn.3tbn.euph.tuba-timp.perc-[mand.4gtr]-[pno]-[str]
Material on hire
SL

The Hunter in his Career

(1903/29) 2'

Chorus: male
pic.2.2.2.2-4.3.3.1-timp.perc-2pno.org-str
Material on hire
Choral score **ED 12516***

I'm Seventeen come Sunday

(1905-12) 3'

Chorus: mixed
4hn.3tpt.3tbn.2tuba/2euph-timp.perc
alt version: pno
Material on hire
Vocal score **ED 11339***

The Immovable Do (1933-40) 5'

Chorus: [mixed/a cappella]
elastic scoring (max):
2pic.2.2.ca.2.bcl.2.cbn-4.3.3.1-timp.perc-str
Material on hire
Choral score **ED 12508**

Irish Tune from County Derry (1902) 4'

Chorus: mixed a cappella
ED 11283

Kipling "Jungle Book" Cycle

(1898-1947) 19'

Chorus: male/mixed
0.2.ca.[3.bcl].2-2.[2.3].0-[timps]-harm/org.pno-[vibrahp.hp]-str(1.1.2.3.1)
Material on hire
SL

The Lads of Wamphray

(1904) 9'

Chorus: male
pic.2.2.ca.Ebcl.3.acl.bcl.2.cbn-6hn.2Ebhn.3Ftpt.3cnt.3.2euph.1-timp.perc-str
Material on hire
SL

The Lads of Wamphray

(1942) 9'

Chorus: male/mixed
pic.2.2.ca.[Ebcl].3.[acl].bcl.2.cbn-4Fhns.2Ebhn/2asax.3tpt.[3cnt].3.euph.2-4timp.perc-str
Material on hire
SL

The Lost Lady Found (1910) 3'

Chorus: mixed/unison/single voice
3hn.2tpt.[tbn]-timp.perc-str(3.0.2.2.1)
alt version : [perc]-[harm].pno-str(3.0.2.2.1)
Material on hire
Vocal score **ED 11284**

Marching Tune (1905) 5'

Chorus: mixed
4hn.2/3tpt.3tbn.tuba-timp.perc
alt. version: pno
Material on hire
SL

Recessional (1905/29) 3'

Chorus: mixed [a cappella]
[org]
ED 12519*

The Running of Shindand

(1901-4?) 1'

Chorus: male a cappella
ED 12505

Scotch Strathspey and Reel

(1901-2) 8'

Chorus: male
[pic].1.1.1.1-0.0.0.0-perc-harm.2gtr/pno-
str
Material on hire
SL

The Sea Wife (1947) 3'

Chorus: mixed
elastic scoring (max):
4hn.3tpt.[bar.euph].tuba-str(2.0.2.2.1)
alt version: pno(2/4hnd)
Material on hire
Vocal score **ED 12114***

Shallow Brown (1910) 5'

Chorus: solo/chorus
[pic.fl].cl.bn.[cbn]-hn/asax.euph-
harm.pno.[2ukelele.2mand.2mandola.2gtr]
-str(2.0.2.2.1)
alt version: pno
Material on hire
Score **ED 12342**

Shallow Brown (1910/25) 5'

Chorus: unison
pno
ED 12342

Sir Eglamore (1904) 5'

Chorus: mixed double
4/6hn.4tpt(or 2cl-2cnt).5tbn(or 2bn-
2tbn.euph).tuba-timp.perc-[1/2hp]-str
Material on hire
SL

Soldier, Soldier (1907-08) 4'

Soloists: 6 soloists
Chorus: mixed
[harm]
ED 12507

There was a Pig went out to Dig (1905) 2'

Chorus: female a cappella (4 prt)
ED 11341

The Three Ravens (1902) 4'

Chorus: mixed
5cl/fl-4cl
Material on hire
Choral score **ED 12520**

We have fed our Seas for a Thousand Years (1900/11) 3'

Chorus: mixed
4hn.2/3tpt.3tbn.euph.tuba-[str(va.vc.db)]
Material on hire
Choral score **ED 12509***

The Widow's Party (1906/23) 4'

Chorus: male
[pic].1.0.1.1-1.2.1.0-timp.perc-
harm.1/2pno-str
alt version: pno (4hnd)
Material on hire
Choral score **ED 12506**

Ye Banks and Braes O'Bonnie Doon (1901/32) 3'

Chorus: mixed
harm/org
alt. version: elastic scoring (max):
pic.2.2.8.saxes.2-2.1.euph.0-harm.org-str
Material on hire
Choral score **ED 12117**

Grandis, Renato de

b.1927

Stage Works

Eduard und Kunegunde

(1970) 20'

Scenic moritate
Text: Brigitte Grossmann
Material on sale
Piano reduction **AVV 98**

Die Schule der Kahlen

(1971) 35'

Comic Opera
Text: Renato de Grandis
Material on hire
AVV

Choral Works

La Commedia Veneziana

(1970) 50'

Text: Corte Carlo Della
Soloists: soprano, bass
Chorus: mixed
perc-harmonica.mand.pno.hp-db
Material on hire
AVV

Gretchaninoff, Alexander Tikhonovich

1864-1956

Chamber & Instrumental Works

Album 16'

pno (4hnd)
ED 1171

Bachkiria, Op. 125 (1927)

fl-hp
ED 2249

Flüchtige Gedanken, Op. 115 (1927) 15'

pno
ED 2071

Glasperlen, Op. 123 (1929) 14'

pno
ED 1518

The Gretchaninoff Collection 30'

pno
SMC 536

Das Großvaterbuch, Op. 119 (1929) 16'

pno
ED 1467

Im Grünen, Op. 99 (1924) 14'

pno
ED 1125

Im Grünen, Op. 99 (1924) 14'

pno (4hnd)
ED 1172

In aller Frühe, Op. 126 15'

vc-pno
ED 8120

In aller Frühe, Op. 126a 15'

vn-pno
ED 2142

In aller Frühe, Op. 126b 15'

vc-pno
ED 2143

The Jester 3'

vn-pno
ED 11871

Das Kinderbuch, Op. 98

(1923)   14'

pno
ED 1100

Morning Stroll

vn-pno
ED 11871

Quatrième Quatuor, Op. 124 (1929)

str qrt
Parts **ED 3158**

Sonata, Op. 113 (1927)   18'

vc-pno
ED 1549

Sonata in G minor, Op. 129 (1931)

vc-pno
ED 1549

Sonatina in F, Op. 110

(1927)   9'

from "Zwei Sonatinen"
pno
ED 1298

Sonatina in G, Op. 110

(1927)   10'

from "Zwei Sonatinen"
pno
ED 1297

Der Tag des Kindes, Op. 109 (1927)   12'

pno
ED 1414

Tautropfen, Op. 127a

(1930)   14'

pno
ED 2176

Grovermann, Carl Hans

b.1905

Orchestral Works

Heitere Tanzszenen   12'

1.1.2.1-2.1.1.0-timp-str
Material on hire
Eu

Grünauer, Ingomar

b.1938

Stage Works

Amleth und Fengo

(1982)   full evening

Opera in 2 Acts after the "Historia Danica"
Text: Ingomar Grünauer
Material on hire
SM

Besichtigung, Versteigerung und Beseitigung von 5 Künstlern   18'

(Inspection, Auction and Disposal of five
Artists)
Soloists: soprano, silent actor
Material on hire
AVV

König für einen Tag (1990)   70'

Opera in 3 Scenes after Calderón
Text: Ingomar Grünauer after Calderón and
Hugo von Hoffmannsthal
Material on hire
SM

Die Mutter (1988)   80'

Chamber Play after Maxim Gorkij
Material on hire
SM

Peer Gynt (1978)   95'

Ballet by Roberto Trinchero after Henrik
Ibsen under using of music by Edvard
Grieg
Material on hire
SM

Die Rache einer russischen Waise (1993)   full evening

Chamber Operetta in 17 Subscenes after
Henri Rousseau
Text: Matthias Kaiser, Ingomar Grünauer
Material on hire
SM

Die Schöpfungsgeschichte des Adolf Wölfli

(1981)   full evening

for 6 singers, string quintet and percussion
Material on hire
SM

Winterreise (1994)   full evening

Opera in 11 Scenes
Text: Francesco Micieli
Material on hire
SM

Grünauer, Ingomar

b. Melk (Austria) 11.8.1938

Ingomar Grünauer was trained at the
Vienna Academy of Music and Performing
Arts, finishing his studies with the artistic
examination in composition and conducting
in 1959. From 1961-68 he worked as musical director, répétiteur and composer of
incidental music at the Heidelberg Theatre;
the next 14 years he was in the teaching
profession, composing at the same time
music for the music theatre and incidental
music. In 1974 he was appointed teacher of
"scenic music" at the University of Salvador
Bahia (Brazil). Since 1982 Grünauer has
been professor of aesthetics and communication at the Frankfurt College (special subjects: theatrical work and cultural animati-
on). Among his prizes and awards are: 1982
Cultural Award of the city of Wiesbaden.

Solo Voice(s) and Instrument(s)/ Orchestra

Besichtigung, Versteigerung und Beseitigung von 5 Künstlern   18'

(Inspection, Auction and Disposal of five
Artists)
Soloists: soprano, silent actor
*cl-perc-pno(rec,gumballs,hard broom)-va-2
tapes-loudspeaker*
Material on hire
AVV

Sinfonietta

Text: Franz Kafka
Soloists: clarinet, mezzo-soprano, tenor
pic.2.2.ca.2.cbn-4.3.3.cbtuba-timp-str
Material on hire
SM

Guilmant, Félix Alexandre

1837-1911

Concertos

Symphony No. 1 in D Minor, Op. 42
27'

Soloist: organ
2.2.2.2-4.2.3.0-timp-str
Material on hire
SL

Symphony No. 2 in A Major, Op. 91
30'

Soloist: organ
2.2.2.2-4.2.3.1-timp-str
Material on hire
SL

Chamber & Instrumental Works

Cantilene
organ solo
ED 11312

Grand Choeur
organ solo
ED 11309

March on a Theme by Handel
organ solo
ED 11311

Morceau Symphonique, Op. 88
ttbn-pno
ED 10484*

Prière et Berceuse
organ solo
ED 11310*

Haas, Joseph

1879-1960

Stage Works

Die Hochzeit des Jobs, Op. 93 (1940-43)
130'

Comic Opera in 4 Acts
Text: Ludwig Andersen
Material on hire
SM

Tobias Wunderlich, Op. 90
(1934-37)
full evening

Opera in 3 Acts
Text: Hermann Heinz Ortner/Ludwig Andersen
Material on hire
Libretto **BN 3313-80**

Orchestral Works

Heitere Serenade, Op. 41
(1913-14)
25'

2.2.2.2-4.2.0.0-timp.perc-str
Material on hire
SM

Lyrisches Intermezzo (1937) 7'
2.2.2.2-4.2.3.0-timp-hp-str
alt. version: 1.1.2.1-2.2.1.0-timp-str
Material on hire
SM

Ouvertüre zu einem frohen Spiel, Op. 95 (1943)
6'

pic.1.2.2.2-4.2.3.0-timp.perc-str
Material on hire
SM

Variationen-Suite, Op. 64
(1924)
40'

About an old Rokoko Theme
1.0.2.2-2.1.0.0-timp.perc-str
Material on hire
SM

Chamber & Instrumental Works

Alte, unnennbare Tage, Op. 42 (1915)
16'

Elegies
pno
ED 2632

Chamber Trio, Op. 38
(1912)
17'

2vn-pno
ED 2635

Haas, Joseph

b. Maihingen/Bavaria 19.3.1879, d. Munich 30.3.1960

Haas studied composition with Max Reger. In 1911 he was appointed composition teacher at the Stuttgart Conservatory and in 1921 at the Munich Academy of Music. That year he founded, with Paul Hindemith among others, the Donaueschingen Festival. After World War II he was appointed the first president of the Munich Conservatory. He wrote in almost all genres with a distiact focus on choral music ranging from simple a-cappella folk-songs to full-length oratorios.

Church Sonata in D Minor, Op. 62/2 (1926) 15'

vn-org
ED 1964

Church Sonata in F Major, Op. 62/1 (1925) 15'

vn-org
ED 1963

Deutsche Reigen und Romanzen, Op. 51 (1919) 21'

pno
ED 2633

Eulenspiegeleien, Op. 39

(1912) 15'

pno
ED 2631

Fantasie-Bilder, Op. 9

(1908) 10'

Three Pieces
pno
SM

Gespenster, Op. 34 (1910) 9'

Three Piano Pieces (Nächtlicher Spuk, Mummenschanz)
pno
ED 2627

Grillen, Op. 40 (1912) 21'

Vols.1 & 2
vn-pno
ED 2634-01/-02

2 Grotesken, Op. 28 (1910) 12'

vc-pno
ED 2636-01/-02

Hausmärchen, Op. 35

(1911) 11'

Vol.1
pno
ED 2628

Hausmärchen, Op. 43

(1916) 15'

Vol.2
pno
ED 2629

Hausmärchen, Op. 53

(1920) 15'

Vol.3
pno
ED 2630

Horn Sonata, Op. 29 (1910) 19'

hn-pno
COR 1

Klangspiele, Op. 99 (1945) 48'

Vols.1 & 2
pno
ED 5273/ED 5274

Ein Kränzlein Bagatellen, Op. 23 (1909) 16'

ob-pno
OBB 31

Piano Sonata No.1 in D major, Op. 61/1 (1923) 16'

ED 1729

Piano Sonata No.2 in A minor, Op. 61/2 (1923) 20'

ED 1730

8 Präludien (1936) 14'

organ solo
ED 2550

Schwänke und Idyllen, Op. 55 (1921) 21'

Ein Zyklus von Fantasietten für Klavier
pno
ED 1728

Ein Sommermärchen, Op. 30a (1910) 25'

vc
ED 2637

4 Sonatinas, Op. 94 (1943) 34'

Vols.1 & 2
pno
ED 3873/ED 3874

String Quartet in A Minor, Op. 50 (1919) 33'

Parts ED 3174

Stücke für die Jugend, Op. 69 (1927) 15'

pno
ED 1405/ED 1409

Wichtelmännchen, Op. 27

(1910) 7'

Six Dance Fairy-tales
pno
ED 2626

Solo Voice(s)/Voice(s) and Piano/Guitar

Christuslieder, Op. 74

(1928) 12'

Text: Reinhard J. Sorge
high voice-pno
ED 2021

Frühling, Op. 59 (1925) 13'

Text: E.A. Herrmann
high voice-pno
ED 2642

6 Gedichte, Op. 48 (1918) 14'

Text: C. Flaischlen
high voice-pno
ED 2641

Gesänge an Gott, Op. 68

(1926) 12'

Text: Jakob Kneip
high/low voice-pno/org
ED 2020/2061/2195

Heimliche Lieder der Nacht, Op. 54 (1920) 12'

Text: E.L. Schellenberg/C. Flaischlen/H. Hesse/R. Dehmel
medium voice-pno
ED 2016

Kuckuckslieder, Op. 37

(1912) 9'

Five Songs for high voice
voice-pno
ED 2640

Lieder der Reife und Ernte, Op. 92 (1940)   15'

Text: Franz Ulbrich
high/low voice-pno
ED 3791/ED 3792

Lieder der Sehnsucht, Op. 77

(1929)   15'

medium voice-pno
ED 2090

Lieder des Glücks, Op. 52

(1919)   12'

Text: Karl Adolf Metz
high/medium voice-pno
ED 2015

Lieder vom Baum und Wald, Op. 97 (1944)   16'

Text: Johannes Linke
high/low voice-pno
ED 4020/ED 4021

Lieder vom Leben, Op. 76

(1928)   12'

Text: Ruth Schaumann
high voice-pno
ED 2022

Schelmenlieder, Op. 71 (1929)

20'

Text: Arthur Maximilian Miller
Chorus: children's choir
solo voice-pno
ED 2140

Trali Trala, Op. 47 (1918)   33'

12 children's songs
Text: Robert Reinick
medium voice-pno
Score **ED 2643**

Unterwegs, Op. 65 (1925)   16'

Text: Hermann Hesse
high voice-pno
ED 2018

Solo Voice(s) and Instrument(s)/ Orchestra

An die Heimat (1939)   5'

Text: A. Sergel
Soloist: mezzo-soprano
str-org/pno/pno (4hnd)/concert band
Material on hire
Score **ED 2854**

Tag und Nacht, Op. 58

(1921-22)   40'

Symphonic Suite
Text: Ernst Ludwig Schellenberg
Soloist: high voice
2.2.2.2-4.2.3.0-timp.perc-hp-str
Material on hire
SM

Choral Works

Alemannischer Liederreigen, Op. 89/1 (1943)   10'

Text: Folk
Chorus: female/children
pno
Score **ED 4296** / Choral score **ED 4296-01**

Bernhardus-Lied (1953)   5'

Text: K. Hofen
Chorus: unisono
org
SM

Der Butzemann   1'

Kanon
Chorus: female
CHBL 530

Chorfeier-Suite, Op. 98 (1950)

10'

Chorus: male a cappella
SM

Christ und die Kinder, Op. 44 (1916)   3'

from "6 Lieder"
Text: anonymous
Chorus: female/children a cappella
C 35149

Christ-König-Messe, Op. 88

(1935)   30'

Text: Wilhelm Dauffenbach
Chorus: unison
Arr I: org
Arr II: [1.0.2.1-2.2.0.0]-str
Arr III (min): fl.ob.3cl.2flhn-4hn.3tpt.3tbn.euph-bass-timp
Material on sale
Score **ED 3290**

Christnacht, Op. 85 (1932)   90'

Christmas Play on Bavarian and Tyrolese Melodies
Text: Wilhelm Dauffenbach
Soloists: 2S,A,T,Bar,B
Chorus: mixed, female
fl.2cl-hn-pno-str
Score **ED 3311** / Parts **ED 3270-14** / Choral score **ED 3270** / Libretto **ED 3270-10**

Deutsche Chormesse, Op. 108 (1958/65)   10'

after "Deutsche Kindermesse"
Arranger: Jörg Spranger
Text: H. Kirchhoff
Chorus: mixed [a cappella]
[org]
Choral score **C 45367** / Organ reduction **ED 4859**

Deutsche Kindermesse, Op. 108 (1958)   15'

Text: Hermann Kirchhoff
Chorus: female
org/harm
Material on sale
Choral score **ED 4859-01** / Organ reduction **ED 4859**

Deutsche Messe (1949)   25'

(Franz Schubert)
Text: J.Ph. Neumann
Soloist: organ
Chorus: unison/female/mixed
1.0.2.0-2.2.1.1-timp-str
alt. version: concert band
Material on hire
Organ reduction **ED 3883**

Deutsche Messe (1961)   15'

(Michael Haydn)
Text: Fr.S. Kohlbrenner
Chorus: female/mixed
org
Organ reduction **ED 5150**

Eine deutsche Singmesse, Op. 60 (1924)   25'

Text: Angelus Silesius
Chorus: mixed a cappella
[org]
SM

Deutsche Vesper, Op. 72

(1929)   35'

Text: Bible
Chorus: mixed a cappella
[org]
SM

Deutsche Weihnachtsmesse, Op. 105 (1954)   21'

Text: Peter Dörfler
Chorus: unison
Arr I: org
Arr II: fl.cl-hn-str
Material on sale
Piano reduction **ED 4475**

Ein deutsches Gloria, Op. 86

(1933)   8'

"Singt dem Herrn ein Lied"
Text: Wilhelm Dauffenbach
Chorus: mixed double a cappella
Score **ED 4228** / Choral score **ED 4228-01/-02**

"Die Linien des Lebens sind verschieden", Op. 79/2

(1930)   4'

from "2 geistliche Motetten"
Text: Friedrich Hölderlin/Willi Vesper
Soloists: baritone
Chorus: male a cappella
C 32756

6 dreistimmige Kanons

(1913)   6'

über alte Sprüchlein Vol. 1+2
Chorus: children's
SM

Ecce Sacerdos Magnus, Op. 80a (1930)   3'

Hymn
Text: Wilhelm Dauffenbach
Chorus: unison
org/wind orch
Parts **ED 3255-10** / Choral score **ED 3255-01** / Organ reduction **ED 3255**

4 Elisabeth-Hymns, Op. 84b

(1931) 16'

from "Die heilige Elisabeth"
Chorus: mixed
org/pno
SM

Es blühen die Maien (1933) 3'

Text: Oberbayern/Tirol
Chorus: female a cappella
CHBL 591

Es ist so still geworden

(1951-52) 3'

From "Das Jahr im Lied" (15th century)
Chorus: mixed a cappella
CHBL 327

Fränkischer Liederreigen, Op. 89/2 (1943) 10'

Text: Folk
Chorus: female/children
pno
Score ED 4297 / Choral score ED 4297-01

Ein Freiheitslied, Op. 78

(1929) 10'

"Es ist nun einmal so, seit wir geboren sind"
Text: Dehmel/Hofmannswaldau/Fahrenkrog
Soloist: baritone
Chorus: male a cappella
C 32349

Freund Husch, Op. 44

(1916) 3'

from "6 Lieder"
Text: R. Dehmel
Chorus: female/children a cappella
C 35150

Frisch auf, ihr Musikanten

(1951-52) 2'

Chorus: mixed a cappella with soli(SATB)
CHBL 302

Gott ist die Liebe (1929) 2'

from "Deutsche Vesper"
Chorus: mixed
SM

Gotteslob, Op. 104 (1954) 10'

Sacred Hymn
Text: Ludwig Schuster
Chorus: mixed, male, children's a cappella
SM

Die heilige Elisabeth, Op. 84

(1931) 120'

Oratorio
Text: Wilhelm Dauffenbach
Soloists: soprano, speaker
Chorus: mixed, male, children's
2(pic).2.2.2-4.2.3.0-timp.perc-org-str
Material on hire
Piano reduction ED 3260 / Libretto BN 3310-30

Heißa, Kathreinerle (1949) 1'

Chorus: female/children a cappella
CHBL 530

Das himmlische Orchester

(1932) 3'

Text: Tirol
Chorus: mixed a cappella
CHBL 291

Hymnen an das Licht, Op. 82 (1930) 6'

Chorus: double (6 prt)/mixed a cappella
SM

Ich bin schon siebenhundert Jahr (1933) 3'

Text: Arthur Maximilian Miller
Chorus: female/chidren a cappella
CHBL 553

Das Jahr im Lied, Op. 103

(1951-52) 120'

A German Folksong-oratorio
Text: Ludwig Andersen
Soloists: S.A.T.B, speaker
Chorus: mixed
2(pic).0.2.0-1.2.0.0-timp.2perc-pno-str
Material on hire
Vocal score ED 4340 / Libretto ED 4340-10

Kanonische Motetten, Op. 75

(1927) 4'

Freund, soll'n wir allesamt
Text: Angelus Silesius
Chorus: mixed a cappella
Score C 32024 / Parts C 32024-01/-02

Kanonische Motetten, Op. 75

(1927) 8'

Gott ist die ew'ge Sonn
Text: Angelus Silesius
Chorus: mixed a cappella
Score C 32025

Der Kiebitz, Op. 44 (1916) 3'

from "6 Lieder"
Text: O. Michaeli
Chorus: female/children a cappella
C 35147

Kleiner Morgenwanderer, Op. 44 (1916) 3'

from "6 Lieder"
Text: O. Michaeli
Chorus: female/children a cappella
C 35148

Kommt ein Kindlein (1952) 3'

after the song op. 76/2
Text: R. Schaumann
Chorus: female
SM

Kommt, laßt uns allesamt, Op. 73 (1930-33) 4'

from "Hymnen an den Frohsinn"
Chorus: female
pno
Score ED 2154 / Parts ED 2154-01 (-03)
(chorus)

Des Lebens Sonnenschein, Op. 73 (1930-33) 4'

from "Hymnen an den Frohsinn"
Chorus: female
pno
Score ED 2153 / Parts ED 2153-01 (-03)
(chorus)

Das Lebensbuch Gottes, Op. 87 (1934) 100'

Oratorio
Text: Angelus Silesius
Soloists: soprano, alto
Chorus: mixed, female
1.0.2.0-2.1.1.0-timp-org(pno)-str
alt. version: pno
Material on hire
Libretto ED 3282-10

Das Lied von der Mutter, Op. 91 (1938-39) 120'

Text: Willi Lindner
Soloists: soprano, baritone
Chorus: mixed, children's
2(pic).2.2.2-4.2.3.1-timp.2perc-org-str
Material on hire
SM

Lieder der Sehnsucht, Op. 77

(1929) 15'

Soloist: voice
Chorus: mixed
pno
Material on hire
SM

Lob der Freundschaft, Op. 109 6'

Hymn
Text: Peter Seifert
Chorus: mixed, youth, children's
1.0.1.0-1.0.0.0-timp.perc-pno/org-str
Material on hire
ED 4988

Lobpreis der heiligen Elisabeth, Op. 84a (1931) 4'

(Prolog)
Chorus: mixed
org/pno
SM

Lobt den Herrn, Op. 60/5

(1924) 3'

Text: Angelus Silesius
Chorus: mixed a cappella
C 31099

Mädel kämm dich, putz dich

(1949) 2'

Text: Folk
Chorus: female/children a cappella
CHBL 501

Mailied, Op. 44 (1916) 3'

from "6 Lieder"
Text: V.v. Blüthgen
Chorus: female/children a cappella
C 35145

Marianische Kantate, Op. 112 (1960) 40'

Old Christian Poem
Text: Richard Zoozmann
Chorus: female with soli(SA)
org/harm
Choral score **ED 5174-01** / Organ reduction
ED 5174

"Mensch, steh still und fürcht mich", Op. 79/1

(1930) 4'

from "2 geistliche Motetten"
Text: Heinrich Laufenberg/Angelus
Silesius
Chorus: male a cappella
C 32755

Morgengloria, Op. 110

(1959) 2'

from "Echolieder-Suite"
Text: J. Kneip
Chorus: male a cappella
C 40056

Morgenlied, Op. 66/2 (1925) 7'

"Wie heimlicherweise ein Engelein leise"
Text: Eduard Mörike
Chorus: male a cappella
C 35156

Münchner Liebfrauen-Messe, Op. 96 (1946) 22'

Text: Erwin Volker
Chorus: unison
Arr I: org
Arr II: [fl.2cl.bn-2hn.2tpt.tbn-timp]-str
Arr III(min): 3cl-3hn.2flhn.euph.btuba-
[fl.ob.bn-tbn-timp]
Material on sale
ED 3900

Nachtwandler, Op. 102

(1951) 9'

Serenade
Text: Gustav Falke
Soloist: tenor
Chorus: male
pno
alt. version: small orchestra
Material on sale
ED 4295

Nur, Op. 110 (1959) 2'

from "Echolieder-Suite"
Text: R.A. Schröder
Chorus: male a cappella
C 40054

Praeconium, Op. 113 (1960) 8'

"Heiß uns willkommen, schöne Stadt"
Text: Gertrud von le Fort
Chorus: mixed, children's
2.0.Ebcl.2.2 4.3.3.2-timp
SM

2 Reiterlieder, Op. 67 (1926) 5'

Chorus: male a cappella
SM

Schelmenlieder, Op. 71

(1929) 20'

Text: Arthur Maximilian Miller
Chorus: children's choir
pno
ED 2140

Schiller-Hymne, Op. 107

(1957) 12'

"Die Worte des Glaubens"
Text: Friedrich Schiller
Soloist: baritone
Chorus: mixed
2.2.2.2-4.2.3.0-timp.perc-str
Material on hire
Vocal score **ED 4771**

Die Seligen, Op. 106 (1956) 100'

Variations on Christ's Sermone on the
Mount
Soloists: soprano, baritone
Chorus: mixed, children's
2(pic).2.2.2-4.2.3.1-timp perc-org-str
Vocal score **ED 4921** / Libretto **BN 3316-20**

Speyerer Domfest-Messe, Op. 80 (1930) 25'

Liturgic Cantata
Text: Wilhelm Dauffenbach
Chorus: unison
Arr I: org
Arr II: fl.ob.3cl.2flhn-
4hn.3tpt.3tbn.euph.bass
(min: 2flhn-3hn.tpt.tbn-bass)
Arr III: 1.2.0.0-2.2.0.0-str-bass
Organ reduction ED 3239 / Parts **C 39722-50**
/ Choral score **C 39722**

Steh auf, Nordwind!, Op. 66/1 (1925) 6'

from "Des Knaben Wunderhorn'
Chorus: male a cappella
C 35154

Still, o Himmel (1933) 3'

Text: Chiemgau/Oberbayern
Chorus: female/children a cappella
CHBL 590

Tanzliedsuite, Op. 63 (1924) 14'

nach altdeutschen Reimen
Chorus: male a cappella
SM

Te Deum, Op. 100 (1945) 30'

Text: Liturgical
Soloists: soprano, baritone
Chorus: mixed
2.2.2.2-4.2.3.0-timp-org-str
Material on hire
Vocal score **ED 3889**

Totenmesse, Op. 101 (1947) 75'

Melodram
Text: E. Wiechert
Soloists: speakers
Chorus: children's, female, male + mixed a
capp.
1(pic).1.2.0-2.1.1.0-timp.perc-hp.pno-str
Material on hire
SM

Trali Trala, Op. 47 (1918) 33'

12 children's songs
Text: Robert Reinick
Chorus: children's unison
pno
SM

Trauungsgesang (1933) 3'

Chorus: female a cappella
CHBL 546

Um ein Mägdlein, Op. 83

(1932) 5'

Serenada
Text: Arthur Maximilian Miller
Chorus: male a cappella
SM

Vom Himmel hoch, da komm ich her (1952) 2'

Text: Martin Luther
Chorus: male a cappella
CHBL 126

Wachtelschlag, Op. 110

(1959) 2'

from "Echolieder-Suite"
Text: J. Kneip
Chorus: male a cappella
C 40055

Wiegenlied 6'

Soloist: mezzo-soprano
Chorus: mixed, male, children's unison a
cappella
SM

Wiegenlied, Op. 44 (1916) 3'

from "6 Lieder"
Text: D.v. Lilienkron
Chorus: female/children a cappella
C 35146

Zueignung, Op. 110 (1959) 2'

from "Echolieder-Suite"
Text: R.A. Schröder
Chorus: male a cappella
C 40053

Zum Lob der Arbeit, Op. 81/4 (1941) 5'

Text: W. Lindner
Chorus: female
pno (2hnd)/pno (4hnd)/org-str
SM

Zum Lob der Musik, Op. 81/1 (1930) 6'

"Was mag doch diese Welt" (17th century)
Chorus: female
pno (2hnd)/pno (4hnd)/str-org/wind orch:
(2.1.3.1-2flhn.5.2.3.euph.2-timp)
Score **ED 2151** / Parts **ED 2151-11 (-15)** /
Choral score **ED 2151-01**

Zum Lob der Natur, Op. 81/2 (1930) 10'

Text: Wilhelm Dauffenbach
Chorus: female
pno (2hnd)/pno (4hnd)/str-org
Material on sale
Vocal score **ED 2152**

Hamel, Peter Michael
b.1947

Orchestral Works

Albatros (1977)　　25'

*Improvisation grp:pno.bass-3perc-[sax.ob-
gtr/vib]*
*Orch:3(pic,afl).3(ca).3(bcl).2asax.1(cbn)-
3.2.4.btuba(cbtuba)-timp.3perc-cel-str(12-
14.8-10.6-9.6-9.3-5)*
Material on hire
SM

Dharana (1972)　　19'

Soloist: [voice]
*4(2afl).1.ca.0.2bcl(cbcl).1.cbn-4.0.4.cbtbn.
cbtuba-3perc-prep pno.eorg/hammondorg.
2hp-str(24.0.12.9.7)*
Material on hire
SM

Diaphainon (1973-74)　　16'

*2(pic,afl).2(ca).2.bcl.0.cbn-
2.2.2.cbtbn.cbtuba-timp.2perc-hp-str
(20-25.8-10.6-12.3-6)*
Material on hire
SM

Hamilton, Iain
b.1922

Orchestral Works

**"1912"- A Light Overture,
Op. 38** (1958)　　6'

2.2.2.2-4.2.3.0-timp.perc-str
Material on hire
Study score **ED 10846***

Arias (1962)　　12'

1.1.1.1-1.1.1.0-str
Material on hire
Study score **ED 11245**

**Bartholomew Fair -
Overture, Op. 17** (1952)　　8'

2.2.2.2-4.3.3.1-timp.2perc-str
Material on hire
Study score **ED 10649**

Cantos (1964)　　17'

2.2.2.2-4.3.3.1-hp-str
Material on hire
Study score **ED 11105***

Ecossaise (1959)　　7'

2.2.2.2-4.2.3.1-timp.2perc-hp-str
Material on hire
Study score **ED 10838**

Hamilton, Iain

b. Glasgow 6.6.1922

**An overtly dramatic tension arising from
bold contrasts of gesture and timbre is central to Hamilton's music, whether in operatic or orchestral works. He was one of the
first British composers to exploit the serial
method, applied with great fluency to large-
scale forms often exploring subjects drawn
from Classical antiquity.**

Jubilee (1964)　　15'

2.2.2.2-4.2.3.1-timp.perc-str
Material on hire
SL

Scottish Dances, Op. 32
(1956)　　16'

2.2.2.2-4.2.3.0-timp.perc-str
Material on hire
Study score **ED 10633***

Sinfonia (1959)　　15'

for 2 orchestras
*orch I: 2.0.2.0-4.0.0.1-perc-cel.hp-
str(vnI,vc)*
*orch II: 0.2.0.2-0.3.3.0-timp-pno-
str(vnII,va,db)*
Material on hire
Study score **ED 10737 (min.)**

**Sonata for Chamber
Orchestra, Op. 34** (1957)　　11'

2.1.1.1-1.1.0.0-cel-str
Material on hire
SL

**Symphonic Variations,
Op. 19** (1953)　　17'

2.2.2.2-4.3.3.1-timp.2perc-hp-str
Material on hire
SL

Symphony No.1, Op. 3
(1948)　　22'

2.2.2.2-4.3.3.1-timp.2perc-hp-str
Material on hire
SL

Symphony No.2, Op. 10
(1950-51)　　30'

3.3.3.3-4.3.3.1-timp.perc-pno.hp-str
Material on hire
Study score **ED 10575***

**Variations on an Original
Theme, Op. 1** (1948)　　22'

str
Material on hire
Study score **ED 10218***

Concertos

Clarinet Concerto, Op. 7
(1949-50)　　27'

Soloist: clarinet
2.2.2.2-4.2.3.0-timp.str
Material on hire
SL

**Jazz Trumpet Concerto,
Op. 37** (1958)　　13'

Soloist: jazz trumpet
2.2.2.2-4.2.3.0-timp.perc-str
Material on hire
Study score **ED 10692***

Organ Concerto (1965/88)　　18'

Soloist: organ
1.1.1.1-1.1.1.0-timp-str
Material on hire
SL

Piano Concerto (1960/67)　　20'

Soloist: piano
2.2.2.2-4.2.3.1-timp.perc-hp-str
Material on hire
Piano reduction **ED 10774***

Violin Concerto, Op. 15
(1952)　　27'

Soloist: violin
2.2.2.2-4.2.3.0-timp-str
Material on hire
Piano reduction **ED 11161***

Chamber & Instrumental Works

Aria (1951)　　5'

hn-pno
ED 10232

Brass Quintet (1964) 10'

hn.2tpt.tbn.tuba
Material on hire or sale
SL

Capriccio (1951) 5'

tpt-pno
ED 10239

Cello Sonata, Op. 39 (1959) 17'

vc-pno
Manuscript score on sale
ED 10606*

Clarinet Sonata, Op. 22

(1953) 18'

cl-pno
ED 10426*

Fanfares and Variants

(1960) 10'

organ solo
ED 10785*

3 Nocturnes, Op. 6 (1950) 12'

cl-pno
ED 10194*

Nocturnes with Cadenzas

(1963) 10'

solo pno
ED 10882*

3 Piano Pieces, Op. 30 (1955) 6'

ED 10547

Piano Sonata, Op. 13 (1951) 6'

ED 10184*

Sextet (1962) 12'

fl.2cl-vn.vc-pno
Material on hire or sale
SL

Sonata for 5 (1966) 10'

fl.ob.cl.bn-hn
Material on hire or sale
SL

Sonata Notturna (1965) 10'

hn-pno
ED 10971

Sonatas and Variants (1963) 15'

1.1.1.1-2.2.1.1
Material on hire
SL

String Quartet No.1, Op. 5

(1949) 25'

ED 10256* / Study score ED 10217*

String Quartet No.2

(1965/72) 12'

Material on sale
SL

Trio, Op. 25 (1954) 15'

vn.vc-pno
ED 10590*

Viola Sonata, Op. 9 (1951) 18'

va-pno
ED 10263*

Solo Voice(s) and Instrument(s)/ Orchestra

Dialogues (1965) 15'

Text: Chateaubriand
Soloist: coloratura soprano
fl-tpt-vc-pno(cel)-perc
Material on hire
SL

5 Love Songs, Op. 36 (1958) 18'

Soloist: high voice
2.2.2.2-4.2.3.1-timp.3perc-cel.hp-str
Material on hire
SL

A Testament of War (1960) 15'

Text: Lucan
Soloist: baritone
1.0.1.0-1.1.1.0-timp.perc-cel-str(1.0.1.1.0)
Material on hire
SL

Choral Works

The Bermudas, Op. 33

(1956) 27'

Text: Hamilton/Silvester/Marvell
Soloist: baritone
Chorus: mixed
3.3.3.3-4.2.4.1-timp.3perc-hp-str
Material on hire
Study score ED 10640* / Vocal score ED 10034*

The Fray of Suport, Op. 21

(1954) 8'

Chorus: mixed a cappella
ED 10295

Nocturnal (1959) 6'

Text: John Donne
Chorus: 4S.2A.2T.3B
ED 10784*

Hand, Colin

b.1929

Orchestral Works

Divertimento (1973)

rec-perc-pno-str
Material on sale
ED 11156

Chamber & Instrumental Works

Aria and Giga (1973) 3'

ob-pno
ED 11140

Fanfare for a Festival, Op. 64 (1968) 2'

2srec.arec.2trec.brec
Material on sale
ED 11814

Fenland Suite (1973) 6'

srec.2arec.trec
Material on sale
ED 11139

Festival Overture (1974) 7'

srec.2arec.trec.brec
Material on sale
ED 11246

Guitar Sonatina No.2 (1979) 8'

ED 11407

Plaint (1973) 4'

arec-hpd/pno
ED 11147

Progressive Pieces (1977)

va-pno
ED 11259

Sonata Breve (1971) 6'

arec-pno
ED 11265

Choral Works

In the Beginning (1970) 70'

Soloists: baritone, male speaker
Chorus: children's
rec-2tpt-6perc-pno.org-str
Material on hire
Piano reduction ED 11231

Hartmann, Karl Amadeus

1905-1963

Stage Works

Simplicius Simplicissimus

(1934-35/1956-57)   85'

3 Operatic Scenes after Grimmelshausen
Text: Scherchen/Petzet/Hartmann
Material on hire
Study score **ED 5019** / Vocal score **ED 4324** /
Libretto **BN 3330-80**

Wachsfigurenkabinett

(1929-30)   75'

5 Little Operas
Text: Erich Bormann
Material on hire
Vocal score **ED 7668** / Libretto **BN 3325-1**

Orchestral Works

Adagio - Symphony No.2

(1948/49)   17'

*3(3pic).3(ca).3(barsax).3(cbn)-4.3.3.1-
timp.4perc-cel.pno.hp-str*
Material on hire
Study score **ED 4405**

Klagegesang (1944-45)   23'

*3(3pic).3(ca).3.3(cbn)-4.3.3.1-timp.4perc-
cel.hp-str*
Material on hire
Study score **ED 7887**

Miserae (1933-34)   14'

Symphonic Poem
2(pic).2(ca).2.2-4.3.3.1-timp.4perc-cel-str
Material on hire
Study score **ED 6766**

3 Orchesterstücke (1945)   20'

On the 2nd version of the Piano Sonata
"27. April 1945"
Arranger: Hans Werner Henze (1995)
*3(2pic,afl).2.ca.heck.2.bcl.asax(tsax).2.cbn-
4.3.3.1-timp.3perc-cel.pno.hp-str*
Material on hire
SM

Simplicius Simplicissimus - Overture (1934-35) 10'

1(pic).0.1.1-0.1.1.0-5perc-hp-str
Material on hire
SM

Simplicius Simplicissimus - Suite (1934-35)   27'

1(pic).0.1.1-0.1.1.0-4perc-hp-str
Material on hire
SM

Hartmann, Karl Amadeus

b. Munich 2.8.1905, d. Munich 5.12.1963

The virtues of Karl Amadeus Hartmann's music, long recognised in his native Germany, are increasingly acknowledged internationally as well. At the heart of his output are eight symphonies: ambitious, dramatically focussed works complemented by the "Concerto funebre" for violin and strings and the chamber opera "Simplicius Simplicissimus". A slow, conscientious worker, he withdrew from musical life during the turbulent war years, re-emerging afterwards to found the celebrated Musica Viva concert series in his native city, and to continue the development of his own music, with its roots in Bartok, Berg and the Second Viennese School.

Sinfonia tragica (1940-43)   25'

*2(2pic).2.2.3(cbn)-4.3.3.1-timp.3perc-
cel.hp-str*
Material on hire
Study score **ED 7790**

String Quartet No.2

(1945-46)   27'

Version for string orchestra
Arranger: Henning Brauel (1994)
str
Material on hire
SM

Symphonic Hymns (1941/43)   30'

*3(3pic).3(ca).3(bcl).3(2cbn)-4.6.6.1-
timp.4perc-cel.pno.hp-str*
Material on hire
Study score **ED 6650**

Symphonic Overture

(1942/62)   15'

*3(3pic).3(ca).3.3(cbn)-4.3.3(2valve
tbn,2btbn).1-timp.4perc-cel.pno.hp-str*
Material on hire
Study score **ED 6761**

Symphony Concertante - Symphony No.5 (1950)   20'

2(pic).2.2.2.cbn-0.2.2.1-str
Material on hire
Study score **ED 4404**

Symphony No.3 (1948-49)   35'

*3(3pic).3.3.3(cbn)-4.3.3.1-timp.2perc-
cel.hp-str*
Material on hire
Study score **ED 4273**

Symphony No.4 (1948)   35'

str
Material on hire
Study score **ED 4564**

Symphony No.6 (1951-53)   27'

*3(3pic).3(ca).3(bcl).2.cbn-4.4.3.1-
timp.6perc-cel.pno(2/4hnd).mand.hp-str*
Material on hire
Study score **ED 4419**

Symphony No.7 (1959-60)   32'

*3(3pic).3.3.3(cbn)-4.3.3.1-2timp.6perc-
cel.pno(4hnd).hp(2)-str*
Material on hire
Study score **ED 5005**

Symphony No.8 (1960-62)   25'

*3(3pic).3.3(bcl).3(cbn)-4.3.3.1-timp.6perc-
cel.pno.hp(2)-str*
Material on hire
Study score **ED 5027**

Concertos

Chamber Concerto (1930/35) 26'

Soloists: clarinet, string quartet
str
Material on hire
SM

Concerto for viola with piano

(1954-55)   30'

Soloists: viola, piano
*3(3pic).0.3(bcl).3(cbn)-0.3.3.0-timp.6perc-
cel*
alt. version: va-pno
Material on hire
Study score **ED 4581** / Piano reduction
VAB 13

Concerto funebre (1939/59)   20'

Soloist: violin
str
Material on hire
Study score **ED 5002** / Piano reduction
ED 5167

II Adagio

39231

Karl Amadeus Hartmann
Concerto funebre (1939/59)

Piano Concerto (1953)   16'

Soloist: piano
3(3pic).0.3.3-0.3.3.0-timp.5perc-cel
Material on hire
Study score **ED 4421**

Chamber & Instrumental Works

Burlesque Music (1931)   11'

1(pic).0.1.1-1.1.1.0-3perc-pno
Material on hire
SM

Dance Suite (1931)   10'

cl.bn-hn.tpt.tbn
Material on sale
Score and parts **ED 6533**

Jazz-Toccata and Fugue
(1928)   14'

pno
ED 6426

Kleines Konzert (1931-32)   9'

Arranger: Henning Brauel
str-4perc
Study score **ED 5849** / Parts **ED 5849-01**

Lied (1932)   5'

Soloist: trumpet
0.0.1.bcl.1.cbn-1.1.1.1
Material on hire
SM

Little Suite No.1 (1924-26)   6'

pno
ED 7689

Little Suite No. 2 (1924-26)   7'

pno
ED 7690

Piano Sonata No.1 (1932)   12'

pno
ED 7885

Scherzo (1956)   4'

10perc
ED 7785

Sonata "27 April 1945"
(1945)   16'

pno
ED 6870

Sonatina (1931)   6'

pno
ED 6258

String Quartet No.1 - Carillon (1933)   20'

Study score **ED 4561** / Parts **ED 4626**

String Quartet No.2
(1945-46)   27'

Study score **ED 4562** / Parts **ED 4627**

2 Suites for Solo Violin
(1927)   26'

violin solo
ED 7531

Violin Sonata No.1 (1927)   15'

violin solo
ED 7520

Violin Sonata No.2 (1927)   15'

violin solo
ED 7521

Solo Voice(s)/Voice(s) and Piano/Guitar

Lamento (1936-37/55)   20'

Text: Andreas Gryphius
soprano-pno
ED 4906

Solo Voice(s) and Instrument(s)/ Orchestra

Gesangsszene (1962-63)   23'

Text: Jean Giraudoux
Soloist: baritone
3(pic,afl).3(ca).3(bcl).3(cbn)-3.4.3.1-
2timp.5perc-cel(pno).pno(4hnd).hp-str
Material on hire
Study score **ED 5506** / Vocal score
ED 5464

Symphony No.1
(1935-36/1954-55)   35'

Attempt of a Requiem
Text: Walt Whitman
Soloist: alto
3(3pic).3.ca.3.bcl.3.cbn-4.4.3.1-timp.4perc-
cel.pno.hp-str
Material on hire
Study score **ED 4577**

Choral Works

Friede Anno 48 (1936)   30'

Text: Andreas Gryphius
Soloist: soprano
Chorus: mixed
pno
Score **ED 6006** / Vocal score **ED 6006-01**

Hartmann, Peter
b.1940

Orchestral Works

Adagio (1964)   14'

3(pic).2.2caEbcl.1.bcl.asax.2.cbn-
4.2.3.euph/tuba.bomb/tuba.0-timp.perc-
cel.pno.2hp-str
Material on hire
AVV

Harvey, Jonathan
b.1939

Choral Works

The Annunciation (1964)   8'

Text: Edwin Muir
Chorus: mixed
org
ED 10931

2 Fragments (1965)   12'

Text: medieval
Chorus: mixed a cappella
ED 10947*

Love (1965)   6'

Text: Georg Herbert
Chorus: mixed a cappella
ED 10947

Haubenstock-Ramati, Roman
b.1919

Orchestral Works

Papageno's Pocket-Size Concerto (1954)   3'

No. 6 from the "Divertimento für Mozart"
2.2.2.2-2.2.0.0-timp.glsp-str
Material on hire
SM (Co-prod: UE)
Copyright USA: EAM/Italy: Ed. Suvini
Zerboni

Heddenhausen, Friedel-Heinz

b.1901

Orchestral Works

Bauerntänze   12'

2.2.2.2-4.3.3.1-timp.perc-str
Material on hire
SM

Heger, Robert

1886-1978

Orchestral Works

Ernstes Präludium und heitere Fuge, Op. 26   17'

2.2.2.2-4.2.3.0-timp.perc.glsp[2players]-hp-str
Material on hire
Eu

Heiden, Bernhard

b.1910

Stage Works

The Darkened City (1961-62)

Opera in 3 Acts
Text: Robert Glynn Kelly
Material on hire
EAM

Heiss, Hermann

1897-1966

Orchestral Works

Configurationen I (1956)   15'

On Picture-titles of Paul Klee
2(pic).1(ca).1.bcl.1.cbn-1.2.1.0-timp.perc-2pno-str(10.10.8.6.4)
Material on hire
AVV

Configurationen II (1956/59) 16'

On Picture-titles of Paul Klee
2(pic).1(ca).1.bcl.1.cbn-1.2.1.0-timp.2perc-2pno-str(10.10.8.6.4)
Material on hire
AVV

Sinfonia giocosa (1954)   20'

1(pic).1(ca).1(bcl).tsax.1(cbn)-2.2.1.1-timp.perc-pno.hp-str
Material on hire
AVV

Helfritz, Hans

1902-1995

Concertos

Organ Concerto   22'

Soloist: organ
str
Material on hire
AVV

Saxophone Concerto (1948) 20'

Soloist: tenor saxophone
2.2.2.2-3.3.2.0-timp.perc-cel.hp-str
Material on hire
AVV

Choral Works

9 Mexican Folksongs (1971) 14'

Chorus: female/children
recs/glsp-perc
Score **B 176** / Parts **B 176-11/-12** / Choral
score **B 176-01**

Heller, Barbara

b.1936

Chamber & Instrumental Works

Anschlüsse (1983)   7'

pno
ED 8616

Freude und Trauer (1980)   3'

pno
ED 8617

Heller, Barbara

b. Ludwigshafen/Rhine 6.11.1936

Barbara Heller studied muisc in Mannheim and in Munich. From 1958 to 1962 she worked at the "Staatliche Hochschule für Musik und Theater", Mannheim, as pianist, piano teacher and composer. After postgraduate studies in composition in Mannheim (Hans Vogt), Munich (Harald Genzmer) and Siena (M. Lavagnino/film music) she moved to Darmstadt, where she lives and works as a free lance composer. She was one of the founders of the "Internationaler Arbeitskreis Frau und Musik" in 1978 and she remained an active member until 1981, furthering the cause of women composers through lectures, concerts and radio broadcasts. She has prepared numerous scores for publication. Since 1986 until 1993 she has been a board member of the "Institut für Neue Musik und Musikerziehung" Darmstadt.
Barbara Heller's compositions have been mainly music for piano and chamber music. However, since 1988 improvisation and experimentation have become essential aspects of her music along with a concept of communication which leads to collective compositions created together with musicians and instrumental groups. She also works on sound installations.

Für jeden Tag (1994)   12'

9 little Pieces, in: Piano Workshop 2
pno
ED 8092

Intervalles (1980/87)   4'

pno
ED 8618

Lalai - Schlaflied zum Wachwerden? (1989)   8'

vc-pno
CB 155

Lalai - Schlaflied zum Wachwerden? (1989) 8'

(in: Frauen komponieren; 13 Stücke für Violine und Klavier)
vn-pno
ED 8132

Nah oder fern (1987) 15'

viola solo
VAB 56

Piano Muziek voor Anje (1980) 2'

(in: Frauen komponieren; 22 Klavierstücke)
pno
ED 7197

Scharlachrote Buchstaben (1984) 15'

pno
ED 8620

Solovioline (1982) 9'

violin solo
VLB 90

Solo Voice(s) and Instrument(s)/ Orchestra

Lalai - Schlaflied zum Wachwerden? (1995) 15'

Arranger: Siegfried Schwab
Soloist: speaker
fl-perc-gtr-va
ED 8619

Helm, Everett
b.1913

Orchestral Works

Symphony (1955) 19'

str
Material on hire
Study score **ED 4583**

Concertos

Concerto (1954) 14'

Soloists: flute, oboe, bassoon, trumpet, violin
2perc-str(6.6.4.4.3)
Material on hire
Study score **ED 4551**

Piano Concerto No.1 in G (1951) 24'

Soloist: piano
pic.2.2.2.2-4.3.2.1-timp.perc-str
Material on hire
Piano reduction **ED 4298**

Chamber & Instrumental Works

Flute Sonata (1952) 6'

fl-pno
ED 4193

Violin Sonata (1950) 10'

vn-pno
ED 4047

Wind Quintet (1969) 17'

fl.ob.cl.bn-hn
Score **ED 5931** / Parts **ED 6007**

Helmschrott, Robert M.
b.1938

Choral Works

Das Äußerste 2'

from "Begegnung"
Text: R. Exner
Chorus: mixed a cappella
C 48177

Begegnung 2'

from "Begegnung"
Text: R. Exner
Chorus: mixed a cappella
C 48175

Bruder Nacht 3'

Abendlied
Text: R. Menzel
Chorus: male a cappella
C 45417

Dann 2'

from "Begegnung"
Text: R. Exner
Chorus: mixed a cappella
C 48176

Leben eines Mannes 3'

Text: Werner Bergengruen
Chorus: male a cappella
C 45171

Manchmal 3'

from "Hesse-Lieder"
Text: Hermann Hesse
Chorus: mixed a cappella
C 46425

Menschenzeit 15'

from "Begegnung"
Text: R. Exner
Chorus: mixed a cappella
C 48235

Morgen 4'

from "Hesse-Lieder"
Text: Hermann Hesse
Chorus: mixed a cappella
C 46426

Nachtgefühl 3'

from "Hesse-Lieder"
Text: Hermann Hesse
Chorus: mixed a cappella
C 46428

Nichts 2'

from "Begegnung"
Text: R. Exner
Chorus: mixed a cappella
C 48175

Schönes Heute 5'

from "Hesse-Lieder"
Text: Hermann Hesse
Chorus: mixed a cappella
C 46427

Schweigen 7'

from "Begegnung"
Text: R. Exner
Chorus: mixed a cappella
C 48178

Unsere Zeit 2'

from "Begegnung"
Text: R. Exner
Chorus: mixed a cappella
C 48174

Wir 2'

from "Begegnung"
Text: R. Exner
Chorus: mixed a cappella
C 48177

Henze, Hans Werner
b.1926

Stage Works

Anrufung Apolls - Symphony No.3 (1949-50) 25'

Ballet in 3 Parts
Material on hire
Study score **ED 4567**

Henze, Hans Werner

b. Gütersloh 1.7.1926

With over a dozen operas to his credit, including "The Bassarids", "Elegy for Young Lovers" and "The English Cat", Henze's art begins and ends in the theatre, yet has taken in the major symphonic genres, ballet and chamber music as well. An innate sense of stagecraft and theatricality is basic to his achievement; an instinct for dramatic structure that gives equal power and dynamism to his music whether written for stage or for the concert hall. A programmatic background adds to the tension of works such as "Tristan" and "Le Miracle de la Rose", and to the profound sense of life reacting with art. In his personal recreation of Baroque, classical and contemporary values Henze is one of the most emblematic figures of our time; and in his prodigious creativity, one of the leading figures of 20th century music.

Ballett-Variationen (1949/92) 16'
Actionless Ballet in 1 Scene
Material on hire
SM

The Bassarids (1964-65/92) 120'
Music Drama in 1 Act after Euripides
Text: W.H. Auden/Chester Kallman
Material on hire
Vocal score ED 8121 /
Libretto BN 3348/3349-90

Boulevard Solitude (1951) 82'
Lyrical Drama in 7 Scenes
Text: Grete Weil
Material on hire
Vocal score ED 6630 / Libretto BN 3352-90

La Cubana oder "Ein Leben für die Kunst" (1973) 87'
Television Opera (Vaudeville) in 5 Scenes
Text: Hans Magnus Enzensberger
Material on hire
Vocal score ED 6279

Le Disperazioni del Signor Pulcinella (1949/95) 50'
Dance Play with Song in 3 Acts
Text: Sergio Sivori
Material on hire
SM

Don Chisciotte (1976) 135'
Comic Opera by Giovanni Battista Lorenzi and Giovanni Paisiello
Text: Giuseppe Di Leva/Hans Werner Henze/Henning Brauel
Material on hire
SM

Elegy for Young Lovers (1961/87) 150'
Opera in 3 Acts
Text: W.H. Auden/Chester Kallman
Material on hire
Study score ED 5040 / Vocal score ED 5100 / Libretto BN 3354-70/3354-50

Das Ende einer Welt (1964) 50'
Opera Buffa in 1 Act
Text: Wolfgang Hildesheimer
Material on hire
Vocal score ED 5673

Das Ende einer Welt (1953/93) 50'
Radio Opera in 2 Acts with Prologue and Epilogue
Text: Wolfgang Hildesheimer
Material on hire
Vocal score ED 5673

The English Cat (1980-83/90) 126'
A Story for Singers and Instrumentalists
Text: Edward Bond
Material on hire
Vocal score ED 7571 / Libretto BN 3364-20

Le Fils de l'air oder L'enfant change en jeune homme (1995-96) 35'
Ballet by Jean Cocteau
Material on hire
SM

Fürwahr...!? (1929/30) 12'
from "5 kleine Opern (Wachsfigurenkabinett)" by Karl Amadeus Hartmann
Arranger: Hans Werner Henze (1988)
Text: Erich Bormann
Material on hire
Vocal score ED 7668 / Libretto BN 3325-1

Der Idiot (1952/90) 40'
Mimodram with scenes from the novel of the same name by Fyodor M. Dostojewsky
Text: Ingeborg Bachmann
Material on hire
Piano reduction ED 4320/7666

Der junge Lord (1964) 137'
Comic Opera in 2 Acts
Text: Wilhelm Hauff/Ingeborg Bachmann
Material on hire
Vocal score ED 5850/5671 / Libretto BN 3361-80/3355-30/3356-01/3357-10

Des Kaisers Nachtigall (1959/70) 17'
Ballet Pantomime by Giulio di Majo after Hans Christian Andersen
Material on hire
Study score ED 5015

Knastgesänge (1984) 70'
3 Music-theatre Pieces for Puppeteers, Singers and Instrumentalists. Variations on 4 Songs by Hans Werner Henze
Arranger: Jörg Widmann (1995)
Text: Hans-Ulrich Treichel
Chorus: mixed
Material on hire
SM

König Hirsch (1953/56) 240'
Opera in 3 Acts after the drama by Graf Carlo Gozzi (1772)
Text: Heinz von Cramer
Material on hire
Vocal score ED 4915 / Libretto BN 3358-80

Labyrinth (1951/96) 25'
Ballet in 1 Act by Mark Baldwin
Material on hire
SM

Ein Landarzt (1964) 33'
Opera in 1 Act
Text: Franz Kafka
Material on hire
Vocal score ED 5674

Ein Landarzt (1951/94) 33'
Radio Opera
Text: Franz Kafka
Material on hire
Vocal score ED 5674

Der langwierige Weg in die Wohnung der Natascha Ungeheuer (1971) 55'
Show with 17
Text: Gastón Salvatore
Material on hire
SM

Der Mann, der vom Tode auferstand (1929/30) 12'
from "5 kleine Opern (Wachsfigurenkabinett)" by Karl Amadeus Hartmann
Arranger: Hans Werner Henze/Günther Bialas (1988)
Text: Erich Bormann
Material on hire
Vocal score ED 7668 / Libretto BN 3325-1

Maratona (1956) 50'
Dance Drama in 1 Scene by Luchino Visconti
Material on hire
Piano reduction ED 4937

Hans Werner Henze
Das verratene Meer (1986-89)

Moralities (1967)   23'

3 Morality Plays after Aesop's Fables
Text: W.H. Auden
Soloists: soloists, speaker
Chorus: mixed
Material on hire
Piano reduction **ED 6033**

Orpheus (1978/86)   110'

Story in 6 Scenes (2 Acts)
Text: Edward Bond
Material on hire
Piano reduction **ED 6819**

Pollicino (1979-80)   85'

Fairytale for Music based on Collodi,
Grimm and Perault
Text: Giuseppe Di Leva
Material on hire
Vocal score **ED 7202**

Der Prinz von Homburg

(1958-59/91)   130'

Opera in 3 Acts (9 Scenes) after Heinrich
von Kleist
Text: Ingeborg Bachmann
Material on hire
Vocal score **ED 5080** / Libretto **BN 3360-10**

Il Re Cervo oder Die Irrfahrten der Wahrheit

(1962)   80'

Opera in 3 Acts after the Drama by Graf
Carlo Gozzi
Text: Heinz von Cramer
Material on hire
Vocal score **ED 5440** / Libretto **BN 3359-60**

Re Teodoro in Venezia

(1991-92)   150'

Dramatic Hero Comedy in 2 Acts
(Giovanni Paisiello, 1784)
Arranger: Hans Werner Henze, David Paul
Graham, Lorenzo Mariani
Text: Giovanni Battista Casti
Material on hire
SM / Libretto **BN 3366-90**

Il ritorno d'Ulisse in patria

(1981)   177'

Opera (Claudio Monteverdi, 1641)
Arranger: Hans Werner Henze
Text: Hans Werner Henze after Giacomo
Badoaro
Material on hire
Vocal score **ED 7367**

Tancredi (1952/64)   50'

Ballet in 2 Scenes by Peter Csobádi
Material on hire
Piano reduction **ED 5659**

Undine (1956-57)   110'

Ballet in 3 Acts by Frederick Ashton (free-
ly adapted from De la Motte Fouqué)
Material on hire
Piano reduction **ED 4767**

Das Urteil der Kalliope

(1964/91)   18'

A Pastoral
Text: W.H. Auden/Chester Kallman
Material on hire
SM / Libretto **BN 3368-50**

Venus und Adonis

(1993-95)   full evening

Opera in 1 Act for singers and dancers
Text: Hans-Ulrich Treichel
Material on hire
Libretto **BN 3367-70**

Das verratene Meer

(1986-89)   108'

Music Drama in 2 Acts. Based on the novel
"Gogo no Eiko" by Yukio Mishima
Text: Hans-Ulrich Treichel
Material on hire
Libretto **BN 3365-00**

Das Vokaltuch der Kammersängerin Rosa Silber (1950/90)   18'

Exercise with Stravinsky about a picture by
Paul Klee. Actionless ballet
Material on hire
SM

We come to the River

(1974-76)   145'

Actions for Music
Text: Edward Bond
Material on hire
Study score **ED 6682** / Libretto **BN 3363-40/3362-60**

Das Wundertheater

(1948/64)   45'

Opera in 1 Scene on an Intermezzo by
Miguel Cervantes
Text: Adolf Graf von Schack
Material on hire
Vocal score **ED 5672**

Das Wundertheater

(1948/65)   45'

Opera in 1 Scene after Miguel Cervantes.
Version for actors and 5 Instrumentalists
Arranger: Henning Brauel (1964)
Text: Adolf Graf von Schack
Material on hire
SM

Orchestral Works

Die Abenteuer des Don Chisciotte (1990)   11'

Suite
Arranger: Norbert Studnitzky
pic.2.1.[ca].Ebcl.3.[acl].bcl.2asax.tsax.[barsax].1-4.2flhn.tflhn.3.3.euph.2-timp.3perc
Score **SHS 1005-10** / Parts **SHS 1005-50**

Antifone (1960)   17'

pic.trec.fl.afl.ssax/cl.asax/cl.tsax /cl.bar-sax/bcl.0-0.2.2.0-timp.4perc-vib.marimb.cel.pno-str (6.0.2.2.1)
Material on hire
Study score **ED 5018**

Apollo trionfante (1979)   15'

2(2pic).3(ob d'am,ca,heck).2(Ebcl,bcl).ssax(bcl).2(cbn)-6.3.3.btuba-timp.4perc-cel.pno-3db
Material on hire
SM

Appassionatamente

(1993-94)   12'

Fantasia sopra "Lo sdegno del mare"
3(2pic,afl).1.ca.0.2bcl(cbcl).ssax.3(cbn-4.3.4.0-timp.5perc-cel.pno.2hp-str
Material on hire
Study score **ED 8428**

Aria de la folía española

(1977)   22'

1(pic).2(ob d'am,ca).1(Ebcl,bcl).2-2.0.0.0-timp.perc-mand.cel.pno-str(9.0.4.4.1)
Material on hire
Study score **ED 6841**

Arien des Orpheus (1979)   25'

gtr.hp.hpd-str(9.0.4.4.3)
alt. version: large string orchestra (1981)
Material on hire
SM

Ballett-Variationen (1949/92)   16'

3(pic).3(ca).2.2.cbn-3.3.3.btuba-timp.2perc-pno.hp-str
Material on hire
SM

Barcarola (1979)   20'

3(3pic,afl).3(ca,heck).3(3Ebcl,bcl,cbcl).ssax.barsax.3(cbn)-6.4.4.1-3perc-cel.pno.2hp-str
Material on hire
Study score **ED 6899**

Los Caprichos (1963)   20'

Fantasy
pic.2.2.ca.bcl.2.cbn-4.3.3.1-timp.3perc-cel.pno.hp-str
Material on hire
Study score **ED 5501**

Deutschlandsberger Mohrentanz No. 1 (1984)   5'

srec.arec.trec.brec-5perc-gtr-solo str(1.1.1.1.0)-str
Material on sale
Score **CON 203** / Parts **CON 203-01 (-06)**

Deutschlandsberger Mohrentanz No. 2 (1985)   4'

srec.arec.trec.brec-5perc-gtr-solo str(1.1.1.1.0)-str
Material on sale
Score **CON 203** / Parts **CON 203-01 (-06)**

3 Dithyrambs (1958)   20'

1.1.1.1-2.1.0.0-timp.2perc-pno.hp-str(min:6.6.4.4.2)
Material on hire
Study score **ED 4597**

Infoline · e-Mail
Schott Musik International
Mainz: Schott.Musik.Com@T-Online.de
London: 101627.166@compuserve.com

Dramatic Scenes from "Orpheus"No. 1 (1979) 50'

2(2pic).3(ob d'am,ca,heck).2(Ebcl,bcl).
ssax(asax,bcl).2(cbn)-6.3.3.btuba-4perc-
cel.pno.hpd.org.hp-str(9.0.4.4.3)
Material on hire
SM

Dramatic Scenes from "Orpheus"No. 2 (1979) 50'

2(2pic,afl,bfl).3(ob d'am,ca,heck).
2(Ebcl,bcl).ssax(asax,tsax,barsax,bcl).
2(cbn) -6.3.3.btuba-4perc-cel.pno.hpd.org.
hp.gtr-str(9.0.4.4.3)
Material on hire
SM

Fandango (1985/92) 12'

On a Bass by Padre Soler
3(pic,afl).2.ca.3(bcl).3(cbn)-4.3.ttbn.btbn.1-
4perc-pno(cel).2hp-str
Material on hire
SM

Fantasia for Strings (1966) 15'

From the film "The young Törless" by
Volker Schlöndorff
str
Material on hire
SM

Finale: Vivace assai 2'

No. 12 from the "Divertimento für Mozart"
2.2.2.2-2.2.0.0-timp-str
Material on hire
SM (Co-prod: UE)
Copyright USA: EAM/Italy: Ed. Suvini
Zerboni

Heliogabalus Imperator

(1972/87) 28'

4(2pic.afl).2.ca.Ebcl.2.bcl.2.cbn-
6.4(Dtpt).3.ttuba.btuba-5perc-cel.hp-str
Material on hire
Study score ED 6331

Hochzeitsmusik - Wedding Music (1957) 10'

from the Ballet "Undine"
2(pic).1.ca.1.bcl.2-4.3.2.1-timp-2hp-vc.db
Material on hire
SM

In memoriam: Die Weiße Rose (1965) 9'

fl.ca.bcl.bn-hn.tpt.tbn-2vn.va.vc.db
Material on hire
SM

Interludes (1964) 15'

from "Der junge Lord'
2(pic).2.2.2-4.2.2.1-timp.4perc-
mand/2mand.cel.pno.hp-str
Material on hire
SM

Katharina Blum (1975) 20'

Concert-Suite
1(pic,afl).1(ca).1(Ebcl,bcl).1(cbn)-1.1.1.0-
2perc-pno(cel)-str
Material on hire
SM

Kleine Elegien (1984-85) 17'

For period Instruments
2srec.2arec.trec.brec-cnt.atbn.ttbn-perc-
lute.zither.org.hp-str(1.0.1.1.0)
Material on hire
SM

Labyrinth (1950) 9'

Fantasy
ob.tsax.bcl-hn.tpt.tbn-3perc-va.vc.db
Material on hire
SM

Mänadentanz (1965) 4'

from the Opera "The Bassarids'
4(2pic,afl).2.2ca.Ebcl.2.bcl(asax).3.cbn-
6.4.3.2-timp.5perc-cel.2pno.2hp-str
Material on hire
SM

Maratona (1956) 30'

Ballet-Suite for 2 Jazz bands and Orchestra
1(pic).1.ca.1.bcl.1-2.2.1.0-timp-hp-str
Jazz bands: fl.asax.tsax-jazztpt.jazztbn-
3perc-pno-db
Material on hire
SM

3 Mozart'sche Orgelsonaten

(1991) 14'

afl.bfl.ob d'am.ca.bcl.bn-hp.gtr-va
d'am.2va.2vc.db
Material on hire
SM

3 Orchesterstücke (1995) 20'

(Karl Amadeus Hartmann, 1945). On the
2nd version of the Piano Sonata "27. April
1945"
3(2pic,afl).2.ca.heck.2.bcl.asax(tsax).2.cbn-
4.3.3.1-timp.3perc-cel.pno.hp-str
Material on hire
SM

5 Piccoli Concerti e Ritornelli (1987) 20'

2(2pic,afl).2(ca,heck).2(Ebcl,Acl,bcl,cbcl).2
(cbn)-2.1.1.0-timp.3perc-cel.pno.hp-
str(6.4.3.3.1)
Material on hire
SM

4 Poemi (1955) 9'

pic.2.2.ca.2.bcl.2.cbn-4.2.2.1-str
Material on hire
Study score ED 4558

Ragtimes and Habaneras

(1975) 14'

Sinfonia for brass
Arranger: Henning Brauel
Ebcnt.8cnt.flhn.3ahn.2aflhn.2ttbn.btbn.2eu
ph.2tuba.2cbtuba
Score SHS 3002 / Parts SHS 3002-70

Ragtimes and Habaneras

(1975/82) 14'

For Symphonic Wind Band
Arranger: Marcel Wengler
pic.1.[2ob].[ca].Ebcl.3.[acl].[bcl].2asax.2t
sax.[barsax].[bn]-
4.2flhn.2tflhn.3.ttbn.bartbn.2euph.2tuba.2bt
uba-timp.perc
Score SHS 1004 / Parts SHS 1004-50

Seconda Sonata per archi

(1995) 9'

str
Material on hire
SM

La selva incantata (1991) 11'

Aria and Rondo
2(pic).2(ca).2(bcl).2(cbn)-3.2.2.0-
timp.2perc-pno-str(8.7.6.5.4)
Material on hire
SM

Sonata for Strings (1957-58) 15'

str(min:8.6.4.4.2)
Material on hire
Study score ED 4591

Spielmusiken (1979-80) 9'

From the Fairytale for Music "Pollicino"
3soprec(2srec).2arec.trec.brec.tcrumhorn/h
n.bcrumhorn/bn/tbn-timp.perc-
sglsp.aglsp.ametph.sxyl.axyl.bxyl.pno.harm
/eorg.2gtr-str
Score CON 194 / Parts CON 194-50

Symphonic Interludes

(1951) 15'

from the lyric drama "Boulevard Solitude'
2(pic).1.ca.1.bcl.2-4.4.3.1-timp.8perc-
pno.mand.hp-str
Material on hire
SM

3 Symphonic Studies

(1956/64) 8'

pic.3.3.ca.Ebcl.2.bcl.ssax.3.cbn-
4.Dtpt.3.2.ttbn.1-timp.4perc-cel.hp-str
Material on hire
SM

Symphony No.1 (1947/63/91) 17'

1(pic).afl(pic).1.ca.0.bcl.0-2.2.0.0-timp-
cel.pno.hp-str
Material on hire
Study score ED 8118

Symphony No.2 (1949) 23'

3(pic).2.ca.2.bcl.2.cbn-4.4.3.1-timp.3perc-
pno.hp-str
Material on hire
Study score ED 4402

Symphony No.3 (1949-50) 25'

pic.2.2.ca.2.bcl.tsax.2.cbn-4.4.3.1-
timp.4perc-cel.pno.hp-str
Material on hire
Study score ED 4567

Symphony No.4 (1955) 20'

In one Movement
pic.2.2.ca.2.bcl.2.cbn-4.3.2.1-timp.3perc-
cel.pno.hp-str
Material on hire
Study score ED 5034

Symphony No.5 (1962) 18'

3(pic).afl.2.2ca.0.0-4.4.4.0-2timp-
2pno.2hp-str
Material on hire
Score ED 54 / Study score ED 5029

Symphony No.6 (1969/94) 40'

for 2 orchestras
2(pic).afl.2.ca.2(Ebcl).bcl.tsax.2(cbn)-
4.3.3.0-timp.4perc-
pno.eorg.hp.gtr(banjo/charango amp)-
str(24 .0.12.12.8)
Material on hire
Study score **ED 6313**

Symphony No.7 (1983-84) 46'

4(2pic,afl).2.ca.heck.4(bcl).cbcl.4(cbn)-
6.4.3ttbn.btbn.cbtbn.btuba-timp.3perc-
cel.pno.hp-str
Material on hire
Study score **ED 7349**

Symphony No.8 (1992-93) 25'

2(pic,afl).2(ca).2(bcl).2(cbn)-
4.2.ttbn.btbn.1-timp.3perc-cel.pno.hp-str
Material on hire
Study score **ED 8276**

Tancredi (1952) 17'

Ballet Suite
1(pic).1.ca.1.bcl.1.cbn-4.2.2.1-timp.3perc-
cel.pno.hp.[trautonium]-str
Material on hire
SM

Tanz- und Salonmusik

(1952/89) 18'

From the mime drama "The Idiot"
1(pic).0.1.1-0.1.1.0-3perc-pno-
str(1.0.1.1.1)
Material on hire
SM

Telemanniana (1967) 12'

In one Movement
3(pic).2.ca.2.bcl.2.cbn-4.3.2.1-timp-cel.hp-
str
Material on hire
Study score **ED 7104**

Trois Pas des Tritons (1958) 13'

from the Ballet "Undine"
2(pic).1.ca.1.bcl.1.cbn-4.3.2.0-timp.3perc-
cel.pno.2hp-str
Material on hire
SM

Undine - First Suite (1958) 26'

2.1.ca.1.bcl.1.cbn-4.3.2.1-timp.3perc-
pno(cel).2hp.gtr-str
Material on hire
SM

Undine - Second Suite

(1958) 21'

In one Movement
2.1.ca.1.bcl.1.cbn-4.3.2.1-timp.3perc-
cel.pno.2hp-str
Material on hire
SM

Voie lactée ô sœur lumineuse

(1995-96) 8'

Toccata
1(pic).0.1.1-1.1.1.0-timp.3perc-
vib.marimb.cel.pno-str(2.0.1.1.1)
Material on hire
SM

Das Vokaltuch der Kammersängerin Rosa Silber (1950/90) 18'

Exercise with Stravinsky. Ballet music
about a picture by Paul Klee
pic1.1.ca.1.bcl.2-2.2.2.1-timp.perc-str
Material on hire
SM

Concertos

An eine Äolsharfe (1985-86) 20'

Soloist: guitar
afl.bfl.ob d'am.ca.bcl.bn-perc-hp-va
d'am.2va.va da gamba.2vc.db
Material on hire
Parts **ED 7460 (solo)**

Chamber Concerto (1946) 12'

Soloists: piano, flute
str
Material on hire
Parts **ED 7161 (soli)**

Concertino (1947) 12'

Soloist: piano
2(pic).2.2.2-2.2.2.1-3timp.2perc
Material on hire
Piano reduction **ED 6988**

Concerto per contrabbasso

(1966) 20'

Soloist: doublebass
2(pic).2(ca).1.bcl.2(cbn)-2.2.1.0-timp-hp-
str(8.0.4.4.2)
Material on hire
Piano reduction **ED 6239**

Doppio concerto (1966) 30'

Soloists: oboe, harp
str(8.0.4.4.2)
Material on hire
Score **ED 7286** / Parts **ED 50 (soli)**

Introduktion, Thema und Variationen (1992) 10'

Soloist: cello
hp-str
Material on hire
Score **ED 8298**

Jeux des Tritons (1956-57/67) 15'

Divertissement from the Ballet "Undine"
Soloist: piano
2(pic).1.ca.1.bcl.1.cbn-4.3.2.1-timp.3perc-
str
Material on hire
SM

Liebeslieder (1984-85) 25'

Soloist: cello
2(pic).afl.2.ca.2.bcl.3(cbn)-
4.3.2ttbn.btbn.btuba-timp.3perc-cel.pno.hp-
str
Material on hire
Parts **ED 7418 (solo)**

Le Miracle de la Rose

(1981) 40'

Imaginary Theatre II
Soloist: clarinet
1(pic).1(ob d'am,ca).0.1([heck])-1.1.1.0-
3perc-pno(cel)-str
Material on hire
Score **ED 7234** / Parts **ED 7124 (solo)**

Music for Viola and 22 Players (1969-70) 26'

"Compases para preguntas ensimismadas"
Soloist: viola
1(pic,afl).arec(trec).1(ca).1(bcl).1-1.0.0.0-
2perc-hpd.pno(cel).hp-str(6.0.0.4.1)
Material on hire
Study score **ED 7311** / Parts **ED 6321 (solo)**

Ode an den Westwind

(1953) 25'

Music for cello and orchestra based on the
poem by Percy Bysshe Shelley
Soloist: cello
2(pic)1.ca.1.bcl.1.cbn-2.2.1.1-3perc-
cel.pno.hp-str(20.0.12.0.8)
Material on hire
Study score **ED 4423** / Piano reduction **ED 4545**

Piano Concerto No.1 (1950) 20'

Soloist: piano
pic.2.2.2.2-4.4.3.2-timp.2perc-str
Material on hire
Piano reduction **ED 4931**

Piano Concerto No.2 (1967) 45'

In one Movement
Soloist: piano
3(2pic).2.ca.2(Ebcl).bcl.2.cbn-4.2.2.1-
timp.7perc-hp-str
Material on hire
Study score **ED 6301** / Piano reduction **ED 5957**

Requiem (1990-92) 90'

9 Sacred Concerti for Chamber Ensemble
Soloists: trumpet, piano
2(2pic,afl).1.ca.1(Ebcl).bcl(cbcl).ssax(asax.
barsax)1(cbn)-2.2.2btpttbn.btbn(cbtbn).0-
timp.3perc-cel.hp-str(4.0.3.3.1)
Material on hire
Study score **ED 8198 "3 Sacred Concertos"
can be performed separately**

3 Sacred Concertos

(1991-92) 28'

from the "Requiem"
Soloist: trumpet
2(2pic,afl).1.ca.1(Ebcl).bcl(cbcl).asax(barsax).1(cbn)-2.2.ttbn.btbn(cbtbn).0-
timp.3perc-cel.pno.hp-str(4.0.3.3.1)
Material on hire
SM

I Sentimenti di Carl Philipp Emanuel Bach (1982)   17'

Transcription of the Clavier-Fantasie
Soloists: flute, harp
str(4.0.2.2.1)
alt. version: solo str(2.0.1.1.0)-str
Material on hire
SM

Tristan (1973)   43'

Soloist: piano
4(2pic,afl).2.ca.Ebcl.2.bcl.ssax.2.cbn-6.4(Dtpt).3.ttuba.btuba-5perc-cel.mand.hp-str-tape
Material on hire
Study score **ED 6629**

Violin Concerto No.1 (1947)   25'

Soloist: violin
2(pic).2.2.2.cbn-3.3.3.1-timp.2perc-cel.pno.hp-str
Material on hire
Piano reduction **ED 4649**

Violin Concerto No.2 (1971)   29'

Text: Hans Magnus Enzensberger
Soloists: violin, bass-baritone
3(3pic).1.ca.2(amp).bcl.2-2.2.1/wagnertuba.0-4perc-2pno(prep).mand.hp.gtr-str(0.0.4.3.2)
Material on hire
Study score **ED 6332** / Piano reduction **ED 6464**

Il Vitalino raddoppiato

(1977)   35'

Chaconne
Soloist: violin
1(pic).1.0.bcl.1-1.0.0.0-hp-str(1.1.1.1.1)
Material on hire
Parts **ED 6924 (solo)**

Chamber & Instrumental Works

6 Absences (1961)   10'

hpd
ED 5380

Adagio, Adagio (1993)   4'

Serenade
vn.vc-pno
ED 8131

Amicizia! (1976)   15'

Quintet
cl-tbn-vc-perc-pno
Score **ED 6712** / Parts **ED 6712-10**

An Brenton (1993)   3'

viola solo
SM

L' Autunno (1977)   20'

1(pic,afl).1(ob d'am).1(Ebcl,bcl).1(cbn)-1([wagnertuba])
Study score **ED 6785** / Parts **ED 6786**

Canzona (1982)   7'

ob-3va.vc-pno.hp
Study score **ED 7447** / Parts **ED 7448**

Capriccio (1976/81)   6'

cello solo
ED 7279

Carillon, Récitatif, Masque

(1974)   13'

mand-gtr-hp
Material on sale
Study score **ED 6470**

Chamber Sonata (1948/63)   15'

vn.vc-pno
Score **ED 5382** / Parts **Ed 5382**

Cherubino (1980-81)   8'

3 Miniatures
pno
ED 7032

Divertimenti (1964)   12'

Interludes from "Der junge Lord"
2pno
ED 5444

Étude Philharmonique

(1979)   4'

violin solo
ED 6948

Euridice (1978/81/92)   6'

Fragments
hpd
ED 6906

Flute Sonata (1947)   10'

fl-pno
FTR 90

Fragmente aus einer Show

(1971)   10'

Movements for brass from "Der langwierige Weg in die Wohnung der Natascha Ungeheuer"
hn.2tpt.tbn.ttuba
Score **ED 6482** / Parts **ED 6482-01**

Für Manfred (1989)   2'

violin solo
SM

Der junge Törless (1966)   15'

Fantasy
3vn.2va.vc
Study score **ED 5514** / Parts **ED 5848**

Des Kaisers Nachtigall

(1959)   17'

fl.bcl-mar.cel.pno-4perc-va.vc
Material on hire
Study score **ED 5015**

Des Kaisers Nachtigall

(1959/70)   17'

Arranger: Henning Brauel
fl(pic)-3perc-cel.pno
Material on hire

Lucy Escott Variations

(1963)   10'

pno
ED 5453

Lucy Escott Variations

(1963)   10'

hpd
ED 5428

La Mano Sinistra (1988)   3'

Piece for Leon
pno(left hnd)
ED 7695

3 Märchenbilder (1980)   15'

From the Fairytale for Music "Pollicino"
Arranger: Reinbert Evers
guitar solo
GA 480

Memorias de El Cimarrón

(1970)   13'

Arranger: Leo Brouwer
guitar solo
ED 6485

Memorias de El Cimarrón

(1996)   13'

Arranger: Jürgen Ruck
2gtr
GA 239

Minette (1993)   12'

Arranger: Andreas Pfeifer
discant-zither
ED 8266

Minette (1996)   12'

Arranger: Jürgen Ruck
2gtr
SM

5 Nachtstücke (1990)   10'

vn-pno
ED 7825

Une Petite Phrase (1984)   2'

pno
ED 7293

Piano Quintet (1990-91)   20'

2vn.va.vc-pno
Score **ED 7831** / Parts **ED 7831**

Piano Sonata (1959)   14'

ED 5084

Piano Variations, Op. 13

(1949)   7'

ED 4046

Piece for Peter (1988)   1'

pno
SM

6 Pieces for Young Pianists

(1980)   20'

From the fairytale for music "Pollicino"
pno
ED 6959

Prison Song   (1971)   6'

Text: Ho Chi Minh
perc-tape
Material on hire or sale
ED 6947

Pulcinella Disperato

(1949/92)   13'

Fantasy
Arranger: Moritz Eggert
pno
ED 8265

Quattro Fantasie   (1958/63)   25'

3 Movements from "Kammermusik 1958"
and "Adagio"
cl.bn-hn-2vn.va.vc.db
Study score **ED 6081** / Parts **ED 6109**

Quintet   (1952)   14'

fl.ob.cl.bn-hn
Study score **ED 4414** / Parts **ED 4480**

Royal Winter Music

(1975-76)   25'

Sonata No.1 on Shakespearean Characters
guitar solo
GA 467

Royal Winter Music   (1979)   20'

Sonata No.2 on Shakespearean Characters
guitar solo
GA 473

S.Biagio 9 Agosto ore 12.07

(1977)   5'

doublebass solo
ED 6914

3 Sacred Concertos

(1991-92)   28'

from the "Requiem'
Arranger: Moritz Eggert
tpt-pno
SM

5 Scenes from the Snow Country   (1978)   10'

marimba solo
BAT 39

Selbst-und Zwiegespräche

(1984-85)   2'

Trio
va-gtr-org/other keyboard-instr
ED 7439

Serenade   (1986)   3'

violin solo
VLB 74

Serenade   (1949)   10'

cello solo
ED 4330

Serenade   (1949)   10'

Arrangement from the original cello version
Arranger: Lucas Drew
doublebass solo
ED 6978

Sonata   (1992)   14'

"Tirsi, Mopso, Aristeo"
violin solo
ED 8115

Sonata for 6 Players   (1984)   12'

*fl(afl,perc).cl(bcl,[cbcl],perc)-
vn(va,perc).vc(perc)-perc-pno(cel)*
Score **ED 7401** / Parts **ED 7409**

Sonata per otto ottoni   (1983)   8'

3tpt.btpt.flhn.2ttbn.btbn
Study score **ED 7209** / Parts **ED 7210**

String Quartet No.1   (1947)   20'

Study score **ED 5503** / Parts **ED 5497**

String Quartet No.2   (1952)   15'

Study score **ED 4410** / Parts **ED 4476**

String Quartet No.3

(1975-76)   19'

Study score **ED 6673** / Parts **ED 6674**

String Quartet No.4   (1976)   37'

Study score **ED 6678** / Parts **ED 6679**

String Quartet No.5   (1976)   25'

Study score **ED 6715** / Parts **ED 6716**

3 Tentos   (1958)   5'

from "Kammermusik 1958"
Arranger: Julian Bream
guitar solo
ED 4886

Toccata mistica   (1994)   4'

pno
ED 8380

Toccata senza Fuga   (1979)   6'

From "Orpheus"
Arranger: Anton Zapf
organ solo
ED 6889

Trombone Sonatina   (1974)   4'

Arranger: Martin Harvey
trombone solo
ED 8155

Trumpet Sonatina   (1974)   4'

trumpet solo
TR 19

Viola Sonata   (1979)   20'

va-pno
ED 6859

Violin Sonata   (1946)   15'

vn-pno
ED 3859

Violin Sonatina   (1979)   10'

From the Fairytale for music "Pollicino"
vn-pno
ED 6958

Solo Voice(s)/Voice(s) and Piano/Guitar

3 Auden Songs   (1983)   10'

Text: W.H Auden
tenor-pno
ED 7181

3 Fragmente nach Hölderlin

(1958)   10'

from "Kammermusik1958"
tenor-gtr
ED 4886

Whispers from Heavenly Death   (1948)   7'

Cantata
Text: Walt Whitman
soprano/tenor-pno
ED 7881

Solo Voice(s) and Instrument(s)/ Orchestra

Apollo et Hyazinthus

(1948-49)   17'

Text: Georg Trakl
Soloist: alto
1.0.1.1-1.0.0.0-hpd-str(1.1.1.1.0)
Material on hire
Study score **ED 4570**

3 Arias from "Elegy for Young Lovers"   (1960/93)   18'

Soloist: baritone
*1(pic).0.ca.0.bcl.asax.1-1.1.1.0-timp.3perc-
vib.marimb.cel.pno.mand.hp.gtr-
str(2.0.1.1.1)*
Material on hire
SM

Ariosi   (1963)   27'

Text: Torquato Tasso
Soloists: soprano, violin
*3(pic).2.ca.2.bcl.2.cbn-4.3.2.1-timp.perc-
cel.hp-str*
Material on hire
Study score **ED 5037** / Vocal score **ED 5454**

Ariosi (1963) 27'

Text: Torquato Tasso
Soloist: soprano
vn-pno (4hnd)
ED 5454

Being Beauteous (1963) 15'

Cantata
Text: Arthur Rimbaud
Soloist: soprano
hp-4vc
Material on hire
Study score **ED 5035** / Piano reduction
ED 5269

El Cimarrón (1969-70) 76'

Recital for 4 musicians
Text: Miguel Barnet/Hans Magnus
Enzensberger
Soloist: baritone
pic(fl,afl,bfl,ryuteki/pic)-gtr-perc
Material on sale
Score **ED 6454** / Study score **ED 6327** /
Parts **ED 6741**

2 Concert Arias from the opera "König Hirsch" (1991)

12'

Text: Heinz von Cramer
Soloist: tenor
1.afl(pic).0.1.bcl.1-cel.pno-str(6.0.3.3.1)
Material on hire
SM

Concert-Suite (1976/78) 22'

From the Comic Opera "Don Chisciotte"
Text: Giuseppe Di Leva, Hans Werner
Henze, Henning Brauel
Soloists: 2 sopranos, tenor, baritone
wind band: 2pic.0.2.Ebcl.ssax.asax.tsax.0-
4.2.tflhn.bflhn.2.2-timp.perc
chamber orchestra: 1(pic,afl).1.1(bcl).
1(cbn)-timp.2perc-pno.org.gtr-va.vc.db
Material on hire
SM

Heilige Nacht (1993) 3'

A Chrismas Song
Soloist: medium voice
rec/fl/ob/vn
ED 8441

Kammermusik 1958

(1958/63) 40'

On the hymn "In lieblicher Bläue"
Text: Friedrich Hölderlin
Soloists: tenor, guitar/harp
cl.bn-hn-str(1.1.1.1.1)
Material on hire
Study score **ED 4599** / Piano reduction
ED 4897

Ein Landarzt (1951/64) 33'

Monodrama
Text: Franz Kafka
Soloist: baritone
1(pic).1(ca).1(bcl).1-1.1.1.0-5perc-
pno(4hnd)/2pno.[org]-str(1.1.1.1.1)
Material on hire
Vocal score **ED 5674**

3 Lieder über den Schnee

(1989) 5'

Text: Hans-Ulrich Treichel
Soloists: soprano, baritone
cl(bcl).bn-hn-solo str(1.1.1.1.1)
Score **ED 7729** / Parts **ED 7729**

Nachtstücke und Arien

(1957) 23'

Text: Ingeborg Bachmann
Soloist: soprano
3(2pic).2.ca.2.bcl.asax.2.cbn-4.3.2.1-
timp.3perc-pno.2hp-str
Material on hire
Study score **ED 4586**

5 Neapolitan Songs (1956) 17'

Drum beat songs to anonymous poems
from the 17th century
Soloist: baritone
2.1.ca.1.bcl.1.cbn-2.1.1.0-hp-str(0.0.4.4.2)
Material on hire
Study score **ED 4579** / Piano reduction
ED 4766

Orpheus - Concert Version

(1978) 120'

Text: Edward Bond
Soloist: speaker
2(2pic,afl,bfl).3(ob d'am,ca,heck).
2(Ebcl,bcl,heck).ssax(asax,tsax,barsax,bcl).
2(cbn) -6.3.3.btuba-4perc-cel.pno.hpd.org.
hp.gtr-str(9.0.4.4.3)
additional: ob.ca.heck.sax-2perc-hp.gtr
Material on hire
SM

Paraphrasen über Dostojewski (1952/90) 32'

Voiced for Prince Myshkin
Text: Ingeborg Bachmann
Soloist: speaker
1(pic).0.1.1-0.1.1.0-perc-pno-[solo]
str(1.0.1.1.1)
Material on hire
SM

El Rey de Harlem (1979) 30'

Imaginary Theatre II
Text: Frederico García Lorca
Soloist: mezzo-soprano
cl(Ebcl,bcl,ssax,barsax,maracas)-
tpt.ttbn(perc)-perc-pno(cel,harm).
egtr(banjo,bgtr)-va(perc).vc(perc)
Material on hire
SM

Il Ritorno d'Ulisse in Patria - Scenes and Arias (1980-82) 49'

(Claudio Monteverdi)
Text: Giocomo Badoaro
Soloists: soprano, alto,tenor,baritone
2(2pic).2afl(2bfl).1.obd'am.2ca(heck).2.2bc
l(cbcl).4(cbn)-4.2Dtpt.2Ctpt.2ttbn.2btbn.0-
timp.4perc-tbanjo.mand.acc/org/harm.cel.
pno.hp.gtr.egtr.bgtr-va d'am.7va.8vc.6db
Material on hire
SM

Songs and Dances (1992-93) 25'

from the Operetta "La Cubana"
Text: Hans Magnus Enzensberger
Soloist: mezzo-soprano
cl.asax(ssax,tsax)-tpt.tbn-pno([prep
pno]).gtr(tbanjo,mand)-db
Material on hire
SM

Das Urteil der Kalliope

(1964/91) 16'

A Pastoral
Arranger: Henning Brauel
Text: W.H. Auden/Chester Kallman
Soloists: soprano, tenor, baritone
mand-hpd
Material on hire
Libretto **BN 3368-50**

Versuch über Schweine

(1968) 20'

Text: Gastón Salvatore
Soloist: baritone
2(pic).1.ca.1.bcl.1.cbn-1.2(Dtpt).ttbn.1-
timp.4perc-eorg.egtr-str(12.0.4.4.2)
Material on hire
Study score **ED 6310**

Voices (1973) 90'

A Collection of Songs
Text: various
Soloists: mezzo-soprano, tenor
pic.fl.afl.bengalfl.inkafl.lotosfl/cl.2 bambo-
ofl.ob.ca.2rec.Ebcl.cl.bcl.bsthn.bn.[cbn]-
1.1.1.1-timp.perc-mand.gtr.egtr.tbanjo.acc.
harm.cel.pno.hammondorg.ocar-vn(va).
va(vn,va d'am).vc.db
Material on hire
Study score **ED 6344**

Wesendonk - Lieder (1976) 15'

(Richard Wagner)
Arranger: Hans Werner Henze
Text: Mathilde Wesendonk
Soloist: alto
1.afl.1.ca.1.bcl.1.cbn-2.0.0.0-hp-
str(6.4.4.4.2)
Material on hire
Study score **ED 7230**

Whispers from Heavenly Death (1948) 7'

Text: Walt Whitman
Soloist: soprano/tenor
tpt-xyl.vib.glsp.cel.hp-vc-perc
Material on hire
SM

Choral Works

Cantata della Fiaba Estrema

(1963) 20'

Text: Elsa Morante
Soloist: soprano
Chorus: chamber
1.ca.1.1-1.1.1.0-hp.gtr-str(1.0.1.1.1)
Material on hire
Study score **ED 5505** / Piano reduction
ED 5465

Chor gefangener Trojer

(1948/64)   15'

Symphonic Movement
Text: Goethe's "Faust", Part II, 3rd Act
Chorus: mixed
2pic.1.2(ca).Ebcl.2.bcl.2.cbn-4.4.3.1-
timp.3perc-pno.hp-str
Material on hire
SM

Das Floß der Medusa

(1968/90)   70'

Oratorio
Text: Ernst Schnabel
Soloists: soprano, baritone, speaker
Chorus: mixed, 9 boy's voices(S,A)
4(2pic,2afl).1.ob d'am.ca.heck.Ebcl.1.
acl/bsthn.bcl.ssax.tsax.2.cbn-4.Dtpt.2btpt.
atbn.ttbn.btbn.aoficl/bomb/tuba in F.wag-
nertuba.btuba.cbtuba-timp.5perc-pno.
eorg.2hp.egtr.begtr-str(12.0.8.6.4)
Material on hire
Study score **ED 6326** / Vocal score
ED 6719

Jephte   (1976)   30'

Oratorio by Giacomo Carissimi
Arranger: Hans Werner Henze
Text: Latin
Soloists: 3 sopranos, alto, tenor, 2 basses
Chorus: mixed (6 prt)
4fl(2pic,afl,bfl)-perc-mand.tbanjo.hp.gtr
Material on hire
SM

Lieder von einer Insel

(1964)   23'

Choral Fantasy
Text: Ingeborg Bachmann
Chorus: mixed
tbn-2vc.db-orgport/small org-timp.2perc
Material on hire
SM

5 Madrigals   (1947)   17'

On poems from the "Great Testament"
Text: François Villon
Chorus: mixed
1(pic).0.1.1-1.1.1.0-str
Material on hire
SM

Musen Siziliens   (1966)   30'

Concerto on fragments of the "Eclogues"
Text: Vergil
Chorus: mixed
2(pic).2.2.2-4.2.2.0-timp-2pno
Material on hire
Study score **ED 5515**

Novae de Infinito Laudes

(1962)   50'

Cantata
Text: Giordano Bruno
Soloists: S.A.T.B
Chorus: mixed
2(2pic).0.2ca.0.2-0.2Dtpt.2.2btpt.4.2-
4timp-2pno.2lute/hpd.2hp-str(0.0.0.4.4)
Material on hire
Study score **ED 5028** / Vocal score
ED 5267

Orpheus behind the Wire

(1981-83)   17'

Text: Edward Bond
Chorus: mixed a cappella (8-12 prt)
SKR 20007

Scenes and Arias   (1956)   14'

from the Opera "König Hirsch"
Soloists: soprano, tenor
Chorus: [children's]
3(pic).2.ca.2.bcl.2.cbn-4.3([pictpt]).2.1-
timp.4perc-cel.pno.mand.hp-str
Material on hire
SM

Vocal Symphony   (1955)   20'

from the Opera "König Hirsch". Sinfonia
in 5 Movements
Text: Heinz von Cramer
Soloists: 5 sopranos, mezzo-soprano, alto,
2 tenors, bass
Chorus: mixed
3(pic).2.ca.2.bcl.2.cbn-4.3.2.1-timp-
glsp.vib.trgl.mand.cel.pno.hp-str
Material on hire
SM

Wiegenlied der Mutter Gottes   (1948)   8'

Text: Lope de Vega
Chorus: children
1.0.1.0-1.1.1.0-hp-va.vc.db
Material on hire
SM

Herrmann, Hugo
1896-1967

Choral Works

Abendfeier   (1952)   3'

Chorus: male a cappella
SM

Anruf   (1957)   2'

Text: K.H.v. Neubronner
Chorus: male a cappella
CHBL 134

Cantata Concertante   (1964)   28'

A Heavenly Concerto
Text: various
Soloists: soprano, baritone
Chorus: mixed
2(pic).2(ca).2.2-4.2.3.1-timp.perc-
cel/pno.hp-str
Material on hire
Study score **ED 5527**

Cantata Primavera   (1954)   32'

Text: Ernst Buschor
Chorus: mixed, children's
2.2.2.2-2.2.2.1-timp.perc-pno.hp-str
Material on hire
Study score **ED 4628**

2 Folk Songs   3'

Chorus: male a cappella
CHBL 189

Nachruf   (1956)   2'

Chorus: mixed a cappella
SM

Rosmarienbaum   (1960)   3'

Text: August Zarnach
Chorus: female a cappella
CHBL 583

Triumph der Liebe   (1966)   32'

Soloist: speaker
Chorus: mixed
2hn.2tpt.2tbn.btuba-timp
Material on hire
SM

Hessenberg, Kurt
1908-1994

Orchestral Works

Konzertante Musik, Op. 39

(1947)   17'

doubled str
Material on hire
Study score **ED 4272**

Musikantenhochzeit   (1939)   8'

Scherzo from Op. 22
pic.2.2.2.2.cbn-4.2.3.1-timp.perc-vn
Material on hire
SM

Der Sturm, Op. 20   (1938-39)   21'

Suite
2.2.2.2-2.2.2.0-timp.perc-cel-str
Material on hire
Eu

Symphony No.2 in A Major, Op. 29   (1943)   50'

pic.2.2(ca).2.bcl.2-4.3.3.1-timp.2perc-str
Material on hire
Study score **ED 3535**

Concertos

Concerto for 2 Pianos, Op. 50   (1950)   21'

Soloists: 2 pianos
0.2.0.2-2.0.0.0-timp-str
Material on hire
SM

Infoline · e-Mail
Schott Musik International
Mainz: Schott.Musik.com@T-Online.de
London: 101627.166@compuserve.com

Hessenberg, Kurt

b. Frankfurt/Main 17.8.1908,
d. Frankfurt/Main 17.6.1994

After composition studies with Günther Raphael in Leipzig, Kurt Hessenberg was first appointed to the Hoch Conservatory, later to the Conservatory of his home town Frankfurt/Main as a teacher of harmony. From 1953 to 1981, he taught composition there. In 1989 he was decorated with the Order of Merit first-class of the Federal Republic. Apart from concertante and chamber music works, his compositions comprise mainly sacred choral works, oratorios and compositions for organ.

Chamber & Instrumental Works

Cello Sonata in C Major, Op. 23 (1942) 12'

vc-pno
ED 3785

Choralpartiten No.1, Op. 43
(1952) 6'

Von Gott will ich nicht lassen
organ solo
ED 4293

Choralpartiten No.2, Op. 43
(1952) 7'

O Welt, ich muß dich lassen
organ solo
ED 4294

Fantasia, Op. 115 (1990) 13'

Ich ruf zu dir, Herr Jesu Christ
organ solo
ED 7692

Flute Sonata in B, Op. 38
(1947) 15'

fl-pno
FTR 109

Kleine Hausmusik, Op. 24
(1942) 16'

pno
ED 2834

7 Little Piano Pieces, Op. 12
(1941) 9'

pno
ED 2882

10 Little Preludes, Op. 35
(1949) 12'

pno
ED 1403

Serenade, Op. 89 (1972) 12'

ob.cl.bn-hn
Score and parts ED 6157

Sinfonietta, Op. 122 15'

2hn.4tpt.2tbn.tuba
Score SHS 3005 / Parts SHS 3005-70

Sonata in C Minor, Op. 34/1
(1944) 10'

pno (4hnd)
ED 1404

String Quartet No.2, Op. 16
(1937) 20'

Score ED 3617 / Parts ED 2856

String Quartet No.3, Op. 33
(1944) 30'

Score ED 3622 / Parts ED 2561

String Quartet No.4, Op. 60
(1954) 30'

Score ED 4592 / Parts ED 4780

String Quartet No.7, Op. 112
(1981) 14'

Partita
Score ED 7025 / Parts ED 7025

String Trio, Op. 48 (1949) 21'

vn.va.vc
Study score ED 4401 / Parts ED 4383

Suite, Op. 77 (1963) 12'

fl-pno
ED 5463

Trio Sonata in B, Op. 56
(1955) 12'

organ solo
ED 4535

Viola Sonata, Op. 94 (1974) 18'

va-pno
VAB 45

Violin Sonata in F Major, Op. 25 (1943) 18'

vn-pno
ED 3787

Solo Voice(s)/Voice(s) and Piano/Guitar

Wenn ich, O Kindlein, vor Dir stehe, Op. 30 (1943/44) 16'

mezzo-soprano-pno
ED 1331

Solo Voice(s) and Instrument(s)/ Orchestra

Fiedellieder, Op. 22
(1939-40) 70'

Text: Theodor Storm
Soloist: tenor
Chorus: mixed
pic.2.2(ca).2.2.cbn-4.2.3.1-timp.2perc-hp-str
Material on hire
SM

3 Lieder, Op. 32a (1948) 9'

Text: Theodor Storm
Soloist: medium voice
1.1.1.1-1.0.0.0-timp-str
Material on hire
SM

10 Lieder, Op. 32 (1944) 21'

Text: Theodor Storm
Soloist: mezzo-soprano/baritone
vn.va-pno
Score ED 4299 / Parts ED 4299

Der Tag, der ist so freudenreich

Soloist: voice
pno-rec
ED 4241

Choral Works

2 Abendlieder (1988) 6'
Text: M. Claudius
Chorus: mixed a cappella
C 46423/46424

2 Choralmotetten, Op. 93
(1976) 13'
Text: J. Neander/G. Tersteegen
Chorus: mixed a cappella
C 44103/44104

4 Choruses, Op. 31 (1944) 18'
Text: various
Chorus: mixed a cappella
C 37933 (-35)/-37

Christmas Cantata, Op. 27
(1942-43) 35'
Text: Matthias Claudius
Soloists: soprano, alto
Chorus: mixed
1.1.ca.1.1-2.1.0.0-timp-org-str
Material on hire
Vocal score **ED 3897-01** / Piano reduction
ED 3897

2 Christmas Songs (1957) 6'
Text: Westfalen
Chorus: male, children's a cappella
C 40652/40653

Christus, der uns selig macht, Op. 118 (1983) 10'
Passionsmotette
Text: M. Weiße
Chorus: mixed a cappella
SKR 20017

Es steht ein Lind in jenem Tal (1965) 2'
from "5 Alte Volkslieder"
Chorus: mixed a cappella
C 41287

Es taget vor dem Walde
(1965) 2'
from "5 Alte Volkslieder"
Chorus: mixed a cappella
C 41286

2 Folksongs (1961) 4'
Chorus: male a cappella
C 40457/40458

4 Geistliche Lieder durch die Tageszeiten, Op. 41 (1947) 16'
Text: various
Chorus: mixed a cappella
C 37422

Lieblich hat sich gesellet
(1965) 4'
from "5 Alte Volkslieder"
Chorus: mixed a cappella
C 41287

Lieder und Epigramme, Op. 47 (1950) 16'
Text: Johann Wolfgang von Goethe
Chorus: male a cappella
C 37581/37582

Maienzeit bannet Lied
(1965) 2'
from "5 Alte Volkslieder"
Chorus: mixed a cappella (5 prt)
C 41285

Mit Lust tret' ich in diesen Tanz (1965) 2'
from "5 Alte Volkslieder"
Chorus: mixed a cappella
C 41288

Morgenlied, Op. 31 (1952) 3'
Text: H. Hoffmann von Fallersleben
Chorus: male a cappella
C 38164

2 Motets, Op. 37 (1951) 18'
Text: Franz von Assisi, Liturgical
Chorus: mixed a cappella
C 37176/37421

4 Poems, Op. 81 (1967) 12'
Text: various
Chorus: mixed a cappella
C 42025 (-28)

3 Poems , Op. 59 (1953) 12'
Text: Gottfried Keller
Chorus: male a cappella
C 38765/38766/39020

Psalm 126, Op. 87 (1971) 8'
Chorus: mixed a cappella
C 43141

Psalm 130, Op. 134 (1989) 6'
Aus der Tiefe rufe ich, Herr, zu Dir
Chorus: mixed
SKR 20024

Psalmen-Triptychon, Op. 36
(1945-46) 105'
Soloists: soprano, baritone
Chorus: mixed double
2.2.2.bcl.2.cbn-4.2.3.0-timp.perc-[org]-str
Material on hire
SM

Das sagt, der Amen heißt, Op. 46 (1952) 8'
Text: Bible
Chorus: mixed double a cappella
Score **ED 4242** / Choral score **ED 4242-01/-02**

Struwwelpeter-Kantate, Op. 49 (1949) 33'
Text: Heinrich Hoffmann
Chorus: chilren's/female
2fl-str-pno
ED 6478/6082

Tröstet mein Volk, Op. 114
(1982) 8'
Text: Erasmus Alberus
Chorus: mixed a cappella
SKR 20005

Vom Wesen und Vergehen, Op. 45 (1948) 30'
Text: Matthias Claudius
Soloists: soprano, baritone
Chorus: mixed
2.2(ca).2.2-0.0.0.0-str
Material on hire
Vocal score **ED 4341-01** / Piano reduction
ED 4341

Die Weihnachtsgeschichte, Op. 54 (1950-51) 13'
Text: Rudolf Alexander Schröder
Soloists: soprano, tenor, baritone
Chorus: mixed
arec-[hpd]-str
Material on sale
Score **ED 77** / Parts **ED 77-11/-17** / Vocal score
ED 77-01

Weinlein, nun gang ein!, Op. 72 (1958-59) 20'
Text: various
Soloist: tenor
Chorus: male
2(pic).1.2.1(-2)-3.1.1.0-timp.perc-str
Material on hire
Vocal score **ED 4994**

Wenn die Bettelleute tanzen
(1958) 2'
Text: Schlesien
Chorus: male a cappella
C 39849

Hiller, Wilfried
b.1941

Stage Works

An diesem heutigen Tage
(1973) 45'
"en ma fin est mon commencement"
Text: Elisabeth Woska, after letters of Mary Stuart
Material on hire
SM

Die Ballade von Norbert Nackendick oder Das nackte Nashorn (1981) 50'
Text: Michael Ende
Material on hire
SM

Chaplin-Ford-Trott
(1929-30) 22'
(K.A. Hartmann: "Wachsfigurenkabinett", No.3)
Material on hire
Vocal score **ED 7668**

Hiller, Wilfried

b. Weißenborn (Swabia) 15.3.1941

At the age of fifteen, Wilfried Hiller began to study piano with Wilhelm Heckmann at the Augsburg Conservatory; in 1963 he continued his musical studies at the Munich Conservatory in composition (with Günther Bialas), opera direction, percussion and as well as music theory. From 1967 Hiller worked as a percussionist in various orchestras. In 1968 he founded the concert series "musik unserer zeit". The following years were influenced by the close acquaintance with Carl Orff whom Hiller met in 1968 and with whom he worked closely together until Orff's death. Since 1971 Hiller has been music editor at Bavarian Radio. In 1989 he became a member of the Bavarian Academy of Fine Arts, in 1991 lecturer at the Munich Conservatory and in 1993 teacher of composition at the Richard Strauss Conservatory of Munich. Among his prizes and awards are 1969 Richard Strauss Award of the city of Munich, 1971 Music Award for further studies of the city of Munich, 1977 Prix Brno, 1977 Villa Massimo Scholarship, 1988 Raiffeisen Award for further studies.

Die Fabel von Filemon Faltenreich oder Die Fußballweltmeisterschaft der Fliegen (1982)   60'

Opera
Material on hire
SM

Die Geschichte vom kleinen blauen Bergsee und dem alten Adler (1995/96)   70'

A Pocket-Opera
Text: Herbert Asmodi
Material on hire
SM

Der Goggolori (1982-83)   150'

Bavarian Opera in 8 scenes
Text: Michael Ende
Material on hire
SM

Ijob (1979)   23'

Monodrama
Text: Martin Buber
Material on hire
SM

Die Jagd nach dem Schlarg

(1987)   90'

Freely adapted from Lewis Carrol
Text: Michael Ende
Material on hire
SM

Knock out (1973-74)   12'

for actors and 2 timpani
Material on sale
SM

Liebestreu und Grausamkeit

(1980)   50'

Ein großes Ritter-Geister-Schau-Rühr- und Spektakelstück
Text: Wilhelm Busch
Material on hire
SM

Der Lindwurm und der Schmetterling oder Der seltsame Tausch (1980)   20'

Musical Fable in 3 Acts
Text: Michael Ende
Material on hire
SM

Niobe (1977)   55'

Opera after fragments from the "Niobe" by Aishylos
Text: Elisabeth Woska/Wilfried Hiller
Material on hire
SM

Der Rattenfänger. Ein Hamelner Totentanz

(1992-93)   120'

Opera
Text: Michael Ende
Material on hire
Libretto BN 3381-20

Tranquilla Trampeltreu, die beharrliche Schildkröte

(1980)   30'

Musikalische Fabel in Rondoform
Text: Michael Ende
Material on hire
SM

Das Traumfresserchen

(1989-90)   90'

Songplay
Text: Michael Ende
Material on hire
Libretto BN 3380-40

Trödelmarkt der Träume

(1979-84)   120'

Scenic Miniatures for 1 mouth and 6 hands
Text: Michael Ende
Material on hire
SM

Die zerstreute Brillenschlange (1979)   7'

Text: Michael Ende
Material on sale
ED 7008

Orchestral Works

Hintergründige Gedanken des Erzbischöflichen Salzburger Compositeurs Heinrich Ignaz Franz Biber beim Belauschen eines Vogelkonzerts (1991)   15'

str
Material on hire
SM

München (1990-91)   20'

Dance Suite
1(afl).pic.2.2.2-4.2.2.1-timp.perc-cel.pno.hp-str-stage music
Material on hire
SM

Concertos

Chagall-Zyklus (1993)   22'

Soloist: clarinet
perc-hpd.hp-str(solo vn-va.vc.db)
Material on hire
SM

Hamelin (1992-93)   14'

Drei Klangbilder from the opera "Der Rattenfänger"
Soloist: clarinet
timp.3perc-pno([cel]).hp-str
Material on hire
SM

Der Josa mit der Zauberfiedel (1985)   45'

Tänze auf dem Weg zum Mond
Text: Janosch
Soloists: speaker, violin
1(pic).0.1.0.1.1.1.1-timp.perc-pno.hp-str
alt. version: timp.perc-pno-vn
Material on hire
ED 7803

Pegasus 51 (1995-96)   16'

Concert
Soloist: jazz-percussion
2(pic).2.2(asax).2-4.3.3.1-timp.3perc-hp-str
Material on hire
SM

Veitstanz (1995) 18'

Soloist: clarinet
3(pic).2.0.2.cbn-4.3.3.1-3timp.3perc-cel.hp-str
Material on hire
SM

Chamber & Instrumental Works

Bestiarium (1978/84) 11'

6vc
Material on sale
SM

Fanfare (1970) 3'

12tpt-timp-perc
Material on hire
SM

Die feindlichen Nachbarn oder Die Folgen der Musik

(1994) 8'

6 Variations and Epitaph on a cycle of pictures by Wilhelm Busch
cello solo
Material on sale
SM

Der Fiedler (1993) 6'

From "Chagall-Zyklus"
vn.va.vc/db
ED 8375

Katalog I (1972-74) 15'

percussion solo
BAT 22

Katalog II (1973) 12'

2perc
BAT 18

Katalog III (1969) 15'

3perc
BAT 5

Katalog IV (1971-73) 16'

4perc
BAT 25

Katalog V (1966-74) 12'

5perc
BAT 6

Lilith (1987) 12'

vn.va.vc.db-pno
Material on sale
Study score **ED 7756**

2 Miniatures for Children

(1984) 3'

in: Neue Klavierstücke für Kinder
pno
ED 7392

Notenbüchlein für Tamino

(1990) 7'

8fl(pic)
Material on sale
FTR 158

Pas de deux (1978) 16'

2pno
SM

Phantasie über ein Thema von J.A. Hiller (1982) 6'

on a cycle of pictures by Wilhelm Busch
pno
ED 7190

Scherzo (1991) 5'

(Karl Amadeus Hartmann, 1956)
10perc-pno (4hnd)
ED 7785

Schildkröten-Boogie (1985) 2'

Arranger: Werner Thomas-Mifune
2vc
CB 127

Schulamit (1990) 6'

altoflute/flute solo
SM

Tarot-Toccatas (1993-95) 13'

organ solo
SM

Zauberfiedel-Suite (1985) 20'

vn-perc-pno
SM

Solo Voice(s) and Instrument(s)/ Orchestra

Muspilli (1978) 12'

Soloist: bass
str qrt-pno-drum
SM

Traum vom verlorenen Paradies (1977) 6'

From "Niobe"
Soloist: tenor
afl-pno/gtr/hp
Material on sale
SM

Choral Works

Das große Lalula (1984-85) 8'

7 Choral-aphorisms
Text: Christian Morgenstern
Chorus: female/children a cappella
C 46435

Schulamit (1977/93) 65'

Songs and Dances of Love - An Erotic Tryptic
Text: Martin Buber
Soloists: female speaker, soprano, bass-baritone, boy's voice
Chorus: mixed
2(pic,afl).0.0.0-3.3.3.1-shofar-timp.4perc-pno(cel).2hp-str
Material on hire
SM

Hindemith, Paul
1895-1963

Stage Works

Cardillac, Op. 39 (1925-26) 90'

Opera in 3 Acts (Original Version)
Text: Ferdinand Lion after E.T.A. Hoffmann
Material on hire
Score **PHA 104 (1-3)** / Study score **ETP 8013** / Vocal score **ED 3219** / Libretto **BN 3377-40**

Cardillac (1952) full evening

Opera in 4 Acts (New version)
Text: Ferdinand Lion/Paul Hindemith
Material on hire
Vocal score **ED 5445** / Libretto **BN 3370**

Der Dämon, Op. 28 (1922) 34'

Dance-Pantomime in 2 Scenes after Max Krell
Material on hire
Piano reduction **ED 3205**

Die Harmonie der Welt

(1956-57) full evening

Opera in 5 Acts
Text: Paul Hindemith
Material on hire
Vocal score **ED 4925** / Libretto **BN 3371-50**

Hérodiade (1944) 22'

Récitation Orchestrale in 1 Scene after Stéphane Mallarmé
Material on hire
Piano reduction **ED 4115**

Hin und Zurück, Op. 45a

(1927) 12'

Sketch with music in 1 Act
Text: Marcellus Schiffer
Material on hire
Score **PHA 106** / Vocal score **ED 3220**

Das lange Weihnachtsmahl

(1960-61) 60'

Opera in 1 Act
Text: Thornton Wilder/Paul Hindemith
Material on hire
Vocal score **ED 5175** / Libretto **BN 3375-80**

Lehrstück (1929) 50'

Text: Bertolt Brecht
Material on hire
Score **PHA 106** / Study score **ED 1500** / Vocal score **ED 1500-01** / Piano reduction **ED 6597**

Hindemith, Paul

b. Hanau 16.11.1895, d. Frankfurt/Main 28.12.1963

As teacher, performer and philosopher Hindemith would have an assured place in musical history quite apart from his over-whelming presence as a leading composer of our century. A moving spirit of 1920's modernism, he looked both forward to the atonality of Schönberg and Webern and backward to the expressive distancing of the baroque. In the masterful "Kammermusik" series and the vast reper-toire of solo sonatas for all the major instru-ments he espoused a common-sense approach to the creation and consumption of music. But his life's quest - witnessed in the heroes of his operas "Mathis der Maler" and "Die Harmonie der Welt", and in his own theoretical writings - was for a univer-sal harmony, reconciling the conflicting demands of music, art and life in compel-ling truth.

Mathis der Maler (1934-35) 185'

Opera in 7 Scenes
Text: Paul Hindemith
Material on hire
Study score ED 4575 / Vocal score ED 5800 / Libretto BN 3372-30

Mörder, Hoffnung der Frauen, Op. 12 (1919) 24'

Opera in 1 Act
Text: Oskar Kokoschka
Material on hire
Score PHA 101 / Vocal score ED 3202

Neues vom Tage

(1928-29) full evening

Comic Opera in 3 Parts
Text: Marcellus Schiffer
Material on hire
Study score ED 3492 / Libretto BN 3373-01

Neues vom Tage

(1928-29/53-54) full evening

Opera in 2 Acts (revised version)
Text: Marcellus Schiffer/Paul Hindemith
Material on hire
Vocal score ED 3233 /
Libretto BN 3373-01

Nobilissima Visione (1938) 48'

Dance Legend in 6 Scenes by Paul Hindemith and Léonide Massine
Material on hire
Piano reduction ED 2786

Das Nusch-Nuschi, Op. 20

(1920) 30'

Puppet Play in 1 Act
Text: Franz Blei
Material on hire
Score PHA 103

Sancta Susanna, Op. 21

(1921) 25'

Opera in 1 Act
Text: August Stramm
Material on hire
Score PHA 103 / Vocal score ED 3204

Theme with 4 Variations - The Four Temperaments

(1940) 29'

Ballet
Soloist: piano
str
Material on hire
Score ED 92 / Study score ED 6309 / Piano reduction ED 1625

Tuttifäntchen (1922) full evening

Christmas Tale in 3 Scenes
Text: Hedwig Michel/Franziska Becker
Material on hire
SM

Wir bauen eine Stadt (1930) 15'

Musical Play for Children
Text: Robert Seitz
Material on sale
Score ED 5424 / Parts ED 5424-11 (-17) /
Choral score ED 5424-01/-02

Orchestral Works

Amor und Psyche (1943) 7'

Overture. (Farnesina)
pic.1.2.2.2-2.2.2.0-timp-perc-str
Material on hire
Score PHA 204

Concerto for Orchestra, Op. 38 (1925) 12'

2(pic).Ebcl.1.bcl.2.cbn-3.2.2.1-timp.3perc-str
Material on hire
Score PHA 201 / Study score ED 3444/
ETP 8036

Der Dämon - Concert Suite, Op. 28 (1923) 25'

1.0.1.0-1.1.0.0-pno-str qnt
Material on hire
Piano reduction ED 3205

Geschwindmarsch von Beethoven from "Symphonia Serena" (1946) 4'

for wind band
pic.6.2.ca.12.bcl.2.cbn-4.10.6.6-timp.perc-cel
Material on sale
Score ED 6845-10 / Parts ED 6845

Geschwindmarsch von Beethoven from "Symphonia Serena" (1946) 4'

for symphonic wind band
Arranger: Juan Vicente MasQuiles
pic.4.2.18.Ebcl.acl.bcl.2asax.2tsax.bar-sax.2-4.6cnt/tpt.3.6euph.4-timp.perc-db
Material on sale
Score BSS 80100

Hérodiade (1944) 22'

Récitation Orchestrale after Stéphane Mallarmé
1.1.1.1-1.0.0.0-pno-str
Material on hire
Piano reduction ED 4115

Im Kampf mit dem Berg

(1921) 60'

Music to the film of the same name by Arnold Fanck
Arranger: Lothar Prox
1(pic).1.1.0-0.1.1.0-timp.perc.pno.harm-str
alt. version: pno-vn (and other instru-ments)
Material on hire
SM

Kammermusik No.1 with Finale 1921, Op. 24/1 (1921) 16'

1(pic).0.1.1-0.1.0.0-perc-pno.acc-str qnt
Material on hire
Study score ED 3436

Konzertmusik, Op. 50

(1930) 19'

Boston Symphony
0.0.0.0-4.4.3.1-0.0.0.0-str(1.0.1.1.1)
Material on hire
Study score ED 3502

Konzertmusik, Op. 41

(1926) 15'

pic.fl.ob.3cl.Ebcl.2flhn(2ssax/ssax.asax)-2nathn.2hn(ttuba/tsax).euph(bcl).3tpt.3tbn.2tuba.perc
Material on hire
Study score ED 6486

Konzertmusik, Op. 50

(1930) 18'

Arrangement for Concert Band
Arranger: Guy M. Duker
pic.2.2.(ca).4.acl.bcl.cbcl.2asax.tsax.bar-sax.2-2.3.cnt.4.3.euph.1-timp.perc-db
Material on hire
EAM

Musica Humana

Paul Hindemith
Symphony "Die Harmonie der Welt" (1951)
beginning of 2nd movement

Der Lindberghflug (1929)

Radio-play in cooperation with Kurt Weill
Text: Bertolt Brecht
1.0.1(Ebcl).1.asax.1-0.2.1.1-timp.perc-
pno.banjo-str
Material on sale
Score **PHA 106**

Ludus tonalis (1942/91) 63'

Studies in Counterpoint
Arranger: Joao Oliver dos Santos
3(2pic,afl).3(ob
d'am,ca).Ebcl.2.bcl.tsax.2.cbn-
4.3(pictpt).btpt(euph).3.1-2timp.5perc-
pno(cel).2hp-str(16.14.12.10.8)
Material on hire
SM

Ludus Tonalis (1942/1991/94) 20'

(First Orchestral Suite)
Arranger: Joao Oliver dos Santos
3(2pic,afl).2.ca.Ebcl.2.bcl.2.cbn-4.3.3.1-
timp.5perc-pno(cel).2hp-str(16.14.12.10.8)
Material on hire
SM

Lustige Sinfonietta, Op. 4

(1916) 39'

Text: Christian Morgenstern
Soloist: narrator
2(pic).2.ca.2.2.cbn-2.2.0.0-timp.perc-
str(8.6.6.6.4)
Material on hire
Score **PHA 201** / Study score **ED 7319**

March from "Symphonische Metamorphosen" (1943) 4'

for large wind band
Arranger: Keith Wilson
pic.2.2.ca.4.Ebcl.2bcl.2asax.tsax.barsax.2.
cbn-4.3cnt.2.3.2euph.tuba-timp.4perc-db
Score **SHS 1012** / Parts **SHS 1012-50**

Marsch über den alten "Schweizerton" (1960) 4'

2(pic).2.2.2-4.2.3.1-timp.perc-str
Material on hire
SM

Neues vom Tage (1929) 8'

Ouvertüre mit Konzertschluß
2(pic).1.ca.2.bcl.asax.2.cbn-1.2.2.1-2perc-
str(6.0.4.4.4)
Material on hire
Study score **ED 3492**

Nobilissima Visione (1939) 48'

Dance Legend in 6 Scenes. Arrangement
for large orchestra
2(pic).2.2.2-4.2.3.1-perc-str
Material on hire
SM

Nobilissima Visione - Suite

(1938) 20'

2.2.2.2-4.2.3.1-timp.3perc-str
Material on hire
Study score **ED 3531**

Nusch-Nuschi - Tänze, Op. 20 (1921) 9'

2(pic).2.ca.Ebcl.2.bcl.2.cbn-2.2.3.1-
timp.3perc-cel.hp-str
Material on hire
SM

Philharmonic Concerto

(1932) 23'

3(pic).2.ca.2.bcl.2.cbn-4.3.3.1-timp.2perc-
str
Material on hire
Score **PHA 202** / Study score **ED 3505**

Pittsburgh Symphony

(1958) 26'

2(pic).2.ca.2.bcl.2.cbn-4.2.3.1-timp.4perc-
str
Material on hire
Score **PHA 207** / Study score **ED 5011**

Plöner Musiktag (1932) 10'

B. Tafelmusik
fl-tpt(cl)-str
Material on sale
ED 1623

Plöner Musiktag (1932) 6'

D. Abendkonzert 1.Einleitungsstücke
high,medium & low parts
Material on sale
ED 1691

Plöner Musiktag (1932) 5'

D. Abendkonzert 6.Quodlibet
high,medium & low parts
Material on sale
ED 1696

Plöner Musiktag (1932) 16'

Suite
Arranger: Willi Draths
1.[1].1.0-1.2.1.0-[perc]-str(1.0.0.vc.[db])
Material on sale
Score **CON 78** / Parts **CON 78-50/-60**

Plöner Musiktag - Suite 16'

1.[1].1.0-1.2.1.0-[perc]-str
Material on sale
CON 78

Ragtime (1921) 4'

(wohltemperiert)
2pic.1.2.3.2-4.2.3.1-timp.perc-str
Material on hire
Score **PHA 201** / Piano reduction **ED 7325**

Schulwerk, Op. 44/2 (1927) 6'

II. 8 Canons
str
Material on sale
ED 1455

Schulwerk, Op. 44/3 (1927) 8'

III. 8 Pieces
str
Material on sale
CON 80

Schulwerk, Op. 44/4 (1927) 10'

IV. 5 Pieces
str
Material on sale
CON 75

Sinfonietta in E (1949-50) 21'

pic.1.2.2.2-3.1.2.1-timp.perc-cel-str
Material on hire
Score **ED 93** / Study score **ED 4070**

Sing-und Spielmusiken, Op. 45/3 (1928) 5'

III. Ein Jäger aus Kurpfalz
str-wind
Material on sale
ED 1464

Spielmusik, Op. 43/1 (1927) 7'

fl.ob-str
Material on hire
Study score **CON 79**

Suite französischer Tänze

(1958) 9'

pic.1.1.ca.0.1-0.1.0.0-lute-str
Material on sale
CON 76

Symphonia Serena (1946) 34'

pic.2.ca.2.bcl.2.cbn-4.2.2.1-timp.3perc-cel-
str
Material on hire
Study score **ED 4422**

Symphonische Metamorphosen über Theme von Carl Maria von Weber

(1943) 25'

2.pic.2.ca.2.bcl.2.cbn-4.2.3.1-timp.3perc-str
Material on hire
Score **ED 78** / Study score **ED 3541/ETP 1394** /
Piano reduction **ED 4124**

Symphonische Tänze (1937) 33'

2(pic).2.2.2-4.2.3.1-timp.3perc-str
Material on hire
Score **PHA 203** / Study score **ED 3525** /
Piano reduction **ED 3717**

Symphony "Die Harmonie der Welt" (1951) 34'

2(pic).2.2.bcl.2.cbn-4.2.3.1-timp.3perc-str
Material on hire
Study score **ED 4061**

Symphony in Bb (1951) 19'

for symphonic wind band
pic.2.2.Ebcl.4.acl.bcl.2asax.tsax.barsax.2-
4.4cnt.2.3.euph.2-timp.3perc
For symphonic band Add:
5basses.2euph.5perc
Score **SHS 1009** / Study score **ED 4063** / Parts
SHS 1009-50

Symphony in Eb (1940) 33'

pic.2.2.ca.2.bcl.2.cbn-4.3.3.1-timp.3perc-str
Material on hire
Score **PHA 204** / Study score **ED 3532**

Symphony "Mathis der Maler" (1934) 26'

2(pic).2.2.2-4.2.3.1-timp.perc-str
Material on hire
Score **PHA 202/ED 69** / Study score
ETP 573/ED 3509 / Piano reduction **ED 3286**

Symphony "Mathis der Maler" (1934) 27'

For Concert Band
Arranger: Guy M. Duker
pic.2.2.ca.4.acl.bcl.cbcl.2asax.tsax.bar-
sax.2-2.3cnt.4.3.euph.1-timp.perc.db
Material on hire
SM

When Lilacs Last in the Door-Yard Bloom'd (1946) 5'

Prelude
2.2.2.2-3.2.2.1-timp.perc-org-str
Material on hire
SM

Concertos

Cello Concerto (1940) 28'

Soloist: cello
2(pic).2.2.bcl.2-4.2.3.1-timp.perc-cel-str
Material on hire
Score **PHA 306** / Study score **ED 4073** /
Piano reduction **ED 2838**

Cello Concerto in Eb Major, Op. 3 (1915) 30'

Soloist: cello
2(pic).2.2.2-4.2.3.0-timp-str(12.12.8.6.6)
Material on hire
Score **PHA 305** / Piano reduction **ED 6790**

Clarinet Concerto (1947) 24'

Soloist: clarinet
pic.2.2.0.2-2.2.2.0-timp.perc-str
Material on hire
Score **PHA 307** / Piano reduction **ED 4025**

Concerto for Trumpet and Bassoon (1949) 17'

Soloists: trumpet, bassoon
str
Material on hire
Score **PHA 308** / Piano reduction **ED 4491**

Concerto for Wind and Harp (1949) 13'

Soloists: flute, oboe, clarinet, bassoon, harp
0.0.0.0-2.2.1.0-str
Material on hire
Score **PHA 308/ED 94** / Study score **ED 4064**

Horn Concerto (1949) 15'

Soloist: horn
1(pic).2.2.2-0.0.0.0-timp-str
Material on hire
Score **PHA 307** / Study score **ED 4068** /
Piano reduction **ED 4024**

Kammermusik No.2 (Piano Concerto), Op. 36/1 (1924) 16'

Soloist: piano
1(pic).1.2.[bcl].1-1.1.1.0-str(1.0.1.1.1)
Material on hire
Study score **ED 3440** / Piano reduction
ED 1857

Kammermusik No.3 (Cello Concerto), Op. 36/2 (1925) 17'

Soloist: cello
1(pic).1.Ebcl.1.1-1.1.1.0-str(1.0.0.1.1)
Material on hire
Study score **ED 3441** / Piano reduction
ED 1987

Kammermusik No.4 (Violin Concerto), Op. 36/3

(1925) 23'

Soloist: violin
2pic.0.0.Ebcl.1.bcl.2.cbn-0.cnt.0.1.1-timp-
str(0.0.4.4.4)
Material on hire
Study score **ED 3442** / Piano reduction
ED 1920

Kammermusik No.5 (Viola Concerto), Op. 36/4

(1927) 12'

Soloist: viola
1(pic).1.Ebcl.1.bcl.2.cbn-1.2.2.1-
str(0.0.0.4.4)
Material on hire
Study score **ED 3443** / Piano reduction
ED 1977

Kammermusik No.6, Op. 46/1 (1927/30) 19'

Soloist: viola d'amore
1.1.1.bcl.1-1.1.1.0-str(0.0.0.3.2)
Material on hire
Study score **ED 6315** / Piano reduction
ED 7162

Kammermusik No.7 (Organ Concerto), Op. 46/2

(1927) 18'

Organ Concerto
Soloist: organ
pic.1.1.1.bcl.2.cbn-1.1.1.0-str(0.0.0.2.1)
Material on hire
Study score **ED 6316** / Piano reduction
ED 1897

Konzertmusik, Op. 48

(1929-30) 20'

Soloist: viola
pic.1.1.ca.1.bcl.2.cbn-3.1.1.0-str(0.0.0.4.4)
Material on hire
Score **PHA 303** / Study score **ED 3491** /
Piano reduction **ED 8488**

Konzertmusik, Op. 49

(1930) 21'

Soloist: piano
4hn.3tpt.2tbn.tuba-2hp/1hp
Material on hire
Piano reduction **ED 3248**

Organ Concerto (1962) 25'

Soloist: organ
pic.2.2.2.2.cbn-2.2.3.1-timp.perc-cel-str
Material on hire
Study score **ED 5033** / Piano reduction
ED 5388

Piano Concerto (1945) 34'

Soloist: piano
pic.1.2.2.bcl.2-2.2.2.1-timp.2perc-str
Material on hire
Piano reduction **ED 3838**

Plöner Musiktag (1932) 3'

D. Abendkonzert 2.Flötensolo
Soloist: flute
str
Material on sale
ED 1692

Plöner Musiktag (1932) 3'

D. Abendkonzert 4.Variationen
Soloist: clarinet
str
Material on sale
ED 1694

Der Schwanendreher (1935) 26'

after old Folksongs
Soloist: viola
2(pic).1.2.2-3.1.1.0-timp-hp-str(0.0.0.4.3)
Material on hire
Study score **ETP 1816** / Parts **ED 2515 (Solo)** /
Piano reduction **ED 4555**

Theme with 4 Variations - The Four Temperaments

(1940) 29'

Soloist: piano
str
Material on hire
Score **ED 92** / Study score **ED 6309** / Piano
reduction **ED 1625**

Trauermusik (1936) 8'

on the dead of King Georg V
Soloist: viola/violin/cello
str
Material on sale
Score **ED 3514** / Parts **ED 3171** / Piano
reduction **ED 2515**

Tuttifäntchen (1922) 20'

Suite
Soloist: violin
1(pic).1.1.1-1.1.0.0-timp.perc-str
Material on sale
Score **CON 77** / Parts **CON 77-50/-60**

Violin Concerto (1939) 30'

Soloist: violin
2(pic).2.2.bcl.2-4.2.3.1-timp.perc-str
Material on hire
Study score **ED 3529** / Piano reduction
ED 3634

Infoline · e-Mail
Schott Musik International
Mainz: Schott.Musik.com@T-Online.de
London: 101627.166@compuserve.com

Chamber & Instrumental Works

3 Anekdoten für Radio (1925)
from "Drei Stücke für 5 Instrumente"
cl-tpt-vn.db-pno

Bassoon Sonata (1938)   9'
bn-pno
ED 3686

Berceuse (1921)   1'
pno
Score PHA 509

2 Canonic Duets (1929)   11'
2vn
ED 2212

Canonic Piece
in: Neue Musik, Vol. 2
2vn
Score ED 2212

Canonic Sonata, Op. 31/3
(1923)   6'
2fl
ED 2002

Cello Sonata, Op. 11/3
(1919/22)   22'
vc-pno
ED 1986 / Score PHA 506

Cello Sonata, Op. 25/3
(1922)   11'
cello solo
ED 1979 / Score PHA 505

Cello Sonata (1948)   20'
vc-pno
ED 3839 / Score PHA 507

Clarinet Quintet, Op. 30
(1923/54)   18'
cl-str qrt
Score ED 4560 / Parts ED 4528 /
Parts ED 4560-50 (1954 version)

Clarinet Sonata (1939)   17'
cl-pno
ED 3641

Cor Anglais Sonata (1941)   11'
ca-pno
ED 3672

Double Bass Sonata (1949)   14'
db-pno
ED 4043 / Score PHA 507

Duett (1934)   4'
va.vc
ED 4765 / Score PHA 505

Duett (1942)   2'
2vc
ED 8338

Duett (1942)   2'
2vc
ED 8186

2 Duette (1927)   2'
bn-db
ED 8509

14 Easy Pieces (1931)   12'
"Neue Musik" Vol.1
2vn
ED 2211

3 Easy Pieces (1938)   8'
vc-pno
ED 2771

Echo (1942)   2'
fl-pno
ED 4916

Etudes for violinists (1926)   14'
violin solo
ED 4687

Flute Sonata (1936)   15'
fl-pno
ED 2522

6 ganz leichte Stücke (1942)   4'
bn-vc
ED 8508

Harp Sonata (1939)   11'
harp solo
ED 3644

Horn Sonata (1939)   18'
hn-pno
ED 3642

In einer Nacht, Op. 15
(1917-19)   26'
...Träume und Erlebnisse...
pno
ED 7904 / Score PHA 509

In Sturm und Eis (1921)
Music to the film "Im Kampf mit dem
Berg" by Arnold Fanck for Saloon-orche-
stra
1(pic).1.1.0-0.1.1.0-timp.perc-pno.harm-str

**Klaviermusik (2 Vols.),
Op. 37** (1925/27)   36'
pno
ED 1299/1300 / Score PHA 509

Klavierstück (1929)   3'
pno
Score PHA 509

**Kleine Kammermusik,
Op. 24/2** (1922)   13'
fl(pic).ob.cl.bn-hn
Score ED 3437 / Parts ED 4389

**Kleine Klaviermusik,
Op. 45/4** (1929)   5'
pno
ED 1466

**Des kleinen Elektromusikers
Lieblinge** (1930)   10'
7 Pieces
3 trautoniums/str trio/wind trio
Score and parts ED 8510

Konzertstück (1933)   8'
2asax
ED 7169

Lied (1921)   2'
pno
Score PHA 509

Little Sonata, Op. 25/2
(1922)   12'
va d'am-pno
ED 2079

Little Sonata (1942)   12'
vc-pno
ED 8186

Ludus Minor (1944)   6'
cl-vc
ED 8341

Ludus Tonalis (1942)   63'
pno
ED 3964/ED 8200 ("Ludi leonum") /
Score PHA 510

Ludus Tonalis (1942)   63'
Arranger: Joachim Dorfmüller
organ solo
ED 7027

Minimax (1923)   21'
str qrt
Score ED 6734 / Parts ED 6735

Movement (1914-15)   3'
vn-pno
Score PHA 506

**Musikalisches
Blumengärtlein und
Leyptziger Allerlei** (1927)   10'
cl-db/vc
ED 8339

Nobilissima Visione (1938)   2'
Meditation
vn-pno
ED 3683

Nobilissima Visione (1938)   2'

Meditation
va-pno
ED 3684

Nobilissima Visione (1938)   2'

Meditation
vc-pno
ED 3685

Oboe Sonata (1938)   12'

ob-pno
ED 3676

Octet (1957-58)   26'

cl.bn-hn-vn.2va.vc.db
Score **ED 4595** / Parts **ED 4686**

Organ Sonata No.1 (1937)   18'

organ solo
ED 2557

Organ Sonata No.2 (1937)   12'

organ solo
ED 2558

Organ Sonata No.3 (1940)   13'

organ solo
ED 3736

Ouvertüre zum Fliegenden Holländer, wie sie eine schlechte Kurkapelle morgens um 7 am Brunnen vom Blatt spielt (1925)   8'

str qrt
Score **ED 8106** / Parts **ED 8106**

Piano Sonata, Op. 17 (1920)   20'

(Reconstruction)
Arranger: Bernhard Billeter
ED 7951 / Score **PHA 509**

Piano Sonata No.1 in A - "Der Main" (1936)   31'

ED 2518 / Score **PHA 510**

Piano Sonata No.2 in G (1936)   14'

ED 2519 / Score **PHA 510**

Piano Sonata No.3 in B (1936)   20'

ED 2521 / Score **PHA 510**

8 Pieces (1927)   7'

flute solo
ED 4760

3 Pieces (1917)   18'

vc-pno
Score and parts **PHA 506**

Pieces (1927)   5'

doublebass solo
ED 8378

3 Pieces for 5 Instruments (1925)   6'

cl-tpt-vn.db-pno
Material on sale
Study score **ED 3312**

Plöner Musiktag (1932)   5'

A. Morgenmusik
2tpt(flhn).2tbn(hn).[tuba]
Material on sale
Study score **ED 1622**

Plöner Musiktag (1932)   4'

D. Abendkonzert 3. 2 Duette
vn-cl
ED 1693

Plöner Musiktag (1932)   8'

D. Abendkonzert 5.Trio
3rec
Score **ED 1695** / Study score **ED 10094-01** / Parts **ED 10094-02**

Quartet (1938)   24'

cl-vn.vc-pno
Score **ED 3180** / Parts **ED 3178/3179**

Ragtime (1921)   6'

pno (4hnd)
ED 7325

Rondo (1925)   4'

2/3gtr
GA 457/412

Schulwerk, Op. 44/1 (1927)   5'

I. 9 Pieces
2vn (solo or group)
ED 1454/B 107

Sing-und Spielmusiken, Op. 45/4 (1929)   5'

IV. Little Piano Music
pno
ED 1466

Sonata (1938)   13'

pno (4hnd)
ED 3716

Sonata (1942)   16'

2pno
ED 3970

Sonata (1943)   11'

altosaxophone/horn
ED 4635

Sonata for 10 Instruments, Op. 10a (1917)

1.0.1.bcl.1-1.0.0.0-str(1.1.1.1.1)
SM

Sonata for 4 Horns (1952)   16'

4hn
Score **ED 4417** / Parts **ED 4492**

Sonata for Wind Quintet (1937)   11'

2tpt.hn.tbn.tuba
Score **ED 6880** / Parts **ED 6881**

String Quartet No. 1 C Major, Op. 2 (1915)   38'

Score **ED 8184** / Parts **ED 8185**

String Quartet No.2 in F Minor, Op. 10 (1918)   29'

Score **ED 3433** / Parts **ED 3115**

String Quartet No.3 in C Major, Op. 16 (1920)   26'

Score **ED 3434** / Parts **ED 3116**

String Quartet No.4, Op. 22 (1921)   25'

Score **ED 3435** / Parts **ED 3117**

String Quartet No.5, Op. 32 (1923)   24'

Score **ED 3438** / Parts **ED 3118**

String Quartet No.6 in Eb (1943)   26'

Score **ED 3537** / Parts **ED 2277**

String Quartet No.7 (1945)   15'

Score **ED 3538** / Parts **ED 3843**

String Trio No.1, Op. 34 (1924)   17'

vn.va.vc
Score **PHA 505/ED 3439** / Parts **ED 3102**

String Trio No.2 (1933)   24'

vn.va.vc
Score **PHA 505/ED 3506** / Parts **ED 3160**

Stücke (1941)   5'

vc/2vc-bn/2bn
ED 6049

Suite "1922", Op. 26 (1922)   22'

pno
ED 1732 / Score **PHA 509**

Symphonische Tänze (1937)   33'

Transcription
pno (4hnd)
ED 3717

Symphony "Mathis der Maler" (1934)   27'

Transcription
pno (4hnd)
ED 3286

Tanz der Holzpuppen (1922)   3'

from "Tuttifäntchen"
pno
ED 1734

INVITATION TO SUBSCRIBE TO A REMARKABLE PUBLICATION!

Paul Hindemith
The Complete Works

The Hindemith edition of complete works is a critical, scientifically sound edition which also takes the needs of the musical practice into account by offering new, philologically sound material.

Subscription conditions

Subscription to the complete edition: obliges the subscriber to take the complete edition. Partial subscription: makes it possible for the subscriber to purchase a complete series. Purchase of individual volumes: is also possible by not subscribing to this edition.

Available volumes

Series I: Stage Works

Vol. 1:
Mörder, Hoffnung der Frauen (1919)
Order No. PHA 101

Vol. 3:
Sancta Susanna (1921)
Order No. PHA 103

Vol. 4:
Cardillac (1926)
Teil A /B / C
Order No. PHA 104-10, 104-20, 104-30

Vol. 6:
• Szenische Versuche:
• Hin und zurück (1927)
• Lehrstück (1929)
• Der Lindberghflug (1929)
Order No. PHA 106

Vol. 11:
Das lange Weihnachtsmahl (1960)
Order No. PHA 111

Series II: Orchestral Works

1917-30
Vol. 1:
• Lustige Sinfonietta d-Moll, op. 4 (1916)
• Rag Time (wohltemperiert) (1921)
• Konzert für Orchester, op. 38 (1925)
• Konzertmusik für Streichorchester und Blechbläser, op. 50 (1930)
Order No. PHA 201

1932-34
Vol. 2:
• Philharmonisches Konzert (1932)
• Symphonie "Mathis der Maler" (1934)
Order No. PHA 202

Vol. 3:
Symphonische Tänze (1937)
Order No. PHA 203

1940-43
Vol. 4:
• Symphonie in Es (1940)
• Amor and Psyche (Farnesina) (1943)
• Poor Lazarus (Fragment) (1941)
Order No. PHA 204

1958-60
Vol. 7:
• Pittsburgh Symphony (1958)
• Marsch über den alten "Schweizerton" (1960)
Order No. PHA 207

Serie III: Solo Concertos

Vol. 3:
• Violin-Konzert (1939)
• Konzertmusik für Solobratsche und größeres

Kammerorchester, op. 48
(early version) (1930)
Order No. PHA 303

Vol. 5:
Violoncello-Konzert Es-Dur, op. 3 (1915/16)
Order No. PHA 305

Vol. 6:
Violoncello-Konzert (1940)
Order No. PHA 306

Vol. 7:
Bläserkonzerte I
• Klarinetten-Konzert (1947)
• Horn-Konzert (1949)
Order No. PHA 307

Vol. 8:
• Bläserkonzerte II
• Concerto für Holzbläser und Orchester 1949)
• Concerto für Trompete (B), und Fagott mit Streichorchester (1949)
Order No. PHA 308

Serie V: Chamber Music

Vol. 5:
Streicherkammermusik II
Order No. PHA 505

Vol. 6:
Streicherkammermusik III
Order No. PHA 506

Vol. 7:
Streicherkammermusik IV
Order No. PHA 507

Vol. 9:
Klaviermusik I
Order No. PHA 509

Vol. 10:
Klaviermusik II
Order No. PHA 510

Serie VI: Lieder

Vol. 1:
Klavierlieder I
Order No. PHA 601

Vol. 2:
Klavierlieder II
Order No. PHA 602

Vol. 4:
Sologesänge mit Instrumenten
Order No. PHA 604

Vol. 5:
Sologesänge mit Orchester
Order No. PHA 605

Serie VII: Choral Works

Vol. 2:
When lilacs last in the door-yard bloom'd. A Requiem "For those we love"
Order No. PHA 702

Vol. 5:
Chorwerke a cappella
Order No. PHA 705

SCHOTT

Tanzstücke, Op. 19 (1919/20) 14'

pno
ED 1418 / Score **PHA 509**

Toccata

for mechanic piano
mechanic piano (4hnd)
ED 8090

Trio, Op. 47 (1928) 15'

va-heck/tsax-pno
ED 3148

Trio (1932) 15'

from "Plöner Musiktag"
srec.2arec
Study score **ED 10094-01** / Parts **ED 10094-02**

Trombone Sonata (1941) 10'

tbn-pno
ED 3673

Trumpet Sonata (1939) 16'

tpt-pno
ED 3643

Tuba Sonata (1955) 11'

tuba-pno
ED 4636

Variation (1941) 5'

vc-pno
ED 4276 / Score **PHA 507**

Variations (1936) 8'

pno
ED 7055

Viola Sonata in F, Op. 11/4

(1919) 16'

va-pno
ED 1976 / Score **PHA 506**

Viola Sonata, Op. 11/5

(1919) 18'

viola solo
ED 1968 / Score **PHA 505**

Viola Sonata, Op. 25/1

(1922) 15'

viola solo
ED 1969 / Score **PHA 505**

Viola Sonata, Op. 25/4

(1922) 15'

va-pno
ED 6740 / Score **PHA 506**

Viola Sonata (1938-39) 24'

va-pno
ED 3640 / Score **PHA 507**

Viola Sonata, Op. 31/4

(1923) 17'

viola solo
ED 8278 / Score **PHA 505**

Viola Sonata (1937) 13'

viola solo
ED 8279 / Score **PHA 505**

Violin Sonata, Op. 31/1

(1924) 10'

violin solo
ED 1901 / Score **PHA 505**

Violin Sonata, Op. 31/2

(1924) 7'

violin solo
ED 1902

Violin Sonata, Op. 11/6

(1917-18)

violin solo
Score **PHA 505**

Violin Sonata in C (1939) 14'

vn-pno
ED 3645 / Score **PHA 507**

Violin Sonata in D, Op. 11/2

(1918) 19'

vn-pno
ED 1919 / Score **PHA 506**

Violin Sonata in E (1935) 10'

vn-pno
ED 2455 / Score **PHA 507**

Violin Sonata in Eb, Op. 11/1

(1918) 10'

vn-pno
ED 1918 / Score **PHA 506**

Walzer, Op. 6 (1916) 8'

pno (4hnd)
ED 8060

Wind Septet (1948) 16'

fl.ob.cl.bcl.bn-hn.tpt
Score **ED 3540** / Parts **ED 919**

Wir bauen eine Stadt (1931) 5'

pno
ED 2200

Solo Voice(s)/Voice(s) and Piano/Guitar

Bal des Pendus (1944) 4'

Ballad
Text: Jean-Arthur Rimbaud
high/medium voice-pno
ED 6896

9 English Songs (1942-44) 24'

Text: various
soprano/mezzo-soprano-pno
ED 6839

3 Hymns, Op. 14 (1919) 10'

Text: Walt Whitman
baritone-pno
ED 7117 / Score **PHA 601**

Das Kind (1922) 1'

Text: Friedrich von Hagedorn
soprano-pno
Score **PHA 601**

La Belle Dame sans Merci

(1942) 5'

Ballad
Text: John Keats
high/medium voice-pno
ED 6895

8 Lieder, Op. 18 (1920) 14'

Text: various
soprano-pno
ED 2023 / Score **PHA 601**

6 Lieder (1933-35) 17'

Text: Friedrich Hölderlin
tenor/low voice-pno
ED 5462/5752

Lustige Lieder in Aargauer Mundart, Op. 5 (1914-16) 9'

high voice-pno
Score **PHA 601**

Das Marienleben, Op. 27

(1922-23) 63'

(Original version)
Text: Rainer Maria Rilke
soprano-pno
ED 2025 / Score **PHA 601**

Das Marienleben, Op. 27

(1922-23/1936-48) 69'

(New version)
Text: Rainer Maria Rilke
soprano-pno
ED 2026

14 Motets (1960) 6'

1. Exit Edictum
soprano/tenor-pno
ED 5085

14 Motets (1944) 4'

2. Pastores Loquebantur
soprano/tenor-pno
ED 4390

14 Motets (1959) 5'

3. Dicebat Jesus scribis et pharisaeis
soprano/tenor-pno
ED 5086

14 Motets (1959) 4'

4. Dixit Jesus Petro
soprano/tenor-pno
ED 5087

14 Motets (1958) 5'

5. Angelus Domini apparuit
soprano/tenor-pno
ED 5088

14 Motets (1959) — 4'
6. Erat Joseph et Maria
soprano/tenor-pno
ED 5089

14 Motets (1958) — 3'
7. Defuncto Herode
soprano/tenor-pno
ED 5090

14 Motets (1941) — 5'
8. Cum natus esset
soprano/tenor-pno
ED 4392

14 Motets (1959) — 4'
9. Cum factus esset Jesus
soprano/tenor-pno
ED 5091

14 Motets (1959) — 4'
10. Vidit Joannes Jesum
soprano/tenor-pno
ED 5092

14 Motets (1944) — 4'
11. Nuptiae factae sunt
soprano/tenor-pno
ED 4391

14 Motets (1960) — 5'
12. Cum descendisset Jesus
soprano/tenor-pno
ED 5093

14 Motets (1943) — 4'
13. Ascendente Jesu in Naviculam
soprano/tenor-pno
ED 5094

Nähe des Geliebten (1914) — 2'
Text: Johann Wolfgang von Goethe
voice-pno
Score **PHA 601**

2 Songs (1917) — 6'
Text: Else Lasker-Schüler, Guido Gezelle
alto-pno
ED 8421 / Score **PHA 601**

2 Songs (1955) — 3'
Text: Oscar Cox
soprano/tenor-pno
ED 4441

7 Songs (1908-09) — 11'
soprano/tenor-pno
Score **PHA 601**

Solo Voice(s) and Instrument(s)/ Orchestra

Es trägt die Nacht (1931) — 5'
from the Oratorio "Das Unaufhörliche'
Text: Gottfried Benn
Soloist: soprano
2.1.1.1-1.0.0.0-str
Material on hire
SM

3 Gesänge , Op. 9 (1917) — 18'
Text: Else Lasker-Schüler, Ernst Wilhelm Lotz
Soloist: soprano
3(pic).2.ca.Ebcl.2.2.cbn-8.4.3.1-timp.perc-2hp-str
Material on hire
Score **PHA 605**

Die junge Magd, Op. 23/2
(1922) — 20'
Text: Georg Trakl
Soloist: alto
fl.cl-str qrt
Material on sale
Study score **ED 2024** / Vocal score **ED 3404**

Lustige Sinfonietta, Op. 4
(1916) — 39'
Text: Christian Morgenstern
Soloist: narrator
2(pic).2.ca.2.2.cbn-2.2.0.0-timp.perc-str(8.6.6.6.4)
Material on hire
Score **PHA 201** / Study score **ED 7319**

Mag Sonne leuchten (1926) — 4'
from "Cardillac'
Soloist: baritone
2.2.3.tsax.3-1.2.2.1-perc-str
SM

Das Marienleben, Op. 27
(1938-59) — 23'
Text: Rainer Maria Rilke
Soloist: soprano
2.2.3.2-2.2.2.0-timp.2perc-str
Material on hire
Vocal score **ED 2026**

Melancholie, Op. 13
(1917-19) — 12'
4 Songs
Text: Christian Morgenstern
Soloist: female voice
str qrt
ED 8410 / Score **PHA 604**

Serenades, Op. 35 (1924) — 20'
Text: various
Soloist: soprano
ob-va.vc
ED 2027 / Score **PHA 604**

6 Songs (1938/59) — 23'
from "Das Marienleben"
Text: Rainer Maria Rilke
Soloist: soprano
2(pic).2.ca.2.bcl.2-2.2.2.0-timp.perc-str
Score **PHA 605**

Des Todes Tod, Op. 23a
(1922) — 16'
Text: Eduard Reinacher
Soloist: female voice
2va.2vc
Score **PHA 604/ED 4493** / Parts **ED 5422**

Was gabst du mir (1952) — 4'
from "Cardillac'
Soloist: soprano
2.2.3.3-1.2.2.1-perc-str
Material on hire
SM

Wie es wär', wenn's anders wär' (1918) — 5'
Text: v. Miris
Soloist: soprano
fl.ob.bn-2vn.va.2vc
ED 8411/8411-10 / Score **PHA 604**

Ein Wille treibt mich (1952) — 4'
from "Cardillac'
Soloist: baritone
2.2.3.tsax.3-1.2.2.1-perc-str
Material on hire
SM

Die Zeit vergeht (1926) — 4'
from "Cardillac'
Soloist: soprano
2.2.3.3-1.2.2.1-perc-str
Material on hire
SM

Choral Works

An eine Tote (1958) — 3'
from "12 Madrigale"
Text: Josef Weinheber
Chorus: mixed a cappella (5 prt)
SKR 20032 / Score **PHA 705** / Study score **C 39901** / Choral score **CHBL 345**

An einen Schmetterling
(1958) — 3'
from "12 Madrigale"
Text: Josef Weinheber
Chorus: mixed a cappella (5 prt)
SKR 20032 / Score **PHA 705** / Study score **C 39901** / Choral score **CHBL 347**

Angst vorm Schwimmunterricht (1930) — 2'
from "Chorlieder für Knaben"
Text: Karl Schnog
Chorus: boy's a cappella
C 32759 / Score **PHA 705**

Apparebit repentina dies

(1947)   17'

Chorus: mixed
4hn.2tpt.3tbn.tuba
Material on hire
Piano reduction ED 4237/136

Art läßt nicht von Art, Op. 33 (1923)   1'

from "Lieder nach alten Texten"
Text: Spervogel
Chorus: mixed a cappella
C 31418 / Score PHA 705

Bastellied (1930)   2'

from "Chorlieder für Knaben"
Text: Karl Schnog
Chorus: boy's a cappella
C 32757 / Score PHA 705

4 Canons (1928/49)   3'

Text: various
Chorus: female a cappella
CHBL 515

6 Chansons (1939)   8'

Text: Rainer Maria Rilke
Chorus: mixed a cappella
Score PHA 705 / Choral score C 43782-01 (-06)

The devil a monk would be

(1937-38)   1'

from "5 Songs on old texts"
Chorus: mixed a cappella
Score PHA 705 / Choral score C 44005

Du mußt dir alles geben

(1930)   2'

Text: Gottfried Benn
Chorus: male a cappella
C 32784 / Score PHA 705

Du Zweifel an dem Sinn der Welt (1958)   3'

from "12 Madrigale"
Text: Josef Weinheber
Chorus: mixed a cappella (5 prt)
SKR 20034 / Score PHA 705 / Study score
C 39901 / Choral score CHBL 352

Eine lichte Mitternacht

(1929)   2'

Text: Walt Whitman
Chorus: male a cappella
C 32546 / Score PHA 705

Eines Narren, eines Künstlers Leben (1958)   3'

from "12 Madrigale"
Text: Josef Weinheber
Chorus: mixed a cappella (5 prt)
SKR 20031 / Score PHA 705 / Study score
C 39901 / Choral score CHBL 342

Es bleibt wohl, was gesagt wird (1958)   3'

from "12 Madrigale"
Text: Josef Weinheber
Chorus: mixed a cappella (5 prt)
SKR 20034 / Score PHA 705 / Study score
C 39901 / Choral score CHBL 350

Erster Schnee (1939)   3'

Text: Gottfried Keller
Chorus: male a cappella
C 37583 / Score PHA 705

Frauenklage, Op. 33 (1923)   1'

from "Lieder nach alten Texten"
Text: Burggraf zu Regensburg
Chorus: mixed a cappella (6 prt)
C 31417 / Score PHA 705

Frühling (1958)   3'

from "12 Madrigale"
Text: Josef Weinheber
Chorus: mixed a cappella (5 prt)
SKR 20032 / Score PHA 705 / Study score
C 39901 / Choral score CHBL 346

Fürst Kraft (1930)   2'

Text: Gottfried Benn
Chorus: male a cappella
C 32783 / Score PHA 705

Galgenritt - The Demon of the Gibbet (1949)   4'

Text: Fritz-James O'Brien
Chorus: male a cappella
C 37535 / Score PHA 705

Heimliches Glück, Op. 33

(1923)   1'

from "Lieder nach alten Texten"
Text: Reinmar
Chorus: mixed a cappella (6 prt)
C 31420 / Score PHA 705

Ite, angeli veloces - Custos quid de nocte (1955)   15'

Cantata in 3 Parts
Text: Paul Claudel/Paul Hindemith
Soloists: mezzo-soprano, alto, tenor
Chorus: mixed
1.1.1.1-1.1.1.1-perc-str
Material on hire
Vocal score ED 4634-01 / Piano reduction
ED 4634

Ite, angeli veloces - Gesang an die Hoffnung (1953)   15'

Cantata in 3 Parts
Text: Paul Claudel/Paul Hindemith
Soloists: mezzo-soprano, alto, tenor
Chorus: mixed
2(pic).2.ca.2.bcl.2.cbn-4.2.3.1-timp.perc-pno-str
wind band: pic.1.0.Ebcl.3.asax.tsax.bar-sax.2-4.3/3cnt.3.euph.2-perc-org
Material on hire
Vocal score ED 4497-01/-02 / Piano reduction
ED 4497

Ite, angeli veloces - Triumphgesang Davids

(1955)   15'

Cantata in 3 Parts
Text: Paul Claudel/Paul Hindemith
Soloists: mezzo-soprano, alto, tenor
Chorus: mixed
2.2.ca.2.bcl.2.cbn-4.2.3.1-timp.perc-pno-str
wind band: pic.1.0.Ebcl.3.asax.tsax.bar-sax.2-4.3/3cnt.3.euph.2-perc-org
Material on hire
Vocal score ED 4623-01/-02 / Piano reduction
ED 4623

Judaskuß (1958)   3'

from "12 Madrigale"
Text: Josef Weinheber
Chorus: mixed a cappella (5 prt)
SKR 20033 / Score PHA 705 / Study score
C 39901 / Choral score CHBL 348

Kraft fand zu Form (1958)   3'

from "12 Madrigale"
Text: Josef Weinheber
Chorus: mixed a cappella (5 prt)
SKR 20034 / Score PHA 705 / Study score
C 39901 / Choral score CHBL 351

Lady's lament (1937-38)   1'

from "5 Songs on old texts"
Chorus: mixed a cappella
Score PHA 705 / Choral score C 44002

Landsknechtstrinklied, Op. 33 (1923)   1'

from "Lieder nach alten Texten"
Chorus: mixed a cappella (6 prt)
C 31421 / Score PHA 705

Der Liebe Schrein, Op. 33

(1923)   1'

from "Lieder nach alten Texten"
Text: H. von Morungen
Chorus: mixed a cappella (5 prt)
C 31419 / Score PHA 705

Lied des Musterknaben

(1930)   2'

from "Chorlieder für Knaben"
Text: Karl Schnog
Chorus: boy's a cappella
C 32758 / Score PHA 705

Lied von der Musik - A Song of Music (1940)   2'

Text: George Tyler
Chorus: 3-prt female/S.S.A
str
Material on sale
Score ED 5416 / Parts ED 5416-11 (-15) /
Choral score ED 5416-01

Lieder für Singkreise, Op. 43/2 (1926)   3'

Text: various
Chorus: mixed a cappella
Material on sale
ED 1451

Infoline · e-Mail

Schott Musik International
Mainz: Schott.Musik.com@T-Online.de
London: 101627.166@compuserve.com

Liedersätze aus dem Kontrapunkt-Unterricht

(1912-14)
Chorus: mixed
Score **PHA 705**

Lügenlied (1928) 1'

Chorus: mixed (SAT)
str-[wind]
C 37723 / Score **B 107**

Mitwelt (1958) 3'

from "12 Madrigale"
Text: Josef Weinheber
Chorus: mixed a cappella (5 prt)
SKR 20031 / Score **PHA 705** / Study score
C 39901 / Choral score **CHBL 341**

Magisches Rezept (1958) 3'

from "12 Madrigale"
Text: Josef Weinheber
Chorus: mixed a cappella (5 prt)
SKR 20033 / Score **PHA 705** / Study score
C 39901 / Choral score **CHBL 349**

Mainzer Umzug (1962) 38'

Text: Carl Zuckmayer/Paul Hindemith
Soloists: soprano, tenor, baritone
Chorus: mixed
2(pic).2.2.2-2.2.2.0-2perc-str
Material on hire
SM / Libretto **BN 3376-60**

Mass (1963) 20'

Chorus: mixed a cappella
ED 5410 / Score **PHA 705**

Nun da der Tag des Tages müde wird (1939) 1'

Text: Friedrich Hölderlin
Chorus: male a cappella
Score **PHA 705** / Choral score **C 37586**

Of Household Rule (1937-38) 1'

from "5 Songs on old texts"
Chorus: mixed a cappella
Score **PHA 705** / Choral score **C 44003**

Old Irish Air (1940) 3'

The Harp that once thro' Tara's Halls
Chorus: mixed
pno/orch(hp-str)
Material on sale
Vocal score **ED 5408** / Piano reduction
ED 5408

Plöner Musiktag (1932) 16'

Cantata
Text: Martin Agricola
Soloists: voice, speaker
Chorus: youth
[wind]-[perc]-str
Material on sale
ED 1624

In Praise of Music (1928/43)

Soloists: mezzo-soprano, baritone
Chorus: mixed
fl-str
Score **AP 42-01** / Parts **AP 42-05**

Schundromane lesen (1930) 2'

from "Chorlieder für Knaben"
Text: Karl Schnog
Chorus: boy's a cappella
C 32760 / Score **PHA 705**

Sing-und Spielmusiken, Op. 45/1 (1928) 7'

I. Frau Musica
Text: Martin Luther
Soloists: mezzo-soprano, baritone
Chorus: mixed
fl-str
Material on sale
Score **ED 1460** / Parts **ED 1460 -05** / Vocal
score **ED 1460-01**

Sing-und Spielmusiken, Op. 45/2 (1928) 7'

II. 8 Canons
Soloists: mixed/female (2 prt)
2vn.va.[vc]
Score **ED 1462** / Parts **ED 1462-11 (-14)** /
Choral score **ED 1462-01**

Sing-und Spielmusiken, Op. 45/5 (1929) 4'

V. Martinslied
Text: Johannes Olorinus
Chorus: unison choir
[fl.ob.cl.bn-vn.va.vc.db]
Score **ED 1570** / Parts **ED 1570-11 (-13)** /
Choral score **ED 1570-01**

Spruch eines Fahrenden

(1928) 2'
Chorus: female a cappella
C 37729/B 107 / Score **PHA 705**

Die Stiefmutter (1939) 1'

Text: Friedrich Hölderlin
Chorus: male a cappella
Score **PHA 705** / Choral score **C 37587**

Der Tod (1931) 2'

Text: Friedrich Hölderlin
Chorus: male a cappella
C 33527 / Score **PHA 705**

Tauche deine Furcht in schwarzen Wein (1958) 3'

from "12 Madrigale"
Text: Josef Weinheber
Chorus: mixed a cappella (5 prt)
SKR 20031 / Score **PHA 705** / Study score
C 39901 / Choral score **CHBL 343**

Trink aus! (1958) 3'

from "12 Madrigale"
Text: Josef Weinheber
Chorus: mixed a cappella (5 prt)
SKR 20031 / Score **PHA 705** / Study score
C 39901 / Choral score **CHBL 344**

Trooper's Drinking Song

(1937-38) 1'
from "5 Songs on old texts"
Chorus: mixed a cappella
Score **PHA 705** / Choral score **C 44004**

True love (1937-38) 1'

from "5 Songs on old texts"
Chorus: mixed a cappella
Score **PHA 705** / Choral score **C 44001**

Über das Frühjahr (1929) 3'

Text: Bertold Brecht
Chorus: male a cappella
C 32545 / Score **PHA 705**

Das Unaufhörliche (1931) 85'

Oratorio in 3 parts
Text: Gottfried Benn
Soloists: soprano, tenor, baritone, bass
Chorus: mixed, children's
pic.2.2.2.2.[cbn]-3.2.2.1-timp.perc-[org]-str
Material on hire
Piano reduction **ED 3258**

Variations on an Old Dance Tune (1939) 6'

Chorus: male a cappella
C 37584 / Score **PHA 705**

Das verfluchte Geld (1939) 1'

Text: Friedrich Hölderlin
Chorus: male a cappella
Score **PHA 705** / Choral score **C 37585**

Vision des Mannes (1930) 3'

Text: Gottfried Benn
Chorus: male a cappella
C 32785 / Score **PHA 705**

Vom Hausregiment, Op. 33

(1923) 1'
from "Lieder nach alten Texten"
Text: Martin Luther
Chorus: mixed a cappella (6 prt)
C 31416 / Score **PHA 705**

Wahre Liebe (1938) 1'

Text: Heinrich V. Veldeke
Chorus: mixed a cappella
C 38418

Wer sich die Musik erkiest

(1952)
Sing-und Spielmusiken
Chorus: female voices
str
Score **B 107** / Parts **B 107-11 (-15)** / Choral
score **B 107-01**

Wer sich die Musik erkiest, Op. 45/2 (1928) 1'

Chorus: mixed (2 prt)
str
Material on sale
Vocal score **C 37723**

When Lilacs Last in the Door-Yard Bloom'd (1946) 60'

A Requiem for those we love
Text: Walt Whitman
Soloists: mezzo-soprano, baritone
Chorus: mixed
pic.1.1.ca.1.bcl.1.cbn-3.2.2.1-timp.3perc-org-str
Material on hire
Score **PHA 702** / Vocal score **ED 3800-01** /
Piano reduction **ED 3800** / Libretto **BN 3374-10**

Wir bauen eine Stadt (1930) 15'

Text: Robert Seitz
Chorus: children's
var. (high.medium.low)-tambourin.drum-
[pno]
Material on sale
Vocal score **ED 5424-01/-02** / Piano reduction
ED 5424

Höffer, Paul
1895-1949

Stage Works

**Der falsche Waldemar,
Op. 39** full evening

Opera in 4 Acts
Material on hire
SM

Orchestral Works

Festliche Ouvertüre 7'

concert band
Study score **FG 12-01** / Parts **FG 12-02**

Heitere Ouvertüre 6'

concert band
Score **FG 14-01** / Parts **FG 14-02**

**Symphonische Variationen,
Op. 47** 35'

3.2.3.2-4.3.3.1-timp.2perc-str
Material on hire
SM

Chamber & Instrumental Works

Tanzvariationen (1937) 22'

pno
ED 2648

Choral Works

Fröhliche Wanderkantate

(1939) 20'

Text: Joseph von Eichendorff
Soloists: alto, baritone
Chorus: mixed
fl-perc-str
SM

**Weihnachtskantate,
Op. 38** 10'

Chorus: mixed double
cl-tpt-pno-str
Material on hire
SM

Holland, Theodore
1878-1947

Orchestral Works

Spring Sinfonietta (1943) 12'

2.2.2.2-4.2.3.0-timp.2perc-cel-str
Material on hire
SL

Höller, Karl
1907-1987

Orchestral Works

Fuge (1948) 12'

str
Material on hire
Study score **ED 5016**

**Sweelinck-Variationen,
Op. 56** (1951) 23'

*pic.2.2(ca).2.2.cbn-4.2.3.1-timp.perc-
cel.hp-str*
Material on hire
Study score **ED 4062**

Chamber & Instrumental Works

Choral Passacaglia, Op. 61

(1963) 14'

organ solo
ED 5288

Ciacona, Op. 54 (1949) 12'

organ solo
ED 4346

**Flute Sonata No.2 in C,
Op. 53** (1948) 12'

fl-pno
FTR 112

Höller, Karl

b. Bamberg 25.7.1907, d. Hausham/Bavaria
14.4.1987

He studied at the Würzburg Conservatory
and at the Munich Academy of Music
where he took his exams in composition and
organ in 1929, and afterwards became a
master-class student of Joseph Haas. From
1931 he was in a practical organ-playing
course and from 1933-37 a teacher at the
Academy. From 1937 he gave lessons at the
Frankfurt/Main Conservatory and in 1949
took over Haas's composition master-class
at the Munich Conservatory where he was
appointed president in 1954. In 1955 he
became a member of the Berlin Academy of
Arts and in 1958 honorary member of the
Bavarian Academy of fine Arts.

2 Piano Sonatinas, Op. 58

(1962) 14'

ED 4817/ED 4818

Tessiner Klavierbuch, Op. 57

(1961) 21'

pno
ED 4750

Viola Sonata in E, Op. 62

(1966-67) 21'

va-pno
VAB 14

Infoline · e-Mail
Schott Musik International
Mainz: Schott.Musik.com@T-Online.de
London: 101627.166@compuserve.com

Höller, York

b.1944

Orchestral Works

Topic (1969-70) 14'

*3(pic).2.ca.2.bcl.2.cbn-2.4.2.0-timp.5perc-
cel.pno.hpd.hp-str(min:8.8.8.8.8)*
Material on hire
AVV

Choral Works

Décollage (1972) 20'

Chorus: 2 speaking chamber (also playing
percussion)
egtr(ebgtr)-vc(amp)-eorg-tape
Material on hire
AVV

Holliger, Heinz

b.1939

Stage Works

Come and Go (1976/77) 35'

Chamber Opera
Text: Samuel Beckett
Material on hire
SM

Der magische Tänzer

(1963-65) 35'

2 Scenes
Text: Nelly Sachs
Soloist: tape Soloists: 2 singers 2 speakers,
2 dancers
Chorus: mixed
Material on hire
SM

Not I (1978-80) 35'

Monodrama for soprano and tape
Text: Samuel Beckett
Material on sale
SM

What Where (1988) 35'

Chamber Opera
Text: Samuel Beckett
Material on hire
SM

Orchestral Works

Ad Marginem (1978-85) 7'

from the "Scardanelli Zyklus"
2fl.2cl-str(1.1.2.2.1)-tape
Material on hire
SM

Holliger, Heinz

b. Langenthal, canton of Berne 21.5.1939

A virtuoso composer who is also a musical
mystic, Holliger belongs to a rich and rare
breed of creative artists which also includes
Liszt and Skryabin amongst its numbers.
As an oboist, Holliger has used his vast
technical expertise to revolutionize and
extend the way other composers view the
instrument's potential. As a composer
himself, Holliger has been inspired by a
range of poets including Holderlin, Trakl and
Celan, and has explored the outer reaches
of musical expression, handling sound as if
a newly discovered medium.

Atembogen (1974-75) 22-25'

3.2afl.0.2.3bcl(cbcl).0-5.0.0.0-str(6.6.6.6.6)
Material on hire
Study score **ED 6848**

Bruchstücke (1978-85) 4'

from the "Scardanelli Zyklus"
*3(pic,afl).2(ca).2(bcl).2-2.1.1.0-timp.perc-
pno.hp-str(1.1.2.2.1)*
Material on hire
SM

Choral à 4 (1983) 3'

from the "Scardanelli Zyklus"
*Arr I: str(1.1.2.2.0)
Arr II: afl.cl-hn-va.vc
Arr III: ca.cl-hn.tbn-2vc*
Material on hire
SM

Choral à 8 (1983) 3'

from the "Scardanelli Zyklus"
cl.bcl-2hn-str(1.1.2.2.0)
Material on hire
SM

Eisblumen (1985) 6'

from the "Scardanelli Zyklus"
str(1.1.2.2.1)
Material on hire
SM

Elis - 3 Nachtstücke (1963/73) 6'

Arrangement of the version for piano
*2(2pic).2.2(bcl).2(cbn)-3.3.2.1-perc-
cel.pno.hp-str(12.10.8.8.6)*
Material on hire
SM

Engführung (1983-84) 8'

from the "Scardanelli Zyklus"
afl.ob d'am.ca.2cl.bn-2.0.0.0-str(1.1.2.2.1)
Material on hire
SM

Der ferne Klang (1983-84) 6'

from the "Scardanelli Zyklus"
*pic.fl.0.ob d'am.ca.2cl.bn-1.0.0.0-
str(1.0.2.1.0)-tape*
Material on hire
SM

2 Liszt-Transkriptionen

(1986) 12'

*2(2pic).(afl).(bfl).2.ca.4.bcl.cbcl.2.cbn-
5.4.4.1-timp.perc-hp-str(14.12.10.8.6)*
Material on hire
Study score **ED 7732**

Ostinato Funebre (1991) 8'

from the "Scardanelli Zyklus"
*2(2pic).2.2(bcl).cbcl.2-2.1.1.0-timp.3perc-
str(1.1.2.2.1)*
Material on hire
SM

Pneuma (1970) 16'

*4.4(2ca).4.4-4.4(4Bbtpt high).4.2-
timp.4perc-pno(eorg)-4 mouth pieces from
srec-shô-3harmonicas (Melodica)-4radios
[4 players[2execute 3rd and 4th flute]]
alt. version (1970): 2/4.2(2ca).2.2-2.2.2.1-
timp.3perc-pno(eorg)-4 mouth pieces from
srec-shô-3harmonicas (Melodica)/Yamaha
Pianica 36-4radios [4 players[2execute 3rd
and 4th flute]]*
Material on hire
Study score **AVV 311**

(S)irató (1992-93) 15'

*3(2pic).3(ca).2.2bcl.cbcl.3(cbn)-4.3.4.1-
timp.5perc-pno.cel.cym.hp-
str(14.12.10.10.6)*
Material on hire
Study score **ED 8439**

Schaufelrad (1983-84) 8'

from the "Scardanelli Zyklus"
Soloists: [4-5 female voices]
*0.afl.0.ob d'am.ca.1.2/2asax-1.1.1.0-
str(1.0.1.1.0)*
Material on hire
SM

Sommerkanon IV (1978) 2'

from the "Scardanelli Zyklus"
*fl/hn.afl.0.ob d'am.ca.1.0-hn/fl.0.0.0-
str(0.0.1.2.0)*
Material on hire
SM

Tonscherben (1985) 12-15'

4(pic,afl).3(ca).4(Ebcl,bcl).3(cbn)-
4.3(Bbtpt high).3.1-timp.4perc-pno.hp-
str(14.12.10.8.6)
Material on hire
Study score **ED 7624**

Concertos

Turm-Musik (1984) 25'

Soloist: flute
2(pic,afl).2(ob d'am,ca).2(bcl).2-2.1(pictpt).1(ttbn.btbn).0-timp.2-3perc-pno.hp-
str(1.1.2.2.1)-tape
Material on hire
Study score **ED 7680**

Violin Concerto (1993-95) 24'

"Hommage à Louis Soutter"
Soloist: violin
3(3pic,afl).3(ca).4(2bcl).2-3.3.3(tsax,bar-
sax).0-timp.5perc-cymb.cel.hp-
str(6.6.4.4.3)
Material on hire
Piano reduction **ED 8524**

Chamber & Instrumental Works

Chaconne (1975) 7'

cello solo
ED 6689

Chinderliecht (1995)

"Kinderleicht". Pieces for little and grown-
up children
pno
Material on sale
SM

Come and go (1976-77) 35'

Chamber music by Samuel Beckett
3cl(bcl,cbcl)
Material on sale
SM

Come and go (1976-77) 35'

Chamber music by Samuel Beckett
3fl(afl,bfl)
Material on sale
SM

Come and go (1976-77) 35'

Chamber music by Samuel Beckett
3va
Material on sale
SM

Duo (1982) 6'

vn.vc
Score **AVV 128**

Duo II (1988/94) 10'

vn.vc
Material on sale
SM

Elis - 3 Nachtstücke (1961/66) 6'

pno
ED 5383

Felicity's Shake-Wag (1988) 1'

vn.vc
Material on sale
SM

„h" for Wind Quintet

(1968) 11'

fl.ob.cl.bn-hn
Study score **AVV 100** / Parts **AVV 100-10**

Kreis (1971-72) 12'

4-7wind instruments or 3-6 wind & 1 str
instrument - [tape]
Study score **AVV 816** / Parts **AVV 816-10**

4 Lieder ohne Worte

(1982-83) 17'

vn-pno
Study score **AVV 131**

Lieder ohne Worte II (1985) 23'

vn-pno
ED 8430

Mobile (1962) 4 -12'

ob-hp
Score **ED 5384**

Piano Quintet (1989) 15'

ob(ca).cl(bcl).bn-hn-pno
Score and parts **ED 7805**

Prelude, Arioso and Passacaglia (1987) 13'

harp solo
ED 7697

Quodlibet pour Aurèle

(1986) 3'

2fl-2vn-hn
ED 7725

Sequenzen über Johannes I,32 (1962) 3'

harp solo
ED 5472

Sonate (in)solit(aire), dite "le Piémontois Jurassien"

(1995) 9'

ou "de Tramelan-dessus à Hameau-dessus"
flute solo
Material on sale
SM

String Quartet (1973) 30-35'

Study score **ED 6538** / Parts **ED 6539**

Studie II (1981) 10'

oboe solo
AVV 118

„(t)air(e)" (1980-83) 14'

flute solo
AVV 133

Trema (1981) 13'

viola solo
AVV 123

Trema (1981) 13'

cello solo
AVV 124

Trema (1983) 13'

violin solo
AVV 132

Trio (1966) 14-15'

ob/ca-va-hp
Score **AVV 306** / Study score **AVV 306**

Solo Voice(s)/Voice(s) and Piano/Guitar

Dörfliche Motive (1960-61/94) 4'

4 Bagatelles
Text: Alexander Xaver Gwerder
soprano-pno
Material on sale
SM

6 Lieder (1956/57) 12'

Text: Christian Morgenstern
soprano-pno
Material on sale
SM

5 Mileva-Lieder (1994) 12'

Text: Mileva Demenga
soprano-pno-[3 instruments]
Material on sale
SM

Variazioni su nulla (1988) 6'

Text: Giuseppe Ungaretti
counter tenor/alto-2 tenors-bass
Material on sale
SM

Solo Voice(s) and Instrument(s)/ Orchestra

Alb-Chehr (1991) 26'

Soloists: speaker and voices ad lib.
vn.db-2cl.2dulcimer-str-perc
Material on hire
SM

"Beiseit" (1990-91)   40'

12 Songs
Text: Robert Walser
Soloist: countertenor (or alto)
cl(bcl).acc.db
Score and parts **ED 7942**

Erde und Himmel (1961)   8'

Text: Alexander Xaver Gwerder
Soloist: tenor
fl-vn.va.vc-hp
Material on hire
Study score **ED 5031**

Glühende Rätsel (1964)   15'

Text: Nelly Sachs
Soloist: alto
fl.bcl(cbcl)-va.cymb.hp-5perc
Material on hire
Study score **ED 5001**

3 Liebeslieder (1960)   9'

Text: Georg Trakl
Soloist: alto
2(pic).2(ca).2(bcl).2(cbn)-2.4.(or 3).2.0-
timp.perc-cel.pno.hp.gtr-str
Material on hire
SM

2 Lieder (1992-93)   14'

Text: Georg Trakl
Soloist: alto
3(2afl).2(2ca).3(bcl).bcl-4.4.2.1-
timp.4perc-cel.pno.hp.gtr-str(14.12.10.8.6)
Material on hire
SM

4 Miniatures (1962-63)   6'

Text: Mechthild von Magdeburg/anony-
mous
Soloist: soprano
ob d'am-cel.hp
Material on sale
SM

Schaufelrad (1983-84)   8'

from the "Scardanelli Zyklus"
Soloists: 4-5 female voices ad lib
0.afl.0.ob d'am.ca.1.2/2asax-1.1.1.0-
str(1.0.1.1.0)
Material on hire
SM

Schwarzgewobene Trauer

(1961-62/66)   6'

Text: Heinz Weder
Soloist: soprano
ob-vc-hpd
Score **AVV 101**

Choral Works

Advent (1959)   12'

Motet after the Mystery-Play "Advent"
Text: August Strindberg
Soloists: soprano, alto
Chorus: mixed
Material on sale
SM

Dona Nobis Pacem (1968-69)   20'

Chorus: 12 solo voices(SSSAAATTTBBB)
a cappella
ED 6455

Gesänge der Frühe (1987)   28'

Text: Friedrich Hölderlin
Chorus: mixed
4(2pic,afl,bfl).3(ob d'am).4(bcl,cbcl).
3(cbn)-5.3.3.1-timp.3perc-pno.hp-
str(14.12.10.8.7)
Material on hire
SM

Die Jahreszeiten

(1975/78/79)   25-75'

Text: Friedrich Hölderlin
Chorus: mixed a cappella
[with instr. colla parte]
ED 6887

Jisei I (1988)   6'

Text: various
Soloists: CT/A, 2 T, Bar
(or four equal voices)
rin/[borduninstrument]
Material on sale
SM

Jisei II (1989)   6'

Text: Saimu
Chorus: CT/A, 2 T, Bar
(or four equal voices)
rin/[borduninstrument]
Material on sale
SM

Jisei III (1992)   6-8'

Text: Heinz Holliger
Soloists: CT/A, 2 T, Bar (or four equal
voices)
4rin/[borduninstruments]
Material on sale
SKR 20023

Der magische Tänzer

(1963-65)   35'

Versuch eines Ausbruchs
Soloists: alto, bass
Chorus: mixed (8 prt)
pic.2(pic).2(ob d'am,ca).2(Ebcl,bcl).2.cbn-
3.3.3.1-perc-cel.pno.2hp-str(10.0.7.6.6)-
tape
Material on hire
SM

Psalm (1971)   12'

Text: Paul Celan
Chorus: mixed a cappella (16 prt)
ED 6487

Scardanelli Zyklus

(1975-85)   150'

(s. also detailed enumeration)
Soloist: flute Soloists: alto, bass
Chorus: mixed
2(pic,afl).2(ca,ob d'am).2(bcl).cbcl.2-
2.1.1.0-timp.3perc-str(1.1.2.2.1)-tape
Material on hire
SM

Siebengesang (1966-67)   21'

Text: Georg Trakl
Soloist: oboe
Chorus: female chamber (4S, 3A)
2(2pic,afl).2(ca).2(Ebcl,bcl).0.cbn-2.2.2.1-
3perc-cel.pno.2hp-str(7.0.5.4.3)-loudspea-
ker
Material on hire
Study score **AVV 310** / Parts **AVV 104 (solo)**

Electronic Works

Cardiophonie (1971)   13'

ob-3 magnetophones
Study score **AVV 806** / Parts **AVV 134**

Introitus (1986)   9'

tape
SM

Not I (1978-80)   35'

Soloist: soprano
tape
SM

5 Pieces (1980)   23'

org-tape
ED 7742

Hopkins, Bill
b.1943

Chamber & Instrumental Works

Studies Vol.1 (1965-66)

pno
ED 11006*

Hormes, Hugo

Orchestral Works

Hungarian Dance

2(pic).2.2.2-4.0.3.0-timp.perc-hp-str
Material on hire
SM

Hosokawa, Toshio
b.1955

Orchestral Works

Medea Fragments I (1996)   8'

Overture
fl(pic,afl).ob(ca).2(bcl)-tbn-2perc-
str(2.0.1.1.1)
Material on hire
SJ

Hosokawa, Toshio

b. Hiroshima 23.10.1955

Hosokawa studied piano and composition in Tokyo. In 1976, he went to West Berlin to study composition with Isang Yun, piano with Rolf Kuhnert and music theory with Witold Szaloneck at the Hochschule der Künste. From 1983 to 1986, he studied at the Staatlichen Hochschule für Musik in Freiburg with Klaus Huber and Brian Ferneyhough. He has received many awards and prizes, including the Composition Prize of "the Young Generation in Europe", and the Energia Music Award. As Artistic Director, he has organized the annual Akiyoshidai International Contemporary Music Seminar and Festival since 1989.

In die Tiefe der Zeit (1994) 18'

vc-acc-str(min 4.4.3.2.1)
Material on hire
SJ

Ferne-Landschaft I (1987) 15'

3(2pic,afl).3.2.bcl.2.cbn-4.3.2.1-4perc-hp-str(14.12.10.8.6) Echo I: tp,tbn Echo II: tp,tbn
Material on hire
Study score SJ 1079

Ferne-Landschaft II (1996) 15'

3(2pic,afl).3.3.2.cbn-4.5.5.1-4perc-pno.hp-str(14.12.10.8.6)
Material on hire
SJ

Garten Lieder I (1995) 14'

*1(pic,afl).1(ca).2(bcl).1(cbn)-2.1.0.0-2perc-pno-str(2.2.2.2.1/4.4.4.2.1)
strings(ad lib.):5.0.2.2.1*
Material on hire
SJ

Hiroshima Requiem 14'

I. Preludio - "Night" (1989)
*3(2pic,afl).3.2.bcl.2.cbn-4.3.3.1-4perc-pno.cel.hp-str(16.14.12.10.8/18.16.14.12.10)
Echo I : hn.tpt.tb
Echo II : hn.tpt.tb*
Material on hire
SJ

Hiroshima Requiem 11'

III. "Dawn" (1992)
2(2pic).2.2(bcl).1.cbn-4.2.2.1-2perc-str(16.14.12.10.8/18.16.14.12.10)
Material on hire
SJ

Landscape VI (1994) 16'

Cloudscapes
1(pic,afl).1(ca).a(bcl).1(bcl).1(cbn)-1.1.0.0-perc-hp-str(min1.1.1.1.1)
Material on hire
SJ

Concertos

Flute Concerto "Per-Sonare"

(1988) 25'
Soloist: fl(pic,afl,bfl)
*2(pic).2.2(bcl).cbn-2.2.1.1-3perc-hp-str(12.10.8.6.4)
Echo I: (fl,pic)-hn.tpt.tbn-perc
Echo II: ob-hn.tpt.tbn-perc*
Material on hire
SJ

Interim (1994) 13'

Soloist: harp
fl(afl).cl-perc-vn.va.vc.db
Material on hire
SJ

Landscape III (1993) 19'

Soloist: violin
2(2pic).2.2(bcl).2(cbn)-2.2.2.1-4perc-hp-str(12.10.8.6.4 / 10.8.6.4.2)
Material on hire
SJ

New Seeds of Contemplation - "Mandara" (1995) 50'

Soloist: shômyô
gagaku ensemble
Material on hire
SJ

Seeds of Contemplation - "Mandara" (1986) 48'

Soloist: shômyô
gagaku ensemble
Material on hire
SJ

Utsurohi-Nagi (1996) 17'

Soloist: shô
*Group A: vn.va.db
Group B: 2vn.vc
Right: 2perc-hp-10vn.4va.3vc.
Left: 2perc-cel-10vn.4va.3vc.2db*
Material on hire
SJ

Chamber & Instrumental Works

Birds Fragments II (1990) 12'

shô-[perc]
Material on hire
SJ

Birds Fragments III (1990) 6'

shô-pic.bfl
Material on hire
SJ

Birds Fragments IV (1991) 9'

vc-perc-shô
Material on hire
SJ

Dan-sô (1984) 16'

vn.vc-pno
Material on hire
SJ

Fragments I (1988) 9'

shakuhachi-koto-sangen
Material on hire
SJ

Fragments II (1989) 12'

afl-str qrt
Material on hire
SJ

Fragments III (1989) 11'

fl.ob.cl.bn-hn
Material on hire
SJ 1094

Im Tal der Zeit... (1986) 16'

2vn.va.vc-pno
Material on hire
SJ

Intermezzo (1991) 9'

lute solo
Material on hire
SJ

Landscape I (1992) 14'

str qrt
SJ 1089

Landscape II (1992) 12'

hp-str qrt
Material on hire
SJ

Infoline · e-Mail
Schott Musik International
Mainz: Schott.Musik.com@T-Online.de
London: 101627.166@compuserve.com

Landscape IV (1993) 18'

str qnt
Material on hire
SJ

Landscape V (1993) 17'

shô-str qrt
Material on hire
SJ

Manifestation (1981) 9'

vn-pno
Material on hire
SJ

Melodia II (1977) 7'

pno
Material on hire
SJ

Nacht Klänge (1994/96) 8'

pno
Material on hire
SJ

Nocturne (1982) 12'

17-stringed koto
Material on hire
SJ

2 Pieces (1993) 4'

vn-pno/hp
Material on hire
SJ 1087

Sen I (1984/86) 12'

flute solo
SJ 1076

Sen II (1986) 13'

cello solo
Material on hire
SJ

Sen III (1988/91) 9'

sangen solo
Material on hire
SJ

Sen IV (1990) 12'

organ solo
Material on hire
SJ

Sen V (1991-92) 10'

accordion solo
SJ 1077

Sen VI (1993) 12'

percussion solo
Material on hire
SJ

Sen VII (1995) 11'

bassoon solo
Material on hire
SJ

Tokyo 1985 (1985) 70'

Soloist: shômyô
gagaku orchestra
Material on hire
SJ

Utsurohi (1986) 16'

shô-hp
Material on hire
SJ

Variations (1994) 12'

for wind ensemble
Soloist: clarinet
2ob.cl.2bn.cbn-2hn
Material on hire
SJ

Vertical Song I (1995) 9'

flute solo
Material on hire
SJ

Vertical Time Study I

(1992) 10'

cl-vc-pno
SJ 1078

Vertical Time Study II

(1993-94) 13'

tsax-pno-perc
Material on hire
SJ

Vertical Time Study III

(94) 12'

vn-pno
SJ 1087

Solo Voice(s)/Voice(s) and Piano/Guitar

Renka I (1986) 13'

Text: from "Manyo-shu"(in Japanese)
soprano-gtr/hp
SJ 1066

Solo Voice(s) and Instrument(s)/ Orchestra

Banka (1989) 12'

Text: from "Manyoshu"(in Japanese)
Soloist: soprano
17-stringed koto
Material on hire
SJ

Birds Fragments I (1990) 7'

Text: Saigyo (in Japanese)
Soloist: mezzo-soprano
afl-hp
Material on hire
SJ

Renka II (1987) 14'

Text: from "Manyo-shu"(in Japanese)
Soloist: soprano
2fl-2perc-cel-2hp
Material on hire
SJ

Renka III (1990) 18'

Text: Izumi-Shikibu (in Japanese)
Soloist: soprano/mezzo-soprano
vn.va da gamba/vc-hp
Material on hire
SJ

Super Flumina Babylonis

(1995) 18'

Soloists: soprano, alto
1(pic,afl).1(ca).2(bcl).1(cbn)-2.1.1.0-3perc-
hp-str(min 1.1.1.1.1)
strings (ad lib.):4.4.4.4.2/6.6.6.4.4
Material on hire
SJ

Choral Works

Ave Maria (1991) 10'

Chorus: mixed a cappella (16 prt)
SJ 1065

Ave Maris Stella (1991) 12'

Chorus: mixed a cappella
SJ 1088

Hiroshima Requiem 18'

II. "Death and Resurrection" (1989)
Text: Dr. Arata Osada (Japanese or English)
Soloists: 3 speakers, S.A.T.B (4 or 8)
Chorus: mixed, children's
3(2pic,afl).3.2.bcl.2.cbn-4.3.3.1-4perc-
pno.cel.hp-
str(16.14.12.10.8/18.16.14.12.10) - [tape]
Echo I : hn.tp.tb - perc (chain)
Echo II : hn.tp.tb - perc (chain)
Material on hire
SJ

Tenebrae (1993) 13'

Chorus: children's a cappella
Material on hire
SJ

Hsiao, Shusien

b.1942

Orchestral Works

Chinesischer Festmarsch 20'

2.2.2.2-3.2.2.0-timp.perc-hp-str
AVV

Huber, Klaus

b.1924

Stage Works

Jot oder Wann kommt der Herr zurück (1972-73) full evening

Opera
Text: Philip Oxman
Material on hire
SM

Orchestral Works

Cantio-Moteti-Interventiones

(1963) 14'

str
Material on hire
SM

Inventionen und Choral

(1956/65) 14'

2(pic).0.ca.2(bcl).1-4.2.2.0-timp.perc-hp.cel-str
alt. version: 2(pic).0.ca.2(bcl)-2.2.1.0-timp.perc-hp.cel-str
Material on hire
SM

Tenebrae (1966-67) 18'

3(2pic,afl).3(ca).4(Ebcl,2bcl).3cbn-4.3.4([cbtbn]).1-timp.4perc-cel.eorg-str
Material on hire
Study score **AVV 304**

Turnus (1973-74) 22'

Soloists: conductor, stage-manager
5(3pic,2afl).4.3.3(cbn).cbn-6.5.4.1-5perc-prep pno.org/eorg-str(6.6.6.6.6)-tape
Material on hire
SM

Concertos

Alveare Vernat (1965) 13'

Soloist: flute (alto flute)
12 solo str(4.3.2.2.1)/str orch
Material on hire
Study score **ED 5509** / Parts **ED 6270 (solo)**

"Erinnere dich an G..."

(1976-77) 20'

Soloist: double bass
afl(pic.fl.bfl.).ca.3Acl(2bcl/[3bcl]).bn(cbn)-3hn.tbn-hp.gtr-timp.perc-3va
Material on hire
Parts **ED 6953 (solo)**

"... ohne Grenze und Rand..."

(1976-77) 12'

Soloist: viola
3.2(2ob d'am).1.bcl.0-2.3.0.0-3perc-str(3.0.0.2.1)
Material on hire
SM

Huber, Klaus

b. Berne 30.11.1924

Klaus Huber studied violin with Steffi Geyer and composition with Wily Bukhard in Zurich, later with Boris Blacher in Berlin. In 1959 he received international attention as a composer with the world premiere of his cantata "Des Engels Anredung an die Seele" at the ISCM world music festival in Rome. From 1960-63 he taught at the Basle Academy of Music. In 1973 Klaus Huber became the sucessor of Wolfgang Fortner at the Conservatory of Freiburg/Breisgau; there he was teacher of composition class and director of the Institute of New Music until 1990. He has been a visiting professor, among other at the McGill University in Montreal, the Accademia Chigiana in Siena and the Bavarian Academy of Fine Arts, of the Berlin Academy of Arts and of the Mannheim Free Academy of Arts. He was been awarded many prizes including: 1959 Award of the Conrad Ferdinand Meyer Foundation of Zurich, 1969 Music Award of the canon of Berne, 1970 Beethoven Prize of the city of Bonn, 1978 Arts Award of the city of Basle, 1986 Premio Italia.

Tempora (1969) 25'

Soloists: violin, violin with scordatura
2(2pic,afl).1(ca).2(Ebcl,bcl).1-2(huntinghn).2(pictpt)tbtbn.btuba([pictuba])-4perc-cel.hpd.mand.hp.gtr-str(3.0.3.2.1)
Material on hire
AVV

Chamber & Instrumental Works

Ascensus (1969) 16'

fl-vc-pno
AVV 44

La Chace (1963) 5'

hpd
ED 5429

Moteti-Cantiones (1962-63) 25'

str qrt
Material on sale
ED 5385

2 Movements for 7 Brass Instruments (1957-58) 7'

2tpt.2hn.2tbn.tuba
Study score **ED 5038** / Parts **ED 5904**

Noctes Intelligibilis Lucis

(1961) 15'

ob-hpd
OBB 11

Sabeth (1966-67) 7'

afl-ca/va-hp
AVV 29

Transpositio ad Infinitum 15'

cello solo
ED 6684

Solo Voice(s)/Voice(s) and Piano/Guitar

Traumgesicht from "... inwendig voller figur ..."

(1971) 4'

Text: Bible
solo voice (baritone)
AVV 108

Solo Voice(s) and Instrument(s)/ Orchestra

... Ausgespannt... (1972) 17-20'

Soloist: baritone
3.1.3.1-3.1.1.0-perc-org.hp.gtr-str(3.0.1.3.1)-tape.loudspeaker
Material on hire
SM

Psalm of Christ (1967) 11'

Text: Psalm 22
Soloist: baritone
cl.bcl-hn.tpt.tbn-vn.va.vc
Score **AVV 305** / Parts **AVV 305-10**

Choral Works

Hiob 19 (1971) 10'

Text: Bible
Chorus: mixed
hn.tpt.tbn-perc-3vc.db
Score **AVV 102** / Parts **AVV 102-10** / Choral
score **AVV 102-01**

„... inwendig voller Figur...“

(1970-71) 24'

Text: Johannes-Apokalypse/Albrecht Dürer
Chorus: mixed
*5(4pic,afl).4.4(Ebcl,Acl,bcl).4(2cbn)-
4.5.5([pictpt]).4cbtbn.3Wagnertuba(dtuba,b
tuba).cbtuba-timp.5perc-2hp-
str(0.0.10.0.8)-tape.loudspeaker*
Material on hire
Study score **AVV 312**

Kanon zum Jahresbeginn

(1977) 1'

Text: Simon Huber
Chorus: mixed a cappella
ED 6714

Humel, Gerald
b.1931

Stage Works

**Die Folterungen der Beatrice
Cenci** (1971) 30'

Ballet
Material on hire
SM

Orchestral Works

**Die Folterungen der Beatrice
Cenci** (1971) 30'

Concert Version
pic.fl.afl.bfl-tpt.flhn-2perc-pno-vn
Material on hire
SM

Lepini (1977) 26'

*4(3pic,afl).2.ca.Ebcl.1.2.cbn-
4.3.btpt.2.btbn.1-timp.4perc-hp-str*
Material on hire
SM

Chamber & Instrumental Works

Arabesque

gtr-perc-vc
Score and parts **ED 6771**

Hummel, Bertold
b.1925

Orchestral Works

Kontraste, Op. 50 (1973) 18'

str
Material on hire
SM

**Symphonic Overture,
Op. 81d** (1987) 8'

*pic.2.2.Ebcl.3.bcl.2asax.tsax.barsax.2-
4.3.3.euph.2-timp.perc-db*
Score **SHS 1001** / Parts **SHS 1001-50**

Visionen, Op. 73 (1980) 22'

*3(pic).2.ca.2.bcl.2.cbn-4.3.3.1-timp.4perc-
hp-str*
Material on hire
SM

Concertos

Percussion Concerto, Op. 70

(1978/82) 32'

Soloist: percussion
*3(pic).2.ca.2.bcl.2-4.3.3.1-timp.3-4perc-hp-
str*
Material on hire
Parts **ED 7267 (solo)** / Piano reduction
ED 7830

Chamber & Instrumental Works

"In Memoriam-", Op. 74

(1980) 14'

perc-org
ED 7182

Invocations, Op. 68a (1978) 22'

tpt-org
ED 6814

Invocations, Op. 68b (1978) 22'

ssax-org
ED 6814-01

Klangfiguren (1972) 10'

solo str(10vn.3va.3vc.db)
Score and parts **ED 6542**

Eine kleine Blasmusik

(1976) 9'

3tpt.3tbn
Score **BLK 314** / Parts **BLK 315/316**

Notturno, Op. 75b (1982) 3'

in: Das neue Klavierbuch, Vol. 3
pno
ED 7095

Sonata Brevis, Op. 87b

(1987) 12'

arec-pno
OFB 169

Sonatina, Op. 75a (1981) 10'

hn-pno
COR 7

Tempo di Valse (1982) 4'

vibraphone solo
BAT 34

Humperdinck, Engelbert
1854-1921

Stage Works

Hänsel und Gretel

(1893) full evening

Fairytale in 3 Scenes
Arranger: Irmen
Text: Adelheid Wette
Material on hire
Score **ED 7400** / Study score **ETP 913/
ED 3423-01** / Vocal score **ED 10281 (engl.)/
ED 8029 (dt.)** / Libretto **ED 10085-01 (engl.)**

Orchestral Works

Abendsegen 3'

Arranger: A. Wolf
*2.2.Ebcl.3.2asax.tsax.barsax.2-3.3thn.
2flhn.2.3.euph.2
alt. version: Ebcl/fl.3cl-
2hn.thn.2flhn.euph.2tuba*
Study score **BSS 42959-01** / Score and parts
BSS 42959

Lied des Sandmännchens, Abendsegen und Traumpantomime (1893) 12'

from the Fairytale "Hänsel und Gretel"
3.2.2.2-4.2.3.1-timp.perc-hp-str
Score **BSS 25751** / Study score **ED 3424** /
Parts **BSS 25751-10**

Overture (1893) 8'

from the Fairytale "Hänsel und Gretel"
3.2.2.2-4.2.3.1-timp.perc-str
Score **ED 3424** / Study score **ETP 1101** /
Piano reduction **BSS 25750**

Overture (1914) 10'

from the opera in 2 Acts
"Die Marketenderin"
3.3.2.2-4.3.3.0-timp.perc-str
SM

Chamber & Instrumental Works

String Quartet in C Major (1920)

Score **ED 3522** / Parts **ED 3172**

Solo Voice(s)/Voice(s) and Piano/Guitar

Abendsegen 3'

Text: Adelheid Wette
medium voice-pno
ED 09713

Abendsegen 3'

Text: Adelheid Wette
soprano-mezzo-soprano-pno
ED 09719

Besenbinderlied

baritone-pno
BSS 25787

Dance Duet

"Brüderchen, komm tanz mit mir"
soprano-mezzo-soprano-pno
ED 09711

Lied des Taumännchens

soprano-pno
BSS 25795

Choral Works

Abendsegen 3'

Text: Adelheid Wette
Arranger: Friedrich Zipp
Chorus: female
pno
CHBL 512

Humpert, Hans
1901-1943

Orchestral Works

Music for Orchestra (1936) 27'

2.2.2.2-4.2.3.1-str
Material on hire
SM

Chamber & Instrumental Works

Prelude and Toccata (1934) 9'

organ solo
ED 2426

Prelude, Canzone and Fugue
(1934) 10'

organ solo
ED 2268

Violin Sonata (1938)

vn-pno
ED 2686

Choral Works

Ich bin vergnügt (1930) 1'

Chorus: mixed a cappella (3 prt)
SM

Husa, Karel
b.1921

Orchestral Works

Divertimento (1949) 16'

str
Material on hire
SM

Fantasies for Orchestra
(1956-57) 20'

pic.1.1.1.0-0.3.0.0-timp.perc-pno-str
Material on hire
SM

Husa, Karel

b. Prague 7.8.1921

Husa studied composition and conducting at the Prague Conservatory, giving performances as a guest in the Prague Radio Orchestra and in public concerts in 1945/46. In 1946 he went to Paris to study composition with Arthur Honnegger and Nadia Boulanger and conducting with Jean Fournet, André Cluytens and Eugéne Bigot. Since 1954 he has been professor of harmony and director of the University Symphony Orchestra at the Cornell University in Ithaca (New York). In 1969 he was awarded the Pulitzer Prize, in 1983 the Kennedy Center Friedheim Award, in 1989 the American Academy of Arts and Letters Award and in 1993 the Grawemeyer Award. In March 1995 he became a member of the American Academy of Arts and Letters; on 28th October 1995 he was awarded the Czech Order of Merit first-class.

4 Little Pieces (1955) 15'

str
Score **CON 84** / Parts **CON 84-70/-71**

Mosaïques pour orchestre
(1960) 15'

pic.1.1.ca.1.bcl.1-2.2.2.0-timp.4perc-cel.pno.hp-str
Material on hire
SM

Musique d'Amateurs (1952) 15'

ob-tpt-perc-str
Material on hire
SM

Nocturno from "Fantasies for Orchestra" (1956-57) 5'

pic.1.1.1.0-0.3.0.0-perc-pno-str(8.7.6.5.4)
Material on hire
SM

Portrait (1953) 11'

str
Material on hire
SM

Symphony No.1 (1953) 28'

*pic.2.2.ca.2.bcl.2.cbn-4.3.3.1-timp.3perc-
pno.hp/2hp-str*
Material on hire
SM

Concertos

Concertino, Op. 10 (1949-50) 16'

Soloist: piano
2.2.2.2-2.2.0.0-timp.perc-str
Material on hire
SM

Poème (1959) 13'

Soloist: viola
0.1.0.0-1.0.0.0-pno-str
Material on hire
Piano reduction **VAB 17**

Chamber & Instrumental Works

8 Böhmische Duette (1955) 17'

pno (4hnd)
ED 4779

Evocations de Slovaquie
(1951) 15'

cl-va.vc
Score **ED 6037** / Parts **ED 6038**

Piano Sonata, Op. 11 (1952) 24'

ED 4348

String Quartet No.1, Op. 8
(1948) 18'

Study score **ED 4262** / Parts **ED 4347**

String Quartet No.2 (1953) 20'

Score and parts **ED 6012**

I

Ichiyanagi, Toshi
b.1933

Orchestral Works

Interspace (1987) 9'

str(6.6.5.5.0/8.8.7.7.0)
Material on hire
Study score **SJ 1047**

Symphonic Movement "Kyoto" (1989) 10'

*pic.2.afl.2.2.2.cbn-4.3.2.btbn.0-4perc-
pno.hp-str(16.14.12.10.8)*
Material on hire
SJ

Symphony for Chamber Orchestra "Time Current"
(1986) 20'

1.1.1.1-1.1.1.0-2perc-pno-str(1.1.1.1.1)
Material on hire
SJ

Voices from the Environment
(1989) 12'

*3(pic).3.3.2.cbn-4.3.2.btbn.1-timp.4perc-
pno-str(16.14.12.10.8/14.12.10.8.6)*
Material on hire
SJ

Concertos

Concerto for Koto and Chamber Orchestra "The Origin" (1989) 17'

Soloist: koto
*2(pic).2.2.2-2.2.0.0-2perc-pno-
str(8.6.4.4.2)*
Material on hire
SJ

Engen (1982) 22'

Soloist: koto
*2.2.ca.2.2-4.2.2.btbn.0-perc-pno(cel).hp-
str(14.14.12.10.6)*
Material on hire
SJ

Existence (1989) 12'

Soloist: organ
*3(pic).2.ca.2.bcl.2.cbn-4.3.2.btbn.0-4perc-
hp-str(14.12.10.8.6)*
Material on hire
SJ

In the Reflection of Lighting Image (1980) 23'

Soloist: percussion
*pic.1.2.1.Ebcl.2-4.2.1.btbn.0-pno(cel).hp-
str(12.10.8.8.6)*
Material on hire
SJ

Ichiyanagi, Toshi

b. Hyogo prefecture 4.2.1933

Ichiyanagi studied composition with Kishio Hirao and John Cage, and piano with Chieko Hara and Beveridge Webster. After attending the Julliard School of Music and the New School for Social Research between 1954-60, he returned to Japan where he introduced many new musical concepts, including Cage's idea of indeterminancy. He has received many awards including the Elizabeth A Coolidge Prize and the Serge Koussevitsky Prize. Currently engaged in musical events for the promotion of contemporary music.

Interplay (1992) 20'
Soloist: flute
str(10.0.4.3.2)
Material on hire
SJ

Luminous Space (1991) 23'
Soloists: shô, ondes martenot
3(pic).3.3.2.cbn-4.3.2ttbn.btbn.0-
timp.3perc-pno(cel)-str(16.14.12.10.8)
Material on hire
SJ

Paganini Personal (1984-86) 13'
Soloist: marimba
pic.2.2.2.2-4.2.2.btbn.0-4perc-pno-
str(14.12.10.10.8)
Material on hire
SJ

Piano Concerto No.1 "Reminiscence of Spaces"
(1981) 14'
Soloist: piano
pic.2.2.ca.2.2.cbn-4.2.2.btbn.0-4perc-
str(14.12.10.10.8)
Material on hire
SJ

Piano Concerto No.2 "Winter Portrait" (1987) 15'
Soloist: piano
pic.2.3.3.2-4.3.2.btbn.0-5perc-
str(14.12.10.8.6)
Material on hire
Study score SJ 1060

Piano Concerto No.3 "Cross Water Roads" (1991) 17'
Soloist: piano
2(pic).2(ca).2.2.cbn-2.2.btbn.0-2perc-
str(12.10.8.8.6 / 8.6.4.4.2)
Material on hire
SJ

Time Surrounding (1984) 12'
Soloist: percussion
pic.2.3.3.2.cbn-4.3.3.1-8perc-pno-
str(12.10.8.8.6)
Material on hire
SJ

Violin Concerto "Circulating Scenery" (1983) 27'
Soloist: violin
pic.2.3.3.3-4.3.2.btbn.0-3perc-pno(cel)-
str(14.12.10.10.8)
Material on hire
Study score SJ 1023

Chamber & Instrumental Works

Accumulation (1984) 10'
shakuhachi-2koto-sangen
Material on hire
SJ

Before Darkness appears
(1981) 12'
acc-pno
Material on hire
SJ

Cloud Atlas I, II, III (1985) 10'
pno
SJ 1025

Cloud Brocade - Cloud Atlas VII (1989) 4'
pno
SJ 1059

Cloud Current - Cloud Atlas IX (1989) 3'
pno
SJ 1059

Cloud Falls - Cloud Atlas VI
(1987) 4'
pno
SJ 1048

Cloud Figures (1984) 9'
oboe solo
SJ 1036

Cloud in the Distance - Cloud Atlas VIII (1989) 3'
pno
SJ 1059

Cloud Rainbow - Cloud Atlas V (1987) 7'
pno
SJ 1048

Cloud Shore, Wind Roots
(1984) 80'
ancient instruments-gagaku ensemble
Material on hire
SJ

Cloud Vein - Cloud Atlas IV
(1987) 3'
pno
SJ 1048

Dimensions (1990) 15'
organ solo
Material on sale
SJ

Distance (1979) 20'
noh dance.noh fl.fl.cl-2perc-pno-vc
Material on hire
SJ

Enenraku (1982) 45'
gagaku ensemble
Material on hire
SJ

Fantasy (1992) 8'
organ solo
SJ 1069

Farewell to ... (1992) 6'
To the Memory of Luigi Nono
pno
Material on sale
SJ

Flowers Blooming in Summer (1982) 7'
hp-pno
SJ 1016

Friends I (1990) 4'
violin solo
Material on sale
SJ

Hikari-nagi (1983) 11'
ryuteki-perc
Material on hire
SJ

Hoshi no Wa (1983) 12'
shô solo
Material on sale
SJ

Imaginary Scenes (1995)   6'

pno
SJ 1093

In Memory of John Cage
(1992-93)   3'

pno
SJ

Inexhaustible Fountain
(1990)   8'

pno
Material on hire
SJ

Inter Konzert (1987)   10'

pno
SJ 1042

Intercross (1993)   12'

vn-pno
SJ 1075

Interrelation (1991)   14'

vc-pno
Material on hire
SJ

Katachi naki Mugen no Yoha
(1987)   11'

koto solo
Material on sale
SJ

Kaze no Iroai (1980)   11'

flute solo
Material on sale
SJ

Multiple Space (1976)   10'

organ solo
Material on sale
SJ 10000

Music for Piano No.6
(1961)   Var.

Material on sale
SJ

Ogenraku (1980)   40'

gagaku ensemble
Material on hire
SJ

Paganini Personal (1982)   11'

marimba-pno
SJ 1013

Perspectives (1986)   6'

violin solo
SJ 1033

Piano Nature (1989)   11'

pno
Material on sale
SJ

Piano Quintet "Prana"
(1985)   14'

fl.cl-vn.vc-pno
Material on sale
SJ 1024

Portrait of Forest (1983)   9'

marimba solo
SJ 1018

Recurrence (1979)   14'

fl.cl-perc-pno.hp-vn.vc
Material on hire
Score SJ 1020

Reigaku Symphony No.2 "Kokai" (1989)   58'

gagaku orch-reigaku orch-shomyo
Material on hire
SJ

Reigaku Symphony "The Shadows Appearing through Darkness" (1987)   50'

*ancient instruments-gagaku orch-shomyo
(Buddhist chanting)*
Material on hire
SJ

Rinkaiikiy (1983)   12'

sangen solo
Material on sale
SJ

Scenes IV (1981)   8'

vn-pno
Material on sale
SJ

Scenes V (1982)   8'

vn-pno
Material on sale
SJ

Sensing the Color in the Wind (1988)   12'

shakuhachi-2koto
Material on hire
SJ

Sonata (1954)   14'

vn-pno
Material on sale
SJ

The Source (1989)   11'

marimba solo
SJ 1061

Still Time I (1986)   21'

shô solo
Material on sale
SJ

Still Time II (1986)   6'

kugo solo
Material on sale
SJ

Still Time III (1987)   6'

harp solo
Material on sale
SJ

String Quartet (1957)   23'

Material on sale
SJ

String Quartet No.2 "Interspace" (1986)   22'

Material on hire
SJ

String Quartet No.3 "Inner Landscape" (1994)   14'

Material on hire
SJ

Ten, Zui, Ho, Gyaku (1988)   18'

shakuhachi-ondes martenot
Material on hire
SJ

Time in Tree, Time in Water
(1981)   22'

perc-pno
Material on sale
SJ

Transfiguration of the Flower (1988)   13'

koto-sangen-shakuhachi
Material on hire
SJ

Transfiguration of the Moon
(1988)   12'

vn-sho
Material on sale
SJ

Transstream (1987)   Var.

18perc
Material on sale
SJ

Trio "Interlink" (1990)   12'

vn-pno-perc
SJ 1068

Troposphere (1990)   13'

ondes martenot-marimba
SJ

Two Existence (1980)   9'

2pno
SJ 1004

Voices of Water (1988)   11'

hitsu
Material on sale
SJ

Wa (1981)   12'

13 stringed koto.17 stringed koto-pno-perc
Material on hire
SJ

Water Relativity (1989) 14'

hitsu-kin
Material on hire
SJ

The Way (1990) 35'

2sho-2hichiriki-shakuhachi-koto-biwa-2perc-dancer
Material on hire
SJ

The Way II (1990) 40'

4shô-u-4hichiriki-o hichiriki-shakuhachi-2koto-biwa-3perc-10shômyo-dance
Material on hire
SJ

Wind Gradation (1989) 11'

ryuteki-pno
Material on sale
SJ

Wind Stream (1989) 9'

flute solo
Material on sale
SJ

Wind Trace (1984) 13'

3 keyboard percussion instruments
SJ 1031

Winter Portrait II (1987) 8'

koto solo
Material on sale
SJ

Yami o Irodoru Mono
(1985) 10'

2vn-pno
Material on sale
SJ

Solo Voice(s)/Voice(s) and Piano/Guitar

Aru Toki (1981) 10'

Text: Santoka (in Japanese)
soprano-pno
Material on hire
SJ

Solo Voice(s) and Instrument(s)/ Orchestra

Music for Art Kites (1989) 7'

Text: Makoto Ooka (in Japanese)
soprano-fl
Material on hire
SJ

Symphony "Berlin Renshi"
(1988) 42'

Text: various
Soloists: soprano, tenor
pic.3(pic).3.3.2.cbn-4.3.2.btbn.0-7perc-pno(cel).hp-str(16.14.12.10.8)
Material on hire
SJ

Choral Works

Genshiryoku Sensuikan "Onagazame" no Seitekina Kokai to Jisatsu no Uta
(1989) 17'

Text: Makoto Ooka (Japanese)
Chorus: mixed a cappella
Material on sale
SJ

Heso no Uta (1984) 15'

Text: Seikyo Muchaku (Japanese)
Chorus: children's a cappella
Material on sale
SJ

Requiem (1985) 23'

Text: Koichi Kihara (Japanese)
Chorus: male a cappella
Material on sale
SJ

Syntax (1986) 20'

Text: Japanese Proverbs (Japanese)
Chorus: mixed a cappella
Material on sale
SJ

Electronic Works

Intoxicant Moon (1991) 12'

ondes martenot
SJ

Music for Living Space
(1970) 10'

electronics
Material on hire
SJ

Parallel Music (1962) 10'

electronics
Material on hire
SJ

Présage (1986) 16'

6 ondes martenot
Material on hire
SJ

Tokyo 1969 (1969) 15'

electronics
Material on hire
SJ

Ince, Kamran
b.1960

Orchestral Works

Before Infrared (1986) 10'

3.2.3.3-4.3.3.1-timp.3perc-hp-str
Material on hire
EAM

Deep Flight (1988) 11'

1.1.1.1-2.2.3.1-timp.perc-pno-str
Material on hire
EAM

Domes (1993) 12'

3(pic,afl).3(ca).3(bcl).3(cbn)-4.3.3.1-3perc-pno.hp-str
Material on hire
Study score **EA 742**

Ebullient Shadows (1987) 14'

4.3.4.4-4.3.3.1-timp.3perc-pno.hp-str
Material on hire
Study score **EA 615X**

Hot, Red, Cold, Vibrant
(1992) 10'

2(pic).3(ca).3(Ebcl,bcl).2-4.3.3.0-3perc-pno.hp-str
Material on hire
EAM

Infrared Only (1985) 10'

3.2.3.3-4.3.3.1-timp.3perc-hp-str
Material on hire
EAM

Lipstick (1991) 22'

2(pic).2.2(Ebcl,bcl).4sax.2-1.2.2.0-3perc-pno.synth.hp-str
Material on hire
EAM

Plexus (1993) 23'

1(pic).0.1.4sax.0-0.2.2.0-drum machine.synth.pno.egtr.ebass-str
Material on hire
EAM

Symphony No.1 (1989) 28'

Castles in the Air
3.3.3.3-4.3.3.1-timp.3perc-pno-str
Material on hire
EAM

Concertos

Piano Concerto (1984) 19'

Soloist: piano
3.2.2.3-4.2.3.1-timp.3perc-str
Material on hire
EAM

Ince, Kamran

b. Montana 1960

Already widely commissioned and with an impressive list of orchestral works to his credit, Kamran Ince received his early musical training in Turkey, at the Ankara and Izmir Conservatories. Later he attended the Oberlin Conservatory and the Eastman School of Music, where he earned a doctorate. His numerous awards include the Prix de Rome, a Guggenheim Fellowship, the Lili Boulanger Prize and the Rose Prize from the Brooklyn Philharmonic.

Chamber & Instrumental Works

The Blue Journey (1982) 12'

pno
Material on sale
EAM

Cross Scintillations (1986) 12'

pno (4hnd)
EA 624X

Fantasy of a Sudden Turtle

(1990) 19'

vn.va.vc-pno
Material on sale
EAM

Hammer Music (1990) 15'

fl(pic).cl(bcl)-perc-synth-vn.va.vc
Material on hire
EAM

Kaç (1983) 9'

Escape
asax-perc-pno
Material on sale
EAM

Köçekçe (1984) 10'

vn-pno
Material on sale
EAM

My Friend Mozart (1987) 3'

pno
EA 591

Night Passage (1992) 19'

fl.bcl(Ebcl)-tpt-drums-synth-vn(amp).vc(amp)-bass
Material on hire
EAM

One Last Dance (1991) 4'

fl.Ebcl.bcl.bn-perc
Material on hire
EAM

Sonnet #395 (1989) 12'

fl(pic,afl).ob.cl.bn-perc-vn.vc
Material on hire
EAM

An Unavoidable Obsession

(1988) 5'

pno
EAM

Waves of Talya (1989) 16'

fl.cl-vn.vc-pno-perc
Material on hire
EAM

Solo Voice(s) and Instrument(s)/ Orchestra

Matinees (1989) 14'

Text: James Merrill
Soloist: speaker
fl(afl,pic).ob(ca).cl(bcl).bn-hn
Material on hire
EAM

Ireland, John

1897-1962

Concertos

Legend (1933) 15'

Soloist: piano
2(pic).1.ca.2.2-4.0.2ttbn.0-timp.perc-str
Material on hire
ED 3528 / Score ED 3302 / Piano reduction
ED 2773

Solo Voice(s)/Voice(s) and Piano/Guitar

Songs sacred and profane

(1929-31)

Text: Meynell, Werner, William Butler Yeats
high voice-pno
ED 11202

Ishii, Kan

b.1921

Choral Works

Gesang eines welken Baumes und der Sonne (1956/66) 12'

Text: K. Nakada
Soloists: tenor
Chorus: male
pno
Score ED 5471 / Choral score ED 5471-01

J

Jarnach, Philipp
1892-1982

Orchestral Works

Morgenklangspiel, Op. 19
(1926)   15'

Romancero II
*3(pic).2.ca.2.bcl.3(cbn)-4.3.3.0-timp.2perc-
hp-str(min:14.14.8.8.6)*
Material on hire
SM

Musik mit Mozart, Op. 25
(1935)   24'

Symphonic Variations
3(pic).2(ca).2.3cbn-3.2.3.0-timp.perc-str
Material on hire
SM

Musik zum Gedächtnis der Einsamen (1952)   15'

str
Study score **ED 4418** / Parts **ED 4494**

Sinfonia brevis, Op. 11
(1923)   22'

*[pic].3.2.ca.2.bcl.3.[cbn]-4.3.3.btuba-
timp.2perc-[cel].hp-str(min:14.14.8.8.6)*
Material on hire
SM

Vorspiel I, Op. 22 (1930)   12'

*3(pic).2.ca.3(bcl).3(cbn)-4.3.3.1-
timp.3perc-pno-str*
Material on hire
SM

Concertos

Concertino in E minor, Op. 31 (1952)   15'

After Giovanni Platti (approx. 1759)
Soloists: 2 violins
str
Material on hire
SM

Chamber & Instrumental Works

Das Amrumer Tagebuch, Op. 30 (1947)   10'

3 Klavierstücke
pno
ED 3958

Ballabible, Op. 17/1 (1924)

pno
ED 1735

Jarnach, Philipp

b. Noisy 21.8.1921, d. Bornsen/Schleswig-Holstein 17.12.1982

From 1907 studied Jarnach piano with Risler and harmony with Lavignac in Paris, was teacher at the Zurich Conservatory from 1918-21, then music critic of the Berlin Börsen-Courier. From 1927-49 he worked as a professor of composition at the Cologne Conservatory; from 1949-59 he was director and from 1959-70 professor of composition of the Hamburg Conservatory. One of his most important students was Kurt Weill. From 1955 he was a member of the Berlin Academy of Arts and of the Hamburg Free Academy of Arts. The refined works of Jarnach who was one of the earliest composers of New Music in Germany show an unfailing strength of form which was part of his Romantic origin and training.

Burlesca, Op. 17/3 (1924)

pno
ED 1737

10 kleine Klavierstücke
(1927)   9'

pno
ED 1410

Konzertstück, Op. 21 (1930)   9'
Romancero III
organ solo
ED 2087

Piano Sonata No.1, Op. 18
(1925)   10'

Romancero I
ED 1738

Piano Sonata No.2 (1952)   23'
ED 4387

Sarabande, Op. 17/2 (1924)

pno
ED 1736

Solo Voice(s)/Voice(s) and Piano/Guitar

Der wunde Ritter, Op. 15/4
(1922)   6'
Text: Heinrich Heine
voice-pno
BSS 30797-04

Jarre, Maurice
b.1924

Orchestral Works

Concertino   3'
No. 11 from the "Divertimento für Mozart"
*2.2.2.2.2bsthn-2.2.2.0-4timp.perc-
str(18.0.4.3)*
Material on hire
SM (Co-prod: UE)
Copyright USA: EAM/Italy: Ed. Suvini
Zerboni

Jirásek, Jan
b.1955

Choral Works

Lukas-Passion (1995)
(Johann Sebastian Bach)
Oratorio
Arranger: Jan Jirásek
Soloists: 2 tenors, 2 basses
Chorus: mixed, boy's
2(pic).2.2.2-2.2.1.0-timp.2perc-hpd(org)-str
Material on hire
SM

Josephs, Wilfried
b.1927

Orchestral Works

The Ants, Op. 7 (1955)   7'
(Die Ameisen). Comedy-Overture
2.2.2.2-4.3.3.1-timp.4perc-xyl-str
Material on hire
Eu

Elegy, Op. 13 (1957)   6'
str
Material on hire
Eu

Concertos

**Meditatio de Beornmundo,
Op. 30** (1961)   15'
Concertante for viola and small orchestra
Soloist: viola
0.2.0.0-2.0.0.0-str(5.4.2.2.1)
Material on hire
Eu

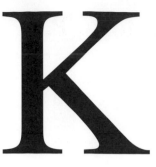

Kadosa, Pál
1903-1983

Orchestral Works

Sérénade, Op. 65 (1967-68)   7'
1.1.1.1-1.0.0.0-str(4.4.2.2.2)
Score **CON 86** / Parts **CON 86-50/-60**

Kai, Naohiko
b.1932

Concertos

Violin Concerto (1969)   11'
Soloist: violin
2.2.3.3-4.3.3.1-perc-cel.hp-str
Material on hire
SJ

Kalabis, Viktor
b.1923

Chamber & Instrumental Works

Sonata, Op. 32 (1970)   12'
tbn-pno
ED 6522

Variations, Op. 31 (1969)   11'
cl-hn
COR 2

Kaminski, Heinrich
1886-1946

Concertos

Concerto for Orchestra with Piano (1936)   26'
Soloist: piano
1.1.0.1-1.1.0.0-str
Material on hire
SM

Choral Works

6 Chorales (1915)   8'
Chorus: mixed a cappella
C 30878

Motet „O Herre Gott" (1918)   6'
Text: Liturgical
Chorus: mixed [a cappella]
org
Score **ED 4195** / Choral score **ED 4195-01**

Psalm 130, Op. 1a (1912)   4'
Text: Bible
Soloist: soprano
Chorus: mixed a cappella
C 30879

Der Tag ist hin (1915)   1'
Text: J.Chr. Ruben
Chorus: mixed a cappella
CHBL 251

Vergiß mein nicht, mein allerliebster Gott (1915)   1'
(Johann Sebastian Bach)
Chorus: mixed a cappella
CHBL 252

Kauffmann, Leo Justinus
1901-1944

Chamber & Instrumental Works

Divertimento (1938)
fl-va da gamba/va-hpd
ED 2688

Little Suite (1938)
va-pno
SM

Kaufmann, Armin
1902-1980

Concertos

Musik, Op. 38   19'
Soloist: trumpet
str
Material on hire
AVV

Kaufmann, Dieter
b.1941

Stage Works

Warten auf Musik   15'
Ballet
Material on hire
AVV

Concertos

Concertomobil, Op. 18 (1971)   20'
Soloist: violin
2.2.2.bcl.2-4.2.3.1-timp.perc-str-tape
Material on hire
AVV

Solo Voice(s) and Instrument(s)/ Orchestra

Semi-Buffa, Op. 23 (1973)   7'
Soloists: 2 sopranos, baritone, opera guide
pic.2.2.2.2.cbn-4.3.3.1-timp.4perc-pno-str(1.1.1.1.1)
Material on hire
AVV

Electronic Works

Pax (1970)   15'
Ceremony
18 voices-loudspeaker
Material on hire
AVV

Kaun, Hugo
1863-1932

Orchestral Works

Symphony No. 2 c-Moll, Op. 85   38'
for large orchestra
3.3.3.3-4.3.3.1-3timp.perc-hp-prg-str
Material on hire
Eu

Kelemen, Milko
b.1924

Orchestral Works

Concerto Giocoso (1957)   13'
2(pic).1.2.2-2.1.0.0-timp.perc-str
Material on hire
AVV

Kleine Streichermusik   5'
str(5.5.3.3.2)
Score **CON 88** / Parts **CON 88-70**

Konstellationen (1959)   8'
1.1.1.1-1.1.1.0-str
Material on hire
AVV

Skolion (1959)   12'
3(pic).2.2.2-4.3.3.1-timp.perc-str
Material on hire
AVV

Symphonic Music 1957
(1957)   20'
2.2.2.2-4.2.3.1-timp.perc-str
Material on hire
AVV

Chamber & Instrumental Works

Etudes Contrapuntiques
(1966)   15'
fl.ob.cl.bn-hn
Score and parts **AVV 10**

Oboe Sonata (1960)   12'
ob-pno
OBB 28

Kelkel, Manfred
b.1929

Stage Works

La Mandragore - Alraune (Mandrake), Op. 17 (1965)   50'
Musical Psychodrama
Text: Marcel le Bourhis
Material on hire
Vocal score **ED 5920**

Concertos

Zagreber Konzert, Op. 19   25'
Soloist: guitar
2(pic).1.ca.2.2-2.2.0.0-3perc-cel.pno.hp-str(6.5.4.3.2)
Material on hire
Piano reduction **ED 6498**

Chamber & Instrumental Works

Suite, Op. 10 (1971)   10'
srec-cel/pno-[perc]
OFB 119

Kerskes, Gerhard

Orchestral Works

La Camarilla - Paso doble
(composed in collaboration with Willi Astroth)
2asax.2tsax-3tpt.2tbn-perc-pno.acc.gtr-3vn.db
Material on hire
SM

Kiehle, Theo

Stage Works

Mitten in der Nacht
(1955)   full evening
Operetta in 5 Scenes
Text: Ted Hartwig
Material on hire
SM

Killmayer, Wilhelm
b.1927

Stage Works

Pas de deux classique (1964)   6'
Ballet
Material on hire
SM

La Buffonata (1959-60)   40'
Ballet-Opera
Text: Tankred Dorst
Material on hire
Piano reduction **ED 5079** / Libretto **BN 3440-01**

Encore (1970)   6'
Ballet-Piece "Schnellpolka"
Material on hire
SM

Une leçon de français
(1964)   22'
Musical Scene
Material on hire
SM

Paradies (Paradise)
(1972-74)   15'
Ballet
Material on hire
SM

La Tragedia di Orfeo
(1960-61)   35'
Opera
Text: after Angelo Poliziano
Material on hire
SM

Yolimba oder Die Grenzen der Magie (1962/70)   70'
Musical Comedy in 1 Act
Text: Tankred Dorst/Wilhelm Killmayer
Material on hire
Vocal score **ED 5268** / Libretto **BN 3441-10**

Orchestral Works

Divertissement (1957)   14'
pic.2.2.2.2-2.2.3.1-timp.perc-glsp.xyl-cel.pno.hp-str
Material on hire
SM

Killmayer, Wilhelm

b. Munich 21.8.1927

The contemporary trends of minimalism and polystylism have a remarkable precedent in Killmayer's work, influenced by the composer's regard for the work of Shakespeare, Hölderlin and Schumann in particular. While he has written in most of the major forms, choral music and song are favourite media.

Encore (1970) 3'

Schnellpolka
pic.2.2.2.2-3.3.3.1-timp.3perc-pno-str
Material on hire
SM

Fin al Punto (1970) 12'

str(8.0.3.3.1)
Material on hire
Study score **ED 7144**

Grande Sarabande (1980) 17'

str(16.0.8.6.4/8.0.3.3.1)
Material on hire
Study score **ED 6944**

Im Freien (1980) 10'

Poème symphonique
2(2pic).2.2(Ebcl,bcl).2(cbn)-2.3.3.0-timp.3-4perc-pno.hp-str
Material on hire
Study score **ED 7067**

La joie de vivre (1996) 14'

0.2.0.1-2.0.0.0-str(6.0.1.1.1)
Material on hire
SM

Jugendzeit (1977) 13'

Poème symphonique
2pic.2.3.Ebcl.2.3(cbn)-4.3.3.0-3perc-hp-str
Material on hire
Study score **ED 6904**

Nachtgedanken (1973) 15'

2(pic).2(ca).3.2-2.1.3.0-2perc-str
Material on hire
Study score **ED 6658**

Pas de deux classique (1964) 6'

pic.2.2.2.2-3.3(Dtpt).3.1-timp.3perc-cel.pno.2hp-str
Material on hire
SM

Symphony No.1 - "Fogli"

(1968) 12'

1.0.2(bcl).0-1.0.0.0-timp.perc-pno.harm.mand.hp-str(6.6.4.4.3)
Material on hire
Study score **ED 6328**

Symphony No.2 - "Ricordanze" (1968-69) 9'

1.1.0.1-0.0.0.0-hpd-str(6.0.2.1.1)
Material on hire
Study score **ED 6328**

Symphony No.3 - "Menschen-Los" (1972-73/88) 23'

4(2pic,afl).3.(ca)4(Ebcl,bcl).3.cbn-6.4(btpt).3(atbn).1(cbtuba)-2perc-cel.2pno.org.mand.zither.2hp-str
Material on hire
Study score **ED 6606**

Überstehen und Hoffen

(1977-78) 10'

Poème symphonique
2pic.2.3.3.4-4.3.3.1-timp.perc-str
Material on hire
Study score **ED 6905**

Verschüttete Zeichen

(1977-78) 12'

Essay symphonique
4(4pic,srec).3.3(Ebcl,bcl).3(cbn)-4.4(cnt).3.1(cbtuba)-5perc-cel.2hp-str
Material on hire
Study score **ED 7066**

Zittern und Wagen (1980) 4'

Waltz
2(pic,rec).2.2.1-2.2.3.1-timp.perc-hp-str
Material on hire
SM

Concertos

The broken Farewell (1977) 5'

Soloist: trumpet
1.1.1.1-1.0.0.0-str
Material on hire
SM

Pezzi ed Intermezzi (1968) 20'

Soloists: piano, cello
2(pic).2.2.2-2.2.3.1-2perc-str
Material on hire
SM

Piano Concerto (1955) 16'

Soloist: piano
0.0.0.0-6.4.3.1-3perc-str
Material on hire
SM

Sostenuto (1984) 8'

Soloist: cello
str(16.0.6.6.4/8.0.3.3.1)
Material on hire
SM

Chamber & Instrumental Works

An John Field (1975) 23'

Nocturnes
pno
ED 6688

8 Bagatellen (1990-91) 20'

vc-pno
ED 7986

Brahms-Bildnis (1976) 12'

vn.vc-pno
ED 6764

Douze Études Transcendentales (1991-92) 10'

pno
ED 8398

Fantasie (1992) 8'

vn-pno
ED 8314

Führe mich, Alter, nur immer in Deinen geschnörkelten Frühlings-Garten! Noch duftet und taut frisch und würzig sein Flor. (1974) 6'

fl.cl-atbn-perc-pno-vn.va.vc
Material on hire
SM

Humoreske (1989) 3'

vn-pno
ED 7768

Kammermusik (1957) 13'

For jazz ensemble
cl.asax.jazztpt-4perc-pno.hpd-vn.db
Material on hire
SM

Kindertage - Kammermusik No.3 (1973) 7'

fl-5perc-pno.eorg.acc.zither.gtr-va
Material on sale
Study score **ED 6473**

5 Neue Klavierstücke

(1986-88) 25'

pno
ED 7743

Paradies (1972) 15'

2pno/pno (3hnds)
ED 6694

Paradies (Paradise)

(1972-74) 15'

pic.1.trec.afl.0.4.ssax.0-4.0.0.0-2glsp-2pno.eorg-amplifier
Material on hire
SM

Per nove strumenti (1968) 8'

ob.cl.bn-hn-2vn.va.vc.db
Score and parts **ED 7302**

3 Pezzi (1968) 5'

tpt-pno
TR 4

3 Piano Pieces (1982) 25'

pno
ED 7167

5 Romancen (1987) 20'

vn-pno
ED 7568

5 Romanzen (1989) 20'

vc-pno
ED 7829

Rundgesänge und Morgenlieder (1993) 13'

A Piano Cycle
pno
ED 8394

Die Schönheit des Morgens

(1994) 14'

5 Romances
va-pno
ED 8345

Schumann in Endenich - Kammermusik No.2 (1972) 8'

5perc-pno.eorg/harm
ED 6431

String Quartet No.1 (1969) 10'

ED 6781

String Quartet No.2 (1975) 10'

Score and parts **ED 6691**

String Trio (1984) 8'

2vn.vc
ED 7266

Tre Dance (1959) 7'

ob-perc
OBB 12

Trois Études blancs

(1990-91) 10'

pno
ED 7987

The Woods so Wilde - Kammermusik No.1 (1970) 12'

fl-3perc-gtr-va
Score **ED 6545** / Study score **ED 6545-01**

Solo Voice(s)/Voice(s) and Piano/Guitar

Blasons anatomiques du corps féminin (Cycle II)

(1991) 14'

Text: various
soprano-pno
ED 8505

3 Gesänge nach Hölderlin

(1965) 8'

Text: Friedrich Hölderlin
baritone-pno
ED 5831

Heine-Porträt

(1994/95) full evening

Song Book
Text: Heinrich Heine
tenor-pno
SM

Hölderlin-Lieder (Cycle I)

(1982-85) 40'

Text: Friedrich Hölderlin
tenor-pno
ED 7421

Hölderlin-Lieder (Cycle II)

(1983-87) 45'

Text: Friedrich Hölderlin
tenor-pno
ED 7572

Hölderlin-Lieder (Cycle III)

(1983-91) 20'

Text: Friedrich Hölderlin
tenor-pno
SM

Huit Poésies de Mallarmé

(1993) 17'

Text: Stephane Mallarmé
soprano-pno
ED 8315

9 Lieder (1993) 11'

Text: Peter Härtling
mezzo-soprano-pno
ED 8507

8 Lieder (1993) 16'

Text: Georg Trakl
tenor-pno
ED 8506

3 Lieder nach Texten von Eichendorff (1991)

Text: Friedrich Hölderlin
tenor-pno
Material on sale
SM

Salvum me fac (1969-71) 11'

Text: Bible
baritone-pno
ED 6411

Die Zufriedenheit (1993) 8'

Text: Friedrich Hölderlin
tenor-pno
Material on sale
SM

Solo Voice(s) and Instrument(s)/Orchestra

Altissimu (1969) 7'

Text: Franz von Assisi
Soloist: soprano
trec-timp.perc
ED 7303

Aussicht (1989) 6'

Text: Friedrich Hölderlin
Soloist: baritone
9 instruments
Score and parts **ED 7757**

Blasons anatomiques du corps féminin (Cycle I)

(1968) 14'

Text: various
Soloist: soprano
cl-vn.vc-pno
Score and parts **ED 6114**

Französisches Liederbuch

(1979-80) 30'

Soloists: soprano, baritone
2(pic)-tpt-4perc-cel-str(2.0.1.1.1)
Material on hire
Study score **ED 7239** / Vocal score **ED 7278**

Hölderlin-Lieder (Cycle I)

(1982-85)   45'

Nach Gedichten aus der Spätzeit
Text: Friedrich Hölderlin
Soloist: tenor
2(2pic).2.2(Ebcl,bcl).2(cbn)-2.0.cnt.2.0-
timp.4perc-cel.hp-str
Material on hire
Vocal score **ED 7421**

Hölderlin-Lieder (Cycle II)

(1983-87)   45'

Nach Gedichten aus der Spätzeit
Text: Friedrich Hölderlin
Soloist: tenor
2(2pic,afl,srec).2(ca).2(bcl).2(cbn)-
4.0.cnt.2.0-timp.perc-hp-str
Material on hire
Vocal score **ED 7572**

Huit Poésies de Mallarmé

(1993/95)   17'

Text: Stephane Mallarmé
Soloist: soprano
2(pic,afl,bfl).1.2(bcl.asax).1-2.1.0.0-2perc-
pno.eorg(hpd).hp-str
Material on hire
Vocal score **ED 8317**

Merlin-Liederbuch (1981/96) 50'

Arranger: Kay Westermann
Soloists: 4 voices
fl(pic)-tpt-perc-vn.va.vc.db
Material on hire
SM

Le petit Savoyard (1956) 15'

French Folksongs
Soloist: soprano
pic.fl-2perc-cel.hpd-vn.vc.db
Material on hire
SM

Preghiere (1969) 10'

Text: Psalm LXVIII
Soloist: baritone
0.afl.3.3.3-3.3.3.0-timp.perc-pno.2hp-
str(0.0.0.8-10.6-8)
Material on hire
SM

Rêveries (1953) 13'

Text: various
Soloist: soprano
perc-pno
Material on hire
Score and parts **ED 7333**

Romances (1954) 15'

Text: Federico Garcia Lorca
Soloist: soprano
3perc-pno
Study score **ED 7332** / Parts **ED 7332-10 (percussion)**

Sappho (1959-60) 16'

Five Greek Songs
Text: Wolfgang Schadewaldt
Soloist: soprano
pic.3-6fl.4-6ob-5perc-pno.2-4hp
alt. version: fl(pic)-2perc-hp/pno
Material on hire
SM

8 Shakespeare Lieder

(1955)   16'

Soloist: tenor
cl.bn-3perc-pno-vn
Material on hire
SM

Tamquam sponsus (1974) 10'

Soloist: soprano
srec.arec.pic.fl.Ebcl.cl.bcl-perc-
acc.pno.gtr-vn.va.vc.db
Material on hire
SM

Tre canti di Leopardi

(1965)   14'

Soloist: baritone
fl.2cl.bn-2hn-perc-hp-str
Material on hire
SM

Choral Works

Antiphone (1967) 8'

Soloist: baritone
Chorus: [male]
3(2pic,afl).2.3(bcl).2-2.4.3.1-timp.perc-
cel.pno-str(12.0.6.4.4)
Material on hire
SM

Cantetto (1971) 6'

"A colomba il sole"
Text: Giuseppe Ungaretti
Chorus: mixed a cappella
C 43265

Canti Amorosi (1953-54) 9'

Text: various
Soloists: soprano, tenor
Chorus: mixed a cappella
C 39799

4 Choruses (1971/90) 13'

Text: Giuseppe Ungaretti, Giovanni Meli,
Joseph von Eichendorff
Chorus: mixed a cappella + soli
SKR 20029

Geistliche Hymnen und Gesänge (1964) 11'

Text: Jean-Baptiste Racine
Chorus: mixed a cappella (6 prt)
C 41320

3 Kanons (1987) 2'

from "Neue Sprichwörter und
Geschichten"
Text: Wilhelm Killmayer
Chorus: mixed a cappella
C 47471

Lauda (1968) 10'

"Amore, Amore che si m'hai ferito"
Text: Jacopone da Todi
Chorus: mixed (8 prt)
[3.3.3.3-4.3.3.0-timp.perc-2pno-str]
Material on hire
C 42263

Laudatu 1 & 2 (1967-69) 10'

Text: Franz von Assisi
Chorus: mixed a cappella (8 prt)
[org/instrument]
C 43363/43364

Lazzi (1977) 10'

Text: Wilhelm Killmayer
Chorus: female a cappella (3-4 prt)
C 45055

Une leçon de français

(1964)   22'

Soloists: 2 speakers
Chorus: mixed
pic1.0.2(Ebcl,bcl).0-0.3.3.1-3perc-db
Material on hire
SM

Das Licht auf dem Scheffel

(1987)   2'

from "Neue Sprichwörter und
Geschichten"
Chorus: mixed a cappella
C 47474

Lieder, Oden und Szenen

(1962)   15'

Text: Johann Wolfgang von Goethe
Chorus: mixed a cappella
ED 5148

Pfannengericht (1987) 2'

from "Neue Sprichwörter und
Geschichten"
Chorus: mixed a cappella
C 47473

Romantische Chorlieder

(1965)   12'

Text: Ludwig Tieck
Chorus: male (2-3 prt)
[hn]
C 41644

7 Rondeaux (1966) 11'

Text: Charles d'Orléans
Soloist: voice
Chorus: female a cappella
C 42178 (-84)

Sonntagsgeschichten - Sonntagnachmittagskaffee

(1982-83)   3'

Text: Wilhelm Killmayer
Chorus: mixed a cappella
SKR 20004

Sonntagsgeschichten - Sonntagsausflug (1983-85) 2'

Chorus: mixed a cappella
C 20013

Sonntagsgeschichten - Sonntagsgedanken (1985) 5'

Chorus: mixed a cappella
C 20014

Speranza (1977) 5'

Text: Wilhelm Killmayer
Chorus: mixed (5 prt) a cappella
C 44379

Spucken und Schlucken

(1987) 2'

from "Neue Sprichwörter und
Geschichten"
Chorus: mixed a cappella
C 47472

...was dem Herzen kaum bewußt... (1995) 20'

8 Songs (Cycle No. 1)
Text: Joseph von Eichendorff
Chorus: male a cappella
SM

Kirchner, Volker David

b.1942

Stage Works

Belshazar (1984-85) 80'

Musical Drama
Text: Harald Weirich
Material on hire
SM

Erinys (1986-89) 75'

Opera in 2 Parts
Text: Volker David Kirchner after
Aischylos
Material on hire
Libretto **BN 3446-00**

Die fünf Minuten des Isaak Babel (1980) full evening

Scenic Requiem in 12 Scenes
Text: Harald Weirich/Volker David
Kirchner
Material on hire
SM

Inferno d'amore (1992) 60'

Scenic Moments
Text: William Shakespeare/Michelangelo
Buonarotti
Soloists: 4 actors, 2 sopranos
Material on hire
SM

Das kalte Herz (1980/87) 70'

Scenic Ballad
Text: Marc Günther after Wilhelm Hauff
Material on hire
Libretto **BN 3445-20**

Die Trauung (1974) full evening

Opera
Text: Witold Gombrowicz/Walter Thiel
Material on hire
SM

Kirchner, Volker David

b. Mainz 25.6.1942

Kirchner studied at the Peter Cornelius Conservatory of Mainz from 1956-59 and at the Cologne State Conservatory from 1959-63. There he also took courses with Bernd Alois Zimmermann. Besides his work as a solo violist with the Cologne Rheinisches Kammerorchester and the Frankfurt Radio Symphony Orchestra among others, he has composed music for more than 20 stage works. He received the Award of the Rhineland-Palatinate for Young Composers for his opera "Die Trauung". In 1977 he received the Arts Award of the Rhineland-Palatinate and in 1995 the composition award of the Lower Saxon Savings-Bank Foundation and the Hanover District Savings Bank.

Orchestral Works

Bildnisse I (1981-82) 17'

2(pic).2.ca.2(bcl).2(cbn)-2.2.2.0-str
Material on hire
Study score **ED 7145**

Bildnisse II (1983-84) 12'

2(pic).2.ca1.bcl.1.cbn-2.2.2.0-pn.hp-str
Material on hire
Study score **ED 7251**

Bildnisse III (1991) 15'

*1.2(ca).0.bcl.2bsthn.0.cbn-
2nathn/2hn.0.0.0.0-perc-str*
Material on hire
Study score **ED 8181**

Der blaue Harlekin (1981) 7'

Hommage à Picasso. A Grotesque
fl.cl.2bn(cbn)-2tpt.2tbn
Score and parts **ED 8015**

3 Fragments (1976)

From the Opera "Die Trauung"
*3(pic).3(ca).3(bcl).3(cbn) -4.4.4.2-
timp.4perc-pno(cel).2hp-str(10.10.7-8.6.5)*
Material on hire
SM

Hortus Magicus (1994) 10'

*pic.3(pic).2.ca.3(bcl).2.cbn-4.3.3.1-
timp.3perc-cel.hp-str*
Material on hire
SM

Kondukt (1989) 5'

Funeral Music
1.2(ca).0.2bsthn.0.cbn-2.0.0.0-perc-str
SM

Orphischer Gesang

(1975-76) 10'

str orch/str sxt: 2vn.2ba.2vc
Material on hire
SM

Schattengesang (1990) 15'

Musical Drama
str
SM

Das Souper des Monsieur Papagenor (1992-93) 4'

Ein musikalisches Hors d'œuvre
2(pic,lotosfl).2(ca).2.2(cbn)-2.2.0.0-perc-str
Material on hire
SM

Symphony No.1 (1980) 20'

„Totentanz"
*4(pic).3.3(Ebcl).bcl.3.cbn-
8(4tuba).4.4.cbtuba-2timp.8perc-
cel.pno.mand.2hp-str(16.14.12.10.8)*
Material on hire
SM

Concertos

Nachtstück (1980-81) 12'

Soloist: viola
2.2.ca.2.2(cbn)-2.2.2.0-str(0.0.6.5.3)
Material on hire
Study score **ED 7290** / Parts **ED 7279 (solo)**

Schibboleth (1989) 10'

Poème Concertante
Soloist: viola
*3.3.3.3-4.4.4.2-timp.perc-cel.pno(4hnd)-
str(12.10.8.6.4)*
Material on hire
Piano reduction **ED 7809**

Violin Concerto (1981-82) 25'

Soloist: violin
*3(pic).3(ca).3(Ebcl,bcl).2.cbn-4.3.3.1-
2timp.perc-str*
Material on hire
Piano reduction **ED 7939**

Chamber & Instrumental Works

Choralvariationen

(1967-68/93)　　　　　10'

solo str(7.0.4.3.1)
Material on hire
Study score **ED 7880**

Dybuk　(1995)　　5'

marimba solo
BAT 43

Exil　(1994)　　　20'

cl-vn.vc-pno
Score **ED 8418**

Gethsemani　(1994)　7'

Notturno
2vn.2va.2vc
ED 8327

Lamento d'Orfeo　(1986)　9'

hn-pno
ED 7527

Mysterion　(1985)　　12'

afl-hn-va d'am.vc-pno
Score and parts **ED 7364**

Piano Sonata　(1985-86)　17'

ED 7463

Saitenspiel　(1993)　　15'

vn.vc
ED 8179

String Quartet　(1982-83)　16'

Score **ED 7184** / Parts **ED 7185**

Stringsextet No. 1　(1976)

2vn.2va.2vc
alt. version: str(1.1.2.2.1)
Material on hire
SM

Stringsextet No. 2　(1976)

2vn.2va.2vc
Material on hire
SM

Tre Poemi　(1986-87)　13'

hn-pno
ED 7675

Trifoglietto per undici musicisti di Kirzehwan - Canonetto　(1981)　7'

Collective composition with Friedrich
Zehm and Friedrich K. Wanek
2fl(pic).2ob.2cl.2bn(cbn)-2hn
Material on hire
SM

Trio　(1979)　　　　16'

vn.vc-pno
ED 7015

Und Salomo sprach　(1987)　4'

cello solo
ED 7641

Solo Voice(s) and Instrument(s)/ Orchestra

3 Gesänge - "Abgesang"

Soloist: low voice
*3(pic).3(ca).3(bcl).3(cbn)-
8(4tuba).4.4.btuba.cbtuba-2timp.3perc-
cel.pno.mand.2hp-str(16.14.12.10.8)*
Material on hire
SM

Golgatha　(1979)　　10'

Text: Bible
Soloists: 3 boy's voices
*pic.fl.ob.2ca/ob da caccia.bn-hi hat-
str(0.0.6.4.2)*
Material on hire
AVV

3 Lieder　(1985-86)　　7'

Text: Johann Wolfgang von Goethe
Soloist: medium voice
hn-vn.vc-pno
Score and parts **ED 7556**

Orfeo　(1986-87)　　22'

Text: Rainer Maria Rilke
Soloist: baritone
hn-pno
Material on sale
Score and parts **ED 7615**

Riten　(1970-71)　　20'

Soloists: soprano, dancer, conductor
perc-pno-db
AVV 94

Symphony No.2　(1991-92)　40'

„Mythen"
Soloists: soprano, mezzo, alto
*4(3pic).3(ca).3(Ebcl).2.cbn-4.3.3.1-
2timp.5perc-cel(pno,org/eorg).hp-
str(14.12.10.8.5)-tape*
Material on hire
SM

Choral Works

Babel-Requiem　(1979)　75'

Text: Latin
Soloists: soprano, bass, speaker
Chorus: double mixed
*3(pic,afl).3(ca).3(3bsthn,Ebcl,bcl).2bsthn.3
(cbn)-4.4.4.euph/tuba.btuba-2timp.5perc-
pno(cel).org.2hp-str(14-16.12-14.10-12.8-
10.6-8)*
Material on hire
SM

Lamento　(1976)

Text: Bible
Chorus: mixed a cappella
Material on hire
SM

Missa (Missa moguntina)

(1992-93)　　　　　55'

Soloists: soprano, mezzo, tenor, 2 basses,
boy's voice
Chorus: mixed, children's
*3(pic).3(ca).3(bcl).2.cbn-
4.4(pictpt).3.1.cbtuba-timp.2perc-org-str*
Material on hire
SM

Passion　(1981-82)　　45'

Text: Liturgical
Soloists: bass, speaker
Chorus: mixed, children's
3.3.3.3-4.3.4.10timp.perc-pno-str
Material on hire
SM

Requiem　(1988)　　45'

Soloists: soprano, mezzo, alto, tenor, bass,
3 trumpets
Chorus: mixed
pic.3.3.3.2.cbn-6.7.3.1-timp.perc-2pno-str
Material on hire
SM

Klebe, Giselher
b.1925

Orchestral Works

Symphony No.1, Op. 12

(1951)　　　　　26'

str(12.10.8.6.6)
Material on hire
SM

Symphony No.2, Op. 16

(1952-53)　　　　18'

*2(pic).2(ca).2(bcl).2(cbn)-4.2.0.1-2timp-hp-
str(12.10.8.6.6)*
Material on hire
SM

Concertos

Concerto for Violin and Cello, Op. 18　(1954)　19'

Soloists: violin, cello
2.2.2(bcl).2-4.2.0.1-timp.2perc-str
Material on hire
SM

Espressioni liriche

No. 7 from the "Divertimento für Mozart"
Soloists: Horn, trumpet, trombone
2.2.2.2-2.2.0.0-timp-str
SM (Co-prod: UE)
Copyright USA: EAM/Italy: Ed. Suvini
Zerboni

Klebe, Giselher

b. Mannheim 28.6.1925

Klebe studied with Boris Blacher in Berlin from 1946 to 1951. He took over the composition class of Wolfgang Fortner at the Detmold Academy of Music in 1957. His expressively pointillistic style is due to both the variable metrics of Blacher and the dodecaphony of Webern.

Scene (1954)   6'

Soloists: 4 violins
6-12vn-pno (4hnd)
Material on hire
Study score **AVV 58**

Chamber & Instrumental Works

Sonata for 2 Pianos, Op. 4

(1952)   11'

2pno
ED 4292

Violin Sonata, Op. 14 (1953)   9'

vn-pno
ED 4478

Solo Voice(s) and Instrument(s)/ Orchestra

Römische Elegien, Op. 15

(1953)   15'

Text: Johann Wolfgang von Goethe
Soloist: speaker
pno.hpd-db
Material on hire
Study score **ED 4576**

Knab, Armin
1881-1951

Stage Works

Das Lebenslicht

(1955)   full evening

Musical Drama in 7 Scenes
Text: Anna Bethe-Kuhn
Material on hire
Score **ED 4443** / Libretto **BN 3450-90**

Chamber & Instrumental Works

Festlicher Reigen (1949)   13'

2vn.va.vc.[db]
Score and parts **ED 3884**

Kleine Musik (1960)   6'

3rec
ED 4892

Lindegger Ländler (1944)   10'

pno
ED 2862

Lindegger Ländler (1944)   10'

vn.vc-pno
Score and parts **ED 2487**

7 Organ Chorales (1941)   11'

organ solo
ED 3728

Piano Chorale (1933)   11'

ED 2346

Piano Sonata in E Major

(1929)   25'

ED 2368

Knab, Armin

b. Neu-Schleichach (Lower Franconia) 19.2.1881, d. Bad Wörishofen 23.6.1951

Armin Knab, who became known as an important music teacher and composer of songs and choral works, was born into a family of teachers. From 1900 he studied law and music theory in Würzburg and Munich. In 1904 he took his doctorate in law, passed the state legal examination in1907 and became judge in the local court of Vilshofen in 1911, judge in the local court of Rothenburg/Tauber in 1913-26 and judge in the regional court of Würzburg in 1927-34. At the same time he gained more and more reputation and popularity as a composer. In 1934 he finally decided in favour of music, taking an appointment to teach music theory and composition at the Berlin Academy of Music Education and Church Music. In 1935 he was made professor and in 1940 was awarded the Max Reger Prize.

Variationen über ein Kinderlied (1931)   7'

str qrt
Material on sale
ED 1569

Volkslied Variationen

(1950)   11'

violin solo
ED 2798

Solo Voice(s)/Voice(s) and Piano/Guitar

12 Lieder (1949) 25'
Text: Johann Wolfgang von Goethe
high voice-pno
ED 3931

Litauische Lieder (1932) 15'
voice-pno
ED 1699

Solo Voice(s) and Instrument(s)/ Orchestra

Liebesklagen des Mädchens
(1922) 8'
Text: various
Soloist: soprano
str
Material on hire
SM

Rosa Mystica (1949) 9'
Text: Angelus Silesius
alto-va
ED 3879

2 Solo Cantatas (1950) 16'
Soloist: soprano
fl-str
Score **ED 4038** / Parts **ED 4038-10**

Choral Works

Brot und Wein (1950) 7'
Text: Albert Korn/Georg Trakl
Chorus: female a cappella (4 prt)
C 37930 (-32)

Ein Brotlaib (1930) 1'
Text: R. Billinger
Chorus: male a cappella
CHBL 1

Den Toten (1951) 3'
Text: Ludwig Andersen
Chorus: male a cappella
CHBL 33

Drei Laub auf einer Linden
(1949) 2'
Chorus: female a cappella
CHBL 620

Es, es, es & es (1949) 2'
Chorus: female a cappella
CHBL 598

Geboren ist uns ein Kindelein (1952) 3'
Chorus: female a cappella
CHBL 520

Grüß Gott, du schöner Maien (1935) 20'
Soloists: voices, speaker
Chorus: youth
rec-vn
ED 2444

Mariä Geburt (1921-23) 7'
Text: Des Knaben Wunderhorn
Soloist: alto
Chorus: female (S,A)
fl.ob.cl-str(1.1.1.1.1)
Score **C 34188** / Parts **C 34189-11 (-18)** / Vocal score **C 34191** / Piano reduction **C 34190**

Mitten wir im Leben sind
(1950) 3'
Text: various
Chorus: female a cappella
CHBL 502

Der Morgenstern (1933) 2'
Chorus: female a cappella
CHBL 550

St. Michael am Meer (1933) 3'
Text: Christof Beck
Chorus: female a cappella
CHBL 549

Weihnachtskantate (1931-32) 4'
Text: Josef Garber
Soloists: soprano, alto, 3 male voices, speaker
Chorus: mixed
0.1.0.0-2.1.0.0-timp-str
alt. version: ob-org-vn
Score **ED 3278-11** / Parts **ED 3278-11 (-25)/ED 4039-00 (-12) reduced version** / Choral score **ED 3278-01** / Vocal score **ED 3278**

Wir zogen in das Feld (1935) 2'
Chorus: male a cappella
C 34249

Köhler, Emil

Orchestral Works

Optimismus
Waltz
2.2.2.2-2.2.2.0-timp.perc-str
Material on hire
SM

Komarova, Tatjana
b.1968

Chamber & Instrumental Works

Sonata (1990) 9'
pno
ED 8299

Komma, Karl Michael
b.1913

Orchestral Works

Concertino (1938) 14'
fl-hpd-str
Material on hire
SM

Korngold, Erich Wolfgang
1897-1957

Stage Works

Das Lied der Liebe
(1931) full evening
Operetta in 3 Acts. Music after Johann Strauß
Text: Ludwig Herzer
Material on hire
SM

Der Ring des Polykrates, Op. 7 (1913-14) 60'
Comic Opera in 1 Act
Text: Heinrich Teweles
Material on hire
SM

Die tote Stadt, Op. 12
(1916-19) 145'
Opera in 3 Scenes
Text: Paul Schott after Georges Rodenbach
Material on hire
Vocal score **ED 3208** / Libretto **BN 3480-00**

Korngold, Erich Wolfgang

b. Brno 29.5.1897, d. Hollywood 29.11.1957

Korngold was a child prodigy who by the age of 20 had already won the admiration of Richard Strauss and Puccini. The acclaim for his third opera, "Die tote Stadt" was as universal as the success of his Oscar-winning film scores for Hollywood. Symphonic works - the Violin Concerto and the Symphony in F# - were less appreciated at the time, but are now regarded as essential texts of late Romaniticism.

Violanta, Op. 8 (1914-15)   80'

Opera in 1 Act
Text: Hans Müller-Einigen
Material on hire
SM

Das Wunder der Heliane, Op. 20 (1924-26)   180'

Opera in 3 Acts
Text: Hans Müller
Material on hire
SM

Orchestral Works

Baby-Serenade, Op. 24

(1925)   20'

2(pic).1.2(Dcl,bcl).2asax.tsax.1-1.3.1.0-timp.perc-[banjo].pno.hp-str
Material on hire
SM

Military March (1917)   8'

2.2.2.2-4.2.3.0-timp.perc-hp-str
Parts **BSS 33017**

Schauspiel-Ouvertüre, Op. 4

(1911)   14'

pic.2.2.2.bcl.2.cbn-4.3.3.1-timp.perc-hp-str
Material on hire
SM

Sinfonietta, Op. 5 (1911-12)   44'

3(pic).2(ca).2.bcl.2.cbn-4.3.3.1-4perc-cel.pianino-2hp-str(16.16.12.12.8)
Material on hire
SM

Straussiana (1953)   6'

[pic].2.[1].2.[1]-[2].2.2.0-timp.perc-pno.[hp]-str(1.1.1.1.1.1)
Material on hire
SM

Symphonic Overture, Op. 13

(1919)   18'

"Sursum Corda!"
3(pic).2.ca.3.bcl.2.cbn-4.3.btpt.3.1-timp.perc-pno.2hp-str(14vnI.8vnII.8vnIII.6vaI.6vaII.6vcI.6vcII.8db)
Material on hire
Score **BSS 30495**

Symphonic Serenade in B Major, Op. 39 (1947-48)   30'

str(16.16.12.12.8)
Material on hire
SM

Symphony in F Sharp, Op. 40 (1951-52)   50'

3(pic).2.2.bcl.2.cbn-4.3.4.1-timp.perc-cel(pno).hp-str(16.14.10.10.8)
Material on hire
SM

Theme and Variations, Op. 42 (1953)   7'

2.1.2.1-2.2.2.0-timp.perc-hp-str(vnI.vnII.vnIII.1.1)
Material on hire
SM

Viel Lärmen um Nichts - Much ado about Nothing, Op. 11 (1918)   25'

Incidental Music
1.1.1.1-2.1.1.0-timp.perc-pno.harm.hp-str
Material on hire
SM

Viel Lärmen um Nichts - Much ado about Nothing, Op. 11 (1919)   16'

Suite
1.1.1.1-2.1.1.0-timp.perc-pno.harm.hp-str
Material on hire
SM

Concertos

Cello Concerto in C Major, Op. 37 (1946)   13'

Soloist: cello
2(pic).2(ca).2.bcl.2(cbn)-2.2.2.1-timp.3perc-cel.pno.hp-str
Material on hire
Piano reduction **ED 4117**

Piano Concerto in C Sharp, Op. 17 (1923)   34'

Soloist: piano-left hand
3(pic).2(ca).2(bcl).2.cbn-4.3.3.0-timp.2perc-cel.hp-str(12.8.6.6.6)
Material on hire
SM

Violin Concerto in D Major, Op. 35 (1936-39/45)   22'

Soloist: violin
2(pic).2(ca).2.bcl.2(cbn)-4.2.1.0-timp.2perc-cel.hp-str
Material on hire
Piano reduction **ED 6713**

Chamber & Instrumental Works

Caprice Fantastique (1908)   4'

vn-pno
BSS 33663

Don Quixote (1909)   13'

Six Character Pieces
pno
ED 8376

Gesang der Heliane (1924-26)   3'

from the Opera "Das Wunder der Heliane", op. 20
vn-pno
ED 1929

Geschichten von Strauß, Op. 21 (1927)   9'

Large Fantasy
pno
ED 2150

Große Fantasie (1916-19)   15'

from the Opera "Die tote Stadt", op. 12
Arranger: F. Rebay
pno
ED 1748

4 kleine fröhliche Walzer

(1914)   10'

pno
ED 8377

1. BILD

Erich Wolfgang Korngold
Die tote Stadt (1916-19)

4 Little Cartoons for Children, Op. 19 (1926) 2'

pno
ED 7392

7 Märchenbilder, Op. 3

(1910) 22'

pno
ED 7580

Mariettas Lied (1916-19) 6'

from the opera "Die Tote Stadt", op. 12
vn-pno
ED 1928

Piano Quintet in E Major, Op. 15 (1920) 30'

2vn.va.vc-pno
Parts ED 3133

Piano Sonata No.2 in E Major, Op. 2 (1910) 26'

ED 1736

Piano Sonata No.3 in C, Op. 25 (1930) 25'

ED 2227

3 Pieces (1918-19) 11'

from the music to Shakespeare's "Viel Lärmen um Nichts"
pno
ED 1740

4 Pieces (1918/19) 12'

from the music to Shakespeare's "Viel Lärmen um Nichts"
vn-pno
ED 1927

Schach Brügge! (1916-19) 10'

from the Opera "Die tote Stadt", op. 12
pno
ED 1749

String Quartet No.1 in A Major, Op. 16 (1922) 31'

Study score ED 8122 / Parts ED 8123

String Quartet No.2 in Eb Major, Op. 26 (1933-35) 18'

Score ED 7726 / Parts ED 7727

String Quartet No.3 in D Major, Op. 34 (1945) 26'

Score ED 6822 / Parts ED 6823

String Sextet in D Major, Op. 10 (1914-16) 35'

2vn.2va.2vc
Study score ED 3446 / Parts ED 3134

Suite, Op. 23 (1930) 18'

2vn.vc-pno(left hand)
Score and parts ED 6812

Tanzlied des Pierrot

(1916-19) 4'

from the Opera "Die tote Stadt", op. 12
pno
ED 1750

Tanzlied des Pierrot

(1916-19) 4'

from the Opera "Die tote Stadt", op. 12
vn-pno
ED 1926

Violanta-Potpourri (2 parts) 12'

In 2 Parts
Arranger: F. Rebay
pno
ED 1751/ED 1752

Violin Sonata in G Major, Op. 6 (1912-13) 30'

vn-pno
VLB 76

Zwischenspiel (1924-26) 11'

from the Opera "Das Wunder der Heliane", op. 20
pno
ED 1754

Solo Voice(s)/Voice(s) and Piano/Guitar

Lied des Pagen (1918-19) 3'

Text: William Shakespeare
soprano-pno
BSS 30590

3 Lieder, Op. 22 (1928-29) 12'

voice-pno
ED 8169

5 Lieder, Op. 38 (1940/47) 16'

Text: various
medium voice-pno
ED 4533

Lieder des Abschieds, Op. 14

(1920-21) 15'

Text: various
alto-pno
Material on hire
ED 2032

Mariettas Lied (1916-19) 5'

"Glück, das mir verblieb" from the Opera "Die tote Stadt", op. 12
high voice-pno
BSS 30639-01

4 Shakespearian Songs, Op. 31 (1937) 12'

from "Othello" and "Wie es euch gefällt"
high voice-pno
ED 7882

Sonett für Wien, Op. 41

(1948) 4'

Text: Hans Kaltneker
mezzo-soprano-pno
BSS 39681

3 Songs, Op. 18 (1924) 11'

Text: Hans Kaltneker
medium voice-pno
ED 2033

Songs of the Clown, Op. 29 (1937) 14'

Five Songs from "Twelfth night" by Shakespeare
high voice-pno
ED 7882

Unvergänglichkeit - The Eternal, Op. 27 (1935) 8'

Text: Eleonore van der Straten
voice-pno
ED 7751

Solo Voice(s) and Instrument(s)/ Orchestra

Einfache Lieder, Op. 9

(1911-16) 23'

Text: various
Soloist: voice
pno/orch: 2.2(ca).2.2-2.2.0.0-timp.perc-cel.pno.hp-str
Material on hire
Vocal score ED 8306

Lieder des Abschieds, Op. 14

(1920-21) 12'

Text: various
Soloist: alto
3.2(ca).2.bcl.2-4.0.0.0-timp.perc-cel.hp-str
Study score BSS 30745 / Piano reduction ED 2032

Mariettas Lied from "Die tote Stadt", Op. 12

(1916-19) 6'

Soloist: soprano
pic.2.2.ca.2.bcl.2.cbn-4.1.btpt.3.btuba-timp-glsp-cel.pno.2hp-str
Material on hire
Vocal score BSS 30639-01

Tanzlied des Pierrot, Op. 12

(1916-19) 3'

from the Opera "Die tote Stadt", op. 12
Arranger: Franz Willms
Soloist: baritone
2(pic).1.2.2-4.1/2.1.0-timp-trgl.cel.hp-str
Material on hire
ED 09723

Choral Works

Passover-Psalm, Op. 30

(1941) 10'

Hymn on Hebrew Prayers from Hagada
Text: Jacob Sonderling
Soloist: soprano
Chorus: mixed
4hn.3tpt-timp.perc-pno.org.hp-str(6.0.2.3.2)
Material on hire
SM

Prayer, Op. 32 (1942) 3'

Soloist: tenor
Chorus: 6/3 sopranos, 6/3 altos
org-hp(pno)
Score **ED 8203-00** / Parts **ED 8203-11 (harp)** /
Vocal score **ED 8203-01**

Kosma, Joseph

1905-1969

Stage Works

Un Amour électronique

(1961) 40'

Opera Buffa in 1 Act
Text: André Kedros
Material on hire
Vocal score **ED 5657**

Chamber & Instrumental Works

Autumn Leaves

pno
ED 011044

Kotonski, Wlodzimierz

b.1925

Orchestral Works

Musica Cameralna (1958) 8'

*1(pic).1.2(bcl).0-1.1.0.0-4perc-
cel.pno.hp.gtr-str(4.0.4.2.1)*
Material on hire
AVV

Musique en Relief (1959) 10'

*2(2pic).3.2.2-2.4.3.1-timp.4perc-
marimb.vib.cel.pno.hp-str(20.0.12.10.8)*
Material on hire
AVV

Kounadis, Arghyris

b.1924

Concertos

Triptychon (1964) 11'

Soloist: flute
perc-cel.pno.hpd-str
Material on hire
SM

Kovách, Andor

b.1915

Stage Works

Medea (1959) 75'

Opera in 1 Act
Text: Jean Anouilh
Material on hire
SM

Orchestral Works

Eurydice (1953)

Overture
*pic.2.2.ca.2.bcl.2.cbn-4.3.2.1-timp.perc-
pno.hp-str*
Material on hire
SM

Concertos

Musique concertante 20'

Soloist: marimba
perc-str(10.10.8.6.6 / 12.12.10.8.6)
Material on hire
SM

Chamber & Instrumental Works

Cello Sonata (1993)

cello solo
SM

Obscur Clair (1981)

vn-pno
SM

Choral Works

Mariennacht 1735, Op. 109

(1976)

Oratorio. (Bruder Martinovich)
Text: Frederic Karinthy, Kurt Neufert
Soloists: tenor, speaker
Chorus: mixed
*2(pic).2.2.2-4.3.3.1-timp.3perc-xyl.hp-
str(2.2.2.2.2/4.4.4.2.2)*
Material on hire
SM

Song of Paradise (1977) 16'

Text: Paul Kreutzer
Soloist: baritone
Chorus: mixed
2.1.ca.2.2-4.2.2.0-timp.perc-hp-str
Material on hire
SM

Kreisler, Fritz

1875-1962

Stage Works

Sissy (1932) full evening

Singspiel in 2 Acts
Text: Ernst Decsey/Gustav Holm/Gustav
Marischka/Hubert Marischka
Material on hire
SM
Copyright not for: A, H

Orchestral Works

Caprice viennois, Op. 2

Arranger: Russ Garcia
2asax.2tsax.barsax-0.4.4.0-gtr.pno-str
Material on hire
SM

Concertos

Schön Rosmarin (1910) 3'

Soloist: violin
1.1.2.1-2.2.1.0-perc-pno-str
SM

Chamber & Instrumental Works

Album mit ausgewählten Stücken

vn-pno
ED 1600

Kreisler, Fritz

b. Vienna 2.2.1875, d. New York 29.1.1962

Fritz Kreisler was one of the most popular and succesful virtuoso violinists of this century. He was trained by Hellmesberger in Vienna and by Massart and Delibes in Paris. Concert tours led him around the globe; numerous recording prove his technical and musical mastery. Even as a composer he gained an international reputation; his transcriptions and original compositions for violin belong to the standard repertoire of every violinist.

Altdeutsches Schäfermadrigal

Originalkompositionen Nr. 9
vn-pno
BSS 31930

Andantino

vc-pno
BSS 29020-01

Aucassin und Nicolette

Kleine Stücke in der 1. Lage Nr. 3
vn-pno
BSS 31218

Berceuse romantique, Op. 9

Originalkompositionen Nr. 5
vn-pno
BSS 30601

Caprice viennois, Op. 2

Originalkompositionen Nr. 2
vn-pno
BSS 29033

Caprice viennois (Cradle song), Op. 2

pno
BSS 29033-01

Liebesfreud

"Altwiener Tanzweisen", No. 1
pno
BSS 29509

Liebesfreud

"Altwiener Tanzweisen", No. 1
vc-pno
BSS 29028

Liebesfreud

"Altwiener Tanzweisen", No. 1
Arranger: Sergej Rachmaninoff
pno
ED 1757

Liebesleid

"Altwiener Tanzweisen", No. 2
pno
BSS 29510

Liebesleid

"Altwiener Tanzweisen", No. 2
Arranger: Sergej Rachmaninoff
pno
ED 1758

Marche Miniature Viennoise

Kleine Stücke in der 1. Lage Nr. 6
vn-pno
BSS 32776

Polichinelle

Originalkompositionen Nr. 7
vn-pno
BSS 30603

Recitativo und Scherzo-Caprice, Op. 6

Originalkompositionen Nr. 4
violin solo
BSS 29500

Romanze, Op. 4

Originalkompositionen Nr. 1
vn-pno
BSS 29031

Rondino über ein Thema von Beethoven

Kleine Stücke in der 1. Lage Nr. 1
vn-pno
BSS 31216

Schön Rosmarin (1910) 3'

"Altwiener Tanzweisen", No. 3
pno
BSS 29511

String Quartet in A Minor

(1922)

Study score ED 3449 / Parts ED 3122

Synocopation

Originalkompositionen Nr. 13
vn-pno
BSS 37968

Tambourin chinois

Originalkompositionen Nr. 3
vn-pno
BSS 29032

Zigeuner-Cappriccio

Originalkompositionen Nr. 10
vn-pno
BSS 31931

Solo Voice(s)/Voice(s) and Piano/Guitar

Caprice viennois (Cradle song), Op. 2

low voice-pno
BSS 30666-03

Křenek, Ernst

1900-1991

Stage Works

Pallas Athene weint

(1952-55)   full evening

Opera in 1 Prelude and 3 Acts
Text: Ernst Křenek
Material on hire
Vocal score ED 4324 / Libretto BN 3490-80
(Co-prod: UE)

Orchestral Works

7 Easy Pieces (1955) 8'

str
Score CON 89 / Parts CON 89-70

Elf Transparente (1954) 20'

2(pic).2.2.2-4.2.2.1-timp.perc-hp-str
Material on hire
Study score ED 5003 (Co-prod: UE)
Copyright USA: EAM/Italy: Ed. Suvini Zerboni

Symphonic Piece, Op. 86

(1939)   16'

str
Material on hire
SM (Co prod: UE)
Copyright USA: EAM/Italy: Ed. Suvini Zerboni

Symphony No.5 (1947-49) 22'

2.2.3.2-4.2.2.1-timp.perc-str
Material on hire
SM (Co-prod: UE)
Copyright USA: EAM/Italy: Ed. Suvini
Zerboni

Symphony "Pallas Athene"

(1954) 22'

2(pic).2.2(bcl).2-4.2.2.0-timp.3perc-cel.pno.hp-str
Material on hire
Study score **ED 5006 (Co-prod: UE)**
Copyright USA: EAM/Italy: Ed. Suvini
Zerboni

Concertos

Capriccio (1955) 10'

Soloist: cello
pic.0.1.0.bcl.1-1.1.1.0-timp.3perc-cel.hp-str(8-10.0.5-6.3-4.2-4.)
Material on hire
SM (Co-prod: UE)
Copyright USA: EAM/Italy: Ed. Suvini
Zerboni

Piano Concerto No.3 (1946) 21'

Soloist: piano
2(pic).2.Ebcl.2.2-4.2.2.1-timp.2perc-hp-str
Material on hire
SM (Co-prod: UE)
Copyright USA: EAM/Italy: Ed. Suvini
Zerboni

Violin Concerto No.2

(1953-54) 25'

Soloist: violin
2.2.2.2-4.2.2.0-timp.2perc-cel.hp-str
Material on hire
SM (Co-prod: UE)
Copyright USA: EAM/Italy: Ed. Suvini
Zerboni

Solo Voice(s)/Voice(s) and Piano/Guitar

5 Lieder , Op. 82 (1958) 9'

Text: Franz Kafka
voice-pno
ED 4794

Choral Works

Cantata for Wartime, Op. 95

(1944/55) 12'

Mitternacht und Tag
Text: Hermann Melville
Chorus: female
2.2.2.2-4.2.2.0-timp.2perc-str
Material on hire
SM (Co-prod: UE)
Copyright USA: EAM/Italy: Ed. Suvini
Zerboni

Guten Morgen, Amerika

(1956) 3'

Text: Carl Sandburg
Chorus: mixed a cappella
C 39551

Ich singe wieder, wenn es tagt (1955) 5'

Text: Walther von der Vogelweide
Chorus: mixed
str
Score **ED 4981** / Parts **ED 4981-11 (-15)** /
Choral score **ED 4981-01 (Co prod: UE)**
Copyright USA: EAM/Italy: Ed. Suvini
Zerboni

Motette zur Opferung

(1957) 13'

Chorus: mixed a cappella
C 39559

Proprium missae (1957) 13'

Chorus: mixed a cappella
C 39419

Psalmverse zur Kommunion

(1957) 13'

Chorus: mixed a cappella
C 39420

Kröll, Georg

b.1934

Orchestral Works

Parodia ad Perotinum

(1971) 10'

Organum for Orchestra
4(afl).3.4(bcl).3.-0.4.4.0-3perc-str(0.0.6.6.3)
Material on hire
AVV

Still leben 15'

4(2pic,afl).3(ca).4(Ebcl,bsthn,bcl).asax.2-4.3.3.0-4perc-2pno(cel).2hp.2gtr-str(20.0.10.8.6)
Material on hire
AVV

Variations (1964-65) 8'

2(2pic, afl).2.2.bcl.asax.2-2.3.2(2cbtbn).2.cbtuba-3perc-2pno(cel).2hp-str(16.0.8.8.4)
Material on hire
AVV

Chamber & Instrumental Works

Estampida (1968) 8'

guitar solo
AVV 43

Invocazioni (1973) 12'

fl.cl.ob.bn-hn
AVV 92

Infoline · e-Mail
Schott Musik International
Mainz: Schott.Musik.com@T-Online.de
London: 101627.166@compuserve.com

L

Lacerda, Osvaldo
b.1927

Chamber & Instrumental Works

Três Miniatures Brasilieras
(1968)
4-5perc
BAT 16

Landré, Guillaume
1905-1968

Orchestral Works

Concert Piece (1938)   10'
pic.2(pic).2.ca.Ebcl.1.bcl.2.cbn-4.3.3.1-timp.perc-str
Material on hire
SM

Lehmann, Hans Ulrich
b.1937

Orchestral Works

Composition for 19
(1964-65)   10'
1(pic).1.ca.1.bcl.1-1.1.1.0-perc-vib.cel.pno.hp-str(1.1.1.1.1)
Material on hire
AVV

Positionen (1971)   13'
3(2pic,afl).2.ca.2(Ebcl).2.cbn-4.3.3.1-timp.4perc-str
Material on hire
AVV

Concertos

Concerto for 2 Wind Instruments and Strings
(1969)   12'
Soloists: flute, oboe/clarinet
str orch/12solo str
Material on hire
AVV

Dis-cantus 1 (1971)   15'
Soloist: oboe
str(6.0.2.2.1)
Material on hire
AVV

Quanti 1 (1962)   13'
Soloist: flute
ca.cl.bcl.bn-tpt.hn.ttbn-vib.marimb.hp-vn.va.vc.db
Material on hire
AVV

Chamber & Instrumental Works

Episodes (1963-64)   11'
fl.ob.cl.bn-hn
AVV 14

Instants for Piano (1968)   5'
AVV 163

Monodie (1970)   5'
wind instrument
Score **AVV 91**

Noten (1964-66)   6'
organ solo
AVV 25

3 Regions (1970)   7'
cl-tbn-vc
Material on sale
Score **AVV 97** / Study score **AVV 96**

Spiele (1966)   6'
fl.ob-hp
AVV 84

Tractus (1971)   9'
fl.ob.cl
AVV 95

Viola Studies (1966)   8'
viola solo
AVV 24

Solo Voice(s) and Instrument(s)/ Orchestra

Dis-cantus 2 (1971)   10'
Text: Bible
Soloist: soprano
2.2.2.1-0.2.2.0-org-str(0.0.0.4.2)
Material on hire
AVV

Rondo (1967)   22'
Text: Helmut Heissenbüttel
Soloist: soprano
3(pic).2.ca.3.bcl.2.cbn-4.3.3ttbn(with fourth valve).1-timp.4perc-2hp-str(20.0.10.8.6)
Material on hire
AVV

Lehmann, Markus
b.1919

Stage Works

Der kleine Bahnhof (1957)   40'
Comic Opera
Text: Peter Steinbach
Material on hire
SM

Lumpacivagabundus oder Das liederliche Kleeblatt   full evening
Incidental music to the farcical Comedy in 9 Scenes by Johann Nestroy/Heinz Hilpert
Arranger: Adolf Müller
Material on hire
SM

Die Wette (1966)   20'
Musical Burlesque in 1 Act
Text: Kurt Neufert
Material on hire
SM

Zwecks Heirat   35'
Comic Opera in 1 Act
Text: Kurt Neufert
Material on hire
SM

Orchestral Works

Sentenzen (1959)   20'
3.3.4.3-4.3.3.1-timp.perc-cel.hp-str
Material on hire
SM

Leighton, Lucas
b.1908

Orchestral Works

Ballet de la Reine   18'
2.2.2.2-2.2.3.0-timp.perc-hp-str
Material on hire
Eu

Lendvai, Erwin
1882-1949

Solo Voice(s) and Instrument(s)/ Orchestra

5 Sonette der Louïze Labé, Op. 33   20'
Text: arranged by Rainer Maria Rilke
Soloist: soprano
1.0.1.1-0.0.0.0-pno-str
Material on hire
SM

Choral Works

Glockenlied, Op. 19/2 (1927)   3'
Text: Carl Spitteler
Chorus: male a cappella
SM

Licht muß wieder werden
(1927)   3'
Chorus: male a cappella
SM

Lhotka, Fran
1883-1962

Stage Works

Der Teufel im Dorf (Djavo u selu) (1935)   full evening
Ballet in 3 Acts
Material on hire
Piano reduction **ED 5442**

Liebermann, Rolf
b.1910

Orchestral Works

Symphony 1949 (1949)   20'
2.2.2(bcl).2-0.3.1.0-timp.perc-pno-str
Material on hire
AVV

Solo Voice(s) and Instrument(s)/ Orchestra

Musik (1949)   21'
Text: Charles Baudelaire/Paul Verlaine
Soloist: speaker
2.2.2(bcl).2-0.3.2.0-timp.perc-pno-str
Material on hire
AVV

Choral Works

Streitlied zwischen Leben und Tod (1950)   30'
Text: Robert Kothe
Soloists: soprano, mezzo-soprano, tenor, bass
Chorus: mixed
2.2.2.bcl.2-0.3.3.1-timp.perc-pno.hp-str
Material on hire
Study score **AVV 57** / Choral score **AVV 3**

Ligeti, György
b.1923

Stage Works

Le Grand Macabre
(1974-77/95)   120'
Opera in 2 Acts
Text: Michael Meschke/György Ligeti
Material on hire
Study score **ED 8522** / Libretto **BN 3501-70**

Rondeau (1976)   30'
One-Man Theatre
Material on hire
SM

Infoline · e-Mail
Schott Musik International
Mainz: Schott.Musik.com@T-Online.de
London: 101627.166@compuserve.com

Ligeti, György

b. Diciosânmartin 28.5.1923

Few composers have been able so success-fully to create and reinvent their own, uni-que sound-world as György Ligeti. From the timeless orchestral landscapes of "Atmosphères" and "San Francisco Polyphony" to the Romanticism of the Horn Trio and the recent, Hungarian inspired concertos for piano and violin, his novel approach to the most basic elements of music has ensured a succession of works that continually challenge the limits of our musical understanding while beguiling the senses with sounds of the utmost transpa-rency and freshness. A vein of sharp, surre-al humour plays its part, heard not only in the music-theatre of "Aventures et Nouvelles Aventures", but also in the opera "Le Grand Macabre". As a teacher, Ligeti is respected for the same qualities as are found in his music: for the insight he brings to the problems of 20th century music, and for the originality of his proposed solutions.

Orchestral Works

Ballad and Dance (1949-50) 3'

After Romanian Folksongs for School orchestra
rec-perc-pno-str
Score **CON 177** / Parts **CON 177-50/-60**

Chamber Concerto

(1969-70) 21'

for 13 instrumentalists
1(pic).1(ob d'am,ca).2(bcl).0-1.0.1.0-hpd(org/harm).pno(cel)-str(1.1.1.1.1)
Material on hire
Study score **ED 6323**

Concert Românesc (1952) 12'

2(pic).2(ca).2.2-3.2.0.0-perc-str
Material on hire
SM

Lontano (1967) 11'

4(2pic,3afl).4(ca).4(bcl,[cbcl]).3.cbn-4.3([Dtpt]).3.1-str
Material on hire
Study score **ED 6303**

Melodien (1971) 13'

1(pic).1(ob d'am).1.1-2.1.1.1-perc-pno(cel)-str(8.7.6.5.4)
Material on hire
Study score **ED 6334**

6 Miniatures (1953) 12'

Arranger: Friedrich K. Wanek (1975)
2fl(pic).2ob(ca).2cl(Ebcl).2bn-2hn
Material on hire
SM

Old Hungarian Dances

(1949) 11'

(Régi magyar társas táncok)
[fl.cl]-str
Score **CON 188** / Parts **CON 188 -11 (-17)**

Ramifications (1968-69) 9'

str(min:7.0.2.2.1)
Material on hire
Study score **ED 6305**

San Francisco Polyphony

(1973-74) 12'

3(2pic,afl).3(ob d'am,ca).3(Ebcl,bcl).2.cbn-2.2.2.btuba-2perc-pno(cel).hp-str(12.12.10.8.6)
Material on hire
Study score **ED 6707**

Concertos

Double Concerto (1972) 15'

Soloists: flute, oboe
3(3pic).3(ob d'am,ca).2(Ebcl).bcl.2.cbn-2.1.1.tbtbn.0-perc-cel.hp-str(0.0.4.6.4)
Material on hire
Study score **ED 6338** / Parts **ED 6599 (solo)**

Piano Concerto (1985-88) 22'

Soloist: piano
1(pic).1.1(ocarina).1-1.1.1.0-2perc-str(8.7.6.5.4)
Material on hire
Score **ED 7746/-01** / Piano reduction **ED 7437**

Violin Concerto (1990-92) 28'

Soloist: violin
2(pic,srec,afl).1(ocarina).2(Ebcl,bcl,2oca-rina).1(ocarina)-2.1.1.0-2perc-str(5.0.3.2.1)
Material on hire
SM

Chamber & Instrumental Works

Andante - Allegretto (1950) 7'

str qrt
ED 8334

6 Bagatelles (1953) 13'

fl.ob.cl.bn-hn
Study score **ED 6409** / Parts **ED 6407**

Ballad and Dance (1950) 3'

Two Violin Duos after a Romanian Folksong
2vn
ED 8371

Capriccio No. 1 (1947) 3'

pno
ED 7807

Capriccio No. 2 (1947) 2'

pno
ED 7807

Cello Sonata (1948/53) 9'

cello solo
ED 7698

Continuum (1968) 4'

hpd
ED 6111

Early Pieces (1942-51) 10'

pno (4hnd)
ED 7955

Étude pour Piano No.14a

(1993) 1'

"Coloana Fara Sfarsit"
player pno (pianist ad lib.)
ED 8399

Étude pour piano No. 15

"White on White"
ED 8541

2 Études for Organ

(1967-69) 12'

"Harmonies", "Coulée"
organ solo
ED 6477

Études pour piano (1985) 19'

Premier livre
No. 1: "Desordre"
No. 2: "Cordes vives"
No. 3: "Touches bloquées"
No. 4: "Fanfares"
No. 5: "Arc-en-ciel"
No. 6: "Automne à Varsovie"
ED 7428/ED 7989

4 SOSTENUTO ESPRESSIVO *)
1/4 (♩ = 64)

Fl.
Cl.
Fg.

4 SOSTENUTO ESPRESSIVO *)
4 (♩ = 64)

Vc. Soli

*) Das Tempo ♩ = 64 ist nur ein Hinweis. Das Stück soll mit vielem Ausdruck gespielt werden: außer den angegebenen rallentandi und accelerandi können weitere Tempaschwankungen ad lib. erfolgen.
The tempo marking ♩ = 64 is only a general indication. The piece must be played with great expression; apart from the indicated rallentandos and accelerandos other fluctuations in tempo are permissible.
**) Fagott-sordino: ein Tuch, in die Schallöffnung gestopft.
Bassoon mute: a cloth placed in the bell of the instrument.
NB. Sämtliche Vn. I, Vn. II und Vcl. nehmen Sordino, die Vle. ebenfalls, außer den 4 ersten Bratschisten, die senza sord. beginnen und erst ab Takt 19 con sord. spielen.
All Vn. I, Vn. II and Vcl. are muted, as are the Vle, except for the first four Violas, which begin senza sord. and play con sord. from bar 19 onwards.

5

Fl.
Ob.
Cl.
Fg.
Cor.
Tr.
Vle. Soli
Vc. Soli

György Ligeti
Lontano (1967)
beginning

151

Études pour Piano (1988-93) 23'

Deuxième livre
No. 7: "Galamb Borong"
No. 8: "Fém"
No. 9: "Vertige"
No. 10: "Der Zauberlehrling"
No. 11: "En suspens"
No. 12: "Entrelacs"
No. 13: "L'Escalier du Diable"
No. 14: "Coloana infinitá"
No. 14a: "Coloana fárá Sfárşit"
SM

Horn Trio (1982) 22'

vn-hn-pno
Score **ED 7309** / Parts **ED 7744**

Hungarian Rock (1978) 5'

hpd
ED 6805

Invenció (1948)

pno
ED 7807

Monument. Selbstportrait. Bewegung (1976) 15'

2pno
ED 6687

Musica Ricercata (1951-53) 24'

pno
ED 7718

Mysteries of the Macabre (1988) 7'

Arranger: Elgar Howarth
tpt-pno
ED 8062

Passacaglia Ungherese (1978) 5'

hpd
ED 6843

10 Pieces for Wind Quintet (1968) 15'

fl.ob.cl.bn-hn
Study score **ED 6304** / Parts **ED 6318**

Ricercare (1953) 4'

organ solo
ED 7745

String Quartet No.1 (1953-54) 21'

Métamorphoses Nocturnes
Score **ED 6476** / Parts **ED 7247**

String Quartet No.2 (1968) 22'

Study score **ED 6639** / Parts **ED 6638**

Viola Sonata (1991-94) 22'

viola solo
ED 8374

Solo Voice(s)/Voice(s) and Piano/Guitar

Két dal (1946-47) 5'

Three Songs
Text: Sándor Weöres
voice-pno
ED 8453

Mysteries of the Macabre (1988) 7'

soprano-pno
SM

Solo Voice(s) and Instrument(s)/ Orchestra

Mysteries of the Macabre (1992) 9'

Soloist: soprano/trumpet
2.3(ca).2(bcl).2(cbn)-4.2.1.1-2perc-cel.pno.eorg.hp.mand-str
Material on hire
Study score **ED 8205**

Mysteries of the Macabre (1991) 9'

Arranger: Elgar Howarth
Soloist: soprano/trumpet
1(pic).1.1(bcl).1(cbn)-1.1.1.0-2perc-pno(cel).mand-str(2.1.1.1)
Material on hire
Study score **ED 8210**

Choral Works

Betlehemi Királyok (1946) 2'

Text: Attila József
Chorus: mixed/female a cappella (2 prt)
C 48128

Bujdosó (1946) 2'

Chorus: mixed a cappella (3 prt)
C 46760

Clocks and Clouds (1972-73) 13'

Chorus: female(4S.4MS.4A)
5(3pic,afl).3.5(bcl).4(cbn)-0.2.0.0-glsp.vib-cel.2hp-str(0.0.4.6.4)
Material on hire
Study score **ED 8204**

Éjszaka - Reggel (1955) 5'

(Night - Morning)
Text: Sándor Weöres
Chorus: mixed a cappella (6-8 prt)
ED 6415

3 Fantasies (1982) 11'

Text: Friedrich Hölderlin
Chorus: mixed a cappella (16 prt)
SKR 20003

Ha folyóvíz volnék (1947-53) 1'

Text: Folk
Chorus: mixed (canon 4 prt)
SM

Haj, ifjuság (1952) 5'

3 Folksongs (Youth)
Chorus: mixed a cappella
C 46762

Hortobágy (1952) 5'

Hungarian Folksongs
Chorus: mixed a cappella
C 46763

Húsvét (1946) 3'

(Easter)
Text: Folk
Chorus: female double a cappella
C 48129

Idegen Földön (Far from Home) (1945-46) 4'

Text: Bálint Balassa
Chorus: female a cappella
C 46165

Inaktelki nóták (1953) 4'

Songs from Inaktelke
Chorus: mixed (2 prt)
C 46759

Kállai kettős (1950) 3'

Doppeltanz aus Kálló
Chorus: mixed a cappella
C 46761

Lakodalmas (1950) 1'

Wedding-dance
Chorus: mixed a cappella
C 46764

Magány (Solitude) (1946) 3'

Text: Sándor Weöres
Chorus: mixed a cappella (3 prt)
SKR 20019

Magas Kősziklának (1946) 2'

Text: Folk
Chorus: mixed a cappella (3 prt)
C 46758

Magyar Etűdök (Hungarian Studies) (1983) 6'

Text: Sándor Weöres
Chorus: mixed a cappella (16 prt)
SKR 20006

Mátraszentimrei Dalok (Songs from Mátraszentimre) (1955) 5'

Chorus: female/children's a cappella (2-3 prt)
C 45593

Nonsense Madrigals

(1988-93)   13'

6 solo male voices(2A.T.2Bar.B) a cappella
ED 7866

Pápainé (Widow Pápai)

(1953)   3'

Chorus: mixed a cappella
SKR 20018

Pletykázó asszonyok   (1952)   1'

(Klatschende Frauen)
Text: Sándor Weöres
Chorus: female a cappella
SM

Scenes and Interludes

(1978)   47'

from "Le Grand Macabre'
Text: Michael Meschke/György Ligeti
Soloists: soprano, mezzo-soprano, tenor,
baritone
Chorus: [mixed]
3(2pic).3(ob d'am,ca).3(Ebcl,asax,bcl).
3(cbn)-4.4(Dtpt).btpt.ttbn.tbtbn.cbtbn.1.
btuba(cbtuba)-3perc-cel(hpd).pno(epno).
eorg.regal.hp-solo str(3.0.2.6.4)
Material on hire
SM

Electronic Works

Artikulation   (1958)   4'

tape
Audio-Score and CD/MC on hire

Glissandi   (1957)   8'

tape
SM

Pièce électronique No.3   (1957)

tape
SM

Poème symphonique

(1962)   20-30'

100 metronomes
SM

Linde, Hans-Martin

b.1930

Concertos

Konzert   (1991)   16'

Soloist: recorder (sopranino, alto, bass)
str
Score **CON 247** / Parts **CON 247-70** / Piano
reduction **OFB 174**

Linde, Hans-Martin

b. Werne 24.5.1930

Hans-Martin Linde grew up in a musical home in Iserlohn, Westphalia. In 1947 he went to study the flute with Gustav Scheck at the Freiburg Conservatory, where he also studied choral conducting and composition with Konrad Lechner. After completing his studies he worked as a flute teacher and choral conductor in his home town. At this time he started to take a keen interest in playing the recorder and the baroque traverse flute. In 1955 he embarked on a long period of work with the Westdeutscher Rundfunk (West German Radio) in Cologne, involving regular chamber music recordings and an appointment as flautist and later as conductor with the Capella Basiliensis in Bâle. From 1976 to 1979 Hans-Martin Linde was head of the senior department of the Basel Academy of Music. From 1979 to 1995 he ran a choral conducting class, taught performance practice and directed the Academy's choirs, besides his international carreer as a flautist (including several CD and vinyl recordings). Since 1983 he has increasingly been working as a conductor of instrumental groups and opera.
Hans-Martin Linde has published articles on performance practice and methods for the recorder, and has composed works for orchestra, chamber and vocal ensembles. His compositions for recorder have become firmly established in the 20th-century repertoire for that instrument. He uses avant-garde playing techniques and experiments with new compositional structures, but a link with tonality and old forms is nevertheless always detectable.

Chamber & Instrumental Works

Amarilli mia bella   (1971)   10'

Hommage à Johann Jacob van Eyck
recorder (S,A,B) solo
OFB 133

Anspielungen

for baroque or modern traverse-flute
flute solo
FTR 150

Das Basler Blockflötenbuch

(1993)   60'

recorder (S,A,T,B) solo
ED 8250

Blockflöte virtuos   (1983)   16'

altorecorder solo
OFB 156

Capriccio   (1963)   9'

*2arec.trec-drum-3va da gamba
alt. version: 3fl-drum-vn.va.vc*
Score **ED 5389** / Parts **ED 5389**

Drei Skizzen   (1990)   10'

arec-vn-pno/hpd
ED 8249

Fantasien und Scherzi

(1963)   5'

altorecorder solo
OFB 46

Fünf Studien   (1974)   5'

arec-pno
OFB 160

3 Jazzy Tunes

arec-pno
OFB 177

Märchen   (1977)   8'

after "Der metaphysische Kanarienvogel"
by Hans von Flesch-Brunningen (1919)
recorder (Sop,A,T,B) solo
OFB 154

Music for a bird   (1968)   4'

altorecorder solo
OFB 48

Music for two   (1983)   11'

arec-gtr
OFB 157

Musica da camera   (1972)   11'

rec (A,B)-gtr
OFB 135

Neuzeitliche Übungsstücke

(1960)

altorecorder solo
ED 4797

Quartett-Übung (1961) 22'

srec.arec.trec.brec
ED 5262

Serenade

recorder (S,T) solo
ED 7848

Serenata à tre (1964) 12'

recorder (S,A,B)-gtr -vc/va da gamba
ED 5536

Sonate

arec-org
ED 8476

Sonate in d moll (1961) 8'

arec-pno
OFB 47

Suite (1993) 11'

srec(arec).arec.trec.brec
OFB 168

Trio (1960) 10'

arec.fl-hpd/pno
ED 5261

Una Follia nouva (1989) 12'

altorecorder solo
OFB 165

Litaize, Gaston
1909-1991

Chamber & Instrumental Works

Diapason 8'

Fantaisie sur le nom de Jehan Alain
organ solo
ED 7886

Diptyque 9'

ob-org
ED 8019

Reges Tharsis 6'

(Méditation sur l'offertoire de l'Epiphanie)
organ solo
ED 7968

Sonata à deux 11'

organ solo (4hnd)
ED 8053

Triptyque 12'

hn-org
ED 7955

Lokschin, Alexander
1920-1987

Solo Voice(s) and Instrument(s)/ Orchestra

3 Scenes from Goethe's Faust (1980) 38'

Soloist: soprano
1.0.ca.2(Ebcl).bcl.2(cbn)-1.1.ttbn.0-timp.perc-hp-str
Material on hire
Score KIN 1002

Lopatnikoff, Nicolai
1903-1976

Orchestral Works

Symphony No.1, Op. 12

(1928) 25'

pic.2.2.ca.2.bcl.2.cbn-4.3.2.1-timp.perc-hp-str
Material on hire
SM

Concertos

Piano Concerto No.2, Op. 15

(1930) 25'

Soloist: piano
pic.2.2.ca.2(Ebcl).2-3.2.2.1-timp.perc-str
Material on hire
Piano reduction ED 2138

Lopes-Graça, Fernando
1906-1994

Orchestral Works

Trois danses portugaises

(1941) 9'

pic.2.2.ca.2.bcl.2.cbn-4.4.3.1-timp.perc-2hp-str
Material on hire
SM

Lörik, Anna

Orchestral Works

Budapester Marsch 8'

pic.1.1.2.1-2.2.3.0-perc-pno-str(3.2.2.2.2)
alt. version: 2(pic).2.3.2ssax.2asax.0-2flhn.4nathn.3.4.euph.2
Material on hire
CRZ 4001

Magjar Vigadò 4'

2.2.2.2-4.2.3.1-timp.perc-pno.hp-str
Material on hire
SM

Rio Chico 4'

Tango for Orchestra
Arranger: Herbert Turba
2.1.2.1-2.2.3.0-timp.perc-pno.[gtr].hp-str(4.3.2.1.1)
Material on hire
SM

Lotz, Hans-Georg
b.1934

Chamber & Instrumental Works

Quartet

srec.arec.trec.brec
OFB 136

Lutschewitz, Martin

b.1922

Chamber & Instrumental Works

2 kleine Festmusiken
0.0.Ebcl.2.0-2flhn.2.2.2thn.euph.2
BLK 200

Lutyens, Elisabeth

1906-1983

Orchestral Works

Chorale for Orchestra, Op. 36 (1956) 4'
2.1.1.1-3.3.2ttbn.btbn.0-hp-3vn.3vc
Material on hire
SL

Music for Orchestra 2, Op. 48 (1962) 11'
2pic.afl.ob.asax.Ebcl.3cl.bn-4tpt.3tbn.sar-rusophone-timp.perc-cel-str(6.0.0.6.4)
Material on hire
Study score **ED 10878***

Music for Orchestra 3, Op. 56 (1963) 14'
3.2.4.3-4.3.4.1-timp.perc-cel.hp-str
Material on hire
SL

Music for Wind, Op. 60 (1964) 11'
2.2.2.2-2.0.0.0
Material on sale
SL

Concertos

Music for Piano and Orchestra, Op. 59 (1964) 10'
Soloist: piano
2.1.1.1-2.2.2.1-timp.perc-hp-str
Material on hire
SL

Lutyens, Elisabeth

b. London 9.7.1906, d. London 14.4.1983

Daughter of Edwardian architect Sir Edwin Lutyens, Elizabeth Lutyens is remembered as a pioneer amongst woman composers, and an early advocate of the twelve-note system in Britain at a time when it was derided and misunderstood. Thought most comfortable in the smaller forms, she created a large output of works for the concert hall in addition to her commercial writing for the cinema. Formal clarity and precision were valued above romantic expression, but her finest music balances classical poise and direction with a turbulent current of genuine emotion.

Symphonies, Op. 46 (1961) 17'
Soloist: piano
3.3.4.3-4.3.3.1-timp.6perc-2hp
Material on hire
Piano reduction **ED 10907**

Chamber & Instrumental Works

5 Bagatelles, Op. 49 (1962) 5'
pno
ED 10893

Capriccii, Op. 33 (1955) 8'
2hp-perc
Material on sale
SL

3 Duos - No.1, Op. 34
(1956-57) 10'
hn-pno
Manuscript score on sale
SL

3 Duos - No.2, Op. 34
(1956-57) 10'
vc-pno
Manuscript score on sale
SL

3 Duos - No.3, Op. 34
(1956-57) 11'
vn-pno
Manuscript score on sale
SL

The Fall of the Leafe (1966) 8'
Soloist: oboe
str qrt
Material on sale
SL

5 Little Pieces, Op. 14/1
(1945) 5'
cl-pno
ED 10930*

Nocturnes, Op. 30 (1955) 6'
gtr-vn.vc
Material on sale
SL

Scena, Op. 58 (1964) 14'
vn.vc-perc
Material on sale
SL

Sinfonia, Op. 32 (1955) 5'
organ solo
Manuscript score on sale
SL

String Quintet, Op. 51
(1963) 21'
2vn.va.2vc
Material on sale
SL

String Trio, Op. 57 (1964) 10'
vn.va.vc
Material on sale
Study score **ED 10945**

Symphonics for Solo Piano
Manuscript score on sale
SL

Wind Trio, Op. 52 (1963) 10'
fl.cl.bn
Material on sale
SL

Infoline · e-Mail
Schott Musik International
Mainz: Schott.Musik.com@T-Online.de
London: 101627.166@compuserve.com

Solo Voice(s) and Instrument(s)/ Orchestra

And Suddenly it's Evening, Op. 66 (1966) 20'

Text: Quasimodo
Soloist: tenor
2tpt.hn.2tbn-perc-cel.hp-vn.vc.db
Study score **ED 11110***

Catena, Op. 44 (1961) 40'

Text: various
Soloist: soprano/tenor
*1.1.3.1-2.1.2.0-timp.2perc-
cel.pno.mand.hp.gtr-str(1.0.1.1.1)*
Material on hire
SL

Choral Works

De Amore, Op. 39 (1957) 40'

Text: Chaucer
Soloists: soprano, tenor
Chorus: mixed
*2(pic).1.2.1-2.2cnt.2.1.0-timp.3perc-
pno/(cel).hp-str*
Material on hire
SL

Encomion, Op. 54 (1963) 17'

Chorus: mixed
0.0.0.0-4.3.3.1-timp.4perc
Material on hire
SL

Excerpta Tractatus logico philosophici, Op. 27 (1952) 10'

Text: Wittgenstein
Chorus: mixed a cappella
ED 10887

The Hymn of Man, Op. 61 (1965/70) 10'

Text: Swinburne
Chorus: mixed a cappella
Material on hire
SL

Magnificat and Nunc Dimitis (1965) 10'

Chorus: mixed a cappella
ED 10936*

Maasz, Gerhard
1906-1984

Orchestral Works

Handwerkertänze (1936) 12'

2.2.2.2-2.2.1.0-timp.perc-[pno]-str
Material on hire
SM

Chamber & Instrumental Works

10 Easy Pieces (1973) 14'

2gtr
GA 431

Little Suite (1954) 13'

rec-pno
ED 4514

Miniatrio (1956) 10'

vn.va.vc
Score **ED 4589** / Parts **ED 4922**

Solo Voice(s) and Instrument(s)/ Orchestra

Klingende Jahreszeiten (1951) 20'

Text: various
Chorus: children's
srec-vn
B 106

Choral Works

Das Hasenspiel (1967) 7'

Text: Christian Morgenstern
Chorus: children's
rec-xyl.glsp-vc/gtr-str(1.1.0.0.0)
Score **B 163** / Parts **B 163-11 (-15)** / Vocal
score **B 163-01**

Wir sind die Musikanten (1977) 15'

Soloist: [speaker]
Chorus: male/[female]
*2(pic).2.ca.2.2(cbn)-2.2.1.[1]-timp.4perc-
pno(cel)-str(4.4.2.2.2)*
Score **CON 184** / Parts **CON 184-10 (-15)** /
Choral score **CON 184-01**

MacCombie, Bruce
b.1943

Orchestral Works

Chelsea Tango (1991)　　11'

3(pic).3(ca).3(bcl).3(cbn)-4.3.3.1-
timp.3perc-pno-str
Material on hire
Study score **EA 743**

Concertos

Nightshade Rounds (1988)　10'

Soloist: guitar
str
Material on hire
EAM-Helicon

Chamber & Instrumental Works

3 Designs for 3 Players
(1979)　　　　　　　　12'

cl-vc-pno
Score and parts **EA 618**

Elegy (1993)　　　　　9'

cl-vn.vc-pno
Material on sale
EAM-Helicon

Gerberau Musics (1979)　10'

pno (partially prepared)
EA 619

Greeting (1993)　　　　8'

fl.cl-vn.vc-pno
Material on hire
EAM-Helicon

Nightshade Rounds (1979)　10'

guitar solo
EA 620

MacCombie, Bruce

b. Providence, Rhode Island 1943

MacCombie's varied career has included periods as Dean of the Julliard School and of the School for Arts at Boston University. The recipient of many prizes and awards, he has been described in the pages of the New York Times as a "deft and evocative craftsman". He is a gifted composer of choral and vocal music, intensely thoughtful and full of passion and colour.

Solo Voice(s) and Instrument(s)/ Orchestra

Leaden Echo, Golden Echo
(1989)　　　　　　　　16'

Text: Gerard Manley Hopkins
Soloist: soprano
1.1.1.0-1.1.1.0-perc-pno-str
alt. version: S-pno
Material on hire
Study score **EA 686**

Choral Works

Color and Time (1988)　12'

Text: Thomas E. Bezanson
Chorus: mixed a cappella
EAM-Helicon

Mainardi, Enrico
1897-1976

Orchestral Works

Music for Strings, Op. 54　20'

str
Material on hire
SM

Concertos

Cello Concerto (1960)　　28'

Soloist: cello
pic.2.2.ca.2.bcl.2-3.2.2.0-timp-str
Material on hire
Piano reduction **ED 5836**

Cello Concerto (1969)　　25'

Soloists: 2 celli
pic.2.2.ca.2.bcl.2.cbn-0.0.0.0-timp.perc-
pno-str(12.10.8.8.6)
Material on hire
SM

Elegy (1957)　　　　　15'

Soloist: cello
str
Material on hire
Study score **ED 5009**

Chamber & Instrumental Works

Ballata della lontananza
(1968)　　　　　　　　8'

cello solo
ED 5763

Cello Sonata (1958)　　20'

vc-pno
ED 4678

Cello Sonata (1959)　　18'

cello solo
ED 5159

Cello Sonata quasi Fantasia
(1962)　　　　　　　　16'

vc-pno
ED 5459

Cello Sonatina (1939)　　7'

vc-pno
ED 3630

Cello Studies and Pieces
(1923-53)　　　　　　　32'

cello solo
ED 4625

Due Tempi Romantici

(1964) 18'

vn.vc-pno
Material on sale
Score and parts **ED 5905**

Piano Trio (1958) 21'

vn.vc-pno
Parts **ED 4770**

7 Preludes (1964) 13'

cello solo
ED 5492

Recitative, Aria and Epilogue

(1966) 12'

vc-pno
ED 6110

Sonata Breve (1942) 9'

cello solo
ED 3783

7 Studi Brevi (1961) 14'

cello solo
ED 5764

Trio (1969) 23'

fl-vc-pno
ED 6227

Violin Sonata (1961) 18'

vn-pno
ED 5178

Majo, Giulio di
b.1933

Orchestral Works

Sinfonia da camera (1933) 10'

1.1.1.1-1.1.0.0-timp.cel.pno.hp-str
Material on hire
AVV

Chamber & Instrumental Works

Caprichos (1959) 5'

pno
ED 5099

Maler, Wilhelm
1902-1976

Orchestral Works

Concerto grosso, Op. 11 (1928)

Orchesterspiel II
Concertino: 1(pic).0.0.1-pno-vn.va.vc
Concerto: str(4.4.3.2.1)
Material on hire
SM

Flämisches Rondo (1937) 25'

2(pic).2(ca).2.2(cbn)-4.2.3.1-timp.2perc-hp-str
Material on hire
SM

Music for String Orchestra

(1937) 27'

str
Material on hire
SM

Orchesterspiel (1930) 5'

2(pic).2.2.2-4.2.3.0-timp-str
Material on hire
SM

Concertos

Concerto, Op. 10 (1927) 18'

Soloist: harpsichord/piano
1(pic).1(ca).1.1-1.0.0.0-perc-str(5.4.3.3.1/7.6.5.4.2)
Material on hire
SM

Triple Concerto (1940) 40'

Soloists: piano, violin, cello
2(pic).2(ca).2.2(cbn)-4.3.3.1-timp.2perc-str
Material on hire
SM

Violin Concert in A-Major

(1932)

Soloist: violin
2(pic).2(ca)-2(bcl).2(cbn)-4.2.3.1-timp-str
Material on hire
SM

Chamber & Instrumental Works

3 Little Piano Pieces on Old Christmas Songs 10'

pno
ED 2772

String Quartet in G-Major

(1942) 20'

Parts **ED 3170**

String Terzett (1938) 20'

vn.va.vc
Parts **ED 2859**

Choral Works

Cantata (1930) 40'

Text: Stefan George
Soloist: bass
Chorus: mixed
2.2.0.0-0.2.3.0-timp-str
Material on hire
SM

Der ewige Strom (1934) 100'

Oratorio
Text: Stefan Andres
Soloists: soprano, tenor, bass
Chorus: mixed
2(pic).2(ca).2(asax, bcl).2(cbn)-4.2.3.1-timp.perc-cel(glsp).hp-str
Material on hire
SM

Malipiero, Gian Francesco
1882-1973

Stage Works

El Mondo novo (1950-51) 26'

Fantasy-Ballet after Tipolo
Material on hire
AVV

Orchestral Works

La Laterna Magica (1955) 21'

Ballet-Suite from "El Mondo novo"
2.2.2.2-4.2.3.1-perc-cel.pno-str
Material on hire
AVV

Quattro Invenzioni (1933) 12'

(La festa degli indolenti)
2.2.2.2-2.1.1.0-3perc-pno(4hnd)-str
Material on hire
Study score **ETP 881**

Malipiero, Riccardo

b.1914

Choral Works

Cantata Sacra (1947) 30'

Text: Katharina von Siena
Soloist: soprano
Chorus: mixed
2(pic).2.2.2-4.3.2.0-timp.perc-str
Material on hire
Study score **AVV 83**

Martinet, Jean-Louis

b.1912

Orchestral Works

Trois mouvements symphoniques (1953-54) 31'

pic.2.2.ca.2.bcl.2(cbn)-4.3.3.1-timp.perc-cel.pno.hp-str
Material on hire
SM

Martinon, Jean

1910-1976

Concertos

Cello Concerto, Op. 52

(1963) 27'

Soloist: cello
2(pic).2.2.2-2.2.1.0-timp.perc-pno(cel).hp-str(12.12.8.6.4)
Material on hire
Piano reduction **ED 5434**

Violin Concerto No. 2, Op. 51 (1958) 33'

Soloist: violin
2(pic).2.2.bcl.2-4.2.2.0-timp.perc-cel.hp-str(12.10.8.6.4)
Material on hire
Piano reduction **ED 5284**

Chamber & Instrumental Works

Duo, Op. 47 (1959) 22'

vn-pno
ED 4791

Sonatina No.6, Op. 49/2

(1958) 11'

violin solo
ED 5063

String Quartet, Op. 43

(1946) 29'

Parts **ED 4199**

Martinů, Bohuslav

1890-1959

Orchestral Works

Partita (1031) 11'

Suite No.1
str
Material on hire
SM

Serenade (1932) 12'

1.2.1.2-2.2.1.0-str(2solo vn-6.6.4.3.2)
Material on hire
SM

Sinfonia concertante (1932) 22'

Orchestra I: 0.3.0.1-2.0.0.0-str
Orchestra II: 2(pic).0.2.1-2.2.3.1-timp-str
Material on hire
Study score **ED 4403**

Concertos

Cello Concerto No. 1 (1955) 27'

Soloist: cello
2.2.2.2-4.2.3.0-timp.perc-str
Material on hire
Piano reduction **ED 4645**

Concerto for String Quartet with Orchestra (1931) 17'

Soloists: string qrt
2.2.2.2-2.2.2.0-timp.perc-str
Material on hire
Study score **ED 4593**

Suite concertante (1955) 23'

Soloist: violin
2.2.2.2-4.2.3.1-timp.perc-str
Material on hire
Piano reduction **ED 4644**

Martinů, Bohuslav

b. Policka, Bohemia 8.12.1890,
d. Liestal/Switzerland 28.8.1959

The neo-classical label neatly describes Martinů's fondness for vigorous contrapunctal forms and baroque rhythms yet leaves everything unsaid about his richly individual melodic voice and the distinctly Czech flavour of his music. An abundance of concertos, quartets and sonatas is ample testimony to the strength of a creative gift that was equally at home in ballets and operas, still holding the stage. Though separated from his native land in later years, he maintained its national spirit in music of unbounded optimism tempered with the genuine pathos of exile - notably in a canon of six symphonies all composed after his move to the United States in 1941.

Chamber & Instrumental Works

Esquisses de Danses (1932) 2'

pno
ED 2327

Piano Trio (1930) 15'

5 Pièces Brèves
vn.vc-pno
Material on sale
Score and parts **ED 2183**

Infoline · e-Mail
Schott Musik International
Mainz: Schott.Musik.com@T-Online.de
London: 101627.166@compuserve.com

Rhythmische Etüden (1931)

violin solo-[pno]
VLB 46

Les Ritournelles (1932)   3'

pno
ED 2326

Choral Works

Ei, steig auf (1948)   2'

from "8 Tschechische Madrigale"
Chorus: mixed a cappella
C 41351

Gram zernagt mein Herzchen (1948)   2'

from "8 Tschechische Madrigale"
Chorus: mixed a cappella
C 41355

Hei! Alle kommt herbei

(1948)   2'

from "8 Tschechische Madrigale"
Chorus: mixed a cappella
C 41354

Ja, noch einmal (1948)   2'

from "8 Tschechische Madrigale"
Chorus: mixed a cappella
C 41358

Sag mir, Gott (1948)   2'

from "8 Tschechische Madrigale"
Chorus: mixed a cappella
C 41353

Unserer Liebe Glück (1948)   2'

from "8 Tschechische Madrigale"
Chorus: mixed a cappella
C 41356

Wandern müssen wir (1948)   2'

from "8 Tschechische Madrigale"
Chorus: mixed a cappella
C 41352

Wie mir ist (1948)   2'

from "8 Tschechische Madrigale"
Chorus: mixed a cappella
C 41357

Martirano, Salvatore
1927-1995

Orchestral Works

Contrasto (1954)   9'

3.3.3.3-4.3.3.1-timp.3perc-cel.hp-str
Material on hire
Study score **ED 10724***

Solo Voice(s)/Voices(s) and Piano/Guitar

Chansons Innocentes

(1957)   14'

Text: E.E. Cummings
soprano-pno
ED 10903*

Choral Works

O that Shakespeherian Rag

(1959)   23'

Chorus: mixed
2cl.asax-tpt.tbn-pno-perc-db
Material on hire
Study score **ED 10726***

Mass (1952-55)

Chorus: mixed double a cappella
Material on hire
SL

Martland, Steve
b.1959

Orchestral Works

Babi Yar (1983)   35'

2pic.1.1.ca.2.bcl.asax.tsax.2-4.3.3.1-7perc-pno.synth.egtr.bgtr-str(32.0.8.10.8)
Material on hire
Study score **ED 12356**

Crossing the Border

(1990-91)   25'

str(min:8.8.4.4.2)
Material on hire
Study score **ED 12402**

Dividing the Lines (1986)   30'

9cnt.flhn.5hn.2tbn.btbn.2euph.4tuba-2perc
Material on hire
SL

Lotta Continua (1981/84)   20'

3(pic).2.2.2-2.2.2.0-5perc-pno-str(8.8.6.6.4)
band: asax.flhn-egtr-jazz kit
Material on hire
SL

Wolf-gang (1991)   15'

6 Mozart Arias
Arranger: Steve Martland
2ob(ca).2cl(ssax,bcl).2bn-2hn
Material on hire or sale
SL

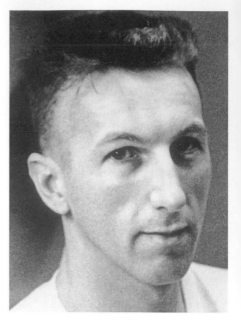

Martland, Steve

b. Liverpool 10.10.1959

Where art impinges on the realities of life, Steve Martland's music speaks with a refreshing directness, raising social issues and philosophical questions of burning importance to our age. Most striking is the rhythmic verve of his work, extending into new areas the discoveries of his teacher Louis Andreissen. But Martland is a lyricist as well, whose melodic style can achieve a rapt, almost spiritual communication. With the exception of his symphonic poem "Babi Yar" he has chosen to avoid the standard concert-hall forms, perferring to write for smaller groups, including his own Steve Martland Band, taking music to schools, to community centres and out into the street.

Concertos

Orc (1984)   20'

Soloist: horn
fl.ob.cl.bn-tpt.tbn-perc-pno.synth-str(max:4.4.2.2.2)
Material on hire
SL

Chamber & Instrumental Works

American Invention (1985)   22'

2fl.2bcl-hn-perc-2pno.bgtr-2vn.va.vc
Material on hire
Study score **ED 12281**

Beat the Retreat (1995) 12'

ssax.ssax/asax.barsax-Ebtpt.tbn-drums.marimb-pno.egtr.bgtr-vn
Material on hire
SL

Big Mac (1987) 6'

asax.tsax-flhn.tbn-synth.vib-vn.db
Material on hire or sale
SL

Crossing the Border

(1991-92) 24'

str qrt-tape
Material on sale
SL

Dance Works (1993) 25'

asax.tsax.barsax.flhn-tbn-keybd-vn-egtr.bgtr
Material on hire
SL

Dance Works (1993) 25'

2pno
Manuscript score on sale
SL

Drill (1987) 27'

2pno
ED 12338

Duo (1982) 15'

tpt-pno
Manuscript score on sale
SL

Full Fathom Five (1993) 15'

brass qnt
Material on sale
ED 12510

Horses of Instruction

(1994/95) 17'

tsax-vc-egtr.bgtr-marimb.pno
alt. version: asax.tsax.barsax.Bbtpt.tbn-pno.egtr.bgtr.marimb-vn
Material on hire or sale
Study score **ED 12482**

Kgakala (1982) 12'

pno
ED 12286

Mr. Anderson's Pavane

(1994) 10'

brec.bcl-tbn-vn-egtr.pno-perc-bass
Material on hire or sale
SL

Patrol (1992) 30'

str qrt
Material on sale
Study score **ED 12415**

Remembering Lennon

(1981/85) 13'

fl.cl-perc-pno-vn.va.vc
Material on hire or sale
SL

Remix (1986) 5'

jazz ensemble (min): asax.tsax/bcl-flhn.tbn-perc-synth/ehpd-vn.bass
Material on hire or sale
Study score **ED 12337**

Shoulder to Shoulder (1986) 15'

fl(pic).asax.tsax.barsax-hn.3tpt.2tbn.btbn-pno/synth.bgtr
Material on hire
Study score **ED 12327**

Toccata and Fugue BWV 565

(1992) 10'

(J.S.Bach)
Arranger: Steve Martland
str qrt
Material on sale
SL

Solo Voice(s)/Voice(s) and Piano/Guitar

Terra Firma (1989) 24'

Text: Stevan Keane
5 solo voices(amp)-video
Material on hire
SL

Solo Voice(s) and Instrument(s)/ Orchestra

El Pueblo Unido Jamas Sera Vencido (1987) 5'

vocals-fl.asax.tsax.barsax-hn.3tpt.2tbn.btbn-pno-bass
Material on hire or sale
SL

Glad Day (1988) 16'

Text: Stevan Keane
Soloist: voice
asax.tsax.barsax-tpt(flhn).tbn-drums-synth.bgtr-2vn.va.vc
Material on hire
SL

The Perfect Act (1991) 5'

Text: Stevan Keane
Soloist: voice
tsax-tbn-brec-drums-keybd(ehpd)-vn(amp)-egtr.bass/bgtr
Material on hire or sale
SL

Principia (1989) 4'

[vocals]-asax.[tsax]-[tpt(flhn)].tbn-[drums]-pno/synth.[egtr]-vn-bass
Material on hire or sale
SL

Choral Works

Skywalk (1989) 8'

Text: Stevan Keane
Chorus: mixed/5voices a cappella
ED 12362

Marx, Karl
1897 1985

Choral Works

Winterlied, Op. 13/4 (1955)

Text: D. Schirmer
Chorus: mixed (3 prt)
Vocal score **CHBL 319**

Maxwell Davies, Sir Peter
b.1934

Orchestral Works

Carolísima (1994) 17'

1(pic).1.1.bcl.1(cbn)-1.1.1.0-perc-str(min: 1.1.1.1.1)
Material on hire
Study score **SL 12491**

First Fantasia on an "In Nomine" of John Taverner

(1962) 11'

2.2.2.2-2.2.2.1-handbells-str
Material on hire
Study score **ED 10818**

Prolation (1958) 20'

3.3.3.2-4.3.4.1-timp.4perc-cel.hp-str
Material on hire
Study score **ED 10709***

Ricercar and Doubles on "To many a well" (1959) 12'

1.1.1.1-1.0.0.0-hpd-va.vc
Material on hire
Study score **ED 10803**

Sinfonia (1962) 20'

1.1.1.1-1.0.0.0-str
Material on hire
Study score **ED 10820**

Sir Charles his Pavan (1992) 4'

2.afl.2.2.bcl.2.cbn-4.2.3.1-timp.perc-hp-str
Material on hire
Study score **ED 12438**

Maxwell Davies, Peter

b. Manchester 8.9.1934

A leading composer on the international arena, Peter Maxwell Davies is also a distinguished conductor and a pioneer in the world of music education. Reflecting the ideals of the "Manchester School", his early works, tough and gritty, owed as much to the example of medieval music as to the precepts of Schönberg. Later essays in music-theatre created a genre of their own. His symphonies and concertos, written over the last decade to a series of distinguished commissions, are acknowledged as significant additions to the repertoire.

St. Michael (1957)　　17'

Sonata for wind
2.2.2.2-3.2.3.1
Material on hire
Study score **ED 10792**

5 Voluntaries (1960)　　10'

(Various Composers)
Arranger: Peter Maxwell Davies
3.3.2.1-2.3.2.0-timp.perc-hpd/pno-
str(3.0.1.1.1)
Material on hire
ED 10994

William Byrd: 3 Dances

(1959)　　4'

Arranger: Peter Maxwell Davis
2.2.2.1-1.2.1.0-perc-hpd.gtr-str
Score and parts **ED 10932**

Chamber & Instrumental Works

Alma Redemptoris Mater

(1957)　　7'

1.1.2.1-1.0.0.0
Material on sale
Study score **ED 10802**

Organ Fantasia from "O Magnum Mysterium"

(1960)　　15'

organ solo
ED 10826

5 Piano Pieces, Op. 2

(1955-56)　　15'

ED 10551

String Quartet No.1 (1961)　13'

ED 10816

Trumpet Sonata, Op. 1

(1955)　　10'

tpt-pno
ED 11067

Solo Voice(s) and Instrument(s)/ Orchestra

Leopardi Fragments (1962)　16'

Text: from Leopardi
Soloists: soprano, alto
1.1.1.1-0.1.1.0-hp-vc
Material on hire
Score **ED 10819**

Choral Works

Alleluia pro Virgine Maria

(1960)　　2'

from "O Magnum Mysterium"
Chorus: mixed
[str qrt]/[woodwinds]
Score **ED 11274**

Alma Redemptoris Mater

(1962)　　7'

Chorus: (equal voices) a cappella (4 prt)
ED 11268

Carol on St. Steven (1962)　　4'

Chorus: mixed a cappella
ED 11269

4 Choruses (1960)

from "O Magnum Mysterium"
Chorus: mixed a cappella
[str qrt]/[woodwinds]
Score **ED 11276**

The Fader of Heven (1960)　2'

from "O Magnum Mysterium'
Chorus: mixed a cappella
ED 11276

Haylle Comly & Clene

(1960)　　2'

from "O Magnum Mysterium'
Chorus: mixed a cappella
ED 11276

Jesus Autem Hodie (1962)　4'

Chorus: mixed a cappella
ED 11270

The Lord's Prayer (1962)　2'

Chorus: mixed a cappella
ED 11277

Nowell (1962)　　7'

Chorus: mixed a cappella
ED 11271

O Magnum Mysterium

(1960)　　40'

Chorus: mixed
1.1.1.1-1.0.0.0-7perc-org-va.vc
Material on sale
Score **ED 10825** / Parts **ED 10825-01/-03**

O Magnum Mysterium

(1960)　　2'

from "O Magnum Mysterium"
Chorus: mixed a cappella
[str qrt]/[woodwinds]
Score **ED 11272**

Te Lucis Ante Terminum

(1961)　　11'

Chorus: mixed
2.1.2.0-0.2.2.0-glsp-gtr-vc
Material on hire
Study score **ED 10817-02** / Vocal score
ED 10817-01

May, Helmut W.
b.1929

Orchestral Works

Spiritual Concerto (1979)　17'

str(5.5.3.3.2)
Score **CON 190** / Parts **CON 190-70** / Piano
reduction **VLB 49**

Meier, Jost

b.1939

Stage Works

Augustin (1988)   full evening

Opera in 5 Scenes
Text: Hansjörg Schneider, Martin Markun
Material on hire
SM

Der Drache (1985)   full evening

Opera in 3 Acts
Text: Jewgenij Lvovich Schwarz, Martin Markun
Material on hire
SM

Sennentuntschi (1983) full evening

Opera in 5 Scenes
Text: Hansjörg Schneider, Martin Markun
Material on hire
SM

La Vie funambulesque - Der Tanz auf dem Seil

(1983-84)   40'

Ballet music in 4 Movements
Material on hire
SM

Mieg, Peter

1906-1990

Orchestral Works

Toccata-Arioso-Gigue

(1959)   13'

str
Material on hire
SM

Concertos

Oboe Concerto (1957) ·   20'

Soloist: oboe
0.0.0.2-2.0.0.0-str(1.1.1.0.1)
Material on hire
Piano reduction **OBB 15**

Meier, Jost

b. Solothurn/Switzerland 15.3.1939

Having grown up with music from earliest childhood - at the age of six he had his first piano lessons, at the age of nine he began to play violoncello. Jost Meier took up a career as a cellist which led him to the Zurich Tonhalle Orchestra, the Moeckli Quartet and the chamber orchestra Camerata Berne.
As a composer he was initially self-taught, then trained with Rolf Loser and Frank Martin.
Jost Meier was active as a teacher in Berne, and from 1969-79 as a conductor at the Städtebund Theatre of Biel/Solothurn and of the orchestral society of Biel, in addition to the Basel theatre from 1979-83. Since then he has worked as a free-lance composer and teacher in Zurich and Basel. Among his prizes and awards are: 1969 Prix de composition ORTF, Paris; 1984 Prix de Festival de Lausanne.

Migot, Georges

1891-1976

Chamber & Instrumental Works

Sonatine nr. 2

srec-pno
OFB 65

Mihalovici, Marcel

1898-1985

Solo Voice(s)/Voice(s) and Piano/Guitar

Abendgesang, Op. 75 (1957)

4 poems
Text: Yvan Goll
high voice-pno
ED 5083

Miller, Franz R.

b.1926

Fanfare und Entrata (1993) 5'

Soloists: 4 trumpets
concert band
Score **SHS 2006** / Parts **SHS 2006-70**

Choral Works

Der Winter ist ein rechter Mann

Text: M. Claudius
Chorus: male a cappella
Vocal score **C 47231**

Moeschinger, Albert

1897-1985

Orchestral Works

Variations and Finale about a Theme by Purcell, Op. 32   20'

timp-str(10-16.10-14.6-8.6-8.3-5)
Material on hire
SM

Concertos

Piano Concerto No.2, Op. 23
(1930)   20'

Soloist: piano
2(pic).1.1.1-2.1.1.0-perc-str(6.6.6.4.2)
Material on hire
Piano reduction **ED 3272**

Mohler, Philipp
1908-1982

Orchestral Works

Heitere Overtüre, Op. 27
(1945)					10'

str
Score **CON 96** / Parts **CON 96-70**

### Shakespeare-Suite					24'
Dance movements
2ob.[2ca].2bn-hpd.gtr/[lute]-str
Score **CON 97** / Parts **CON 97-50**

### Symphonische Fantasie, Op. 20 (1941)					16'
2.2.2.2-4.2.3.1-timp.perc-cel.hp-str
Material on hire
SM

### Symphonisches Vorspiel, Op. 18 (1939)					15'
3.3.2.3-4.3.3.1-timp.perc-str
Material on hire
SM

Chamber & Instrumental Works

### Capriccio, Op. 19a (1940)					6'
fl-pno
ED 4384

### Konzertante Sonate, Op. 31					24'
va-pno
VAB 21

Choral Works

### Ach, wie flüchtig, ach, wie nichtig, Op. 15 (1936)					5'
Text: Johann M. Franck
Chorus: male a cappella
C 34600

### Es geht wohl anders als du meinst, Op. 33/1 (1960)					5'
Gesänge aus den Wandersprüchen
Text: Joseph von Eichendorff
Chorus: mixed a cappella
C 40261

Mohler, Philipp

**b. Kaiserslautern 26.11.1908,
d. Frankfurt/Main 11.09.1982**

Philipp Mohler studied composition with Joseph Haas, and referred to Paul Hindemith as his leading inspiration besides Haas. In 1940 he succeeded Hugo Distler as a teacher, becoming professor of composition and conducting at the Stuttgart Conservatory in 1943. In 1958 he was appointed director of the Frankfurt Conservatory; he held this post until his retirement in 1975. Within these years he expanded this institute, helping it to gain an international reputation. He was awarded among other the following prizes: 1943 Stamitz Music Award, 1961 Arts Award of the Rhineland-Palatinate, 1974 Order of Merit of the Federal Republic Germany, 1975 Goethe Medal of the state of Hessen. The Pfälzischer Sängerbund has established the Philipp Mohler Medal, which is bestowed on high-ranking politicians for their furtherance of choral music.

Das Ewige ist Stille, Op. 42/3
(1963)					5'
Text: Wilhelm Raabe
Chorus: male a cappella
C 40947

Festliche Liedkantate, Op. 37
(1956)					12'
Chorus: male/mixed
brass(4.3.3.1)-timp
Parts **C 39528** / Vocal score **C 39527**

### Ein freier Mut (1953)					3'
Chorus: female a cappella
CHBL 538

Die Gedanken sind frei
(1950)					3'
Chorus: female a cappella
CHBL 503

### Hausspruch, Op. 42/1 (1959)					2'
Text: various
Chorus: male a cappella
C 40036

### Im Frühtau zu Berge (1950)					2'
Chorus: female a cappella
CHBL 584

### Laetare, Op. 43 (1967-68)					15'
Cantata
Text: Carl Zuckmayer
Soloist: high soprano
Chorus: male,[children's]
2/3(pic).2.2.2-4.3.3.[1]-timp.perc-hp-str
Material on hire
Vocal score **ED 6015-01** / Piano reduction **ED 6015**

Nachtmusikanten, Op. 24
(1949)					30'
Serenade
Text: Abraham a Santa Clara
Soloist: tenor
Chorus: mixed
1(pic).0.1.1-1.1.0.0-timp.2perc-str
Material on hire
Vocal score **ED 3898-01** / Piano reduction **ED 3898**

Der Postillion, Op. 33/2
(1960)					5'
Gesänge aus den Wandersprüchen
Text: Joseph von Eichendorff
Chorus: mixed a cappella
C 40262

### Singend sei dein Tag, Op. 29/2 (1954)					2'
Chorus: male a cappella
CHBL 78

Spanische Szenen, Op. 45
(1975)					25'
Lyric Cantata
Text: Lope de Vega
Chorus: mixed
2(pic).2(ca).2.2-2.2.1.0-timp.3perc-hp-str
alt. version: perc-2pno
Material on hire
Score **ED 6703** / Parts **ED 6703-11/-12
(percussion)** / Vocal score **ED 6703-01**

### Der Tod von Flandern, Op. 9/1 (1936)					4'
Text: Elsa L. Wolzogen
Chorus: male a cappella
C 34197

Ein Traum ist unser Leben
(1951)					4'
Text: Johann Gottfried Herder
Chorus: male a cappella
C 37838

Trost, Op. 32/1 (1952) 25'

Text: Hans Leip
Chorus: male a cappella
C 38519

Vergangen ist die Nacht, Op. 14 (1942) 25'

Cantata on Folksongs
Chorus: children's/female
fl-str
Score **ED 3740** / Parts **ED 3740-11 (-16)** /
Vocal score **ED 3740-01**

Viva la Musica, Op. 41

(1961) 25'

Text: various
Soloist: soprano/tenor
Chorus: male
[3tpt]-str
Score **ED 5260** / Parts **ED 5260-10** / Vocal
score **ED 5260-01**

Viva la Musica, Op. 41a

(1961) 25'

Text: various
Soloist: soprano/tenor
Chorus: male
2.2.2.2-4.3.3.1-timp.perc-hp-str
Material on hire
Vocal score **ED 5260-01**

Wandspruch Kantate, Op. 29

(1963) 7'

Text: Fritz Brunner
Chorus: mixed
pno/brass(4.3.3.1)-timp
Score **C 40740** / Parts **C 39579-10 (brass)** /
Vocal score **C 38057/-58**

Wandspruch Kantate, Op. 29a (1963) 7'

Text: Fritz Brunner
Chorus: male
pno/brass(4.3.3.1)-timp
Choral score **C 43840-01**

Zum Abschied (1952) 2'

Chorus: female a cappella
CHBL 537

Moran, Robert

b.1937

Orchestral Works

L' Après-midi du Dracoula

(1966) 13'

flexible
AVV 90

Elegant Journey with Stopping Points of Interest

(1965)

chamber orchestra/percussion
Material on hire
Score **AVV 90**

Silver and the Circle of Messages (1969-70) 12'

1.0.1.bcl.1-1.0.1.0-perc-hp-str(1.0.1.1.1/3.0.2.1.1)
Material on hire
AVV

Mori, Kurodo

b.1950

Orchestral Works

Premier beau Matin de Mai

(1987) 12'

1.1.1.1-1.1.1.0-pno-str(1.0.1.1.1)
Material on hire
SJ

Concertos

In Process of Time (1986) 13'

Soloist: percussion
2.2.2.2-3.2.3.0-hp.cel-str(7.6.5.4.3)
Material on hire
SJ

Chamber & Instrumental Works

Difference (1985-86) 11'

Soloists: 2 violins
2vn
SJ 1037

Mors, Rudolf

1920-1988

Stage Works

Der Kreidekreis

(1977-82) full evening

Opera in 4 Acts
Text: Klabund
Material on hire
SM

Mossolow, Alexandr Wassiljevich

1900-1973

Orchestral Works

Symphony No. 5 (1965) 35'

pic.2.2.ca.2.bcl.2.cbn-4.3.3.1-timp.6perc-cel(hpd,pno).hp-str
Material on hire
Score **KIN 1001**

de la Motte, Diether

b.1928

Choral Works

Festliche Kantate (1961) 21'

Text: various
Chorus: mixed
2.0.1.0-0.2.0.0-timp.perc-pno-str
Score **ED 4972** / Parts **ED 4972-10** / Vocal
score **ED 4972-01**

2 French Folksongs (1960) 6'

Chorus: male a cappella
C 40298

Ständchen für Don Quixote

(1960) 9'

Text: Miguel Cervantes
Soloists: tenor, 3 speakers
Chorus: male a cappella
Score **ED 5134** / Vocal score **ED 5134-01/-02**

Müller, Karl-Josef

b.1937

Choral Works

Omnia translata omnia

(1984) 11'

Text: Ovid
Chorus: male
speaker-2pno
SM

Infoline · e-Mail

Schott Musik International
Mainz: Schott.Musik.com@T-Online.de
London: 101627.166@compuserve.com

Müller, Sigfrid Walther
1905-1946

Orchestral Works

Böhmische Musik, Op. 55   21'
3.2.2.2-4.3.3.0-timp.perc-str
Material on hire
Eu

Heitere Musik, Op. 43   25'
2.2.2.2-3.2.2.0-timp.perc-str
Material on hire
Eu

Concertos

Concert in B Major, Op. 62   22'
Soloist: flute
2ob-2hn-str
Material on hire
Eu

Concerto grosso in D-Major, Op. 50   15'
Soloist: trumpet
2.2.2.2-2.0.0.0-timp.perc-str
Material on hire
Eu

Concerto in F Major, Op. 56   18'
Soloist: bassoon
1.1.2.0-1.1.0.0-timp.perc-str
Material on hire
Eu

Müller-Siemens, Detlev
b.1957

Stage Works

Genoveva oder Die weiße Hirschkuh   (1977)   60'
Drama in 4 Scenes and 1 Interlude
Text: Julie Schrader
Material on hire
AVV

Die Menschen   (1989-90)   120'
Opera in 2 Acts
Text: Detlev Müller-Siemens after Walter Hasenclever
Material on hire
Libretto BN 3550-70

Müller-Siemens, Detlev
b. Hamburg 30.7.1957

Müller-Siemens is the author of an impressive list of works that already includes a symphony, various concertos, and the remarkable series of instrumental pieces collectively entitled "Under Neonlight". Literature and philosophy are important sources of inspiration in his music, the composer responding through his art to some of the central paradoxes of our time. A pupil of Messiaen and Ligeti, Müller-Siemens is himself a professor of composition at the Musikhochschule, Basel.

Orchestral Works

Carillon   (1991)   20'
3(3pic).3(ca).3(bcl).3(cbn)-4.3.3.1-pno-str
Material on hire
AVV

Concerto for 19 Players
(1975)   13'
1(pic).1.1.bcl.1.cbn-1.0.0.1-timp.2perc-cel.pno.hp-str(2.0.1.1.2)
Material on hire
AVV

Enigma   (1992)   12'
1.1.1.1-1.1.1.0-perc-pno-str
Material on hire
AVV

Passacaglia   (1978)   17'
pic.3.3.3.3(cbn)-4.3.3.1-timp-str
Material on hire
AVV

Pavane   (1988)   8'
3.3.3.3.4.2.3.0-2perc-str
Material on hire
AVV

Phoenix 1   (1993)   14'
1.1.1(bcl).1-1.1.1(btbn).0-pno-str(1.1.1.1.1)
Material on hire
AVV

Phoenix 2   (1994)   14'
1.1.1(bcl).1-1.1.1(btbn).0-pno-str(1.1.1.1.1)
Material on hire
AVV

Phoenix 3   (1995)
1.1.1.1-1.1.1.0-pno-str(1.1.1.1.1)
Material on hire
AVV

2 Pieces   (1976-77)   9'
Concerto No. 2
2.2.2.2-2.0.0.0-str(3.0.1.1.1)
Material on hire
AVV

Quatre passages   (1988-89)   24'
3(pic).3.3.3-4.2.3.0-perc-str
Material on hire
AVV

Scherzo and Adagio patetico
(1976)   8'
3(pic)3(ca).3.(bcl).3(cbn)-4.3.3.1-perc-str
Material on hire
AVV

Symphony No.1   (1978-80)   45'
pic.3.3.3.3(cbn)-4.3.3.1-timp.perc-str
Material on hire
AVV

Tom-a-Bedlam   (1990/93)   27'
1(pic).1(ca).1(bcl).ssax.asax.tsax.1(cbn)-1.flhn.0.1.euph.0-str(1.1.1.1.1)
Material on hire
AVV

Under Neonlight 1   (1981)   15'
1.1.1.1-1.1.1.0-perc-pno.(eorg)-str
Material on hire
Study score AVV 315

Concertos

Double Concerto   (1992)   24'
Soloists: violin, viola
2(pic).2(ca).2(bcl).2(cbn)-2.2.0.0-perc-str
Material on hire
AVV

Horn Concerto   (1988-89)   20'
Soloist: horn
pic.2.2.2.bcl.2.cbn-2.2.2.1-perc-str(12.10.8.6.4)
Material on hire
Study score AVV 321

Piano Concerto (1980-81)   20'

Soloist: piano
3.3.3.3-4.3.3.0-perc-eorg-str
Material on hire
AVV

Viola Concerto (1983-84)   18'

Soloist: viola
2(pic).4.2.asax.2-4.3.2.1-2perc-pno-str(6.0.0.4.4)
Material on hire
Parts **AVV 125 (solo)**

Chamber & Instrumental Works

Nocturne (1975)   8'

vn-pno
Manuscript score on sale
AVV

Octet (1988-89)   20'

cl.bn-hn-2vn.va.vc.db
Score and parts **AVV 320**

Pavane (1984-85)   11'

1.1.1.1-0.0.0.0-pno-str(1.1.1.1.0)
Material on hire
AVV

Phantasie (1988)   13'

vn.vc-pno
Score and parts **AVV 149**

Les Sanglots longs des Violons de l'Automne

(1975)   10'

(Verlaine)
fl.ob.cl.bn-hn
Study score **AVV 105** / Parts **AVV 111**

Sextett (1993)   24'

fl(pic).ob.cl(bcl)-str trio
AVV 322

String Quartet No.1

(1989-90)   28'

AVV 153

Under Neonlight 2 (1980-83) 34'

pno
AVV 117

Under Neonlight 3 (1987) 15'

pno
AVV 141

Variationen über einen Ländler von Schubert

(1977-78)   18'

1(pic).1.1.1-1.0.0.0-str(1.1.1.2.0)
Material on hire
AVV

Solo Voice(s) and Instrument(s)/ Orchestra

Songs and Pavanes (1984-85) 35'

Text: Franz Kafka
Soloist: tenor
3(pic).2.ca.3(bcl).3(cbn)-4.3(Dtpt).3.1-str
Material on hire
AVV

Tom-a-Bedlam (1990-91)   27'

Text: anonymous
Soloists: 2S.MS.T.Bar.B
1(pic).1(ca).1(bcl).1(cbn)-1.0.0.0-str(1.1.1.1.1)
Material on hire
AVV

Choral Works

Arioso (1986)   8'

Text: Franz Kafka
Soloists: soprano, tenor, horn
Chorus: mixed (16 prt)
pic.2.2.ca.2.bcl.2.cbn-4.3.3.1-str
Material on hire
AVV

Müller-Zürich, Paul

1898-1993

Orchestral Works

Marienleben, Op. 8   25'

8 Pieces for chamber orchestra
fl.ob.cl-hn-str(1.1(va).1.1.1)
Material on hire
SM

Concertos

Organ Concerto, Op. 28

(1938)   20'

Soloist: organ
str
Material on hire
SM

Viola Concerto in F Minor, Op. 24 (1934)   20'

Soloist: viola
ob.bn-tpt-timp-str
Material on hire
Piano reduction **ED 3289**

Violin Concerto in G Major, Op. 25 (1936)   20'

Soloist: violin
1.1.0.1-1.1.0.0-timp-str
Material on hire
Piano reduction **ED 2513**

Chamber & Instrumental Works

Prelude and Fugue in E Minor, Op. 22 (1934)   6'

organ solo
ED 2337

Toccata in C Major, Op. 12

(1925)   5'

organ solo
ED 2116

Toccata No.3 in A, Op. 50

(1952)   7'

organ solo
ED 4536

Choral Works

Chor der Toten, Op. 16

(1931)   5'

Text: Conrad Ferdinand Meyer
Chorus: male
0.2.2.2-4.3.3.1-perc-db
alt. version: org
Material on hire
SM

Te Deum, Op. 11 (1924)   33'

Soloists: soprano, bass
Chorus: mixed
2.2.2.2-4.3.3.1-timp-[org]-str
Material on hire
SM

Mussorgsky, Modest

1839-1881

Orchestral Works

Tableaux d'une Exposition

(1874)   32'

Critical edition by Arbie Orenstein
Arranger: Maurice Ravel (1922)
3(2pic).3(ca).2.bcl.asax.2.cbn-4.3.3.1-timp.perc-cel.2hp-str
Material on hire
Study score **ETP 8022 (British Commonwealth only)**

N

Nancarrow, Conlon
b.1912

Orchestral Works

Study No. 1 (1995)   3'

Arranger: Yvar Mikhashoff
*pic.0.1.1.ssax(bcl).1-1.1.1.0-timp-
xyl.marimb(vib).pno.hpd (amp)(cel
amp)/synth.[gtr]-str*
Material on hire
SM

Study No. 2 (1995)   4'

Arranger: Yvar Mikhashoff
*1.1(ca).1.bcl.ssax.1-1.1.1.0-
xyl(marimb).vib.cel (amp)(hpd amp)-
str(1.0.1.1.1)*
Material on hire
SM

Study No. 3c (1995)   3'

Arranger: Yvar Mikhashoff
*1(pic).1.Ebcl.0.bcl.cbcl.ssax(cl).tsax.
1(cbn)-0.1.0.0-marimb.pno.hpd
(amp)/synth-db*
Material on hire
SM

Study No. 5 (1995)   3'

Arranger: Yvar Mikhashoff
*pic.ob/cl.bcl/tsax.bn/bcl-3Btpt/3Ctpt-
xyl.marimb.2pno-2vn.va/vc/gtr.vc/db.db/vc*
Material on hire
SM

Study No. 6 (1995)   4'

Arranger: Yvar Mikhashoff
*1.1(ca).1(bcl).0-1.0.0.0-
glsp.marimb.cel.2pno.-2vn.va.2db*
Material on hire
SM

Study No. 7 (1995)   10'

Arranger: Yvar Mikhashoff
*pic.0.1.2(Ebcl,bcl,asax,tsax).1-1.1.1.0-
xyl.marimb.pno.hpd (amp)(cel)-str*
Material on hire
SM

Study No. 9 (1995)   4'

Arranger: Yvar Mikhashoff
*pic.0.1.Ebcl.bcl.1-1.1.1.0-
xyl.marimb.pno(cel).hpd (amp)-
str(1.0.1.1.1)*
Material on hire
SM

Study No.12 (1995)   8'

Arranger: Yvar Mikhashoff
*pic.0.1(ca).1(Ebcl).bcl(asax).1-1.1.0.0-
marimb(xyl.vib).acc.pno(cel).hpd
(amp).gtr-2vn(mand).va.vc.db*
Material on hire
SM

Nancarrow, Conlon

b. Texarkana/Arkansas 27.10.1912

**Nancarrow's compositions for player-piano,
combining the most stunning rhythmic
intricacies with popular styles such as blues
and flamenco, are amongst the most complex musical works to have emerged this
century. Though looking back to the
Stravinsky transcriptions for mechanical
piano, they also break fresh ground in deve-
loping the relationship between music and
machines.**

Chamber & Instrumental Works

**Studies for Player Piano
Vol.1** (1950-68)   55'
SM

**Studies for Player Piano
Vol.2** (1950-68)   55'
(Study No 41)
ED 7684

**Studies for Player Piano
Vol.3** (1950-68)   21'
(Study No.37)
ED 7685

**Studies for Player Piano
Vol.4** (1950-68)   20'
(Study No.3)
ED 7686

**Studies for Player Piano
Vol.5** (1950-68)   54'

(Studies Nos. 2,6,7,14,20,21,24,26,33)
ED 7687

**Studies for Player Piano
Vol.6** (1950-68)   50'

(Studies Nos. 4,5,9,10-12,15-18)
ED 7688

Study No. 14 (1995)   3'

Arranger: Y. Mikhashoff
bcl-cel.hpd (amp)-db
Material on hire
SM

Study No. 16 (1995)   3'

Arranger: Y. Mikhashoff
ob.bn-hn-vib.marimb.cel.hpd (amp)-vc
Material on hire
SM

Study No. 17 (1995)   2'

Arranger: Y. Mikhashoff
xyl.vib-hpd (amp)
Material on hire
SM

Study No. 18 (1995)   2'

Arranger: Y. Mikhashoff
xyl-hpd (amp)
Material on hire
SM

Study No. 19 (1995)   1'

Arranger: Y. Mikhashoff
xyl.marimb-pno.hpd (amp)
Material on hire
SM

Naoumoff, Emile
b.1962

Concertos

Piano Concerto No.2 (1982) 25'

Soloist: piano
2.2.2.2-2.2.2.0-str
Material on hire
AVV

Pictures at an Exhibition

(1993)   40'

(Modeste Mussorgsky)
Arranger: Emile Naoumoff
Soloist: piano
*3(pic,afl).2.ca.2(Acl,Ebcl).bcl.2.cbn-
4.3.3.0-timp.perc-str*
Material on hire
SM

Triptyque (1979)   12'

Soloist: violin
str
Material on hire
SM

Naoumoff, Emile

b. Sofia 20.2.1962

After eight years of studies with Nadia
Boulanger from 1971 to 1979, he passed his
exams with distinction and received several
prizes. After his conducting studies with
Pierre Dervaux, he first became the assi-
stant of Nadia Boulanger in 1979 and in
1980, after her death professor at the Ecole
Normale de Musique in Paris. Since 1984 he
has been professor at the Conservatoire
National Supérieur de Musique, Paris.

Chamber & Instrumental Works

13 Anecdotes (1991)   18'

pno
ED 7755

3 Bilder aus der Kindheit

(1983)   13'

fl-pno
FTR 129

3 Elegies (1988)   6'

bn-pno
FAG 21

Fantasy for Organ (1986)   8'

organ solo
ED 7510

Impasse (1982)   12'

pno
ED 7193

Impression (1993)

bn-pno
FAG 24

Petite Suite   8'

va-pno
VAB 51

Piano Sonata (1981)   18'

ED 7004

3 Pieces (1982)   12'

cl-pno
KLB 26

4 Preludes (1988)   11'

pno
ED 7749

Rhapsodie (1993)   15'

pno
ED 8328

Sur le nom de Bach (1985)   12'

Piano Suite
AVV 130

Natschinski, Gerd
b.1928

Stage Works

**Hoffmann's
Erzählungen**   full evening

Phantastic Ballet after Jacques Offenbach
Text: Bernd Köllinger after J. Barbier and
E.T.A. Hoffmann
Material on hire
SM

Negri, Gino
b.1919

Choral Works

Antologia di Spoon River

(1945)   29'

Text: E.L. Masters
Soloists: soprano, mezzo-soprano, alto,
tenor, baritone, bass
Chorus: mixed
*1.1.1.sax.0-1.0.0.0-glsp-hp-pno.cel.hpd-
str(5.0.3.2.1)*
Material on hire
SM

Newson, George

b.1932

Orchestral Works

27 Days for Orchestra

(1969-70)   30'

13.7.6.5-10.3.4.1-timp.4perc-pno.hp-str
Material on hire
SL

June is a Month in the Summer (1969)   17'

2ob.bn-timp-str
Material on hire
SL

Niculescu, Stefan

b.1927

Orchestral Works

Hétéromorphie (1967)   14'

4.4.4.4-6.4.4.1-str(24.0.8.8.8)
Material on hire
AVV

Unisonos (1970)   10'

3.3.3.3-4.3.3.0-timp.2perc-str
Material on hire
AVV

Niederste-Schee, Wolfgang

b.1910

Orchestral Works

Humoresken   12'

1.1.1.1-0.2.1.0-perc-str(4.3.2.2.2)
Material on hire
SM

Nono, Luigi

1924-1990

Stage Works

Intolleranza (1960-61)   full evening

Opera in 2 Parts
Text: Alfred Andersch
Material on hire
Study score AVV 75 / Libretto BN 3620-10

Nono, Luigi

b. Venice 29.1.1924, d. Venice 8.5.1990

Luigi Nono was amongst the first postwar modernists to address the problem of opera, which he did with striking success in "Intolleranza 1960". The left-wing approach shown in much of his work, the result of deeply held beliefs in the bond between music, social justice and revolution, was tempered in his later output to include subject matter of a more personal and philosophical nature. The oeuvre is diverse and ambitious, though for all its complexity, not without an innately Italian sense of lyricism.

Polifonica-Monodia-Ritmica

(1951)   12'

Material on hire
Study score AVV 76

Der rote Mantel (1953)   35'

Ballet
Text: Federico García Lorca
Material on hire
AVV

Orchestral Works

Canti per 13 (1955)   12'

1(pic).1.1.bcl.ssax.1-1.1.1.0-str(1.0.1.1.1)
Material on hire
AVV

Composizione per Orchestra No.1 (1951)   20'

pic.2.2.ca.Ebcl.2.bcl.ssax.asax.2.cbn-4.2.3.1-timp.perc-cel.pno.hp-str
Material on hire
AVV

Composizione per Orchestra No.2 (1958)   12'

Diario pollaco "58
4.4.4.4-8.4.4.0-4timp.16perc-str(16.0.8.8.8)
Material on hire
Study score AVV 66

Due espressioni (1953)   15'

3(pic).3.3.bcl.3-6.4.3.1-perc-hp-str
Material on hire
AVV

Incontri (1955)   7'

2(pic).2.2.2-2.1.1.0-2timp-str(2.2.2.2.2)
Material on hire
Study score AVV 52

Polifonica-Monodia-Ritmica

(1951)   12'

1.0.1.bcl.asax.0-1.0.0.0-perc-pno
Material on hire
Study score AVV 76

Der rote Mantel - Concert Suite (B) (1953) 18'

3(pic).2.4(asax,bcl).2-4.3.2.0-timp.perc-glsp.marimb.vib.cel.2hp-str
Material on hire
AVV

Concertos

Epitaffio No.2 (1952-53)   12'

Y su sangre ya viene cantando
Text: Federico García Lorca
Soloist: flauto
perc-vib.cel.xyl.hp-str(6.6.6.6.6)
Study score AVV 313

Varianti (1957)   16'

Soloist: violin
3fl.3cl-str(10.0.8.8.6)
Material on hire
Study score AVV 51

Solo Voice(s) and Instrument(s)/ Orchestra

Canti di vita e d'amore

(1962)   18'

sul ponte di Hiroshima
Text: various
Soloists: soprano, tenor
3.3.3.3-4.4.4.0-timp.4-6perc-str(8.8.8.6.6)
Material on hire
Study score AVV 78

Choral Works

Canciones a Guiomar

(1962)   12'

Text: Antonio Machado
Soloist: soprano
Chorus: female
va.vc.db-cel.gtr-7perc
Material on hire
AVV

Il canto sospeso (1955-56)   28'

Passages from farwell letters of European
partisans who were sentenced to death
Text: various
Soloists: soprano, alto, tenor
Chorus: mixed
*4(pic).2.2.bcl.2-6.5.4.0-3timp.perc-cel.2hp-
str*
Material on hire
Study score **AVV 50/ETP 8029**

Cori di Didone (1958)   12'

from Giuseppe Ungaretti's "La terra pro-
mesa"
Chorus: mixed (16 prt) double
6perc
Material on hire
Study score **AVV 54**

Epitaffio No.1 (1952-53)   13'

España en el corazón
Text: Federico García Lorca/Pablo Neruda
Soloists: soprano, baritone
Chorus: mixed (speaking)
*2.0.Ebcl.1.bcl.0-0.0.0.0-3perc-
vib.cel.pno.hp-str(5.0.4.3.0)*
Material on hire
Study score **AVV 313**

Epitaffio No.1, 2 & 3

(1952-53)   45'

(s. detailed enumeration)
Material on hire
Study score **AVV 313**

Epitaffio No.3 (1952-53)   12'

Memento
Text: Federico García Lorca
Soloist: female speaker
Chorus: mixed (speaking)
*pic.2.2.Ebcl.2.bcl.2-4.3.4.1-timp.perc-
glsp.2xyl.cel.2hp-str*
Material on hire
Study score **AVV 313**

"Ha Venido" (1960)   4'

Text: Antonio Machado
Soloist: soprano
Chorus: 6 sopranos a cappella
Score **AVV 6**

Intolleranza - Concert Suite

(1960)   18'

Soloist: soprano
Chorus: mixed(on tape)
3.3.3(2bcl).3-6.4.4.0-timp.perc-cel.hp-str
Material on hire
AVV

Liebeslied (1954)   6'

Chorus: mixed
timp.2perc-hp
Material on hire
Study score **AVV 60**

Der rote Mantel - Concert Suite (A) (1954)   29'

Soloists: soprano, baritone
Chorus: mixed
*3(pic).2.3(asax).bcl.2-4.3.2.0-timp.perc-
glsp.marimb.vib.cel.2hp-str*
Material on hire
AVV

Sarà dolce tacere (1960)   10'

Text: Cesare Pavese
Chorus: 8 solo voices a cappella
AVV 5

La terra e la compagna

(1958)   8'

Text: Cesare Pavese
Soloists: soprano, tenor
Chorus: mixed (24 prt)
4.0.0.0-0.4Dtpt.4.0-7-8perc-str(5.0.5.4.4)
Material on hire
Study score **AVV 56**

La victoire de Guernica

(1954)   13'

Text: Paul Eluard
Chorus: mixed
3.3.3.bcl.3-4.4.3.1-2timp.perc-cel.2hp-str
Material on hire
Study score **AVV 69**

Nussio, Otmar
b.1902

Orchestral Works

Escapades musicales (1949)   11'

2.2.2.2-2.2.1.0-timp.perc-str
Material on hire
Study score **ETP 900**

Infoline · e-Mail
Schott Musik International
Mainz: Schott.Musik.com@T-Online.de
London: 101627.166@compuserve.com

Ohana, Maurice
1914-1992

Stage Works

Études choréographiques
(1959/63)   10'

4perc/6perc
Material on hire
Study score **ED 6534**

Olah, Tiberiu
b.1928

Chamber & Instrumental Works

Espace et Rhytme (1964)

3 groups of percussions
AVV 36

Orff, Carl
1895-1982

Stage Works

Antigonae (1949)   140'
A Tragedy
Text: Friedrich Hölderlin after Sophokles
Material on hire
Study score **ED 5025** / Vocal score **ED 4026** /
Libretto **BN 3630-70**

Astutuli (1948)   50'
A Bavarian Comedy
Material on hire
Study score **ED 7398** / Libretto **BN 3631-50**

Die Bernauerin (1946)   100'
A Bavarian Play
Material on hire
Study score **ED 6856** / Vocal score **ED 3997** /
Libretto **BN 3632-30**

Carmina Burana (1935-36)   65'
Cantiones Profanae
Material on hire
Score **ED 85** / Study score **ED 4425/ETP 8000**
/ Vocal score **ED 2877** / Libretto **BN 3633-01**

Catulli Carmina (1942)   45'
Ludi Scaenici
Material on hire
Score **ED 75** / Study score **ED 4565** / Vocal
score **ED 3990** / Libretto **BN 3634-10**

Orff, Carl

b. Munich 10.7.1895, d. Munich 29.3.1982

Baroque opera and Greek tragedy are the twin foundations of Orff's art, which draws theatre, music, dance and spectacle into a unity recalling Wagner's concept of "Gesamtkunstwerk", but with a very different identity of its own. "Carmina Burana" established and perpetuates his reputation. Another major achievement was the "Schulwerk", an educational method that is still widely used. The essence of Orff's music, heard in a series of large-scale choral and scenic works, is a hedonistic rhythmic impulse fulfilling a deep-rooted need in his many admirers.

Comoedia de Christi Resurrectione (1955)   40'
An Easter Play
Text: Carl Orff
Material on hire
Vocal score **ED 4932** / Libretto **BN 3635-80**

Klage der Ariadne (1927) (Claudio Monteverdi)
(1925/40)   12'

from "Lamenti-Trittico Teatrale"
Arranger: Carl Orff
Material on hire
Vocal score **ED 2874/4311** / Libretto **BN 3637-40**

Die Kluge (1941-42)   90'
The Story of the King and the Wise Woman
Material on hire
Score **ED 6631** / Study score **ED 4580** / Vocal
score **ED 4580** / Libretto **BN 3636-60**

"Lamenti-Trittico Teatrale"
(1924/40)   100'

(s. also detailed enumeration)
Material on hire
SM

1. O Fortuna

Carl Orff
Carmina Burana (1936)

Ludus de Nato Infante Mirificus (1960) 45'

A Christmas Play
Material on hire
Vocal score ED 5265 / Libretto BN 3638-20

Der Mond (1938/71) 90'

A Little World Theatre
Material on hire
Study score ED 6481 / Vocal score ED 6529 /
Libretto BN 3639

Oedipus der Tyrann

(1957-59) 160'

A Tragedy
Text: Friedrich Hölderlin after Sophokles
Material on hire
Study score ED 5525 / Vocal score ED 4996 /
Libretto BN 3640-40

Orpheus (Claudio Monteverdi) (1924/39) 60'

from "Lamenti-Trittico Teatrale"
Arranger: Carl Orff
Text: Dorothee Günther
Material on hire
Vocal score ED 3188 / Libretto BN 3637-40

Prometheus (1963/67) 130'

A Tragedy
Text: Aischylos
Material on hire
Study score ED 6337 / Vocal score ED 5840 /
Libretto ED 5940

Ein Sommernachtstraum - A Midsummer Night's Dream

(1917/62) full evening

A Sharespearean Drama
Text: Carl Orff after William Shakespeare
Material on hire
Vocal score ED 3992

Tanz der Spröden (Claudio Monteverdi) (1925/40) 30'

from "Lamenti-Trittico Teatrale"
Arranger: Carl Orff
Text: Dorothee Günther
Material on hire
Vocal score ED 3186

De temporum fine comoedia

(1971/79/81) 65'

Scenic Cantata
Material on hire
Score ED 7365 / Study score ED 5407 / Vocal
score ED 6527 / Libretto BN 3643-90

Trionfo di Afrodite (1950-51) 45'

Concerto Scenico
Material on hire
Study score ED 4566 / Vocal score ED 4306 /
Libretto BN 3629-30

Die Weihnachtsgeschichte

(1948) 30'

from "Orff-Schulwerk Jugendmusik"
Arranger: Gunild Keetman
Score ED 3565 / Parts ED 3565-11 (-14) /
Vocal score ED 3565-01/-09 /
Libretto ED 3565-02 (-07)

Orchestral Works

Als die Treue ward geborn

(1941-42) 4'

from "Die Kluge"
Arranger: Friedrich K Wanek
2(pic).2.2.2(cbn)-2.1.1.0
Material on hire
SM

4 Burlesque Scenes (1938) 11'

from the Opera "Der Mond"
Arranger: Hermann Regner (1991)
2(pic).2.Ebcl.3.bcl.2asax.2tsax.[barsax].1-
4.thn.2flhn/2cnt.3.euph.2-timp.4perc-
zith/keyb
Score SHS 1017 / Parts SHS 1017-50

Carmina Burana (1935-36) 24'

Suite for concert band
Arranger: John Krance
pic.2.2.Ebcl.3.Acl.bcl.2asax.tsax.barsax.2-
4.3cnt.2.3.bar/euph/thn.2-
2timp.5perc-[cel].[2pno]-db
Score SHS 1015 / Parts SHS 1015-50

Carmina Burana (1935-36) 20'

Suite for concert band
Arranger: Jos Moerenhout
2.2.Ebcl.4.Acl.bcl.2asax.2tsax.barsax-
4.2thn.2cnt/2flhn-2.3.bar/euph.2-
timp.3perc-db
FG 22-10 / Parts FG 22

Catulli Carmina (1943) 45'

for symphonic concert band
Arranger: Guy M. Duker
pic.2.2.ca.Ebcl.3.Acl.bcl.cacl.cbcl.2asax.
tsax.barsax-4.3cnt.2.3.bar/euph.2-timp.11-
12perc-[pno]-db
Material on hire
SM

Entrata (1928/40) 12'

(William Byrd)
6.4.2ca.0.2.cbn-6.11.4.2-4timp-perc-
2cel.4pno.org.2hp-str
Material on hire
SM

Entrata (1940/54) 12'

(Wiiliam Byrd) Reduced versions
Arranger: Robert Wagner
4.4.(2ca).0.2.cbn-4.8.3.1-2timp.perc-pno
4hnd(cel,glsp).org.2hp-str
alt. version: 3.3.(2ca).0.2.cbn-4.6.3.1-
2timp.perc-pno 4hnd(cel,glsp).org.2hp-str
Material on hire
SM

Entrata (1940/54) 12'

(William Byrd) Symphonic wind band
version
Arranger: Guy M. Duker
6.4.4.2acl.2bcl.2cbcl.2asax.2barsax.2.cbn-
6.2thn.3cnt.8.4.2euph.5-2timp.5perc-
cel.pno(4hnd).org-2db
Material on hire
EAM

Kleines Konzert (1937) 13'

1(pic).2.0.2-2.1.1.0-timp.2perc-cel.hp-
str(0.0.4-6.4.2)
Material on hire
SM

3 Tänze und Schlußszene

(1938/71) 13'

from "Der Mond"
Arranger: Friedrich K Wanek
2(pic).2.2.2(cbn)-2.1.1.0
Material on hire
SM

Tanzende Faune, Op. 21

(1914) 15'

Orchestral Play
4.2.ca.3.3-4.2.0.0-timp.perc-
cel(pno(4hnd))-2hp-str(8.8.4.4.2)
Material on hire
SM

Uf dem Anger (1935-36) 2'

from "Carmina burana"
3.2.ca.Ebcl.2.2-4.3.3.0-timp.perc-str
Material on hire
SM

Chamber & Instrumental Works

Carmina Burana (1981) 13'

5 Movements for 10 Winds
Arranger: Friedrich K Wanck
2(pic).2.(ca)2.2(cbn)-2.0.0.0
Score ED 6950 / Parts ED 6951

Carmina Burana (1935-36) 13'

Arranger: Hermann Regner
2pno
ED 09766

Ecce gratum (1935-36) 3'

from Carmina Burana
Arranger: Hilger Schallehn
Chorus: mixed
pno (4hnd)
Vocal score ED 6996

Einzug und Reigen (1952) 5'

from "Orff-Schulwerk Jugendmusik"
3srec.2arec.trec.brec-timp.perc-gtr-vc.db
Score ED 3564

Kleines Konzert (1927/75) 15'

fl(pic).ob.bn-tpt.tbn-timp.perc-hpd
Score and parts ED 6618

Orff-Schulwerk

Refer to Separate Catalogue
SM

5 Pieces for Brass 7'

From the "Orff-Schulwerk"
Arranger: Hermann Regner
4tpt.2hn.4tbn.tuba-[timp]
Score SHS 3004 / Parts SHS 3004-70

Quartettsatz (1914) 9'

2vn.va.vc
ED 7816

Solo Voice(s)/Voice(s) and Piano/Guitar

Early Songs (1911-21)

Text: Beer-Hofmann, Lingg, Lenau,
Nietzsche, Klabund, Werfel
voice-pno
ED 7024

Choral Works

Aufruf - Komm, Sintflut der Seele (1930) 1'

from the cantata "Fremde sind wir"
Arranger: Friedrich K Wanek
Text: Franz Werfel
Chorus: male a cappella
Material on hire
C 41921

Ave Maria (1912-14) 2'

Chorus: mixed a cappella
C 47005

Cantus-Firmus-Sätze (1929)

Chorus: mixed
[instruments]
Score **ED 4454**

Carmina Burana (1935-36) 65'

Cantiones Profanae
Text: Benedictbeurian manuscript
Soloists: soprano, tenor, baritone
Chorus: mixed, boy's
3(2pic).3(ca).3(Ebcl,2Acl,bcl).2.cbn-4.3.3.1-timp.5perc-cel.2pno-str
Material on hire
Score **ED 85** / Study score **ED 4425/ETP 8000** /
Vocal score **ED 2877** / Libretto **BN 3633-01**

Carmina Burana (1935-36) 65'

Version for School performance
Arranger: Wilhelm Killmayer
Soloists: soprano, tenor, baritone
Chorus: mixed, boy's
pno (4hnd)/2pno-perc
Score **ED 4920** / Parts **ED 4920-10
(percussion)** / Vocal score **ED 4920-01/-02** /
Piano reduction **ED 4920**

Carmina Burana (1935-36) 65'

Arranger: Juan Vicente Mas Quiles
Soloists: soprano, tenor, baritone
Chorus: mixed, boy's
*3(pic).3(ca).Ebcl.3.acl.bcl.[cbcl].2asax.tsax.
barsax.2.cbn-4.thn.2flhn.3.3.euph.2-
timp.6perc-cel.2pno-db*
Material on hire
Study score **SHS 8001**

Catulli Carmina (1943) 45'

Ludi Scaenici
Soloists: soprano, tenor
Chorus: mixed (SSAATTBB)
timp.10-12perc-4pno
Material on hire
Score **ED 75** / Study score **ED 4565** / Vocal
score **ED 3990** / Libretto **BN 3634-10**

3 Choruses 2'

From the "Orff-Schulwerk"
Chorus: equal voices
Vocal score **C 42618**

4 Choruses from Catulli Carmina (1943) 6'

Soloist: tenor
Chorus: mixed a cappella (7 prt)
C 37774

Concento di voci - Laudes Creaturarum (1954) 3'

Chorus: mixed a cappella (8 prt)
C 39560

Concento di voci - Sirmio (1930) 8'

Tria Catulli Carmina
Chorus: mixed a cappella (6 prt)
C 38748

Concento di voci - Sunt lacrimae rerum (1956) 13'

Cantiones Seriae
Text: Orlando di Lasso,
Liber Ecclesiastes III, anonymous
Soloists: tenor, baritone, bass
Chorus: male a cappella (6 prt)
C 39534-02

Dithyrambi (1955-56/81) 22'

"Die Sänger der Vorwelt" - "Nänie und
Dithyrambe"
Text: Friedrich Schiller
Chorus: mixed (4-6 prt)
6fl-3tbn-timp.9perc-4pno.2hp-db
Material on hire
Vocal score **ED 4939**

Fremde sind wir (1930/68) 4'

Cantata
Text: Franz Werfel
Chorus: mixed (6 prt)
2pno
Score **ED 6022** / Vocal score **ED 6022-01**

Der gute Mensch (1930/68) 11'

Cantata
Text: Franz Werfel
Chorus: mixed double
2/3pno-2timp.6perc
Score **ED 6021** / Parts **ED 6021-11
(percussion)** / Vocal score **ED 6021-01**

In taberna quando sumus (1935-36) 5'

from "Carmina Burana"
Chorus: male
pno (4hnd)
Score **ED 5844** / Vocal score **ED 5844-01**

Lugete o Veneres (1930) 3'

Chorus: mixed a cappella (6 prt)
C 44687

Odi et amo (1943) 2'

Chorus: mixed a cappella
CHBL 398

Pieces for Speaking Chorus (1969)

Chorus: speaking
fl-timp.perc-vc
ED 5583

Rota (1972) 4'

"Sumer is icumen in" (old english
Summer-Canon)
Chorus: mixed (S.T.Bar), boy's
*[bn]-4tpt/4srec.2tbn/2va da gamba/va-
timp.perc-2gtr-vc.db*
Score **ED 6412** / Parts **ED 6412-11 (-27)** /
Vocal score **ED 6412-01**

2 Sacred Choruses 1'

from the "Orff-Schulwerk"
Chorus: equal voices a cappella
Vocal score **C 42403**

Si puer cum puellula (1936) 1'

from Carmina Burana
Chorus: male a cappella
CHBL 79

Sonnengesang des heiligen Franziskus (1954) 3'

Chorus: equal voices a cappella
C 42186

Sprechstücke (1976)

Text: various
Soloists: speakers
Chorus: speaking
timp.perc-2pno(4hnd)
Score **ED 6711**

Trionfo di Afrodite (1950-51) 45'

Concerto Scenico
Text: Carl Orff
Soloists: 2 sopranos, 2 tenors, bass
Chorus: male,female,mixed
*3(3pic).3(2ca).3.3(cbn)-6.3.3.2-timp.10-
12perc-2pno.2hp-3gtr-str(12-14.12-
14.12.12.8)*
Study score **ED 4566** / Vocal score **ED 4306** /
Libretto **BN 3629-30**

Des Turmes Auferstehung (1921) 14'

Text: Franz Werfel
Chorus: male
*5(2pic).afl.4.ca.heck.0.5(cbn).cbn-
0.[8].4.0-timp.3perc-
6pno/3pno.org.6hp/3hp-str*
Material on hire
SM

Veni creator spiritus

(1930/68)   10'

Cantata
Text: Franz Werfel
Chorus: mixed
2/3pno-3timp.5perc
Score **ED 6020** / Parts **ED 6020-11**
(percussion) / Vocal score **ED 6020-01**

Vom Frühjahr, Öltank und vom Fliegen (1931/68)   11'

Cantata
Text: Bertolt Brecht
Chorus: mixed
3pno/2pno-6-9perc
Score **ED 6023** / Parts **ED 6023-11**
(percussion) / Choral score **ED 6023-01**

Von der Freundlichkeit der Welt (1930/73)   6'

Cantata
Text: Bertolt Brecht
Chorus: mixed
4timp.8perc-2-3pno(4hnd)
Material on hire
Score **ED 5706** / Parts **ED 5706-11**
(percussion) / Choral score **ED 5706-01**

Ott, Günther

Stage Works

Blues Giselle   full evening

Ballet
Arranger: Herbert Heise
Material on hire
SM

Pals, Leopold von der

1884-1966

Concertos

Konzertstück   12'

Soloist: violin
2.2.2.2-4.2.0.0-timp-str
Material on hire
Eu

Papandopoulo, Boris

1906-1991

Orchestral Works

Sinfonietta, Op. 79 (1938)   25'

str
Material on hire
SM

Pauels, Heinz

1908-1985

Stage Works

Capriccio   12'

Ballet in 4 Movements
Material on hire
SM

Mardi Gras   12'

Ballet in 2 Movements after the Concert-
Piece of the same name
Material on hire
SM

Moll Flanders   full evening

Music Ballad in 9 Scenes
Text: Daniel Defoe, Ernst Gärtner
Material on hire
SM

O Hyazinthia   50'

Ridiculous Opera in 1 dramatic Act
Text: Kurt Neufert
Material on hire
SM

Pauels, Heinz

b. Oberhausen 1.3.1908, d. Bergheim
10.2.1985

Pauels studied composition at the Munich
Academy of Music. At the age of 17, he had
already taken his diploma. The first prize
that Pauels won for his string quartet op.4
at the Bruinier Competition in 1932 led to
numerous successful performances in
Europe and the USA. From 1948-73 Pauels
was director of incidental music at the
theatres of Cologne; where he wrote his
numerous, frequently performed incidental
musics, operas and ballets for Cologne,
Wuppertal, Darmstadt and Saarbrücken in
particular. Among other awards, in 1984 he
was given the Order of Merit of the Federal
Republic of Germany.

Paulus, Stephen

b.1949

Stage Works

Harmoonia (1991) 45'

Children's Opera in 1 Act
Text: Michael Dennis Browne
Material on hire
EAM

The Postman always Rings Twice (1982) 120'

Opera in 2 Acts
Text: Colin Graham
Material on hire
Vocal score **EA 602** / Libretto **EA 503**

The Village Singer (1979) 60'

Opera in 1 Act
Text: Michael Dennis Browne
Material on hire
Vocal score **EA 454**

The Woodlanders

(1985) full evening

Romantic Tragedy in 3 Acts
Text: Colin Graham
Material on hire
Libretto **EA 1001**

Orchestral Works

Concertante (1989) 11'

3(pic).3.3.3-4.3.2.btbn.1-timp.3perc-pno-str
Material on hire
Study score **EA 678**

Concerto for Orchestra

(1983) 27'

*3(pic).3(ca).3.3(cbn)-4.4.2.btbn.1-
timp.3perc-pno/cel.hp-str*
Material on hire
Study score **EA 512**

Ground Breaker (1987) 7'

*2(pic).2.2.2-4.3.2.btbn.1-timp.perc-4 wor-
kers with power tools-str*
Material on hire
EAM

Ordway Overture (1985) 5'

3(pic).3.3.3-4.3.3.1-timp.2perc-str
Material on hire
Study score **EA 669X**

Reflections: 4 Movements on a Theme of Wallace Stevens

(1985) 22'

1.2.1.2-2.1.0.0-timp.perc-pno-str
Material on hire
EAM

7 Short Pieces for Orchestra

(1984) 13'

*3(pic).3.3(bcl).3(cbn)-4.3.2.btbn.1-
timp.3perc-pno/cel.hp-str*
Material on hire
EAM

Sinfonietta (1991) 15'

3.3.3(bcl).3-4.3.2.btbn.1-timp.3perc-hp-str
Material on hire
EAM

Street Music (1990) 4'

2.2.2.2-4.3.3.1-timp.2perc-str
Material on hire
EAM

Suite from "The Postman always Rings Twice" (1986) 22'

*3(pic).3.3.asax.3-4.3.2.btbn.1-timp.3perc-
pno.hp-str*
Material on hire
EAM

Paulus, Stephen

b. Summit, New Jersey 24.8.1949

An experimental operatic composer with
a considerable list of major works to his
credit, Stephen Paulus hails from a family
of musicians and began writing music at an
early age before beginning formal studies at
the University of Minnesota. He has been a
resident composer at numerous festivals
including the Tanglewood Festival, the
Santa Fe Chamber Music Festival and the
Aspen Music Festival. His opera, "The
Postman Always Rings Twice" (1982) was
the first American opera-production ever to
be presented at the Edinburgh Festival.

Symphony for Strings

(1989) 22'

str
Material on hire
EAM

Symphony in 3 Movements

(1986) 30'

Soliloquy
*3(pic).3.3.3-4.3.3.1-timp.3perc-pno/cel.hp-
str*
Material on hire
EAM

Translucent Landscapes

(1982) 18'

*2.1.2.1-2.1.1.0-timp.perc-pno.hp-
str(8.6.5.4.2)*
Material on hire
EAM

Infoline · e-Mail

Schott Musik International
Mainz: Schott.Musik.com@T-Online.de
London: 101627.166@compuserve.com

Concertos

Divertimento (1983) 12'
Soloist: harp
1.1.1.1-timp.perc-str(6.6.4.4.2)
Material on hire
EAM

Double Concerto (1993) 25'
Soloists: violin, cello
3(pic).3(ca).3(bcl).3-4.3.2.btbn.1-timp.3perc-pno/cel.hp-str
Material on hire
EAM

Ice Fields (1990) 20'
Soloist: guitar
2.2.2.2-4.2.2.1-timp.2perc-str
Material on hire
EAM

Organ Concerto (1992) 21'
Soloist: organ
timp.perc-str
Material on hire
Parts **EA 767 (solo)**

Trumpet Concerto (1991) 25'
Soloist: trumpet
3.3.3.3-4.3.3.1-timp.3perc-pno/cel.hp-str
Material on hire
EAM

Violin Concerto No.1 (1987) 25'
Soloist: violin
3.3.3.3-4.3.2.1-timp.3perc-pno.hp-str
Material on hire
EAM

Violin Concerto No.2 (1992) 21'
Soloist: violin
2.2.2.2-2.2.1.0-timp.2perc-pno.hp-str
Material on hire
EAM

Chamber & Instrumental Works

Air on Seurat (The Grand Canal) (1992) 7'
vc-pno
Material on sale
EAM

American Vignettes (1988) 18'
vc-pno
Material on sale
EAM

Bagatelles (1990) 12'
vn-pno
Material on sale
EAM

Banchetto Musicale (1981) 12'
vc-pno
Material on sale
EAM

Berceuse
harp solo
EA 501

Concerto for Brass Quintet (1991) 15'
EA 710X

Courtship Songs (1981) 15'
fl.ob-vc-pno
Material on sale
EAM

Dance (1986) 3'
pno
EA 591

Duo for Clarinet and Piano (1974) 5'
cl-pno
Material on sale
EAM

Fantasy in Three Parts (1989) 15'
fl-gtr
EA 702X

Landmark Fanfare (1978) 1'
brass qnt
Material on sale
EAM

Life Motifs (1988) 12'
vn.vc-pno
Material on sale
EAM

7 Miniatures (1990) 21'
vn.va.vc
EA 685X

Music for Contrasts (1980) 15'
str qrt
Material on sale
EAM

Music of the Night (1992) 15'
vn.vc-pno
Material on sale
EAM

Ordway Fanfare (1984) 2'
brass qnt
Material on sale
EAM

Partita (1986) 22'
vn-pno
Material on sale
EAM

Preludes, Vol. 1
pno
EA 760

Quartessence (1990) 20'
str qrt
Material on sale
EAM

Seven for the Flowers near the River (1988) 19'
va-pno
EA 699X

String Quartet No.2 (1987) 20'
Material on sale
EAM

Translucent Landscapes (1979) 21'
pno
EA 498X

Solo Voice(s)/Voice(s) and Piano/Guitar

All my Pretty Ones (1984) 26'
Text: Michael Dennis Browne
soprano-pno
EA 554X

Artsongs (1983) 27'
Text: various
tenor-pno
EA 555X

Bittersuite (1988) 16'
Text: Ogden Nash
baritone-pno
EA 713X

3 Elizabethan Songs (1973) 5'
Text: various
soprano-pno
Material on sale
EAM

Mad Book, Shadow Book: Michael Morley's Songs (1977) 25'
Text: Michael Dennis Browne
tenor-pno
Material on sale
EAM

Songs of Love and Longing
soprano-pno
EA 756

Solo Voice(s) and Instrument(s)/ Orchestra

Letters from Collette (1986) 30'

Soloist: soprano
perc-pno-str qrt
Material on hire
EAM

Mad Book, Shadow Book: Michael Morley's Songs

(1978) 25'

Text: Michael Dennis Browne
Soloist: tenor
fl.cl-perc-pno-vn.va.vc
Material on hire
EAM

Night Speech (1989) 20'

Soloist: baritone
3(pic).3.3.3-4.3.2.btbn.1-timp.3perc-pno.hp-str
Material on hire
EAM

Suite from "Harmoonia"

(1991) 5'

Text: Michael Dennis Browne
Soloist: speaker
2.2.2.2-4.3.2.1-timp.3perc-pno.hp-str
Material on hire
EAM

Voices from the Gallery

(1991) 30'

Soloist: speaker
1.1.1.1-1.1.0.0-timp.perc-str
Material on hire
EAM

Choral Works

A child my choice

Chorus: mixed a cappella
EA 482

An American Medley

(1988) 15'

Text: Traditional Folk
Chorus: mixed
brass qnt
Material on hire
EAM

The Angels and the Shepherds 2'

Text: Helen A. Dickenson
Chorus: mixed a cappella
EA 610

Angels we have Heard on High 3'

Text: anononymous
Chorus: mixed
org
EA 613

Barbara Allen 2'

Chorus: mixed
gtr
Material on hire
EAM

Bring a Torch, Jeannette Isabella 1'

Chorus: mixed
gtr
EA 611

Built on a Rock 4'

Text: Gruntvig/Paulus
Chorus: mixed
org/pno
EA 466

Canticles: Songs and Rituals for the Easter and the May

(1977) 35'

Text: Michael Dennis Browne
Soloists: soprano, mezzo-soprano, speaker
Chorus: mixed
1.1.1.1-2.2.1.0-timp.perc
Material on hire
EAM

Canticum Novum (1990) 30'

Text: Traditional
Chorus: mixed
fl.ob-perc-hp
Material on hire
EAM

Cats, Friends & Lovers 10'

Text: Stevie Smith
Chorus: female a cappella
EA 744

Christmas Eve Carol 5'

Chorus: mixed a cappella
Material on sale
EAM

Christmas Tidings: 5 Carols

(1989) 15'

Text: Traditional
Chorus: mixed
str
Material on hire
EAM

Come Life, Shaker Life

(1991) 3'

Chorus: mixed a cappella
Material on sale
EAM

Echoes Between the Silent Peaks (1984) 25'

Text: Tu-Fu
Chorus: mixed
fl.ob-perc-hp-vn.vc
Material on hire
EAM

Evensong (1990) 3'

Chorus: mixed a cappella
Material on sale
EAM

The First Nowell 3'

Chorus: mixed a cappella
EA 544

For all Saints (1990) 12'

Text: various
Chorus: mixed
org
EAM

Fountain of My Friends

(1977) 10'

Text: Michael Dennis Browne
Chorus: female
pno
EAM

Hallelu! 2'

Chorus: mixed (2 prt)
keybd
EA 511

I Gave my Love a Cherry 3'

Soloist: soprano
Chorus: mixed
hp
EAM

In the Moon of Wintertime

(1990) 3'

Chorus: female
hp
EAM

Jesu Carols (1985) 10'

Chorus: mixed
hp
EA 601

Lately arrived from London

(1980)

from "Letters for the Times'
Chorus: mixed
accompaniment
Study score EA 467

Let All Creation Praise

(1991) 4'

Text: Psalm 150/Hildegard
Chorus: mixcd
org
EAM

Infoline · e-Mail
Schott Musik International
Mainz: Schott.Musik.com@T-Online.de
London: 101627.166@compuserve.com

Letters for the Times (1980) 15'

Text: 17th/18th Century Newspapers
Soloists: soprano, tenor, baritone
Chorus: mixed
1.1.0.1-0.0.0.0-3perc-pno-str(1.1.1.1.0)
Material on hire
EAM

Love Letters (1986) 15'

Soloists: soprano, alto
Chorus: female
fl-perc
Material on hire
EAM

Madrigali Di Michelangelo

(1987) 20'

Text: Michelangelo
Chorus: mixed a cappella
EAM

Marginalia (1977) 10'

Text: 13th Century Irish scribes
Chorus: mixed
fl-perc
EAM

North Shore (1977) 35'

Text: Michael Dennis Browne
Soloists: mezzo-soprano, baritone
Chorus: mixed
2.0.2.1-2.2.1.0-timp.2perc-pno/cel.hp-str(1.0.0.1.1)
Material on hire
EAM

Now is the Gentle Season

(1978) 4'

Text: anonymous
Chorus: mixed a cappella
EA 524

O Little Town of Bethlehem 3'

Text: Phillip Brooks
Chorus: mixed
hp-ob
Study score **EA 578**

Peace (1990) 5'

Text: G.M. Hopkins
Chorus: mixed a cappella
EAM

Personals (1975) 5'

Chorus: mixed
fl-perc
EAM

Pium Paum 3'

Text: Melva Rorem
Chorus: mixed a cappella
EA 550

4 Preludes on Playthings of the Wind (1990) 10'

Text: Carl Sandburg
Chorus: mixed a cappella
EAM

Run, Shepherds, run!

Chorus: mixed
pno
EA 481

Sacred Songs (1990) 21'

Chorus: mixed
fl.ob-perc-org
Material on hire
EAM

Shall we gather at the River 3'

Chorus: mixed a cappella
EA 515

Silver the River 3'

Text: Michael Dennis Browne
Soloist: treble
Chorus: mixed (2 prt)
keybd
EA 525

Sing hevin imperial

Chorus: mixed
pno
EA 483

Single Girl 3'

Text: Traditional American Folk
Chorus: mixed
hp
EAM

So Hallow'd is the Time

(1980) 40'

Text: various
Soloists: treble, soprano, tenor, bass
Chorus: mixed
1.1.1.1-1.3.1.0-timp.2perc-org.hp-str
Material on hire
Study score **EA 488** / Vocal score **EA 479**

This is the Month

Chorus: female
pno
EA 480

Too many Waltzes (1986) 10'

Text: Wallace Stevens
Chorus: male
chimes.timp-hp
EAM

Visions from Hildegard

(1992) 15'

Part 1
Text: Hildegard von Bingen
Chorus: mixed
fl.ob-timp.perc-org
Material on hire
EAM

Visions from Hildegard

(1992) 12'

Part 2
Text: Hildegard von Bingen
Chorus: mixed
perc-brass qnt
Material on hire
EAM

Voices (1988) 40'

Text: Rainer Maria Rilke
Soloists: soprano, tenor
Chorus: mixed
3(pic).3.3.3-4.3.3.1-timp.3perc-pno.hp-str
Material on hire
EAM

Wassail Song 2'

Chorus: mixed a cappella
EA 612

The Water is wide 3'

Soloists: soprano, baritone
Chorus: mixed
hp
Material on hire
EAM

We give Thee but Thine Own 4'

Text: Howe/Paulus
Chorus: S.A.B.
keybd
Study score **EA 522**

Whitman's Dream 11'

Text: Walt Whitman
Chorus: mixed double
4hn.3tpt.3tbn.tuba-timp
Material on hire
SM

Peixe, Guerra

Orchestral Works

Nonette 16'

1.0.1.1-0.1.1.0-pno-stre(1.0.1.1.0)
AVV

Penderecki, Krzysztof

b.1933

Stage Works

Paradise Lost

(1976-78) full evening

Sacra Rappresentazione. Opera
Text: Christopher Fry after John Milton
Material on hire
Libretto **BN 3649-80/3648-10**

Die schwarze Maske

(1984-86) full evening

Opera in 1 Act
Text: Gerhart Hauptmann
Material on hire
Vocal score **ED 7614** / Libretto **BN 3651-10**

Penderecki, Krzysztof

b. Debica 23.11.1933

A composer who has been a centre of international attention since his first works were received with a mixture of awe and notoriety in 1959, Krzysztof Penderecki is at heart an experimentalist, whether in the progressive scores of the early 1960's, in the stark expressionism of "The Devils of Loudun" of 1969, or the more romantically orientated works of the 1970's and 80's in concerto form. He takes a primal attitude to music, conceiving it as a sound continuum encompassing expressive gestures from the purest white noise to the most complex pitch structures. For the last three decades he has been, and seems likely to remain, Poland's leading composer.

Die Teufel von Loudun

(1968-69)   full evening

Opera
Text: Krzysztof Penderecki after Aldous
Huxley
Material on hire
Study score **ED 6225** /
Libretto **BN 3645-50/3646-30**

Ubu Rex (1990-91)   full evening

Opera Buffa
Text: Jerzy Jarocki/Krzysztof Penderecki
Material on hire
Libretto **BN 3652-80**

Orchestral Works

Adagietto from "Paradise Lost" (1979)   5'

2.2(ca).2.2(cbn)-4.3.3.1-timp.perc-str
Material on hire
Study score **ED 6902**

Adagio - Symphony No.4

(1989)   33'

*pic.2.2.ca.Ebcl.2.bcl.2.cbn-5.3.4.1-
timp.2perc-str back stage: 3tpt*
Material on hire
Study score **ED 8064**

"Als Jakob erwachte" (1974)   8'

aus dem Schlaf, sah er, dass Gott dagewesen war. Er hat es aber nicht bemerkt."
*3(2pic,3ocar).3(ca,3ocar).3(3ocar).
3(cbn,3ocar)-5.3.3.1-timp.perc-
str(24.0.10.10.8)*
Material on hire
Study score **ED 6623**

Burleske Suite from "Ubu Rex" (1995)   16'

Arranger: Henning Brauel
*pic.2.2.ca.Ebcl.2.bcl.2.cbn-4.3.3.1-
timp.perc-cel-db*
Material on hire
Score **SHS 1019**

Canon (1962)   10'

str(24.0.8.8.6)-tape
Material on hire
Study score **ED 6342**

De natura sonoris No.2

(1971)   12'

*0.0.0.0-4.0.4.1-timp.5perc-pno.harm-
str(24.0.8.8.6)*
Material on hire
Study score **ED 6335**

Drei Stücke im alten Stil

(1963)   6'

From the film music to "Tagebuch von
Saragossa"
str
Score **CON 241** / Parts **CON 241-70**

Intermezzo (1973)   6'

str(12.0.6.4.2)
Material on hire
SM

Musik aus "Ubu Rex"

(1994)   25'

Arranger: Henning Brauel
*pic.2.2.ca.Ebcl.2.bcl.2.cbn-4.3.3.1-
timp.4perc-cel-str*
Material on hire
SM

Prélude (1971)   8'

*3(2pic,afl).3(ca).3(Ebcl).bcl.2.cbn-
3.3(Dtpt).4.1-timp.3perc-cel.pno.harm-4db*
Material on hire
SM

Sinfonietta per archi (1992) 12'

str
Material on hire
Study score **ED 8117**

Symphony No.1 (1972-73)   30'

*3(2pic).3(ca).3(Ebcl).bcl.3(cbn)-5.3.4.1-
timp.6perc-cel.pno.harm.hp-str(24.0.8.8.6)*
Material on hire
Study score **ED 6614**

Symphony No.2 (1979-80)   35'

Christmas Symphony
*pic.2.2.ca.3(Ebcl,bcl).2.cbn-5.3.3.1-
timp.4perc-cel-str*
Material on hire
Study score **ED 7323**

Symphony No. 3 (1988/95)   50'

*pic.2.2.ca.3(Ebcl,Acl).bcl.3.cbn-
5.3.btpt.4.1-timp.3perc-cel-str*
Material on hire
SM

Symphony No.4 (1989)   33'

s. Adagio - Symphony No. 4

Symphony No.5 (1991-92)   35'

*4(pic).4(ca).4(Ebcl).bcl.3.cbn-5.3.4.1-
timp.4perc-cel-str(16.14.12.12.10)*
Material on hire
SM

Concertos

Cello Concerto No.2 (1982) 35'

Soloist: cello
*pic.2.2.2.bcl.2(cbn)-4.3.2.1-timp.5perc-cel-
str*
Material on hire
Study score **ED 7566** / Piano reduction
ED 7187

Concerto (1992)   25'

per flauto or clarinet ed orchestra da camera
Soloist: flute/clarinet
*2(pic).2(ca).2(bcl).2(cbn)-2.2.0.0-2perc-
cel-str(8.6.4.4.2)*
*version for clarinet and orchestra da
camera (1995)*
Material on hire
Piano reduction **ED 8108**

Partita (1971/91)   29'

Soloists: hpd.egtr.bgtr.hp-db
*2(pic).2.2.bcl.1.cbn-2.2.2.0-timp.6perc-cel-
str(12.0.4.4.2)*
Material on hire
Study score **ED 6339**

Sinfonietta No. 2 (1994)   20'

Soloist: clarinet
str
Material on hire
Study score **ED 8343**

Viola Concerto (1983/84)   22'

Soloist: viola/cello/clarinet (with small
accompaniment)
2(pic).2.2.2(cbn)-2.2.2.0-timp.3perc-cel-str
alt. version: timp.perc-cel-str
Material on hire
Study score **ED 7573** / Piano reduction
ED 7519

Violin Concerto

(1976-77/1988)   40'

Soloist: violin
3.3.5.3-4.3.3.1-timp.perc-cel.hp-str
Material on hire
Study score **ED 6917** / Piano reduction
ED 7716

Krzysztof Penderecki
2nd Symphony (1979-80)
beginning of 1st movement

Violin Concerto No. 2

(1992/95)   35'

Soloist: violin
2(pic).2(ca).2(bcl).2(cbn)-4.2.3.0-
timp.3perc-cel-str
Material on hire
Piano reduction **ED 8451**

Chamber & Instrumental Works

Actions   (1971)   17'

fl/bcl-tsax/cl.tsax/ssax.barsax-
tpt/flhn2tpt(Dtpt).2tbn-perc-gtr.bgtr.org-db
Material on hire
SM

Cadenza   (1984)   8'

violin solo
ED 7649

Cadenza   (1984)   8'

viola solo
VAB 52

Capriccio   (1980)   6'

tuba solo
ED 7446

Capriccio per Siegfried Palm

(1968)   6'

cello solo
ED 6072

Clarinet Quartet   (1993)   18'

cl-str trio
Score and parts **ED 8229**

Divertimento   (1994)   10'

cello solo
CB 158

Entrata   (1994)   4'

0.0.0.0-4.3.3.1-timp
Material on hire
SM

Per Slava   (1985-86)   6'

cello solo
ED 7538

Prelude   (1987)   2'

clarinet solo
ED 7567

String Quartet No.2   (1968)   8'

Score and parts **ED 6235** / Study score
ED 6302

String Trio   (1990-91)   12'

vn.va.vc
Score and parts **ED 7879**

Der unterbrochene Gedanke

(1988)   3'

str qrt
ED 7640

Violin Sonata   (1953)   9'

vn-pno
ED 7797

Choral Works

Agnus Dei from the "Polish Requiem"   (1981)   5'

Chorus: mixed a cappella (8 prt)
SKR 20002

Benedicamus Domino   (1992)   3'

Chorus: male a cappella (5 prt)
C 47592

Canticum Canticorum Salomonis   (1970-73)   17'

Chorus: mixed
2(afl).2.ca.1.bcl.1-1.1.2.0-4perc-
cel.harm.hp.gtr-str(9.0.4.3.1)
Material on hire
Study score **ED 6131**

Ecloga VIII   (1972)   15'

Text: Publius Vergilius
Chorus: male a cappella/6 solo voices
Study score **ED 6341**

Kosmogonia   (1970)   20'

Soloists: soprano, tenor, bass
Chorus: mixed
4(2pic).4.3.bcl.2asax.barsax.3.cbn-
6.4(Dtpt).4.2-timp.5perc-
vib.cel.pno.harm.org.hp-bgtr-
str(24.0.10.10.8)
Material on hire
Study score **ED 6324/BN 3647-01** / Libretto
ED 6324/BN 3647-01

Lacrimosa from the "Polish Requiem"   (1980)   6'

Soloist: soprano
Chorus: mixed
2.2.2.2.cbn-5.3.3.1-timp.perc-str
Material on hire
Study score **ED 7075**

Magnificat   (1973-74)   40'

Soloist: bass
Chorus: 7 male voices, two mixed (24 prt),
childrens
3(2pic, afl).3(ca).4(bcl).3(cbn)-
5.3.2Bachtpt.3.1-timp.perc-
glsp.cel.pno.harm.hp.-str(24.0.8.8.8)
Material on hire
Study score **ED 6646**

Polish Requiem   (1980-84/93)   95'

Soloists: soprano, alto, tenor, bass
Chorus: mixed
3(pic).3.3(2Acl).bcl.3.cbn-6.4.4.1-
timp.2perc-str
Material on hire
Study score **ED 7731**

Prelude, Visions and Finale from "Paradise Lost"

(1979)   40'

Soloists: soprano, mezzo-soprano, 2 tenor,
2 bass
Chorus: mixed
pic.2.3(ca).ssax.3.bcl.cbcl.2.cbn-5.3.4.1-
timp.perc-cel.org.hp-str
Material on hire
SM

Sanctus from "Polish Requiem"   15'

Soloists: alto, tenor
Chorus: mixed
3(pic).2.3.2.cbn-5.3.3.0-timp.3perc-str
Material on hire
SM

Die schwarze Maske - 2 Scenes and Finale   (1988)   30'

Soloists: soprano, mezzo-soprano
Chorus: mixed
3(pic).2.ca.3(Ebcl).bcl.ssax.2asax.2.cbn-
4.3.3.1-2timp-4perc-cel.org-str
on stage: 2pic.srec.arec.trec.0.2Ebcl.0-
0.3.3.0-perc-hpd-vc
Material on hire
SM

Song of Cherubim   (1986)   8'

Chorus: mixed a cappella (8 prt)
SKR 20020

Te Deum   (1979-80)   35'

Soloists: soprano, mezzo-soprano, tenor,
bass
Chorus: mixed
pic.2.2.ca.2.bcl.2.cbn-5.3.3.1-timp.2perc-
cel-str
Material on hire
Study score **ED 7107**

Utrenja I   (1969-70)   50'

Grablegung Christi
Text: Bible
Soloists: soprano, alto, tenor, bass,
basso profondo
Chorus: two mixed choruses
4(2pic,afl).3.3(Ebcl).bcl.cbcl.2asax.
2barsax.3.cbn-.6.5.4.2-timp.3perc-
pno.vib.marimb.harm.bgtr-str(24.0.10.10.8)
Material on hire
Study score **ED 6314**

Utrenja II   (1970-71)   35'

Auferstehung
Text: Bible
Soloists: soprano, alto, tenor, bass,
basso profondo
Chorus: two mixed, children's
4(2pic,afl).4(ca).4(Ebcl,bcl).cbcl.3.cbn-
6.4(Dtpt).4.2-timp.perc-bxyl/marimb.
marimb.xyl.vib.cel.pno.harm-
str(24.0.10.10.8)
Material on hire
Study score **ED 8308**

Veni Creator   (1987)   8'

(Hrabanus Maurus)
Chorus: mixed a cappella (8 prt)
SKR 20021

Pepping, Ernst
1901-1981

Orchestral Works

Invention (1930) 4'

2.2.2.2-2.2.0.0-str
Material on hire
SM

Lust hab ich g'habt zur Musika (1936) 13'

Variations
1.1.1.1-1.1.0.0-str
Score CON 112 / Parts CON 112-50/-70

Partita (1934) 20'

2.3.3.3-4.2.2.1-timp.perc-str
Material on hire
SM

Prelude (1929) 6'

2.3.3.3-4.3.2.1-str
Material on hire
SM

Symphony No.1 (1939) 32'

2.2.2.2-4.3.2.1-timp.perc-str
Material on hire
SM

Symphony No.2 (1942) 40'

2.3.3.3-4.3.2.1-timp.perc-str
Material on hire
SM

Chamber & Instrumental Works

Choralpartita (1932) 6'

„Wer nur den lieben Gott läßt walten"
organ solo
ED 2246

Choralpartita (1933) 6'

„Wie schön leuchtet der Morgenstern"
organ solo
ED 2247

Fugue on B-A-C-H (1943) 11'

pno
ED 3959

4 Fugues in C,D Eb and F
(1942) 9'

organ solo
ED 3816

2 Fugues in C Sharp (1943) 7'

organ solo
ED 3817

Pepping, Ernst

b. Duisburg 12.9.1901, d. Berlin 1.2.1981

For Ernst Pepping the severe discipline of musical expression set within strict limits of form and counterpoint was a lifelong ideal. Naturally drawn to choral music in an austere, neo-baroque idiom, he wrote a cappella masses as well as music for the Protestant liturgy and a considerable quantity of organ music, chiefly fugues and chorale preludes. His deliberately singleminded cultivation of archaic styles is remarkable in the stylistically pluralistic 20th-century.

3 Fugues on B-A-C-H
(1943) 11'

organ solo
ED 3818

Great Organ Book (1939)

Vols.1,2 & 3
organ solo
ED 3729 (-31)

Little Organ Book (1940)

organ solo
ED 3735

25 Organ Chorales (1960)

organ solo
ED 4723

Organ Concerto No.1
(1941) 20'

organ solo
ED 3733

Organ Concerto No.2
(1941) 17'

organ solo
ED 3734

Piano Sonata No.1 (1937) 21'

ED 2584

Piano Sonata No.2 (1937) 18'

ED 2585

Piano Sonata No.3 (1937) 13'

ED 2623

Praeludia-Postludia zu 18 Chorälen (1969) 23'

Vols.1 & 2
organ solo
ED 6040/ED 6041

2 Romanzen (1935) 4'

pno
ED 2478

Sonatina (1931) 11'

pno
ED 2180

String Quartet (1943) 25'

Study score ED 3534 / Parts ED 2988

Tanzweisen und Rundgesang
(1938) 15'

pno
ED 3715

Toccata and Fugue (1941) 10'

from the Chorale „Mitten wir im Leben sind"
organ solo
ED 3737

Variations and Suite (1932) 6'

2vn
Piano reduction ED 2218

Choral Works

Alle Vögel sind schon da
(1944) 2'

Text: Folk
Chorus: female a cappella
CHBL 557

Auf einem Baum ein Kuckuck saß (1944) 2'

Chorus: female a cappella
CHBL 558

Bauerngarten (1942) 12'

from "Der Wagen" No.1
Text: Josef Weinheber
Chorus: mixed a cappella
ED 3902

Bei Tag und Nacht (1942) 18'

3 Folk Songs
Chorus: mixed a cappella (5 prt)
ED 3910

Choralsuite Part 1 (1929)　12'

Text: M. Luther
Chorus: mixed double a cappella (4/8 prt)
C 32473

Choralsuite Part 2 (1929)　9'

Text: various
Chorus: mixed a cappella (3-8 prt)
C 32474 (-76)

Choralsuite Part 3 (1929)　12'

Text: various
Chorus: mixed a cappella (3-8 prt)
C 32477 (-79)

Christmas Songs (1938)　5'

Text: various
Chorus: equal voices a cappella
Choral score **ED 3594**

3 Evangelien-Motetten

(1937-38)　15'

Chorus: mixed a cappella (4-6 prt)
C 35565 (-67)

Folksongs (1943)　4'

Chorus: children's/female a cappella
ED 3899

German Choral Mass

(1928)　21'

Chorus: mixed a cappella (6 prt)
ED 3241

German Mass (1938)　22'

Chorus: mixed a cappella
ED 3546

Das gute Leben (1936)　8'

Text: various
Chorus: mixed a cappella
C 34769

Der Herd (1942)　13'

from "Der Wagen" No.3
Text: Josef Weinheber
Chorus: mixed a cappella
ED 3904

Herr Walther von der Vogelweide (1942)　14'

from "Der Wagen" No.6
Text: Josef Weinheber
Chorus: mixed a cappella
ED 3907

Das Jahr (1940)　36'

Text: Josef Weinheber
Chorus: mixed a cappella
ED 2913

Jahraus - jahrein (1942)　13'

from "Der Wagen" No.4
Text: Josef Weinheber
Chorus: mixed a cappella
ED 3905

Das Licht (1942)　12'

from "Der Wagen" No.2
Text: Josef Weinheber
Chorus: mixed a cappella
ED 3903

Mitten wir im Leben (1931)　4'

Text: Martin Luther
Chorus: male
CHBL 110

Der Morgen (1942)　13'

5 Folksongs
Chorus: mixed a cappella
ED 3909

Prediger-Motetten (1938)　12'

Chorus: mixed a cappella
C 35359

Psalm 90 (1934)　20'

Text: Bible
Chorus: mixed a cappella (6 prt)
ED 3275

Schlaf, Kindlein, schlaf

(1944)　2'

Text: Folk
Chorus: female a cappella
CHBL 557

Spandauer Chorbuch (1934-93)

Chorus: mixed/female a cappella
SM

Uns ist ein Kind geboren

(1936)　5'

Chorus: mixed a cappella
C 34927

Der Wagen (1942)　78'

(s. also detailed enumeration)
Text: Josef Weinheber
Chorus: mixed a cappella
ED 3902 (-07)

Im Weinland (1942)　14'

from "Der Wagen" No.5
Text: Josef Weinheber
Chorus: mixed a cappella
ED 3906

Wohlan, die Zeit ist kommen

(1944)　2'

Text: Franken
Chorus: female a cappella
CHBL 559

Petridis, Petro

b.1892

Orchestral Works

Greek Suite　20'

3.3.3.3-4.2.3.1-timp.perc.glsp.xyl-h.cel-str
Material on hire
SM

Ionische Suite　19'

3.3.3.3-4.2.3.1-3timp-hp-str
SM

Petsch, Hans

1891-1978

Orchestral Works

5 kurze Geschichten　18'

2.2.2.2-2.2.2.0-timp.2perc-str
Material on hire
SM

Palatia　20'

2.2.2.2-2.2.2.0-timp.perc-str
Material on hire
SM

Pfitzner, Hans

1869-1949

Stage Works

Palestrina (1912-15)　201'

Musical Legend in 3 Acts
Text: Hans Pfitzner
Material on hire
Score **ED 135** / Study score **ETP 8034** / Vocal score **ED 4316** / Libretto **BN 3650-01**

Orchestral Works

Palestrina - 3 Preludes

(1912-15)　22'

4(2pic).2(ca).3(Ebcl).3.cbn-6.4.4.1-
timp.perc-hp-str
Red. version (arr. Zanotelli) :
3(pic).2.ca.2.bcl.3(cbn)-4.3.3.1-timp.perc-
hp-str
Material on hire
Study score **ED 4557**

Concertos

Cello Concerto in A Minor

(1888)　25'

Soloist: cello
2.2.2.2-2.2.3.0-timp-str
Material on hire
Study score **ETP 1821** / Piano reduction
ED 6791

Cello Concerto in G Major, Op. 42 (1935)　16'

Soloist: cello
2(pic).2.2.2(cbn)-4.2.3.1-timp.perc-hp-str
Material on hire
Study score **ED 3512** / Piano reduction
ED 6828

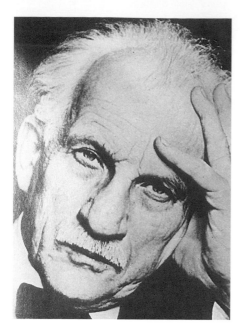

Pfitzner, Hans

b. Moscow 23.4.1869, d. Salzburg 22.5.1949

Son of a violinist, but musical heir to the nineteenth-century school of Brahms and Wagner, Pfitzner is amongst music's most renowned conservatives. His outstanding composition, and testament to his beliefs in the traditional role of music, is the opera "Palestrina", an immediate success after its première in 1917. But there are other distinguished scores, including symphonies and concertos, many of which have been revived with success in recent years.

Chamber & Instrumental Works

Piano Trio in B Major

(1886) 18'

vn.vc-pno
ED 6963

Solo Voice(s)/Voice(s) and Piano/Guitar

Complete Songs

Vols.1 & 2
Text: various
voice-pno
ED 6701/ED 6709

Picker, Tobias
b.1954

Orchestral Works

Dedication Anthem (1984) 5'

military band
Material on hire
EAM-Helicon

2 Fantasies (1991) 11'

3.2.2.3-4.3.3.1-timp.perc-pno-str
Material on hire
EAM-Helicon

Old and Lost Rivers (1986) 6'

3(pic).2.3(bcl).3-6.3.0.1-timp.perc-pno.hp-str
Material on hire
Study score **EA 673**

Seance-Homage a Sibelius
(1991) 4'

4.1.ca.2.3-4.0.3.0-timp.perc-pno-str
Material on hire
EAM-Helicon

Symphony No.1 (1982) 28'

3(pic).3(ca).3(bcl).3-4.2.3.1-timp.perc-pno.2hp-str
Material on hire
EAM-Helicon

Symphony No.3 (1989) 24'

str
Material on hire
EAM-Helicon

Concertos

Bang! (1992) 4'

Soloist: piano
3.2.2.3-4.3.4.1-timp.perc-cel.hp-str
Material on hire
EAM-Helicon

Keys to the City (1983) 19'

Piano Concerto No.2
Soloist: piano
2(pic).2.2(ssax,asac,bcl).2(cbn)-4.2.4.1-timp.2perc-str
Material on hire
Study score **EA 535**

Keys to the City (1987) 19'

Soloist: piano
ob.cl.bn-str(2.1.1.1)
Material on hire
EAM-Helicon

Piano Concerto No.1 (1980) 20'

Soloist: piano
2(pic,afl).2(ca).2(bcl).2-4.2.4.1-timp-str
Material on hire
EAM-Helicon

Picker, Tobias

b. New York City 18.7.1954

Following studies with Charles Wuorinen, Elliott Carter and Milton Babbitt, Tobias Picker established a glowing early reputation when, aged 24, he was described by the New Yorker as „a genuine creator with a fertile, unforced vein of invention". In 1985 he was invited to become Composer-in-Residence of the Houston Symphony Orchestra, the youngest American composer ever chosen for such a prestigious post. Combining urban vigor with a romantic affinity with the natural world, his orchestral works, including a sequence of symphonies, have been widely played by many of the major American orchestras.

Piano Concerto No.3 (1986) 24'

Kilauea
Soloist: piano
3.3.3.3-4.3.4.1-timp.perc-2hp-str
Material on hire
EAM-Helicon

Romances and Interludes
(1990) 25'

Soloist: oboe
2.1(ca).2.2-4.0.0.0-timp.perc-pno/cel.hp-str
Material on hire
EAM-Helicon

Violin Concerto (1981) 22'

Soloist: violin
2.2(ca).3(bcl).2-4.2.3.1-timp-pno.hp-str
Material on hire
EAM-Helicon

Chamber & Instrumental Works

The Blue Hula (1981) 10'
fl.cl-vib(fl/marac)-vn.vc-pno
Material on hire
EAM-Helicon

The Blue Hula (1990) 3'
pno
EAM-Helicon

Invisible Lilacs (1991) 20'
vn-pno
Material on sale
EA 761

3 Lullabies (1990) 6'
violin solo
Material on sale
EAM-Helicon

Nova (1979) 12'
vn.va.vc.db-pno
Material on hire
EAM-Helicon

Octet (1978) 11'
ob.bcl.hn-vib/marimb-hp-vn.vc.db
Material on hire
EAM-Helicon

Old and Lost Rivers (1986) 6'
pno
EA 591

3 Piano Pieces (1989) 10'
EAM-Helicon

Pianorama (1984) 10'
2pno (4hnd)
Material on sale
EA 562

Rhapsody (1978) 12'
vn-pno
EA 532X

Romance (1979) 12'
vn-pno
Material on sale
EAM-Helicon

Serenade (1983) 12'
pno-wind qnt
Material on hire
EAM-Helicon

Sextet No.3 (1976) 13'
fl-vn.vc.db-glsp/vib-pno
Material on hire
EAM-Helicon

String Quartet No.1 (1987) 24'
New Memories
Material on sale
EAM-Helicon

String Quartet with Bass (1988) 24'
str qrt-db
Material on hire
EAM-Helicon

When Soft Voices die (1977) 15'
pno
Material on sale
EAM-Helicon

Solo Voice(s)/Voice(s) and Piano/Guitar

Aussöhnung (1984) 3'
Text: Johann Wolfgang von Goethe
soprano-pno
Material on sale
EAM-Helicon

Half a Year Together (1987) 3'
Text: Richard Howard
soprano-pno
Material on sale
EAM-Helicon

Native Trees (1992) 4'
Text: W.S. Merwin
soprano-pno
Material on sale
EAM-Helicon

Remembering (1987) 3'
Text: Edna St.Vincent Milay
soprano-pno
Material on sale
EAM-Helicon

To the Insects (1992) 5'
Text: W.S. Merwin
soprano-pno
Material on sale
EAM-Helicon

When we meet again (1985) 2'
Text: Edna St.Vincent Milay
soprano-pno
Material on sale
EAM-Helicon

Solo Voice(s) and Instrument(s)/ Orchestra

The Encantadas (1983) 27'
Text: Herman Melville
Soloist: speaker
2(pic).2(ca).2(bcl).2-4.2.3.1-timp.perc-pno.hp-str
Material on hire
EAM-Helicon

The Encantadas (1986) 27'
Text: Herman Melville
Soloist: speaker
2(pic).2(ca).2(bcl).2-2.2.0.0-timp.perc-pno.hp-str
Material on hire
EAM-Helicon

Symphony No.2 (1986) 30'
Aussöhnung
Soloist: soprano
3(pic).3(ca).3(bcl).3(cbn)-4.3.3.1-timp.2perc-pno.hp-str
Material on hire
EAM-Helicon

Pillney, Karl Hubert
1896-1980

Orchestral Works

Konzertwalzer nach Lanner (1926) 11'
2.2.2.2-4.2.3.0-timp.perc-hp-str
Material on hire
SM

Pironkoff, Simeon
b.1927

Orchestral Works

Requiem (1968) 10'
für einen jungen Unbekannten Menschen
str(7.0.3.2.1)
Material on hire
AVV

Infoline · e-Mail
Schott Musik International
Mainz: Schott.Musik.com@T-Online.de
London: 101627.166@compuserve.com

Concertos

Music (1973) 10'

Soloists: 2 pianos
*3(pic).2.ca.2.bcl.2.cbn-4.2.2.1-timp.2perc-
str*
Material on hire
AVV

Poos, Heinrich
b.1928

Chamber & Instrumental Works

Greensleeves (1970)

Variations on an Old English Song
arec-hpd/pno
ED 6234

Choral Works

Abseits (1975) 2'

from "Sechs Gedichte"
Text: Theodor Storm
Chorus: male a cappella
C 44054

Der Abt, der reit' (1988) 3'

Text: Johann Hermann Schein
Chorus: mixed a cappella (6 prt)
C 46446

Alalá (1973) 9'

Song cycle
Chorus: female a cappella (4 prt)
C 43462

An die Freunde (1975) 2'

from "Sechs Gedichte"
Text: Theodor Storm
Chorus: male a cappella
C 44054

Annerle, wo warst du?
(1967) 3'

No.1 from "Drei Madrigale nach slowaki-
schen Liebesliedern"
Chorus: mixed a cappella (8 prt)
C 41867

Ansprache des Bauern an seinen Ochsen (1991) 3'

Text: Bertolt Brecht
Chorus: male a cappella
C 47258

Poos, Heinrich

b. Seibersbach 25.12.1928

Poos studied composition and musicology
as his main subjects at Berlin. After various
positions as a church musician he was
appointed professor of music theory at the
Academy of Arts in 1971. Most important
to his development as a composer was the
influence of his teacher Ernst Pepping. IIe
composes almost exclusively choral music.
The outstanding feature of his works is a
sort of "pleasing artistry" so that even
seemingly simple compositions are characterized by diverse relations with regard to
text and music.

Des Antonius von Padua Fischpredigt (1974) 7'

Text: Joseph von Eichendorff
Chorus: mixed
fl.cl.bn-hpd/pno
Material on sale
Score **C 43769** / Parts **C 43771** / Choral score
C 43770

Ave Maria (1981) 10'

Text: Latin
Soloist: soprano
Chorus: mixed
org
Score **ED 6997** / Vocal score **ED 6997-01**

Chanson (1975) 3'

No.1 from "Suite on French Folksongs"
Chorus: mixed a cappella
Choral score **C 43847**

3 Choruses (1965) 9'

Text: Bertolt Brecht
Chorus: mixed a cappella
C 41525

Cock a doodle doo (1979) 3'

No.6 from "Suite on English Folksongs"
Chorus: mixed a cappella
Choral score **C 44526**

Dona nobis pacem (1928) 3'

Chorus: mixed (6 prt)
C 48686

Ei Baur, was kost dei Heu
(1984) 3'

No.1 from "Vier deutsche Volkslieder"
Chorus: female a cappella
C 45471

Ein Jäger längs dem Weiher ging (1970) 3'

from "Vom edlen Jägerleben"
Text: Zuccalmaglio
Chorus: male a cappella
Score **C 42564** / Parts **C 42565-01/-02** (chorus)

Erntedank (1970) 2'

Text: Anton Velser
Chorus: mixed [a cappella]
[2tpt.3tbn/pno]
Material on sale
Score **C 42729** / Parts **C 42731** / Choral score
C 42730

Es ist ein Gesang in meinen Sommer gefallen (1980) 19'

Text: various
Chorus: female
2hn-hp/pno
Score **ED 6933** / Parts **ED 6933-11** (-13) /
Vocal score **ED 6933-01**

Es kribbelt und wibbelt weiter (1988) 2'

Text: Theodor Fontane
Chorus: male a cappella
C 46355

Es muß geschieden sein
(1993) 5'

3 old Folk-Songs
Text: Wilhelm von Zuccalmaglio/
anonymous
Chorus: female a cappella
C 48288

Fein sein, beinander bleibn
(1984) 3'

No.2 from "Vier deutsche Volkslieder"
Chorus: female a cappella
C 45472

Frisch auf zum fröhlichen Jagen (1970) 2'

From "Vom edlen Jägerleben"
Chorus: male a cappella
Score **C 42562** / Parts **C 42562-01/-02** (chorus)

Gavotte (1975) 3'

No.2 from "Suite on French Folksongs"
Chorus: mixed a cappella
Choral score **C 43848**

Gebet (1979) 1'

Text: Gustav Falke
Chorus: male a cappella
CHBL 230

Gestern bei Mondenschein

(1984) 3'

No.3 from "Vier deutsche Volkslieder"
Chorus: female a cappella
C 45473

Gigue (1975) 5'

No.5 from "Suite on French Folksongs"
Chorus: mixed a cappella (6 prt)
Choral score **C 43851**

Gloria Patri (1988) 5'

Text: Latin
Chorus: mixed
org/2pno
ED 7620

Greensleeves (1982) 4'

Chorus: male a cappella
C 45119

Gute Nacht (1975) 2'

from "Sechs Gedichte"
Text: Theodor Storm
Chorus: male a cappella
C 44055

Hat mein Lieb ein Schlehlein

(1967) 2'

Czech Folksong
Text: Heinrich Poos
Chorus: male a cappella
C 41956

Hochzeit hielt das Mückelein

(1963) 3'

No.4 from "Mährische Volkslieder"
Chorus: male a cappella
C 40819

Hochzeit hielt das Mückelein

(1974) 3'

Chorus: mixed a cappella
C 43584

Hypostasis vel Somnium Jacob 16'

Sinfonia on Genesis and Johannes
Text: Bible
Chorus: mixed double
SKR 20035

Ich will truren fahren Ian

(1970) 10'

Chorus: mixed (6 prt)
fl-pno-db
Score **ED 6255** / Parts **ED 6255-11/-12** /
Choral score **ED 6255-01**

In der Frühe (1975) 2'

from "Sechs Gedichte"
Text: Theodor Storm
Chorus: male a cappella
C 44056

Ein jegliches hat seine Zeit

(1973) 40'

Text: Bertolt Brecht
Soloists: soprano, speaker
Chorus: male
0.0.2.1-3.0.2.0-perc-str
Material on hire
Score **ED 6648** / Choral score **ED 6648-01**

Ein jegliches hat seine Zeit

(1973) 40'

Text: Bertolt Brecht
Soloists: soprano, speaker
Chorus: male
2pno-timp.perc
Score **ED 6634** / Parts **ED 6634-11/-12** /
Choral score **ED 6648-01**

The Keel Row (1979) 3'

No.1 from "Suite on English Folksongs"
Chorus: mixed a cappella
Choral score **C 44521**

The Keeper (1979) 3'

No.3 from "Suite on English Folksongs"
Chorus: mixed a cappella
Choral score **C 44523**

Kommt, wir gehn auf schmalem Wege (1967) 3'

No.3 from "Drei Madrigale nach slowaki-
schen Liebesliedern"
Chorus: mixed a cappella
C 41869

Lieder im Rosenhag (1993) 6'

3 Christmas Folk-Songs
Text: various
Chorus: female a cappella
C 48289

Die Linien des Lebens

(1985) 4'

Text: Friedrich Hölderlin
Chorus: male a cappella
C 45833

Magnificat (1973) 6'

Text: Latin
Soloists: soprano
Chorus: mixed [a cappella] (6 prt)
org
C 43430

The Miller of Dee (1979) 3'

No.5 from "Suite on English Folksongs"
Chorus: mixed a cappella
Choral score **C 44525**

Mir entfloh die Wachtel

(1963) 3'

No.1 from "Mährische Volkslieder"
Chorus: male a cappella
C 40816

Musikanten (1985) 2'

Text: Heinrich Poos
Chorus: male a cappella
C 45684

Musikanten, warum schweigt ihr (1961) 3'

No.1 from "Drei mährische Volkslieder"
Chorus: mixed a cappella
C 40561

Musikanten, warum schweigt ihr (1984) 3'

No.3 from "Drei Liebesmadrigale nach
tschechischen Volksliedern"
Text: Heinrich Poos
Chorus: female a cappella
C 45470

Nachklänge - Das Alter

(1987) 4'

Text: Joseph von Eichendorff
Chorus: mixed a cappella (6 prt)
C 46449

Nachklänge - Der Kehraus

(1989) 3'

Text: Joseph von Eichendorff
Chorus: mixed a cappella (6 prt)
C 46774

Nachklänge - Der Soldat (Epilogue) (1989) 2'

Text: Joseph von Eichendorff
Chorus: mixed a cappella (6 prt)
C 46776

Nachklänge - Der traurige Jäger (1987) 3'

Text: Joseph von Eichendorff
Chorus: mixed a cappella (6 prt)
C 46447

Nachklänge - Klang um Klang (1984) 3'

Text: Joseph von Eichendorff
Chorus: mixed a cappella (6 prt)
C 45500

Nachklänge - Nachtgruß

(1984) 1'

Text: Joseph von Eichendorff
Chorus: mixed a cappella (6 prt)
C 45501

Nachklänge - Umkehr

(1989) 3'

Text: Joseph von Eichendorff
Chorus: mixed a cappella (6 prt)
C 46775

Nachklänge - Weltlauf

(1987) 4'

Text: Joseph von Eichendorff
Chorus: mixed a cappella (6 prt)
C 46448

Nacht und Träume (1975) 8'

Text: Clemens von Brentano
Chorus: female
pno
Score **C 44063** / Choral score **C 44064**

Die Nachtigall (1975) 2'

from "Sechs Gedichte"
Text: Theodor Storm
Chorus: male a cappella
C 44056

O Liebe, Liebe (1984) 3'

No.2 from "Drei Liebesmadrigale nach
tschechischen Volksliedern"
Chorus: female a cappella
C 45469

O Liebe, Liebe (1963) 3'

No.3 from "Mährische Volkslieder"
Chorus: male a cappella
C 40817

The old True Love (1979) 3'

No.2 from "Suite on English Folksongs"
Chorus: mixed a cappella
Choral score C 44522

Pater noster (1981) 10'

Text: Latin
Soloist: baritone
Chorus: mixed
org/pno
Score ED 7006 / Choral score ED 7006-01

Pavane (1975) 3'

No.3 from "Suite on French Folksongs"
Chorus: mixed a cappella
Choral score C 43849

Pax et Bonum (1983) 30'

Triptych
Text: Bible
Soloist: baritone
Chorus: mixed (6 prt)
4hn.3tpt.3tbn.tuba-timp.perc-org-db
Material on hire
SM

Psalm 126 (1976) 8'

Text: Martin Luther
Soloist: tenor
Chorus: male a cappella (6 prt)
C 44267

Psalm 23 (1976) 4'

Soloist: baritone
Chorus: male a cappella
C 44266

Psalm 77 (1991) 6'

Chorus: male a cappella
C 47520

Rosen im Tal (1993) 6'

3 German Folk-Songs
Chorus: female a cappella
C 48290

Seht es regnen, seht es gießen

(1967/74) 2'

Text: Heinrich Poos
Chorus: mixed a cappella
C 43585

Sing mir, o Nachtigall (1961) 3'

No.2 from "Drei mährische Volkslieder"
Chorus: mixed a cappella (5 prt)
C 40562

Singen heißt verstehen

(1976) 7'

Arranger: Gerhard Weihe
Text: Heinrich Poos
Soloists: soprano, alto, tenor, bass
Chorus: mixed unison
tpt.tsax.tbn-gtr.bass-epno
Choral score C 44131

Singet dem Herrn ein neues Lied (1971) 4'

Psalm 98
Chorus: male a cappella
C 43106

Die Sonn' ist untergegangen

(1987) 3'

Chorus: male a cappella
C 46011

Sphragis (1984) 9'

Text: Ovid
Chorus: mixed a cappella (6 prt)
SKR 20009

Spiele mir, Geigerlein (1963) 3'

No.2 from "Mährische Volkslieder"
Chorus: male a cappella
C 40817

Stehn zwei Stern am hohen Himmel (1984) 3'

No.3 from "Vier deutsche Volkslieder"
Chorus: female a cappella
C 45474

Suite on English Folksongs

(1979) 18'

(see also detailed enumeration)
Chorus: mixed a cappella
Choral score C 44521-10

Tambourin (1975) 3'

No.4 from "Suite on French Folksongs"
Chorus: mixed a cappella (5 prt)
Choral score C 43850

Tanzlied (1979/82) 3'

Ritmo di Joropo
Chorus: mixed a cappella
C 45387

Tanzlied (1979/82) 3'

Ritmo di Joropo
Chorus: male a cappella
C 44566

Tanzlied (1979/82) 3'

Ritmo di Joropo
Chorus: female a cappella
C 44567

There's None to soothe

(1979) 3'

No.4 from "Suite on English Folksongs"
Chorus: mixed a cappella
Choral score C 44524

Die Tochter der Heide (1988) 3'

Text: Eduard Mörike
Chorus: female a cappella
CHBL 621

Totenklage um Samogonski

(1973) 7'

Fantasy
Text: Werner Bergengruen
Soloist: speaker
Chorus: male double a cappella
Choral score C 43490

Über die Heide (1975) 2'

from "Sechs Gedichte"
Text: Theodor Storm
Chorus: male a cappella
C 44055

Um Jaroschau fließen zwei der Bäche (1984) 3'

No.1 from "Drei Liebesmadrigale nach
tschechischen Volksliedern"
Text: various
Chorus: female a cappella
C 45468

Um Jaroschau fließen zwei der Bäche (1967) 3'

No.2 from "Drei Liebesmadrigale nach
tschechischen Volksliedern"
Chorus: mixed a cappella
C 41868

Das Weltgericht (1980) 10'

Text: Martin Luther
Chorus: male a cappella
C 44824

Wenn ich durch die Berge meiner Heimat (1961) 5'

No.3 from "Drei mährische Volkslieder"
Chorus: mixed a cappella (6 prt)
C 40562

Wie lieblich schallt durch Busch und Wald (1970) 3'

From "Vom edlen Jägerleben"
Text: v. Schmid
Chorus: male a cappella
C 42563

Zeichen am Weg (1980) 15'

6 Miniatures
Text: various
Chorus: male
pno (4hnd)
Score ED 6892 / Choral score ED 6892-01

Zu Bethlehem geboren

(1967) 3'

Text: various
Chorus: female a cappella
CHBL 594

Poot, Marcel
1901-1988

Orchestral Works

Divertimento (1952)　　13'

1.1.1.0-1.1.0.0-str
Eu

Impromtu　　7'

En forme de Rondo
1.1.1.1-2.2.2.0-timp.perc-pno-str
Material on hire
Eu

Petite Suite (1961)　　16'

2.2.2.2-2.2.2.0-timp.perc-pno-str
Eu

Concertos

Konzertstück (1942)　　16'

Soloist: violin
2.2.2.2-2.2.2.0-timp-str

Pütz, Eduard
b.1911

Orchestral Works

Fantasy in Blue　　10'

*3(pic).2.2.bcl.asax.barsax.2-4.4.3.1-
timp.2perc-epno.hp.egtr-str*
Score **CON 245** / Parts **CON 245-50/-60**

Chamber & Instrumental Works

Blue Waltz　　4'

fl-pno
ED 8515

Blues for Benni　　6'

vn-pno
ED 8070

How about that, Mr. Offenbach!　　3'

Can-Can Fantasy
pno
ED 8496

Jazz Sonata (1988)　　10'

pno/hpd
ED 7954

Pütz, Eduard

b. Illerich/Mosel 13.2.1911

Eduard Pütz studied school music and mathematics at the Musikhochschule and at the University in Cologne. His composition teachers were Heinrich Lemacher and Kaspar Roeseling. From 1950 to 1965 he was a secondary school teacher in Rheinbach and from 1965 to 1979 he was lecturer in music theory and composition at the "Rheinische Musikschule" in Cologne. Eduard Pütz deals with crossing the boundaries between so-called "serious" and light music. His compositions, many of which are written with pedagogical aims for children and young people, therefore incorporate stylistic characteristics of jazz and pop music. Eduard Pütz has composed for all musical genres: his work includes one opera, symphonic music, chamber music, choral music and piano music.

3 Jazz Waltzes　　8'

Arranger: Fritz Emonts
pno (4hnd)
ED 8543

Let's swing, Mr. Bach　　12'

6 Piano Pieces in Play-Bach-Style
pno/hpd
ED 8003

Mr. Clementi goin' on Holidays　　10'

Little Study Pieces in Blues- and Rock-Style
pno
ED 6662

Nachtstücke　　12'

pno
ED 8545

Short Stories　　16'

10 Little Pieces
vc-pno
ED 7533

Tango Passionato　　4'

4vc
CB 159

Twilight Dream　　5'

vn-pno
ED 8420

Valsette

pno
ED 011028

Infoline · e-Mail
Schott Musik International
Mainz: Schott.Musik.com@T-Online.de
London: 101627.166@compuserve.com

R

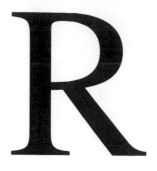

Rainier, Priaulx
1903-1986

Orchestral Works

Aequora Lunae (1966-67) 30'

3.3.3.2-2.2.2.1-timp.perc-str
Material on hire
SL

**Dance Concerto
"Phala-phala"** (1960-61) 14'

3.2.3.2-2.2.2.1-timp.4perc-[cel].hp-str
Material on hire
SL

Sinfonia da Camera (1947) 21'

str
Material on hire
SL

Concertos

Cello Concerto (1964) 21'

Soloist: cello
2.2.2.2-2.2.1.0-timp.3perc-str
Material on hire
Study score **ED 10913*** / Piano reduction **ED
10913-01/-02***

Concertante for 2 Winds

(1977-80) 18'

Soloists: oboe, clarinet
2.1.0.1-2.2.2.0-timp.2perc-str
Material on hire
Study score **ED 12082***

Due Canti e Finale (1976-77) 23'

Soloist: violin
3.3.2.2-2.2.0.1-timp.perc-str
Material on hire
Study score **ED 12132***

Chamber & Instrumental Works

Barbaric Dance Suite

(1949) 12'

pno
ED 10394

Grand Duo (1980-82)

vc-pno
Manuscript score on sale
SL

5 Keyboard Pieces (1955) 10'

pno
Manuscript score on sale
SL

Rainier, Priaulx

b. Howick, Natal 3.2.1903,
d. Besse-en-Chandesse, Auvergne 10.10.1986

A composer with a slender yet distinguished
output, Rainier was a pioneering female
musician, a violinist, and a much loved teacher. Her musical roots lay within the broad
stream of neo-classicism, owing a particular
debt to Bartok, but also showing the influence of her South African upbringing.

Organ Gloriana (1972) 13'

organ solo
Manuscript score on sale
SL

Pastoral Triptych (1958-59) 9'

oboe solo
ED 10636

6 Pieces (1957) 18'

fl.ob.cl.bn-hn
Material on sale
Study score **ED 10740***

Primordial Canticales (1974)

organ solo
Manuscript score on sale
SL

Primordial Canticles (1974)

organ solo
Manuscript score on sale
SL

Quanta (1961-62) 12'

ob-str trio
Material on sale
Study score **ED 10843***

Quinque (1971) 12'

hpd
Manuscript score on sale
SL

String Quartet (1939)   16'

Study score **ED 10210*** / Parts **ED 10250***

String Trio (1965-66)   15'

vn.va.vc
ED 11117

Suite (1943)   16'

cl-pno
ED 10409

Suite (1963-65)   10'

viola/cello solo
Manuscript score on sale
SL

Viola Sonata (1945)   10'

va-pno
ED 10410*

Solo Voice(s)/Voice(s) and Piano/Guitar

Cycle for Declamation

(1953)   9'

Text: John Donne
soprano/tenor solo
ED 10299

Dance of the Rain (1947)   10'

Text: Eugène Marais
soprano/tenor-gtr
ED 10902

3 Greek Epigrams (1937)   6'

soprano/tenor-pno
ED 10181

Ubunzima (1948)   4'

Text: Zulu
soprano/tenor-gtr
ED 11064

Solo Voice(s) and Instrument(s)/ Orchestra

The Bee Oracles (1969)   18'

Text: Edith Sitwell
Soloist: tenor/baritone
fl.ob-hpd-vn.vc
Material on hire
SL

Choral Works

Requiem (1955-56)   27'

Text: David Gascoyne
Soloist: tenor
Chorus: mixed a cappella
Material on hire
SL

Rasch, Kurt
1902-1986

Orchestral Works

Concerto for Orchestra, Op. 25   13'

3.2.2.tsax.2-4.2.3.1-perc-hp-str
Material on hire
Eu

Toccata, Op. 27   10'

3.2.2.2-4.3.3.1-timp.3perc-hp-str
Material on hire
Eu

Ravel, Maurice
1875-1937

Orchestral Works

Alborado del Gracioso

(1905)   10'

3.3.2.3-4.2.3.1-timp.perc-2hp-str
Material on hire
Study score **ETP 8001**
(British Commonwealth only)

Une Barque dur L'Océan

(1906)   8'

pic.2.2.ca.2.bcl.2-4.2.3.1-timp.perc-cel.2hp-str
Study score **ETP 8002**
(British Commonwealth only)

Boléro (1928)   16'

Critical edition by Arbie Orenstein
pic.2(pic).2(ob d'am)ca.Ebcl.2.bcl.ssax. tsax.2.cbn-4.4.3.1-timp.perc-cel.hp-str
Material on hire
Study score **ETP 8023**
(British Commonwealth only)

Pavane pour une infante défunte (1899)   8'

2.1.2.2-2.0.0.0-hp-str
Material on hire
SL (British Commonwealth only)

Chamber & Instrumental Works

Le Jardin féerique

Arranger: Roger Brison
fl-pno
ED 12431

Jeux d'Eau (1901)

pno
ED 12359 (British Commonwealth only)

Miroirs (1904-05)

pno
ED 12360 (British Commonwealth only)

Pavane pour une Infante défunte (1904-05)

Arranger: Stefan Nesyba
fl-gtr
ED 12214

Pavane pour une Infante défunte (1904-05)

Arranger: G. Drouet/Georges Pitch
va/vc-pno
ED 11345

Pavane pour une Infante défunte (1904-05)

srec.arec.trec.brec-pno
Score **ED 11372** / Parts **ED 11372-10**

Raxach, Enrique
b.1932

Orchestral Works

Syntagma (1965)   17'

4(2pic).3.ca.Ebcl.2.bcl.3.cbn-6.4.3.2-timp.4perc-2hp-str
Material on hire
AVV

Rees, Howard

Chamber & Instrumental Works

Doug's New Flute Thing (1970)

fl-tape
SM

Regner, Hermann
b.1928

Orchestral Works

Spielmusik aus Schwaben
1.0.Ebcl.2.2asax.2tsax.0-3.2thn.2flhn.2.
euph.2-perc
Parts **BLK 201-11 (-33)** / Score and parts
BLK 201

Chamber & Instrumental Works

Bläserübung I
for trumpets, horns or other brass instruments
ED 5420

Bläserübung II
brass-perc
ED 5421

Changing Patterns
4perc
BAT 28

5 Duos
percussion solo
BAT 8

15 Easy Duets
2vc
ED 7780

6 Easy Percussion Trios
percussion solo
BAT 20

Es war einmal ein König
(1995)   21'
pno
ED 8546

50 Etudes
1-3perc
BAT 29

Intrade   2'
12hn
Score **SHS 3003** / Parts **SHS 3003-70**

Klangspiele
pno (4hnd)-4perc
WKS 5

Regner, Hermann

b. Marktoberdorf/Allgäu 12.5.1928

Hermann Regner studied conducting and composition at the Augsburg Conservatory, going on to study musicology and folk traditions at the University of Munich, where he received his Doctorate in 1957. After a time as a lecturer at the Musikhochschule in Trossingen, in 1964 Regner became Professor of Musical Education at the Orff Institute of the "Mozarteum" Academy of Music and Performing Arts in Salzburg, where he continued to work until emeritus status was conferred upon him in 1993. Regner worked in close colaboration with Carl Orff. As a lecturer and writer he spread Orff's ideas about music teaching in courses all over the world and in numerous publications. His teaching work encompassed several areas of study: music teaching methods, composition, ensemble playing, conducting, aural training, teaching practice, improvisation at the piano, music and choreography; he also directed the Camerata Vocale of the Orff Institute. In addition, Regner produced a wide range of work as a composer, as well as a series of works designed for use in teaching.

Meditations
3 Pieces
sopranorecorder solo
OFB 180

Mein Lieblingslied von gestern
and other curious pieces
vc-pno
ED 8194

8 Miniatures
srec/arec-axyl.ametph/bmetph (1/2 players)
OFB 146

Mondzeit   (1995)   15'
7 Pieces
srec(arec,trec,brec)-gtr
OFB 179

7 Trios
7perc
BAT 27

Solo Voice(s) and Instrument(s)/ Orchestra

"mit musik"
5 Poems
Text: Ernst Zandl
Soloist: speaker
flutes.recs-2tpt/2cl-perc-pno-vc.db
Score and parts **WKS 21**

Choral Works

Choral Studies
Vocalises in graphic notation
Chorus: mixed a cappella
WKS 11

I Dream a World   6'
Text: Langston Hughes
Chorus: mixed
perc
Score and parts **ED 12307**

Reifner, Vinzenz
1878-1922

Orchestral Works

Aus deutschen Märchen - Nr. 1 Dornröschen, Op. 17   15'
Symphonic Fairytale Fantasy
3.2.3.2-4.3.3.1-timp.perc.glsp-hp-str
Material on hire
Eu

Frühling, Op. 12   16'
Symphonic Poem
3.2.2.2-4.3.3.1-timp.perc.glsp-hp-str
Material on hire
Eu

Reimann, Aribert

b.1936

Stage Works

Chacun sa Chimère (1981) 30'

Poème visuel - Ballet
Text: Charles Baudelaire
Material on hire
SM

Die Gespenstersonate

(1983) 90'

Opera. Arranged for Music bei Aribert
Reimann and Uwe Schendel
Text: August Strindberg
Material on hire
Study score **ED 8021** / Libretto **BN 3687-00**

Lear (1976-78) 185'

Opera in 2 Parts
Text: Claus H. Henneberg after William
Shakespeare
Material on hire
Study score **ED 6857** / Libretto **BN 3689-
70/3688-90**

Melusine (1970) 100'

Opera in 4 Acts
Text: Claus H. Henneberg after Yvan Goll
Material on hire
Libretto **BN 3690-00**

Das Schloß (1990-92) 165'

Opera
Text: Franz Kafka/Max Brod/Aribert
Reimann
Material on hire
Libretto **BN 3685-40**

Ein Traumspiel (1964) 120'

Opera
Text: Carla Henius, after August Strindberg
Material on hire
Vocal score **AVV 20**

Troades (1985) 120'

Opera
Text: Gerd Albrecht/Aribert Reimann after
Euripides/Franz Werfel
Material on hire
Libretto **BN 3686-20**

Die Vogelscheuchen (1970) 60'

Ballet in 3 Acts after Günther Grass
Material on hire
SM

Reimann, Aribert

b. Berlin 4.3.1936

Plays by Shakespeare, Euripides and
Strindberg have found operatic form in
Reimann's output - an achievement that
places him at the forefront of contemporary
composers in any country exploring the
boundaries of music theatre. A gifted pianist
whose recital work with Fischer-Dieskau is
legendary, he possesses a profound understanding of the voice; like Britten, he writes
with a deep awareness of the individual
psychological and vocal characteristics
of his performers. Darkly pessimistic, his
style reflects the trauma of a childhood in
wartime Germany.

Orchestral Works

7 Fragmente für Orchester

(1988) 11'

In memoriam Robert Schumann
*pic.1.afl.1.ca.Ebcl.1.bcl.2.cbn-4.4.2.1-hp-
str(12.10.8.8.6)*
Material on hire
SM

Invenzioni (1979) 17'

*1(pic,afl).1(ca).1(bcl).1-1.1.1.0-
str(1.1.1.1.1)*
Material on hire
SM

Loqui (1969) 11'

*pic.1.afl.1.ca.Ebcl.1.bcl.1.cbn-4.3.2.1-
timp.perc-str(12.10.8.6.5)*
Material on hire
SM

Musik aus dem Ballett "Die Vogelscheuchen" (1970) 30'

Suite
*pic.1.afl.1.ca.1.Ebcl.bcl.2.cbn-4.4.3.1-
timp.perc-str(12.12.10.8.6)*
Material on hire
SM

Neun Stücke für Orchester

(1993) 23'

*pic.1.afl.1.ca.Ebcl.1.bcl.1.cbn-4.3.2.1-
timp.3perc-pno.hp-str(12.10.8.6.5)*
Material on hire
Study score **ED 8444**

Rondes (1967) 12'

str(5.4.3.2.1)
Material on hire
Study score **AVV 302**

Symphony (1964) 30'

From the opera "Ein Traumspiel"
*3(pic)2.ca.2.bcl.2.cbn-4.3.3.1-timp.perc-
cel.pno.hpd.hp-str*
Material on hire
SM

Variations (1975) 17'

*pic.1.afl.1.ca.1.Ebcl.bcl.2.cbn-4.4.3.1-
timp.perc-str(12.10.8.6.5)*
Material on hire
Study score **ED 6720**

Concertos

Concerto for Violin and Cello (1988-89) 25'

Soloists: violin, cello
*pic.1.afl.1.ca.heck.Ebcl.1.bcl.2.cbn-4.3.2.1-
timp.perc-2hp-6db*
Material on hire
SM

Piano Concerto No.1 (1961) 30'

Soloist: piano
2(pic)1.ca.2.2-3.2.2.1-timp.perc-cel.hp-str
Material on hire
SM

Piano Concerto No.2 (1972) 20'

Soloist: piano
*1.1.Ebcl.0.bcl.1.cbn-0.2.1.0-perc-
str(4.0.2.2.1)*
Material on hire
SM

Chamber & Instrumental Works

Auf dem Weg, Vol. 1

(1989/93) 15'

3 Pieces
pno
ED 8289

Aribert Reimann
Neun Stücke für Orchester (1993)
beginning

Canzoni e Ricercari (1961) 17'

fl-va.vc
AVV 11

Cello Sonata (1963) 21'

vc-pno
AVV 16

Dialog 1 (1963) 8'

organ solo
ED 4822

Nocturnos (1965) 10'

vc-hp
AVV 32

Reflexionen (1966) 11'

fl.ob.bn-vn.va.vc-hpd
Material on hire
SM

Solo for Cello (1981) 8'

cello solo
ED 7099

Spektren (1967) 9'

pno
AVV 31

String Trio (1987) 25'

vn.va.vc
Score **ED 7562** / Parts **ED 7581**

Variations for Piano (1979) 22'

pno
ED 7106

Solo Voice(s)/Voice(s) and Piano/Guitar

Drei Sonnette von William Shakespeare (1964) 12'

Text: William Shakespeare
baritone-pno
AVV 13

Eingedunkelt (1992) 15'

Text: Paul Celan
alto solo
ED 8445

Engführung (1967) 20'

Text: Paul Celan
tenor-pno
AVV 34

Entsorgt (1989) 13'

Text: Nicolas Born
baritone solo
ED 7884

5 Gedichte von Paul Celan
(1960) 15'

Text: Paul Celan
baritone-pno
AVV 35

Impression IV (1961) 8'

Text: E.E. Cummings
soprano-pno
ED 7683

Kinderlieder (1961) 10'

Text: Werner Reinert
soprano-pno
ED 7682

Lady Lazarus (1992) 14'

Text: Syliva Plath
soprano solo
ED 8074

Nacht-Räume (1988) 14'

Text: Rainer Maria Rilke
soprano-pno (4hnd)
ED 7883

Nachtstück (1966) 11'

Text: Joseph von Eichendorff
baritone-pno
AVV 26

Nachtstück II (1978) 17'

Text: Joseph von Eichendorff
baritone-pno
AVV 116

Neun Sonnette der Louïze Labé (1986) 36'

Text: Louïze Labé
mezzo-soprano-pno
ED 7528

Nightpiece (1992) 15'

Text: James Joyce
soprano-pno
SM

Parerga (1971/87) 8'

To "Melusine"
Text: Yvan Goll
soprano solo
ED 8051

Die Pole sind in uns (1995) 8'

Text: Paul Celan
baritone-pno
ED 8574

Shine and Dark (1989) 20'

Text: James Joyce
baritone-pno(left hnd)
ED 7767

Six Poems (1975) 27'

Text: Sylvia Plath
soprano-pno
ED 6968

Tre Poemi di Michelangelo
(1985) 15'

baritone-pno
ED 7430

Wir, die wie der Strandhafer Wahren (1994) 6'

Text: Paul Celan
mezzo-soprano-pno
Material on sale
SM

Solo Voice(s) and Instrument(s)/ Orchestra

Ein apokalyptisches Fragment (1987) 25'

Text: Karoline von Günderrode
Soloists: mezzo-soprano, piano
1.afl(pic).1.ca.heck.1.bsthn.bcl.1.cbn-2.0.0.0-timp.perc-hp-str(6.6.6.0.6)
Material on hire
SM

Chacun sa Chimère (1981) 30'

Text: Charles Baudelaire
Soloist: tenor
2(pic).afl.bfl.0.1.Ebcl.bcl.cbcl.0-6vc.6db
Material on hire
SM

Denn Bleiben ist nirgends
(1968) 20'

First Duenese Elegy
Text: Rainer Maria Rilke
Soloist: speaker
pic.1.afl.1.ca.Ebcl.1.bcl.1.cbn-4.2.2.1-timp.perc-hp-str(12.10.8.6.5)
Material on hire
SM

Drei Lieder (1980-82) 30'

Text: Edgar Allan Poe
Soloist: soprano
1.afl.1.ca.1.bcl.1.cbn-2.1.1.0-2hp-str(6.6.5.4.3)
Material on hire
Study score **ED 7097**

Epitaph (1965) 16'

Text: Percy Bysshe Shelley
Soloist: tenor
fl.ca-cel.hp-va.vc.db
Material on hire
SM

Finite Infinity (1994-95) 35'

Text: Emily Dickinson
Soloist: soprano
pic.1.afl.1.ca.Ebcl.1.bcl.1.cbn-0.3.3.0-pno.hp-str(10.8.6.6.4)
Material on hire
Study score **ED 8497**

Infoline · e-Mail
Schott Musik International
Mainz: Schott.Musik.com@T-Online.de
London: 101627.166@compuserve.com

Fragments from "Lear"

(1976-78) 42'

Text: William Shakespeare
Soloist: baritone
3(3pic).afl.2.ca.2(Ebcl).bcl.2.cbn-6.4.3.1-
timp.perc-2hp-str(24.0.10.8.6)
Material on hire
SM

Fragments from "Melusine"

(1970) 35'

Text: Claus H. Henneberg, after Yvan Goll
Soloists: soprano, baritone
1(pic).afl.1.ca.1(Ebcl).bcl.1.cbn-2.2.2.0-
timp-cel.hp-str(4.4.3.3.2)
Material on hire
SM

Gedichte der Maria Stuart, Op. 135 (1988) 9'

(Robert Schumann)
Arranger: Aribert Reimann
Soloist: mezzo-soprano
1.afl.0.ca.1.1.cbn-1.0.0.0-str(0.0.4.3.2)
Material on hire
SM

Hölderlin-Fragmente (1963) 20'

Soloist: soprano
2(pic).1.ca.1.b cl.1.cbn-3.2.2.1-timp.4perc-
cel.pno.hp-str
Material on hire
Study score **AVV 74**

Inane (1968) 24'

Text: Manuel Thomas
Soloist: soprano
2pic.1.afl.0.Ebcl.1.2bcl.2.2cbn-0.4.0.0-
timp.perc-str(0.0.0.8.6)
Material on hire
Study score **AVV 314**

Lines (1973) 14'

Text: Percy Bysshe Shelley
Soloist: soprano
str(4.4.3.2.1)
Material on hire
SM

Mignon (1995) 19'

(Franz Schubert)
Arranger: Aribert Reimann
Text: Johann Wolfgang von Goethe
Soloist: soprano
str qrt
ED 8466

Sechs Gesänge, Op. 107

(1994) 10'

(Robert Schumann)
Arranger: Aribert Reimann
Soloist: soprano
str qrt
ED 7683

Ein Totentanz - Suite (1960) 15'

Text: Aribert Reimann
Soloist: baritone
1.1.1.1-1.0.0.0-hpd.hp-str
Material on hire
Study score **AVV 71** / Vocal score **AVV 7**

Trovers (1967) 14'

Soloist: speaker
cl.bn-tpt.tbn-vn.db-cymbal
Material on hire
SM

Unrevealed (1979-80) 30'

Text: Lord Byron
Soloist: baritone
str qrt
Score **ED 6941** / Parts **ED 6942**

Wolkenloses Christfest

(1974) 35'

(Requiem)
Text: Otfried Büthe
Soloists: baritone, cello
pic.1.afl.1.ca.2(Ebcl,bcl).2bcl.2.2cbn-
0.4.3.0-timp.perc-2hp-str(0.0.10.0.6)
Material on hire
Study score **ED 6619**

Zyklus (1971) 26'

Text: Paul Celan
Soloist: baritone
pic.1.afl.bfl.1.ca.1.Ebcl.bcl.2.cbn-4.3.3.1-
timp.perc-2hp-str(0.0.8.8.6)
Material on hire
Study score **AVV 310**

Choral Works

Auf verschleierten Schaukeln

(1957) 10'

Text: Hans Arp
Chorus: mixed a cappella
SKR 20010

John III, 16 (1976) 11'

Text: Bible
Chorus: mixed a cappella (8 prt)
ED 6669

Nunc dimittis (Canticum Simeonis) (1984) 10'

Soloist: baritone
Chorus: mixed (8 prt)
bfl
Parts **SKR 20524-11 (flute)** / Choral score
SKR 20524

Requiem (1980/82) 90'

Text: Latin
Soloists: soprano, mezzo-soprano, baritone
Chorus: mixed
2(2pic).afl(pic).bfl(pic).2.ca.2(Ebcl).bcl.2.c
bn-0.4.4.1-timp.perc-2hp-str(0.0.10.8.6)
Material on hire
SM

Verrà la morte (1966) 35'

Cantata
Text: Cesare Pavese
Soloists: soprano, tenor, baritone
Chorus: mixed double
2(2pic).afl.2.ca.2.bcl.2.cbn-0.0.0.0-
timp.perc-cel.hpd.2hp-str(0.0.8.6.5)
Material on hire
SM

Rein, Walter
1893-1955

Chamber & Instrumental Works

Divertimento (1961) 13'

horn qrt
Score and parts **ED 5164**

Piano Music on Folksongs 23'

ED 4619

Spielbuch (1950) 11'

3vn/4vn
ED 4134

Waldmusik (1961) 6'

4hn
Score and parts **ED 5165**

Choral Works

Ade zur guten Nacht (1950) 2'

Chorus: male a cappella
CHBL 16

Alles ist Liebe (1955) 24'

Text: Alexander M. Miller
Chorus: mixed,female,children's
1.1.1.1-1.1.0.0-perc-str
Material on hire
Piano reduction **ED 4527**

Aufregung im Hühnerhof

(1954) 2'

Chorus: female a cappella
CHBL 560

Biergesängel (1954) 3'

Chorus: male a cappella
C 38623

Blüh auf! (1930) 3'

No.2 from "Drei ernste Gesänge"
Text: Angelus Silesius
Chorus: female a cappella
C 32627

Chor der Bauern (1932) 4'

Chorus: male a cappella
SM

Chor der Kaufleute (1932) 3'

Chorus: male a cappella
SM

Das Echo (1952) 3'

Text: Walter Rein
Chorus: male a cappella + solo qrt
C 38176

Dreimol oms Städele (1956) 2'

Chorus: male a cappella
C 39592

Drunten im Unterland

(1950) 2'

Text: Schwaben
Chorus: mixed a cappella
C 39630

Dunkle Wolken (1946)

Chorus: mixed a cappella
SM

Es ist Weihnacht (1954) 7'

Cantata after a French Christmassong
Soloist: soprano
Chorus: female
str qnt
Score **ED 4982** / Parts **ED 4982-11 (-15)** /
Vocal score **ED 4982-01**

Es schläft in allem Ding

(1950) 4'

Text: Paul Rohleder
Chorus: male a cappella
SM

Es sungen drei Engel

Chorus: mixed a cappella
SM

Es wollt ein Jägerlein jagen

(1950) 3'

Chorus: male a cappella
CHBL 5

Es wollt ein Jägerlein jagen

(1949) 3'

Chorus: female a cappella (4 prt)
CHBL 589

Freiheit, die ich meine

(1955) 5'

Text: M. v. Schenkendorf
Chorus: male [a cappella]
[2tpt.3tbn]
CHBL 101

Frisch auf in Gottes Namen

(1933) 2'

Chorus: female a cappella
CHBL 548

Gegenwart

Chorus: mixed (S.A.T)
SM

Genialisches Treiben (1930) 3'

Chorus: mixed a cappella
SM

Gesellen der Nacht

Text: Ernst Moritz Arndt
Chorus: children's (2-3 prt)
fl-2vn.vc
SM

Die Gezeiten (1930) 3'

No.1 from "Drei ernste Gesänge"
Text: Johann Gottfried Herder
Chorus: female a cappella
C 32626

Handwerksburschen Abschied 3'

Chorus: male a cappella
C 39623

Hausspruch (1933) 1'

Chorus: female a cappella
SM

Heija, im frischen Mai

Chorus: male a cappella (4 voices)
SM

Heimat (1954) 9'

Cantata
Text: Jochen Hoffbauer
Chorus: male, children's/female
1.3.Ebcl.0.0-4.2flhn.2.2.euph.2-[timp]
Score **ED 4512** / Parts **ED 4512-10** /
Vocal score **ED 4512-01/-02**

Heimat (1954) 9'

Cantata
Text: Jochen Hoffbauer
Chorus: male, children's/female
2hn-str
Score **ED 4512** / Parts **ED 4512-11 (-15)** /
Vocal score **ED 4512-01/-02**

Herr, schicke, was du wilt

(1930) 3'

No.3 from "Drei ernste Gesänge"
Text: Eduard Mörike
Chorus: female a cappella
C 32628

Hochzeits-Madrigal

Chorus: male a cappella
SM

Der Hufschmied

Chorus: mixed a cappella
SM

Ich wollt, daß ich daheime wäre

Text: H. von Laufenberg
Chorus: mixed a cappella
SM

Jägerlied (1950) 2'

Text: Franken
Chorus: male a cappella
CHBL 18

Junggesellen (1952) 3'

Text: Hermann Löns
Chorus: male a cappella
C 37622

Kein Feuer, keine Kohle

(1951) 2'

Text: various
Chorus: female a cappella
CHBL 517

Komm, Trost der Nacht, o Nachtigall (1958) 4'

Text: H.J. Christoffel v. Grimmelshausen
Chorus: mixed, children's, male
[2tpt.3tbn.tuba]
Score **C 39346** / Parts **C 39349** / Vocal score **C 39447/-48**

Komm, Trost der Welt, du stille Nacht (1952) 4'

Text: Joseph von Eichendorff/Paul Gerhardt
Chorus: male, children's
C 38297

Laßt uns glauben (1953) 18'

Text: Arthur Maximilian Miller
Chorus: mixed, children's
2.2.2.2-2.2.2.0-timp-str
Material on hire
Score **ED 4232** / Vocal score **ED 4332-01/-02**

Der liebste Buhle (1950) 2'

Chorus: male a cappella
CHBL 4

Lied der Sonne

Text: Christian Morgenstern
Chorus: children's (2-3 prt)
fl-2vn.vc
SM

Lob des Herings

Chorus: male a cappella
SM

Ein Mädchen und ein Gläschen Wein (1950) 3'

Text: Johann Wolfgang von Goethe
Chorus: male a cappella
CHBL 22

Minnelied (1953) 4'

Text: Walter Rein
Chorus: male a cappella
CHBL 76

Mit Mädchen sich vertragen

(1955) 2'

Text: Johann Wolfgang Goethe
Chorus: male a cappella
SM

Mörike-Zyklus (1953) 25'

Chorus: male
3hn
Score **ED 4236** / Parts **ED 4236-10/ ED 4236-01 (-04) (chorus)**

Musik und Jägerei (1952) 7'

Text: Valentin Rathgeber
Chorus: male
fl-hn.tpt-2vn.vc.[db]
Score **ED 4263** / Parts **ED 4263-10**

Muß i denn (1949) 3'

Chorus: male a cappella
CHBL 8

Nach grüner Farb mein Herz verlangt (1955) 4'

Chorus: male, children's/female a cappella
C 39067

O Heiland, reiß die Himmel auf (1952) 2'

Chorus: male a cappella
SM

O Lamentatione!

Chorus: mixed a cappella
SM

Der Obadrauf (1956) 1'

Chorus: male a cappella
SM

Sandmännchen (1954) 2'

Chorus: female a cappella
SM

Sängerwettstreit (1955) 3'

Text: Leo Petri
Soloists: 2 tenors, 2 basses
Chorus: male a cappella
Score **C 39101** / Choral score **C 39102/-03**

Schneider Courage

Text: Johann Wolfgang von Goethe
Chorus: mixed a cappella
SM

Sommerdörfchen

Chorus: male
SM

Spaßige Geschichte (1954) 6'

Text: Margarete Staats
Chorus: female a cappella
SM

Stehn zwei Stern am hohen Himmel (1950) 2'

Text: Westerwald
Chorus: male a cappella
CHBL 15

Streit zwischen Löffel und Gabel (1954) 2'

Chorus: female a cappella
SM

Stundenruf des Wächters (1952) 3'

Text: various
Soloist: baritone
Chorus: male, children's
CHBL 55

Der Tambour (1953) 3'

Text: Eduard Mörike
Chorus: male a cappella
C 38477

Tanz rüber (1949) 2'

Chorus: female a cappella
SM

Trinklied (1953) 3'

Text: Johann Günther
Chorus: male a cappella
CHBL 77

Tummel dich, guts Weinlein (1927) 2'

Chorus: male a cappella
SM

Türmerlied (1932) 4'

Text: from Goethe's "Faust"
Chorus: male
3tpt.3tbn
Score **C 33449** / Parts **C 33561**

Und in dem Schneegebirge (1952) 2'

Text: Schlesien
Chorus: male a cappella
CHBL 37

Und in dem Schneegebirge (1952) 2'

Text: Schlesien
Chorus: female a cappella
CHBL 524

Wach auf, mein Herzens Schöne (1956) 2'

Chorus: male a cappella
C 39591

Weihe der Nacht (1952) 4'

Hymnic Cantata
Text: Friedrich Hebbel
Chorus: male, children's
1.0.Ebcl.3.0-2.2thn.2flhn.2.2.euph.2
Parts **ED 4448-10** / Choral score
ED 4448-01/-02 / Vocal score **ED 4448**

Der Weinfuhrmann (1957) 1'

Text: Lothringen
Chorus: male a cappella
CHBL 130

Wer sich die Musik erkiest (1950) 5'

Text: Martin Luther
Chorus: mixed a cappella
C 37918

Der Winter 15'

Text: Walter Rein
Soloists: alto, baritone
Chorus: mixed, children's
0.1.0.0-1.0.0.0-str
SM

Wunderlichstes Buch der Bücher (1952) 3'

Text: Johann Wolfgang Goethe
Chorus: male a cappella
C 38480

Zum Tanze, da geht ein Mädel (1951) 2'

Chorus: mixed a cappella
CHBL 278

Zum Tanze, da geht ein Mädel (1952) 2'

Chorus: female a cappella
CHBL 523

Zur Ernte (1952) 3'

Chorus: male a cappella
SM

Reizenstein, Franz
1911-1968

Chamber & Instrumental Works

Partita (1938)

arec-hpd
OFB 1014

Reutter, Hermann
1900-1985

Stage Works

Die Brücke von San Luis Rey (1954) 75'

Dramatic Scene after Th. Wilder
Text: Gerhard Reutter
Material on hire
Vocal score **ED 4318**

Doktor Johannes Faust, Op. 47 (1936/55) 180'

Opera in 3 Acts
Text: Ludwig Andersen
Material on hire
Libretto **BN 3692-70**

Reutter, Hermann

b. Stuttgart 17.6.1900, d. Heidenheim/Brenz 1.1.1985

Hermann Reutter studied piano, singing and composition with Walter Courvoisier at the Munich Academy of Music. From 1923 concert tours led him through Germany and abroad. As a composer, he first received notice at the music festivals of Donaueschingen and Baden-Baden (1923, 1926, 1927/1928). In 1932 Reutter took an appointment to teach composition at the Stuttgart Conservatory, from 1936-1945 he was director of the Hoch Conservatory in Frankfurt/Main. In 1952 he became professor of composition and lied interpretation at the Stuttgart Conservatory where in 1956 he was appointed director until his retirement in 1966. He then took over a master class in lied interpretation at the Munich Conservatory until 1974.

Don Juan und Faust, Op. 75

(1950)   115'

Opera after Chr.D. Grable
Text: Ludwig Andersen
Material on hire
Vocal score **ED 4031** / Libretto **BN 3693-50**

Hamlet (1979-80)   145'

Opera in 5 Acts
Text: August Wilhelm
Material on hire
SM

Die Kirmes von Delft, Op. 48

(1937)   35'

Ballet in 3 Scenes
Material on hire
SM

Der Lübecker Totentanz, Op. 35 (1948)   18'

Musical Drama
Text: Old inscriptions of the Lübecker Marienkirche
Material on hire
SM

Notturno Montmartre

(1953)   45'

Ballet in 4 Scenes
Material on hire
Piano reduction **ED 4313**

Odysseus, Op. 55 (1942)   180'

Opera in 3 Acts
Text: Rudolf Bach
Material on hire
SM

Die Prinzessin und der Schweinehirt (1938)   130'

Musical Drama in 10 Scenes
Text: Else Hellmund after Hans Christian Andersen
Material on hire
SM

Die Rückkehr des verlorenen Sohnes, Op. 34 (1952)   50'

Revised version of the Opera of the same title (1929)
Text: Rainer Maria Rilke
Soloists: mezzo-soprano, tenor, 2 baritone, bass
Chorus: mixed
2.2.2.asax.2-2.2.0.0-timp.perc-pno-str
Material on hire
SM

Saul, Op. 33 (1928/48)   45'

Musical Drama in 1 Act
Text: A. Lernet-Holenia
Material on hire
Vocal score **ED 3982**

Der Tod des Empedokles

(1966)   55'

Scenic Concerto in 2 Acts
Text: Friedrich Hölderlin
2(pic).2(ca).2(asax).2(cbn)-2.2.2.0-timp.perc-pno(cel).hp-str (min 4.4.4.4.2)
Material on hire
Vocal score **ED 5765** / Libretto **BN 3691-90**

Topsy, Op. 76 (1950)   45'

Spiel (Ballet)
Text: Fred Schmitz
Material on hire
SM

Der verlorene Sohn, Op. 34

(1929)   45'

Opera in 5 Scenes
Text: André Gide
Material on hire
SM

Der Weg nach Freudenstadt, Op. 66 (1948)   40'

Ballad of the Main Road in 5 Scenes
Text: Sonja Korty
Material on hire
Vocal score **ED 3984**

Die Witwe von Ephesus

(1954/66)   70'

Opera in 1 Act
Text: Ludwig Andersen after Petronius
Material on hire
Vocal score **ED 4317/4317-01** / Libretto **BN 3694-30**

Orchestral Works

Dance Variations, Op. 76

(1951)   20'

2(pic).2(ca).2(bcl).asax.2-4.2.2.0-tlmp.3perc-pno(cel)-str
Material on hire
SM

Figurinen (1972)   18'

2(pic).2(ca).2(asax).2(cbn)-4.3.3.1-timp.perc-cel.hp-str
Material on hire
SM

Die Kirmes von Delft, Op. 48

(1937)   35'

Ballet Suite
2(pic).2(ca).2.2(cbn)-4.2.3.1-timp.2perc-cel.hp-str
Material on hire
SM

Notturno Montmartre - Suite

(1952)   22'

3(2pic).2(ca).3(Ebcl).2.cbn-4.3Ctpt.3.1-timp.perc-cel.pno.hp-str
Material on hire
SM

Symphony (1960)   25'

str
Material on hire
SM

Concertos

Capriccio, Aria and Finale

(1964)   25'

Soloist: piano
2.2.ca.2.2-4.3.3.0-timp.perc-str(min:12.10.8.6.4)
Material on hire
Piano reduction **ED 5396**

Concert Variations (1952)   22'

Soloist: piano
2(pic).2(ca).2.1.cbn-4.2.3.0-timp.2perc-str
Material on hire
SM

Concertino, Op. 69 (1947)   22'

Soloist: piano
str
Material on hire
SM

Concerto in Eb for 2 Pianos, Op. 63 (1950)   17'

Soloists: 2 pianos
2.2.2.2.cbn-4.3.3.0-timp.perc-str
Material on hire
SM

Epitaph für Ophelia (1970)   22'

Soloist: violin
1.2(ca).1.1-1.0.0.0-str(4.4.3.2.1)
Material on hire
Piano reduction **ED 6815**

Piano Concerto No.1, Op. 19

(1926)   22'

Soloist: piano
pic.1.1.1.1-1.1.0.0-timp.perc-str(8.6.4.3.2)
Material on hire
SM

Piano Concerto No.2, Op. 36

(1929)   25'

Soloist: piano
2.2.2.2-4.2.3.0-timp.perc-str
Material on hire
SM

Piano Concerto No.4, Op. 62

(1948)   30'

Soloist: piano
2.2.2.2-4.3.3.0-timp.perc-str
Material on hire
SM

Prozession (1958)   22'

Soloist: cello
2(pic).1.ca.2(asax).1.cbn-4.3.3.0-timp.perc-pno(cel).hp-str
Material on hire
Piano reduction **ED 4759**

Symphonic Fantasy, Op. 50

(1938)   35'

Piano Concerto No.3
Soloist: piano
2(pic).2(ca).2.2-4.2.3.1-timp.perc-str
Material on hire
SM

Violin Concerto, Op. 39

(1933)   20'

Soloist: violin
2.2.2.2-2.2.0.0-timp.perc-cel-str(2.0.0.2.2)
Material on hire
SM

Chamber & Instrumental Works

Abendangelus - Bolero - Fandango   4'

Arranger: Turnagoel
guitar solo
GA 502

Cinco Caprichos sobre Cervantes (1968)   17'

viola solo
VAB 47

Cinco Caprichos sobre Cervantes (1968)   17'

Arranger: Turnagoel
guitar solo
GA 487

Dance Suite, Op. 29

pno
ED 1416

Fantasia Apocalyptica, Op. 7 (1926)

pno
ED 1790

Fantasiestücke, Op. 28   14'

guitar solo
GA 500

Little Piano Pieces, Op. 28

(1928)

pno
ED 1415

Music (1951)   25'

va-pno
VAB 24

Die Passion in 9 Inventionen, Op. 25 (1930)   14'

pno
ED 2137

Die Passion in 9 Inventionen, Op. 25 (1930)   14'

Arranger: Turnagoel
guitar solo
GA 488

Pfingstmusik, Op. 41/2 (1932/68)

2vn
SM

Pièce concertante (1968)   11'

asax-pno
ED 5893

Rhapsody, Op. 51 (1939)

vn-pno
ED 3690

Sonata Monotematica

(1972)   17'

bn-pno
ED 6425

Sonata Monotematica

(1972)   17'

vc-pno
ED 6424

Variations, Op. 15   2'

pno
ED 1791

Violin Sonata, Op. 20

(1926)   20'

vn-pno
SM

Solo Voice(s)/Voice(s) and Piano/Guitar

3 altägyptische Gedichte

(1962)

bass-pno
SM

Bogenschützen (1971)

Text: Federico García Lorca/Enrique Beck
high voice-pno
ED 6496

Chamber Music (1972)   9'

4 selected Poems
Text: James Joyce
low voice-pno
ED 6494

Christmas Cantilena (1952)   18'

Text: Matthias Claudius
medium voice-pno
ED 4487 / Piano reduction **ED 4487**

Epitaph für einen Dichter

(1962)   14'

Text: William Faulkner
high voice-pno
ED 5289

5 Fragmente nach Friedrich Hölderlin (1965)   10'

tenor-pno
ED 5532

Ein Füllen ward geboren

(1962)

Chanson Variée
Text: Saint-John Perse
medium voice-pno
ED 5299

Hamlet's first and second Monologue 6'
Text: William Shakespeare
baritone-pno
ED 7085

Hymne an Deutschland
(1950) 3'
Text: Rudolf Alexander Schröder
voice-pno
BSS 37879

Die Jahreszeiten
Text: Friedrich Hölderlin
medium voice-pno
ED 4799

6 Late Poems (1972)
Text: Ricarda Huch
medium voice-pno
ED 4798

4 Lieder, Op. 54 (1941)
Text: Friedrich Rückert
voice-pno
ED 3793

5 Lieder, Op. 58 (1948)
Text: Theodor Storm
low voice-pno
ED 3675

3 Lieder, Op. 60 (1947)
Text: Matthias Claudius
high voice-pno
ED 3872

3 Lieder, Op. 61 (1947)
Text: Clemens von Brentano
high voice-pno
ED 3871

12 Lieder, Op. 65 (1948) 27'
Text: Hans Heinrich Ehrler
high voice-pno
ED 3667

3 Lieder, Op. 67 (1947)
Text: Friedrich Hölderlin
voice-pno
ED 3851

9 Lieder (1971) 16'
Text: Ricarda Huch
voice-pno
ED 6492

4 Lieder (1972) 6'
Text: Nelly Sachs
medium voice-pno
ED 6493

5 Lieder (1972)
Text: Marie Luise Kaschnitz
medium voice-pno
ED 6495

Lieder der Liebe (1951) 12'
Text: Ricarda Huch
soprano-pno
ED 4298

3 Lieder der Ophelia (1980) 7'
Text: William Shakespeare
soprano-pno
ED 6981

9 Lieder und Gesänge, Op. 59 (1948)
Text: Gottfried Keller
high voice-pno
ED 3668

Meine dunklen Hände 10'
Text: Hughes/Bontemps
baritone-pno
ED 4761

6 Poems, Op. 73 (1949)
Text: Johann Wolfgang von Goethe
soprano-baritone-pno
ED 4118

Russische Lieder, Op. 21
(1927) 3'
Text: various
high voice-pno
ED 2042

Russische Lieder, Op. 68 (1949)
medium voice-low voice-pno
ED 3297

Russische Lieder, Op. 23 (1930)
Text: various
medium voice-pno
ED 2139

3 Lieder, Op. 56 (1944) 6'
Text: Friedrich Hölderlin
low voice-pno
ED 3738

7 Lieder, Op. 64 (1948) 24'
Text: Hans Heinrich Ehrler
bass-pno
ED 3666

Triptychon "Sankt Sebastian" (1968) 12'
Text: E.F. Sommer
baritone-pno
ED 6112

Die Weise von Liebe und Tod, Op. 31 (1947) 18'
Text: Rainer Maria Rilke
medium voice-pno
ED 3852

Das zeitgenössische Lied
Songs by Various Composers
Arranger: Hermann Reutter
Text: various
soprano/mezzo-soprano/tenor/baritone
ED 5745 (-48)

3 Zigeunerromanzen (1956) 20'
Text: Federico García Lorca/Enrique Beck
voice-pno
ED 4943

Solo Voice(s) and Instrument(s)/ Orchestra

Andalusiana (1962) 26'
Arien and Intermezzi
Text: Federico García Lorca
Soloist: soprano
2(pic).1.ca.2(bcl).asax.2(cbn)-4.2.0.0-
timp.perc-hp.pno(cel)-str(12.10.8.6.4)
Material on hire
Piano reduction **ED 5286**

5 antike Oden, Op. 57 (1948)
Text: Rudolf Bach after Sappho
Soloist: mezzo-soprano
va-pno
ED 3674

Aus dem Hohelied Salomonis
(1956) 35'
"Concerto grosso"
Text: Bible
Soloists: alto, viola, piano
2(pic).2(ca).2(bcl).asax.2(cbn)-4.3.3.0-
timp.perc-cel.hp-str
Material on hire
SM

Hamlet Symphony (1982) 90'
Text: William Shakespeare
Soloists: S.MS.2T.2Bar.speaker
Chorus: 2 single voices
3(2pic).2.ca.2(bcl).asax.2.cbn-4.4.3.1-
timp.3perc-pno(cel).hp-str
Material on hire
SM

Der himmlische Vagant
(1951) 25'
Lyric Portrait of François Villon
Soloists: alto, baritone
1.pic.1.ca.1.asax.1.cbn-0.0.0.0-timp.perc-
pno-str(1.0.1.1.1)
Material on hire
SM

Kleine Ballade von den drei Flüssen (1960) 7'
Text: Federico García Lorca
Soloist: soprano
2.2.2.asax.2-2.2.0.0-timp.perc-hp-str
Material on hire
Piano reduction **ED 5169**

Kleines geistliches Konzert
(1953)
alto-va
ED 4486

Ein kleines Requiem (1961) 14'
Text: Federico García Lorca
Soloist: bass
vc-pno
ED 5190

Der Liebe will ich singen

(1977) 12'

Soloists: soprano, baritone
2(pic).2(ca).2cl(asax).2(cbn)-3.2Ctpt.2.0-timp.perc-hp-str(12.10.8.6.4)
Material on hire
Vocal score **ED 6702**

Liebeslied aus dem Chinesischen des Sao Han

(1975) 4'

Text: Hans Bethge
speaker-fl
ED 6652

Lyrical Cantata, Op. 70

(1948) 24'

Text: Eckart Peterich
Soloist: soprano
fl-timp-pno-str
Material on hire
SM

Missa Brevis, Op. 22 (1930) 22'

Text: various
Soloist: alto
vn.vc
ED 3153

Monolog der Iphigenie, Op. 74 (1949) 15'

Text: Johann Wolfgang von Goethe
Soloist: female voice
2.3.3.3-4.3.3.0-timp.perc-hp-str
Material on hire
SM

3 Monologe des Empedokles

(1966) 18'

Text: Friedrich Hölderlin
Soloist: baritone
2(pic).2(ca).2(asax).2(cbn)-2.2.2.0-timp.perc-cel.pno.hp-str
Material on hire
Piano reduction **ED 6264**

3 Nocturnes (1975) 11'

Text: Friedrich Nietzsche
Soloist: bass/baritone
fl.ob.cl.bn-hn-pno
Score **ED 6651** / Parts **ED 6651-01**

Prediger Salomo (12,1-9)

(1973) 12'

Text: Bible
Soloist: low voice
fl-pno/org
ED 6423

Solo Cantata, Op. 45 (1948) 12'

Text: Matthias Claudius
Soloist: alto
va-pno/org
Study score **ED 3853**

3 Lieder, Op. 3 (1937) 25'

Text: Friedrich Hölderlin
Soloist: medium voice
str(qrt/orch)
Material on hire
SM

Spanischer Totentanz

(1953) 15'

Text: Federico García Lorca
Soloists: 2 medium voices
1(pic).1.ca.2(bcl).asax.2-2.2.0.0-timp.3perc-pno(cel)-str(8.6.4.3.2)
Material on hire
Vocal score **ED 5756**

Szene und Monolog der Marfa (1966) 10'

Text: Friedrich Schiller
Soloist: soprano
1.pic.1.ca.2.asax.2.cbn-4.3.3.0-timp.perc-hp-str
Material on hire
Vocal score **ED 5923**

Weltlicht (1959) 22'

Text: Halldór Laxness/Ernst Harthern
Soloist: bass/baritone
1.1.ca.1.asax.1-2.2.1.0-timp.perc-pno-str(4.4.3.3.2)
Material on hire
Study score **ED 5014**

Choral Works

Bauernhochzeit (1950) 25'

8 Poems from "Stimmen der Völker"
Text: Johann Gottfried Herder
Chorus: mixed
2(pic).1.ca.2.2(cbn)-2.0.0.0-hp-str(min:10.8.6.4.2)
Material on hire
SM

4 Bettellieder, Op. 38b (1930)

Chorus: mixed a cappella
C 32740

Choral Fantasy, Op. 52

(1939) 60'

Text: Johann Wolfgang von Goethe
Soloists: soprano, baritone
Chorus: mixed
2(pic).2(ca).2(bcl).2-4.2.3.1-timp.2perc-cel/pno.hp-str(14.12.10.8.6)
Material on hire
Vocal score **ED 2915**

Christmas Cantilena (1952) 18'

Text: Matthias Claudius
Soloist: medium voice
Chorus: mixed
pno/org
Material on hire
Vocal score **ED 4487/5903**

Gesang des Deutschen, Op. 49 (1937) 23'

Text: Friedrich Hölderlin
Soloists: soprano, baritone
Chorus: mixed
2(pic).2(ca).2.2-4.3.3.0-timp.perc-str
Material on hire
SM

Gleichnis vom barmherzigen Samariter (1959) 6'

Text: Bible
Chorus: mixed a cappella
C 40228

Gleichnis vom Saemann

(1959) 6'

Text: Bible
Chorus: mixed a cappella
C 40226

Gleichnis von den Jungfrauen (1959) 6'

Text: Bible
Chorus: mixed a cappella
C 40227

Der glückliche Bauer, Op. 44

(1932) 15'

Text: Matthias Claudius
Chorus: mixed/male
2(pic).0.2.1-1.2.0.0-timp.perc-str
Material on hire
Study score **ED 3315**

Der große Kalender, Op. 43

(1930-32/70) 106'

Text: Ludwig Andersen
Soloists: soprano, baritone
Chorus: mixed,children's
2(pic).2(ca).2(asax).2(cbn)-2.2.2.1-timp.2perc-[org]-str
Material on hire
SM

Das große Welttheater

(1951) 20'

6 Choruses
Text: Calderón de la Barca
Chorus: mixed
3.2.ca.3.asax.2.cbn-4.3.3.1-timp.3perc-pno
Material on hire
SM

Hochzeitslieder, Op. 53

(1941) 25'

Text: Johann Gottfried Herder
Chorus: mixed
pno
Vocal score **ED 3908**

Hymne an Deutschland

(1950) 3'

Text: Rudolf Alexander Schröder
Chorus: mixed [a cappella]/female/children's/male
[2.2.2.2-4.3.2.0-timp-pno.org-str]
Material on hire
Parts **C 37888** / Choral score **C 37886**

Hymne an Deutschland

(1950) 3'

Text: Rudolf Alexander Schröder
Chorus: male a cappella
[2hn.3tpt.3tbn.tuba-timp]
Score **C 39123** / Choral score **CHBL 92**

Jesu Nachtgespräch mit Nikodemus (1976) 5'

Text: Bible
Chorus: mixed a cappella
C 42544

3 Madrigals, Op. 71 (1949)

Text: Euripides, Friedrich Hölderlin, Johann Wolfgang von Goethe
Chorus: mixed a cappella
C 37733

Der neue Hiob, Op. 37 (1930)

Text: Robert Seitz
Soloists: 2T.2Bar.2B
Chorus: mixed
pno-str
Material on hire
SM

Pandora, Op. 72 (1949) 30'

Text: Johann Wolfgang von Goethe
Soloists: soprano, baritone
Chorus: mixed
3.3.3.3-4.3.3.1-timp.perc-cel.pno.hp-str
Material on hire
Vocal score **ED 4027**

Phyllis and Philander
(1970) 20'

Text: Peter Squentz
Chorus: mixed
fl.ob.cl.bn-hn.tpt-pno
Material on hire
Score **ED 147** / Parts **ED 147-10** / Vocal score
ED 147-01

Tres Laudes - Charon (1964)

Carmina Latina
Text: Josef Eberle
Chorus: mixed a cappella
C 41167

Tres Laudes - Laudes Francisci (1964)

Carmina Latina
Text: Josef Eberle
Chorus: mixed a cappella
C 41174

Tres Laudes - Multas novit amor vias (1964)

Carmina Latina
Text: Josef Eberle
Chorus: mixed a cappella
C 41166

Triptychon (1959) 23'

Text: Friedrich Schiller
Soloist: tenor
Chorus: mixed
2(pic).1.ca.2.asax.1.cbn-4.3.3.1-timp.perc-str
Material on hire
SM

Trost der Nacht (1976) 9'

Text: H.J. Christoffel v. Grimmelshausen
Chorus: mixed [a cappella]
[fl-pno]
Score and parts **ED 6670 (flute)** / Vocal score
ED 6671

Reznicek, Emil Nikolaus von
1860-1945

Chamber & Instrumental Works

Donna Diana (1894/1908/33)

Overture
Arranger: Lutz
5acc-timp
Score **ASH 12** / Parts **ASH 12-01(-06)**

Richter, Nico
1915-1945

Stage Works

Kannitverstan (Cannot understand) 25'

Ballet-Mimodrama freely adapted from the fairytale by Hebel
1.1.1.1-1.1.1.0-perc-pno-str
Material on hire
AVV

Ridil, Christian
b.1943

Choral Works

Nachts 8'

Text: H. Lange
Chorus: mixed a cappella (8 prt)
SKR 20001

Rietz, Johannes
1905-1976

Choral Works

Chorische Tänze (1959) 25'

Text: Komma/Weidenheim
Soloist: mezzo-soprano
Chorus: mixed
2.2.2.2-4.3.2.1-timp.2perc-pno-str
alt. version: pno
Material on hire
SM

Rivier, Jean
1896-1987

Orchestral Works

Symphony No.2 in C (1937) 19'

str
Material on hire
SM

Rodgers, Philip
b.1916

Chamber & Instrumental Works

Elisabethan-Melodies

Vol. 1
Arranger: Duarte
guitar solo
GA 217

Elisabethan-Melodies

Vol. 2
Arranger: Duarte
guitar solo
GFA 218

Sight Reading Exercises

sopranorecorder solo
ED 10563

20 Simple Tunes

srec-pno
ED 10273

Rodrigo, Joaquín
b.1901

Stage Works

Pavana Real (1954) 30'

Ballet in 3 Acts
Material on hire
Score **ED 8366** / Piano reduction **ED 8487**

Orchestral Works

A la Busca del Más Allá
(1977) 17'

pic.2.ca.2.2-4.3.3.1-timp.perc-cel.hp-str
Material on hire
Study score **ETP 1455**

Rodrigo, Joaquín

b. Sagunto, Valencia 22.11.1901

Popularly considered to be a "one-work" composer - justly famed for the "Concierto de Aranjuez", premièred in Barcelona in 1939 and today surely one of the world's best loved pieces of classical music – Rodrigo is in fact the author of a richly varied musical oeuvre. Though blind from the age of 3, he has evoked Spanish sights and sounds in his music with singular distinction, yet has responded to other, more significant elements than the merely picturesque. The "Fantasia para un gentil-hombre", written for Segovia, is based on music by the seventeenth-century composer Gaspar Sanz, while the cantata Ausencias de Dulcinea is a hommage to the national hero Cervantes. But these are just two works from a list of some three-hundred instrumental, vocal and choral compositions, all of which deserve reconsideration.

Homenaje a la Tempranica
(1939)   4'
pic.1.1.1.1-2.2.0.0.0-timp.perc-hp-str
Material on hire
Study score **ED 8361**

Juglares (1923)   5'
3(pic).2(ca).2.2-4.3.3.1-timp.perc-hp-str
Material on hire
Score **ED 8362** / Piano reduction **ED 8317**

Música para un Jardin
(1957)   12'
pic.1.1.ca.1.0-1.1.0.0.0-perc-cel.hp-str
Material on hire
Score **ED 8363**

Pallilos y Panderetas (1982)   12'
2(pic).2.2.2-2.2.0.0.0-timp.perc-str
Material on hire
Score **ED 8369**

5 Piezas Infantiles (1924)   12'
3(pic).3(ca).3(bcl).2-4.3.3.1-timp.perc-cel.hp-str
Material on hire
Score **ED 8356**

Preludio para un Poema a la Alhambra (1928)   8'
pic.2.2.ca.2.2-4.3.3.1-timp.perc-hp-str
Material on hire
Score **ED 8365**

2 Spanish Dances (1969)   9'
2(pic).2.2.2-2.2.0.0.0-str
Material on hire
Score **ED 8359**

Tres Viejos Aires de Danza
(1922/29)   8'
1.1.1.1-2.0.0.0-str
Material on hire
Score **ED 8364**

Concertos

Cançoneta (1923)   3'
Soloist: violin
str
Score **CON 209** / Parts **CON 209-70** / Piano reduction **VLB 78**

Concierto Andaluz (1967)   25'
Soloists: 4 guitars
2(pic).2.2.2-4.2.0.0-str
Material on hire
Study score **ETP 8026** / Piano reduction **ED 7992**

Concierto como un Divertimento (1981)   21'
Soloist: cello
2(pic).2.2.0-1.2.0.0.0-xyl-cel-str(5.4.3.2.1)
Material on hire
Score **ED 8370** / Piano reduction **ED 7394**

Concierto de Aranjuez
(1939)   20'
Soloist: guitar
2(pic).2(ca).2.2-2.2.0.0.0-str
Material on hire
Study score **ED 1809** / Parts **ED 7242-01 (solo)** / Piano reduction **ED 7242**

Concierto de Aranjuez
(1939/74)   20'
Soloist: harp
2(pic).2(ca).2.2-2.2.0.0.0-str
Material on hire
Study score **ETP 1809** / Parts **ED 7369 (solo)** / Piano reduction **ED 7242**

Concierto Galante (1949)   20'
Soloist: cello
2(pic).2.2.2-2.2.0.0.0-str
Material on hire
Score **ED 8357** / Piano reduction **ED 8158**

Concierto Madrigal (1966)   30'
Soloists: 2 guitars
pic.1.1.1.1-1.1.0.0.0-str
Material on hire
GA 528 / Study score **ETP 1824** / Parts **ED 7391 (soli)** / Piano reduction **ED 7390**

Concierto para una Fiesta
(1982)   27'
Soloist: guitar
pic.1.1.ca.1.1-1.1.0.0.0-perc-str
Material on hire
Score **ED 8352** / Parts **ED 7289-01 (solo)** / Piano reduction **ED 7289**

Concierto Pastoral (1977)   25'
Soloist: flute
0.1(ca).1.0-1.1.0.0.0-str
Material on hire
Piano reduction **ED 11489**

Fantasia para un Gentilhombre (1954)   22'
Soloist: guitar
pic.1.1.0.1-0.1.0.0.0-str
Material on hire
Study score **ETP 1823** / Piano reduction **GA 208**

Fantasia para un Gentilhombre (1978)   22'
Arranger: James Galway
Soloist: flute
0.1.1.1-1.1.0.0.0-str
Material on hire
Piano reduction **ED 11488**

Chamber & Instrumental Works

A L'Ombre de Torre Bermeja (1954)   4'
pno
ED 7454

Atardecer (1970-72/87)   8'
pno (4hnd)
ED 7541

Bagatella (1926)   3'
pno
ED 7914

2 Berceuses (1923/28)   5'
pno
ED 7915

Joaquín Rodrigo
Concierto de Aranjuez (1939)
2nd movement

7 Cançiones Valencianes

(1982) 15'

vn-pno
VLB 77

Capriccio (1944) 7'

violin solo
ED 7846

Como una Fantasia (1979) 8'

cello solo
CB 136

Dos Piezas caballerescas

(1945) 6'

vc ensemble
Score **CON 210** / Parts **CON 210-10**

Dos Piezas caballerescas

(1945) 6'

Arranger: Germer (1986)
4gtr
GA 530

2 Esbozos (1923) 5'

vn-pno
ED 7916

3 Evocaciones (1981) 10'

pno
ED 7540

Juglares (1923) 5'

pno (4hnd)
ED 8317

Music

19 Pieces
pno
SMC 540

5 Piezas del Siglo XVI

(1937) 10'

pno
ED 7537

5 Piezas Infantiles (1924) 12'

2pno
ED 11451

Preludio al Gallo Mañanero

(1926) 4'

pno
ED 7938

The Rodrigo Collection

Arranger: Hinson
pno
SMC 535

Serenata al Alba del Dia

(1982) 7'

fl/vn-gtr
GA 489

Serenata Española (1931) 4'

pno
ED 7917

Sonata a la Breve (1978) 10'

vc-pno
CB 137

Sonatas de Castilla (1950-51) 22'

con Toccata a modo de pregón
pno
ED 7453

3 Spanish Dances (1941) 5'

pno
ED 7452

3 Spanish Pieces (1954) 10'

guitar solo
GA 212

Suite para Piano (1923) 10'

ED 7918

Triptic for Guitar (1979) 12'

GA 492

Un Tiempo fue Italica Famosa (1981) 5'

guitar solo
GA 515

Solo Voice(s)/Voice(s) and Piano/Guitar

Arbol (1987) 2'

from "Cançiones de dos èpocas"
Text: Fina de Calderón
voice-pno
ED 8395

Barcarola (1938) 3'

Text: Victoria Kamhi
voice-pno
SM

Canción del Cucú (1937) 3'

Text: Victoria Kamhi
voice-pno
SM

Canción del Grumete (1938) 2'

Text: anonymous
voice-pno
SM

Cançiones (1934/64) 28'

voice-pno
ED 7598

Canço del Teuladí (1934) 2'

Text: Teodoro Llorente
voice-pno
SM

Canticel (1938) 3'

Text: Josep Carner
voice-pno
SM

Cantiga (1925) 3'

from "Cançiones de dos èpocas"
Text: Gil Vicente
voice-pno
ED 8395

Coplas del Pastor Enamorado (1935) 3'

Text: Lope de Vega
voice-pno/gtr
ED 7603

Esta Niña se Lleva la Flor

(1934) 7'

Text: Francisco de Figueroa
voice-pno
SM

Estribillo (1937) 2'

Text: S.J.Polo de Medina
voice-pno
SM

Fino Cristal (1934) 3'

Text: C.Rodríguez Pinto
voice-pno
SM

Folias Canarias (1948) 3'

voice-pno
ED 10600

Folias Canarias (1948) 3'

voice-gtr
ED 10600

La Grotte (1962) 4'

Hommage à Debussy
soprano-pno
ED 7601

12 Popular Spanish Songs

(1951) 15'

voice-pno
Piano reduction **ED 10675**

Por qué te llamaré? (1987) 2'

from "Cançiones de dos èpocas"
Text: Fina de Calderón
voice-pno
ED 8395

Romance de la Infantina de Francia (1928) 5'

from "Cançiones de dos èpocas"
Text: anonymous
voice-pno
ED 8395

Romancillo (1954) 3'

Text: anonymous
voice-pno
SM

Serranilla (1928) 3'

from "Cançiones de dos èpocas"
Text: Marqués de Santillana
voice-pno
ED 8395

Sobre el Cupey (1965) 3'

Text: L.Hernández Aquino
voice-pno
SM

Soneto (1950) 3'

Text: J. Bautista de Mesa
voice-pno
SM

35 Songs

voice-pno
SMC 541

3 Spanish Songs (1951) 6'

voice-gtr
ED 10601

Un Home, San Antonio!

(1951) 3'

Text: Rosalía de Castro
voice-pno
SM

Villancicos (1952) 7'

medium voice-gtr
ED 12378

Villancicos (1952) 7'

medium voice-pno
ED 12406

Solo Voice(s) and Instrument(s)/ Orchestra

Cantico de la Esposa (1934) 4'

Text: San Juan de la Cruz
Soloist: soprano
1.1.ca.0.1-1.0.0.0-3perc-str
Material on hire
Score **ED 8355**

Cuatre Cançons en llengua catalana (1935) 12'

Text: various
Soloist: voice
2(pic).1.1.1-2.2.0.0-timp.perc-2hp-str
Material on hire
Score **ED 8358** / Vocal score **ED 7591**

Despedida y Soledad (1980) 3'

from "Liricas Castellanas"
Text: anonymous
Soloist: soprano
pic-cnt-vihuela
Score and parts **ED 7597**

Duérmete, Niño (1952) 3'

from "Villancicos y canciones de Navidad"
Text: Victoria Kamhi
Soloists: soprano, baritone
ob.ca-str
Material on hire
Score **ED 8360** / Piano reduction **ED 7596**

Espera del Amado (1980) 3'

from "Liricas Castellanas"
Text: anonymous
Soloist: soprano
pic-cnt-vihuela
Score and parts **ED 7597**

La Espera (1952) 3'

from "Villancicos y Canciones de Navidad"
Text: Victoria Kamhi
Soloist: soprano
fl.ca-hp-str
Material on hire
Score **ED 8351**

Rosaliana (1965) 12'

Text: Rosalía de Castro
Soloist: soprano
1.1.1.0-1.0.0.0-perc-str
Material on hire
Score **ED 8367** / Piano reduction **ED 7719**

San Juan y Pascua (1980) 3'

from "Liricas Castellanas"
Text: anonymous
Soloist: soprano
pic-cnt-vihuela
Score and parts **ED 7597**

Serranilla (1928) 3'

Text: Marqués de Santillana
Soloist: soprano
1.1.1.1-2.1.0.0-str(1.1.1.1.0)
Material on hire
Score **ED 8355**

Triptic de Mosén Cinto

(1936) 12'

Text: Mosen Jacinto Verdaguer
Soloist: voice
2(pic).1.ca..1.1-2.2.0.0-perc-cel.hp-str
Material on hire
Score **ED 8350** / Piano reduction **ED 8475**

Villancicos (1952) 7'

Text: various
Soloist: mezzo-soprano
2.1(ca).1.1-2.1.0.0-perc-hp-str
Material on hire
Piano reduction **ED 10676/10678**

Villancicos y Canciones de Navidad (1952) 15'

(s. detailed enumeration)
Text: various
Soloist: soprano
2(pic).1.ca.0.0-2.0.0.0-timp-hp-str
Material on hire
SM

Choral Works

A la Chiribirivuela (1952) 3'

from "Villancicos y Canciones de Navidad"
Text: anonymous
Soloists: S.A.T.B.
Chorus: mixed a cappella
C 47827

A la Clavelina (1952) 2'

from "Villancicos y Canciones de Navidad"
Text: Lope de Vega
Soloist: soprano
Chorus: chidren's a cappella (2 prt)
[gtr]
C 47842

Cantan por Belén Pastores

(1952) 4'

from "Villancicos y Canciones de Navidad"
Text: Victoria Kamhi
Soloist: soprano
Chorus: mixed
pic.1.1.ca.0.0-2.0.0.0-perc-hp-str
Material on hire
Score **ED 8354** / Piano reduction **ED 7728**

Cántico de San Francisco de Asis (1981) 18'

Chorus: mixed
2,2,2,0-4,2,3,1-timp.perc-cel-str
Material on hire
Score **ED 8353**

Himnos de los Neófitos de Qumran (1965/75) 10'

Soloists: 3 sopranos
Chorus: male
2fl.bn-timp.perc-cel.hp-str
Material on hire
Score **ED 8368**

Triste estaba el Rey David

(1950) 4'

Text: anonymous
Chorus: mixed a cappella
C 47826

Roehr, Walter
1890-1964

Chamber & Instrumental Works

Im Duett

12 small Pieces
srec.arec
ED 4851

Sonatina No. 1 in F Major

srec-pno
ED 3919

Sonatina No. 2 in F Major

srec-pno
ED 3891

Sonatina No. 3 in F Major

srec-pno
ED 4368

Sonatina No. 4 B-Dur

srec-pno
ED 4889

Wir musizieren zu dreien

2srec.arec
ED 5223

Roslawez, Nikolaj Andrejevich

1881-1944

Orchestral Works

V Casy Novolunija - In den Stunden des Neumonds

(1912-13)   15'

pic.2.2.ca.2.bcl.2-4.3.3.1-timp.perc-cel.hp-str
Material on hire
Study score **ED 8107**

Concertos

Violin Concerto No.1 (1925) 45'

Soloist: violin
3(pic).2.ca.2.bcl.2.cbn-4.3.3.1-timp.perc-pno.hp-str
Material on hire
Study score **ED 7823** / Piano reduction
ED 7824

Chamber & Instrumental Works

Cello Sonata No.1 (1921) 13'

vc-pno
ED 8038

Cello Sonata No.2 (1922) 13'

vc-pno
ED 8039

3 Dances (1923) 10'

vn-pno
ED 8261

Legende 7'

vn-pno
ED 8261

Meditation (1921)

vc-pno
ED 8037

Roslawez, Nikolaj Andrejevich

b. Dushatino 4.1.1881, d. Moscow 23.8.1944

Coming from a rural background, he was initially self-taught and later received his musical education at the Moscow Conservatory. His compositions were of an experimental kind. He achieved a new harmonic ordering, which was not diatonic and which he referred to as the "synthetic chord" technique. He developed the technique in piano miniatures, sio that it became a 12-note system embracing concepts of 12-note serialims and mirror symetry. In the 1920s Roslawez was one of the leaders of Russian musical life. As a convinced Marxist he defended an aesthetic of "musical positivism", which opposed the idea of an objectively definable emotional quality. After 1930 his name disappeared from Soviet dictionaries and concert programmes.

Nocturne (1913) 6'

ob-2vn.vc-hp
Material on sale
Study score **ED 8129**

Piano Pieces (1914-22)

SM

Piano Sonata No.1 (1914) 12'

ED 7941

Piano Sonata No.2 (1916) 12'

ED 8391

Piano Sonata No.5 (1923) 14'

ED 8392

5 Pieces (1919-21) 11'

pno
ED 7907

24 Préludes (1941-42) 24'

vn-pno
ED 7940

String Quartet No.1 (1913) 12'

ED 8126

String Quartet No.3 (1920) 8'

ED 8127

String Quartet No.5 (1942) 22'

ED 8128

Tanz der weissen Jungfrauen

(1912) 5'

vc-pno
ED 8045

Trio No.2 (1920) 16'

vn.vc-pno
Material on sale
ED 8059

Trio No.3 (1921) 15'

vn.vc-pno
Material on sale
ED 8035

Trio No.4 (1927) 28'

vn.vc-pno
Material on sale
ED 8036

Viola Sonata No.1 (1926) 12'

va-pno
ED 8177

Viola Sonata No.2 (1930) 19'

va-pno
ED 8178

Violin Sonata No.1 (1913) 10'

vn-pno
ED 8042

Violin Sonata No.2 (1917) 12'

vn-pno
ED 8043

Violin Sonata No.4 (1920) 10'

vn-pno
ED 8044

Violin Sonata No.6 16'

vn-pno
ED 8431

Solo Voice(s)/Voice(s) and Piano/Guitar

Lieder und Romanzen I 30'

voice-pno
ED 8435

Lieder und Romanzen II 35'

voice-pno
ED 8436

Lieder und Romanzen III 35'

voice-pno
ED 8437

Choral Works

Komsomolija (1928) 18'

Chorus: mixed
2pic.3.3.ca.Dcl.3.bcl.3.cbn-6.2cnt.4.4.1-
timp.perc-xyl.pno.2hp-str(16.16.14.8.6)
Material on hire
Study score **ED 8256**

Rouse, Christopher
b.1949

Orchestral Works

Gorgon (1984) 16'

3(3pic).3(ca).3(bcl).3(cbn)-4.3.3.1-
timp.4perc-pno/cel.hp-str
Material on hire
Study score **EA 521**

The Infernal Machine (1981) 5'

3(3pic).3.Ebcl.2.bcl.2.cbn-4.3.3.1-5perc-
cel.hp-str
Material on hire
Study score **EA 492**

Thor (1980) 15'

3(2pic).3.2.Ebcl.bcl.cbcl.3-6.4.4.2-
timp.4perc
Material on hire
EAM-Helicon

Chamber & Instrumental Works

Ku-Ka-Ilimoku (1978) 5'

4perc
Score **EA 456** / Parts **EA 456-10**

Rouse, Christopher

b. Baltimore, Maryland 15.2.1949

As a rock-music historian and writer on musical subjects as well as one of the most noted composers of his generation, Christohper Rouse is a leading figure in American musical life. He has written for many of the renowned soloists and ensembles of our time. He numbers George Crumb, Karel Husa and Richard Hoffmann amongst his major teachers, and is himself a highly regarded teacher whose influence on America's younger generation of composers has been considerable.

Lares Hercii (1983) 5'

vn-hpd
EA 526

Liber Daemonum (1980) 17'

organ solo
EA 517

Little Gorgon (1986) 2'

pno
EA 591

Morpheus (1980) 8'

cello solo
EA 513

Ogoun Badagris (1976) 5'

5perc
EA 457

Rotae Passionis (1982) 18'

fl(pic,afl).cl(Ebcl,bcl)-pno-perc-vn.va.vc
Material on hire
EAM-Helicon

String Quartet No.1 (1982) 17'

Study score **EA 519**

The Surma Ritornelli

(1983) 13'

*fl.pic.cl/bcl-hn.tpt.tbn-2perc-pno/perc-
vn.vc.db*
Material on hire
Study score **EA 528**

Trarames (1983) 5'

carillon solo
EAM-Helicon

Trombone Concerto (1991)

Soloist: trombone
0.0.0.2.cbn-4.3.3.1-timp.4perc-hp-str
Material on hire
EAM

Roux, Maurice le
b.1923

Concertos

Allegro moderato 3'

No. 9 from the "Divertimento für Mozart"
Soloist: glockenspiel
2.2.2.2-2.2.0.0-perc-str
Material on hire
SM (Co-prod: UE)
Copyright USA: EAM/Italy: Ed. Suvini
Zerboni

Rózsa, Miklós
1907-1995

Orchestral Works

3 Hungarian Sketches, Op. 14 (1958) 19'

2.2.2.2-4.2.3.0-timp.perc-hp.cel-str
Material on hire
Study score **ETP 1309**

Theme, Variations and Finale, Op. 13 17'

2.2.2.2-3.2.3.0-timp.perc-hp.cel-str
Material on hire
Eu

Infoline · e-Mail
Schott Musik International
Mainz: Schott.Musik.com@T-Online.de
London: 101627.166@compuserve.com

Rudzinski, Zbigniew
b.1935

Orchestral Works

Moments musicaux III
(1968)   9'

3(pic).3.3(bcl).3-4.3.3.1-4perc-pno-
str(16.16.12.12.0)
Material on hire
Study score **AVV 308**

Chamber & Instrumental Works

Quartet
2perc-2pno
WKS 6

Choral Works

Requiem   (1971)   20'
Den Opfern der Kriege
Soloist: speaker
Chorus: mixed (8 prt)
3(2pic).3.3.3-4.3.3.1-4perc-pno-str
Material on hire
AVV

S

Sackman, Nicholas
b.1950

Stage Works

Simplicia   (1980)   90'
Musical for Schools in 2 Acts
Text: Grimmelshausen/Tony Purcell
Material on hire
Vocal score **ED 11861** / Libretto **ED 11862**

Orchestral Works

Alap   (1979-81)   20'
2(2pic).afl.1.ca.1.Ebcl.bcl.1.cbn-3.3.2.1-
timp.3perc-str(12.12.10.8.6)
Material on hire
SL

Hawthorn   (1991-93/94)   26'
3.3.ca.3.asax.3.cbn-6.4.3.1-timp.4perc-
pno(cel).hp-str
Material on hire
SL

Paraphrase   (1987/90)   12'
3(pic).2.ca.3.2.cbn-4.3.3.1-pno
Material on hire
SL

Concertos

Ellipsis   (1974-76)   20'
Soloist: piano
fl(afl).cl(Ebcl).ssax(tsax)-hn.2tpt-3perc-
prep pno.eorg.hp-vn.va.2db
Material on hire
SL

Ensembles and Cadenzas
(1972)   16'

Soloist: cello
fl(pic,afl)-tbn(ttbn,btbn)-2perc-pno
Material on hire
SL

Flute Concerto   (1988-89)   20'
Soloist: flute(pic,afl)
str(6.6.4.4.2)
Material on hire
SL

Sackman, Nicholas

b. London 12.4.1950

A modernist by nature, but one given to a particularly trenchant and direct form of musical speech, Sackman composes slowly, but with a dedication and concern for detail that gives each work an enduring quality and substance. His best known work is a fine piano sonata, but he is versatile in all the major forms.

Chamber & Instrumental Works

Corranach (1985)　　　　20'
fl(pic,afl).cl(Ebcl)-hn-perc-pno-vn.vc
Material on hire
Study score **ED 12355**

Doubles (1977-78)　　　23'
2fl(2pic).2ob.ca.Ebcl.ssax.tsax-2hn.tpt.tbn-3perc
Material on hire
SL

Holism (1982)　　　　13'
va.vc
Manuscript score on sale
SL

Piano Sonata (1983-84)　　19'
ED 12283

String Quartet No.1
(1978-79)　　　　　　　17'
Material on sale
Study score **ED 11487**

String Quartet No.2
(1990-91)　　　　　　　24'
Material on sale
SL

Time-Peace (1982-83/86)　　14'
2tpt.hn.tbn.tuba
Material on sale
SL

Trombone Sonata (1986)　　12'
tbn-pno
SL

Solo Voice(s) and Instrument(s)/ Orchestra

And the World-A Wonder Waking (1981)　　　11'
Text: Bill MacCormick
Soloist: mezzo-soprano
fl.ob.cl-tpt.tbn-perc-vn.vc
Material on hire
SL

A Pair of Wings (1970-73)　　18'
Text: Stephen Hawes
Soloists: 3 sopranos
fl(pic,afl)-ttbn/btbn-2perc-hp-va(perc)
Material on hire
ED 11377*

Sadler, Helmut
b.1921

Stage Works

Der Wettermacher　　　60'
Ballet by Kurt Neufert
Material on hire
SM

Concertos

Concertino (1970)
Soloist: clarinet
str
Material on hire
SM

Sakamoto, Yoshitaka
1898-1968

Choral Works

Kyushu Tanko Bushi - Kohlengräberlied (1966)　　1'
Chorus: male a cappella
C 41731

Sansa Sigure - Tanzlied
(1966)　　　　　　　2'
Chorus: male a cappella
C 41730

Shimotzui Bushi - Der fröhliche Schiffer (1966) 1'
Chorus: male a cappella
C 41732

Soran Bushi-Lied des Fischers (1966)　　　2'
Chorus: male a cappella
C 41729

Sato, Somei
b.1947

Orchestral Works

Journey through Sacred Time (1986)　　　14'
shô-2perc-2hp-str(8.8.6.4.2)
Material on hire
SJ

Sauer, Emil von
1862-1942

Orchestral Works

Concerto No. 2 c-Moll　　30'
2.2.2.2-4.2.3.1-timp.perc-str
Material on hire
SM

Infoline · e-Mail
Schott Musik International
Mainz: Schott.Musik.com@T-Online.de
London: 101627.166@compuserve.com

Saux, Gaston

b.1886

Chamber & Instrumental Works

Quartet No.1 in F

srec.arec.trec.brec
Parts **ED 10753**

Quartet No. 2 in G

srec.arec.trec.brec
SM

Schallehn, Hilger

b.1936

Choral Works

Abkühlung (1985)   2'

from "Drei Tanzlieder"
Text: G. Deesen
Chorus: female a cappella
C 45626

Altes Marschlied (1979)   3'

from "Drei Landsknechtslieder"
Chorus: male a cappella
C 45647

Das Buch der Weihnachtslieder

Chorus: mixed
[pno/org]/[instruments]
Score **ED 7061** / Choral score **C 45701-
C 45701** / Parts **ED 7061-11 (-28)**

Down by the Riverside

(1993)   3'

from "Drei Negro-Songs"
Chorus: female (4 prt)
C 48304

Freundinnen (1985)   2'

from "Drei Tanzlieder"
Text: G. Deesen
Chorus: female a cappella
C 45628

Go down Moses (1991)   4'

(Negro-Spiritual)
Chorus: female (4 prt)
C 47522

Good News (1991)   2'

(Negro-Spiritual)
Chorus: female (4 prt)
C 47521

Hallo Kinder, hört mal her

(1991)   2'

Text: H. Schallehn
Chorus: children's unison
combo
Parts **C 47301 (chorus)**

Herr, dein Wort (1985)   2'

Spruchmotette
Chorus: mixed a cappella
CHBL 435

Irische Liebesgeschichten

(1985)   12'

Chorus: male
pno/[fl.cl.bn.gtr.acc.mand.va.vc.db]
Score **ED 7517-10** / Parts **ED 7517-11** / Choral
score **ED 7517-01** / Vocal score **ED 7517**

Ein kleines Lied (1985)   2'

Text: Ebner-Eschenbach
Chorus: mixed a cappella
CHBL 434

Landser-Frömmigkeit (1979) 3'

from "Drei Landsknechtslieder"
Chorus: male a cappella
C 45647

Landsknechts Trinkrunde

(1979)   3'

from "Drei Landsknechtslieder"
Chorus: male a cappella
C 45648

Little David, Play on your Harp (1993)   3'

from "Drei Negro-Songs"
Chorus: female a cappella (4 prt)
Vocal score **C 48306**

O lux beata Trinitas (1985)   6'

Chorus: mixed a cappella
C 45964

Rock my Soul (1991)   3'

(Negro Spiritual)
Chorus: female (4 prt)
C 47523

Selig sind die Toten (1994)   6'

Apok. 14,13
Chorus: female a cappella
C 48333

Singen ist das Atmen der Seele (1987)   4'

Chorus: male/mixed a cappella
C 48052

Sometimes I Feel like a Motherless Child (1993)   2'

from "Drei Negro-Songs"
Chorus: female (4 prt)
Vocal score **C 48305**

Sommermorgenlied (1985)   3'

Text: Theodor Fontane
Chorus: mixed a cappella
C 45968

Steht auf und singt (1985)   4'

Text: M. Barthel
Chorus: mixed a cappella
C 44634

Stimmen (1985)   2'

from "Drei Tanzlieder"
Text: G. Deesen
Chorus: female a cappella
C 45627

Das Vespergeläut - Les cloches des vêpres

(1990)   3'

Chorus: female a cappella
C 47189

Schaub, Hans Ferdinand

1880-1965

Orchestral Works

Abendmusik (1921)   10'

2(pic).2.2.2-4.2.3.0-timp.2perc-[cel].[hp]-str
Material on hire
SM

Scherer, Johann

Chamber & Instrumental Works

Sonate in B Major, Op. 1/1

3arec
OBF 84

Sonate in F Major, Op. 1/2

3arec
OBF 84

Schidlowsky, Leon
b.1931

Chamber & Instrumental Works

String Quartet (1967)
Score and parts **AVV 307**

Choral Works

Requiem (1968)   12'
Text: Latin
Chorus: mixed (12 prt)
AVV 49

Schilling, Hans Ludwig
b.1927

Choral Works

Legende vom Weisen und Zöllner (1968)   15'
Text: Bertolt Brecht
Soloists: narrator, speaker, soprano, tenor, baritone
Chorus: mixed
3.1.2.asax.0-2.3.3.0-timp.4perc-cel.pno.hpd.2gtr-str(8-10.6-8.6.6.3)
Material on hire
Score **ED 5528** / Vocal score **ED 5528-01**

Schmidt, Werner Albert
b.1925

Orchestral Works

3 Dramatic Pieces   15'
str
Material on hire
SM

Schnabel, Gottfried
b.1930

Orchestral Works

Lyrical Fantasy   10'
str
Material on hire
AVV

Statics (1969)   12'
3(afl,2bcl).1(ca).2(bcl).asax.tsax.barsax.0-0.3.3.0-4perc-cel.2pno(4hpd).2hp-str
Material on hire
AVV

Schnebel, Dieter
b.1930

Stage Works

Jowaegerli (1982-83)   60'
Tradition IV. Alemanic Words and Pictures
Text: Johann Peter Hebel
Material on hire
SM

ki-no (1963-67)   15'
Räume I. Nightmusic
Material on hire
SM

Körper-Sprache (1979-80)   15-90'
Organkomposition
Material on sale
ED 7166

Maulwerke (1968-74)   15-90'
mouths-electronics
ED 7083 / Score and parts **ED 7135**

St. Jago (1981-91/95)   85'
Tradition IV(2). Music and Pictures to Kleist
SM

Zeichen-Sprache (1987-89)   60'
Music for Gestures and Voices
SM

Orchestral Works

Beethoven Symphony
(1985)   10'
Re-Visionen I(2)
1.0.1.1-1.1.0.0-perc-str(1.0.1.1.1)
Material on hire
SM

Schnebel, Dieter
b. Lahr/Schwarzwald 14.3.1930

From 1949-52 Schnebel studied music in Freiburg and attended the Kranichstein Summer Courses for New Music (Varese, Adorno, Leibowitz, Křenek, Scherchen, Nono, Boulez, Henze, Stockhausen). From 1952-1956 he studied theology, philosophy and musicology (Barth, Bultmann, Bloch) in Tübingen. At various times he has worked in Kaiserslautern, as a teacher of religion in Frankfurt and as a teacher of religion and music in Munich. In 1976 he became professor of experimental music and musicology in Berlin. In 1991 he received the cultural award of Lahr and became a member of the Berlin Academy of Arts.

Blendwerk (1978)   18'
from Re-Visionen I(5)
str(9.8.8/4.4/2.2/1)
Material on hire
SM

Canones (1975-77/93-94)   32'
2(afl).2(ca).2(bcl).2(cbn)-2.2.2.1-timp-acc.marimb.hp-str
Material on hire
SM

Compositio (1955-56/64-65)   12'
Versuche IV
2(pic).2(ca).2(Ebcl).bcl.2(cbn)-2.ttbn.btbn.btuba-timp.perc-pno.hp.egtr-str(8.0.6.4.2)
Material on hire
Study score **ED 6336**

Diapason (1977)   9'
Tradition I(2). Canon à 13
0.2.2.bcl.2-2(cnt).2.ttbn.btbn.btuba-perc-cel.pno.vib.marimb.glsp.gtr.[hpd]-str(12.0.8.8.4)
Material on hire
SM

Drei-Klang (1976-77)   90'

Räume 4
Ens I: 1wind-1str-1perc
Ens II: vnI.vnII(fl/cl)-va(bcl/tbn)-vc-pno
Ens III: egtr.bgtr-2perc-eorg
Material on hire
SM

Inter (1994)

2.2.2.2-2.2.2.1-hp-str
Material on hire
SM

Janácek-Moment (1991-92)   2'

Re-Visionen II(1)
0.3/3tpt.3/2tpt.0-0.3.2.1-timp.perc-hp-str(1.1.1.1.0)
Material on hire
SM

Körper-Sprache (1979-80) 15-90'

Organkomposition
3-9 performers
Material on sale
ED 7166

Mahler-Moment (1985)   3-5'

Re-Visionen II(4)
str(16.14.12.10.8/6.6.6.4.2/3.3.2.2.2)
Material on hire
SM

Mozart-Moment (1988-89)   1'

Re-Visionen II(3)
1-2.1-2.1-2.1 2-2.0.0.0-2perc-str(2-8.2-8.2-6.2-4.1-2)
Material on hire
SM

Orchestra (1974-77)   75'

Symphonische Musik für mobile Musiker
3.3.2.bcl.3.-6.3.3.btuba-timp.perc-str(12.12.10.8.6)
Material on hire
SM

Schubert-Phantasie

(1978/89)   18-25'

Re-Visionen I(5) for divided large orchestra
Orchestra I:3(2pic).3(ca).3(Ebcl,bcl).2.cbn-4(2wagnertuba).3.3(ttbn,2btbn).btuba-timp.perc-hp-str(2/4.2/4.2/4.2.2)
Orchestra II: str(9.8.8.4.2)
Material on hire
SM

Sinfonie-Stücke (1984-85)   10'

2(2pic).afl(fl,lotosfl).2.ca.2.bcl.3(cbn)-4.3.3.1-timp.perc-hp-str(12.10.10.8.6)
Material on hire
SM

Verdi-Moment (1989)   3'

Re-Visionen II(5)
1-2pic.0.afl.1-2.ca.3.1-2.cbn-2-4.2-3.2-3.1-2perc-str(16-10.14-8.12-6.10-4.8-2)
Material on hire
SM

Concertos

Hymnus - Piano Concerto

(1989-92)   18'

from Sinfonie X-II (3)
Soloist: piano
3(pic,afl).3.3.3-4.3.3.1-3perc-acc.hp.ondes martenot/asax-str(14.12.10.8.6)
Material on hire
SM

Chamber & Instrumental Works

Analysis (1953)   5'

Versuche I
timp.2perc-pno.hp-2vn.2va.2vc
Score **ED 6541** / Study score **ED 6336**

anschläge - ausschläge

(1965-66)   20'

Modelle No.5. Scenic Variations
fl-vc-hpd
Study score **ED 6641**

Auguri (1987-93)   15'

pno
ED 8248

Bagatellen (1986)   20'

pno
ED 7530

Chorale Prelude I/II

(1966/69)   40'

Für Stimmen IV
org(1player,1registrar)-additional instr (2 players)-tape(amp)-tbns(min:4)
Material on hire
Score **ED 6532**

Circe (1988)   15'

harp solo
SM

concert sans orchestre

(1964)   20'

Modelle No.3
pno-audience
Piano reduction **ED 5703**

espressivo (1961-63)   15'

Modelle No.2
pno-audience
Piano reduction **ED 6467**

Fragment (1955)   2'

Versuche III
1.1.1.1-1.1.1.0-timp.perc-pno.hp
Alt vers: S-fl.bn-tpt.tbn-timp.perc-xyl.pno.hp
Material on hire
Study score **ED 6336**

Handwerke - Blaswerke I

(1977)   20'

for archaic and exotic instruments
1wind-1str-1perc
SM

Harmonik (1979)   20'

variable orch: 5-12 players (wind, strings or mixed)
SM

In motu proprio (1975)   12'

Tradition I(1). Canon à 7
7vc/7cl(Ebcl, bcl)
Score **ED 6659**

5 Inventions (1987)   8-9'

cello solo
ED 7748

Kontrapunkt (1975)   5-12'

from Schulmusik
variable (e.g.2wind-2str-pno)
SM

Marsyas (1987)   12'

shawm(s)-[accompaniment]
SM

Medusa (1989-93)   15'

accordion solo
SM

Museumsstücke I, II (1993) 110'

8 actors
WKS 24/25

Nostalgie (1962)   15-20'

Modelle No.1
conductor
ED 5704

Pan (1978/88)   18-30'

flute solo(variable flute-instruments)-accompaniment(e.g: vc)
ED 7783

Pan (1978/88)   18-30'

flute solo
FTR 126

Quintet in B Major

(1976-77)   17-22'

Tradition II(1)
vnI.vnII/fl/cl.va/bcl/tbn.vc-pno
Score and parts **ED 6952**

raum-zeit y (1958-59)   5'

Projekte I
indefinite number of instruments with percussion
SM

raum-zeit y (1958-59/92-93) 25'

octet-version
cl(Ebcl).bn-hn-perc(conductor)-2vn.va.vc.db
SM

réactions (1960-61)   7-20'

Abfälle I(1)
1instr/voice-audience
ED 6483

Rhythmen (1977)   30'

from Schulmusik
egtr.bgtr-perc-marimb.vib-eorg
SM

Sisyphos (1990)   12'

ob/ca/cl-bcl/bn/tbn
Score **ED 7993**

Stück III (1991)   4'

from "4 Stücke for Violin and Piano"
violin solo
ED 7988

Stücke (1954-55)   5'

Versuche II
str(1.1.1.1.0/2.2.2.2.0)
Score **ED 6541** / Study score **ED 6336**

4 Stücke (1991)   20'

vn-pno
ED 7988

Stuhlgewitter (1987)   15'

Erfahrungen II(2)
min: 12 performers
SM

Toccata mit Fugen (1995-96)   21'

organ solo
SM

Übungen mit Klängen   20'

from Schulmusik
variable instr/voices (min: 6 players)
WKS 18

visible music I (1960-62)   10-20'

Abfälle 1(2)
conductor-one instrument
Piano reduction **ED 6484**

Zahlen für (mit) Münzen

(1985)   15'

Erfahrungen II(1); from Schulmusik
4 performers/4 groups
SM

Zeichen-Sprache (1987-89)   60'

Music for Gestures and Voices
4-10 actors
SM

Zwischenfugen (1979-82/85)   20'

Tradition V(1)
organ solo [+registrar]
ED 8193

Solo Voice(s)/Voice(s) and Piano/Guitar

Kaschnitz-Gedichte (1994)   15'

Text: Marie Luise Kaschnitz
voice(alto)-pno
ED 8416

Lamento di Guerra (1991)   12'

mezzo-soprano-org/synth
ED 7994

Laut - Gesten - Laute

(1984-88)   20-40'

1-4 solo voices
SM

lectiones (1964-74)   20-50'

Abfälle II(2)
4 speakers and listener
SM

Mein Herz ruht müde (1994)   3'

Text: Else Lasker-Schüler
alto-pno
SM

Quintessenz (1994)   12'

vocal qrt-pno
SM

Solo Voice(s) and Instrument(s)/ Orchestra

Baumzucht (1992/95)   10'

Musical Recital
Text: Johann Peter Hebel
Soloist: speaker (amp)
3wind(high/medium/low)-perc-pno-3str-tape-[2 walkmen]
alt. version: speaker-melody instrument-harmony instrument
Material on hire
Score **ED 8456**

glossolalie (1959-60)   10'

Projekte III
2-4 speakers-2-4 instruments
SM

Glossolalie 61 (1960-61)   40'

Projekte IV
3-4speakers-3-4instr(harm.pno-2perc.add instr)
ED 6414

Jowaegerli (1982-83)   60'

Tradition IV. Alemanic Words and Pictures
Text: Johann Peter Hebel
Soloists: S, A/S, T/B, B
ca.tpt.btpt-acc-gtr-3perc-vc
Material on hire
SM

Lieder ohne Worte (1980/86)   15'

Tradition III(3)
soprano/vn-bcl/vc-pno/gtr/acc
Material on sale
SM

Metamorphosen des Ovid oder Die Bewegung von den Rändern zur Mitte hin und umgekehrt (1987)   120'

Soloists: solo voices
str(5.0.3.2.1)
Material on hire
SM

Metamorphosenmusik

(1986-87)   35'

Soloist: mezzo-soprano
0.afl.0.ca.1(bcl).0-0.1.0.0-str(5.0.3.2.1)
Material on hire
SM

Mit diesen Händen (1992)   40'

Text: Heinrich Böll
voice-vc
ED 8175

O Liebe! - süßer Tod

(1984/95)   15'

5 sacred songs after Bach
(from:"Schemellis Musikalischem Gesangbuch")
Soloist: mezzo-soprano
Chorus: [mixed chamber]
2(afl).2(ca).2(bcl).2-2.2.2.1-[acc/org].cymb.hp-str(4.4.4.4.2)
Material on hire
SM

Sinfonie X (1987-92)   156'

Soloist: alto
3(2pic,afl).4(ca).4(2Ebcl,bcl)-sax/bn.(3cbn)-5(3wagnertuba).4.3.1-timp.10perc-pno.acc.hp-str(18.12.14.10.8)-tape
Material on hire
Study score **ED 8326**

St. Jago (1981-91/95)   85'

Tradition IV(2). Music and Pictures to Heinrich von Kleist
Soloists: 3 speakers(M.F.M) soprano, alto, tenor, bass
0.afl(pic).0.1.bcl(cbcl).0-0.1.1.0-timp.perc-synth.hp.egtr-str(1.1.1.1.1)tape
Material on hire
SM

Thanatos-Eros (1979-82/85)   35'

Tradition III(1). Symphonic Variations
Soloists: soprano/mezzo-soprano, bass/baritone
3(2pic,afl).2ca.2bcl.3(cbn)-4(2tuba).3.3.1-timp.3perc-pno.hp-str(12.10.10.8.6)
Material on hire
SM

Das Urteil (1959)   10-30'

Projekte II
Text: Franz Kafka
Soloists: natural voices
degenerate instruments-other sound sources
Material on hire
SM

Wagner-Idyll (1980) 10'

Re-Visionen I(4)
Soloist: voice
afl.ssax(asax)-tpt-2perc-harm/org.hp/2gtr-va.vc
Material on hire
SM

Choral Works

Amazones (1993) 15'

Text: Heinrich von Kleist
Chorus: female a cappella/5 solo voices
ED 8397

Blasmusik (1973) 10-20'

from Schulmusik
Chorus: mixed (min: 10 voices)
WKS 17

Contrapunctus I (1972-76) 7'

Re-Visionen I(1); Bach-Contrapuncti
Chorus: 5S.5A.5T.5B
ED 6420

Contrapunctus VI (1972-76) 7'

Re-Visionen I(1); Bach-Contrapuncti
Chorus: 5S.5A.5T.5B
ED 6680

Contrapunctus XI (1972-76) 7'

Re-Visionen I(1); Bach-Contrapuncti
Chorus: 5S.5A.5T.5B
ED 6681

Für Stimmen (...missa est)

(1956-69) 30-50'

(s. also detailed enumeration)
Chorus: 5S.4A.4T.5B (can be doubled or trebled)
SM

Gesums (1974) 10-20'

from Schulmusik
Chorus: mixed (min 10 voices)
WKS 17

Harmonik (1979) 8-20'

from Schulmusik
Chorus: 5-12 voices
SM

I dt 31,6 (1956-58) 5-8'

from "Für Stimmen (...missa est)"
Chorus: 12 vocal groups (4S.4A.4T.4B)
ED 6458/ED 6640 (large choir)

II amn (1958/66-67) 14-25'

from "Für Stimmen (...missa est)"
Chorus: 7 vocal groups (4S.4A.4T.4B)
ED 6456

III :! (madrasha II)

(1958/67-68) 10-17'

from "Für Stimmen (...missa est)"
Chorus: 3 choral groups (5S.4A.4T.5B)
[tape]
ED 6457

In motu proprio (1975) 12'

Tradition I(1)
Chorus: 7S.7B
Score ED 6659

Missa (1984-87) 90'

Dahlemer Messe
Soloists: S.A.T.B
Chorus: mixed double
3(2pic,afl).3(ca).3(bcl).3(cbn)-4.3.3.1-timp.perc-org.hp.cymb-str(1.1.1.1.1)
Material on hire
SM

Motetus 1 10'

Chorus: mixed double
SKR 20028

Schumann-Moment (1989) 2'

Re-Visionen II(2)
4S.4A.4T.4B-hp-2perc
alt. version: 2.2.1.bcl.2-2.1.0.0-hp-2perc
Material on hire
SM

Totentanz (1994) 36'

Soloists: 2 speakers (female, male), soprano, bass
Chorus: mixed
3(pic,afl).3.3(Ebcl,bcl).3(cbn)-4.3.3.btuba(cbtuba)-4perc-glsp.xyl(marimb).pno.hp-str(12.12.12.10.10)-live electronics
Material on hire
SM

Das Urteil (1959/90) 40'

Projekte II
Text: Franz Kafka
Chorus: mixed
1.1.2.2(cbn)-0.2.2.1-2perc-str(5(1,3,5perc).0.3(perc).2(perc).1(perc))-tape
Material on hire
SM

Electronic Works

Environments (1972) Var.

Gehörgänge (Räume 3). Concept of a music for inquiring ears
radios-record player-tape recorder-live ensembles
SM

Hörfunk - Radiophonien I-V

(1969-70) 40-60'

tape
SM

ki-no (1963-67) 15'

Räume I. Nightmusic
2-4 slide projectors-screen-speaker-perc-tape
SM

Languido (1993) 20'

bfl-live electronic
SM

Maulwerke (1968-74) 15-90'

mouths-electronics
Piano reduction ED 7083/7135

Monotonien No. 1-7

(1988-89) 70'

pno-live electronics
ED 7906

No - ein Hörspiel (1979-80) 60'

tape
SM

Schneider, Norbert
b.1950

Chamber & Instrumental Works

Toccata "Schlafes Bruder"

organ solo
ED 8525

Schneider, Otto
b.1912

Chamber & Instrumental Works

5 Miniaturen (1985)

bn-pno
FAG 20

Theme and Variations

arec-pno
OFB 171

Schoeller, Philippe

b.1957

Orchestral Works

Winter Dance (1993-94)   15'

Chamber Symphony No.1
1(pic).1.1.bcl.1-1.1.1.0-2perc-pno(cel).hp-
str qnt-str(6.5.4.4.3)
Material on hire
SM

Solo Voice(s) and Instrument(s)/ Orchestra

Légendes I. Water (1993)   25'

4 Méditations symphoniques
Text: Jean-Luc Parant
Soloist: [speaker]
2(pic).0.ob d'am.ca .2.bcl.2-4.3.2.btbn.0-
3perc-pno(cel).hp-str(8.8.6.6.4)
Material on hire
SM

Schönberg, Arnold

1874-1951

Stage Works

Moses und Aron

(1930-32)   full evening

Opera in 3 Acts
Text: Arnold Schönberg
Material on hire
Score **AS 1008** / Study score **ETP 8004** / Vocal
score **ED 4935** / Libretto **BN 3810-50**
Copyright not for: USA, CDN, C

Von Heute auf Morgen, Op. 32 (1928-29)   60'

Opera in 1 Act
Text: Max Blonda
Material on hire
Score **AS 1007** / Vocal score **ED 5077**
Copyright not for: USA, CDN, C

Orchestral Works

Kaiserwalzer   12'

(Johann Strauß; Op. 437)
fl.cl-pno-str(1.1.2.1.0)
Material on hire
SM
Copyright not for: USA, CDN, MEX, C

Schönberg, Arnold

b. Vienna 13.9.1874, d. Los Angeles 13.7.1951

The Schönbergian enigma is of a composer who was at once both a deeply intuitive artist and a profoundly practical thinker. His passionate yearning for musical unity found its rational imperative in the serial method. In the opera "Moses und Aron" and the unfinished oratorio "Die Jakobsleiter" Schönberg extended this quest to the sources for coherence in life as well, with results that placed him amongst this centry's greatest artists. Paradoxically, the plurality of today's contemporary music may also be a legacy of his influential manifesto. The difficulty of his work is apocryphal, and for the sensitive performer it contains opportunities for elegance as well as inwardness.

Choral Works

Dreimal tausend Jahre, Op. 50a

Text: D.D. Runes
Chorus: mixed a cappella
Choral score **SKR 19007**

Der erste Psalm "O du mein Gott", Op. 50c (1950-51)   7'

Text: Arnold Schönberg
Soloist: speaker
Chorus: mixed
2(pic).2(ca).Ebcl.1.bcl.2-2.2.1.0-perc-str
Material on hire
BSS 39328

Friede auf Erden, Op. 13

(1912)   8'

Text: Conrad Ferdinand Meyer
Chorus: mixed a cappella (8 prt)
[2.2.2.2-2.0.0.0-str]
Material on hire
Choral score **SKR 19008**

Der Tanz um das goldene Kalb (1930-32)   25'

from "Moses und Aron"
Text: Arnold Schönberg
Soloists: soprano, alto, 2 tenors, baritone
Chorus: mixed
3(pic).3.Ebcl.2.bcl.3(cbn)-4.3.3.1-
timp.perc-cel.pno.2mand.hp-str
Material on hire
SM
Copyright USA, CDN, C, MEX: Belmont
Music Publishers

Schoff, Manfred

b.1936

Chamber & Instrumental Works

2 Impromptus

bn-pno
FAG 25

Schroeder, Hermann

1904-1984

Orchestral Works

Concerto for Strings, Op. 23   20'

str
Material on hire
SM

Symphonic Hymns, Op. 29

(1943)   25'

3(pic).2.2.bcl.2.cbn-4.3.3.1-timp.perc-str
Material on hire
SM

Symphony in D minor

(1940)   40'

3(pic).2.2(bcl).2-4.3.3.1-timp.perc-str
Material on hire
SM

I. Akt

Arnold Schönberg
Moses und Aron (1930-32)

INVITATION TO SUBSCRIBE TO A REMARKABLE PUBLICATION!

Arnold Schönberg
The Complete Works

Arnold Schönberg is the central figure in the musical life of this century. His significance became evident while he was still alive, and his influence after his death has become tremendous.
His works ushered in a fundamental change of the world's musical conception.

This edition claims to serve both research and musical practice. It is published in two series:

Series A
contains the finished works, the piano scores created by the composer, the performable though unfinished works and fragments.

Series B
contains early versions, sketches and drafts as well as Critical Reports and geneses of the relevant works.

Available volumes
Series A and B

I Lieder
Vol. 1, 2: Lieder mit Klavierbegleitung I
Vol. 1, 2: Kritische Berichte, Fassungen, Skizzen, Fragmente (Text- / Notenteil))
Vol. 3: Orchesterlieder
Vol. 3: Kritischer Bericht, Skizzen, Fragmente

II Piano and Organ Music
Vol. 4: Werke für Klavier zu zwei Händen
Vol. 4: Kritischer Bericht, Skizzen, Fragmente
Vol. 5: Werke für Orgel; Werke für zwei Klaviere zu vier Händen; Werke für Klavier zu vier Händen
Vol. 5: Kritischer Bericht, Skizzen, Fragmente

I Stage Works
Vol. 7, 1: Von heute auf morgen, score
Vol. 7, 1: Text und Skizzen
Vol. 7, 2: Klavierauszug
Vol. 7, 2: Kritischer Bericht
Vol. 8, 1: Moses und Aron, I. Akt
Vol. 8, 1: Kritischer Bericht, Skizzen
Vol. 8, 2: Moses und Aron, Zwischenspiel, II. Akt, Text zum III. Akt

IV Orchestral Works
Vol. 11: Kammersymphonien
Vol. 11: Frühfassungen, Kritischer Bericht, Skizzen, Fragmente
Vol. 12: Orchesterwerke I
Vol. 12: Kritischer Bericht, Skizzen
Vol. 13: Orchesterwerke II
Vol. 13: Kritischer Bericht, Skizzen
Vol. 14, 1: Orchesterwerke III
Vol. 14: Kritischer Bericht, Skizzen
Vol. 14, 2: Orchesterfragmente
Vol. 14, 2: Kritischer Bericht, Skizzen
Vol. 15: Konzerte
  • für Geige und Orchester, op. 36
  • für Klavier und Orchester, op. 42
Vol. 15: Kritischer Bericht, Skizzen, Fragmente

V Choral Works
Vol. 18: Chorwerke I
Vol. 18: Fragmente von Chorwerken und Kanons, Kritischer Bericht, Skizzen
Vol. 19: Chorwerke II
Vol. 19: Kritischer Bericht, Skizzen, Fragmente

Subscription conditions
All volumes of series A and B can be obtained only by subscription to the complete edition.

The purchase of individual volumes or a single series is not possible.

VI Chamber Music
Vol. 20: Streichquartette I
Vol. 20: Kritischer Bericht, Skizzen, Fragmente
Vol. 21: Streichquartette II; Streichtrio
Vol. 21: Kritischer Bericht, Skizzen, Fragmente

VII Arrangements
Vol. 25: Bearbeitungen I
  Johann Sebastian Bach: Zwei Choralvorspiele, Präludium und Fuge Es-Dur — Carl Loewe: Der Nöck — Heinrich van Eyken: Lied der Walküre — Bogumil Zepler: Mädchenreigen
Vol. 26: Bearbeitungen II
  Johannes Brahms: Klavierquartett g-Moll, op. 25, für Orchester gesetzt
Vol. 26: Kritische Berichte, Fragmente
Vol. 27: Instrumentalkonzerte nach Werken alter Meister
  Konzert D-Dur für Violoncello und Orchester, nach M. G. Monn — Konzert B-Dur für Streichquartett und Orchester, nach G. F. Händel
Vol. 27: Ausgaben für Violoncello mit Klavierbegleitung; Kadenzen
Vol. 27: Kritischer Bericht, Skizzen

VIII Supplements
Vol. 29: Die Jakobsleiter. Oratorio (Fragment)

SCHOTT

Schroeder, Hermann

b. Bernkastel-Kues (Mosel) 26.3.1904,
d. Bad Orb 7.10.1984

Hermann Schroeder studied at the Cologne Musikhochschule (1926-30) with Heinrich Lemacher and Walter Braunfels (composition), Hans Bachem (organ), Hermann Abendroth (conducting) and Dominicus Johner (Gregorian chant). He was music teacher in Cologne (1930-38) and cathredal organist in Trier (1938/39). From 1946-1981 he taught music theory at the Cologne Musikhochschule and was director of Cologne's Bach Society (1947-1962). With H. Lemacher, Schroeder has published several textbooks on harmony, counterpoint and musical form, which have gained wide currency in German-speaking countries. In 1952 he was awarded the Robert Schumann Prize of the City of Düsseldorf, in 1955 the first prize in the organ competition at Haarlem/the Netherlands, in 1956 he received the Arts Prize from the state of Rheinland-Pfalz and in 1974 he was appointed honorary doctor by the University of Bonn. Schroeder is one of the most important German composers of the 20th century for organ. His music combines elements of the Middle Ages (fauxbourdon, ostinato technique, Gregorian modes), 20th century polyphony and a linear writing in extended tonality similar to Hindemith. Chamber music for organ and other instruments constituted a special field of his musical activity.

Concertos

Cello Concerto, Op. 24

(1937)   26'

Soloist: cello
2(pic).2.2.2-4.2.3.1-timp-str
Material on hire
SM

Organ Concerto, Op. 25

(1938)   18'

Soloist: organ
0.0.0.0-0.3.3.1-timp-str
Parts **ED 2559 (solo)**

Chamber & Instrumental Works

Concertino (1965)   10'

vn-ob-org
ED 5907

Concerto piccolo (1977)   8'

organ solo
ED 6776

3 Dialogues (1973)   7'

ob-org
ED 6418

Duo, Op. 28 (1951)   9'

vn-pno
ED 4122

Duplum (1967)   10'

hpd-org/2pno/2 positives
ED 6233

5 German Christmas Carols, Op. 18 (1936)   12'

pno (4hnd)
ED 2509

Kleine Intraden (1960)   10'

organ solo
ED 5071

Little Preludes and Intermezzi (1932)   9'

organ solo
ED 2221

Die Marianische Antiphone

(1954)   11'

organ solo
ED 4538

Minnelieder (1939)   13'

pno
ED 3720

6 Organ Chorales, Op. 11

(1934)   8'

organ solo
ED 2265

Organ Fantasy, Op. 56

(1930)   9'

organ solo
ED 2188

Organ Sonata No.1 (1957)   11'

organ solo
ED 4941

Organ Sonata No.2 (1966)   11'

organ solo
ED 5493

Organ Sonata No.3 (1970)   10'

organ solo
ED 6229

Orgel Ordinarium "Cunctipotens genitor Deus"

(1964)   9'

organ solo
ED 5281

Orgelchoräle im Kirchenjahr

(1964)   8'

organ solo
ED 5426

Partita "Veni Creator Spiritus" (1959)   12'

organ solo
ED 4989

Piano Sonata No.1 in A Minor (1946)   10'

ED 4123

Piano Sonata No.2 (1953)   11'

ED 4540

Piano Trio, Op. 33 (1959)   10'

vn.vc-pno
Parts **ED 4764**

Piano Trio No.2, Op. 40

(1967)   11'

vn-hn-pno
Parts **ED 5651**

Piano Trio No.3, Op. 43

(1969)   11'

cl-vc-pno
Parts **ED 6008**

5 Pieces (1954)   11'

vn-org
ED 4911

Praeambeln und Interludien

(1954)   12'

organ solo
ED 4539

Prelude and Fugue (1930)   8'

"Christ lag in Todesbanden"
organ solo
ED 2554

Prelude, Canzone and Rondo

(1938)   13'

vn-org
ED 3680

Quartet, Op. 38 (1963) 11'

ob-vn.va.vc
Study score **ED 5219** / Parts **ED 5185**

Sextet, Op. 36 (1961) 11'

fl.ob.cl.hn.bn-pno
Score and parts **ED 4998**

5 Sketches (1978) 9'

organ solo
ED 6858

Sonata (1977) 10'

fl-org
ED 8386

Sonata (1966) 11'

vc-org
ED 6107

String Quartet in C Minor, Op. 26 (1940) 13'

Score **ED 3615** / Parts **ED 3183**

String Quartet No.2, Op. 32 (1954) 12'

Score **ED 4552** / Parts **ED 4541**

String Trio, Op. 14/2 (1949) 8'

2vn.va
Score **ED 3624** / Parts **ED 1589**

String Trio in E Minor, Op. 14/1 (1933) 9'

vn.va.vc
Score **ED 3507** / Parts **ED 3161**

Susani (1948) 15'

pno
ED 3882

Variations on the "Tonus Peregrinus" (1975) 9'

organ solo
ED 6625

Solo Voice(s)/Voice(s) and Piano/Guitar

3 Christmas Carols (1948) 7'

Text: Fassbinder
high voice-pno
ED 3880

Choral Works

Als ich bei meinen Schafen wacht (1968) 2'

from "Fünf Weihnachtslieder"
Chorus: male, children's/female a cappella
C 42417

Ave Maria, gratia plena

(1933) 2'

Chorus: female a cappella
CHBL 542

Carmen mysticum, Op. 30

(1949) 50'

Cantata after Goethe's Faust
Text: Johann Wolfgang von Goethe
Soloists: soprano, baritone, speaker
Chorus: mixed
2(pic).2(ca).2.2-4.3.3.0-timp.perc-org-str
Material on hire
SM

3 Christmas Carols (1938) 5'

Chorus: mixed a cappella
C 35732

6 Christmas Carols (1947) 12'

Chorus: female
pno.org
Score **ED 3887** / Vocal score **ED 3887-01**

Einst liebt' ich ein Mädchen

(1969) 3'

from "Zwei Volkslieder"
Chorus: mixed a cappella
C 42413

Engel haben Himmelslieder

(1968) 2'

from "Fünf Weihnachtslieder"
Chorus: male, children's/female a cappella
C 42415

Freu dich, Erd und Sternenzelt (1968) 2'

from "Fünf Weihnachtslieder"
Chorus: male, children's/female a cappella
C 42416

Leben und Bestehen 9'

Text: Joseph von Eichendorff/Matthias Claudius
Chorus: mixed/female
2afl.[fl]-glsp.xyl-pno-str
Score **ED 5200** / Parts **ED 5200-11 (-18)** / Choral score **ED 5200-01**

Lustig, ihr Brüder (1968) 3'

Chorus: male, children's a cappella
C 42465

Mazurka (1969) 3'

from "Zwei Volkslieder"
Chorus: mixed a cappella
C 42414

6 Mörike-Chöre (1964) 13'

Text: Eduard Mörike
Chorus: mixed a cappella
C 40995

Der römische Brunnen

(1951) 2'

from "Römische Brunnen"
Text: Conrad Ferdinand Meyer
Chorus: mixed a cappella
C 37990

Römische Fontäne (1951) 2'

from "Römische Brunnen"
Text: Rainer Maria Rilke
Chorus: mixed a cappella
C 37991

Schön ist die Welt (1968) 3'

Chorus: male, children's a cappella
C 42466

Spruch (1951) 2'

from "Römische Brunnen"
Text: Friedrich Rückert
Chorus: mixed a cappella
C 37992

Te Deum, Op. 16 (1933) 9'

Chorus: mixed [a cappella]
[org]/[2tpt.3tbn.tuba]
Score **ED 33726** / Parts **ED 33727-01 (-04)** (chorus)/**ED 33728 (brass)**

Vom Himmel hoch, o Engel kommt (1968) 2'

from "Fünf Weihnachtslieder"
Chorus: male, children's/female a cappella
C 42418

Zu Bethlehem geboren

(1968) 2'

from "Fünf Weihnachtslieder"
Chorus: male, children's/female a cappella
C 42419

Schüler, Johannes
1894-1966

Orchestral Works

5 Orchestral Movements 12'

2pic.2.2.ca.2.bcl.tsax.2.cbn-4.3.3.1-timp.2perc.cel.hp-str
Material on hire
Study score **ED 4594**

Solo Voice(s) and Instrument(s)/ Orchestra

Die fünf Marienlieder des Kuno Kohn 10'

Text: Alfred Lichtenstein
Soloist: baritone
2pic.2.2.ca.2.bcl.tsax.2cbn-4.3.3.1-timp.2perc-cel.hp-str
Material on hire
SM

Schulhoff, Erwin

1894-1942

Stage Works

Flammen (1924-29) 120'

Opera in 2 Acts
Text: Karel Josef Beneš
Material on hire
Libretto **BN 5710-90**

Die Mondsüchtige (1925) 25'

Dance Grotesque in 1 Scene
Text: Vítzslav Nezval/Karel Josef Beneš
Material on hire
SM

Orchestral Works

Suite for Chamber Orchestra

(1921) 20'

*1(pic).1.ca.1(Ebcl).bcl.1-2.1.0.0-4perc-hp-
str(1.1.1.1.1 / 3.3.2.1.1)*
Material on hire
SM

Symphony No.2 (1932) 23'

*pic.1.1.ca.1.bcl(asax).1.cbn-2.1.0.0-timp-
banjo-str(8.6.4.4.3)*
Material on hire
SM

Symphony No. 7 - Eroica

(1941) 45'

Arranger: Henning Brauel (1995)
*3(pic).2.ca.2.bcl(Acl).2.cbn-4.3.3.1-
timp.3perc-str*
Material on hire
SM

Concertos

Hot-Sonate (1930) 14'

Arranger: Detlef Bensmann (1994)
Soloist: alto saxophone
*2.2.ca.2.bcl.1.cbn-4.3.2.1-2timp.3perc-
cel.hp-str(10.8.6.6.3)*
Material on hire
SM

Piano Concerto (1923) 21'

Soloist: piano
*pic.1.1.ca.1(Ebcl).bcl.1.cbn-2.1.0.0-
timp.4perc-hp-str(8.8.6.6.6)*
Material on hire
SM

Schulhoff, Erwin

b. Prague 8.6.1894, d. Wülzburg/Bavaria
(Concentration-Camp) 18.8.1942

**An ardent modernist, Schulhoff was a cos-
mopolitan figure whose natural association
with the avant-garde movement after the
First World War made him an influential
figure in advanced musical circles. A gifted
pianist, he specialised in jazz and in the the
quarter-tone repertoire of Haba and his
pupils. Stage works, symphonies, chamber
music and songs of high quality all point to
a creative life cut tragically short.**

Chamber & Instrumental Works

Baßnachtigall (1922) 4'

contrabassoon solo
FAG 22

Cello Sonata (1914) 22'

vc-pno
CB 151

Divertissement (1926) 15'

ob.cl.bn
Score **ED 7736** / Parts **ED 7737**

Hot-Sonate (Jazz-Sonate)

(1930) 14'

asax-pno
Score **ED 7739**

11 Inventions, Op. 36 (1921) 7'

pno
ED 8066

Ironien, Op. 34 (1920) 10'

pno (4hnd)
ED 8099

5 Pieces (1923) 13'

str qrt
Score **ED 7734** / Parts **ED 7735**

Suite No.3 (1926) 15'

pno(left hnd)
ED 8105

Violin Sonata No.2 (1927) 15'

vn-pno
ED 7738

Solo Voice(s)/Voice(s) and Piano/Guitar

5 Songs (1919) 10'

Text: anonymous
high/medium voice-pno
ED 8104

Solo Voice(s) and Instrument(s)/ Orchestra

Die Wolkenpumpe, Op. 40

(1922) 8'

Soloist: baritone
Ebcl.bn.cbn-tpt-3perc
Score **ED 8072** / Parts **ED 8072**

Choral Works

H.M.S. Royal Oaks (1930) 40'

Jazz Oratorio
Text: Otto Rombach
Soloists: speaker, soprano, jazz
singer(tenor)
Chorus: mixed
*jazz orchestra: ssax.asax.tsax-
3cnt.2tbn.sous-perc-pno.cel.banjo.2acc*
Material on hire
SM

Schuller, Gunther
b.1925

Stage Works

**The Visitation
(Die Heimsuchung)**

(1965-66)   full evening

Opera in 3 Acts
Text: Gunther Schuller after Franz Kafka
Material on hire
Libretto **BSS 90301 (Co-prod: AMP)**

Orchestral Works

**Concert Suite from
"The Visitation"** (1970)   41'

3.3.3.2-4.3.3.1-timp.perc-cel.pno.hpd.hp-str
Material on hire
SL (Co-prod: AMP)
Copyright not for: USA, CDN, LAT AM, JAP

Contours (1955-58)   21'

1.1.2.1-1.1.1.0-perc-hp-str
Material on hire
Study score **ED 10701 (min.)***

Contrasts (1961)   19'

2.afl.3.3.3-3.3.3.1-timp.3perc-cel/pno.hp-str
Material on hire
SL

Spectra (1958)   17'

4.4.3.bcl.4-4.4.3.1-timp.4perc-hp-str
Material on hire
Study score **ED 10798**

Concertos

Piano Concerto (1962)   20'

Soloist: piano
pic.2.2.ca.2.bcl.2.cbn-4.3.3.1-timp.3perc-str
Material on hire
Piano reduction **ED 10895**

Chamber & Instrumental Works

Woodwind Quintet (1984)   12'

Study score **ED 10943 / Parts ED 11013**

Schuller, Gunther

b. New York 22.11.1925

Conductor, horn player, editor, virtuoso orchestrator, teacher and many things besides, Schuller has enjoyed a full career as musical polymath even before adding the role of self-taught composer who in 1957 devised "third-stream" music, fusing serialism and jazz improvisation. One of the most admired of American composers outside his native land, he is a natural experimenter who in "The Visitation" of 1966 also produced one of the most controversial and provocative of post-war American operas.

Schulthess, Walter

1894-1971

Orchestral Works

Serenade in B Major, Op. 9   30'

2.2.ca.2.2-2.2.0.0-timp-str
Material on hire
SM

Concertos

Violin Concertino in A Major, Op. 7   14'

Soloist: violin
2.2.2.2-2.0.0.0-hp-str
Material on hire
SM

Solo Voice(s)/Voice(s) and Piano/Guitar

Lieder (1967)   5'

Text: Christian Morgenstern
high voice-pno
ED 5838

Lieder (1967)   7'

Text: Karl Stamm
medium voice-pno
ED 5837

Schwantner, Joseph
b.1943

Stage Works

Through Interior Worlds

(1992)   25'

Ballet
*3(pic).3(ca).3.(bcl).3(cbn)-4.3.3.1-
timp.3perc-pno/cel.hp-str*
Material on hire
EAM-Helicon

Orchestral Works

...And the Mountains rising nowhere (1977)   11'

*6(2pic).4(2ca).2.4-4.4.4.1-timp.5perc-
pno(amp)-db*
Study score **EA 375 / Parts EA 375-10**

Freeflight (1989)   6'

Fanfares and Fantasy
*3(pic).3.3(bcl).3(cbn)-4.3.3.1-timp.3perc-
pno.hp-str*
Material on hire
Study score **EA 736**

From a Dark Millennium

(1981)   12'

*3(2pic).2.ca.3(Ebcl,2bcl).3-4.3.4.1-
timp.4perc-pno(amp).cel(amp)-2db*
Score **EA 470 / Parts EA 470-10**

Schwantner, Joseph

b. Chicago 22.3.1943

Schwantner is a much admired figure in American music - a Professor of Composition at the Eastman School of Music who has also served on the faculty of the Julliard School. He received his musical and academic training at the Chicago Conservatory and Northwestern University, completing a doctorate in 1968. Performed by major artists and orchestras worldwide, his works have won many awards, including a 1979 Pulitzer Prize for "Aftertones of Infinity" and a 1981 Kennedy Center Friedheim Award, first prize, for "Music of Amber".

A Sudden Rainbow (1984) 18'
3(pic).3(ca).3(bcl).3(cbn)-4.3.3.1-
timp.3perc-pno.cel.hp-str
Material on hire
Study score **EA 558**

Toward Light (1987) 22'
3(pic).3.3.3-4.3.3.1-timp.3perc-2pno.hp-str
Material on hire
Study score **EA 701**

Concertos

Distant Runes and Incantations (1984) 15'
Soloist: piano (amp)
2(pic).2(ca).2(bcl).2-2.2.0.0-2perc-cel-str
Material on hire
Study score **EA 541**

Dreamcaller (1984) 22'
Text: Schwantner
Soloists: soprano, violin
1(afl).2(ca).1(bcl).2-2.1.0.0-perc-pno/cel-str
Material on hire
EAM-Helicon

...From Afar (1987) 16'
Soloist: guitar
3(pic).3(ca).3(bcl).3(cbn)-4.3.3.1-
timp.3perc-pno/cel-str
Material on hire
EAM-Helicon

Percussion Concerto (1992) 20'
Soloist: percussion
3(pic).3(ca).3(bcl).3(cbn)-4.3.3.1-
timp.3perc-pno/cel.hp-str
Material on hire
EAM-Helicon

Piano Concerto (1988) 29'
Soloist: piano
2(pic).2(ca).2(bcl).2-2.2.2.1-cel-2perc-str
Material on hire
Study score **EA 698**

A Play of Shadows (1990) 15'
Soloist: flute
2(pic).2.2(bcl).2-2.1.1.0-3perc-pno.hp-str
Material on hire
Study score **EA 715**

Chamber & Instrumental Works

Consortium 2 (1971) 12'
fl.cl-vn.vc-pno-perc
Material on hire
EAM-Helicon

Distant Runes and Incantations (1987) 15'
fl.cl-2vn.va.vc-pno-perc
Material on hire
Study score **EA 541**

In Aeternum (1975) 14'
Consortium 4
Soloist: cello
afl(fl,pno,perc).bcl(cl,perc)-va(vn,perc)-
perc
Score **EA 196** / Parts **EA 196-10**

In Aeternum 2 (1972) 10'
organ solo
EA 169

Music of Amber (1981) 22'
fl.cl(bcl)-vn.vc-pno-perc
Material on hire
Study score **EA 485**

Soaring (1986) 3'
fl-pno
EA 733

Veiled Autumn (1987) 4'
Kindertodeslied
pno
EA 591

Velocities (1990) 12'
Moto Perpetuo
marimba solo
EA 704

Solo Voice(s)/Voice(s) and Piano/Guitar

2 Poems of Agueda Pizarro
(1980) 15'
soprano-pno
EA 476

Solo Voice(s) and Instrument(s)/ Orchestra

Evening Land (1995) 30'
Symphony for Chorus and Orchestra
Text: Par Lagerkvist
Soloist: soprano
3(pic).3(ca).3(bcl).3(cbn)-4.3.3.1-
timp.2perc-pno/hpd.hp-str
Material on hire
EAM-Helicon

Magabunda (Witchnomad)
(1983) 32'
Text: Agueda Pizarro
Soloist: soprano
4(afl,pic).3(ca).3(Ebcl,bcl).3(cbn)-4.3.3.1-
timp.3perc-pno/cel(amp).hp-str
Material on hire
Study score **EA 516**

New Morning for the World
(1982) 23'
Daybreak of Freedom
Text: Martin Luther King, Jr.
Soloist: speaker
4(2pic).3(ca).3(bcl).2-4.3.4.1-timp.4perc-
pno(amp).cel(amp).hp-str
Material on hire
Study score **EA 484**

Sparrows (1979) 20'
Text: Issa
Soloist: soprano
fl(pic).cl-vn.va.vc-perc-pno.hp
Material on hire
Study score **EA 450**

Choral Works

Evening Land (1992) 30'

Symphony for Chorus and Orchestra
Text: Par Lagerkvist
Chorus: mixed
3(pic).3(ca).3(bcl).3(cbn)-4.3.3.1-
timp.3perc-pno/cel.hp-str
Material on hire
EAM-Helicon

Scott, Cyril
1879-1970

Stage Works

The Alchemist (1917) full evening

Opera in 3 Scenes
Material on hire
SM

Orchestral Works

Aubade, Op. 77 (1952) 18'

3(pic).2.ca.2.bcl.2-4.2.3.1-timp.perc-2hp-
str(4.0.1.1.1)
Material on hire
SM

Noël 10'

Christmas Overture
Chorus: mixed
3(pic).2.ca.bcl.2.cbn-4.3.3.1-timp.perc-
cel.pno.org.hp/[2hp]-str
Material on hire
SM

2 Passacaglias (1916) 7'

4(pic).3.ca.4.bcl.4.cbn-6.4.3.1-timp.3perc-
cel.pno.org.2hp-str
Material on hire
SM

Concertos

Piano Concerto in C Major
(1915) 25'

Soloist: piano
2.1.2.2-0.0.0.0-timp.perc-cel.hp.woodhar-
monica-str
Material on hire
Piano reduction **BSS 30764**

Scott, Cyril

b. Oxton, Cheshire 27.9.1879, d. Eastbourne
31.12.1970

Scott's progressive stance gained the admiration of Debussy and of German music cri-
tics, and he was the first British composer
to apply the techniques of musical impres-
sionism in his work. Though songs and
piano pieces form the bulk of his output,
there are memorable symphonies and operas that merit rediscovery.

Chamber & Instrumental Works

Arabesque

pno
ED 1796*

Aubade (1974) 6'

fl/arec/vn-pno/hpd
Study score **ED 10330**

Bumble Bees

violin solo
ED 1949*

Butterfly Waltz

pno
ED 1800*

Carillon (1913) 2'

pno
ED 1797*

Cherry Ripe, Old English Air (1911) 3'

vn-pno
ED 1948*

Cherry Ripe, Old English Air (1911) 3'

pno
ED 11977*

Concerto

vc-pno
ED 1940*

Cornish Boat Song (1931) 3'

vn.vc-pno
ED 2181*

3 Country Dances

pno
ED 1441*

Danse élegiaque, Op. 74/1

pno
ED 1801*

Danse from "Deux Préludes"

vc-pno
ED 1945*

Danse langoureuse, Op. 74/3

pno
ED 1803*

Danse negre, Op. 58/5 2'

pno
ED 1805*

Danse orientale, Op. 74/2

pno
ED 1802*

Egypt

An Album of 5 Impressions
pno
ED 1436*

Élégie, Op. 73/1

vc-pno
ED 1941*

The Extatic Shepherd 2'

flute solo
FTR 142 (ED 2001*)

The Gentle Maiden (Irish Air)

vc-pno
ED 1947*

Idyll

violin solo
ED 1950*

Impressions from the Jungle Book

pno
ED 1437*

Indian Suite (1922)   8'

pno
ED 1438*

Little Folk Dance (1931)   3'

vn.vc-pno
ED 2182*

Lotusland, Op. 47/1 (1905)   3'

pno
ED 1804*

Miniatures (1915)   5'

pno
ED 1439*

Miss Rennington (Scherzo)

pno
ED 1435*

Old China Suite (1918)   5'

pno
ED 1435*

A Pageant (1920)   6'

3 Dances
pno
ED 1442*

Pastoral and Reel

vc-pno
Ed 1992*

Piano Sonata, Op. 66

ED 1449*

Pierrot amoureux, Andante   5'

vc-pno
ED 1991*

Poème Erotique from "Deux Préludes"

vc-pno
ED 1944*

Poems (1912)   10'

pno
ED 1440*

Rainbow Trout (1916)   4'

pno
ED 1799*

Romance, Op. 73/2

vc-pno
ED 1942*

Sonnet Nos. 1 & 2

vc-pno
SM

Suite No. 2, Op. 75   7'

pno
ED 1443*

3 Symphonic Dances

Arranger: Percy Grainger
2pno
ED 1855*

Tallahassee Suite (1911)   6'

vn-pno
ED 1450*

The Melodist and the Nightingales (1930)   7'

vc-pno
ED 2130*

Toy Box

pno
ED 2334*

Trio No. 2

vn.vc-pno
ED 10416*

Violin Sonata No.1, Op. 59

(1910)   16'

vn-pno
ED 1449*

Zoo (1930)   6'

pno
ED 2115*

Searle, Humphrey

1915-1982

Stage Works

The Diary of a Madman, Op. 35 (1958)   20'

Opera in 1 Act
Text: Humphrey Searle after Nikolai Gogol
Material on hire
Vocal score **ED 10686*** / Libretto **ED 10686-01***

Dualities, Op. 39 (1963)   20'

Ballet in 6 Scenes
Material on hire
SL

The Great Peacock, Op. 34a

(1959)   20'

Ballet in 1 Act
Material on hire
SL

Les Noctambules, Op. 30

(1956)   30'

Ballet in 1 Act
Material on hire
SL

The Photo of the Colonel, Op. 41 (1963)   full evening

Opera in 3 Acts
Text: Eugène Ionescos
Material on hire
Vocal score **ED 10869*** /
Libretto **ED 10869-01***

Searle, Humphrey

b. Oxford 1915, d. London 12.5.1982

An expert on the music of Liszt, Searle was the first British compsoer to base a mature oeuvre in the serial method. Powerfully Romantic, his music speaks at its clearest in a fine Piano Sonata and in the triptych of choral works: "Gold Coast Customs", "The Riverrun" and "The Shadow of Cain".

Orchestral Works

Les Noctambules - Suite, Op. 30 (1955-56)   14'

3(pic).2.2.2-4.3.3.1-timp.4perc-pno(cel).hp-str
Material on hire
SL

Scherzi, Op. 44 (1964)   9'

2(pic).2.2.2-2.2.0.0-perc-str
Material on hire
SL

Symphony No.1, Op. 23

(1952-53)   25'

2(pic).2.2(bcl).2(cbn)-4.2.3.1-timp.perc-str
Material on hire
SL

Symphony No.2, Op. 33

(1958)   20'

2(pic).2.2.2-4.2.3.1-timp.3perc-cel.pno-str
Material on hire
Study score **ED 10711***

Symphony No.3, Op. 36

(1960)   22'

3.3.3.3-4.2.3.1-timp.3perc-str
Material on hire
SL

Symphony No.4, Op. 38

(1962)   20'

*2(pic).2(ca).2(bcl).2(cbn)-4.2.3.1-timp.
3-4perc-pno(cel).hp-str*
Material on hire
SL

Symphony No.5, Op. 43

(1964)   25'

*2(2pic).2(ca).2(bcl).2(cbn)-4.2.3.1-timp.
3-4perc-pno(cel).hp-str*
Material on hire
Study score **ED 10926**

Variations and Finale, Op. 34

(1958)   18'

pic.ob.cl.bn-hn-2vn.va.vc.db
Material on hire
Study score **ED 10628**

Concertos

Aubade, Op. 28 (1955)   6'

Soloist: horn
str
Material on hire
Piano reduction **ED 10500***

Concertante, Op. 24 (1954)   6'

Soloist: piano
timp.perc-str
Material on hire
Study score **AVV 61**

Divertimento, Op. 26a

(1954)   8'

Soloist: flute
str
Material on hire
Piano reduction **ED 10474**

Piano Concerto No.2, Op. 27

(1954-55)   23'

Soloist: piano
2(pic)2.2.2-4.2.3.1-timp.3perc-str
Material on hire
SL / Piano reduction **ED 10397***

Chamber & Instrumental Works

Gonderliera, Op. 19 (1950)   3'

ca-pno
ED 10529*

Suite, Op. 32 (1956)   11'

cl-pno
ED 10487*

Suite, Op. 29 (1955)   6'

pno
ED 10547

Toccata alla Passacaglia, Op. 31 (1957)   5'

organ solo
ED 10580*

Solo Voice(s) and Instrument(s)/ Orchestra

The Riverrun, Op. 20

(1951)   30'

Text: James Joyce
Soloist: speaker
*2(pic).2(ca)2(bcl).2(cbn)-4.2.3.1-timp.perc-
pno(cel).hp-str*
Material on hire
AVV

Choral Works

The Shadow of Cain, Op. 22

(1951)   25'

Soloist: speaker
Chorus: mixed
2.2.2.2-4.2.3.1-timp.perc-str
Material on hire
SL

Song of the Sun, Op. 42

(1966)   12'

Text: Náhuatl poems (transl. Irene
Nicholson)
Chorus: mixed a cappella
ED 10905

Segovia, Andrés
1893-1987

Chamber & Instrumental Works

Estudio sin luz

gtr
GA 179

Estudios

gtr
GA 178

Sehlbach, Erich
1898-1985

Stage Works

Signor Caraffa, Op. 21

(1938)   75'

Comic Opera in 3 Acts
Material on hire
SM

Seiber, Mátyás
1905-1960

Stage Works

The Invitation (1960)   56'

Ballet in 5 Scenes
Material on hire
SL

Orchestral Works

Besardo-Suite No.2 (1942)   14'

str
Material on hire
Study score **ED 10222**

Improvisations (1959)   11'

Arranger: Johnny Dankworth
*jazzband: 2asax.2tsax.barsax.4tpt.4tbn-
perc-pno-db*
*orch: 2(pic).2.2(bcl).2-4.3.3.1-timp.3perc-
hp-str*
Material on hire
Study score **ED 10728**

Orchestral Suite from "The Invitation" (1960)   20'

2.2.2.2-4.3.3.1-timp.3perc-cel.pno.hp-str
Material on hire
SL

Renaissance Dance Suite

(1959)   20'

2(pic).2.2.2-3.2.0.0-perc-hp-str
Material on hire
SL

Concertos

Concertino (1951)   17'

Arrangement from the "Divertimento"
Soloist: clarinet
str
Material on hire
Piano reduction **ED 10341**

Seiber, Mátyás

b. Budapest 4.5.1905, d. Krüger Nationalpark (South Africa) 25.9.1960

Seiber's compositional background as pupil of Kodaly and specialist in Schönberg and jazz made him the most versatile, gifted yet enigmatic emigre to settle in Britain between the wars. Serialism is combined with baroque forms in the James Joyce cantata "Ulysses" (1950). Folksong arrangements, easy piano pieces and solo works for woodwind and orchestra show the lighter side of his musical character.

Elegy (1953)   8'

Soloist: viola
2(pic).1.1.bcl.1-2.3.0.0-timp.perc-str
Material on hire
Study score **ED 4585*** / Piano reduction
ED 10422

Fantasia Concertante

(1943-44)   16'

Soloist: violin
str
Material on hire
Study score **AVV 64** / Piano reduction **AVV 2**

Notturno (1944)   8'

Soloist: horn
str
Material on hire
Study score **ED 10204*** / Piano reduction
ED 10336

Pastorale and Burlesque

(1942)   8'

Soloist: flute
str
Material on hire
Study score **ED 10211*** / Piano reduction
ED 10185*

Tre pezzi (1956)   20'

Soloist: cello
2(pic).2.2(bcl).2-4.2.2.0-timp.4perc-
pno(cel).hp-str
Material on hire
Piano reduction **ED 10379***

Chamber & Instrumental Works

Andantino Pastorale (1949)   3'

cl-pno
ED 10527*

77 Breaks for Percussion

(1932)
ED 2078*

Concert Piece (1953-54)   7'

vn-pno
ED 10429

Dance Suite

(Arrangement of Easy Dances)
Arranger: De Haan
cl-pno
ED 12423

Dance Suite

(Arrangement of Easy Dances)
Arranger: De Haan
asax-pno
ED 12424

Dance Suite

(Arrangement of Easy Dances)
Arranger: De Haan
tpt-pno
ED 12425

Dance Suite

(Arrangement of Easy Dances)
Arranger: De Haan
fl-pno
ED 12426

Dance Suite

(Arrangement of Easy Dances)
Arranger: De Haan
fl.ob.cl.bn/asax
ED 12429

Dance Suite Vol.1 (1984)   10'

(Arrangement of Easy Dances)
Arranger: Denis Bloodworth
srec.arec.trec.brec
ED 12251

Dance Suite Vol.2 (1984)   10'

(Arrangement of Easy Dances)
Arranger: Denis Bloodworth
srec.arec.trec.brec
ED 12252

Dance Suite Vol.3 (1989)   10'

(Arrangement of Easy Dances)
Arranger: Denis Bloodworth
srec.arec.trec.brec
ED 12347

8 Dances (1956)

guitar solo
ED 10399

Divertimento (1926)   17'

cl-str qrt
Material on hire
Piano reduction **ED 10341**

Easy Dances (1932)   1'

accordion solo
Manuscript score on sale
SL

Easy Dances (1932)   1'

pno
ED 2234/2546 (2 Vols.)

Easy Dances (1932)   1'

pno (4hnd)
ED 2529

Fantasy (1941)   6'

vc-pno
Manuscript score on sale
SL

Improvisation (1957)   4'

ob-pno
ED 10648

Pastorale (1941)

trec-str trio
ED 10251* / Study score **ED 10313***

Permutazioni a Cinque

(1958)   8'

fl.ob.cl.bn-hn
ED 10693* / Study score **ED 10685 (min.)***

Rhythmical Studies (1933)   5'

pno
ED 2328

Scherzando Capriccioso

(1944)   5'

pno
ED 10247*

String Quartet No.3

(1948-51)   23'

(Quartetto Lirico)
ED 10257* / Study score **ED 10206**

Violin Sonata (1960)   18'

vn-pno
ED 10747*

Solo Voice(s)/Voice(s) and Piano/Guitar

The Owl and the Pussy-Cat

(1953)   4'

Text: Edward Lear
high voice-pno
ED 10689*

Quatre chansons populaires françaises (1948)   11'

high voice-gtr
ED 10637

To Poetry (1953)   15'

Text: Var.
high voice-pno
ED 10329*

Solo Voice(s) and Instrument(s)/ Orchestra

The Owl and the Pussy-Cat

(1953)   4'

Text: Edward Lear
Soloist: high voice
vn-gtr
Material on hire
ED 10638*

Quatre chansons populaires françaises (1948)   11'

Soloist: soprano
str
Material on hire
Vocal score **ED 4630**

Choral Works

Alle Leut' sind ausgegangen

(1929)   2'

Arranger: Hilger Schallehn
Chorus: female/male a cappella
C 46028/46029

Cantata Secularis (1949-51)   20'

The Four Seasons
Chorus: mixed
2(pic).2(ca).2(bcl).2-4.3.3.1-timp.5-6perc-pno(cel).hp-str
Material on hire
Vocal score **ED 10714***

3 Fragments from "A Portrait of the Artist as a Young Man" (1958)   19'

Text: James Joyce
Soloist: speaker
Chorus: mixed
fl.cl.bcl-vn.va.vc-pno-timp.perc
Material on hire
Vocal score **ED 10656***

Ulysses (1946-47)   45'

Text: James Joyce
Soloist: tenor
Chorus: mixed
3(2pic).2(ca).2(bcl).2.[cbn]-4.3.3.1-timp.3perc-pno(cel).hp-str
Material on hire
Vocal score **ED 10280***

Sekles, Bernhard
1872-1934

Chamber & Instrumental Works

String Quartet, Op. 31

Study score **ED 3460**

Senfter, Johanna
1879-1961

Concertos

Piano Concerto, Op. 90

(1938)   40'

2.2.2.2.-4.2.0.0-timp-str
Material on hire
SM

Chamber & Instrumental Works

Berceuse   4'

Schott Piano Collection Johanna Senfter
pno
ED 8275

2 Choralvorspiele   4'

in: Choralvorspiele von Reger-Schülern
organ solo
ED 7769

Fugues, Nos. 4, 5 & 7 (1907-09)

Schott Piano Collection Johanna Senfter
pno
ED 8275

3 Klavierstücke, Op. 83 (1937-38)   11'

Schott Piano Collection Johanna Senfter
pno
ED 8275

2 Klavierstücke, Op. 129 (1956)   8'

Schott Piano Collection Johanna Senfter
pno
ED 8275

Klavierstudie (1898)

Schott Piano Collection Johanna Senfter
pno
ED 8275

6 kleine Stücke für Anfänger (1898-1903)

Schott Piano Collection Johanna Senfter
pno
ED 8275

Mazurka   3'

Schott Piano Collection Johanna Senfter
pno
ED 8275

Melodie und Elegie, Op. 13

in: Frauen komponieren
vn-pno
ED 8132

Passacaglia, Nos. 5, 7 & 9 (1907-09)

Schott Piano Collection Johanna Senfter
pno
ED 8275

Scherzo (1907)

Schott Piano Collection Johanna Senfter
pno
ED 8275

Violin Sonata G Minor, Op. 61   18'

violin solo
VLB 89

Vogelweise   4'

Schott Piano Collection Johanna Senfter
pno
ED 8275

Infoline · e-Mail
Schott Musik International
Mainz: Schott.Musik.com@T-Online.de
London: 101627.166@compuserve.com

Sgambati, Giovanni

1841-1914

Orchestral Works

Berceuse-Réverie, Op. 42/2

Arranger: Massenet
2.0.ca.1.1-1.0.0.0-timp-hp-str
Material on hire
SM

Concertos

Piano Concerto, Op. 15　　35'

Soloist: piano
2.2(ca).2.2-4.2.3.1-timp-str
Material on hire
Piano reduction **BSS 23366**

Chamber & Instrumental Works

Piano Etude, Op. 10/2 (1878-80)

pno
BSS 23290

Choral Works

Missa da Requiem, Op. 38

(1897-98)　　70'

Soloist: baritone
Chorus: mixed
2.2.3.2-4.3.3.1-timp.perc-hp.org-str
Material on hire
SM

Shchedrin, Rodion

b.1932

Orchestral Works

Khorovody-Reigen (1989)　　23'

Concerto No. 4
4(2pic,afl).arec.2.ca.3(Ebcl,bcl).3-4.3(Btpt high).3.1-timp.5perc-cel(pno).hpd.hp-str(16.14.12.10.8)
Material on hire
Score **KIN 1003**
(Co-prod: Kompositor International, Mainz)
SM

Shchedrin, Rodion

b. Moscow 16.12.1932

Rodion Shchedrin has established himself as one of the major figures in contemporary Russian composition, and is regarded as one of the principal successors of Prokofiev and Shostakowich. The treatment of Russian folklore in contemporary music has been his active concern since his earliest mature works and a large proportion of his works involve the synthesis of traditional forms or extra-musical inspirations with contemporary composition techniques. His music spans a wide range of genres, and in particular he has made a considerable contribution to the repertory of modern musical theatre. Most of his works are large-scale compositions, scintillating, suggestive and brilliantly orchestrated. In addition to opera and ballet, he has written for orchestra, piano and chorus, often using Russian poems as his text. He is aslo an active concert pianist and organist.

Kristallene Gusli (1994)　　10'

pic.2.2.2.2-3.3.3.1-2perc-pno.hp-str(16.14.12.10.8)
Material on hire
SM

Old Russian Circus Music

(1989)　　25'

Concerto No.3 for Orchestra
4(2pic).2.ca.4.2.cbn-4.3.3.1-timp.5perc-pno(cel)-str(16.14.12.10.8)
Material on hire
Score **ED 8182**

Russische Photographien

(1994)　　23'

String Music
str
Material on hire
Score **ED 8429**

Shepherd's Pipes of Vologda

(1995)　　6'

Hommage a Bártók
ob.ca-hn-str
Material on hire
SM

Veličanie (1995)　　8'

Songs of praise
str
Material on hire
SM

Concertos

Cello Concerto (1994)　　30'

"sotto voce concerto"
Soloist: cello
3(pic,afl).rec.2.ca.2.2.cbn-4.2.3.1-timp.3perc-hp-str(16.14.12.10.8)
Material on hire
Piano reduction **ED 8283**

Trumpet Concerto (1993)　　20'

Soloist: trumpet
3(pic,afl).3(ca).2.2-3.2.2.1-timp.2perc-str(16.14.12.10.8)
Material on hire
Piano reduction **ED 8252**

Chamber & Instrumental Works

Echos (1994)　　9'

based on a Cantus Firmus by Orlando di Lasso
soprec-org
ED 8415

Piano Terzetto (1995)　　20'

vn.vc-pno
SM

Choral Works

The Sealed Angel (1993)　　62'

Text: russian liturgy
Soloists: soprano, alto, tenor, 2 boy's voices
Chorus: mixed
fl
Score **ED 8517** / Parts **ED 8517-11 (flute)**

Sheinkman, Mordechai

b.1926

Orchestral Works

Passi 9'

3(pic).2.2.2-4.2.3.1-3-4perc-str
Material on hire
Study score **ED 4563**

Siegl, Otto

1896-1978

Choral Works

Das Gebirge 35'

Text: Johannes Linke
Chorus: male
2.2.2.2-4.2.3.1-timp.perc-[hp]-str
Material on hire
SM

Silvestri, Constantin

1913-1969

Chamber & Instrumental Works

Sonate, Op. 21/1 (1940)

harp solo
ED 5386

Silvestrow, Valentin

b.1937

Orchestral Works

Eschatophonie (1966) 23'

2pic.2.3.ca.Ebcl.2.bcl.3.cbn-4.4.3.1-
timp.perc-cel.pno.2hp-str(16.12.12.10.8)
Material on hire
AVV

Singleton, Alvin

b.1940

Stage Works

Dream Sequence "76"

(1976) 68'
Opera in 2 Parts
Text: Singleton
Material on hire
EAM

Orchestral Works

After Fallen Crumbs (1987) 7'

3.2.ca.3.2.cbn-4.3.2.1-timp.perc-hp-str
Material on hire
Study score **EA 626**

Again (1979) 12'

1(pic).1.1(bcl).1-1.1.1.0-perc-pno-
str(2.0.1.1.1)
Material on hire
EAM

56 Blows (1994) 12'

(Quis Custodiet Custodies?)
3(pic).3(ca).3(bcl).3(cbn)-4.3.3.1-3perc-
pno.hp-str
Material on hire
Study score **EA 757**

Cara Mia Gwen (1993) 15'

2.2.2(Ebcl).2-4.2.2.0-str
Material on hire
EAM

Durch Alles (1992) 15'

3(pic,afl).3(ca).3(bcl).3(cbn)-4.3.3.1-str
Material on hire
EAM

Even Tomorrow (1991) 15'

3(2pic).3.3(Ebcl).3(cbn)-4.3.3.1-
timp.4perc-pno(cel).hp-str
Material on hire
EAM

Eine Idee ist ein Stueck Stoff

(1988) 10'
str
Material on hire
EAM

Shadows (1987) 20'

3(pic,afl).3(ca).3(Ebcl,bcl).3(cbn)-4.3.3.1-
2timp.2perc.mar.xyl-hp-str
Material on hire
Score **EA 670**

Sinfonia Diaspora (1991) 12'

3(pic).3(ca).3(bcl).3(cbn)-4.3.3.1-hp-str
Score **EA 711X**

Singleton, Alvin

b. Brooklyn 28.12.1940

Singleton has written for a wide range of intrumental ensembles, and has also composed solo works for piano, cello, flute, viola, harpsichord, bass clarinet and marimba. Stage pieces include the opera "Dream Sequence "76" (1976) and the satirical "Necessity is a Mother...". A pupil of Petrassi, he has been praised for his music's sensitive display of tone colour and contrast, and for its exhilarating command of dynamic flow that extends from episodes of extreme stillness to passages of high rhythmic energy.

A Yellow Rose Petal (1982) 20'

2(2pic,afl).2(ca).2(bcl).2(cbn)-2.2.1.0-
2perc-cel-str(min:10.8.6.5.3)
Material on hire
Score **EA 563**

Concertos

Kwitana (1974) 17'

Soloists: piano, doublebass, percussion
1.0.1.1-0.2.2.0-str(1.0.1.1.0)
Material on hire
EAM

Chamber & Instrumental Works

Again (1975-79) 12'

str
EAM

Akwaaba (1985) 29'/19'

fl.cl.bn-perc-pno-vn.vc
Material on hire
EAM

Apple (1984) 20'

Ebcl.2Bcl.bcl
Material on sale
EAM

Argoru 1 (1970) 4'

pno
EAM

Argoru 2 (1970) 13'

cello solo
EA 692

Argoru 3 (1971) 5'

flute solo
EA 694

Argoru 4 (1978) 10'

viola solo
EA 695X

Argoru 5a (1984) 13'

bassclarinet solo
EA 696X

Argoru 5b (1984) 13'

altoflute solo
EA 697X

Argoru 6 (1988) 6'

marimba solo
EA 718

Argoru 7 (1994) 6'

vibraphone solo
EAM

Be Natural (1974) 10'

any combination of 3 bowed str
Material on sale
EAM

Changing Faces 3'

pno
EA 591

Cinque (1969) 7'

pno
EAM

Et Nunc (1980) 13'

afl.bcl-db
Material on sale
EAM

Extension of a Dream

(1977/87) 18'

2perc
EA 38X

La Flora (1983) 14'

fl(afl).cl-2perc-vn.vc
EAM

Inside-Out (1983-84) 20'

pno (4hnd)
EAM

Intezar (1994) 19'

va.vc.db
Material on sale
Score and parts **EA 758**

Mutations (1966) 10'

pno
EAM

Secret Desire to be Black 20'

str qrt
Material on sale
Score **EA 709X** / Parts **EA 709X**

String Quartet No.1 (1967) 13'

Material on sale
EAM

Such a Nice Lady (1979) 15'

cl-vn.va.vc-pno
Material on sale
EAM

Le Tombeau du Petit Prince

(1978) 7'

hpd
EAM

Woodwind Quintet (1968-69) 12'

EAM

Solo Voice(s) and Instrument(s)/ Orchestra

Necessity is a Mother (1981) 30'

Text: Singleton
3voices-db(amp)
Material on sale
EAM

A Seasoning (1971) 12'

Text: Singleton
Soloist: male/female voice
fl(perc).asax(perc)-tbn(perc)-db(perc)-perc
Material on hire
EAM

Choral Works

Alleluia (1987) 7'

Chorus: female a cappella
EAM

Epitaph (1966) 2'

Text: Sir Walter Raleigh
Chorus: mixed double a cappella
EAM

Fallen Crumbs (1987) 7'

Text: Singleton
Chorus: male a cappella
EAM

Gloria (from Messa) (1975) 10'

Text: Catholic Liturgy
Soloist: soprano
Chorus: 4S.4A.4T.4B
fl-2gtr-eorg-vc.db
Material on hire
EAM

Messa (1975) 26'

Soloist: soprano
Chorus: 4S.4A.4T.4B
fl-2gtr-eorg-vc.db
Material on hire
EAM

The World is here with me

(1990) 5'

Text: Susan Kouguell
Chorus: female
pno
EAM

Sitt, Hans
1850-1922

Concertos

Concertino in A minor, Op. 28 28'

Soloist: violin
2.2.2.2-4.2.3.0-3perc-str
Material on hire
Eu

Concerto in A Minor, Op. 68 29'

Soloist: viola
2.2.2.2-2.2.3.0-perc-str
Material on hire
Eu

Concerto No.2 in D Minor, Op. 38 30'

Soloist: cello
2.2.2.2-4.2.3.0-perc-str
Material on hire
Eu

Concerto No. 3 in D minor, Op. 111 30'

Soloist: violin
2.2.2.2-4.2.3.1-3perc-str
Material on hire
Eu

Konzertstück in G Minor, Op. 46 16'

Soloist: viola
2.2.2.2-2.2.3.0-perc-str
Material on hire
Eu

Chamber & Instrumental Works

20 Studies, Op. 62

violin solo
Eu

Skrowaczewski, Stanislaw

b.1923

Orchestral Works

Suite for Strings from 6 Concerts en Sextuor (1977) 14'

(Jean-Philippe Rameau)
Arranger: Skrowaczewski
str
Material on hire
EAM

Toccata and Fugue in D Minor, Op. S.565 15'

(J.S. Bach)
Arranger: Skrowaczewski
4(pic).4(ca).4(2bcl).4(cbn)-4.4.3.1-timp.perc-pno.hp-str
Material on hire
EAM

Concertos

Clarinet Concerto (1980) 23'

Soloist: clarinet
3(pic).0.0.0.bcl.2(cbn)-2.0.4.0-timp.3perc-cel.hpd(amp)-str(10.8.6.6.4)
Material on hire
Piano reduction **EA 487**

Concerto for Cor Anglais

(1969) 17'

Soloist: cor anglais
3(pic).0.0.0-3.3.3.0-timp.3perc-pno-str(10.0.8.8.6)
Material on hire
EAM

Ricercari Notturni (1977) 25'

Soloist: sax/clarinet
3(pic).0.0.2-2.2.3.1-timp.3perc-hpd(amp)-str(10.8.6.6.4)
Material on hire
Piano reduction **EA 432**

Slavenski, Josip

1896-1955

Orchestral Works

Balkanophonia, Op. 10

(1927) 18'

2(pic).2(ca).2.2-4.2.3.0-timp.2perc-hp-str
Material on hire
SM

Chamber & Instrumental Works

Aus dem Dorfe, Op. 6 (1925)

fl.cl-vn.va.db
BSS 31360

Jugoslawische Suite, Op. 2

(1921) 18'

pno
BSS 31626

Piano Sonata, Op. 4 (1924) 13'

BSS 31651

Choral Works

Herbstnächte - Jesenske noci

(1927) 2'

from "Sechs serbische Volkslieder"
Chorus: mixed a cappella
C 32456

Hochzeitslied - Svtovska

(1927) 2'

from "Sechs serbische Volkslieder"
Chorus: mixed a cappella
C 32453

Klagelied des Blinden - Slepacka (1927) 2'

from "Sechs serbische Volkslieder"
Chorus: mixed a cappella
C 32454

Kolo (1932) 4'

Improvisations
Chorus: female
str qnt/orch
Score **C 33415** / Parts **C 33417-11 (-15)** / Vocal score **C 33416**

Liebeslied - Dilberka (1927) 2'

from "Sechs serbische Volkslieder"
Chorus: mixed a cappella
C 32457

Scherzlied (1930) 2'

Text: Hermann Roth
Chorus: male a cappella
C 32654

Scherzlied - Saljivka (1927) 2'

from "Sechs serbische Volkslieder"
Chorus: mixed a cappella
C 32455

Spottlied (1930) 2'

Text: Hermann Roth
Chorus: male a cappella
C 32655

Spottlied - Rugalica (1927) 2'

from "Sechs serbische Volkslieder"
Chorus: mixed a cappella
C 32458

Smith Brindle, Reginald

b.1917

Concertos

Guitar Concerto (1980-81) 10'

Soloist: guitar
1.1.1.1-0.0.0.0-perc-pno.eorg-str(5.4.3.2.1)
Study score **ED 11421** / Parts **ED 11421-01**

Chamber & Instrumental Works

Chaconne and Interludes

(1981) 9'

2gtr
ED 11431

Concerto "Cum Jubilo"

(1983) 13'

3gtr
ED 11850

Concerto de Angelis (1974) 15'

4gtr
ED 11371

Las Doce Cuerdas (1981) 9'

2gtr
ED 11853

El Polifemo de Oro (1956) 9'

guitar solo
ED 11846

Etruscan Preludes (1953) 6'

guitar solo
ED 11458

Fuego Fatuo (1948) 3'
guitar solo
ED 11454

Guitar Sonata No.3 (1980) 12'
The Valley of Esdralon
ED 11423

Guitar Sonata No.4 (1980) 7'
La Brevé
ED 11424

Guitar Sonata No.5 (1983) 10'
ED 11430

Guitarcosmos Vols.1-3
Progressive Studies
guitar solo
ED 11387 (-89)

Hathor at Philae (1982) 9'
arec-gtr
ED 12155

Nocturne (1947) 2'
guitar solo
ED 11455

Pagan Dance
guitar solo
ED 11453

The Pillars of Karnak (1955) 7'
2gtr
ED 11432

4 Poems of Garcia Lorca
(1978) 12'
guitar solo
ED 11368

5 Sketches (1959) 9'
vn-gtr
ED 11391

Sonatina Fiorentina (1948)
guitar solo
ED 11457

Ten-String Music (1957) 6'
vc-gtr
ED 11392

Vita Senese (1948) 3'
guitar solo
ED 11456

Soler, Josep
b.1935

Chamber & Instrumental Works

Sonidos de la noche - Klänge der Nacht
6perc
Score **BAT 9** / Parts **BAT 9-01**

Sollima, Eliodoro
b.1926

Chamber & Instrumental Works

Sonata (1971) 15'
arec-pno
OFB 127

Souster, Tim
b.1943

Solo Voice(s) and Instrument(s)/ Orchestra

Poem in Depression Wei Village 8'
Soloist: male voice
fl-va.vc-pno
Material on hire
SL

Staeps, Hans-Ulrich
1909-1988

Chamber & Instrumental Works

Reihe kleiner Duette (1950)
2arec
OFB 94

Virtuose Suite (1961)
altorecorder/violin solo
OFB 95

Stein, Egon
b.1903

Orchestral Works

Sinfonietta 15'
for brass ensemble
Material on hire
Eu

Steinbrenner, Wilfried
1943-1975

Concertos

Imago I (1973) 15'
Soloist: violin
str(16.16.12.12.8)
Material on hire
AVV

Solo Voice(s) and Instrument(s)/ Orchestra

Kristall (1973) 20'
Lyric Paradoxon
Text: Paul Celan
Soloist: soprano
1(pic).afl.1.ca.2.2(cbn)-0.0.0.0-2perc-org.hp-3str qnt(each 2.0.1.1.1)
Material on hire
AVV

Stephan, Rudi

1887-1915

Stage Works

Die ersten Menschen

(1914)   full evening

Opera in 2 Acts
Text: Otto Borngraeber
Material on hire
SM

Orchestral Works

Music for Orchestra (1912) 19'

3/pic.2.2.ca.3/2.bcl.2.cbn-4.3.3.1-timp.perc-hp-str
Material on hire
Study score **ED 3462**

Musik für 7 Saiteninstrumente (1911) 25'

Original version
pno.hp-solo str(1.1.1.1.1)
Material on hire
SM

Musik für 7 Saiteninstrumente (1911) 25'

Arranger: G.E. Lessing
pno.hp-str orch
Material on hire
Study score **ED 3463**

Symphonischer Satz (1910) 37'

3(2pic).1.ob d'am.ca.3.bcl.3.cbn-6.4.3.1-timp.perc-cel.hp.org-str
Material on hire
SM

Concertos

Music for Violin and Orchestra (1912) 19'

Soloist: violin
3(pic).3(ca).3(bcl).2.cbn-4.3.2.1-timp.perc-hp-str
Material on hire
Piano reduction **ED 1953**

Chamber & Instrumental Works

Groteske (1911) 8'

vn-pno
VLB 65

Stephan, Rudi

b. Worms 29.7.1887, d. nr. Tarnopol, Galacia 29.9.1915

A war victim, Stephan was killed in action on the Eastern front, a premature end to a career that had already shown great promise. Reger and the new classicism were strong influences on his development, reflected in the plain, abstract titles of works such as "Music for Orchestra" and "Music for Viola and Orchestra". Had he lived, Stephan would undoubtedly have been a potent force in post-war European music.

Solo Voice(s)/Voice(s) and Piano/Guitar

2 ernste Gesänge (1913-14) 4'
voice-pno
BSS 30668

Ich will Dir singen (1913-14) 12'
voice-pno
ED 2051

7 Lieder (1913-14) 16'
voice-pno
ED 2049

Up de eensame Hallig (1914) 3'
Text: Detlef Liliencron
low voice-pno
ED 2050

Solo Voice(s) and Instrument(s)/ Orchestra

Abendlied (1914) 2'

Text: Gustav Falke
Soloist: voice
ob.2cl.bcl-str(1.1.1.1.0)
Material on hire
Piano reduction **BSS 36245/ED 2908**

Dir (1914) 2'

Text: Hinrich Hinrichs
Soloist: voice
str
Material on hire
SM

Liebeszauber (1913) 15'

Text: Friedrich Hebbel
Soloist: baritone
3(pic).2.ca.3(bcl).3(cbn)-4.3.2.1-timp.2perc-cel.hp-str
Material on hire
SM

Pantherlied 1'

Text: Gerda von Robertus
Soloist: voice
2(pic).2(ca).2.2-4.2.3.0-timp.perc-cel.hp-str
Material on hire
SM

Sternberg, Erich Walter

1881-1974

Solo Voice(s) and Instrument(s)/ Orchestra

The Raven (1953) 25'

Text: Edgar Allan Poe
Soloist: bass-baritone
3(2pic).2(ca).Ebcl.2.bcl.tsax.2.cbn-4.2.3.1-timp.perc-hp-str
Material on hire
AVV

Infoline · e-Mail
Schott Musik International
Mainz: Schott.Musik.com@T-Online.de
London: 101627.166@compuserve.com

Stockmeier, Wolfgang

b.1931

Chamber & Instrumental Works

Sonatine (1963)

arec-pno
OFB 96

Straus, Oscar

1870-1954

Orchestral Works

Serenade for Strings in G Minor, Op. 35   19'

str
Material on hire
SM

Strauss, Richard

1864-1949

Orchestral Works

Concert Overture in C Minor (1883)   13'

2.2.2.2-4.2.3.1-timp-str
Material on hire
Study score **ETP 1135**

Serenade in G Major, o. Op. AV 32 (1877)   20'

2.2.2.2-2.2.0.0-timp-str
Material on hire
SM

Symphony in D Minor

(1880)   34'

2.2.2.2-4.2.3.0-timp-str
Material on hire
SM

Strauss, Richard

b. Munich 11.6.1864,
d. Garmisch-Partenkirchen 8.9.1949

Though he was the unrivalled master of the modern orchestra and was at one time a byword for sumptuous excess, Richard Strauss, both as craftsman and as musical dramatist, was a true heir of his beloved Mozart. Fired by the example of Liszt and Wagner, he imparted a new and heightened expressive weight to instrumental music through a sequence of revolutionary symphonic poems, then composed some of the world's most oustanding operas as well. Perhaps the last composer gifted with a truly intuitive musical creativity, he spanned the entire modern history of music, in the Indian Summer of his old age composing neo-classical works that were contemporary in time with the pioneering scores of Boulez and Stockhausen.

Concertos

Romance in E Flat Major, o. Op. AV 61 (1879)   10'

Soloist: clarinet
0.2.0.2-2.0.0.0-str
Material on hire
Study score **ETP 1399** / Piano reduction **KLB 35**

Romance in F Major (1883)   12'

Soloist: cello
2.2.2.2-2.0.0.0-str
Material on hire
Study score **ETP 1399** / Parts **CB 134 (solo)**

Chamber & Instrumental Works

Arabischer Tanz, o. Op. AV 182 (1893)   2'

vn.va.vc-pno
Score and parts **ED 8458**

Festmarsch, o. Op. AV 178

(1881)   6'

vn.va.vc-pno
Score and parts **ED 8458**

Introduktion, Thema und Variationen, o. Op. AV 52

(1878)   12'

Soloist: clarinet
hn-pno
COR 14

Liebesliedchen, o. Op. AV 182 (1893)   5'

vn.va.vc-pno
Score and parts **ED 8458**

Ständchen, o. Op. AV 168

(1881)   5'

vn.va.vc-pno
Score and parts **ED 8458**

Trio No.1 A-Dur, AV 37

(1877)   14'

pno-vn.vc
ED 8443

Trio No.2 D-Dur, AV 53

(1878)   26'

pno-vn.vc
ED 8446

Variationen über "s'Deandl is harb auf mi" (1882)   7'

vn.va.vc
ED 8270

Solo Voice(s) and Instrument(s)/ Orchestra

Alphorn, o. Op. AV 29

(1876)   4'

Text: J. Kerner
Soloist: soprano
hn-pno
ED 8389

Study Scores of the Complete Stage Works

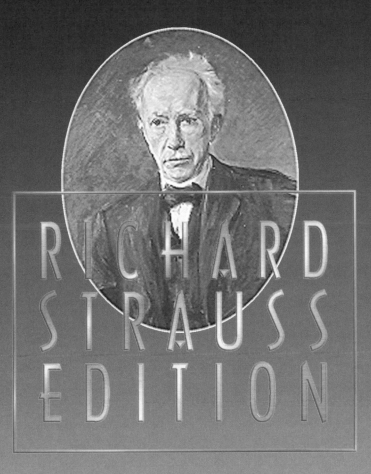

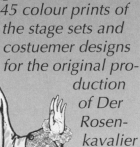

Ganymed, o. Op. AV 187

(1897) 7'

On a song by Franz Schubert (Op. 19/3)
Arranger: Richard Strauss
Soloist: voice
2.2.2.2-4.0.0.0-str
Material on hire
SM

Choral Works

Lied der Freundschaft, Op. 45/2 (1898) 4'

Text: S. Dach
Chorus: male a cappella
C 47538

Stravinsky, Igor
1882-1971

Some of the Stravinsky works listed below may not be available in your country through Schott. Please ask your local Schott representative.

Stage Works

Danses concertantes

(1941-42) 20'

Ballet
Material on hire
Study score **ED 4275**

Jeu de Cartes (1936) 24'

Ballet
Material on hire
Score **ED 56** / Study score **ETP 1392** /
Vocal score **ED 3296**

L' Oiseau de Feu (1909-10) 40'

Ballet in 2 Scenes after the Russian
Folk-Fairytale
Text: Michel Fokine
Material on hire
Score **ED 6461** / Study score **ETP 8043** /
Piano reduction **ED 3279**

L' Oiseau de Feu (1909-10) 40'

Ballet in 2 Scenes after the Russian
Folk-Fairytale
New critical edition by: Herbert Schneider
Text: Michel Fokine
Material on hire
Study score **ETP 8043**

L' Oiseau de Feu (1909-10) 40'

Ballet in 2 Scenes (reduced version, 1993)
Arranger: Henning Brauel
2(pic).2.2.2-4.2.3.1-timp.perc-pno.hp-str
Material on hire
SM

Scènes de Ballet (1944) 18'

Ballet Scenes
Material on hire
Study score **BSS 90300**

Stravinsky, Igor

b. Oranienbaum 5.(17.)6.1882,
d. New York 6.4.1971

If Schönberg supplied the intellect of twentieth-century music, Stravinsky supplied its nerves and reflexes. His return to classicism after the savagery and neo-primitivism of his earlier music influenced a generation of composers, just as the "Rite of Spring" and "Les Noces" had pushed forward the boundaries of art before the First World War. Russian-period works such as "The Firebird" have long been established as pillars of the orchestral repertoire. But compositions of the 30's and 40's, including "Dumbarton Oaks", the Violin Concerto and the Symphony in C have also acquired permanent concert-hall status.

Orchestral Works

Circus Polka (1944) 4'

Symphonic Version
pic.1.2.2.2-4.2.3.1-timp.perc-str
Material on hire
Study score **ED 4274** / Piano reduction
ED 10155

Circus Polka (1942) 4'

*fl(pic).4cl.asax.barsax-
2hn.5cnt.4tbn.2euph.2tuba-
perc-hammondorg*
Score and parts **SMC 130**

Concerto in Eb "Dumbarton Oaks" (1938) 15'

1.0.1.1-2.0.0.0-str(3.0.3.2.2)
Material on hire
Score **ED 2851** / Study score **ED 3527**/
ETP 1813

Danses concertantes

(1941-42) 20'

1.1.1.1-2.1.1.0-timp-str(6.0.4.3.2)
Material on hire
Study score **ED 4275**

Feu d'artifice, Op. 4 (1908) 4'

Fantasy
*pic.2.2(ca).3(bcl).2-6.3.3.1-timp.perc-
cel.2hp-str(16.14.12.10.8)*
Material on hire
Study score **ETP 1396/ETP 8039** /
Piano reduction **ED 962**

Jeu de Cartes (1936) 24'

Suite
*2(pic).2(ca).2.2-4.2.3.1-timp.perc-
str(12.10.8.6.6)*
Material on hire
Score **ED 56** / Study score **ED 3511** / Piano
reduction **ED 3296**

4 Norwegische Impressionen

(1942) 8'

2(pic).2(ca).2(Acl).2-4.2.2.1-timp-str
Material on hire
Study score **ED 6333**

Ode (1943) 11'

Tryptic for orchestra
3(pic).2.2.2-4.2.0.0-timp-str
Material on hire
Study score **ED 5942**

L' Oiseau de Feu (1912) 28'

Suite
*3(2pic).3.ca.3(3Dcl).bcl.3(cbn).cbn-4.3.3.1-
timp.perc-cel.pno.3hp-str(16.16.14.8.6)*
Material on hire
SM

L' Oiseau de Feu (1919) 20'

Suite
2(pic).2.2.2-4.2.3.1-timp.perc-pno.hp-str
Material on hire
Study score **ED 3467**

L' Oiseau de Feu (1945) 28'

Ballet Suite
2(pic).2.2.2-4.2.3.1-timp.perc-pno.hp-str
Material on hire
Study score **ED 73/ED 4420/ETP 1389**

L' Oiseau de Feu (1909/10/45) 28'

Arranger: Henning Brauel
2(pic).2.2.2-4.2.3.1-timp.perc-pno.hp-str
Material on hire
SM

Pas de deux (1941) 6'

after Piotr Ilyich Tschaikovskij
1.1.2.1-1.2.2.0-timp-pno-str(5.0.4.3.2)
Material on hire
Study score **ED 4409**

Scènes de Ballet (1944) 18'

Symphonic Version
2.2.2.1-2.3.3.1-timp-pno-str
Material on hire
Score **ED 8174**

Igor Stravinsky
L'Oiseau de Feu (1909-10)
Danse de 17 Suite de Kastchéi

Scherzo à la Russe (1944) 4'

pic.2.2.2.2-4.3.3.1-timp.perc-pno.hp-str
Material on hire
Score **ED 4553** / Study score **ED 4553/
ETP 8035**

Scherzo à la Russe (1944) 4'

Version for Jazz orchestra
2(pic).1.0.2asax.2tsax.barsax.0-1.3.3.1-
timp.perc-pno.hp.gtr-str
Material on hire
Score **ED 8175** / Study score **ED 8175**

Scherzo fantastique, Op. 3

(1908) 16'

(Der Bienenflug)
pic.3(pic,afl).2.ca.3(Dcl).bcl.2.cbn-
4.2.atpt..0.0-perc-cel.3hp-str
Material on hire
Study score **ED 3501/ETP 8017**

Symphony en ut (1940) 30'

pic.2.2.2.2-4.2.3.1-timp-str
Material on hire
Score **ED 3840** / Study score **ED 3536/
ETP 1511**

Symphony in 3 Movements

(1945) 24'

pic.2.2.3(bcl).2.cbn-4.3.3.1-timp.perc-
pno.hp-str
Material on hire
Score **ED 99** / Study score **ED 4075/ETP 574**

Tango (1940) 3'

3.2.2.bcl.2sax.tsax.2-2.3.3.1-perc-pno.gtr-
str
Material on hire
SM (G, A, British Commonwealth)

Tango (1953) 3'

4cl.bcl-4tpt.3tbn-gtr-str(3.0.1.1.1)
Material on hire
Study score **ED 4569 (G, A, British
Commonwealth)**

Concertos

Concerto en Ré (1931) 22'

Soloist: violin
pic.2.2.ca.Ebcl.2.3(cbn)-4.3.3(btbn).1-
timp.-str(8.8.6.4.4)
Material on hire
Score **ED 49** / Study score **ED 3504/
ETP 1815** / Piano reduction **ED 2190**

Chamber & Instrumental Works

Berceuse (1909-10) 3'

from "L' Oiseau de Feu"
pno
ED 2547

Berceuse (1909-10) 3'

from "L' Oiseau de Feu"
vn-pno
ED 2081

Berceuse (1909-10) 3'

from "L' Oiseau de Feu"
Arranger: Dushkin
vn-pno
ED 2186

Circus Polka (1942) 4'

pno
ED 4282

Circus Polka (1942) 4'

Arranger: Victor Babin
2pno
ED 4283

Circus Polka (1942) 3'

Arranger: Sol Babitz
vn-pno
ED 8113

Concerto for 2 Pianos

(1935) 20'

2pno
ED 2520

Concerto in Eb (1938) 15'

Dumbarton Oaks
2pno
ED 2791

Danse infernale, Berceuse, Finale (1909-10) 12'

from "L' Oiseau de Feu"
Arranger: Agosti
pno
ED 2378

Danses concertantes

(1941-42) 20'

Arranger: Ingolf Dahl
2pno
SM

Elegy (1946) 5'

violin/viola solo
VLB 47

Feu d'artifice (1908) 4'

pno (4hnd)
ED 962

Pastorale (1908) 4'

Lied ohne Worte
vn-ob.ca.cl.bn
ED 3313 / Piano reduction **ED 2294**

Prélude et Ronde (1909-10) 4'

from "L' Oiseau de Feu"
vn-pno
ED 2080

Ronde des Princesses

(1909-10) 4'

from "L' Oiseau de Feu"
Arranger: Agosti
pno
ED 2548

Scherzo (1909-10) 3'

from "L' Oiseau de Feu"
Arranger: Dushkin
vn-pno
ED 2250

Scherzo à la Russe (1944) 4'

2pno
ED 10646

Sonata for 2 Pianos

(1943-44) 10'

2pno
ED 4015

Tango (1940) 3'

pno
ED 4917

Tango (1940) 3'

Arranger: Victor Babin
2pno
ED 4720

Solo Voice(s)/Voice(s) and Piano/Guitar

Pastorale (1908) 4'

Lied ohne Worte
soprano-pno
ED 2295

Solo Voice(s) and Instrument(s)/ Orchestra

Pastorale (1908) 4'

Lied ohne Worte
Soloist: soprano
ob.ca.cl.bn
ED 3399

Choral Works

Babel (1944) 7'

Cantata after Genesis I, 11(1-9)
Soloist: narrator
Chorus: male
3(pic).2.2.bcl.2.cbn-4.3.3.0-timp-hp-str
Material on hire
Study score **ED 4412** / Vocal score
ED 4342-01 / Piano reduction **ED 4342**

Unterschale (1914-17) 10'

Soloist: male voice
Chorus: male
[4hn]
Score **ED 39491** / Parts **ED 39491-10** / Choral
score **C 32640**

Critical New Edition
in the Eulenburg Study Scores
IGOR STRAVINSKY

This edition is based on all currently available sources (sketches, manuscripts, first prints with corrections by the composer himself), particularly from the Paul Sacher Foundation in Basle and from the publisher's own archives.

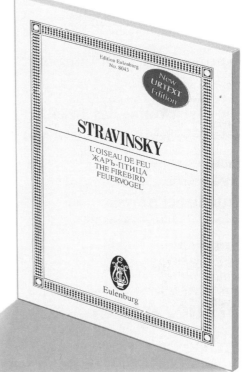

Published:

The Firebird – Ballet 1910

The publisher commissioned Dr. Herbert Schneider, professor of musicology at the Frankfurt Conservatory, to prepare a critical new edition for the performance practice on the basis of all available source materials in accordance with scientific editorial principles. The starting-point of this edition is the autograph of the ballet score written in 1909/10. Other sources are a handwritten copy by an unknown copyist with autograph entries, the correction proofs of the original edition of the score by Jurgenson, a copy of this score owned by Robert Craft, the original performance material – part of it newly discovered – of the Ballets Russes as well as the orchestral parts used by Diaghilev for the world premiere. In the course of this work, numerous parts were newly discovered in Paris. Also used by way of comparison were the autograph piano version already written before the instrumentation and all known approval copies of the composer.

- **Performance material is available for hire.**
- **Study score, Order No. ETP 8043**
- **Critical Report, Order No. ETP 8044 (in preparation)**

1997 publications:

Fireworks, Op. 4
Fantasy for large orchestra (1908)
Edited by Ulrich Mosch
Order No. ETP 8039

Scherzo à la Russe (1944)
Edited by Christoph Flamm
• **for orchestra**
Order No. ETP 8035
• **for jazz band**

Planned publications:

Pastorale (1907) / **Scherzo fantastique, Op. 3** (1908) / **Pastorale** (1927) / **Jeu de Cartes** (1936) / **Concerto in Es „Dumbarton Oaks"** (1938) / **Concerto en Ré** (1940) / **Symphony en Ut** (1940) / **Tango,** Orchestralversion for bass Clarinet (1940) / **Tango,** Version for clarinets, bass clarinet, 4 trumpets, 3 trombones, guitarre, strings (1953) / **Pas de deux** (1941) / **Dances concertantes** (1941/42) / **Scènes de ballet** (1944) / **Symphony in three movements** (1945)

Edition Eulenburg

Streul, Eberhard
b.1941

Stage Works

Das Geheimnis der Wolfsschlucht (1983)   90'
(Carl Maria von Weber). Children's Musical
Text: Eberhard Streul
Material on hire
SM

Die Leiche im Sack (1985)   100'
Opera in 1 Act
Arranger: Franz Wittenbrink
Text: Eberhard Streul
Material on hire
SM

Papageno spielt auf der Zauberflöte (1980)   90'
(W.A. Mozart). Children's Musical
Text: Eberhard Streul
Material on hire
SM

Die Sternstunde des Josef Bieder (1984-85)   full evening
for Actor/Baritone and Piano or Tape
Arranger: Syri/Schenk
Libretto **on hire**

Stunde bei Aloysia (1991)   90'
Monologue for two female singers
Text: Eberhard Streul
Material on hire
Libretto **on hire**

Stroe, Aurel
b.1932

Stage Works

Ça n'aura pas le Prix Nobel (1969)   90'
Opera in 3 Parts
Text: Paul Sterian
Material on hire
AVV

Choral Works

Musique pour "Oedipe à Colone de Sophocle" (1963)   8'
Soloist: mezzo-soprano
Chorus: male
2.2.2.0-4.3.3.0-4perc
Material on hire
AVV

Strohbach, Siegfried
b.1929

Choral Works

All that Glisters is not gold   3'
from "Seven Songs from Shakespeare's Comedies"
Text: William Shakespeare
Chorus: mixed a cappella
C 47852

Come away, Death   3'
from "Seven Songs from Shakespeare's Comedies"
Text: William Shakespeare
Chorus: mixed a cappella
C 47852

Hey, Robin, jolly Robin   3'
from "Seven Songs from Shakespeare's Comedies"
Text: William Shakespeare
Chorus: mixed a cappella
C 47850

If she be made of white and red   3'
from "Seven Songs from Shakespeare's Comedies"
Text: William Shakespeare
Chorus: mixed a cappella
C 47851

It was a Lover and his Lass   3'
from "Seven Songs from Shakespeare's Comedies"
Text: William Shakespeare
Chorus: mixed a cappella
C 47853

O Mistress mine   3'
from "Seven Songs from Shakespeare's Comedies"
Text: William Shakespeare
Chorus: mixed a cappella
C 47850

Take, o take those Lips away   3'
from "Seven Songs from Shakespeare's Comedies"
Text: William Shakespeare
Chorus: mixed a cappella
C 47851

Stürmer, Bruno
1892-1958

Orchestral Works

Tänzerische Spielmusik
[1].0.[Ebcl].2.0-2.2thn.2flhn.1/2.euph.1/2-perc
Score **FG 17** / Parts **FG 17-10**

Tanzsuite, Op. 24   10'
1.1.1.1-1.1.0.0-timp.perc-pno-str(4.4.2.2.2)
Material on hire
SM

Zeitgesichte, Op. 25   10'
1(pic).1(ca).1.0-1.1.0.0-timp.3perc-pno-str(4.4.2.2.2)
Material on hire
SM

Chamber & Instrumental Works

3 kleine Hausmusiken
(1937)   12'
vc-pno
ED 2685

Little Sonata, Op. 103   7'
pno
ED 2682

Sonatina in C (1938)   6'
vn-pno
ED 2795

Choral Works

Narren überall, Op. 90/3
(1953)   2'
Text: D.G. Morhof
Chorus: mixed/male a cappella
C 34642/38411

Subotnick, Morton

b.1933

Orchestral Works

A Desert Flowers (1989)   25'

1.0.1.1-1.1.1.1-marimb.1perc-pno-str-computer
Material on hire
EAM

Place (1979)   20'

3.3.3.3-5.3.3.1-timp.3perc-mand.cel.hp-str
Material on hire
EAM

Two Butterflies (1974)   14'

amplified orchestra: 1.2.3.2-3.3.0.1-timp.perc-hp-str
Material on hire
EAM

Concertos

Axolotl (1982)   17'

for Cello, Electronic Ghost Score & Orch
Soloist: cello
1.0.2.0-0.0.2.0-2perc-pno.hp-8vc.4db
Material on hire
EAM

Before the Butterfly (1975)   20'

Soloists: tpt.tbn-perc-hp-vn.va.vc (all amp)
2.2.2.2-3.2.2.1-timp.3perc-cel-str
Material on hire
EAM

The Double Life of Amphibians (1984)   90'

Soloists: 2 male voices, female voice, dancer
chamber orch-elec
Material on hire
EAM

In Two Worlds (1987)   35'

Saxophone Concerto
Soloist: saxophone
chamber orch-computer
Material on hire
EAM

Chamber & Instrumental Works

After the Butterfly (1979)   18'

Soloists: trumpet, electronic ghost score
2cl-2tbn-2vc-perc
Material on hire
EAM

Subotnick, Morton

b. Los Angeles 14.4.1933

Enlarging the relationship between live performers and technology has been a longterm project for Subotnick since his early days as a pioneer of electronic music. In recent pieces such as the opera "Jacob's Room" and "The Key to Songs", an electronic media opera collaboration with video artist Ed Emshwiller, computerized sound generation and specially designed "intelligent" software offer highly sophisticated forms of interaction that make him one of the international leaders in this field. In addition to writing for electronic media, Subotnick has also composed extensively for the orchestra. He tours widely as a composer/performer, and is much in demand as a lecturer.

And the Butterflies begin to sing (1988)   35'

2vn.va.vc.db-keybd.computer
Material on hire
EAM

Ascent into Air (1981)   26'

2vc-cl.bcl-tbn.btbn-4perc-2pno-computer
Material on hire
EAM

The First Dream of Light (1980)   18'

tuba solo-electric ghost score
Material on hire
EAM

A Fluttering of Wings (1982)   25'

str qrt-[electric ghost score]
Material on hire
EAM

The Key to Songs (1985)   25'

2pno-2perc-va.vc-electric sounds
Material on hire
EAM

Liquid Strata (1977)   27'

pno-electric ghost score
Material on hire
EAM

Mandolin (1961-63)   14'

va-tape-film
Material on hire
EAM

Parallel Lines (1978)   16'

Soloists: piccolo, electronic ghost score
ob/ca.cl/bcl-tpt.tbn-hp-2perc-va.vc
Material on hire
EAM

Passages of the Beast (1978) 18'

cl-electric ghost score
Material on hire
EAM

Play! No.3 (1965)   2'

pno/mime-tape-film
Material on hire
EAM

Ten (1963/76)   12'

fl.ob-tpt.tbn-3perc-pno-va.db
Material on hire
EAM

Trembling (1983)   17'

vn-pno-tape-electric ghost score
Material on hire
EAM

Solo Voice(s) and Instrument(s)/ Orchestra

Hungers (1986)   90'

Soloist: voice
keybd-mallets-vc-dancer-video.lights-computer
Material on hire
EAM

The Last Dream of the Beast (1979)   17'

Soloist: soprano
vc ensemble-tape-ghost electronics
Material on hire
EAM

2 Life Histories (1977)   24'

Text: Greek/Old Testament
Soloist: male voice
cl-elec ghost score
Material on hire
EAM

Play! No.4 (1965)   17'

Soloist: soprano
vib-vc-4'game players'-2'game conductors'-2films
Material on hire
EAM

Sugár, Rezsö

1919-1988

Orchestral Works

6 Small Pieces   8'

str(5vnI.5vnII.4vnIII.3vc.3db)
Score **CON 144** / Parts **CON 144-70**

Concertos

Variations   9'

Soloist: violin
pno-str(5vnI.5vnII.4vnIII.3vc.3db)
Score **CON 145** / Parts **CON 145-01**
(solo)/CON 145-70

Sutermeister, Heinrich

1910-1995

Stage Works

Das Dorf unter dem Gletscher (1937)   70'

Ballet
Material on hire
SM

Die Füße im Feuer und Fingerhütchen (1949)   20'

2 Dramatic Scenes
Text: Conrad Ferdinand Meyer
Material on hire
SM

Das Gespenst von Canterville (1962-63)   60'

Spiel with Music for Television
Text: Heinrich Sutermeister after Oscar Wilde
Material on hire
SM

Madame Bovary

(1967)   full evening

Opera in 1 Prologue and 2 Acts
Text: Heinrich Sutermeister after Flaubert
Material on hire
Vocal score **ED 5835** / Libretto **BN 3760-50**

Sutermeister, Heinrich

b. Feuerthalen, canton of Schaffhausen 12.8.1910, d. Morges, canton of Waadt 16.3.1995

The bulk of Sutermeister's output consists of stage works, indebted to the example of Orff in their simplicity and directness, yet also displaying a personal dramatic formula in their attention to Italian theatrical models. Concertos and chamber music complement the operatic achievement. Sutermeister's choral pieces are enduringly popular.

Max und Moritz (1951)   25'

Ballet
Text: After Wilhelm Busch
Material on hire
Score **ED 4211** / Vocal score **ED 4211-01**

Niobe (1946)   full evevning

Monodrama in 2 Acts
Text: Peter Sutermeister
Material on hire
Libretto **BN 3761-30**

Raskolnikoff (1945-47)   140'

Opera in 2 Acts
Text: Peter Sutermeister after Fjodor M. Dostojevski
Material on hire
Vocal score **ED 3980** / Libretto **BN 3762-01**

Le Roi Bérenger (1981-83)

Prologue and 18 Scenes
Text: Heinrich Sutermeister after Eugène Ionesco
Material on hire
SM

Romeo and Juliet (1940)   105'

Opera in 2 Acts
Text: Heinrich Sutermeister after William Shakespeare
Material on hire
Piano reduction **ED 3978** / Libretto **BN 3763-10**

Der rote Stiefel (1951)   full evening

Musical Scene in 2 Parts
Text: Heinrich Sutermeister after Wilhelm Hauff
Material on hire
Libretto **BN 3765-60**

Die schwarze Spinne (1936) 55'

Opera in 1 Act
Text: Albert Roesler after Jeremias Gotthelf
Material on hire
Vocal score **ED 3978**

Seraphine (Die stumme Apothekerin) (1959)   55'

Opera buffa in 1 Act
Text: Heinrich Sutermeister after Rabelais
Material on hire
Libretto **BN 3764-80**

Titus Feuerfuchs oder Liebe, Tücke und Perücke

(1958)   full evening

Opera in 2 Acts
Text: Heinrich Sutermeister after Johann Nestroy
Material on hire
Vocal score **ED 4936** / Libretto **BN 3766-40**

Die Zauberinsel

(1942)   full evening

Opera in 1 Prelude and 2 Acts
Text: Heinrich Sutermeister after William Shakespeare
Material on hire
SM

Orchestral Works

Aubade pour Morges (1979) 11'

2.2.2.2-2.2.0.0-str
Material on hire
SM

Divertimento No.1 (1936)   25'

str
Material on hire
Study score **ED 5004**

Divertimento No.2 (1959-60) 25'

2(pic).2.2.2-2.2.0.0-timp.2perc-pno-str
Material on hire
Study score **ED 5017**

Marche fantasque (1950)   15'

3(2pic).2.ca.2.bcl.2.cbn-4.3.3.1-timp.2perc-1/2pno-str
Material on hire
Study score **ED 4406**

Modeste Mignon (1974)   8'

after a Waltz by Honoré de Balzac
2(pic).2.2.2(cbn)-2.0.0.0
Score **ED 6500** / Parts **ED 6500-10**

Poème funèbre - En mémoire de Paul Hindemith (1965) 7'

str
Material on hire
SM

Romeo and Juliet - Suite

(1940) 18'

3(pic).2(ca).2(bcl).2(cbn)-4.3.3.1-
timp.3perc-cel.pno.hp-str
Material on hire
SM

Sérénade pour Montreux

(1970) 13'

0.2.0.0-2.0.0.0-str
Material on hire
Study score **ED 6383**

Concertos

Cello Concerto No.1

(1954-55) 30'

Soloist: cello
pic.2.2.ca.2.bcl.2.cbn-4.3.3.1-timp.2perc-
hp-str
Material on hire
Piano reduction **ED 4429**

Cello Concerto No.2 (1971) 30'

Soloist: cello
2(pic).2.2.2-2.2.0.0-perc-str(9.8.6.5.4)
Material on hire
Piano reduction **ED 6153**

Clarinet Concerto (1975) 22'

Soloist: clarinet
2(pic).2(ca).0.2(cbn)-2.2.0.0-timp.perc-
str(10.8.6.5-6.4-5)
Material on hire
Piano reduction **KLB 19**

Concertino (1932) 13'

Soloist: piano
cl.bn-hn.tpt.ttbn-pno
Material on sale
Score and parts **ED 8079**

Piano Concerto No.1 (1943) 36'

Soloist: piano
3(2pic).2(ca).2(bcl).2(cbn)-2.2.0.0-
timp.2perc-str
Material on hire
Piano reduction **ED 3669**

Piano Concerto No.2 (1953) 26'

Soloist: piano
2(pic).2.2.2-2.2.0.0-timp-str
Material on hire
Piano reduction **ED 4548**

Piano Concerto No.3

(1961-62) 33'

Soloist: piano
3(2pic).2.ca.2.bcl.2.cbn-4.3.3.1-timp.2perc-
hp-str
Material on hire
Piano reduction **ED 4819**

Quadrifoglio (1976-77) 26'

Soloists: flute, oboe, clarinet, bassoon
2(pic).2(ca).Ebcl.1.2(cbn)-4.3.3.1-
timp.2perc-hp-str
Material on hire
Study score **ED 6787**

Chamber & Instrumental Works

Bergsommer (1941) 14'

8 little Pieces
pno
ED 2881

Capriccio (1947) 5'

clarinet solo
ED 10401

Gavotte de Concert (1950) 5'

tpt-pno
TR 18

Hommage à Arthur Honegger (1955) 10'

pno
ED 5755

Serenade No.1 (1949) 12'

2cl.bn-tpt
Material on hire
Score **ED 4573**

Serenade No.2 (1961) 14'

fl.ob.cl.bn-hn.tpt
Score **ED 5218** / Parts **ED 5184**

Sonatina in Eb (1948) 13'

pno
ED 4119

String Quartet No. 3 (1933) 23'

Material on sale
SM

Winterferien 11'

pno
ED 6821

12 zweistimmige Inventionen

(1932) 23'

pno
ED 8004

Solo Voice(s)/Voice(s) and Piano/Guitar

4 Lieder (1945)

Text: various
high voice-pno
ED 4017

4 Lieder (1967)

Text: Swiss Troubadors
baritone-pno
ED 6119

Max und Moritz (1953) 25'

Text: Wilhelm Busch
vocal qrt-pno (4hnd)
Vocal score **ED 4211**

The Seventieth and Eighty Sixth Psalm (1947) 10'

'Eile, Gott mich zu erretten'
low voice-org
ED 4049

Solo Voice(s) and Instrument(s)/ Orchestra

Die Alpen (1948) 23'

Fantasy on Swiss Folk Songs
Text: Albrecht von Haller
Soloist: speaker
2(pic).2(ca).2(bcl).2(cbn)-4.2.3.1-
timp.2perc-str
Material on hire
SM

Consolatio philosophiae

(1977) 18'

Scène dramatique
Text: Boetius
Soloist: high voice
3(pic).3(ca).3(bcl).3(cbn)-4.3.3.1-
timp.3perc-hp-str
Material on hire
Vocal score **ED 6817**

7 Liebesbriefe (1947) 22'

Text: various
Soloist: tenor
2(pic).2(ca).2.2(cbn)-4.2.3.0-timp.2perc-
cel.pno.hpd/harm.hp-str
Material on hire
SM

6 Liebesbriefe (1980) 20'

Text: various
Soloist: soprano
2(pic).2.2.2-4.2.0.0-timp.perc-hpd.hp-str
Material on hire
Vocal score **ED 6913**

4 Lieder (1967)

Soloist: baritone
fl.ob.bn-vn-hpd
Material on hire
ED 5968

Romeo and Juliet - Juliet's Aria (1940) 4'

"Ich reise weit"
Soloist: soprano
3(2pic).1.ca.2(Ebcl,bcl).1.cbn-4.3.3.1-
timp.2perc-str
Material on hire
SM

Choral Works

Dem Allgegenwärtigen - Cantata No.3 (1957-58) 35'

after the Ode of the same title and the"Great Hallelujah"
Text: Friedrich Gottlieb Klopstock
Soloists: soprano, baritone, bass
Chorus: mixed
2(2pic).2(ca).2(bcl).2(cbn)-4.3.3.1-timp.2perc-pno.hp-str
Material on hire
Vocal score **ED 4790-01** / Piano reduction **ED 4790**

2 Barocklieder (1953) 8'

Text: various
Soloists: vocal quartet
Chorus: mixed a cappella
C 39028

Cantata No.1 - "Andreas Gryphius" (1935-36) 25'

Seven Choruses
Text: Andreas Gryphius
Chorus: mixed a cappella
C 34999

Cantata No.2 (1944) 30'

Text: various
Soloist: alto
Chorus: mixed
2pno
Score **ED 2560** / Vocal score **ED 2560-01**

3 Choruses (1960) 10'

Text: Joachim Ringelnatz
Chorus: female/children's
pno
Score **ED 6444** / Choral score **ED 6444-01**

Ecclesia (1973-74) 20'

Cantata
Text: Pierre-Alain Tâsche/Heinrich Sutermeister
Soloists: soprano, bass
Chorus: mixed
3(pic).2.ca.2.bcl.2.cbn-4.3.3.1-timp.2perc-hp.org-str
Score **ED 6627** / Parts **ED 6628** / Vocal score **ED 6363-10** / Piano reduction **ED 6363**

Erkennen und Schaffen - Cantata No.6 (1963) 15'

(Croire et Créer)
Text: Friedrich von Schiller
Soloists: soprano, baritone
Chorus: mixed
2(pic).2.2.2(cbn)-2.3.2.0-timp.2perc-cel(pno).hp-str
Material on hire
Vocal score **ED 5294-01** / Piano reduction **ED 5294**

Gloria (1988) 14'

Soloist: soprano
Chorus: mixed (8 prt)
2hn.2tpt.2tbn-timp.perc-str
Score **ED 7699** / Parts **ED 7699-50** / Vocal score **ED 7699-01** / Piano reduction **ED 7699-10**

Gratias agimus tibi (1988) 4'

from the "Gloria"
Text: Latin
Chorus: male a cappella
C 47593

Das Hohelied - Cantata No.4 (1960) 11'

Text: Christian Morgenstern
Soloists: soprano, baritone
Chorus: mixed
2(pic).2(ca).2(bcl).2-4.3.3.1-timp.2perc-cel.hp-str
Material on hire
Vocal score **ED 5161-01** / Piano reduction **ED 5161**

Der Kaiser von China (1969) 5'

Text: Hugo von Hofmannsthal
Chorus: male a cappella
C 42733

Die Landsknechte (1968) 2'

from "2 Männerchöre"
Chorus: male a cappella
C 42329

3 Lieder (1961) 7'

Text: Georg Britting
Chorus: male a cappella
Score **C 40699** / Parts **C 40700-01/-02 (chorus)**

2 Madrigals (1951) 6'

from the opera "Der rote Stiefel"
Text: P. Meylan
Chorus: mixed a cappella
C 40980

Mass in Eb (1948)

Chorus: mixed a cappella
C 37559

Missa da Requiem (1957) 45'

Text: Latin
Soloists: soprano, baritone/bass
Chorus: mixed
3(pic).2.ca.2.bcl.3(cbn)-4.3.3.1-timp-pno.hp-str
Material on hire
Study score **ED 5012** / Vocal score **ED 4516**

Ode auprès des Roseaux (1987) 5'

Chorus: male a cappella
C 46375

Omnia ad unum - Cantata No.8 (1965-66) 17'

Text: Gottfried Wilhelm Leibnitz/Albrecht von Haller
Soloist: baritone
Chorus: mixed
pic.2.2.ca.2.bcl.2.cbn-4.3.3.1-timp.2perc-cel.pno.hp-str
Material on hire
Vocal score **ED 5762**

Der Papagei aus Kuba - Cantata No.5 (1961) 34'

Seven Tales after La Fontaine and Friedrich von Hagedorn
Text: Heinrich Sutermeister
Chorus: mixed
1(pic).1(ca).1(bcl).1-1.1.0.0-timp.perc-pno/hpd-str
Material on hire
Vocal score **ED 5293-01** / Piano reduction **ED 5293**

Schilflieder (1968) 5'

from "2 Männerchöre"
Text: Nikolaus Lenau
Chorus: male a cappella
Score **C 42327** / Parts **C 42328-01/-02 (chorus)**

Sonnenhymne des Echnaton - Cantata No.7 (1965) 11'

"Anbetung dem Gotte"
Text: Heinrich Sutermeister
Chorus: male
2hn.3tpt.2tbn.tuba-timp.perc-pno
Material on hire
Vocal score **ED 5761-01** / Piano reduction **ED 5761**

Les Soudards

Text: J.S. Curtet
Chorus: male a cappella
Vocal score **C 42349-01**

Te Deum 1975 (1974) 24'

Soloist: soprano
Chorus: mixed
pic.2.2.ca.2.bcl.2.cbn-4.3.3.1-timp.perc-hp.org-str(6.5.4.4.3)
Material on hire
SM

Szelényi, István
1904-1972

Orchestral Works

Heitere Suite 15'

str
Score **CON 146** / Parts **CON 146-70**

Chamber & Instrumental Works

Chamber Music

2tpt.2hn.2bn
Score and parts **ED 6039**

Colorit

pno (4hnd)
ED 8465

Duos and Sonatine
2vn
VLB 30

Improvisation (1947) 2'
vn/fl-pno
ED 09767

Kinderwelt auf vier Saiten
vn-pno
ED 5771

Little Suite
4violins (chor/soli)
Score **CON 148** / Parts **CON 148-70/-71**

Musikalisches Bilderbuch
pno
ED 5770

Nocturne 6'
pno
ED 8406

Piano Sonata (1970) 14'
pno (4hnd)
ED 8577

Sinfonietta a tre per violini
3vn (soli/chor)
Score **CON 147** / Parts **CON 146-70**

Suite
2tpt.2tbn
Score and parts **BLK 312**

Suite
2bn
FAG 9 (Co-prod: Edition Musica Budapest)

Tambourin
2 Suites
pno/hpd-perc-[gtr]-str
Score **CON 149** / Parts **CON 149-50/-60**

Tajcevic, Marko
b.1900

Orchestral Works

7 Balkantänze (1927) 14'
2(pic).2.ca.2.3-4.2.3.0-timp.perc-cel.hp-str
Material on hire
Piano reduction **ED 6256**

Chamber & Instrumental Works

Balkantänze (1957) 9'
pno
ED 4930

Takahashi, Yuji
b.1938

Chamber & Instrumental Works

Ji(t) (1978) 10'
fl-pno
SJ 1039

Sieben Rosen hat ein Strauch
(1979) 7'
violin solo
SJ 1003

Takemitsu, Toru
1930-1996

Orchestral Works

Archipelago S. (1993) 14'
for 21 players
1(afl).1(ob d'am).2.1-2.1.2.0-2perc-cel.hp-str(2.0.2.2.1)
Material on hire
Study score **SJ 1084**

Day Signal (1987) 3'
- Signals from Heaven I -
2hn.pictpt.4tpt.4tbn.tuba
Material on hire
SJ

Takemitsu, Toru

b. Tokyo 8.10.1930, d. Tokyo 20.2.1996

As a Japanese composer spanning East and West in a way inconceivable earlier this century Toru Takemitsu is truly a child of his time. Versed in Western music, yet freed by the challenge of modernism from imitating classical models in the manner of earlier oriental composers, he created an inimitable style reflecting the pursuit of nature and number symbolism. A steady flow of commissions from leading international orchestras is testament of his legendary ear for the most subtle balance of colour and texture, and for the creation of improvisatory forms having the spontaneity and allusiveness of dream. Piano works and ensemble pieces bear the same hallmark of immaculately placed sonorities. Owing allegiance to no school, and creating none of his own, he remains a unique figure in world music.

Dream/Window (1985) 15'

3(2pic,afl).3(ca).3(bcl).3(cbn)-4.3.3.0-4perc-str(24.0.12.8.8)-fl.cl-cel.2hp.gtr-str qrt
Material on hire
Study score **SJ 1044**

Dreamtime (1981) 14'

3(2pic,afl).3(ca).3(bcl).2.cbn-4.3.3.1-3perc-cel.2hp-str(16.14.12.10.8)
Material on hire
Study score **SJ 1027**

3 Film Scores (1994) 12'

Transcription for String Orchestra of his Music for Films
1. Music of Training and Rest (from Jose Torres)
2. Funeral Music (from Black Rain)
3. Waltz (from Face of Another)
str
Material on hire
SJ

How slow the Wind (1991) 11'

1.pic(afl).2(ca).2(bcl).2(cbn)-2.0.0.0-2perc-pno(cel).hp-str(8.6.4.4.2)
Material on hire
Study score **SJ 1083**

In an Autumn Garden

(1973) 16'

4th part of complete version
Gagaku orchestra
Material on hire
SJ

In an Autumn Garden

(1979) 45'

Complete Version
Gagaku orchestra
Material on hire
SJ

Night Signal (1987) 3'

Signals from Heaven II
4hn.cnt.2tpt.3tbn.tuba
Material on hire
SJ

Rain Coming (1982) 10'

1(afl).1.1.1-1.1.1.0-perc-pno(cel)-str(1.1.1.1.1)
Material on hire
Study score **SJ 1012**

Spirit Garden (1994) 15'

3(pic,afl).3(ob d'am,ca).3(Ebcl,bcl).sax.2.cbn-4.3.3.0-5perc-2hp.cel.pno-str(14.12.10.8.6)
Material on hire
SJ

Star-Isle (1982) 6'

3(pic,afl).3(ca).3(Ebcl,bcl).2.cbn-4.cnt.3.3.1-4perc-cel.2hp-str(16.14.12.10.8)
Material on hire
Study score **SJ 1035**

Tree Line (1988) 12'

1(afl).1.2(bcl).1(cbn)-2.1.1.0-2perc-pno(cel).hp-str(1.1.1.1.1)
Material on hire
Study score **SJ 1058**

Twill by Twilight (1988) 12'

- In Memory of Morton Feldman -
4(2pic,2afl).3.(ca)4(Ebcl,bcl).3(cbn)-4.pictpt.3.3.1-5perc-cel.pno.2hp-str(16.14.12.10.8)
Material on hire
Study score **SJ 1053**

Visions (1990) 13'

4(2pic,afl,bfl).3(ob d'am,ca).3(Ebcl,bcl).cbcl.3(cbn)-4.3.btpt.3.0-4perc-cel.pno.2hp-str(16.14.12.10.8)
Material on hire
Study score **SJ 1073**

A Way a Lone II (1981) 14'

str
Material on hire
Study score **SJ 1026**

Concertos

Ceremonial (1992) 8'

An Autumn Ode
Soloist: shô
3(pic).3.3.bcl.3-4.3.3.0-3perc-cel.hp-str(14.12.10.8.6)
Material on hire
SJ

Fantasma/Cantos (1991) 18'

Soloist: clarinet
3(pic,afl).3(ob d'am,ca).3(Ebcl,bcl).cbcl.2cbn-4.3.3.0-4perc-cel.hp-str(14.12.10.8.6)
Material on hire
Study score **SJ 1080**

Fantasma/Cantos II (1994) 11'

Soloist: trombone
2(pic,afl).2(ob d'am,ca).2(bcl).2(cbn)-3.1.0.0-2perc-hp.cel-str(6.6.4.4.2)
Material on hire
SJ

Far calls. Coming, far!

(1980) 15'

Soloist: violin
3(pic,afl).3(ca).4(Ebcl,bcl).2.cbn-4.3.2.1-timp.4perc-cel.2hp-str(16.14.12.10.8)
Material on hire
Study score **SJ 1005**

From me flows what you call Time (1990) 31'

Soloists: 5 percussionists
3(2pic,afl).3(ob d'am,ca).4(Ebcl.bcl.cbcl).3(cbn)-4.3.3.0-cel.2hp-str(14.12.10.8.6)
Material on hire
SJ

Gémeaux (1971-86) 30'

for two orchestras and two conductors
Soloists: oboe, trombone
Orchestra I:
2(2pic,afl).1(ca).2(Ebcl,bcl,cbcl).2(cbn)-3.2.2.0-3perc-cel.hp.mant-str(12.0.6.5.4)
Orchestra II:
2(pic,afl).0.2(Ebcl,bcl).2(cbn)-3.2.2.0-3perc-pno.hp.gtr-str(12.0.6.5.4)
Material on hire
SJ

I hear the Water Dreaming

(1987) 11'

Soloist: flute
2(pic,afl).2(ca).2(bcl).2(cbn)-2.3.2.0-3perc-cel.2hp-str(14.12.10.8.6)
Material on hire
Study score **SJ 1052**

Nostalghia (1987) 11'

- In Memory of Andrei Tarkovskij -
Soloist: violin
str(8.6.4.4.2)
Material on hire
Study score **SJ 1045**

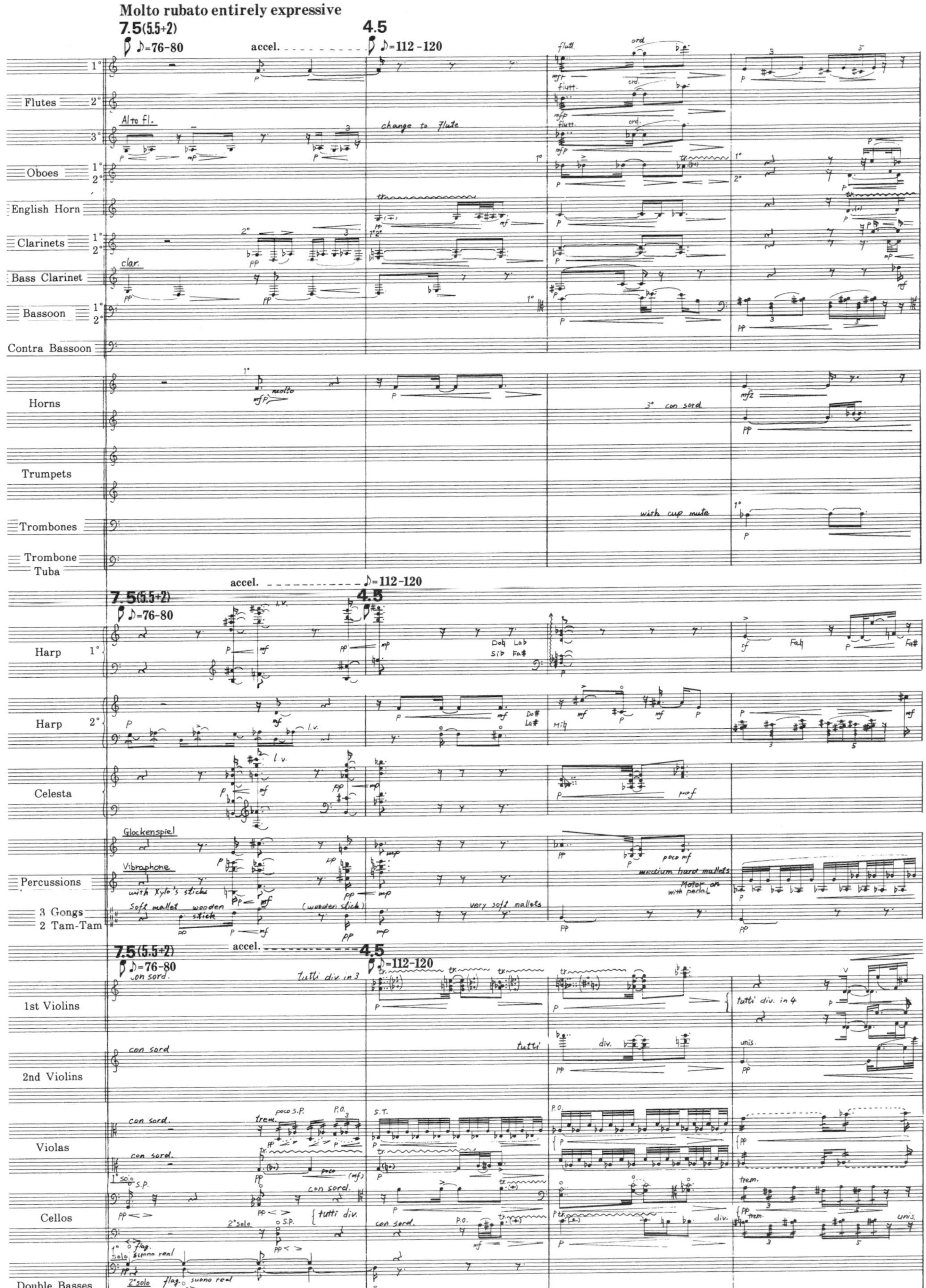

Toru Takemitsu
Dreamtime for Orchestra (1981)
beginning

Orion and Pleiades (1984) 26'

Soloist: cello
*pic.2(afl).2(ca).ob d'am.3(Ebcl,bcl).3(cbn)-
4.3.3.1-4perc-cel.2hp-str(14.12.10.8.6)*
Material on hire
Study score **SJ 1030**

Quotation of Dream (1991) 17'

- Say sea, take me! -
Soloists: 2 pianos
*3(pic,afl).3(ca).3(pic,bcl).3(cbn)-4.3.3.0-
4perc-cel.hp-str(12.12.10.8.6)*
Material on hire
SJ

riverrun (1984) 14'

Soloist: piano
*3(pic,afl).3(ca).3(Ebcl).cbcl.3(cbn)-
4.2.Dtpt.3.0-4perc-cel.2hp-str(14.12.10.8.6)*
Material on hire
Study score **SJ 1040**

Scene (1959) 5'

Soloist: cello
str(10.8.6.6.4/8.6.4.4.2)
Material on hire
SJ

Spectral Canticle (1995) 15'

Soloists: violin, guitar
*3(pic,afl).3(ca).3.bcl.ssax.3(cbn)-4.3.3.0-
4perc-cel.hp-str(14.12.10.8.6)*
Material on hire
SJ

A String around Autumn (1989) 18'

Soloist: viola
*3(pic,afl).3(ob d'am,ca).3(Ebcl,bcl).
cbcl.2.cbn-4.3.3.0-4perc-pno(cel).2hp-
str(14.12.10.8.6)*
Material on hire
Study score **SJ 1064**

To the Edge of Dream (1983) 13'

Soloist: guitar
*3(2pic).3(ca).3(bcl)3(cbn)-4.2.3.0-4perc-
cel.2hp-str(14.12.10.8.6)*
Material on hire
Study score **SJ 1022**

Toward the Sea II (1981) 15'

Soloists: alto flute, harp
str
Material on hire
Study score **SJ 1046**

Vers, l'arc-en-ciel, Palma (1984) 15'

Soloists: guitar, oboe d'amore
*3(pic,afl).3(ca).3(Ebcl,bcl).3(cbn)-4.3.3.0-
4perc-cel.2hp-str(14.12.10.8.6)*
Material on hire
Study score **SJ 1054**

Chamber & Instrumental Works

Air (1995) 7'

flute solo
SJ 1096

All in Twilight (1987) 12'

guitar solo
SJ 1051

And then I knew 'twas Wind (1992) 13'

fl-va-hp
SJ 1071

Bad Boy (1961/93) 3'

2gtr
SJ 1074

Between Tides (1993) 18'

vn.vc-pno
SJ 1091

A Bird came down the Walk (1994) 5'

va-pno
SJ 1092

Distance de Fée (1951/89) 8'

vn-pno
SJ 1050

Entre-temps (1986) 11'

ob-str qrt
SJ 1038

Equinox (1993) 5'

guitar solo
SJ 1090

Le Fils des Étoiles (1992) 5'

Prélude du 1er Acte "La vocation"
Arranger: Toru Takemitsu after a solo
pianowork by Erik Satie
fl-hp
SJ 1067

From far beyond Chrysanthemums and November Fog (1983) 8'

vn-pno
SJ 1014

Herbstlied (1993) 4'

Transcription of a Work by Peter Iljich
Tschaikowsky
Arranger: Toru Takemitsu
cl-str qrt
Material on hire
SJ

In the Woods (1995) 14'

Three Pieces
guitar solo
SJ

Itinerant (1989) 6'

- In Memory of Isamu Noguchi -
flute solo
SJ 1055

Litany (1950/89) 10'

- In Memory of Michael Vyner -. Re-com-
position of "Lento in due movimenti"
pno
SJ 1057

Orion (1984) 12'

vc-pno
SJ 1019

Paths (1994) 5'

- In Memoriam Witold Lutoslawski -
trumpet solo
SJ 1085

Rain Dreaming (1986) 7'

hpd
SJ 1032

Rain Spell (1982) 10'

fl(afl).cl-pno.hp.vib
SJ 1011

Rain Tree (1981) 12'

3perc/3keybd
SJ 1006

Rain Tree Sketch (1982) 3'

pno
SJ 1010

Rain Tree Sketch II (1992) 5'

- In Memoriam Olivier Messiaen -
pno
SJ 1072

Rocking Mirror Daybreak (1983) 13'

2vn
SJ 1017

Toward the Sea (1981) 13'

afl-gtr
SJ 1007

Toward the Sea III (1989) 12'

afl-hp
SJ 1049

A Way a Lone (1981) 13'

str qrt
SJ 1008

Les yeux clos II (1988) 7'

pno
SJ 1056

Solo Voice(s) and Instrument(s)/ Orchestra

Family Tree (1992)   25'

"Musical Verses for Young People".
Text: Shuntaro Tanikawa
Soloist: narrator
3(pic,afl).2(ca).4(bcl).3(cbn)-4.3.3.0-3perc-
hp.cel.acc-str(14.12.10.8.6)
Material on hire
SJ

Choral Works

Grass (1982)   5'

Text: Shuntaro Tanikawa (English)
Chorus: male a cappella
SJ 1009

Handmade Proverbs (1987)   5'

4 pop songs
Text: Shuzo Takiguchi (English)
Chorus: 6 male voices a cappella
SJ 1041

My Way of Life (1990)   17'

- In Memory of Michael Vyner -
Text: Ryuichi Tamura (English)
Soloist: baritone
Chorus: mixed
3(pic,afl).2(ob d'am).3(Ebcl,bcl).2(cbn)-
4.3.3.0-4perc-cel.hp-str(14.12.10.8.6)
Material on hire
SJ

Songs I (1979-92)   21'

Text: various
Chorus: mixed a cappella
SJ 1070

Songs II (1979-92)   21'

Text: various
Chorus: mixed a cappella
SJ 1081

Wind Horse (1961-66)   20'

Text: Kuniharu Akiyama (Japanese)
Chorus: mixed
SJ 1082

Electronic Works

A Minneapolis Garden

(1986)   16'

tape
Material on hire
SJ

The Sea is Still (1986)   20'

tape
Material on hire
SJ

Sky, Horse and Death (1958)   4'

magnetic tape
Material on hire
SJ

Static Relief (1955)   7'

magnetic tape
Material on hire
SJ

Wavelength (1984-)   27'

*2percussion players-2dancers-video instal-
lation*
Material on hire
SJ

Tardos, Béla

1910-1966

Chamber & Instrumental Works

Divertimento

fl.ob.cl.bn
Score and parts **BKL 309**

Tcherepnin, Alexander Nikolajevich

1899-1977

Orchestral Works

Georgiana, Op. 92   17'

2.2.2.2-4.2.3.1-timp.perc-str
Material on hire
Study score **ETP 1310**

Musica Sacra, Op. 36   9'

Arrangement of the String Quartet No. 1,
op. 36
str
Material on hire
SM

Concertos

Concerto da Camera in D Major, Op. 33 (1924)   12'

Soloists: flute, violin
2cnt.2hn-timp-str qnt
Material on hire
Piano reduction **ED 3111**

Piano Concerto No.3, Op. 48

(1932)   17'

Soloist: piano
2.2.2.2-4.2.3.1-timp.perc-str
Material on hire
SM

Chamber & Instrumental Works

Clarinet Sonata (1939)   4'

In one Movement
cl-pno
KLB 22

Concert Studies, Op. 52

(1934-36)   18'

pno
ED 4277 (-81)

String Quartet No.1, Op. 36

(1922)   5'

Parts **ED 3129**

Tcherepnin, Iwan

1873-1945

Chamber & Instrumental Works

9 Wheelwinds

2fl.afl.ob.ca.cl.bcl.bn
Score **AV 112** / Parts **AV 113**

Thuille, Ludwig

1861-1907

Stage Works

Gugeline (1901)   full evening

Musical Scene in 5 Acts
Text: Otto Julius Bierbaum
Material on hire
SM

Lobetanz (1898)   full evening

Musical Scene in 3 Acts
Text: Otto Julius Bierbaum
Material on hire
SM

Tippett, Michael
b.1905

Stage Works

The Ice Break (1973-76) 70'
Opera in 3 Acts
Text: Michael Tippett
Material on hire
Vocal score **ED 11253** / Libretto **ED 11253-01/-02**

King Priam (1958-61) 125'
Opera in 3 Acts
Text: Michael Tippett
Material on hire
Vocal score **ED 10787** / Libretto **ED 10787-10**

The Knot Garden (1966-70) 80'
Opera in 3 Acts
Text: Michael Tippett
Material on hire
Vocal score **ED 11075** / Libretto **ED 11075-10**

The Midsummer Marriage
(1947-52) 150'
Opera in 3 Acts
Text: Michael Tippett
Material on hire
Study score **ED 11158** / Vocal score
ED 10778-01 / Libretto **ED 10778-11**

New Year (1985-88) 102'
Opera in 3 Acts
Text: Michael Tippett
Material on hire
Study score **ED 12369** / Vocal score **ED 12333** /
Libretto **ED 12333-01**

Orchestral Works

Concerto for Double String Orchestra (1938-39) 23'
minimum per orch: (4.4.4.4.2)
Material on hire
Score **ED 11106** / Study score **ETP 1331**

Concerto for Orchestra
(1962-63) 31'
2.1.ca.1.bcl.1.cbn-3.2.2.1-timp.3perc-pno.hp-str(min: 6.0.4.5.4)
Material on hire
Study score **ED 10844**

Divertimento on "Sellinger's Round" (1953-54) 16'
1.1.1.1-1.1.0.0-str
Material on hire
Study score **ED 10307**

Fanfare No.5 (1987) 2'
from "The Mask of Time"
Arranger: Meirion Bowen
4hn.4tpt.2tbn.btbn.tuba-perc
Score and parts **ED 12489**

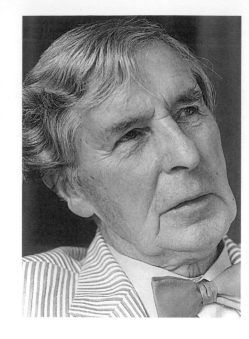

Tippett, Sir Michael

b. London 2.1.1905

All Michael Tippett's music is concerned with the dynamic interaction of opposites, and in choral and operatic works, with the tensions between art and science, the individual and society, dream and reality. A unique fusion of madrigalian counterpoint and Beethovenian sonata archetypes formed the substance of his first mature works such as the Double Concerto and the Corelli Fantasia. However, with his second opera "King Priam", and compositions thereafter, he explored a more block-like idiom of mosiaic constructions, though often involving a synthesis with his earlier style. The essence of his music and its message is a compassionate humanism, expressed most fully in his wartime oratorio "A Child of Our Time" and the choral-orchestral "The Mask of Time".

Fantasia Concertante on a Theme of Corelli (1953) 16'
str(concertino: 2vn.vc (min players): 6.0.2.3.2)
Material on hire
Study score **ETP 1395**

Festal Brass with Blues
(1983) 11'
brass band
ED 12222 / Study score **ED 12221**

Little Music (1946) 10'
str(min: 4.4.2.2.1)
Material on hire
Score **ED 11107** / Study score **ETP 1332**

New Year Suite (1989) 30'
3.2.ca.2.bcl.asax.tsax.barsax(ssax).2.cbn-4.4.3.1-5perc-hp.2egtr-str(min: 4.4.4.4.2)-tape
Material on hire
Study score **ED 12369**

Prelude for Brass, Bells and Percussion (1962) 6'
6hn.Dtpt.2Ctpt.3tbn.2tuba-bells-3perc
Material on hire
Study score **ED 10827**

The Rose Lake (1991-93) 25'
3(3pic).2.ca.2.bcl.2.cbn-6.3.3.1-perc-2hp-str(min: 10.10.6.6.4)
Material on hire
Study score **ED 12435**

The Shires Suite (1965-70/95) 18'
Arranged for Orchestra alone
Arranger: Meirion Bowen
3(pic).2.ca.2.bcl.2(cbn)-4.3.3.1-timp.7perc-cel.pno.hp.egtr-4hunting hns-str additional instrumental groups: 4 fl (m in),4cl (min), hn, tpt
Material on hire
Study score **ED 12439**

Suite for the Birthday of Prince Charles (1948) 16'
Suite in D
2(2pic).2.2.2-4.2.3.1-timp.perc-hp-str
Material on hire
Study score **ETP 1342**

Suite for the Birthday of Prince Charles (1948) 16'
Arranger: Brian Bowen
brass band
ED 12224 / Study score **ED 12223**

Symphony No.1 (1944-45) 35'
3(3pic).2.2.2.cbn-4.3.3.1-timp.perc-str
Material on hire
Study score **ED 10567**

Symphony No.2 (1956-57) 32'
2(2pic).2.2.2-4.2.3.1-timp.perc-pno([cel]).hp-str
Material on hire
Study score **ED 10620**

Symphony No.4 (1976-77) 32'
2(2pic).2.ca.2.bcl.2.cbn-6.3.3.2-timp.4perc-pno.hp-str-synth/tape
Material on hire
Study score **ED 11395**

Triumph (1992) 15'
3(3pic).2.ca.3.bcl.2ssax(2asax).2tsax(asax, barsax)2.cbn-2cnt.3tpt.6hn.2ttbn.btbn. 2euph.2tuba-timp.perc
Material on hire or sale
Study score **ED 12428**

Water out of Sunlight
(1988) 23'
Arranged from "String Quartet No. 4"
Arranger: Meirion Bowen
str(min: 8.0.4.3.2)
Material on hire
Study score **ED 12401**

ACT I

Scene 1

S & Co. 5885

Michael Tippett
The Midsummer Marriage (1947-52)

Concertos

Fantasia on a Theme of Handel (1939-41) 16'

Soloist: piano
2(2pic).2.2.2-4.2.3.0-timp.perc-pno-str
Material on hire
Study score **ED 12365** / Piano reduction
ED 10122

Piano Concerto (1953-55) 32'

Soloist: piano
2.2.2.2-4.2.3.0-timp-cel-str
Material on hire
Study score **ED 10925** / Piano reduction
ED 10592

Triple Concerto (1978-79) 32'

Soloists: violin, viola, cello
1(pic,afl).1.ca(bob).2(Acl).2bcl.1.cbn-
4.2.2.0-timp.7perc-cel.hp-str(min:
8.8.6.4.4)
Material on hire
Study score **ED 11860**

Chamber & Instrumental Works

The Blue Guitar (1982-83) 17'

guitar solo
ED 12218

Fanfare No.1 (1943) 3'

4hn.3tpt.3tbn
ED 11086

Fanfare No.2 (1953) 2'

4tpt
ED 11854

Fanfare No.3 (1953) 1'

3tpt
ED 11854

4 Inventions (1954) 9'

srecs.arecs
ED 11835

Piano Sonata No.1

(1936-37/44) 21'

ED 10123

Piano Sonata No.2 (1962) 14'

ED 10815

Piano Sonata No.3 (1972-73) 22'

ED 11162

Piano Sonata No.4 (1984) 35'

ED 12250

Prelude: Autumn (1991) 4'

From "Crown of the Year"
Arranger: Meirion Bowen
ob-pno
Manuscript score on sale
SL

Prelude, Recitative and Aria

(1964) 5'

fl.ob-hpd/pno
Material on sale
SL

Preludio al Vespro Di Monteverdi (1946) 4'

organ solo
ED 11209

Sonata for 4 Horns (1955) 20'

4hn
Study score **ED 10538** / Parts **ED 10716**

String Quartet No.1

(1934-35/43) 20'

Study score **ED 10568** / Parts **ED 10258**

String Quartet No.2

(1941-42) 21'

Study score **ED 10209** / Parts **ED 10252**

String Quartet No.3

(1945-46) 31'

Study score **ED 10201** / Parts **ED 10254**

String Quartet No.4

(1977-78) 23'

Study score **ED 11420** / Parts **ED 11420a**

String Quartet No.5

(1990-91) 25'

Study score **ED 12400** / Parts **ED 12400-01**

The Wolf Trap Fanfare

(1980) 2'

3tpt.2tbn.tuba
Material on sale
ED 11866

Solo Voice(s)/Voice(s) and Piano/Guitar

Boyhood's End (1943) 12'

Text: W.H. Hudson
tenor/baritone-pno
ED 10279 (high)/**12331(low)**

The Heart's Assurance

(1950-51) 17'

Text: Sidney Keynes/Alun Lewis
high voice-pno
ED 10158

Songs for Achilles (1961) 14'

Text: Michael Tippett
tenor-gtr
ED 10874

Songs for Ariel (1962) 5'

Text: William Shakespeare
medium voice-pno/hpd
Material on hire
Vocal score **ED 10871**

Solo Voice(s) and Instrument(s)/ Orchestra

Byzantium (1989-90) 25'

Text: William Butler Yeats
Soloist: soprano
3(3pic).2.ca.3(Ebcl,3bcl).2.cbn-4.2.3.1-
7perc-cel.2hp.eorg-str
Material on hire
Study score **ED 12383** / Vocal score **ED 12376**

The Heart's Assurance

(1950-51/90) 17'

Arranger: Meirion Bowen (orchestration)
Text: Sydney Keyes/Alun Lewis
Soloist: high voice
1.1.1.1-4.1.0.0-perc-hp-str(min: 3.3.2.2.1)
Material on hire
Study score **ED 12382**

Songs for Ariel (1962) 5'

Text: William Shakespeare
Soloist: medium voice
fl/pic.cl-hn-[perc]-hpd
Material on hire
Vocal score **ED 10871**

Songs for Dov (1970) 26'

Text: Michael Tippett
Soloist: tenor
2(2pic).1.ca.1.bcl.1.cbn-3.1.1.0-timp.6perc-
pno.hp.egtr.ehpd-str(4.0.2.3.2)
Material on hire
Study score **ED 11135**

Sosostris' Aria (1947-52) 11'

from "The Midsummer Marriage'
Soloist: soprano
2.2.2.2-4.2.3.0-timp.perc-cel.hp.gtr-str
Material on hire
SL

Suite: The Tempest (1971/95) 25'

Arranger: Meirion Bowen
Text: William Shakespeare
Soloists: tenor, baritone
1(pic).0.1(bcl).0-1.1.1.0-perc-pno(cel).hp-
str(1.1.1.1.1)
Material on hire
Study score **ED 12496**

Symphony No.3 (1970-72) 55'

Text: Michael Tippett
Soloist: soprano
3(2pic).2.ca.2[Ebcl].bcl.2.cbn-
4.2(flhn).3.1-timp.7perc-cel.pno.hp-str
Material on hire
Study score **ED 11148**

"Words for Music Perhaps"

(1960)   14'

Text: William Butler Yeats
Soloists: speaking voice(s)
bcl-tpt-gong.xyl.vn.vc-pno
Material on hire or sale
SL

Choral Works

Bonny at Morn (1956)   3'

Text: Northumbrian folk-song
Chorus: unison
2srec.arec
ED 12051*

A Child of Our Time

(1939-41)   66'

Text: Michael Tippett
Soloists: S.A.T.B
Chorus: mixed
2.2.ca.2.2.cbn-4.3.3.0-timp.perc-str
Material on hire
Study score **ED 10899** / Vocal score **ED 10065** /
Libretto **ED 10065-01/-10***

Crown of the Year (1958)   28'

Text: Christopher Fry
Chorus: female
recs/fl.ob.cl-cnt/tpt-str qrt-perc-hand bells-pno
Material on hire
Study score **ED 10668**

Dance, Clarion Air (1952)   5'

Text: Christopher Fry
Chorus: mixed a cappella
ED 10437

Lullaby (1959)   6'

Text: William Butler Yeats
Soloist: alto/counter-tenor
Chorus: mixed/chamber a cappella
ED 10721

Magnificat and Nunc Dimittis (1961)   7'

Chorus: mixed
org
ED 10873

The Mask of Time (1980-82)   95'

Text: Michael Tippett
Soloists: S.MS.T.Bar
Chorus: mixed
3(3pic).2.ca.2.bcl.ssax.asax.2.cbn-6.3.3.1-timp.6perc-pno.hp.eorg-str
Material on hire
Vocal score **ED 12196** / Libretto **ED 12197**

Music (1960)   4'

Text: Percy Bysshe Shelley
Chorus: unison/mixed
[str]-pno
Material on sale
Study score **ED 10717*** / Vocal score **ED 10718***

5 Negro Spirituals (1939-41) 14'

From "A Child of our Time"
Chorus: mixed a cappella
ED 10585

Plebs Angelica (1943)   4'

Text: Latin
Chorus: double a cappella
ED 11288

Ritual Dances (1947-52)   29'

from "The Midsummer Marriage"
Chorus: mixed with soloists ad lib.
2(2pic).2.2.2-4.2.3.0-timp.perc-cel.hp-str
Material on hire
Study score **ED 10207**

The Shires Suite (1965-70)   18'

Chorus: mixed
3(pic)2.ca.2.bcl.2(cbn)-4.3.3.1-timp.7perc-cel.pno.hp.egtr-4hunting hns-str
Material on hire
Study score **ED 12439**

4 Songs from the British Isles

(1956)   14'

Chorus: mixed a cappella
ED 11346 (-49)

The Source (1942)   3'

Text: Edward Thomas
Chorus: mixed a cappella
ED 11289

The Vision of St. Augustine

(1965)   35'

Text: Michael Tippett after Augustine
Soloist: baritone
Chorus: mixed
2(2pic).1.ca.1.bcl.1.cbn-4.2.3.1-timp.6perc-cel.pno.hp.xyl/marimb-str(8.8.6.4.4)
Material on hire
Study score **ED 10897** / Vocal score **ED 10898**

The Weeping Babe (1944)   3'

Text: Edith Sitwell
Soloist: soprano
Chorus: mixed a cappella
ED 11290

The Windhover (1942)   2'

Text: G.M. Hopkins
Chorus: mixed a cappella
ED 11291

Toch, Ernst
1887-1964

Stage Works

Egon und Emilie, Op. 46

(1928)   15'

No family Drama
Text: Christian Morgenstern
Material on hire
SM

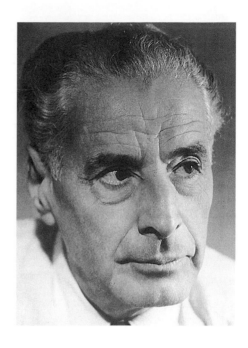

Toch, Ernst

b. Vienna 7.12.1887, d. Los Angeles 1.10.1964

A host of distinguished musicians were associated with Toch's music during his lifetime: Klemperer conducted the first performance of the „merry overture" "Pinocchio" in 1936, and Toch's Pulitzer Prize-winning Third Symphony, for orchestra and a variety of unusual percussion instruments, was premiered by William Steinberg and the Pittsburgh Symphony in 1955. The relative neglect of Toch's work since his death has deprived audiences of a lively and individual voice blending twentieth-century innovation with nineteenth-century craft. From his diverse output, worthy of reassessment in its entirety, a fine Piano Quintet and the orchestral variations "Big Ben" particularly merit revival.

Der Fächer, Op. 51

(1930)   full evening

Opera-Capriccio in 3 Acts
Text: Ferdinand Lion
Material on hire
SM

Die Prinzessin auf der Erbse, Op. 43 (1927)   48'

Musical Fairy Tale in 1 Act
Text: Benno Elkan after Hans Christian Andersen
Material on hire
SM

Orchestral Works

Bunte Suite, Op. 48 (1928)   18'

(Motley Suite)
2(pic).1.ca.2.2-2.2.1.0-timp.perc-pno-str
Material on hire
SM

Das Kirschblütenfest (1928) 19'

Music to the Play of the same title by
Klabund
harm-perc-str(1.1.1.1.0)
Material on hire
SM

Kleine Theater-Suite, Op. 54

(1931) 16'

pic.2.2.Ebcl.2.2-2.2.3.1-2perc-[hp]-str
Material on hire
SM

Komödie, Op. 42 (1927) 12'

For orchestra in one Movement
*pic.2.1.ca.Ebcl.2.2-2.2.ttbn.btbn.cbtbn-
timp.2perc-cel.hp-str qnt-str*
Material on hire
SM

Little Overture, Op. 51

(1930) 6'

to the Opera "Der Fächer"
2.0.1.1-1.1.0.0-4perc-str(1.1.1.1.0)
Material on hire
SM

Miniature Overture (1932) 3'

2.1.1.bcl.1-0.2.1.0-perc
Material on hire
AVV

Peter Pan, Op. 76 (1956) 13'

Fairy Tale for Orchestra in 3 Parts
2(pic).1.2.1-4.1.2.0-timp.perc-hp-str
Material on hire
Study score **ED 4582**

**5 Pieces for Chamber
Orchestra, Op. 33** (1924) 20'

2fl.cl.bcl-perc-str
Material on hire
SM

**Spiel für Blasorchester,
Op. 39** (1926) 8'

*2fl(pic).ob.Ebcl.4cl.bn-4.thn.bar.2flhn.4tpt.
3tbn.btuba-timp.3perc*
Score **SHS 1003** / Parts **SHS 1003-70**

Symphony No.1, Op. 72

(1950-51) 39'

*3(pic).3(ca).3(bcl).2-3.3.3.1-timp.3perc-
cel.hp-str*
Material on hire
Study score **ED 4270**

Vorspiel zu einem Märchen

(1927) 7'

"Die Prinzessin auf der Erbse", op. 43
2(pic).1.1.1-1.1.0.1-timp.perc-str
Material on hire
SM

Concertos

Cello Concerto, Op. 35

(1925) 25'

Soloist: cello
1.1.1.1-1.0.0.0-timp.perc-str
Study score **ED 3473** / Piano reduction **ED
1993**

Fanal, Op. 45 (1928) 8'

(Beacon)
Soloist: organ
*pic.2.1.ca.Ebcl.2.2.cbn-4.4.3.1-timp.perc-
org-str*
Material on hire
SM

Piano Concerto, Op. 38

(1926) 26'

Soloist: piano
3.2.4.3-3.3.3.1-timp.3perc-org-str
Material on hire
Piano reduction **ED 1859**

Symphony for Piano and
Orchestra, Op. 61 (1932) 26'

Piano Concerto No.2
Soloist: piano
2.0.2.2-2.2.0.0-timp.2perc-str
Piano reduction **ED 3277**

Chamber &
Instrumental
Works

5 X 10 Etüden,
Op. 55-59 (1931)

pno
ED 2161/2162/2166/2196/2197/2199

Burlesques, Op. 31 (1923)

pno
ED 1822

5 Capriccetti, Op. 36 (1925) 5'

pno
ED 1825

Cello Sonata, Op. 50 (1929) 12'

vc-pno
ED 2084

Dance Suite, Op. 30 (1924) 20'

fl.cl-vn.va.db-perc
Material on hire
SM

Divertimento for Violin and
Viola, Op. 37 (1926) 10'

from "2 Divertimenti for String Duo"
vn.va
ED 1909

Divertimento No.1 for Violin
and Cello, Op. 37 (1926) 10'

from "2 Divertimenti for String Duo"
vn.vc
ED 1910

Der Jongleur, Op. 31/3 (1923)

pno
ED 1823

Kleinstadtbilder, Op. 49

(1929) 11'

Echoes from a small Town - 14 easy Pieces
pno
ED 2082

3 Piano Pieces, Op. 32

(1925) 7'

pno
ED 1824

Piano Sonata, Op. 47 (1928) 12'

ED 2065

String Quartet No.11, Op. 34

(1924) 32'

Material on sale
Study score **ED 3128**

Tanz und Spielstücke, Op. 40

(1927) 12'

pno
ED 1412

Violin Sonata, Op. 44

(1928) 12'

vn-pno
ED 1240

# Solo
Voice(s)/Voice(s)
and Piano/Guitar

9 Songs, Op. 41 (1926)

Text: various
soprano-pno
ED 2055

Solo Voice(s) and
Instrument(s)/
Orchestra

Die Chinesische Flöte, Op. 29

(1922/49) 26'

Text: Hans Bethge
Soloist: soprano
2fl(pic).cl(Ebcl).bcl(Ebcl)-timp.3perc-cel-str
Material on hire
SM

Music for Orchestra and Baritone, Op. 60 (1932) 17'

Text: Rainer Maria Rilke
Soloist: baritone
2.2.Ebcl.2.2-2.2.2.0-timp.perc-str
Material on hire
SM

Choral Works

Der Tierkreis, Op. 52 (1930) 4'

Text: Wilhelm Busch
Chorus: female
SM

Das Wasser, Op. 53 (1930) 25'

Cantata
Text: Alfred Döblin
Soloists: tenor, baritone, speaker
Chorus: mixed
fl-tpt-perc-6-12vn.4-6vc.db
Material on hire
Study score **ED 3244**

Toldi, Julius
d.1965

Concertos

Concerto 18'

Soloist: horn
1.1.1.0-0.1.0.0-timp.perc-str(10.10.8.8.6)
Material on hire
AVV

Torrent, Jaume
b.1953

Chamber & Instrumental Works

Secuencias estivales 12'

guitar solo
GA 532

Tableaux 14'

guitar solo
GA 527

Turina, Joaquin
1882-1949

Orchestral Works

Evangelio de Navidad, Op. 12 (1915) 15'

pic.2.2.ca.2.bcl.2.cbn-4.3.3.1-timp.2perc-hp-str
SM

Miniaturen

concert band
FG 23

Chamber & Instrumental Works

El Circo, Op. 68 (1931)

Suite
pno
ED 2226

En la Zapatería - Chez le Cordonnier, Op. 71 (1932)

pno
ED 2231

Fandanguillo, Op. 36 (1926)

guitar solo
GA 102

Homenaje a Tárrega, Op. 69 (1932)

guitar solo
GA 136

Miniaturas, Op. 52 (1929)

pno
ED 2106

Miniaturas (1929)

guitar solo
GA 496

Radio Madrid, Op. 62 (1931)

pno
ED 2148

Ràfaga, Op. 53 (1930)

guitar solo
GA 128

Sonata

guitar solo
GA 132

Sonate Espagnole (1908)

vn-pno
VLB 85

Tarjetas postales, Op. 58 (1930)

pno
ED 2146

The Turina Collection

20 Piano Works
Arranger: Hinson
SMC 534

Viaje maritimo

pno
ED 2107

Turnage, Mark-Anthony
b.1960

Stage Works

Greek (1986-88) 90'

Opera in 2 Acts
Text: Steven Berkoff
Material on hire
Vocal score **ED 12348** / Libretto **ED 12348-01**

Killing Time (1991) 30'

Scene for 2 baritone soloists and ensemble
(Television version)
Text: various
Material on hire
SL

Orchestral Works

Drowned Out (1992-93) 22'

3(pic,2afl).3(ca).3(2bcl).2ssax(2barsax).2.cbn-4.4.3.1-5perc-pno.hp-str(16.16.12.12.8)
Material on hire
Study score **ED 12446**

Momentum (1990-91) 10'

3.3.3(Ebcl,2bcl).2asax(ssax).3(cbn)-4.3.2.btbn.0-2perc-pno.hp.[bgtr]-str(16.14.12.12.8)
Material on hire
Study score **ED 12416**

On All Fours (1985) 13'

1(bfl).1(ca,[bob]).1(bcl).1-0.1(flhn,perc).asax(ssax,perc).1(perc).0-perc-pno([epno])-str(3.0.3.2.1) or solo strings
Material on hire
Study score **ED 12280**

Three Screaming Popes
(1988-89) 15'

3(3pic,3afl).3(3ca).3(Ebcl,3bcl).2ssax(2asax).3(cbn)-6.3.3.euph.1-4perc-cel.pno(epno).hp-str(12.12.10.10.8)
Material on hire
Study score **ED 12377**

Turnage, Mark-Anthony

b. Essex 10.6.1960

At the heart of Turnage's music is a sense of theatre; not just music-theatre - though the international success of his first opera "Greek" amply demonstrated his skill in this area - but of the dramatic possibilities latent in performance style, idiom, and the tensions of musical structure. Where jazz influence occurs, as in the saxophone concerto "Your Rockaby", it is subsumed within his own, distinctive manner. Vocal works such as "Her Anxiety" and "Some Days" infuse echoes of the blues with a highly individual lyric voice. "Three Screaming Popes" and "Drowned Out", products of his three years as Composer in Association with the City of Birmingham Symphony Orchestra, working with Simon Rattle, confirmed his reputation as one of Britain's leading composers in any field.

Concertos

Blood on the Floor (1993-96) 80'

Soloists: e-guitar, jazz kit, saxophone
2(2afl).2(2ca).2(2bcl).2ssax(2asax).2(2cbn)
-2.2.2.euph.1-2perc-pno(epno/cel).bgtr(db)-
str(2.2.2.2.1)
Material on hire
SL

Dispelling the Fears

(1993-95) 20'

Soloists: 2 trumpets
2(2afl).2(2ca).2(2bcl).2ssax.2(2cbn)-
2.0.2.euph.1-2perc-cel/pno.hp-str
Material on hire
SL

Kai (1989-90) 18'

Soloist: cello
fl(afl).bcl(cl).ssax(asax).asax(ssax).bn(cbn)
-2tpt.tbn-perc-pno.hp.bgtr-
2vn(perc).va(perc).vc.db
Material on hire
Study score **ED 12397**

Night Dances (1980-81) 14'

Soloists: cel.ob.tpt.hp.str qrt
2(2pic).0.2.1-2.1.0.0-2perc-str(12.12.8.8.4)
Material on hire
Study score **ED 12309**

Your Rockaby (1993-94) 24'

Soloist: soprano saxophone
3(2afl).3.2(bcl).cbcl.2.cbn-4.3.3.1-5perc-
cimbalon.pno(cel).hp-str(16.16.12.12.8)
Material on hire
Study score **ED 12448**

Chamber & Instrumental Works

A Deviant Fantasy (1993) 3'

4cl
Material on sale
SL

Entranced (1982) 8'

pno
Manuscript score on sale
SL

Release (1987) 8'

ssax(perc).asax(ssax,bcl).bcl-tpt(perc).ttbn-
perc-pno-db(amp)
Material on hire or sale
Study score **ED 12366**

Sarabande (1985) 4'

ssax-pno
ED 12417

Set to (1992-93) 12'

4tpt.hn.3tbn.euph.tuba
Material on hire or sale
SL

Sleep on (1992) 11'

vc-pno
ED 12447

This Silence (1992-93) 15'

cl.hn.bn-str qrt
Material on hire or sale
SL

3 Farewells (1990) 12'

fl.cl-hp-str qrt
Material on hire or sale
Study score **ED 12398**

2 Elegies Framing a Shout

(1994) 14'

ssax-pno
ED 12492

Solo Voice(s) and Instrument(s)/ Orchestra

Greek - Suite (1989) 25'

Text: Steven Berkoff
Soloists: mezzo-soprano, tenor
1(pic,afl).2(2ca).2(Ebcl,2bcl).ssax(asax,bar
sax)-2.1.1.0-2perc-pno(epno).hp-va.2vc.db
N.B: Most players double on perc
Material on hire
SL

Her Anxiety (1991) 12'

Text: William Butler Yeats
Soloist: soprano
ob(ca).cl(bcl).bn-hp-vn.va.db
Material on hire
SL

Lament for a Hanging Man

(1983) 9'

Text: Jeremiah/Sylvia Plath
Soloist: soprano
ssax(perc).2bcl(ssax,2perc)-perc-hp
Material on hire
Study score **ED 12336**

Some Days (1989) 15'

Text: various
Soloist: mezzo-soprano
3cl(Ebcl,2bcl).3bn(2cbn)-hp-
str(12.12.8.8.4)
Material on hire
Study score **ED 12384**

Choral Works

Leaving (1990/92) 25'

Text: various
Soloists: soprano, tenor
Chorus: mixed
3(3afl).0.2(2bcl).bcl.3asax(3ssax).1(cbn)-
0.3.0.1-timp.perc-pno(cel).hp.bgtr-
str(0.0.0.8.4)
Material on hire
SL

Ueter, Karl
b.1900

Orchestral Works

Symphony No.1   17'
2.2.2.2-4.3.3.0-timp-str
Material on hire
SM

Symphony No.2   19'
2.2.2.2-4.3.3.1-timp.perc-str
Material on hire
SM

Uhl, Alfred
1909-1992

Orchestral Works

Symphonic March (1942)   5'
2.2.2.2-4.3.2.1-timp.perc-str
Material on hire
SM

Chamber & Instrumental Works

Andante semplice
cl-pno
KLB 39

15 Bassoon Studies (1972)
bassoon solo
FAG 15

Divertimento (1952)   13'
3cl-bcl
Score **ED 4574** / Parts **ED 4437**

48 Etudes Vols. 1&2 (1938)
clarinet solo
KLB 12/13

Sonata Classica (1937)   12'
guitar solo
GA 164

Suite
viola solo
VAB 42

30 Viola Studies (1975)
viola solo
VAB 44

20 Viola Studies
viola solo
VAB 40

Ullmann, Viktor
1898-1944

Stage Works

Der Kaiser von Atlantis oder die Todverweigerung (1943) 60'
Opera in 1 Act
Text: Peter Kien
Material on hire
Vocal score **ED 8197**

Der Sturz des Antichrist, Op. 9 (1936)   full evening
Opera in 3 Acts
Text: Albert Steffen
Material on hire
Libretto **BN 3900-40**

Der zerbrochene Krug, Op. 36 (1941)   60'
Opera with Prelude in 1 Act
Text: Heinrich von Kleist
Material on hire
Vocal score **ED 8434**

Orchestral Works

Don Quixote tanzt Fandango
(1944)   15'
Overture
Arranger: Bernhard Wulff (1994)
pic.2(pic).3(ca).3(Ebcl,bcl).3(cbn)-4.3.3.1-timp.3perc-hpd.hp-str
Material on hire
SM

Symphony No.1, Op. 45
(1943)   19'
"Von meiner Jugend"
Arranger: Bernhard Wulff (1992/94)
3(pic).3(ca).3(Ebcl,bcl).3(cbn)-4.3.3.1-timp.3perc-mand.cel.hp-str
Material on hire
SM

Symphony No.2 in D Major
(1944)   23'
Arranger: Bernhard Wulff (1989)
3(2pic).3(ca).3(Ebc,bcl).3(cbn)-4.3.3.1-timp.perc-hpd.cel.hp-str
Material on hire
SM

Variations, Fantasy and Doublefugue (1934)   13'
on a little piano-piece (op. 5) by Arnold Schönberg
2(pic).1.ca.2(bcl).2(cbn)-3.2.1.0-timp-hp-str(14.10.8.8.6)
Material on hire
SM

Ullmann, Viktor

b. Prague 1.1.1898, d. Auschwitz 18.10.1944

A pupil of Arnold Schönberg and a composer-resident of the notorious Terezin fortress, Ullmann was an Austro-Hungarian composer of great promise who was active in the musical life of Bohemia both as an accompanist and a conductor. He studied quarter-tone composition with Haba at the Prague Conservatoire, but used the techniques of microtonality only intermittently within an overall style that showed a sensitive application of Schönbergian principles within the broad tradition of Germanic-Bohemian music.

Concertos

Piano Concerto, Op. 25

(1939)   19'

Soloist: piano
3(pic).2.ca.3(Ebcl).bcl.2.cbn-4.3.3.1-
timp.3perc-tbanjo.hp-str
Material on hire
SM

Chamber & Instrumental Works

Piano Sonatas Nos. 1-4

(1936-44)   64'

ED 8281

Piano Sonatas Nos. 5-7

(1936-44)   55'

ED 8282

String Quartet No.3, Op. 46

(1943)   14'

Material on sale
Parts **ED 8211**

Variations and Doublefugue

(1925-34)   13'

on a theme (op. 3a) by Arnold Schönberg
pno
ED 8433

Solo Voice(s)/Voice(s) and Piano/Guitar

Complete Songs

Text: various
voice-pno
ED 8199

Solo Voice(s) and Instrument(s)/ Orchestra

Herbst - Lied der Tröstung

(1943-44)   6'

2 Songs
Text: Georg Trakl/Albert Steffen
Soloist: medium voice
str trio
ED 8284

6 Songs, Op. 17   (1937)   14'

Arranger: Geert van Keulen (1994)
Text: Albert Steffen
Soloist: soprano
2(pic).1(ca).1.bcl.1-1.0.0.0-cel.hp-str
Material on hire
SM

Die Weise von Liebe und Tod des Cornet Christoph Rilke

(1944)   25'

Arranger: Henning Brauel
Text: Rainer Maria Rilke
Soloist: speaker
3(pic).2.ca.2.bcl.2.cbn-4.2.3.1-timp.3perc-
pno(cel).hp-str
Material on hire
Piano reduction **ED 8285**

V

Vasks, Pēteris

b.1946

Orchestral Works

"Balsis" - Symphony for Strings ("Voices") (1991)   27'

str(6.5.4.3.2)
Material on hire
Study score **ED 8032**

Cantabile per archi (1979)   8'

str
Material on hire
SM

Lauda (1986)   21'

3(pic,afl).3.3(bcl).3-4.3.3.1-timp.4perc-pno.hp-str(16.14.12.10.8)
Material on hire
SM

Musica dolorosa (1983)   14'

str
Material on hire
SM (Co-prod: Sikorski)

Vestijums - Message (1982)   14'

4perc-2pno-str(16.14.12.10.8)
Material on hire
SM (Co-prod: Sikorski) / Study score Sikorski Ed. 1826

Concertos

Cello Concerto (1993-94)   33'

Soloist: cello
pic.2(afl).2.2.2-4.3.3.1-timp.3perc-pno.cel.hp-str
Material on hire
Piano reduction **ED 8470**

Concerto (1989)   20'

Soloist: cor anglais
2(pic).2.2.2-2.0.0.0-timp.perc-str
Material on hire
SM (Co-prod: Schirmer) / Schirmer only for USA and Canada

Concerto (1979/86)   12'

Soloist: timpani
4perc
Material on hire
SM

Vasks, Pēteris

b. Aizpute, Latvia 16.4.1946

A new voice from Latvia, Vasks's emotionally direct musical language combines an awareness of modern trends with the timeless modality of composers such as Sibelius. The tribulations of his native land and the voice of nature reflecting the optimism of the human spirit are two important strands in his work. By training as a double-bass player, he writes with particular sympathy for the string orchestra.

Chamber & Instrumental Works

Autumn Music (1981)   13'

quasi una sonata - Die Jahreszeiten IV
pno
SM (Co-prod: Sikorski) ED 8050 / Sikorski Ed. 1883 (in: Ausgewählte Klavierwerke)

Cantata (1980)   5'

hpd
ED 8027

Cantus ad pacem (1984)   15'

organ solo
ED 8048

Drei Blicke (1979)   4 -12'

Spring Sonata
free choice of instruments
SM

Episodi e Canto perpetuo (1985)   26'

vn.vc-pno
ED 8100

Fantasia - "Izdegusas zemes ainavas" (1992)   15'

Landscapes of the Burnt-out Earth
pno
ED 8102

Gramata cellam - The Book (1978)   12'

cello solo
SM

In Memoriam (1977)   9'

2pno
SM

Landscape with Birds (1980)   8'

flute solo
SM

A Little Night Music (1978)   13'

pno
SM (Co-prod: Sikorski) ED 8046 / Sikorski Ed. 1883 (in: Ausgewählte Klaviermusik)

Masa vasaras muzika - Little Summer Music (1985)   10'

vn-pno
VLB 88

Moments musicaux (1977)   10'

clarinet solo
SM (Co-prod: Sikorski) Schott KLB 41

Music (1974)   12'

2pno
SM

Musica Seria (1988)   16'

organ solo
ED 8049

Partita (1974)   13'

vc-pno
Material on hire
SM

Pavasara Muzika - Spring Music (1995)   18'

quasi una sonata - Die Jahreszeiten II
pno
SM

Pavasara Sonate (1987)   18'

Spring Sonata
2vn.2va.2vc
SM

Quintet - "In Memory of a Friend" (1982)   10'

fl.ob.cl.bn-hn
SM (Co-prod: Sikorski) / Score Sikorski Ed. 1884

Quintet - "Music for Fleeting Birds" (1977) 8'
fl.ob.cl.bn-hn
SM

Sonata (1992) 10'
altoflute/flute solo
FTR 163

Sonata (1986) 16'
doublebass solo
SM

String Quartet No.1 (1977) 14'
SM

String Quartet No.2 "Vasaras dziedajumi" (1984) 23'
Summer Tunes
Material on sale
ED 8512

String Quartet No.3 (1995) 24'
SM

Te Deum (1991) 13'
organ solo
ED 8052

Toccata (1977) 5'
2pno
SM

Touchings (1982) 7'
oboe solo
SM (Co-prod: Sikorski) Schott OBB 37

Tris Skandarbi - Three Pieces (1973) 9'
cl-pno
KLB 42

Vientulibas Sonate (1990) 14'
The Sonata of Loneliness
guitar solo
GA 526

White Scenery (1980) 7'
Die Jahreszeiten I
pno
SM (Co-prod: Sikorski) ED 8047 / Sikorski
Ed. 1883 (in: Ausgewählte Klavierwerke)

Solo Voice(s)/Voice(s) and Piano/Guitar

3 Poems (1995) 14'
Text: Czeslaw Milosz
counter tenor-2 tenors-baritone
SKR 20036

Solo Voice(s) and Instrument(s)/ Orchestra

Latvija (1987) 12'
Chamber Cantata
Text: Anna Rancane
Soloist: soprano
fl/afl-bells-pno
SM

Choral Works

Baltais fragments - White fragment (1978) 5'
Poem
Text: Maris Caklais
Chorus: male a cappella
SM

Concerto vocale (1978) 16'
Text: Maris Caklais
Chorus: mixed a cappella
SM

Ganu dziesma - Shepherd's Song (1981/89) 4'
Chorus: female a cappella
SM

Kekatu dziesma - Carnival Song (1981) 3'
Arrangement of a folksong
Chorus: female a cappella
SM

Klusas dziesmas - Silent Songs (1979/92) 10'
Text: various
Chorus: mixed a cappella
SM

Liepa - The Lime-Tree (1975/92) 5'
Text: Peteris Zirnitis
Chorus: female a cappella
SM

Liténe (1992-93) 11'
Ballad
Text: Uldis Berzina
Chorus: mixed a cappella (12 prt)
SKR 20030

Madrigal (1976) 4'
Text: Claude de Pontoux
Soloist: soprano
Chorus: mixed a cappella
SM

Mate saule - Mother Sun (1975) 5'
Text: Janis Peters
Chorus: mixed a cappella
SM

Mazi silti svetki (1988) 2'
Text: Janis Baltvilks
Chorus: female a cappella
SM

Musu dziesma - Our Song (1988) 4'
Chorus: female a cappella
SM

Musu masu vardi - Our Mothers's Names (1977) 6'
Text: Maris Caklais
Chorus: male a cappella
SM

Ne tikai lirika (1977) 8'
Cycle
Text: Vitauts Ludens
Chorus: female a cappella
SM

Pater noster (1991/95) 4'
Text: liturgic
Chorus: mixed a cappella
SM

Sava tauta - In his nation (1990) 3'
Text: Andrejs Eglitis
Chorus: mixed a cappella
SM

Skumja mate - Sad Mother (1980/91) 4'
Text: Gabriele Mistral
Chorus: female a cappella
SM

Ugunssargs (1982) 7'
Poem
Text: Maris Caklais
Chorus: mixed a cappella
SM

Varonis - The Hero (1989) 6'
Text: Zinaida Lazda
Chorus: mixed a cappella
SM

Vasara (1978) 3'
Text: Leons Briedis
Chorus: female a cappella
SM

Zemgale 25'
Dramatic Poem
Text: Mara Zalite
Chorus: mixed (12 prt)
SKR 20037

Ziles zina - Message of a Titmouse (1981) 6'
Text: Uldis Berzins
Chorus: female a cappella
SM

Vieru, Anatol
b.1926

Orchestral Works

Sonnenuhr (1968)   13'

3.0.0.0-0.3.4.0-perc-str
Material on hire
AVV

Vogel, Wladimir
1896-1984

Chamber & Instrumental Works

Musette (1979)   3'

guitar solo
GA 459

Choral Works

An die Jugend der Welt
(1954)   8'

Chorus: mixed
[1].0.2.1-0.2.1.0-timp.[perc]-str
Material on hire
Study score **AVV 67**

Arpiade (1954)   28'

Text: Hans Arp
Soloist: soprano
Chorus: mixed speaking
fl.cl-va.vc-pno
Material on hire
AVV

Wahren, Karl-Heinz
b.1933

Orchestral Works

Auf der Suche nach dem verlorenen Tango (1979)   21'

Symphonic Poem
2.2(ca).2.asax.2-4.4.4.0-2perc-cel.pno.hp-str
Material on hire
SM

Wallace, William
1860-1940

Orchestral Works

Passing of Beatrice (1892)   13'

Symphonic Poem No.1
2.2.2.2-4.2.3.1-hp-str
Material on hire
SM

Walter, Fried
b.1907

Stage Works

Die Dorfmusik (1943)   full evening

Comic Opera in 4 Acts
Text: P. Beyer/E. Tram
Material on hire
Vocal score **ED 3985**

Kleopatra, Op. 22   70'

Dance-Play in 3 Scenes
Text: Alice Zickler
Material on hire
Vocal score **ED 3986**

Orchestral Works

Bauernhochzeit (1943)   9'

Incidental Music from Act 2 of the opera
"Die Dorfmusik"
pic.1.2.2.2-4.2.3.1-timp.perc-str
Material on hire
SM

Die Dorfmusik - Country Dances (1943)   5'

2(pic).2.2.2-4.2.3.1-timp.perc-str
Material on hire
SM

Symphonische Tänze (1942) 26'

*3(3pic).3(ca).3(Ebcl,bcl).3(cbn)-4.3.3.1-
timp.perc-hp-str*
Material on hire
SM

Wand, Günter

b.1912

Solo Voice(s) and Instrument(s)/ Orchestra

Odi et amo (1949) 6'

Text: Catull
Soloist: coloratura-soprano
1.1.1.1-0.1.0.0-timp.perc-pno-str(4.0.3.3.3)
Material on hire
SM

Wanek, Friedrich K.

1929-1991

Orchestral Works

Divertimento (1975) 10'

2.2/2cl.0.2-2.1.0.0-str(6-8.6-8.4-6.4-6.2)
Material on hire
SM

4 Grotesques (1973) 10'

2.2.2.2-2.1.0.0-perc
Score ED 6667 / Parts ED 6668

Tableau symphonique

(1988-89) 11'

*2(2pic).2.2(bcl).2(cbn)-4.3.3.0-timp.2perc-
str*
Material on hire
SM

Concertos

Chamber Concerto (1980) 17'

Soloist: trumpet
hpd(epno)-str(10.8.4.4.2-3)
Material on hire
SM

Harpsichord Concerto

Soloist: harpsichord
1.1.1.1-1.0.0.0-str(8.8.8.5.3)
Material on hire
SM

Wanek, Friedrich K.

b. Lugoj 11.11.1929, d. Mainz 13.4.1991

Wanek studied composition at the Bucharest
Conservatory and was editor of contemporary music at the Mainz publishing house
B.Schott's Söhne from 1966; in addition, he
taught composition at the faculty of music
education of the University of Mainz from
1980-82. From 1984 he was teacher of a
composition class at the Mainz Conservatory.
The style of his compositions, most of
which are freely tonal, cannot be assigned
to a certain movement; contemporary elements are combined with traditional.

Musique concertante (1984) 18'

Soloists: 2 harpsichords
1.1.1.1-1.1.0.0-str(8.8.8.6.3)
Material on hire
SM

4 Pièces brèves (1985) 10'

Soloists: 4 harpsichords
str(6.6.4.2.1)
Material on hire
SM

Chamber & Instrumental Works

A propos Haydn (1979) 6'

pno
ED 6909

7 Aphorismen (1989) 11'

2vc
CB 154

3 Burlesque Pieces (1976) 6'

fl-bn
FTR 106

4 Dialogues (1979) 6'

2cl
KLB 23

Divertimento (1973) 10'

2fl(pic).2ob.2cl.2bn(cbn)-2hn
Material on hire
SM

5 Epigrammes (1987) 13'

str qrt
Score ED 7618 / Parts ED 7619

10 Essays (1974) 15'

guitar solo
GA 438

3 Etudes (1985) 12'

pno(6hnd)
ED 7611

Finaletto (1981) 3'

from "Trifoglietto"
2fl(pic).2ob.2cl.2bn(cbn)-2hn
Material on hire
SM

Flute Sonata (1989) 10'

fl-pno
FTR 154

5 Impromptus (1982) 11'

bn-gtr
ED 7093

Klangspiegel (1988) 8'

pno (4hnd)
Material on hire
ED 8195

6 Miniatures (1953/75) 12'

Arranger: Friedrich/György Ligeti
2.2.2.2-2.0.0.0
Material on hire
SM

Musique pour Deux à deux Instruments à Clavier

(1974) 12'

2pno
ED 7593

Nocturnes and Capriccios

(1981) 14'

pno
ED 7594

Präambel - Passacaglia - Toccata (1984) 12'

2pno
ED 7608

Ragtime - Fantasy (1977) 18'

pno
ED 7610

21 Soli (1985) 273'

clarinet solo
KLB 27

Sonata (1990) 12'

db-pno
ED 8304

String Quartet (1985) 12'

Score **ED 7616** / Parts **ED 7617**

3 Studies (1985) 12'

pno(6hnd)
ED 7611

Violin Sonata (1985) 10'

violin solo
VLB 86

Violin Sonata (1989) 11'

vn-pno
ED 8382

Zyklus (1975) 20'

pno
ED 7612

Solo Voice(s) and Instrument(s)/ Orchestra

Due Sonetti (1975) 12'

Text: Michelangelo Buonarrotti
Soloist: mezzo-soprano
str(8.0.2.2.1)
Material on hire
SM

Choral Works

Ammenuhr (1983) 3'

from "Des Knaben Wunderhorn"
Text: Adalbert von Chamisso
Chorus: female a cappella
C 45625

Wartisch, Otto
1893-1969

Orchestral Works

Rondo 9'

2.2.2.2-4.2.3.0-timp.perc-hp-str
Material on hire
Eu

Weill, Kurt
1900-1950

Stage Works

Der Kuhhandel (1934) full evening

"Horse-Trading". Operetta in 2 Acts
Material on hire
Copyright USA: EAM/All other territories: SM

Die sieben Todsünden

(1933) 35'

Ballet chanté in nine scenes
Text: Bertolt Brecht
Material on hire
Vocal score **ED 6005**
Copyright USA: EAM/French speaking areas:
L'Arche/All other territories: SM

Orchestral Works

Hatikvah (1947) 4'

Arrangement for orchestra of the Israeli
National Anthem
3.2.3.2-4.3.3.1-timp.perc-hp-str
Material on hire
Copyright all territories: EAM

The Judgement of Paris

(1938) 30'

Arrangement for ballet of the music from
"Die Dreigroschenoper"
Arranger: Tudor/Cooke
*1(pic).1.1(tsax).asax(cl).1-0.2.2.0-perc-
pno-str*
Material on hire
Copyright all territories: EAM

Symphony No.1 (1921) 25'

"Berliner Symphonie"
2(pic).1.2(bcl).2-2/4.1.1.0-timp.perc-str
Material on hire
Study score **ED 5937**
Copyright USA: EAM/All other territories: SM

Symphony No.2 (1933) 28'

2(2pic).2.2.2-2.2.2.0-timp.-str
Material on hire
Study score **ED 5512 (Co-prod: Heugel)**
Copyright G, PL, A, CZ, SK, CR, UK,
BCW [except CDN]: SM

Concertos

Bastille Music (1922) 15'

Suite from the incidental music for
"Gustav III" (1927), play by August
Strindberg
Arranger: David Drew (1975)
Soloist: violin
pic.0.2-2.2.1.0-perc-glsp-pno.harm
Material on hire
Copyright all territories: EAM

Weill, Kurt

b. Dessau 2.3.1900, d. New York 3.4.1950

**Kurt Weill wrote two symphonies and a
violin concerto in addition to modern classics
such as "Der Dreigroschenoper" and
"Mahogonny". He was a pupil of Busoni,
and in his early years a modernist who
experimented with avant-garde styles. The
more popular vein of his later works was a
clarification of his ideas concerning the
need for music to relate to the life of its
time. But Weill's music, like all great art,
also transcended its period, assuring his
status as one of the twentieth-century's
outstanding composers.**

Chamber & Instrumental Works

Cello Sonata (1920) 23'

vc-pno
EA 490X
Copyright all territories: EAM

2 Movements for String Quartet (1922-23) 10'

Copyright all territories: EAM

String Quartet in B Minor

(1918) 20'

Material on hire
Score **EA 681** / Parts **EA 682**
Copyright USA, UK, BCW: EAM

Solo Voice(s)/Voice(s) and Piano/Guitar

Early Songs (1913-19)   10'
Text: various
voice-pno
EA 723X
Copyright all territories: EAM

2 Folksongs of the New Palestine (1938)   7'
Text: various
voice-pno
Copyright all territories: EAM

Langsamer Fox and Algi-Song (1920-21)   4'
voice-pno
Copyright all territories: EAM

Maikaterlied, Abendlied
(1918)   6'
Duets
Text: Otto Julius Bierbaum
Soloists: 2 sopranos
2 sopranos-pno
EA 724X
Copyright all territories: EAM

Ofrah's Lieder (1916)   10'
Text: Jehuda Halevi
voice-pno
EA 684X
Copyright all territories: EAM

Propaganda Songs (1942)   15'
Text: various
voice-pno
EA 493
Copyright all territories: EAM (except: "Song of the Free")

Rilkelieder (1921)   9'
3 Songs
Text: Rainer Maria Rilke
voice-pno
EA 725X
Copyright all territories: EAM

The Unknown Kurt Weill
(1925-1943)   full evening
14 Songs
Text: various
voice-pno
EA 493
Copyright all territories: EAM

Solo Voice(s) and Instrument(s)/ Orchestra

Klops Lied (1925)   1'
Song on a traditional Berlin text
Soloist: high voice
2pic.bn
Copyright all territories: EAM

Die Sieben Todsünden
(1933)   35'
Text: Bertolt Brecht
Soloists: soprano, 2 tenors, baritone, bass
2(2pic).1.2.1-2.2.1.1-timp.perc-pno.hp.banjo/(gtr)-str
Material on hire
Vocal score **ED 6005**
Copyright USA: EAM/French speaking areas: L'Arche/All other territories: SM

5 Songs from Huckleberry Finn (1950)   20'
Arranger: Robert Russell Bennett (1952)
Text: Maxwell Anderson
Soloist: voice
2.2.2.1-4.2.3.1-timp.perc-pno-str
Copyright all territories: EAM

4 Walt Whitman Songs
(1942/47)   18'
Soloist: voice
2.1.2(bcl).1-2.2.2.0-timp.perc-hp-str
Material on hire
Vocal score **EA 584**
Copyright all territories: EAM

Choral Works

Ballad of Magna Carta
(1940)   15'
Text: Maxwell Anderson
Soloists: bass, speaker
Chorus: mixed
2(2pic).1(ca).2asax(cl,bcl).2tsax(cl).1-0.3.2.0-timp.per-pno.gtr.hp-str
Material on hire
Vocal score **EA 585**
Copyright all territories: EAM

Divertimento, Op. 5 (1922)   24'
Arranger: David Drew/Christopher Shaw (1971)
Chorus: male
0.0.1.1-1.0.2.0-str
Material on hire
Copyright all territories: EAM

Kiddush (1946)   5'
Text: Kiddush
Soloist: tenor
Chorus: mixed
org
EA 399
Copyright all territories: EAM

Recordare, Op. 11 (1923)   17'
Text: Bible
Chorus: mixed, children's a cappella
Score **EA 495** / Parts **EA 496 (children's choir)**
Copyright all territories: EAM

Weismann, Julius
1879-1950

Stage Works

Die pfiffige Magd, Op. 125 (1937/38)
Comic Opera in 3 Acts
Text: Ludwig Holberg
Material on hire
Libretto **BN 3941-01**

Schwanenweiß, Op. 75
(1919/20)   full evening
Opera in 3 Acts
Text: Julius Weismann
Material on hire
SM

Orchestral Works

Die pfiffige Magd, Op. 125
(1937/38)   7'
Overture
2.2.2.2-2.2.0.0-timp.perc-str
Material on hire
SM

Symphony, Op. 131 (1940)   37'
2.2.2.2-4.2.0.0-timp.str
Material on hire
SM

Symphony in B Major, Op. 130 (1940)   37'
2(pic).2.2.2-4.2.0.0-timp-str
Material on hire
SM

Chamber & Instrumental Works

Piano Sonata in A Minor, Op. 87 (1923)   11'
ED 2898

Weismann, Julius

b. 26.12.1879 Freiburg/Breisgau,
d. Singen/Hohentwiel 22.12.1950

Weismann was a student of Dimmler, Rheinberger, Bußberger, von Herzogenberg and Thuille. Initially he wrote lieder and piano works whose subjective style - partly rhapsodic, partly bound by the form of the variant - often reflect natural occurrences. Later however he turned to larger forms.

Weiss, Harald
b.1949

Stage Works

Amanda's Traum

(1988-91)   full evening

Music-Theatre in 2 acts and 1 interval
Material on hire
SM

Das Gespenst (1995-96) full evening

Music-Theatre in 2 acts and 1 interval for children and adults
Material on hire
SM

Concertos

Nachtmusik   15'

Soloist: guitar
2perc-7gtr-str
Score **CON 180** / Parts **CON 180-16**
(solo)/CON 180-50/-60

Chamber & Instrumental Works

My Blue Diary

16 Piano Pieces
pno
ED 8288

Wellesz, Egon
1885-1974

Orchestral Works

Symphony No.1, Op. 62

(1945)   37'

3.3.3.2-4.3.3.1-timp.perc-str
Material on hire
SL

Chamber & Instrumental Works

String Quartet No.5, Op. 60

(1943)   21'

Material on sale
Study score **ED 10212**

Solo Voice(s)/Voice(s) and Piano/Guitar

The Leaden and the Golden Echo, Op. 61 (1944)   12'

Text: Gerard Manely Hopkins
voice-pno
ED 10068*

Wellesz, Egon

b. Vienna 21.10.1885, d. Oxford 9.11.1974

Though chiefly influenced by German late-romanticism, Wellesz absorbed a variety of influences: Byzantine chant, 17th-century opera and other theatrical and religious impulses. A composer of opera, symphonies and string quartets, he was also a distin-guished academic who settled in Britain and became Professor of Music at Oxford University.

Solo Voice(s) and Instrument(s)/ Orchestra

The Leaden and the Golden Echo, Op. 61 (1944)   12'

Text: Gerard Manely Hopkins
Soloist: soprano
cl.vn.va-pno
Study score **ED 10300*** / Parts **ED 10300-10***

Werdin, Eberhard
1911-1991

Orchestral Works

Europäische Tänze (1967)

2fl-glsp.axyl-gtr-str(1.1.0.1.[1])
B 167

Festliche Musik (1957)

2tpt.2tbn-str
Score and parts **CON 169**

Kommt, ihr G'spielen (1951)

Folksongs
recs-perc-glsp.xyl-str(1.0.0.0.0)
B 105

Concertos

Concertino (1961)

Soloists: 2 alto recorders/2 flutes
str
Score and parts **ED 5258**

Chamber & Instrumental Works

Concertino

srec.arec/fl-recorder qrt/str qrt-[gtr]
Score **CON 193** / Parts **CON 193-50/-51** /
Piano reduction **OFB 149**

Kleine Suite (1962)

4recs/str
ED 4824

Serenade (1973)

3tpt-2tbn(2hn, thn)
SM

Slawische Tanzweisen mit Variationen (1953)

pno (4hnd)
ED 4495

Suite (1958)

arr I: 3tpt.2tbn
arr II: 2srec.arec.2trec.2brec
arr III: 3vn.va.2vc
SM

Choral Works

Es stund ein frowe alleine (1951)   3'

from "Drei Chöre nach mittelhoch-
deutschen Texten"
Chorus: female a cappella
SM

Ich will truren varen lan

(1951)   2'

from "Drei Chöre nach mittelhoch-
deutschen Texten"
Chorus: female a cappella
SM

Reigen der verschmähten Mädchen (1951)   1'

from "Drei Chöre nach mittelhoch-
deutschen Texten"
Chorus: female a cappella
SM

2 Trinklieder nach alten Texten (1965)   6'

Chorus: male
pno
Score **ED 5544** / Choral score **ED 5544-01**

Verzierte Volksliedsätze (1960)

Chorus: mixed (3 prt)
fl
B 137

Vier Kinderchöre (1955)

Text: Heinrich H. Roggendorf
Chorus: children's
SM

Westergaard, Peter

b.1931

Chamber & Instrumental Works

Quartet

cl(Acl)-vib-vn.vc
Material on sale
Score and parts **AVV 9**

Solo Voice(s) and Instrument(s)/ Orchestra

Cantata No.2 (1958)   5'

Text: Dylan Thomas
Soloist: bass
pic.afl.0.0.0-0.2.2.0-perc-pno.hp
Material on hire
AVV

Cantata No.3 (1961)   4'

Text: William Butler Yeats
Soloist: mezzo-soprano
cl-va-marimb.vib
Material on hire
AVV

Widor, Charles-Marie

1844-1937

Concertos

Symphony No.3, Op. 69

(1936)   29'

Soloist: organ
pic.2.2.2.2-4.3.3.1-timp.perc-str
Material on hire
SM

Chamber & Instrumental Works

Symphonie gothique, Op. 70

organ solo
ED 1894

Wilckens, Friedrich

1899-1986

Stage Works

Die Weibermühle   50'

Burlesque Dance Comedy in 3 Scenes
Text: Alice Zickler
Material on hire
SM

Wildberger, Jacques

b.1922

Solo Voice(s) and Instrument(s)/ Orchestra

Liebestoto   4'

No. 10 from the "Divertimento für Mozart"
Text: Hans Arp
Soloist: soprano
2.2.2.2-2.2.2.0-perc-str
SM (Co-prod: UE)
Copyright USA: EAM/Italy: Ed. Suvini
Zerboni

Willi, Herbert

b.1956

Stage Works

Schlafes Bruder

(1994-95)   full evening

Opera
Text: Robert Schneider/Herbert Willi
Material on hire
Libretto **BN 3957-80**

Orchestral Works

Concerto for Orchestra

(1991-92)   10'

*3(3pic).3(ca).2.bcl.ssax.3(cbn)-3.3.3.1-
timp.3perc-hp-str(14.12.10.8.6)*
Material on hire
Study score **ED 8348**

Für 16 (1990)   12'

*1(pic).1.1.bcl.1-1.1.1.0-2perc-pno-
str(1.1.1.1.1)*
Material on hire
Study score **ED 8016**

Räume (1991)   10'

*2(2pic).1(ca).3(2Ebcl,bcl).ssax(asax).0-
0.4.4.0-timp.2perc-str*
Material on hire
SM

Concertos

Flute Concerto (1993)   15'

Soloist: flute
*2(pic,afl).2(ca).2(bcl).2-2.2.1.0-timp.2perc-
hp-str(12.10.8.6.4)*
Material on hire
Piano reduction **ED 8344 (solo part included)**

Chamber & Instrumental Works

Horn Trio (1992)   8'

vn-hn-pno
Score and parts **ED 8139**

Piece (1985-86)   5'

flute solo
FTR 153

Willi, Herbert

b. Vorarlberg 7.1.1956

Willi studied school mucis and theology at the University od Innsbruck (Master of Philosophy). At the same time, he studied bassoon and piano at the Innsbruck Conservatory. From 1983 composition studies with Helmut Eder at the Salzburg Mozarteum, diploma in composition and Master of Arts, afterwards further studies with Boguslav Schaeffer. In 1985 and 1986 he was granted the Austrian State Scholarship for Rome in 1987/88, the Rolf Liebermann Schoarship for Opera Composers in 1990 and the Award for Young Composers of the Ernst-von-Siemens Foundation in 1991. In 1992, he was appointed composer-in-residence at the Salzburg Festival; from 1996 till 1998 he will be composer-in-residence at the Salzburg Camerata Academica.

Willms, Franz

1893-1946

Stage Works

Die Klugen und die Törichten   24'

Dance Play in 4 Parts
Material on hire
SM

Die Stunde der Fische   45'

Chinese Dance Play in 5 Scenes
Material on hire
SM

Wimberger, Gerhard

b.1923

Stage Works

La Battaglia oder Der rote Federbusch (1960)   full evening

Comic Opera in 8 Scenes
Text: Eric Spiess
Material on hire
Vocal score **ED 5081** / Libretto **BN 3960-80**

Dame Kobold (1964)   full evening

Musical Comedy freely after Calderon
Text: Hugo von Hofmannsthal/Gebhard
Wimberger/Wolfgang Rennert
Material on hire
Vocal score **ED 5373**

Hero und Leander (1963)   35'

Dance Drama after an old legend by Imre
Keres
Material on hire
SM

Schaubudengeschichte

(1954)   full evening

Opera in 6 Scenes
Text: Eric Spiess
Material on hire
Vocal score **ED 4319**

Orchestral Works

Allegro Giocosa (1956)   4'

No. 8 from the "Divertimento für Mozart"
2(pic).2.2.2-2.2.0.0-timp-str
Material on hire
SM (Co-prod: UE)
Copyright USA: EAM/Italy: Ed. Suvini
Zerboni

Chronique (1969)   20'

*2(pic).afl.1.ca.1.bcl.asax .1.cbn-1.1.1.0-
str(12.0.6.6.4)*
Material on hire
SM

Etude dramatique (1961)   12'

3.2.ca.3.2-4.3.3.1-timp.perc-hp-str
Material on hire
SM

Figuren und Phantasien

(1957)   20'

*3(2pic).2.ca.Ebcl.1.bcl.2.cbn-4.3.3.1-
timp.2perc-cel.pno.hp-str*
Material on hire
SM

Hero und Leander (1963)   20'

Suite after the Dance Drama of the same title
*3(2pic).3.3(bcl).2.cbn-4.3.3.1-timp.3perc-
cel.hp.gtr-str*
Material on hire
SM

Wimberger, Gerhard

b. Vienna 30.8.1923

Over many years Gerhard Wimberger has been closely associated with the Mozarteum, Salzburg both as a student and subsequently as a lecturer and director of master classes. He was awarded the Austrian State Prize for Composition in 1967, and has written for voices, choir and orchestra in a varied output that in a number of successful stage works, including ballet and comic operas, has drawn inspiration from classical mythology.

Partita Giocosa (1961) 18'
1.1.2.1-1.1.1.0-2perc-str
Material on hire
SM

Risonanze (1966) 16'
2.2.1.bcl.1.cbn-3.2.3.0-cel.pno.2hp.gtr-str
Material on hire
SM

Stories (1962) 18'
3.2.ca.2.bcl.2.cbn-4.3.3.1-timp.3perc-db
Material on hire
Study score ED 7194

Concertos

Piano Concerto (1955) 20'
Soloist: piano
[2perc]-str(4.4.3.3.1)
Material on hire
SM

Solo Voice(s)/Voice(s) and Piano/Guitar

8 Chansons (1962) 15'
Text: Erich Kästner
medium voice-pno
BSS 40720

Kästner Liederbuch
(1952-61) 16'
Text: Erich Kästner
medium voice-pno
ED 6901

Solo Voice(s) and Instrument(s)/ Orchestra

3 Lyrical Chansons (1957) 21'
Text: Jacques Prévert/Kurt Kusenberg
Soloist: voice
1.0.ca.1.bcl.asax.0-1.0.0.0-2perc-pno.hpd.hp-str([2vn.va.vc].db)
Material on hire
Vocal score ED 4978

Singsang (1970) 10'
Text: Gerhard Wimberger
Soloist: high voice
jazz combo
ED 6502-01 / Score ED 6502

Choral Works

Ars Amatoria (1967) 28'
Text: Ovid
Soloists: soprano, baritone
Chorus: mixed
fl(pic).cl.asax-jazztpt-jazzperc-cel.hp.vib.egtr-6vn
Material on hire
SM

Heiratspost Kantate (1957) 15'
Text: anonymous
Chorus: mixed
hpd-db
Score ED 4773 / Parts ED 4773-01/-02 (chorus)

4 Sätze nach deutschen Volksliedern (1966) 15'
Soloist: soprano
Chorus: mixed
jazz-combo
ED 5841

Windsperger, Lothar
1885-1935

Orchestral Works

Concert Overture in G Major, Op. 17 18'
3(pic).3(ca).3(bcl).3(cbn)-4.3.3.[2ttuba].cbtuba-timp-str
Material on hire
SM

Concert Overture No.3, Op. 61 (1933) 12'
Lützow
2(2pic).2(ca).2(bcl).2(cbn)-4.3.3.1-timp.2perc-str
Material on hire
SM

Vorspiel zu einem Drama, Op. 29 (1921) 12'
3(pic).2.ca.2.bcl.2.cbn-4.3.3.1-timp-str
Material on hire
SM

Concertos

Piano Concerto, Op. 30
(1925) 30'
Soloist: piano
2.2.2.2-4.2.0.0-timp.perc-str
Material on hire
SM

Violin Concerto, Op. 39
(1928) 35'
Soloist: violin
2(pic).2(ca).2(bcl).2(cbn)-4.3.3.1-timp.perc-hp-str
Material on hire
SM

Wittenbrink, Franz
b.1948

Stage Works

Die Leiche im Sack (1985) 100'
Opera-parody in 1 Act
Text: Eberhard Streul
Material on hire
SM

Wohlgemut, Gerhard

b.1920

Chamber & Instrumental Works

Sonatine

arec-pno
OFB 117

Wolf-Ferrari, Ermanno

1876-1948

Stage Works

Der Kuckuck von Theben

(1943)   full evening

Opera in 3 Acts
Text: Ludwig Andersen/Mario Ghisalberti
Material on hire
Libretto **BN 3980-20**

Wunsch, Hermann

1884-1954

Orchestral Works

Fest auf Monbijou, Op. 50

14'

Suite in 5 Movements
2.2.2.2-2.2.0.0-perc-str
Material on hire
Eu

Kleine Lustspiel-Suite, Op. 37

10'

2.2.2.2-4.2.3.0-timp.perc-str
Material on hire
Eu

Concertos

Chamber Concerto, Op. 22

14'

Soloist: piano
1.1.1.1-2.0.0.0-str
Material on hire
Eu

Wyttenbach, Jürg

b.1935

Orchestral Works

Anrufung und Ausbruch

(1966)   13'

*pic.2(pic,afl).2.ca.0.2bsthn(cl).cbcl(bcl).
3.cbn-4.3.4.4*
Material on hire
AVV

Concertos

Piano Concerto   (1963-64/66)   15'

Soloist: piano
*pic.2.1.ca.1(bsthn).bcl.1.cbn-4.3.2.1-
timp.4perc-2hp-str(12.0.6.6.6)*
Material on hire
AVV

Chamber & Instrumental Works

Divisions   (1964)   10'

Soloist: piano
solo str(4.0.2.2.1)/large str orch
Material on hire
Study score **AVV 73**

Execution ajournée 11

(1970)   30'

str qrt
AVV 93

Kunststücke, die Zeit totzuschlagen   (1972)

Hör- und Sehstück für Musiker
ED 6417

Nachspiel in 3 Teilen   (1966)

2pno
AVV 87

Paraphrase   (1969)

fl-pno
AVV 303

3 Pieces   (1969)

pno
AVV 39

3 Sätze   (1963)

ob-hp-pno
AVV 27

Serenade

fl.cl
FTR 121

Solo Voice(s) and Instrument(s)/ Orchestra

De Metalli   (1965-66/1979)   12'

from "Profezie"
Text: Leonardo da Vinci
Soloist: bass
*1.0.3.2-3.3.2.1-timp.2perc-pno.hp-
str(0.0.0.4.3)*
Material on hire
AVV

Choral Works

Sutil and Laar   (1962-63)   16'

10 Gay Songs
Text: H.P. Matter
Chorus: mixed
pno (4hnd)
Score **ED 5675** / Choral score **ED 5675-01**

Infoline · e-Mail
Schott Musik International
Mainz: Schott.Musik.com@T-Online.de
London: 101627.166@compuserve.com

Xiaogang, Ye

b.1955

Orchestral Works

Strophe (1985)   12'

for 16 musicians
1.1.1.1-1.1.1.0-2perc-pno.hp-str(1.1.1.1.1)
SM

Winter, Op. 28 (1988)

3(pic).2.2.2-4.2.3.1-3perc-hp-str
SM

Concertos

**The Last Paradise,
Op. 24** (1993)

Soloist: violin
3(pic).3(ca).2.2.cbn-5.3.3.1-5perc-hp-str
SM

The Scent of Black Mango

(1994-95)   17'

Soloist: piano
3.2.2.3-4.3.3.1-4perc-hp-str
SM

**The Silence of the
Sakyamuni, Op. 29**

Soloist: shakuhachi
3(pic).2(ca).2.2-4.3.3.1-timp.5perc-cel.hp-str
SM

Chamber & Instrumental Works

Ballade (1988)   9'

pno
SM

Enchanted Bamboo Shoots

(1989-90/94)   10'

2vn.va.vc-pno
SM

Nine Horses (1993)   9'

for 10 musicians
fl.ob.cl-2perc-pno-vn.va.vc.db
SM

Xiaogang, Ye

b. 23.9.1955

From 1978 till 1983 he studied at the Central Conservatory of Music in China. In 1982 he won the first prize at the Alexander Tcherepnin Composition Competition. In 1983 he was appointed composer-in-residence and teacher at the Central Conservatory in China. From 1987 he studied at the Eastman School of Music of the University of Rochester and took his Master's degree there. Ye Xiaogang is one of the best known composers in China.

Solo Voice(s) and Instrument(s)/ Orchestra

Purple Fog & White Poppy

(1991)   14'

Text: Beidao/Mang Ke
Soloist: soprano
2.2.2.2-4.3.3.1-4perc-hp-str
SM

Y

Yuasa, Joji

b.1929

Orchestral Works

Chronoplastic (1972) 13'

3.3.4.3-6.4.2.btbn.1-5perc-2pno(cel).hp-
str(14.14.12.10.8)
Material on hire
Study score **ED 6347**

A Dirge by Bach (1983) 3'

for the sick soul. From J.S. Bach:
Präludium XXII, Fuga XXII a 5 voci
3(pic).2.ca.3(bcl)2.cbn-4.3.3.1-timp.vib-
pno(cel).hp-str(12.10.8.7.7)
Material on hire
SJ

Eye on Genesis II (1992) 13'

3(afl,pic,bfl).3(ca).4(Ebcl,bcl).3(cbn)-
4.3.3(btbn).1-5perc-pno.cel.hp-
str(16.14.12.10.8)
Material on hire
SJ

Hommage à Sibelius (1991) 7'

The Midnight Sun
3(pic,afl).3(ca).3(Ebcl,bcl).3(cbn)-
4.3.3(btbn).0-cel.pno.hp-2perc-
str(16.14.12.10.8)
Material on hire
SJ

A Perspective for Orchestra

(1983) 14'

3.3.3.3-4.3.3.1-4perc-pno(cel).hp-
str(14.12.10.8.7)
Material on hire
SJ

Requiem for Orchestra

(1980) 24'

3.3.3.3-4.3.3.1-5perc-cel.pno.hp-
str(12.10.8.6.6)
Material on hire
SJ

Suite - Scenes from Bashô

(1980-89) 24'

3.2.3.2-4.3.2.0-4perc-pno.cel.hp-
str(12.12.10.8.6)
Material on hire
Study score **ED 7060**

Symphonic Suite (1995) 20'

"The Narrow Road into the Deep North:
Bashô"
3(pic,afl).3(ca).3(Ebcl,bcl).3(cbn)-4.3.3.0-
4perc-hp.pno.cel-str(16.14.12.10.8)
Material on hire
SJ

TIME of Orchestral Time

(1975-76) 19'

4.4.4.4-6.6.4.1-5perc-pno(cel).hp-
str(12.12.12.10.8)
Material on hire
Study score **ED 6820**

Yuasa, Joji

b. Koriyama 12.8.1929

Japan's leading composer after Takemitsu,
Yuasa played a crucial role in the development of electronic music in the 1950's, and
has remained an important influence on the
experimental movement to the present day.
Reflecting the composer's exceptional sensitivity to sonority, his music is also the pro-
duct of a rigorous and probing logic, resul-
ting in refined, impressionist soundscapes
that reveal a highly individual approach to
problems of form and structure. The recipient of many international prizes, Yuasa is
also the composer of distinguished scores
for several documentary and experimental
films.

Concertos

Nine Levels by Ze-Ami

(1988) 35'

Soloist: tape
2.1.2.0-1.1.1.0-2perc-cel(epno).pno-
str(1.1.1.1.1)
Material on hire
SJ

Revealed Time (1986) 16'

Soloist: viola
3(3pic).2(ca).3(Ebcl,bcl).2(cbn)-4.3.3.0-
3perc-pno(cel).hp-str(12.10.8.8.6)
Material on hire
Study score **SJ 1063**

Infoline · e-Mail
Schott Musik International
Mainz: Schott.Musik.com@T-Online.de
London: 101627.166@compuserve.com

Chamber & Instrumental Works

Clarinet Solitude (1980) 8'
clarinet solo
SJ 1015

Cosmos Haptic II (1986) 12'
Transfiguration
pno
SJ 1034

Cosmos Haptic III (1990) 13'
Kokuh
nijugen koto-shakuhachi
Material on hire
SJ

Domain (1978) 9'
flute solo
SJ 1002

Interpenetration No.2
(1983) 10'
2perc
SJ 1021

Ishibutai Ko (1981) 20'
ryuteki.3shakuhachi.jushichigen-2perc
Material on hire
SJ

Mai-Bataraki from Ritual for Delphi (1979) 8'
shakuhachi-perc
Material on hire
SJ

Mai-Bataraki II (1987) 9'
afl/noh-fl
SJ 1043

My Blue Sky, No.3 (1977) 12'
violin solo
SJ 1001

Projection Esemplastic
(1961) 9'
pno(s)
Material on hire
SJ

Projection for Electric Guitar(s) (1968) Var.
Arrogance of the Dead
Material on hire
SJ

Projection for Seven Players
(1955) 17'
fl(pic).ob.cl(bcl)-hn.tpt-vc-pno
Material on hire
SJ

Subliminal Hey J. (1990) 4'
Transcriptions for Piano on "Hey, Jude" by J. Lennon and P. McCartney
pno
Material on hire
SJ

Terms of Temporal Detailing
(1989) 12'
Homage to David Hockney
bassflute solo
SJ 1062

To the Genesis (1988) 12'
shô solo
Material on hire
SJ

Viola Locus (1995) 9'
viola solo
SJ

A Winter Day -Homage to Bashô- (1981) 18'
fl.cl-perc-pno.hp
Material on sale
SJ 1028

Solo Voice(s)/Voice(s) and Piano/Guitar

Kansoku (1965) Var.
solo voices
Material on hire
SJ

Solo Voice(s) and Instrument(s)/ Orchestra

Mutterings (1988) 12'
Text: R.D. Laing
Soloist: mezzo-soprano
fl(afl).cl(bcl)-vn(va).vc-perc-pno.gtr
Material on hire
SJ

Observations on Weather Forecasts (1983) 8'
baritone-tpt
SJ 1029

Suite Fushi Gyo-Un (1988) 24'
Text: Makoto Ooka (Japanese)
Soloists: alto, tenor
sho.fl(shinobue/noh-kan).2shakuhachi.kokyu.futozao.shamisen-2perc.2koto.2jushichigen
Material on hire
SJ

Choral Works

Composition on Ze-Ami's Nine Grades (1984) 20'
Text: Ze-Ami (Japanese)
Chorus: male a cappella
Material on sale
SJ

Projection Onomatopoetic
(1979) 18'
Chorus: mixed a cappella
Material on hire
SJ

Shin Kiyari Kanda Sanka
(1984) 20'
Chorus: male
5 or more shakuhachi
Material on hire
SJ

Uta Asobi (Play Songs) on Onomatopoeia (1985) 15'
Chorus: children's a cappella
Material on hire
SJ

Electronic Works

Aoi no Ue (1961) 27'
Musique Concrete
electronic
SJ

Icon on the Source of White Noise (1967) 13'
5 channel electronic music
SJ

Music for Space Projection
(1970) 15'
6 channel music for tape
SJ

My Blue Sky, No.1 (1975) 16'
stereophonic tape
SJ

My Blue Sky, No.2 (1976) 6'
In Southern California
4 channel computer-electronic music
SJ

A Study in White (1987) 10'
computer music
SJ

Towards "The Midnight Sun" (1984) 18'
homage to Ze-Ami
quadraphonic computer-generated tape-amplified pno
SJ

Voices Coming (1969) 19'
stereophonic tape
SJ

Zádór, Eugen
b.1894

Orchestral Works

Dance Symphony   23'
3.3.3.3-4.3.3.1-timp.perc-hp-str
Material on hire
Eu

Hungarian Capriccio   10'
3.2.2.2-4.2.3.0-perc-str
Material on hire
Eu

Chamber & Instrumental Works

Divertimento   15'
for brass ensemble
Material on hire
Study score **ETP 1301**

Zbinden, Julien-François
b.1917

Concertos

Concertino, Op. 6 (1946)   8'
Soloist: trumpet
str-small drum
Material on hire
Piano reduction **ED 4979**

Divertissement, Op. 10
(1948-49)   14'
Soloist: doublebass
2(pic).2.2.2-2.2.2.0-timp.perc-str
Material on hire
Piano reduction **ED 4781**

Chamber & Instrumental Works

Sonatina, Op. 5 (1945)   9'
fl-pno
ED 4110

Zehden, Hans
b.1912

Orchestral Works

Les Chansons (1951)   21'
1(pic).1.1.1-1.1.1.0-3perc-cel.pno-str
Material on hire
SM

Zehm, Friedrich
b.1923

Orchestral Works

Alla Danza (1978)   12'
orch/str/instrumental ensemble
Score **ED 6755** / Parts **ED 6755-11 (-19)**

Rhythmophonie (1970)   10'
2.0.2.1-2.2.1.0-2perc-[pno.egtr(gtr)]-str
Score **CON 170** / Parts **CON 170-11 (-29)**

Schwierigkeiten & Unfälle mit einem Choral (1974)   10'
Satire
*2fl(pic).2ob.2cl(Ebcl).2bn(cbn)-2hn +
various doublings on perc*
Material on hire
Study score **ED 6655**

Concertos

Capriccio (1968)   16'
Soloist: percussion
1.1.1.1-1.1.0.0-perc-str
Material on hire
Piano reduction **BAT 11**

Concerto da Camera (1967)   16'
Soloist: oboe
str
Material on hire
Piano reduction **OBB 26**

Concerto in Pop (1972-73)   17'
Soloists: eorg, egtr, electric bass, drums
2.0.2.[1]-1.1.1.0-perc-str
Material on hire
SM

Infoline · e-Mail
Schott Musik International
Mainz: Schott.Musik.com@T-Online.de
London: 101627.166@compuserve.com

Zehm, Friedrich

b. Neusalz Oder, Silesia 22.1.1923

The Hindemith tradition of "Gebrauchsmusik" and refined contrapuntal writing
has been the chief influence on Friedrich
Zehm's music. Flavoured with a personal
blend of lyricism and with a sense of harmonic indulgence that includes the exotic
and complex chords of jazz, his music dis-
plays a fine sensitivity to incisive instrumental doublings and to other textural subtle-
ties. Contributions to all the major genres
are included in his list of works.

Chamber & Instrumental Works

Ballad (1981) 9'

hn-pno
Material on sale
Score **COR 8**

Canto e Rondo (1968) 8'

tpt-pno
TR 9

6 Caprices (1966) 18'

2fl
FTR 85

Divertimento Ritmico

(1970) 16'

Modern Dance-Rhytms
rec choir/orch/str-perc-[vc/db or gtr/bgtr]
Study score **ED 6164** / Parts **ED 6164-11 (-21)**

4 Easy Pieces (1990) 12'

vc-pno
CB 147

3 Elegies (1987) 15'

va-pno
VAB 54

Hindemith Variations

(1979) 13'

2ob.ca
OBB 30

Intermezzo (1979) 4'

in: Das neue Klavierbuch
pno solo
ED 7095

Klarinetten im Duett (1975) 16'

8 Pieces
2cl
KLB 18

Little Suite (1974) 5'

in: Leichte Klavierstücke und Sonatinen
des 17.-20.Jahrhunderts
pno solo
ED 6806

Modern Dances (1986) 12'

2vc
CB 128

Musica notturna (1980) 14'

4 Pieces
guitar solo
GA 476

Neue Bläserstücke 11'

4 brass instruments
Score **BLK 105** / Parts **BLK 105-11 (-18)**

Neue Duettstudien (1972) 30'

2fl
FTR 98

Ommagio a Domenico Scarlatti (1985) 15'

Due sonate per pianoforte
ED 7415

Pentameron (1968) 16'

5 pieces
bn-pno
FAG 13

6 Preludes and Fugues

(1980) 21'

guitar solo
GA 486

Rhapsodische Sonate (1982) 16'

vn-pno
VLB 66

Scherzino in Fis (1981) 3'

from "Trifoglietto"
2fl(pic).2ob.2cl.2bn(cbn)-2hn
Material on hire
SM

Serenade (1969) 9'

fl-gtr
GA 443

Sonata Brevis (1985) 10'

tpt-pno
TR 16

Sonatille (1985) 6'

in: Neue Klavierstücke für Kinder
pno solo
ED 7392

Sonatina (1980) 11'

mand-gtr
GA 474

Sonatina giocosa (1973) 7'

cl-pno
KLB 17

11 Stücke für den Anfang

(1980)

(Kreidler Gitarren-Studio)
2/3gtr
ED 6984

Wie spät ist es, Signor Haydn? (1982) 8'

About the Andante from the Symphony
Hob. I/101"Die Uhr"
pno (4hnd)
ED 7013

Solo Voice(s)/Voice(s) and Piano/Guitar

Ein Bündel Chansons

(1967-68) 39'

Text: Fritz Grasshoff
medium voice-pno
ED 6036

Choral Works

Alter Spruch (1969) 2'

from "4 heitere Chorlieder"
Text: Mag. Martinus
Chorus: mixed double a cappella
C 42464

Grasshoffiade (1969) 16'

4 gay songs
Text: Fritz Grasshoff
Chorus: male
piano
Score **C 42338/42340** / Parts **C 42339-01/-02**
C 42341-01/-02 (chorus)

Inserat (1969) 2'

from "4 heitere Chorlieder"
Text: Theodor Storm
Chorus: mixed a cappella
C 42462

Nonstop-Songs (1969) 20'

Cantata after contemporary nonsens-verses
Soloist: speaker
Chorus: youth
wind player.brass player-perc-glsp.pno.gtr-str
Parts **ED 6257-11 (-21)** / Choral score
ED 6257-01

Spruch (1969) 2'

from "4 heitere Chorlieder"
Text: Johann Wolfgang von Goethe
Chorus: mixed a cappella
C 42462

Zur Verlobung (1969) 2'

from "4 heitere Chorlieder"
Text: Wilhelm Busch
Chorus: mixed a cappella
C 42463

Zender, Hans
b.1936

Concertos

Chamber Concerto (1959) 15'

Soloist: flute
hpd.hp-str(1.1.1.1.0)
Material on hire
SM

Zgraja, Krystof
b.1950

Chamber & Instrumental Works

Modern Flutist I

10 easy concert-pieces
fl-pno
ED 8422

Modern Flutist II

20 Duets
2fl
ED 8423

Modern Flutist III

14 Trios
3fl
ED 8424

3 virtuose Flamenco-Studien

14 Trios
flute solo
ED 8425

Zilcher, Hermann
1881-1948

Orchestral Works

Dance-Fantasy, Op. 71 16'

3.2.2.2-4.3.3.1-timp.perc-cel.hp-str
Material on hire
Eu

Zillig, Winfried
1905-1963

Stage Works

Die Windsbraut

(1941) full evening

Opera in 3 Scenes
Text: Richard Billinger
Material on hire
SM

Zimmermann, Bernd Alois
1918-1970

Stage Works

Alagoana (1950-55) 29'

Ballet. "Caprichos Brasileiros"
Material on hire
Piano reduction **ED 4929**

Concerto pour violoncelle et orchestre en forme de "pas de trois" (1965-66) 24'

Ballet
Material on hire
Study score **ED 6329** / Piano reduction **ED 7164**

Kontraste (1953) 10'

Music to an Imaginary Ballet. Idea by Fred Schneckenburger
Material on hire
SM

Des Menschen Unterhaltsprozeß gegen Gott

(1952) 90'

Radio Opera in 3 Acts
Text: Pedro Calderón de la Barca/Hubert Rüttger
Material on hire
SM

Zimmermann, Bernd Alois

b. Bliesheim 20.3.1918, d. Königsdorf nr. Cologne 10.8.1970

Though relatively few in mumber, the compositions of Bernd Alois Zimmermann hold a key position in the history of post-war German music. A late-starter, he not only absorbed the disciplines of serialism and the rigours of the Darmstadt avant-garde, but also merged these influences with jazz and with quotations from earlier composers in a way that strikingly anticipates post-modern techniques. His concept of the "Imaginary ballet", abstract scenarios imposed on often strictly worked formal schemes, accounts for moments of ravishing fantasy within his music. The implicit contrast between order and imagination reflected, perhaps, the conflicts in his own troubled mind. His untimely death occurred when the success of the opera "Die Soldaten", and the "Requiem for a Young Poet" was bringing him ever greater international recognition.

Perspektiven (1955/56) 15'

Music to an Imaginary Ballet for 2 pianos
Material on hire
Piano reduction **ED 4910**

Présence (1961) 30'

Ballet
Text: Paul Pörtner
Material on hire
ED 6733

Die Soldaten (1957-65) 110'

Opera in 4 Acts
Text: Jakob Michael Reinhold Lenz
Material on hire
Study score **ED 6343** / Vocal score **ED 5076-01** / Piano reduction **ED 5067** / Libretto **BN 3990-10**

Bernd Alois Zimmermann
Symphony in one Movement (1953)

Orchestral Works

Alagoana (Caprichos Brasileiros) (1950-55) 29'

Ballet Suite
3(pic).2.ca.Ebcl.bcl.2asax.tsax.2.cbn-
3.3.2.btuba(cbtuba)-2timp.5perc-
pno.hpd(cel).hp.gtr-str
Material on hire
Piano reduction **ED 4929**

Caboclo (1950-55) 4'

From "Alagoana"
2(2pic).2(ca).2.asax.tsax.bsax2-
3.2.2.cbtuba-2timp.6perc-pno.hpd.gtr.hp-
str(3.3.3.3.1)
Material on hire
Piano reduction **ED 4929**

Concerto for Orchestra

(1948) 17'
3(pic).2.ca.2.bcl.3(cbn)-4.3.3.1-timp.4perc-
pno-str
Material on hire
SM

Concerto for Strings (1948) 13'

Arrangement of the "Trio" for strings
(1944)
str
Material on hire
SM

Kontraste (1953) 10'

Music to an Imaginary Ballet. Idea by Fred
Schneckenburger
1(pic).0.1.1-1.1.1.0-timp.4perc-
cel.pno.hpd.hp-str
Material on hire
SM

Metamorphose (1954) 25'

Music to the film of the same name by
Michael Wolgensinger
1(pic).1(ca).1.asax.1-1.1.0.0-timp.3perc-
pno(hpd,eorg,[hammondorg]).hp.egtr-
str(4.0.2.2.1)
Material on hire
SM

Un "Petit Rien" (1964) 6'

3fl(3pic,afl)-3perc-cel.hpd.gtr-str(3.0.2.1.1)
Material on hire
SM

Photoptosis (1968) 13'

Prelude
4(pic). 3(ob d'am,ca).4(bsthn,bcl)3(cbn)-
5(btuba).4.4(cbtbn).cbtuba-timp.2perc-
pno(cel).hp.org-str(12.10.7.6.5)
Material on hire
Study score **ED 6311**

Rheinische Kirmestänze

(1950/62) 6'
2(2pic).2.2.2(cbn)-2.1/cnt.1.cbtuba
Score **CON 176** / Parts **CON 176-10**

Sinfonia prosodica (1945) 40'

3(pic).3(ca).2.3(cbn)-4.3.3.1-timp.3perc-
2hp-str
Material on hire
SM

Söbensprung (1950) 6'

2(pic).2.2.2-2.2.2.1-timp.perc
Material on hire
SM

Stille und Umkehr (1970) 10'

Sketches
4.3.ca.4(bcl).asax.0.cbn-4.2.1.cbtbn.0-
5perc-hp.acc-str(1.0.1.3.3)
Material on hire
Study score **ED 6319**

Suite aus "Gelb und Grün"

(1952) 9'
Music to a puppet play
1(pic).0.1(Dcl).1-1.1.1(tbtbn+ fourth
valve).0-timp.2perc-pno(cel).hpd.hp-
str(1.1.1.1.1)
Material on hire
SM

Symphonic Variations and Fugue on "In Dulci Jubilo"

(1949) 35'
2(pic).2(ca).2.2-4.3.3.1-timp.perc-cel.hp-str
Material on hire
SM

Symphony in one Movement

(1953) 17'
3(pic).3(ca).3(bcl).3(cbn)-4.3.3.1-2timp.
4perc-cel(pno).2hp-str(12vnI.10vnII.
10vnIII.6vaI.6vaII.10vc.8db)
Material on hire
Study score **ED 4568**

Concertos

Canto di speranza (1957) 19'

Soloist: cello
3(pic).2.ca.3(bcl).asax.1-1.2.0.0-
timp.3perc-cel(pno).hp-str(0.0.9.6.4)
Material on hire
Study score **ED 4588** / Parts **ED 6986 (solo)**

Concerto pour violoncelle et orchestre en forme de "pas de trois" (1965-66) 24'

Soloist: cello
3(pic).3(ob d'am).3(bcl).asax(ssax).3(cbn)-
2(Bhn high).2(cnt).2(cbtbn).cbtuba-
timp.5perc-pno(hpd).hp.gtr(egtr).dulci-
mer(hungarian)/prep pno.glasshp/cel-
str(7.7.6.5.4)
Material on hire
Study score **ED 6329** / Piano reduction
ED 7164

Dialoge (1960/65) 18'

Soloists: 2 pianos
5(5pic,afl).3(ca).5(Ebcl,bcl).2asax(tsax,bar
sax).3(cbn)-5.4.4(cbtbn).1(cbtuba)-
3timp.9perc-cel.hp.gtr-str(14.12.10.8.7)
Material on hire
Study score **ED 7134**

Oboe Concerto (1952) 15'

Soloist: oboe
1(pic).0.1.1-1.1.0.1-timp.2perc-pno.hp-str
Material on hire
Piano reduction **ED 6408**

Trumpet Concerto (1954) 15'

Nobody knows de trouble I see
Soloist: trumpet
1(pic).1(ca).jazzcl.3asax.tsax.barsax.1-
1.3jazztpt.jazztbn.btuba-timp.3perc-pno
(hammondorg/xyl).hp.gtr-str
Piano reduction **ED 7163**

Violin Concerto (1950) 18'

Soloist: violin
3.3.3.3-4.3.3.1-timp.perc-cel.pno.hp-str
Material on hire
Piano reduction **ED 6463**

Chamber & Instrumental Works

Enchiridion (1949/52) 27'

Little Pieces.(Part I, II, appendix)
pno
ED 4214

Intercomunicazione

(1967) 12'-24'
vc-pno
ED 6004

Konfigurationen (1954/56) 10'

pno
ED 4942

Little Suite (1942) 8'

vn-pno
ED 7564

Monologe (1964) 18'

2pno
ED 5427

Perspektiven (1955/56) 15'

Music from the Imaginary Ballet
2pno
ED 4910

String Trio (1944) 12'

vn.va.vc
ED 7563

Tempus Loquendi (1963) 12'

fl.afl.bfl
Score **ED 5395** / Parts **ED 5413**

Viola Sonata (1955) 10'

viola solo
VAB 37

Violin Sonata (1950) 15'

vn-pno
ED 4485

Violin Sonata (1951) 13'

violin solo
ED 4907

Solo Voice(s)/Voice(s) and Piano/Guitar

5 Lieder (1942-46)   10'

Text: various
medium voice-pno
ED 7607

3 Sacred Songs (1946)   8'

Text: Ernst Bertram
medium voice-pno
ED 7565

Solo Voice(s) and Instrument(s)/ Orchestra

Die fromme Helene (1957)   40'

Text: Wilhelm Busch
Soloist: voice
fl(pic).ob.cl.bn-tpt.cbtuba-vn.vc
Material on hire
SM

"Ich wandte mich und sah an alles Unrecht, das geschah unter der Sonne" (1970)   20'

Ecclesiastische Aktion
Soloist: bass
*2speaker-3(3pic,afl).3(ca).3.3-
5.3.6(cbtbn).1-timp.6perc-hp.egtr-str*
Material on hire
Study score **ED 6330**

Die Soldaten (1957-63)   30'

Vocal Symphony
Soloists: S.MS.A.T.Bar.B
*4(4pic,afl).3(ca).4(Ebcl,acl,bcl).asax.3(cbn)-
5(btuba).4Ctpt(Ftpt,Bbtpt,Atpt,btpt).4(cbtb
n).cbtuba-timp.6-8perc-glsp.xyl.marimb.
vib.cel.pno(hpd).hp.org.gtr-
str(14.12.10.8.7)*
Material on hire
SM

Choral Works

Bei meines Buhlen Haupte
(1947)   3'

Text: German Folksong
Chorus: mixed a cappella
C 47825

Die Brünnlein, die da fließen
(1947)   30'

Soloists: alto, baritone
Chorus: mixed
1.2.0.2-2.0.0.0-hp-str(1.1.1.0)
Material on sale
ED 7559

Lob der Torheit (1948)   28'

Burlesque Cantata
Text: Johann Wolfgang von Goethe
Soloists: soprano, tenor, bass
Chorus: mixed
*3(pic).2.ca.2/Ebcl9.bcl.3(cbn)-4.3.3.1-
timp.4perc-2pno.cel/pno.hp-str
alt. version (1959): fl.cl.bcl-timp.6perc-
2pno(cel).hp-vn.va.vc*
Material on hire
SM

Requiem für einen jungen Dichter (1967-69)   65'

Lingual
Text: various
Soloists: speaker, soprano, baritone
Chorus: mixed
*4(4pic).4(ob
d'am,ca).4(bcl).asax.tsax(ssax,barsax).
3(cbn)-5(ttuba).4.btpt.5(cbtbn).cbtuba-
3timp.perc-2pno.hp.org.acc.mand-
str(0.0.0.10.8)-live electronic
jazz qnt: sax-cnt-pno-perc-bass*
Material on hire
SM

Electronic Works

Tratto (1965-67)   15'

live electronics
Material on hire
SM

Tratto 2 (1970)   12'

electronics
Material on hire
SM

Zipp, Friedrich
b.1914

Chamber & Instrumental Works

Sonatine, Op. 23a   10'

arec/fl/vn-hpd/pno
OFB 118

Zoll, Paul
1907-1978

Choral Works

Abendlied (1953)   3'

Text: Matthias Claudius
Chorus: male a cappella
CHBL 65

Ach, du Liebste mein (1972)   2'

from "4 heitere Chorlieder"
Chorus: male a cappella
C 43313

Aus weiter Ferne (1960)   4'

Chorus: male a cappella
C 40294

Bei den Klängen des Fandango (1959)   15'

Spanish Song-play
Text: various
Chorus: male
pno
ED 4986 / Parts **ED 4986-01/-02 (chorus)**

Eia, mein Kindchen (1955)   3'

Chorus: female a cappella (4 prt)
CHBL 570

3 Folksongs (1958)   8'

Chorus: mixed
pno
ED 4782 (piano) / Parts **ED 4782-01/-02
(chorus)**

Im Frühlingsregen (1962)   3'

Chorus: male a cappella
C 40771

Frühmorgens auf der Jagd
(1965)   3'

Chorus: male a cappella
C 41380

Das Glöckchen (1951)   2'

from "3 russische Volkslieder"
Chorus: male a cappella
C 37857

Hat zwei Fenster meine Seele (1967)   2'

from "3 Chöre"
Text: russian
Chorus: female a cappella
C 41865

Iberisches Liederspiel
(1963)   17'

Chorus: female (4 prt)
pno-[perc]
Score **ED 5297** / Vocal score **ED 5297-01**

Im Garten die Beere, die rote (1951)   3'

from "3 russische Volkslieder"
Chorus: male a cappella
C 37858

Ein Jäger wollt' zum Jagen gehn (1952)   3'

Chorus: male a cappella, [children's]
CHBL 71

Jenseits des Tales standen ihre Zelte (1969)   3'

Text: Börries v. Münchhausen
Chorus: male a cappella
C 42582

Der Kuckuck ruft im grünen Wald (1952) 2'

Text: M. Barthel
Chorus: female a cappella + 2 solo voices
CHBL 539

Laridah (1972) 4'

from "4 heitere Chorlieder"
Text: O.J. Bierbaum
Chorus: male a cappella
C 43316

Die Lerche (1955) 3'

Text: M. Barthel
Chorus: female a cappella (4 prt)
CHBL 570

Lied in den Rosen (1952) 3'

Text: M. Barthel
Chorus: male a cappella
CHBL 61

Lobt den Herrn, ihr Wesen all (1962) 7'

Little Cantata
Text: A. Stiefenhofen/F.W. Weber
Chorus: mixed/male + boy's
org(pno)/hn.tpt.2tbn
Score **ED 5462** / Parts **ED 5264-10** /
Vocal score **ED 5462-01 (-03)**

Lumpenlied (1972) 4'

from "4 heitere Chorlieder"
Text: C. Flaischlen
Chorus: male a cappella
C 43314

Der Marsch der Könige (1956) 4'

Chorus: male a cappella
C 39501

Meine Heimat (1965) 4'

Text: S.v. Vegesack
Chorus: male a cappella
C 41379

Nach Süden nun sich lenken (1954) 3'

Text: Joseph von Eichendorff
Chorus: male a cappella
C 38916

Nobody knows (1959) 4'

from "4 amerikanische Volkslieder"
Chorus: male a cappella
C 40110

Nun ruhen alle Wälder (1953) 3'

Text: P. Gerhardt
Chorus: male a cappella
CHBL 65

Old Kentucky home (1959) 4'

from "4 amerikanische Volkslieder"
Chorus: male a cappella
C 40111

Pferde zu vieren traben 3'

Chorus: male a cappella
CHBL 56

Die Prinzessin und der Trommler (1954) 2'

Rondo
Chorus: male a cappella
C 38658

Requiem (1978/87) 55'

Arranger: Hilger Schallehn/Norbert
Studnitzky
Soloists: alto, tenor
Chorus: mixed, children's
1.1.2.1-3.2.3.0-timp.perc-str
Material on hire
SM

Rheinisches Fuhrmannslied (1954) 3'

Chorus: male a cappella
C 39350

Ringsum leuchten Apfelblüten (1951) 3'

from "3 russische Volkslieder"
Chorus: male a cappella
C 37866

Sing, kleine Nachtigall (1961) 4'

Chorus: male a cappella
C 40481

Spanisches Liederspiel (1960) 20'

Chorus: mixed
pno.[perc]
Score **ED 5073** / Parts **ED 5073-01/-02**
(chorus)

Swanee Ribber (1959) 4'

from "4 amerikanische Volkslieder"
Chorus: male a cappella
C 40112

Swing low, sweet chariot (1959) 4'

from "4 amerikanische Volkslieder"
Chorus: male a cappella
C 40109

Das verlassene Mägdelein (1952) 2'

Chorus: female a cappella (4 prt)
CHBL 525

Das Waldkonzert (1952) 6'

Text: Chr. Dieffenbach
Chorus: male a cappella
C 38104

Wär ich Mädchen ohne Mann geblieben (1967) 2'

from "3 Chöre"
Text: russian
Chorus: female a cappella
C 41866

Wiegenliedchen (1967) 5'

from "3 Chöre"
Text: russian
Chorus: female a cappella
C 41865

Wohlauf, Gesellen, seid froh und munter (1961) 2'

Chorus: male a cappella
CHBL 181

Wohlauf, in Gottes schöne Welt (1952) 3'

Chorus: male a cappella
CHBL 72

Zu Regensburg auf der Kirchturmspitz (1960) 4'

Chorus: male a cappella
C 40249

Zwei Spielleut (1972) 4'

from "4 heitere Chorlieder"
Text: A. von Bernus
Chorus: male a cappella
C 43315

Infoline · e-Mail
Schott Musik International
Mainz: Schott.Musik.com@T-Online.de
London: 101627.166@compuserve.com

Index by Category

Stage Works

Opera

Albert, Eugen d'
Liebesketten 14
Tragaldabas 14

Andreae, Volkmar
Abenteuer des Casanova, Op. 34 14

Antheil, George
Transatlantic - The People's Choice.... 14

Arlan, Dennis
The Ballad of the Bremen Band 14

Bittner, Julius
Der Musikant 23
Die rote Gred 23

Blomdahl, Karl-Birger
Aniara 23
Herr von Hancken 24

von Bose, Hans-Jürgen
63: Dream Palace 25
Blutbund 25
Chimäre 25
Das Diplom 25
Die Leiden des jungen Werthers 25

Brandts-Buys, Jan
Der Mann im Mond 25
Die Schneider von Schönau 25

Brehme, Hans
Liebe ist teuer 28
Der Uhrmacher
von Straßburg, Op. 36 28

Bresgen, Cesar
Brüderlein Hund 28
Der Igel als Bräutigam 28
Der Mann im Mond 28
Das Urteil des Paris 28

Bryars, Gavin
Medea 31

Casken, John
Golem 34

Castiglioni, Niccolò
Sweet 36

Cowie, Edward
Commedia, Op. 12 38

Dessau, Paul
Die Verurteilung des Lukullus 42

Egk, Werner
Columbus 45
Der Fuchs und der Rabe 45
Die Historie vom Ritter Don Juan
aus Barcelona 45
Irische Legende 46
Der Löwe und die Maus 46
Peer Gynt 46
Der Revisor 46
Siebzehn Tage und vier Minuten
(Circe) 46
Die Verlobung in San Domingo 46
Die Zaubergeige 46

Eisenmann, Will
Bethsabé 48
Der König der dunklen Kammer 48
Leonce und Lena 48

Fortner, Wolfgang
Bluthochzeit 50
Corinna 51
Creß ertrinkt 51
Elisabeth Tudor 51
In seinem Garten liebt
Don Perlimplín Belisa 51
That Time 51

Françaix, Jean
Le Diable boiteux 54

Gál, Hans
„Die beiden Klaas", Op. 42 62

Gerster, Ottmar
Enoch Arden 67
Die Hexe von Passau 67
Madame Liselotte 67
Die Mondschein-Prinzessin 67
Das verzauberte Ich 67

Gilbert, Anthony
The Scene-Machine
(Das Popgeheuer), Op. 18 68

Goehr, Alexander
Arden muss sterben -
Arden Must Die, Op. 21 70
Arianna, Op. 58 70
Behold the Sun -
Die Wiedertäufer, Op. 44 70
Naboth's Vineyard, Op. 25 70
Shadowplay, Op. 30 70
Sonata about Jerusalem, Op. 31 70

Grandis, Renato de
Eduard und Kunegunde 79
Die Schule der Kahlen 79

Grünauer, Ingomar
Amleth und Fengo 80
Besichtigung, Versteigerung und
Beseitigung von 5 Künstlern 80
König für einen Tag 80
Die Mutter 80
Die Rache einer russischen Waise 80
Die Schöpfungsgeschichte
des Adolf Wölfli 80
Winterreise 80

Haas, Joseph
Die Hochzeit des Jobs, Op. 93 81
Tobias Wunderlich, Op. 90 81

Hartmann, Karl Amadeus
Simplicius Simplicissimus 88
Wachsfigurenkabinett 88

Heiden, Bernhard
The Darkened City 91

Henze, Hans Werner
The Bassarids 93
Boulevard Solitude 93
La Cubana oder
'Ein Leben für die Kunst' 93
Don Chisciotte 93
Elegy for Young Lovers 93
Das Ende einer Welt - Opera buffa 93
Das Ende einer Welt - Radio Opera 93
The English Cat 93
Fürwahr...!? 93
Der junge Lord 93
Knastgesänge 93
König Hirsch 93
Ein Landarzt - Opera 93
Ein Landarzt - Radio Opera 93
Der langwierige Weg in die Wohnung
der Natascha Ungeheuer 93
Der Mann, der vom Tode auferstand ... 93
Moralities 95
Pollicino 95
Der Prinz von Homburg 95
Il Re Cervo oder
Die Irrfahrten der Wahrheit 95
Re Teodoro in Venezia 95
Il ritorno d'Ulisse in patria 95
Das Urteil der Kalliope 95
Venus und Adonis 95
Das verratene Meer 95
We come to the River 95
Das Wundertheater 95
Das Wundertheater - reduced version... 95

Hiller, Wilfried
An diesem heutigen Tage 103
Die Ballade von Norbert Nackendick
oder Das nackte Nashorn 103
Chaplin-Ford-Trott 103
Die Fabel von Filemon Faltenreich
oder Die Fußballweltmeisterschaft
der Fliegen 104
Die Geschichte vom alten Adler und
dem kleinen blauen Bergsee 104
Der Goggolori 104
Ijob 104
Die Jagd nach dem Schlarg 104
Liebestreu und Grausamkeit 104
Der Lindwurm und der Schmetterling
oder Der seltsame Tausch 104
Niobe 104
Der Rattenfänger.
Ein Hamelner Totentanz 104
Tranquilla Trampeltreu,
die beharrliche Schildkröte 104
Das Traumfresserchen 104
Trödelmarkt der Träume 104
Die zerstreute Brillenschlange 104

Hindemith, Paul
Cardillac (New version) 105
Cardillac - (Original Version), Op. 39 ... 105
Die Harmonie der Welt 105
Hin und Zurück, Op. 45a 105
Das lange Weihnachtsmahl 105
Lehrstück 105
Mathis der Maler 106
Mörder, Hoffnung der Frauen, Op. 12... 106
Neues vom Tage 106
Neues vom Tage, revised Version 106
Das Nusch-Nuschi, Op. 20 106
Sancta Susanna, Op. 21 106
Tuttifäntchen 106
Wir bauen eine Stadt 106

Höffer, Paul
Der falsche Waldemar, Op. 39 117

Holliger, Heinz
Come and Go 118
Der magische Tänzer 118
Not I 118
What Where 118

Huber, Klaus
Jot oder
Wann kommt der Herr zurück 123

Humperdinck, Engelbert
Hänsel und Gretel 124

Kelkel, Manfred
La Mandragore -
Alraune (Mandrake), Op. 17 134

Kiehle, Theo
Mitten in der Nacht 134

Killmayer, Wilhelm
La Buffonata (Ballet-Opera) 134
Une leçon de français 134
La Tragedia di Orfeo 134
Yolimba oder Die Grenzen der Magie .. 134

Kirchner, Volker David
Belshazar 138
Erinys 138
Inferno d'amore 138
Das kalte Herz 138
Die Trauung 138

Knab, Armin
Das Lebenslicht 140

Korngold, Erich Wolfgang
Das Lied der Liebe 141
Der Ring des Polykrates, Op. 7 141
Die tote Stadt, Op. 12 141
Violanta, Op. 8 142
Das Wunder der Heliane, Op. 20 142

Kosma, Joseph
Un Amour électronique 145

Kovách, Andor
Medea 145

Kreisler, Fritz
Sissy 145

Křenek, Ernst
Pallas Athene weint 146

Lehmann, Markus
Der kleine Bahnhof 149
Die Wette 149
Zwecks Heirat 149

Ligeti, György
Le Grand Macabre 149
Rondeau 149

Meier, Jost
Augustin 163
Der Drache 163
Sennentuntschi 163

Mors, Rudolf
Der Kreidekreis 165

Müller-Siemens, Detlev
Genoveva oder Die weiße Hirschkuh .. 166
Die Menschen 166

Nono, Luigi
Intolleranza 170

Orff, Carl
Antigonae 172
Astutuli 172
Die Bernauerin 172
Carmina Burana 172
Catulli Carmina 172
Comoedia de Christi Resurrectione 172
Klage der Ariadne (1927)
(Claudio Monteverdi) 172

Die Kluge 172
„Lamenti-Trittico Teatrale" 172
Ludus de Nato Infante Mirificus 174
Der Mond 174
Oedipus der Tyrann 174
Orpheus (Claudio Monteverdi) 174
Prometheus 174
Ein Sommernachtstraum -
A Midsummer Night's Dream 174
Tanz der Spröden
(Claudio Monteverdi) 174
De temporum fine comoedia 174
Trionfo di Afrodite 174
Die Weihnachtsgeschichte 174

Pauels, Heinz
Moll Flanders 176
O Hyazinthia 176

Paulus, Stephen
Harmoonia 177
The Postman always Rings Twice 177
The Village Singer 177
The Woodlanders 177

Penderecki, Krzysztof
Paradise Lost 180
Die schwarze Maske 180
Die Teufel von Loudun 181
Ubu Rex 181

Pfitzner, Hans
Palestrina 185

Reimann, Aribert
Die Gespenstersonate 195
Lear 195
Melusine 195
Das Schloß 195
Ein Traumspiel 195
Troades 195

Reutter, Hermann
Die Brücke von San Luis Rey 200
Doktor Johannes Faust, Op. 47 200
Don Juan und Faust, Op. 75 201
Hamlet 201
Der Lübecker Totentanz, Op. 35 201
Odysseus, Op. 55 201
Die Prinzessin und der Schweinehirt ... 201
Die Rückkehr
des verlorenen Sohnes, Op. 34 201
Saul, Op. 33 201
Der Tod des Empedokles 201
Der verlorene Sohn, Op. 34 201
Der Weg nach Freudenstadt, Op. 66 ... 201
Die Witwe von Ephesus 201

Sackman, Nicholas
Simplicia 212

Schnebel, Dieter
Jowaegerli 215
ki-no 215
Körper-Sprache 215
Maulwerke 215
St. Jago 215
Zeichen-Sprache 215

Schönberg, Arnold
Moses und Aron 219
Von Heute auf Morgen, Op. 32 219

Schulhoff, Erwin
Flammen 224
Die Mondsüchtige 224

Schuller, Gunther
The Visitation (Die Heimsuchung) 225

Scott, Cyril
The Alchemist 227

Searle, Humphrey
The Diary of a Madman, Op. 35 228
The Photo of the Colonel, Op. 41 228

Sehlbach, Erich
Signor Caraffa, Op. 21 229

Singleton, Alvin
Dream Sequence '76 233

Stephan, Rudi
Die ersten Menschen 237

Streul, Eberhard
Das Geheimnis der Wolfsschlucht 244
Die Leiche im Sack 244
Papageno spielt auf der Zauberflöte 244
Die Sternstunde des Josef Bieder 244
Stunde bei Aloysia 244

Stroe, Aurel
Ça n'aura pas le Prix Nobel 244

Sutermeister, Heinrich
Die Füße im Feuer und Fingerhütchen ... 246
Das Gespenst von Canterville 246
Madame Bovary 246
Niobe 246
Raskolnikoff 246
Le Roi Bérenger 246
Romeo and Juliet 246
Der rote Stiefel 246
Die schwarze Spinne 246
Seraphine (Die stumme Apothekerin) ... 246
Titus Feuerfuchs oder
Liebe, Tücke und Perücke 246
Die Zauberinsel 246

Thuille, Ludwig
Gugeline 253
Lobetanz 253

Tippett, Michael
The Ice Break 254
King Priam 254
The Knot Garden 254
The Midsummer Marriage 254
New Year 254

Toch, Ernst
Egon und Emilie, Op. 46 257
Der Fächer, Op. 51 257
Die Prinzessin auf der Erbse, Op. 43 ... 257

Turnage, Mark-Anthony
Greek 259
Killing Time 259

Ullmann, Viktor
Der Kaiser von Atlantis oder
die Todverweigerung 261
Der Sturz des Antichrist, Op. 9 261
Der zerbrochene Krug, Op. 36 261

Walter, Fried
Die Dorfmusik 265

Weill, Kurt
Der Kuhhandel 267

Weismann, Julius
Die pfiffige Magd, Op. 125 268
Schwanenweiß, Op. 75 268

Weiss, Harald
Amanda's Traum 269
Das Gespenst 269

Willi, Herbert
Schlafes Bruder 271

Wimberger, Gerhard
La Battaglia oder
Der rote Federbusch 271
Dame Kobold 271
Schaubudengeschichte 271

285

Wittenbrink, Franz
Die Leiche im Sack 272
Wolf-Ferrari, Ermanno
Der Kuckuck von Theben.................... 273
Zillig, Winfried
Die Windsbraut 279
Zimmermann, Bernd Alois
Des Menschen Unterhaltsprozeß
gegen Gott 279
Die Soldaten 279

Ballet

Badings, Henk
Orpheus und Eurydike 15
Bamert, Matthias
Once Upon an Orchestra 16
Bate, Stanley
Perseus 18
Beck, Conrad
Der große Bär 20
Blomdahl, Karl-Birger
Minotauros.. 24
Sisyphos 24
von Bose, Hans-Jürgen
Die Nacht aus Blei.............................. 25
Werther-Szenen.................................. 25
Brauel, Henning
Die Kaiserin von Neufundland............ 27
Bresgen, Cesar
Die schlaue Müllerin 28
Degen, Helmut
Der flandrische Narr 41
Dunhill, Thomas Frederick
Gallimaufry, Op. 86 44
Egk, Werner
Abraxas.. 45
Casanova in London 45
Die chinesische Nachtigall 45
Danza 45
Französische Suite nach Rameau 45
Joan von Zarissa 46
Ein Sommertag 46
Einem, Gottfried von
Glück, Tod und Traum, Op. 17............ 48
Pas de Cœur oder Tod und
Auferstehung einer Ballerina, Op. 16 ... 48
Fortner, Wolfgang
Ballet blanc.. 50
Carmen (Bizet-Collages) 51
Mouvements 51
Die Weiße Rose 51
Die Witwe von Ephesus 51
Françaix, Jean
Les Demoiselles de la Nuit................. 54
Le Jeu sentimental 54
Le Jugement d'un Fou 54
Die Kamelien 54
La Lutherie enchantée 54
Les Malheurs de Sophie 54
Pierrot ou les Secrets de la Nuit 55
Le Roi nu - Des Kaisers neue Kleider.... 55
Scuola di Ballo 55
Verreries de Venise 55
Frommel, Gerhard
Der Gott und die Bajadere, Op. 12...... 61
Gerster, Ottmar
Der ewige Kreis 67
Goehr, Alexander
La Belle Dame sans Merci 70

Grünauer, Ingomar
Peer Gynt 80
Henze, Hans Werner
Anrufung Apolls - Symphony No.3 92
Ballett-Variationen............................. 93
Le Disperazioni del Signor Pulcinella... 93
Le Fils de l'air oder
L'enfant change en jeune homme........ 93
Der Idiot... 93
Des Kaisers Nachtigall 93
Labyrinth 93
Maratona 93
Orpheus.. 95
Tancredi 95
Undine 95
Das Vokaltuch der
Kammersängerin Rosa Silber 95
Hindemith, Paul
Der Dämon, Op. 28 105
Hérodiade 105
Nobilissima Visione.......................... 106
Theme with 4 Variations -
The Four Temperaments 106
Humel, Gerald
Die Folterungen der Beatrice Cenci 124
Kaufmann, Dieter
Warten auf Musik 133
Killmayer, Wilhelm
Encores 134
Paradies (Paradise) 134
Pas de deux classique 134
Kirchner, Volker David
Die fünf Minuten des Isaak Babel 138
Lehmann, Markus
Lumpacivagabundus oder
Das liederliche Kleeblatt 149
Lhotka, Fran
Der Teufel im Dorf (Djavo u selu) 149
Malipiero, Gian Francesco
El Mondo novo 158
Meier, Jost
La Vie funambulesque -
Der Tanz auf dem Seil....................... 163
Natschinski, Gerd
Hoffmann's Erzählungen 169
Nono, Luigi
Polifonica-Monodia-Ritmica 170
Der rote Mantel 170
Ohana, Maurice
Études choréographiques 172
Ott, Günther
Blues Giselle..................................... 176
Pauels, Heinz
Capriccio... 177
Mardi Gras 177
Reimann, Aribert
Chacun sa Chimère........................... 195
Die Vogelscheuchen.......................... 195
Reutter, Hermann
Die Kirmes von Delft, Op. 48 201
Notturno Montmartre 201
Topsy, Op. 76................................... 201
Richter, Nico
Kannitverstan (Cannot understand).... 205
Rodrigo, Joaquín
Pavana Real 205

Sadler, Helmut
Der Wettermacher.............................. 213
Schwantner, Joseph
Through Interior Worlds 225
Searle, Humphrey
Dualities, Op. 39................................ 228
The Great Peacock, Op. 34a.............. 228
Les Noctambules, Op. 30 228
Seiber, Mátyás
The Invitation 229
Stravinsky, Igor
Danses concertantes........................... 240
Jeu de Cartes..................................... 240
L' Oiseau de Feu 240
L' Oiseau de Feu
(New edition by Schneider)................ 240
Scènes de Ballet................................. 240
Sutermeister, Heinrich
Das Dorf unter dem Gletscher............ 246
Max und Moritz 246
Walter, Fried
Kleopatra, Op. 22 265
Weill, Kurt
Die sieben Todsünden........................ 267
Wilckens, Friedrich
Die Weibermühle 270
Willms, Franz
Die Klugen und die Törichten 271
Die Stunde der Fische 271
Wimberger, Gerhard
Hero und Leander 271
Zimmermann, Bernd Alois
Alagoana... 279
Concerto pour violoncelle et orchestre
en forme de „pas de trois"................. 279
Kontraste... 279
Perspektiven...................................... 279
Présence 279

Orchestral Works

Large Orchestra

Andreae, Helmut
Suite for Orchestra............................. 14
Atterberg, Kurt Magnus
Ballad and Passacaglia, Op. 38 15
Auric, Georges
Symphonic Suite from
„Chemin de Lumière 15
Badings, Henk
Symphony No.2................................. 15
Symphony No.5................................. 15
Bamert, Matthias
Keepsake 16
Mantrajana 16
Once Upon an Orchestra 16
Septuria Lunaris 16
Banks, Don
Assemblies.. 17
Divisions 17
Dramatic Music for Young Orchestra... 17
Fanfare and National Anthem 17
Intersections...................................... 17
Meeting Place 17
Nexus 17
4 Pieces 17
Prospects... 17

Bantock, Granville
The Frogs - Comedy Overture 18

Barraud, Henry
Poème 18

Beaser, Robert
Double Chorus 19

Beck, Conrad
Aeneas Silvius Symphonie 20
Concertato 20
Concerto for Orchestra 20
Fantasie 20
Hommages 20
Hymn 20
Innominata 20
Nachklänge 20
Ostinato 20
Sonatina 20
Suite 20
Suite concertante 20
Symphony No.5 20
Symphony No.6 20

Benguerel, Xavier
Dialogue orchestrale 22

Biersack, Anton
Fantasia fugata 23
Symphonic Music 23

Blech, Leo
Waldwanderung, Op. 8 23

Bloch, Augustyn
Enfiando 23

Blomdahl, Karl-Birger
Fioriture 24
Forma Ferritonans 24
Minotauros 24
Sisyphos 24
Spiel für Acht 24
Symphony No.3 - „Facetter" 24

Borck, Edmund von
5 Orchestral Pieces, Op. 8 24
Präludium und Fuge, Op. 10 25

von Bose, Hans-Jürgen
Idyllen 25
Labyrinth I 25
Morphogenesis 25
Musik für ein Haus voll Zeit 25
Scene 25
Suite 25
Symphony No.1 26
Travesties in a Sad Landscape 26
Two Studies 26

Brandts-Buys, Jan
Bilder aus dem Kinderleben 27

Brauel, Henning
Notturno 27
Optophon 27
4 Orchestral Pieces 27
Symphonic Paraphrases 27

Brehme, Hans
Liebe ist teuer, Op. 39 28
Triptychon, Op. 33 28
Variationen über eine
mittelalterliche Weise, Op. 38 28

Bresgen, Cesar
Tänze vom Schwarzen Meer 29

Brod, Max
2 Israelische Bauerntänze, Op. 30 30

Brouwer, Leo
Exaedros I 30
Sonograma II 30

Brüll, Ignaz
Serenade in E Major, Op. 36 31

Bryars, Gavin
The Sinking of the Titanic 31

Busch, Adolf
Capriccio, Op. 46 34

Casken, John
Maharal Dreaming 34
Orion Over Farne 34
Sortilège 34
Tableaux des Trois Ages 34

Castiglioni, Niccolò
Caractères 36
Concerto 36
Décors 36
Rondels 36

Ciry, Michel
Pietà 37

Cowie, Edward
Atlas 38
Concerto for Orchestra 38
Fifteen Minute Australia 38
Symphony 38

Dahl, Ingolf
Hymn 40

Dallapiccola, Luigi
Piccola Musica Notturna 41

Dankworth, Johnny
Improvisations 41

Degen, Helmut
Capriccio, Op. 90 41
Concerto sinfonico 41
Festliches Vorspiel 41
Heitere Suite 42
Hymnische Feiermusik 42
Symphonic Concerto 42
Variationen über ein Geusenlied 42

Dianda, Hilda Fanny
Ludus-I 42

Dohnányi, Ernst von
Symphony in D minor, Op. 9 43

Dombrowski, Hansmaria
Böhmische Sinfonie 43

Duffy, John
American Fantasy Overture 43
David and Bathsheba 43
Heritage Waltz 43
2 Jewish Dances 43
3 Jewish Portraits 43

Dunhill, Thomas Frederick
Gallimaufry, Op. 86 44

Durme, Jef van
Symphony No.5 44

Egk, Werner
Abraxas - Concert Suite 46
Allegria 46
„Englische Suite" from
the ballet „Casanova in London" 46
Französische Suite nach Rameau 46
Georgica 46
Joan von Zarissa - Triptychon 46
Little Symphony 46
Moira 46
Nachtanz, Op. posth. 46
Overture 46
Sonata for Orchestra 46
Sonata for Orchestra No.2 46
Spiegelzeit 46

Variationen über
ein Karibisches Thema 46
Walzer für Orchester 47
Die Zaubergeige - Overture 47

Einem, Gottfried von
Introduktion: „Wandlungen", Op. 21 ... 48
Meditationen, Op. 18 48
Pas de Cœur -
Orchestral Suite, Op. 16 48

Enríquez, Manuel
Ixamatl 49
Trayectorias 49

Evangelatos, Antiochos
Variations and Fugue 49

Ferrari, Luc
Allo! Ici la Terre 50

Fetler, Paul
Celebration 59

Fortner, Wolfgang
Bluthochzeit - Interludes 51
Capriccio and Finale 51
La Cecchina 51
Impromptus 51
Lysistrata 51
Marginalien 51
Prolegomena 51
Symphony 51
Triptychon 51
Variations 51
Die Weiße Rose - Concert Suite 52

Foss, Lukas
Baroque Variations 54
Phorion 54

Françaix, Jean
Les Bosquets de Cythère 55
Cassazione 55
La douce France 55
L' Histoire de Babar 55
Ouverture anacréontique 55
Le Roi nu - Des Kaisers neue Kleider ... 55
Scuola di Ballo 55
Thème et Variations 55
La Ville mystérieuse 56
Les Zigues de Mars 56

Fricker, Peter Racine
Comedy Overture, Op. 32 59
Dance Scene, Op. 22 59
Fantasy 59
Rondo Scherzoso 59
Symphony No.1, Op. 9 59
Symphony No.2, Op. 14 59
Symphony No.3, Op. 36 59
Symphony No.4, Op. 43 59
Symphony No.5, Op. 74 59

Frommel, Gerhard
Concert-Suite 61
Scherzo 61
Sinfonisches Vorspiel, Op. 23 61
Suite, Op. 11 61
Symphony in E Major, Op. 13 61

Gál, Hans
Burlesque, Op. 42b 62
„Scaramuccio"- Ballet Suite, Op. 36 ... 62

Genzmer, Harald
Festliches Vorspiel 63
Kokua 63
Konzert in C 63
Symphony No.1 63

Gerster, Ottmar
Enoch Arden - Overture 67
Ernste Musik.. 67
Festliche Musik 67
Festliche Tanzmusik from
'Madame Liselotte' 67
Festliche Toccata 67
Symphony No. 1 67

Gilbert, Anthony
Ghost and Dream Dancing, Op. 25 68
Regions, Op. 6 68
Symphony, Op. 22 68
Tree of Singing Names 69

Girnatis, Walter
Festmusik der Schiffergilde................. 70
Gartenmusik.. 70

Goehr, Alexander
Colossos or Panic, Op. 55 70
2 Etudes, Op. 43 70
Fantasia, Op. 4 71
Hecuba's Lament, Op. 12 71
Metamorphosis / Dance, Op. 36 71
Pastorals, Op. 19.................................. 71
Symphony in One Movement, Op. 29 ... 71
Symphony with Chaconne, Op. 48...... 71

Goldmark, Karl
Im Frühling, Op. 36.............................. 72
In Italien, Op. 49 73
Ländliche Hochzeit, Op. 26................. 73
Sakuntala, Op. 13 73

Goldschmidt, Berthold
Komödie der Irrungen 73

Gotovac, Jakov
Guslar, Op. 22....................................... 73
Oraci (Die Pflüger), Op. 18................. 73
Symphonischer Kolo, Op. 12 73

Graener, Paul
Comedietta, Op. 82............................... 74
Feierliche Stunde, Op. 106.................. 74
Prinz Eugen, der edle Ritter, Op. 108 ... 74
Salzburger Serenaden, Op. 115 74
Sinfonia breve, Op. 96......................... 74
Turmwächterlied, Op. 107................... 74
Wiener Sinfonie, Op. 110 74

Grainger, Percy Aldridge
Blithe Bells (J.S.Bach) 74
Children's March:
Over the Hills and Far Away 74
Colonial Song 74
Country Gardens................................... 74
Country Gardens (Stokowski version) ... 74
Early one Morning............................... 74
Eastern Intermezzo 74
English Dance 74
Green Bushes 74
Handel in the Strand (large version) ... 75
Handel in the Strand
(Stokowski version)............................. 75
Harvest Hymn....................................... 75
The Immovable Do............................... 75
'In a Nutshell' Suite............................. 75
Irish Tune from County Derry
(arrangement by Adolf Schmid) 75
Irish Tune from County Derry
("County Derry Air")........................... 75
Irish Tune from County Derry
(Stokowski version).............................. 75
Jutish Medley....................................... 75
Mock Morris 75
Mock Morris (Stokowski version) 75

Molly on the Shore.............................. 75
Molly on the Shore
(Stokowski version).............................. 75
„The Nightingale" and
„The Two Sisters"................................ 75
The Power of Love 75
Shepherd's Hey..................................... 75
Shepherd's Hey (Stokowski version).... 75
Spoon River 75
To a Nordic Princess............................ 75
The Warriors 75
Ye Banks and Braes O'Bonnie Doon .. 75
Youthful Suite 75

Haas, Joseph
Heitere Serenade, Op. 41..................... 81
Lyrisches Intermezzo........................... 81
Ouvertüre
zu einem frohen Spiel, Op. 95............ 81

Hamel, Peter Michael
Albatros 86
Dharana... 86
Diaphainon.. 86

Hamilton, Iain
'1912' - A Light Overture, Op. 38....... 86
Bartholomew Fair - Overture, Op. 17... 86
Cantos 86
Ecossaise 86
Jubilee 86
Scottish Dances, Op. 32 86
Sinfonia 86
Symphonic Variations, Op. 19............. 86
Symphony No.1, Op. 3......................... 86
Symphony No.2, Op. 10....................... 86

Hartmann, Karl Amadeus
Adagio - Symphony No.2..................... 88
Klagegesang.. 88
Miserae 88
3 Orchesterstücke 88
Simplicius Simplicissimus - Overture.... 88
Simplicius Simplicissimus - Suite....... 88
Sinfonia tragica.................................... 88
Symphonic Hymns 88
Symphonic Overture............................. 88
Symphony Concertante -
Symphony No.5..................................... 88
Symphony No.3..................................... 88
Symphony No.6..................................... 88
Symphony No.7..................................... 88
Symphony No.8..................................... 88

Hartmann, Peter
Adagio 90

Haubenstock-Ramati, Roman
Papageno's Pocket-Size Concerto 90

Heddenhausen, Friedel-Heinz
Bauerntänze 91

Heger, Robert
Ernstes Präludium und heitere Fuge,
Op. 26 91

Heiss, Hermann
Configurationen I................................. 91
Configurationen II 91

Henze, Hans Werner
Antifone.. 95
Apollo trionfante 95
Appassionatamente 95
Aria de la folía española...................... 95
Ballett-Variationen............................... 95
Barcarola... 95
Los Caprichos 95
3 Dithyrambs 95

Dramatic Scenes from
'Orpheus' No. 1 96
Dramatic Scenes from
'Orpheus' No. 2 96
Fandango 96
Finale: Vivace assai............................. 96
Heliogabalus Imperator 96
Hochzeitsmusik - Wedding Music....... 96
Interludes 96
Kleine Elegien 96
Mänadentanz 96
Maratona... 96
3 Orchesterstücke 96
5 Piccoli Concerti e Ritornelli............ 96
4 Poemi 96
La selva incantata 96
Symphonic Interludes 96
3 Symphonic Studies 96
Symphony No.1..................................... 96
Symphony No.2..................................... 96
Symphony No.3..................................... 96
Symphony No.4..................................... 96
Symphony No.5..................................... 96
Symphony No.6..................................... 97
Symphony No.7..................................... 97
Symphony No.8..................................... 97
Tancredi 97
Tanz- und Salonmusik 97
Telemanniana.. 97
Trois Pas des Tritons 97
Undine - First Suite 97
Undine - Second Suite......................... 97
Das Vokaltuch der
Kammersängerin Rosa Silber 97

Hessenberg, Kurt
Der Sturm, Op. 20 101
Symphony No.2 in A Major, Op. 29 ... 101

Hiller, Wilfried
München 104

Hindemith, Paul
Amor und Psyche 106
Concerto for Orchestra, Op. 38 106
Konzertmusik, Op. 50 106
Ludus tonalis 106
Ludus tonalis 108
Lustige Sinfonietta, Op. 4 108
Marsch über den
alten „Schweizerton" 108
Neues vom Tage 108
Nobilissima Visione............................. 108
Nobilissima Visione - Suite................. 108
Nusch-Nuschi - Tänze, Op. 20 108
Philharmonic Concerto 108
Pittsburgh Symphony 108
Ragtime... 108
Sinfonietta in E.................................... 108
Symphonia Serena 108
Symphonische Metamorphosen über
Theme von Carl Maria von Weber 108
Symphonische Tänze............................ 108
Symphony „Die Harmonie der Welt".. 108
Symphony in Eb 108
Symphony „Mathis der Maler" 109
When Lilacs Last in the
Door-Yard Bloom'd (Prelude)............ 109

Höffer, Paul
Symphonische Variationen, Op. 47 117

Holland, Theodore
Spring Sinfonietta................................. 117

Höller, Karl
Sweelinck-Variationen, Op. 56............ 117

Höller, York
Topic 118

Holliger, Heinz
Atembogen....................................... 118
Bruchstücke..................................... 118
Elis - 3 Nachtstücke........................ 118
2 Liszt-Transkriptionen 118
Ostinato Funebre 118
Pneuma 118
(S)irató 118
Tonscherben.................................... 119

Hormes, Hugo
Hungarian Dance 120

Hosokawa, Toshio
In die Tiefe der Zeit.......................... 121
Ferne-Landschaft I........................... 121
Ferne-Landschaft II 121
Garten Lieder I 121
Hiroshima Requiem 121
Medea Fragments I 121

Hsiao, Shusien
Chinesischer Festmarsch 122

Huber, Klaus
Inventionen und Choral 123
Tenebrae... 123
Turnus.. 123

Humel, Gerald
Lepini 124

Hummel, Bertold
Visionen, Op. 73 124

Humperdinck, Engelbert
Lied des Sandmännchens, Abend-
segen und Traumpantomime 125
Overture („Die Marketenderin") 125
Overture („Hänsel und Gretel") 125

Humpert, Hans
Music for Orchestra........................... 125

Husa, Karel
Fantasies for Orchestra 125
Mosaïques pour orchestre.................. 125
Nocturno
from 'Fantasies for Orchestra' 126
Symphony No.1................................. 126

Ichiyanagi, Toshi
Symphonic Movement „Kyoto"......... 126
Voices from the Environment............. 126

Ince, Kamran
Before Infrared 129
Deep Flight 129
Domes 129
Ebullient Shadows 129
Hot, Red, Cold, Vibrant 129
Infrared Only 129
Lipstick 129
Plexus.. 129
Symphony No.1................................ 129

Jarnach, Philipp
Morgenklangspiel, Op. 19 131
Musik mit Mozart, Op. 25 131
Sinfonia brevis, Op. 11 131
Vorspiel I, Op. 22 131

Jarre, Maurice
Concertino 132

Josephs, Wilfried
The Ants, Op. 7 132

Kadosa, Pál
Sérénade, Op. 65 133

Kaun, Hugo
Symphony No. 2 c-Moll, Op. 85......... 134

Kelemen, Milko
Skolion 134
Symphonic Music 1957...................... 134

Killmayer, Wilhelm
Divertissement................................. 135
Encore 135
Im Freien 135
Jugendzeit 135
Nachtgedanken 135
Pas de deux classique 135
Symphony No.1 - 'Fogli' 135
Symphony No.2 - 'Ricordanze'........... 135
Symphony No.3 - 'Menschen-Los' 135
Überstehen und Hoffen...................... 135
Verschüttete Zeichen 135
Zittern und Wagen 135

Kirchner, Volker David
Bildnisse I 138
Bildnisse II 138
Bildnisse III 138
3 Fragments 138
Hortus Magicus 138
Das Souper des Monsieur Papagenor.. 138
Symphony No.1................................ 138

Klebe, Giselher
Symphony No.2, Op. 16..................... 139

Köhler, Emil
Optimismus...................................... 141

Korngold, Erich Wolfgang
Baby-Serenade, Op. 24...................... 142
Military March.................................. 142
Schauspiel-Ouvertüre, Op. 4 142
Sinfonietta, Op. 5............................ 142
Symphonic Overture, Op. 13.............. 142
Symphony in F Sharp, Op. 40............ 142

Kotonski, Wlodzimierz
Musica Cameralna 145
Musique en Relief 145

Kovách, Andor
Eurydice... 145

Křenek, Ernst
Elf Transparente............................... 146
Symphony No.5................................. 147
Symphony „Pallas Athene" 147

Kröll, Georg
Parodia ad Perotinum 147
Still leben 147
Variations 147

Landré, Guillaume
Concert Piece 149

Lehmann, Hans Ulrich
Positionen 149

Lehmann, Markus
Sentenzen 149

Leighton, Lucas
Ballet de la Reine 149

Liebermann, Rolf
Symphony 1949................................. 149

Ligeti, György
Concert Românesc 150
Lontano 150
Melodien 150
San Francisco Polyphony 150

Lopatnikoff, Nicolai
Symphony No.1, Op. 12..................... 154

Lopes-Graça, Fernando
Trois danses portugaises.................... 154

Lörik, Anna
Budapester Marsch 154
Magjar Vigadò 154
Rio Chico 154

Lutyens, Elisabeth
Music for Orchestra 2, Op. 48............ 154
Music for Orchestra 3, Op. 56............ 154

Maasz, Gerhard
Handwerkertänze 156

MacCombie, Bruce
Chelsea Tango.................................. 157

Maler, Wilhelm
Flämisches Rondo 158
Orchesterspiel 158

Malipiero, Gian Francesco
La Laterna Magica............................. 158
Quattro Invenzioni 158

Martinet, Jean-Louis
Trois mouvements symphoniques 159

Martinů, Bohuslav
Serenade.. 159
Sinfonia concertante 159

Martirano, Salvatore
Contrasto... 160

Martland, Steve
Babi Yar 160
Lotta Continua 160

Maxwell Davies, Sir Peter
Carolísima 161
First Fantasia on an 'In Nomine'
of John Taverner 161
Prolation 161
Sir Charles his Pavan 161
5 Voluntaries 162
William Byrd: 3 Dances 162

Mohler, Philipp
Symphonische Fantasie, Op. 20 165
Symphonisches Vorspiel, Op. 18........ 165

Moran, Robert
L' Après-midi du Dracoula 165

Mossolow, Alexandr Wassiljevich
Symphony No. 5 165

Müller, Sigfrid Walther
Böhmische Musik, Op. 55 166
Heitere Musik, Op. 43 166

Müller-Siemens, Detlev
Carillon 166
Passacaglia 166
Pavane.. 166
2 Pieces 166
Quatre passages 166
Scherzo and Adagio patetico 166
Symphony No.1................................. 166
Tom-a-Bedlam.................................. 166

Mussorgsky, Modest
Tableaux d'une Exposition 167

Newson, George
27 Days for Orchestra....................... 170

Niculescu, Stefan
Hétéromorphie 170
Unisonos 170

Niederste-Schee, Wolfgang
Humoresken..................................... 170

Nono, Luigi
Composizione per Orchestra No.1 170
Composizione per Orchestra No.2 170
Due espressioni.................................. 170
Incontri... 170
Der rote Mantel - Concert Suite (B).... 170

Nussio, Otmar
Escapades musicales........................... 171

Orff, Carl
Entrata.. 174
Kleines Konzert 174
Tanzende Faune, Op. 21 174
Uf dem Anger.................................... 174

Paulus, Stephen
Concertante....................................... 177
Concerto for Orchestra 177
Ground Breaker 177
Ordway Overture 177
7 Short Pieces for Orchestra............... 177
Sinfonietta... 177
Street Music...................................... 177
Suite from
'The Postman always Rings Twice' 177
Symphony in 3 Movements................. 177
Translucent Landscapes...................... 177

Penderecki, Krzysztof
Adagietto from 'Paradise Lost' 181
Adagio - Symphony No.4.................... 181
„Als Jakob erwachte"......................... 181
De natura sonoris No.2....................... 181
Musik aus „Ubu Rex" 181
Symphony No.1 181
Symphony No.2 181
Symphony No.3 181
Symphony No.4 181
Symphony No.5 181

Pepping, Ernst
Invention 184
Partita... 184
Prelude 184
Symphony No.1 184
Symphony No.2 184

Petridis, Petro
Greek Suite 185
Ionische Suite 185

Petsch, Hans
5 kurze Geschichten 185
Palatia 185

Pfitzner, Hans
Palestrina - 3 Preludes....................... 185

Picker, Tobias
2 Fantasies 186
Old and Lost Rivers........................... 186
Seance-Homage a Sibelius 186
Symphony No.1 186
Symphony No.2 186

Pillney, Karl Hermann
Konzertwalzer nach Lanner................. 187

Poot, Marcel
Petite Suite.. 191

Pütz, Eduard
Fantasy in Blue.................................. 191

Rainier, Priaulx
Aequora Lunae 192
Dance Concerto „Phala-phala".......... 192

Rasch, Kurt
Concerto for Orchestra, Op. 25 193
Toccata, Op. 27.................................. 193

Ravel, Maurice
Alborada del Gracioso 193
Une Barque dur L'Océan 193
Boléro 193
Pavane pour une infante défunte 193

Raxach, Enrique
Syntagma 193

Reifner, Vinzenz
Aus deutschen Märchen -
Nr. 1 Dornröschen, Op. 17 194
Frühling, Op. 12 194

Reimann, Aribert
7 Fragmente für Orchester.................. 195
Loqui... 195
Musik aus dem Ballett
„Die Vogelscheuchen".................... 195
Neun Stücke für Orchester 195
Symphony 195
Variations 195

Reutter, Hermann
Dance Variations, Op. 76.................... 201
Figurinen... 201
Die Kirmes von Delft, Op. 48 201
Notturno Montmartre - Suite.............. 201

Rodrigo, Joaquín
A la Busca del Más Allá 205
Juglares 206
Pallilos y Panderetas.......................... 206
5 Piezas Infantiles 206
Preludio para
un Poema a la Alhambra.................. 206
2 Spanish Dances............................... 206

Roslawez, Nikolaj Andrejevich
V Casy Novolunija -
In den Stunden des Neumonds........... 210

Rouse, Christopher
Gorgon 211
The Infernal Machine 211

Rózsa, Miklós
3 Hungarian Sketches, Op. 14............. 211
Theme, Variations and Finale, Op. 13.... 211

Rudzinski, Zbigniew
Moments musicaux III......................... 213

Sackman, Nicholas
Alap 213
Hawthorn 213

Sato, Somei
Journey through Sacred Time.............. 213

Sauer, Emil von
Concerto No. 2 c-Moll 213

Schaub, Hans Ferdinand
Abendmusik.. 214

Schnabel, Gottfried
Statics.. 215

Schnebel, Dieter
Canones 215
Compositio... 215
Diapason 215
Inter... 216
Janácek-Moment................................. 216
Mozart-Moment.................................. 216
Orchestra.. 216
Schubert-Phantasie............................. 216
Sinfonie-Stücke.................................. 216
Verdi-Moment.................................... 216

Schoeller, Philippe
Légendes I. Water 219
Winter Dance 219

Schroeder, Hermann
Symphonic Hymns, Op. 29 219
Symphony in D minor......................... 219

Schüler, Johannes
5 Orchestral Movements 223

Schulhoff, Erwin
Suite for Chamber Orchestra............... 223
Symphony No.2................................... 224
Symphony No. 7 - Eroica.................... 224

Schuller, Gunther
Concert Suite from 'The Visitation'.... 225
Contrasts 225
Spectra 225

Schulthess, Walter
Serenade in B Major, Op. 9................. 225

Schwantner, Joseph
Freeflight 225
A Sudden Rainbow 226
Toward Light 226

Scott, Cyril
Aubade, Op. 77................................... 227
Noël 227
2 Passacaglias 227

Searle, Humphrey
Les Noctambules -Suite, Op. 30......... 228
Scherzi, Op. 44 228
Symphony No.1, Op. 23...................... 228
Symphony No.2, Op. 33...................... 228
Symphony No.3, Op. 36...................... 229
Symphony No.4, Op. 38...................... 229
Symphony No.5, Op. 43...................... 229

Seiber, Mátyás
Improvisations 229
Orchestral Suite from 'The Invitation' ... 229
Renaissance Dance Suite..................... 229

Shchedrin, Rodion
Khorovody-Reigen 232
Kristallene Gusli 232
Old Russian Circus Music................... 232

Sheinkman, Mordechai
Passi 233

Silvestrow, Valentin
Eschatophonie..................................... 233

Singleton, Alvin
After Fallen Crumbs........................... 233
56 Blows 233
Cara Mia Gwen 233
Durch Alles.. 233
Even Tomorrow 233
Shadows... 233
Sinfonia Diaspora 233
A Yellow Rose Petal 233

Skrowaczewski, Stanislaw
Toccata and Fugue
in D Minor, (Op. S.565) 235

Slavenski, Josip
Balkanophonia, Op. 10........................ 235

Stephan, Rudi
Music for Orchestra............................ 237
Symphonischer Satz 237

Strauss, Richard
Concert Overture in C Minor 238
Serenade in G Major, o.Op. AV 32...... 238
Symphony in D Minor......................... 238

Stravinsky, Igor
Circus Polka.............................. 240
Concerto in Eb 'Dumbarton Oaks'...... 240
Danses concertantes.................. 240
Feu d'artifice, Op. 4 240
Jeu de Cartes.......................... 240
4 Norwegische Impressionen 240
Ode.................................... 240
L' Oiseau de Feu, Suite 1912.......... 240
L' Oiseau de Feu, Suite 1919.......... 240
L' Oiseau de Feu, Suite 1945.......... 240
Pas de deux 240
Scènes de Ballet...................... 240
Scherzo à la Russe.................... 242
Scherzo fantastique, Op. 3............ 242
Symphony en ut........................ 242
Symphony in 3 Movements............... 242
Tango, 1940 242
Tango, 1953 242

Stürmer, Bruno
Tanzsuite, Op. 24 244
Zeitgesichte, Op. 25.................. 244

Subotnick, Morton
Place................................. 245
Two Butterflies 245

Sutermeister, Heinrich
Aubade pour Morges 246
Divertimento No.2 246
Marche fantasque...................... 246
Romeo and Juliet - Suite 247

Tajcevic, Marko
7 Balkantänze 249

Takemitsu, Toru
Archipelago S. 249
Dream/Window.......................... 250
Dreamtime 250
How slow the Wind 250
Spirit Garden 250
Star-Isle............................. 250
Twill by Twilight 250
Visions 250

Tcherepnin, Alexander Nikolajevich
Georgiana, Op. 92..................... 253

Tippett, Michael
Concerto for Orchestra 254
New Year Suite 254
The Rose Lake......................... 254
The Shires Suite...................... 254
Suite for the Birthday of
Prince Charles........................ 254
Symphony No.1 254
Symphony No.2 254
Symphony No.3 254
Symphony No.4 254

Toch, Ernst
Bunte Suite, Op. 48 257
Kleine Theater-Suite, Op. 54.......... 258
Komödie, Op. 42 258
Little Overture, Op. 51 258
Peter Pan, Op. 76 258
Symphony No.1, Op. 72................. 258

Turina, Joaquín
Evangelio de Navidad, Op. 12 259

Turnage, Mark-Anthony
Drowned Out 259
Momentum.............................. 259
On All Fours 259
Three Screaming Popes 259

Ueter, Karl
Symphony No.1 261
Symphony No.2 261

Uhl, Alfred
Symphonic March 261

Ullmann, Viktor
Don Quixote tanzt Fandango............ 261
Symphony No.1, Op. 45................. 261
Symphony No.2 in D Major 261
Variations, Fantasy and Doublefugue... 261

Vasks, Pēteris
Lauda 263

Vieru, Anatol
Sonnenuhr............................. 265

Wahren, Karl-Heinz
Auf der Suche nach
dem verlorenen Tango 265

Wallace, William
Passing of Beatrice 265

Walter, Fried
Bauernhochzeit........................ 265
Die Dorfmusik - Country Dances........ 265
Symphonische Tänze.................... 266

Wanek, Friedrich K.
Divertimento.......................... 266
Tableau symphonique 266

Wartisch, Otto
Rondo................................. 267

Weill, Kurt
Hatikvah.............................. 267
Symphony No.1 267
Symphony No.2 267

Weismann, Julius
Die pfiffige Magd, Op. 125............ 268
Symphony, Op. 131..................... 268
Symphony in B Major, Op. 130 268

Wellesz, Egon
Symphony No.1, Op. 62................. 269

Willi, Herbert
Concerto for Orchestra 271
Räume 271

Wimberger, Gerhard
Allegro Giocosa 271
Chronique 271
Etude dramatique 271
Figuren und Phantasien 271
Hero und Leander 271
Risonanze 272

Windsperger, Lothar
Concert Overture in G Major, Op. 17... 272
Concert Overture No.3, Op. 61 272
Vorspiel zu einem Drama, Op. 29 272

Wunsch, Hermann
Fest auf Monbijou, Op. 50 273
Kleine Lustspiel-Suite, Op. 37 273

Xiaogang, Ye
Winter, Op. 28 274

Yuasa, Joji
Chronoplastic 275
A Dirge by Bach 275
Eye on Genesis II 275
Hommage à Sibelius 275
Nine Levels by Ze-Ami 275
A Perspective for Orchestra........... 275
Requiem for Orchestra 275
Suite - Scenes from Bashô 275
Symphonic Suite....................... 275
TIME of Orchestral Time 275

Zádór, Eugen
Dance Symphony........................ 275
Hungarian Capriccio................... 275

Zilcher, Hermann
Dance-Fantasy, Op. 71 279

Zimmermann, Bernd Alois
Alagoana (Caprichos Brasileiros)...... 281
Caboclo 281
Concerto for Orchestra 281
Kontraste............................. 281
Metamorphose 281
Un „Petit Rien" 281
Photoptosis........................... 281
Sinfonia prosodica 281
Söbensprung 281
Stille und Umkehr 281
Symphonic Variations and
Fugue on 'In Dulci Jubilo' 281
Symphony in one Movement 281

Chamber Orchestra

Banks, Don
Elizabethan Miniatures 17
Episode 17
Equation III.......................... 17

Beck, Conrad
Chamber Concerto 20
Lichter und Schatten.................. 20

Biersack, Anton
Bagatelles............................ 23

Bloch, Augustyn
Dialoghi 23

von Bose, Hans-Jürgen
Concertino per il H.W.H............... 25
Prozess............................... 25

Brauel, Henning
Les Fenêtres simultanées.............. 27

Brouwer, Leo
Dos conceptos del tiempo 30

Bryars, Gavin
The Archangel Trip.................... 31
Jesus' Blood Never Failed Me Yet 31

Casanova, André
Symphony No.2, Op. 7 34

Casken, John
Vaganza............................... 34

Cowie, Edward
Leonardo, Op. 20...................... 38

Degen, Helmut
Chamber Symphony 41

Donatoni, Franco
Musica per orchestra da camera........ 43
Musica per orchestra da camera........ 43

Egk, Werner
Music for Small Orchestra 46

Elgar, Edward William
Dream Children, Op. 43 48

Fortner, Wolfgang
Concertino 51
Suite for Orchestra................... 51

Françaix, Jean
85 Mesures et un Da capo 55
Pavane pour un Génie vivant 55
Sérénade.............................. 55
Symphonie en sol majeur 55

Frommel, Gerhard
Suite, Op. 11 61

Gebhard, Hans
Ländliche Suite, Op. 23 62

Genzmer, Harald
Pachelbel Suite 63

Gerster, Ottmar
Oberhessische Bauerntänze 67

Gilbert, Anthony
Crow-Cry, Op. 27 68
Mozart Sampler with Ground 68
Peal II, Op. 12 68
Sinfonia, Op. 5 68

Goehr, Alexander
...a musical offering
(J.S.B. 1985)..., Op. 46 70
Concerto for Eleven, Op. 32 71
Little Symphony, Op. 15 71
Sinfonia, Op. 42 71
Still Lands 71

Graener, Paul
Die Flöte von Sanssouci, Op. 86 74

Grainger, Percy Aldridge
Handel in the Strand
(chamber version) 75
Lord Peter's Stable Boy 75
Shepherd's Hey (Stakowski) 75
Shepherd's Hey (Wright) 75
Ye Banks and Braes O'Bonnie Doon... 75

Grovermann, Carl Hans
Heitere Tanzszenen 80

Haas, Joseph
Lyrisches Intermezzo 81
Variationen-Suite, Op. 64 81

Hamilton, Iain
Arias 86
Sonata
for Chamber Orchestra, Op. 34 86

Hand, Colin
Divertimento 87

Heiss, Hermann
Sinfonia giocosa 91

Henze, Hans Werner
Arien des Orpheus 95
Deutschlandsberger Mohrentanz No.1 ... 95
Deutschlandsberger Mohrentanz No.2 ... 95
In memoriam: Die Weiße Rose 96
Des Kaisers Nachtigall 96
Katharina Blum 96
Labyrinth 96
3 Mozart'sche Orgelsonaten 96
Spielmusiken 96
Voie lactée ô sœur lumineuse 97

Hessenberg, Kurt
Musikantenhochzeit 101

Hindemith, Paul
Der Dämon - Concert Suite, Op. 28.... 106
Hérodiade 106
Im Kampf mit dem Berg 106
In Sturm und Eis 106
Kammermusik No.1
with Finale 1921, Op. 24/1 106
Der Lindberghflug 108
Plöner Musiktag 108
Plöner Musiktag
(Abendkonzert 1.Einleitungsstücke) ... 108
Plöner Musiktag
(Abendkonzert 6.Quodlibet) 108
Plöner Musiktag - Suite 108
Plöner Musiktag - Suite
(Willi Draths version) 108
Plöner Musiktag (Tafelmusik) 108
Sing-und Spielmusiken, Op. 45/3 108
Spielmusik, Op. 43/1 108
Suite französischer Tänze 108

Holliger, Heinz
Ad Marginem 118
Choral à 8 118
Engführung 118
Der ferne Klang 118
Pneuma 118
Schaufelrad 118
Sommerkanon IV 118

Hosokawa, Toshio
Landscape VI 121

Humel, Gerald
Die Folterungen der Beatrice Cenci 124

Husa, Karel
Musique d'Amateurs 125

Ichiyanagi, Toshi
Symphony for Chamber Orchestra
„Time Current" 126

Ince, Kamran
Hammer Music 130
Night Passage 130

Kelemen, Milko
Concerto Giocoso 134
Konstellationen 134

Kerskes, Gerhard
La Camarilla - Paso doble 134

Killmayer, Wilhelm
La joie de vivre 135
Paradies (Paradise) 135

Kirchner, Volker David
Kondukt 138

Komma, Karl Michael
Concertino 141

Korngold, Erich Wolfgang
Straussiana 142
Theme and Variations, Op. 42 142
Viel Lärmen um Nichts -
Much ado about Nothing, Op. 11 142
Viel Lärmen um Nichts -
Much ado about Nothing, Op. 11 142

Kreisler, Fritz
Caprice viennois, Op. 2 145

Lehmann, Hans Ulrich
Composition for 19 148

Ligeti, György
Ballad and Dance 150
Chamber Concerto 150

Lutyens, Elisabeth
Chorale for Orchestra, Op. 36 155

Majo, Giulio di
Sinfonia da camera 158

Maler, Wilhelm
Concerto grosso, Op. 11 158

Martland, Steve
American Invention 160

Maxwell Davies, Sir Peter
Ricercar and Doubles on
'To many a well' 161
Sinfonia 161

Mohler, Philipp
Shakespeare-Suite 164

Moran, Robert
Elegant Journey with
Stopping Points of Interest 165
Silver and the Circle of Messages 165

Mori, Kurodo
Premier beau Matin de Mai 165

Müller-Siemens, Detlev
Concerto for 19 Players 166
Enigma 166
Pavane 166
Phoenix 1 166
Phoenix 2 166
Phoenix 3 166
Under Neonlight 1 166

Müller-Zürich, Paul
Marienleben, Op. 8 167

Nancarrow, Conlon
Study No. 1 168
Study No. 2 168
Study No. 3c 168
Study No. 5 168
Study No. 6 168
Study No. 7 168
Study No. 9 168
Study No. 12 168

Newson, George
June is a Month in the Summer.......... 170

Nono, Luigi
Canti per 13 170
Polifonica-Monodia-Ritmica 170

Paulus, Stephen
Reflections: 4 Movements
on a Theme of Wallace Stevens 177

Peixe, Guerra
Nonette................................. 180

Pepping, Ernst
Lust hab ich g'habt zur Musika.......... 184

Poot, Marcel
Divertimento 191
Impromtu 191

Reimann, Aribert
Invenzioni 195

Rodrigo, Joaquín
Homenaje a la Tempranica 206
Música para un Jardin................... 206
Tres Viejos Aires de Danza 206

Rouse, Christopher
The Surma Ritornelli 211

Sackman, Nicholas
Doubles................................. 213

Schnebel, Dieter
Beethoven Symphony................... 215
Drei-Klang 216
Körper-Sprache 216
Schumann-Moment 216

Schönberg, Arnold
Kaiserwalzer 219

Schulhoff, Erwin
Suite for Chamber Orchestra............ 224

Schuller, Gunther
Contours................................ 225

Searle, Humphrey
Variations and Finale, Op. 34 229

Sgambati, Giovanni
Berceuse-Réverie, Op. 42/2............. 232

Shchedrin, Rodion
Shepherd's Pipes of Vologda 232

Singleton, Alvin
Again 233

Stephan, Rudi
Musik für 7 Saiteninstrumente
(G.E. Lessing version).................. 237
Musik für 7 Saiteninstrumente
(Original version) 237

Subotnick, Morton
A Desert Flowers 245

Sutermeister, Heinrich
Sérénade pour Montreux 247

Takemitsu, Toru
In an Autumn Garden 250
Rain Coming 250
Tree Line 250

Tippett, Michael
Divertimento on 'Sellinger's Round' ... 254

Toch, Ernst
Das Kirschblütenfest 258
5 Pieces
for Chamber Orchestra, Op. 33 258
Vorspiel zu einem Märchen 258

Vasks, Pēteris
Vestijums - Message 263

Weill, Kurt
The Judgement of Paris 267

Werdin, Eberhard
Europäische Tänze 269
Festliche Musik 270
Kommt, ihr G'spielen 270

Willi, Herbert
Für 16 271

Wimberger, Gerhard
Partita Giocosa 272

Xiaogang, Ye
Nine Horses 274
Strophe 274

Zehden, Hans
Les Chansons 277

Zehm, Friedrich
Alla Danza 277
Divertimento Ritmico 278
Rhythmophonie 277

Zimmermann, Bernd Alois
Suite aus 'Gelb und Grün' 281

String Orchestra

Badings, Henk
Trio Cosmos (Nos.1-16) 16

Bamert, Matthias
Ol-Okun 16

Beck, Conrad
Little Suite 20
Symphony No.3 20

Benguerel, Xavier
Musica Riservata 22

Bialas, Günter
Concerto 23

Biersack, Anton
Skizzen 23

von Bose, Hans-Jürgen
Variations 26

Burkhard, Willy
Concerto, Op. 50 33
Fantasy, Op. 40 33
Kleine Serenade, Op. 42 33

Casken, John
Darting the Skiff 34

Ciry, Michel
Pietà 37
Stèle pour un Héros, Op. 43 37

Cowie, Edward
L' Or de la Trompette d'Été 38

Degen, Helmut
Concerto for Strings 41
Serenade 42

Dianda, Hilda Fanny
Impromptus 42

Egk, Werner
Music for String Instruments -
Passacaglia 46
Die Nachtigall 46

Fortner, Wolfgang
Concerto for Strings 51
Immagini 51
6 Madrigals 52
Streichermusik II 51

Françaix, Jean
6 Preludi 55
Sérénade B E A 55
Symphonie d'Archets 55

Fricker, Peter Racine
Litany, Op. 26 59
Prelude, Elegy and Finale, Op. 10 59

Genzmer, Harald
Divertimento di Danza 63
Sinfonietta 63
Sinfonietta Seconda 63
Symphony No.2 63

Goehr, Alexander
Fugue on the Notes
of the Fourth Psalm, Op. 38b 71
Little Music for Strings, Op. 16 71

Gotovac, Jakov
Lied und Tanz
aus dem Balkan,Op. 16 73

Grainger, Percy Aldridge
Irish Tune from County Derry 75
Mock Morris 75
Molly on the Shore 75

Hamilton, Iain
Variations
on an Original Theme, Op. 1 86

Hartmann, Karl Amadeus
String Quartet No.2 88
Symphony No.4 88

Helm, Everett
Symphony 92

Henze, Hans Werner
Fantasia for Strings 96
Seconda Sonata per archi 96
Sonata for Strings 96

Hessenberg, Kurt
Konzertante Musik, Op. 39 102

Hiller, Wilfried
Hintergründige Gedanken des Erzbi-
schöflichen Salzburger Compositeurs
Heinrich Ignaz Franz Biber beim
Belauschen eines Vogelkonzerts 104

Hindemith, Paul
Schulwerk, Op. 44/2 108
Schulwerk, Op. 44/3 108
Schulwerk, Op. 44/4 108

Höller, Karl
Fuge 117

Holliger, Heinz
Choral à 4 118
Eisblumen 118

Huber, Klaus
Cantio-Moteti-Interventiones 123

Hummel, Bertold
Klangfiguren 124
Kontraste, Op. 50 124

Husa, Karel
Divertimento 125
4 Little Pieces 125
Portrait 126

Ichiyanagi, Toshi
Interspace 126

Jarnach, Philipp
Musik zum Gedächtnis der Einsamen.... 131

Josephs, Wilfried
Elegy, Op. 13 132

Kelemen, Milko
Kleine Streichermusik 134

Killmayer, Wilhelm
Fin al Punto 135
Grande Sarabande 135

Kirchner, Volker David
Orphischer Gesang 138
Schattengesang 138
Stringsextett No. 1 139

Klebe, Giselher
Symphony No.1, Op. 12 139

Korngold, Erich Wolfgang
Symphonic Serenade
in B Major, Op. 39 142

Křenek, Ernst
7 Easy Pieces 146
Symphonic Piece, Op. 86 146

Ligeti, György
Old Hungarian Dances 150
Ramifications 150

Mainardi, Enrico
Music for Strings, Op. 54 157

Maler, Wilhelm
Music for String Orchestra 158

Martinů, Bohuslav
Partita 159

Martland, Steve
Crossing the Border 161

May, Helmut W.
Spiritual Concerto 162

Mieg, Peter
Toccata-Arioso-Gigue 163

Moeschinger, Albert
Variations and Finale
on a Theme by Purcell, Op. 32 163

Mohler, Philipp
Heitere Overtüre, Op. 27 164

Papandopoulo, Boris
Sinfonietta, Op. 79 176

Paulus, Stephen
Symphony for Strings 177

Penderecki, Krzysztof
Canon 181
Drei Stücke im alten Stil 181
Intermezzo 181
Sinfonietta per archi 181

Picker, Tobias
Symphony No.3 186

Pironkoff, Simeon
Requiem 187

Rainier, Priaulx
Sinfonia da Camera 192

Reimann, Aribert
Rondes 195

Reutter, Hermann
Symphony 201
Rivier, Jean
Symphony No.2 in C 205
Schmidt, Werner Albert
3 Dramatic Pieces 215
Schnabel, Gottfried
Lyrical Fantasy 215
Schnebel, Dieter
Blendwerk.. 215
Mahler-Moment 216
Stücke 217
Schroeder, Hermann
Concerto for Strings, Op. 23 219
Seiber, Mátyás
Besardo-Suite No.2 229
Shchedrin, Rodion
Russische Photographien 232
Velicanie 232
Singleton, Alvin
Again 233
Eine Idee ist ein Stueck Stoff 233
Skrowaczewski, Stanislaw
Suite for Strings
from 6 Concerts en Sextuor 235
Straus, Oscar
Serenade for Strings in G Minor,
Op. 35 238
Sugár, Rezsö
6 Small Pieces 246
Sutermeister, Heinrich
Divertimento No.1 246
Poème funèbre -
En mémoire de Paul Hindemith 247
Szelényi, István
Heitere Suite 248
Little Suite 249
Sinfonietta a tre per violini 249
Takemitsu, Toru
3 Film Scores 250
A Way a Lone II 250
Tcherepnin, Alexander Nikolajevich
Musica Sacra, Op. 36 253
Tippett, Michael
Concerto for Double String Orchestra... 254
Fantasia Concertante
on a Theme of Corelli.......................... 254
Little Music 254
Water out of Sunlight 254
Vasks, Pēteris
„Balsis" -
Symphony for Strings („Voices") 263
Cantabile per archi............................. 263
Musica dolorosa................................. 263
Zehm, Friedrich
Alla Danza 277
Zimmermann, Bernd Alois
Concerto for Strings 281

Wind Orchestra

Banks, Don
Music for Wind Band 17
Beckerath, Alfred von
Symphony for Wind Orchestra........... 22
Cowie, Edward
Cathedral Music.................................. 38
Egk, Werner
Divertissement 46
Die Zaubergeige - Overture................ 47
Einem, Gottfried von
Alpbacher Tanzserenade..................... 48
Erbse, Heimo
Allegro-Lento-Allegro......................... 49
Fortner, Wolfgang
Music for Wind Band 51
Foss, Lukas
For 24 Winds 54
Françaix, Jean
7 Dances 55
Danses exotiques 55
Elégie 55
Huit Pièces pittoresques 55
3 Marches militaires 55
9 Pièces caractéristiques 55
Quasi Improvvisando 55
Gál, Hans
Promenadenmusik für Blasorchester... 62
Gerster, Ottmar
Oberhessische Bauerntänze 67
Gilbert, Anthony
Dream Carousels 68
Goehr, Alexander
Chaconne for Wind, Op. 34................ 70
3 Pieces
from 'Arden Must Die', Op. 21a........ 71
Grainger, Percy Aldridge
'The Duke of Marlborough' Fanfare ... 74
Irish Tune from County Derry (1918).... 75
Lincolnshire Posy 75
Mock Morris (1911/50) 75
Shepherd's Hey (1908/49) 75
Henze, Hans Werner
Die Abenteuer des Don Chisciotte 95
Ragtimes and Habaneras (for brass).... 96
Ragtimes and Habaneras
(for symphonic wind band) 96
Hindemith, Paul
Geschwindmarsch von Beethoven
from 'Symphonia Serena'
(for symphonic wind band) 106
Geschwindmarsch von Beethoven
from 'Symphonia Serena'
(for wind band) 106
Konzertmusik, Op. 41 106
Konzertmusik, Op. 50 106
March from
„Symphonische Metamorphosen"....... 108
Symphony „Mathis der Maler"
(for concert band) 109
Symphony in B flat 108
Höffer, Paul
Festliche Ouvertüre 117
Heitere Ouvertüre 117
Hummel, Bertold
Symphonic Overture, Op. 81d............ 124
Humperdinck, Engelbert
Abendsegen 124
Kirchner, Volker David
Der blaue Harlekin 138
Ligeti, György
6 Miniatures....................................... 150
Lörik, Anna
Budapester Marsch 154
Lutyens, Elisabeth
Music for Wind, Op. 60...................... 155
Martland, Steve
Dividing the Lines 160
Wolf-gang 160
Maxwell Davies, Sir Peter
St. Michael Sonata............................. 162
Miller, Franz R.
Fanfare und Entrata 163
Orff, Carl
Als die Treue ward geborn 174
4 Burlesque Scenes............................ 174
Carmina Burana (for concert band;
John Crance version)......................... 174
Carmina Burana (for concert band;
Jos Moerenhout version) 174
Catulli Carmina (for symphonic
concert band; Guy M. Duker version).... 174
Entrata 174
Entrata
(symphonic wind band version) 174
3 Tänze und Schlußszene 174
Penderecki, Krzysztof
Burleske Suite from „Ubu Rex" 181
Prélude.. 181
Picker, Tobias
Dedication Anthem 186
Regner, Hermann
Spielmusik aus Schwaben 194
Rouse, Christopher
Thor 211
Sackman, Nicholas
Paraphrase... 212
Schwantner, Joseph
...And the Mountains rising nowhere .. 225
From a Dark Millennium..................... 225
Stravinsky, Igor
Circus Polka....................................... 240
Stürmer, Bruno
Tänzerische Spielmusik...................... 244
Sutermeister, Heinrich
Modeste Mignon................................. 246
Takemitsu, Toru
Day Signal 249
Night Signal 250
Tippett, Michael
Fanfare No.5 254
Festal Brass with Blues 254
Prelude for Brass,
Bells and Percussion.......................... 254
Suite for the Birthday
of Prince Charles 254
Triumph 254
Toch, Ernst
Miniature Overture 258
Spiel für Blasorchester, Op. 39 258
Turina, Joaquín
Miniaturen 259
Wanek, Friedrich K.
4 Grotesques 266
Wimberger, Gerhard
Stories 272
Wyttenbach, Jürg
Anrufung und Ausbruch 273
Zehm, Friedrich
Schwierigkeiten & Unfälle
mit einem Choral 277
Zimmermann, Bernd Alois
Rheinische Kirmestänze 281

Jazz Orchestra

Banks, Don
Meeting Place 17
Nexus 17
Dankworth, Johnny
Improvisations 41
Gilbert, Anthony
Peal II, Op. 12 68
Henze, Hans Werner
Maratona 96
Seiber, Mátyás
Improvisations 229
Stravinsky, Igor
Scherzo à la Russe 242

Solo Instrument(s) with Orchestra

Piano

Arnell, Richard
Piano Concerto, Op. 44 14
Beaser, Robert
Piano Concerto 19
Beck, Conrad
Concertino for Piano 21
Piano Concerto 21
Bentzon, Niels Viggo
Brillantes Concertino 22
Blomdahl, Karl-Birger
Chamber Concerto 24
Borck, Edmund von
Piano Concerto, Op. 20 25
Brehme, Hans
Piano Concerto, Op. 32 28
Bresgen, Cesar
Mayenkonzert 29
Piano Concerto 29
Chisholm, Erik
Piano Concerto No.2 37
Ciry, Michel
Piano Concerto 37
Cowie, Edward
Piano Concerto 38
Degen, Helmut
Kleines Konzert No.1 42
Piano Concerto 42
Elgar, Edward William
Sursum Corda, Op. 11 48
Fortner, Wolfgang
Mouvements 52
Françaix, Jean
Concertino 56
L' Heure du Berger 56
Piano Concerto 56
Fricker, Peter Racine
Piano Concerto, Op. 19 59
Toccata, Op. 33 60
Gebhard, Hans
Piano Concerto, Op. 25 63
Genzmer, Harald
Piano Concerto 63
Gervais, Terence White
Konzert 68

Gilbert, Anthony
Towards Asavari 69
Goehr, Alexander
Konzertstück, Op. 26 71
Piano Concerto, Op. 33 71
Hamilton, Iain
Piano Concerto 86
Hartmann, Karl Amadeus
Piano Concerto 90
Helm, Everett
Piano Concerto No.1 in G 92
Henze, Hans Werner
Concertino 97
Jeux des Tritons 97
Piano Concerto No.1 97
Piano Concerto No.2 97
Tristan 98
Hindemith, Paul
Kammermusik No.2
(Piano Concerto), Op. 36/1 ... 109
Konzertmusik, Op. 49 109
Piano Concerto 109
Theme with 4 Variations -
The Four Temperaments 109
Husa, Karel
Concertino, Op. 10 126
Ichiyanagi, Toshi
Piano Concerto No.1
„Reminiscence of Spaces" 127
Piano Concerto No.2
„Winter Portrait" 127
Piano Concerto No.3
„Cross Water Roads" 127
Ince, Kamran
Piano Concerto 129
Ireland, John
Legend 130
Kaminski, Heinrich
Concerto for Orchestra with Piano ... 133
Killmayer, Wilhelm
Piano Concerto 135
Korngold, Erich Wolfgang
Piano Concerto in C Sharp, Op. 17 ... 142
Křenek, Ernst
Piano Concerto No.3 147
Ligeti, György
Piano Concerto 150
Lopatnikoff, Nicolai
Piano Concerto No.2, Op. 15 ... 154
Lutyens, Elisabeth
Music for Piano and
Orchestra, Op. 59 155
Symphonies, Op. 46 155
Maler, Wilhelm
Concerto, Op. 10 158
Moeschinger, Albert
Piano Concerto No.2, Op. 23 ... 163
Müller-Siemens, Detlev
Piano Concerto 167
Naoumoff, Emile
Piano Concerto No.2 169
Pictures at an Exhibition 169
Picker, Tobias
Bang! 186
Keys to the City (1983) 186
Keys to the City (1987) 186
Piano Concerto No.1 186
Piano Concerto No.3 186

Reimann, Aribert
Piano Concerto No.1 195
Piano Concerto No.2 195
Reutter, Hermann
Capriccio, Aria and Finale 201
Concert Variations 202
Concertino, Op. 69 202
Piano Concerto No.1, Op. 19 ... 202
Piano Concerto No.2, Op. 36 ... 202
Piano Concerto No.4, Op. 62 ... 202
Symphonic Fantasy, Op. 50 ... 202
Sackman, Nicholas
Ellipsis 212
Schnebel, Dieter
Hymnus - Piano Concerto 216
Schulhoff, Erwin
Piano Concerto 224
Schuller, Gunther
Piano Concerto 225
Schwantner, Joseph
Distant Runes and Incantations ... 226
Piano Concerto 226
Scott, Cyril
Piano Concerto in C Major 227
Searle, Humphrey
Concertante, Op. 24 229
Piano Concerto No.2, Op. 27 ... 229
Senfter, Johanna
Piano Concerto, Op. 90 231
Sgambati, Giovanni
Piano Concerto, Op. 15 232
Sutermeister, Heinrich
Concertino 247
Piano Concerto No.1 247
Piano Concerto No.2 247
Piano Concerto No.3 247
Takemitsu, Toru
riverrun 252
Tcherepnin, Alexander Nikolajevich
Piano Concerto No.3, Op. 48 ... 253
Tippett, Michael
Fantasia on a Theme of Handel ... 256
Piano Concerto 256
Toch, Ernst
Piano Concerto, Op. 38 258
Symphony for Piano and
Orchestra, Op. 61 258
Ullmann, Viktor
Piano Concerto, Op. 25 262
Wimberger, Gerhard
Piano Concerto 272
Windsperger, Lothar
Piano Concerto, Op. 30 272
Wunsch, Hermann
Chamber Concerto, Op. 22 273
Wyttenbach, Jürg
Divisions 273
Piano Concerto 273
Xiaogang, Ye
The Scent of Black Mango 274

Two or More Pianos

Castiglioni, Niccolò
Ode.. 36

Degen, Helmut
Concertino for 2 Pianos.................. 42

Fortner, Wolfgang
Phantasie über die Tonfolge b-a-c-h.... 52
Triplum... 52

Françaix, Jean
Concerto for 2 Pianos.................... 56

Fricker, Peter Racine
Concertante No.2, Op. 15................ 59

Hessenberg, Kurt
Concerto for 2 Pianos, Op. 50........... 101

Pironkoff, Simeon
Music... 188

Reutter, Hermann
Concerto in Eb for 2 Pianos, Op. 63 ... 202

Takemitsu, Toru
Quotation of Dream....................... 252

Zimmermann, Bernd Alois
Dialoge... 281

Harpsichord

Bamert, Matthias
Rheology...................................... 16

Degen, Helmut
Kleines Konzert No.6...................... 42

Fortner, Wolfgang
Harpsichord Concerto..................... 52

Françaix, Jean
Harpsichord Concerto..................... 56

Maler, Wilhelm
Concerto, Op. 10 158

Wanek, Friedrich K.
Harpsichord Concerto..................... 266

Organ

Benguerel, Xavier
Organ Concerto............................. 22

von Bose, Hans-Jürgen
Symbolum..................................... 26

Degen, Helmut
Organ Concerto............................. 42

Elgar, Edward William
Sursum Corda, Op. 11 48
Sursum Corda
(Adolf Schmid version), Op. 11 48

Fortner, Wolfgang
Organ Concerto............................. 52

Guilmant, Félix Alexandre
Symphony No. 1 in D Minor, Op. 42.... 81
Symphony No. 2 in A Major, Op. 91 81

Hamilton, Iain
Organ Concerto............................. 86

Helfritz, Hans
Organ Concerto............................. 91

Hindemith, Paul
Kammermusik No.7
(Organ Concerto), Op. 46/2............... 91
Organ Concerto............................. 109

Ichiyanagi, Toshi
Existence...................................... 126

Müller-Zürich, Paul
Organ Concerto, Op. 28 167

Paulus, Stephen
Organ Concerto............................. 178

Schroeder, Hermann
Organ Concerto, Op. 25 222

Toch, Ernst
Fanal, Op. 45 258

Widor, Charles-Marie
Symphony No.3, Op. 69 270

Violin

Arnell, Richard
Violin Concerto, Op. 9 14

Banks, Don
Violin Concerto 17

Beck, Conrad
Chamber Concerto......................... 20

Brauel, Henning
Mercurio....................................... 28

Bresgen, Cesar
Jagdkonzert.................................. 29

Bryars, Gavin
The Old Tower of Löbenicht.............. 32

Casken, John
Violin Concerto 35

Dahl, Ingolf
Elegy Concerto 40

Degen, Helmut
Kleines Konzert No. 2 42

Donatoni, Franco
Divertimento................................. 43

Dutilleux, Henri
L' Arbre des songes 44

Egk, Werner
Geigenmusik................................. 47

Fairchild, Blair
Rhapsody 50

Fortner, Wolfgang
Violin Concerto 52

Françaix, Jean
Suite.. 56
Violin Concerto No.1....................... 56
Violin Concerto No.2....................... 57

Fricker, Peter Racine
Rhapsodia Concertante, Op. 21.......... 60
Violin Concerto, Op. 11................... 60

Genzmer, Harald
Violin Concerto 63

Goehr, Alexander
Violin Concerto, Op. 13 71

Graener, Paul
Violin Concert, Op. 104 74

Hamilton, Iain
Violin Concerto, Op. 15 86

Hartmann, Karl Amadeus
Concerto funebre 88

Henze, Hans Werner
Violin Concerto No.1....................... 98
Violin Concerto No.2....................... 98
Il Vitalino raddoppiato..................... 98

Hindemith, Paul
Kammermusik No.4
(Violin Concerto), Op. 36/3.............. 109
Tuttifäntchen................................. 109
Violin Concerto 109

Holliger, Heinz
Violin Concerto 119

Hosokawa, Toshio
Landscape III................................ 121

Ichiyanagi, Toshi
Violin Concerto „Circulating Scenery"... 127

Kai, Naohiko
Violin Concerto 133

Kaufmann, Dieter
Concertomobil, Op. 18 133

Kirchner, Volker David
Violin Concerto 138

Korngold, Erich Wolfgang
Violin Concerto in D Major, Op. 35 ... 142

Kreisler, Fritz
Schön Rosmarin.............................. 145

Křenek, Ernst
Violin Concerto No.2....................... 147

Ligeti, György
Violin Concerto 150

Maler, Wilhelm
Violin Concert in A-Major 158

Martinon, Jean
Violin Concerto No. 2, Op. 51 159

Martinů, Bohuslav
Suite concertante 159

Müller-Zürich, Paul
Violin Concerto in G Major, Op. 25 ... 167

Naoumoff, Emile
Triptyque...................................... 169

Nono, Luigi
Varianti.. 170

Pals, Leopold von der
Konzertstück................................. 176

Paulus, Stephen
Violin Concerto No.1....................... 178
Violin Concerto No.2....................... 178

Penderecki, Krzysztof
Violin Concerto 181
Violin Concerto No. 2 182

Picker, Tobias
Violin Concerto 186

Poot, Marcel
Konzertstück................................. 191

Rainier, Priaulx
Due Canti e Finale.......................... 192

Reutter, Hermann
Epitaph für Ophelia 202
Violin Concerto, Op. 39 202

Rodrigo, Joaquín
Cançoneta 206

Roslawez, Nikolaj Andrejevich
Violin Concerto No.1....................... 210

Schulthess, Walter
Violin Concertino in A Major, Op. 7... 225

Seiber, Mátyás
Fantasia Concertante 230

Sitt, Hans
Concertino in A minor, Op. 28 234
Concerto No. 3 in D minor, Op. 111 ... 234

Steinbrenner, Wilfried
Imago I.. 236

Stephan, Rudi
Music for Violin and Orchestra.......... 237

Stravinsky, Igor
Concerto en Ré 242

Sugár, Rezsö
Variations 246

Takemitsu, Toru
Far calls. Coming, far!.......................... 250
Nostalghia... 250
Weill, Kurt
Bastille Music...................................... 267
Windsperger, Lothar
Violin Concerto, Op. 39 272
Xiaogang, Ye
The Last Paradise, Op. 24 274
Zimmermann, Bernd Alois
Violin Concerto 281

Viola

Bate, Stanley
Viola Concerto, Op. 46...................... 18
Beck, Conrad
Viola Concerto.................................... 19
Bryars, Gavin
The North Shore 32
The Old Tower of Löbenicht 32
Degen, Helmut
Kleines Konzert No. 3 42
Forsyth, Cecil
Viola Concerto in G Minor................. 50
Françaix, Jean
Rhapsodie 56
Fricker, Peter Racine
Viola Concerto, Op. 18...................... 60
Gerster, Ottmar
Concertino, Op. 16 68
Henze, Hans Werner
Music for Viola and 22 Players 97
Hindemith, Paul
Kammermusik No.5
(Viola Concerto), Op. 36/4 109
Konzertmusik, Op. 48 109
Der Schwanendreher 109
Trauermusik.. 109
Huber, Klaus
„... ohne Grenze und Rand...".............. 123
Husa, Karel
Poème 126
Josephs, Wilfried
Meditatio de Beornmundo, Op. 30...... 132
Kirchner, Volker David
Nachtstück 138
Schibboleth 138
Müller-Siemens, Detlev
Viola Concerto.................................... 167
Müller-Zürich, Paul
Viola Concerto in F Minor, Op. 24 167
Penderecki, Krzysztof
Viola Concerto.................................... 181
Seiber, Mátyás
Elegy... 230
Sitt, Hans
Concerto in A Minor, Op. 68.............. 234
Konzertstück in G Minor, Op. 46........ 234
Takemitsu, Toru
A String around Autumn 252
Yuasa, Joji
Revealed Time..................................... 275

Viola d'amore

Hindemith, Paul
Kammermusik No.6, Op. 46/1 109

Violoncello

Bresgen, Cesar
Cello Concerto in D............................ 29
Bryars, Gavin
Cello Concerto.................................... 31
The North Shore 32
Casken, John
Cello Concerto.................................... 34
Degen, Helmut
Cello Concerto.................................... 42
Kleines Konzert No. 4 42
Dianda, Hilda Fanny
Resonancias-III.................................... 42
Egk, Werner
Canzone 47
Fortner, Wolfgang
Cello Concerto.................................... 52
Zyklus 52
Foss, Lukas
Cello Concerto.................................... 54
Françaix, Jean
Fantaisie.. 56
Introduction et Polonaise
brillante, Op.3.................................... 56
Variations de Concert 56
Genzmer, Harald
Cello Concerto.................................... 63
Goehr, Alexander
Romanza, Op. 24 71
Grainger, Percy Aldridge
Youthful Rapture 76
Henze, Hans Werner
Introduktion, Thema und Variationen.... 97
Liebeslieder 97
Ode an den Westwind......................... 97
Hindemith, Paul
Cello Concerto.................................... 109
Cello Concerto in Eb Major, Op. 3 109
Kammermusik No.3
(Cello Concerto), Op. 36/2 109
Killmayer, Wilhelm
Sostenuto 135
Korngold, Erich Wolfgang
Cello Concerto in C Major, Op. 37..... 142
Křenek, Ernst
Capriccio... 147
Mainardi, Enrico
Cello Concerto (1960)......................... 157
Cello Concerto (1969)......................... 157
Elegy 157
Martinon, Jean
Cello Concerto, Op. 52....................... 159
Martinů, Bohuslav
Cello Concerto No. 1.......................... 159
Penderecki, Krzysztof
Cello Concerto No.2............................ 181
Viola Concerto (version for cello)....... 181
Pfitzner, Hans
Cello Concerto in A Minor.................. 185
Cello Concerto in G Major, Op. 42..... 185
Rainier, Priaulx
Cello Concerto.................................... 192
Reutter, Hermann
Prozession... 202
Rodrigo, Joaquín
Concierto como un Divertimento........ 206
Concierto Galante................................ 206

Sackman, Nicholas
Ensembles and Cadenzas.................... 212
Schroeder, Hermann
Cello Concerto, Op. 24....................... 222
Seiber, Mátyás
Tre pezzi 230
Shchedrin, Rodion
Cello Concerto.................................... 232
Sitt, Hans
Concerto No.2 in D Minor, Op. 38 234
Strauss, Richard
Romance in F Major............................ 238
Subotnick, Morton
Axolotl.. 245
Sutermeister, Heinrich
Cello Concerto No.1............................ 247
Cello Concerto No.2............................ 247
Takemitsu, Toru
Orion and Pleiades.............................. 252
Scene... 252
Toch, Ernst
Cello Concerto, Op. 35....................... 258
Turnage, Mark-Anthony
Kai 260
Vasks, Pēteris
Cello Concerto.................................... 263
Zimmermann, Bernd Alois
Canto di speranza 281
Concerto pour violoncelle et orchestre
en forme de „pas de trois"................. 281

Double bass

Bryars, Gavin
By the Vaar 31
Casken, John
Erin 35
Françaix, Jean
Double Bass Concerto 56
Mozart New-Look 57
Henze, Hans Werner
Concerto per contrabbasso 97
Huber, Klaus
„Erinnere dich an G..."........................ 123
Zbinden, Julien-François
Divertissement, Op. 10....................... 277

Flute

Beaser, Robert
Song of the Bells 19
Berkeley, Lennox
Sonatina 22
Borck, Edmund von
Concertino, Op. 15b 25
Castiglioni, Niccolò
Le Chant du Signe 36
Consonante 36
Françaix, Jean
Divertimento 56
Flute Concerto 56
Impromptu 56
Genzmer, Harald
Flute Concerto 63
Hindemith, Paul
Plöner Musiktag
(Abendkonzert 2.Flötensolo).............. 109

Holliger, Heinz
Turm-Musik 119
Hosokawa, Toshio
Flute Concerto 'Per-Sonare' 121
Huber, Klaus
Alveare Vernat 123
Ichiyanagi, Toshi
Interplay 127
Kounadis, Arghyris
Triptychon 145
Lehmann, Hans Ulrich
Quanti 1 148
Müller, Sigfrid Walther
Concert in B Major, Op. 62 166
Nono, Luigi
Epitaffio No.2 170
Penderecki, Krzysztof
Concerto 181
Rodrigo, Joaquín
Concierto Pastoral 206
Fantasia para un Gentilhombre 206
Sackman, Nicholas
Flute Concerto 212
Schwantner, Joseph
A Play of Shadows 226
Searle, Humphrey
Divertimento, Op. 26a 229
Seiber, Mátyás
Pastorale and Burlesque 230
Takemitsu, Toru
I hear the Water Dreaming 250
Willi, Herbert
Flute Concerto 271
Zender, Hans
Chamber Concerto 279

Recorder

Cooke, Arnold
Recorder Concerto 38
Gilbert, Anthony
Igorochki 69
Linde, Hans-Martin
Konzert 153

Oboe

Beck, Conrad
Concert Music for Oboe 20
Concertino for Oboe 20
von Bose, Hans-Jürgen
„....other echoes inhabit the garden" 26
Bryars, Gavin
The East Coast 31
Casken, John
Masque 35
Fortner, Wolfgang
Aulodie 52
Genzmer, Harald
Chamber Concerto 63
Holliger, Heinz
Siebengesang 120
Lehmann, Hans Ulrich
Dis-cantus 1 148
Mieg, Peter
Oboe Concerto 163
Picker, Tobias
Romances and Interludes 186

Zehm, Friedrich
Concerto da Camera 277
Zimmermann, Bernd Alois
Oboe Concerto 281

Cor anglais

Bamert, Matthias
Concertino 16
Fricker, Peter Racine
Concertante No.1, Op. 13 59
Skrowaczewski, Stanislaw
Concerto for Cor Anglais 235
Vasks, Pēteris
Concerto 263

Clarinet/Bassethorn

Beck, Conrad
Clarinet Concerto 20
Berio, Luciano
Variazioni 22
Cowie, Edward
Clarinet Concerto 38
Grünauer, Ingomar
Sinfonietta 81
Hamilton, Iain
Clarinet Concerto, Op. 7 86
Henze, Hans Werner
Le Miracle de la Rose 97
Hiller, Wilfried
Chagall-Zyklus 104
Hamelin 104
Veitstanz 105
Hindemith, Paul
Clarinet Concerto 109
Plöner Musiktag
(Abendkonzert 4.Variationen) 109
Penderecki, Krzysztof
Sinfonietta No. 2 181
Viola Concerto (version for clarinet) 181
Sadler, Helmut
Concertino 213
Seiber, Mátyás
Concertino 229
Skrowaczewski, Stanislaw
Clarinet Concerto 235
Ricercari Notturni 235
Strauss, Richard
Romance in E Flat Major,
o.Op. AV 61 238
Sutermeister, Heinrich
Clarinet Concerto 247
Takemitsu, Toru
Fantasma/Cantos 250

Saxophone

Borck, Edmund von
Saxophone Concerto, Op. 6 25
Bryars, Gavin
The Green Ray 32
Dahl, Ingolf
Saxophone Concerto 40
Helfritz, Hans
Saxophone Concerto 91
Schulhoff, Erwin
Hot-Sonate 224

Skrowaczewski, Stanislaw
Ricercari Notturni 235
Subotnick, Morton
In Two Worlds 245
Turnage, Mark-Anthony
Your Rockaby 260

Bassoon

Brauel, Henning
Notturno 28
Françaix, Jean
Bassoon Concerto 56
Divertissement 56
Müller, Sigfrid Walther
Concerto in F Major, Op. 56 166

Horn

Banks, Don
Horn Concerto 17
Hindemith, Paul
Horn Concerto 109
Martland, Steve
Orc 160
Müller-Siemens, Detlev
Horn Concerto 166
Searle, Humphrey
Aubade, Op. 28 229
Seiber, Mátyás
Notturno 230
Toldi, Julius
Concerto 259

Trumpet

Egk, Werner
Der Revisor - Concert Suite 47
Hamilton, Iain
Jazz Trumpet Concerto, Op. 37 86
Henze, Hans Werner
3 Sacred Concertos 97
Kaufmann, Armin
Musik, Op. 38 133
Killmayer, Wilhelm
The broken Farewell 135
Ligeti, György
Mysteries of the Macabre 152
Müller, Sigfrid Walther
Concerto grosso in D-Major, Op. 50 ... 166
Paulus, Stephen
Trumpet Concerto 178
Shchedrin, Rodion
Trumpet Concerto 232
Wanek, Friedrich K.
Chamber Concerto 266
Zbinden, Julien-François
Concertino, Op. 6 277
Zimmermann, Bernd Alois
Trumpet Concerto 281

Trombone

Françaix, Jean
Trombone Concerto 56
Rouse, Christopher
Trombone Concerto 211
Takemitsu, Toru
Fantasma/Cantos II 250

Guitar

ApIvor, Denis
Concertino, Op. 26 14

Bresgen, Cesar
Chamber Concerto.............................. 29

Castelnuovo-Tedesco, Mario
Guitar Concerto No.1
in D Major, Op. 99 36
Guitar Concerto No.2
in C Major, Op. 160............................ 36
Sérénade in D minor, Op. 118............ 36

Fetler, Paul
3 Impressions..................................... 50

Françaix, Jean
Guitar Concerto 56

Henze, Hans Werner
An eine Äolsharfe.............................. 97

Kelkel, Manfred
Zagreber Konzert, Op. 19................... 134

MacCombie, Bruce
Nightshade Rounds............................ 157

Paulus, Stephen
Ice Fields 178

Rodrigo, Joaquín
Concierto de Aranjuez 206
Concierto para una fiesta.................... 206
Fantasia para un Gentilhombre........... 206

Schwantner, Joseph
...From Afar 226

Smith Brindle, Reginald
Guitar Concerto 235

Takemitsu, Toru
To the Edge of Dream 252

Weiss, Harald
Nachtmusik.. 269

Harp(s)

Cowie, Edward
La Prima Vera 38

Françaix, Jean
Chaconne 56
Concerto for 2 Harps 56
Jeu poétique en six Mouvements 56

Hosokawa, Toshio
Interim 121

Paulus, Stephen
Divertimento...................................... 178

Rodrigo, Joaquín
Concierto de Aranjuez 206

Percussion

Brouwer, Leo
Exaedros II.. 30

Hiller, Wilfried
Pegasus 51 104

Hummel, Bertold
Percussion Concerto, Op. 70.............. 124

Ichiyanagi, Toshi
In the Reflection of Lighting Image.... 126
Paganini Personal 127
Time Surrounding............................... 127

Kovách, Andor
Musique concertante........................... 145

Mori, Kurodo
In Process of Time............................. 165

Roux, Maurice le
Allegro moderato................................ 211

Schwantner, Joseph
Percussion Concerto 226

Takemitsu, Toru
From me flows what you call Time 250

Zehm, Friedrich
Capriccio.. 277

Timpani

Donatoni, Franco
Concertino 43

Gerster, Ottmar
Capriccietto.. 67

Vasks, Pēteris
Concerto... 263

Mixture Trautonium

Genzmer, Harald
Trautonium Concerto.......................... 63

Tape

Yuasa, Joji
Nine Levels by Ze-Ami....................... 275

Japanese Solo Instruments

Hosokawa, Toshio
New Seeds of Contemplation -
„Mandara" 121
Seeds of Contemplation - „Mandara".... 121
Tokyo 1985 122
Utsurohi-Nagi 121

Ichiyanagi, Toshi
Concerto for Koto and
Chamber Orchestra „The Origin"........ 126
Engen 126

Takemitsu, Toru
Ceremonial... 250

Xiaogang, Ye
The Silence of the Sakyamuni, Op. 29 ... 274

Accordion

Françaix, Jean
Concerto pour Accordéon
et Orchestre.. 56

Two or More Strings

Fortner, Wolfgang
Ballet blanc 52
Klangvariation 52

Françaix, Jean
Divertissement.................................... 56

Goehr, Alexander
Romanza on the Notes
of the Fourth Psalm, Op. 38c 71

Huber, Klaus
Tempora 123

Jarnach, Philipp
Concertino in E minor, Op. 31 131

Klebe, Giselher
Concerto for Violin and Cello, Op. 18 ... 140
Scene.. 140

Martinů, Bohuslav
Concerto for String Quartet
with Orchestra 159

Müller-Siemens, Detlev
Double Concerto................................. 166

Paulus, Stephen
Double Concerto................................. 178

Reimann, Aribert
Concerto for Violin and Cello 195

Tippett, Michael
Triple Concerto.................................. 256

Two or More Harpsichords

Wanek, Friedrich K.
Musique concertante........................... 266
4 Pièces brèves 266

Mixed Wind/Brass

Beck, Conrad
Concertino for Clarinet and Bassoon... 20
Concerto for Wind Quintet
and Orchestra..................................... 21
Serenade... 21

Françaix, Jean
Double Concerto................................. 56
Quadruple Concerto............................ 56

Frommel, Gerhard
Concertino, Op. 24 61

Genzmer, Harald
Divertimento Giocoso 63

Goehr, Alexander
Cambridge Hocket, Op. 57................. 71

Hindemith, Paul
Concerto for Trumpet and Bassoon..... 109
Symphony in Bb................................. 109

Klebe, Giselher
Espressioni liriche 139

Lehmann, Hans Ulrich
Concerto for 2 Wind Instruments
and Strings 148

Ligeti, György
Double Concerto................................. 150

Rainier, Priaulx
Concertante for 2 Winds..................... 192

Sutermeister, Heinrich
Quadrifoglio.. 247

Takemitsu, Toru
Gémeaux 250

Werdin, Eberhard
Concertino 270

Two or More Guitars

Rodrigo, Joaquín
Concierto Andaluz.............................. 206
Concierto Madrigal............................. 206

String and Keyboard

Genzmer, Harald
Concertino No.1 63

Hartmann, Karl Amadeus
Concerto for viola with piano............. 88

Killmayer, Wilhelm
Pezzi ed Intermezzi 135

Maler, Wilhelm
Triple Concerto.................................. 158

Wind/Brass and Keyboard

Genzmer, Harald
Concertino No.1 63

Henze, Hans Werner
Chamber Concerto 97
Requiem 97

Two or More Trumpets

Turnage, Mark-Anthony
Dispelling the Fears 260

Other Mixed

Beck, Conrad
Concerto for String Quartet
and Orchestra 21

Dahl, Ingolf
Symphony Concertante 40

Fortner, Wolfgang
Prismen 52

Foss, Lukas
Elytres 54

Françaix, Jean
Concerto for 15 Soloists
and Orchestra 56
Concerto Grosso 56
Musique de Cour 56

Hartmann, Karl Amadeus
Chamber Concerto 88

Helm, Everett
Concerto 93

Henze, Hans Werner
Doppio concerto 97
I Sentimenti
di Carl Philipp Emanuel Bach 98

Hindemith, Paul
Concerto for Wind and Harp 109

Ichiyanagi, Toshi
Luminous Space 127

Penderecki, Krzysztof
Partita 181

Singleton, Alvin
Kwitana 233

Subotnick, Morton
Before the Butterfly 245

Takemitsu, Toru
Spectral Canticle 252
Toward the Sea II 252
Vers, l'arc-en-ciel, Palma 252

Tcherepnin, Alexander Nikolajevich
Concerto da Camera
in D Major, Op. 33 253

Turnage, Mark-Anthony
Blood on the Floor 260
Night Dances 260

Zehm, Friedrich
Concerto in Pop 277

Choral Music

Mixed a cappella

Beaser, Robert
Psalm 119 20

von Bose, Hans-Jürgen
Karfreitags-Sonett 27
4 Madrigals 27

Bresgen, Cesar
Arra alá, drunten in Baranya 29
Es brennt die grüne Linde 29
Hum fauler Lenz 30
Lino, Leano 30
Nulla vita sine musica 30
Wenn sich junge Herzen heben 30

Casken, John
A Gathering 35
The Land of Spices 35
Sunrising 35
To Fields We Do Not Know 36

Cowie, Edward
Elizabethan Madrigals
Books 1, 2 & 3 39
Gesangbuch 39

Eben, Petr
Verba Sapientiae - De circuitu aeterno ... 45
Verba Sapientiae - De tempore 45
Verba Sapientiae - Laus mulieris 45

Egk, Werner
Joan von Zarissa -
3 Choruses from the Ballet 47

Fortner, Wolfgang
The 46th Psalm 53
Agnus Dei 53
Eine deutsche Liedmesse 53
Glaubenslied 54
4 Petrarca-Sonette 54
3 Sacred Songs 54

Françaix, Jean
3 Poèmes de Paul Valéry 59

Fricker, Peter Racine
Rollant et Oliver, Op. 6 61

Gál, Hans
4 British Folk Songs 62

Genzmer, Harald
Am Abend 65
An ihren Genius 65
Du bist min 65
Finnisches Lied 65
Gebet für einen Unbelehrbaren 65
5 Gesänge 65
Hälfte des Lebens 65
Herz, wo warst du in der Nacht 65
Der Hoffnungslose 65
Hyperions Schicksalslied 65
Ich will truren fahren lan 65
Klageliche not 65
Lebenslauf 66
Lied des Vogelstellers (1958) 66
Lied des Vogelstellers (1979) 66
Mandalay 66
Mistral über den Gräbern 66
Nachts 66
Rechenstunde 66
Der schwarze Mond 66
Sensemayá 66
Sonnenuntergang 66

Stadturlaub (1958) 66
Stadturlaub (1979) 66
Swel man ein guot wip hat 66
Tagelied 66
Tanzende 66
Tanzliedchen 66
Tristissima Nox 66
Tropus ad Gloria 66
Über die Geburt Jesu 66
Ungeheuer und rot
erscheint die Wintersonne 66
Weiße Verlassenheit 67
Wie man einen Vogel malt 67
Wurzel des Waldes 67

Gilbert, Anthony
Missa Brevis 70

Goehr, Alexander
Carol for St. Steven 72
2 Choruses, Op. 14 72
2 Imitations of Baudelaire, Op. 47 72

Grainger, Percy Aldridge
At Twilight 78
Australian Up-Country Song 78
Brigg Fair 78
The Immovable Do 78
Irish Tune from County Derry 78
Recessional 79

Haas, Joseph
Deutsche Chormesse, Op. 108 83
Eine deutsche Singmesse, Op. 60 83
Deutsche Vesper, Op. 72 83
Ein deutsches Gloria, Op. 86 83
Es ist so still geworden 84
Frisch auf, ihr Musikanten 84
Gott ist die Liebe 84
Gotteslob, Op. 104 84
Das himmlische Orchester 84
Hymnen an das Licht, Op. 82 84
Kanonische Motetten, Op. 75 84
Lobt den Herrn, Op. 60/5 84
Wiegenlied 85

Hamilton, Iain
The Fray of Suport, Op. 21 87
Nocturnal 87

Harvey, Jonathan
2 Fragments 90
Love 90

Helmschrott, Robert M.
Das Äußerste 92
Begegnung 92
Dann 92
Manchmal 92
Menschenzeit 92
Morgen 92
Nachtgefühl 92
Nichts 92
Schönes Heute 92
Schweigen 92
Unsere Zeit 92
Wir 92

Henze, Hans Werner
Orpheus behind the Wire 101

Herrmann, Hugo
Nachruf 101

Hessenberg, Kurt
2 Abendlieder 103
2 Choralmotetten, Op. 93 103
4 Choruses, Op. 31 103
Christus, der uns selig macht, Op. 118 ... 103
Es steht ein Lind in jenem Tal 103
Es taget vor dem Walde 103

4 Geistliche Lieder
durch die Tageszeiten, Op. 41 103
Lieblich hat sich gesellet 103
Maienzeit bannet Lied 103
Mit Lust tret' ich in diesen Tanz.......... 103
2 Motets, Op. 37 103
4 Poems, Op. 81 103
Psalm 126, Op. 87 103
Psalm 130, Op. 134 103
Das sagt, der Amen heißt, Op. 46 103
Tröstet mein Volk, Op. 114 103

Hindemith, Paul
Art läßt nicht von Art, Op. 33 115
6 Chansons 115
The devil a monk would be 115
Frauenklage, Op. 33 115
Heimliches Glück, Op. 33 115
Lady's lament 115
Landsknechtstrinklied, Op. 33............. 115
Der Liebe Schrein, Op. 33................... 115
Lieder für Singkreise, Op. 43/2 115
Liedersätze aus dem
Kontrapunkt-Unterricht 116
12 Madrigals (An eine Tote) 114
12 Madrigals (An einen Schmetterling)... 114
12 Madrigals (Du Zweifel
an dem Sinn der Welt) 115
12 Madrigals (Eines Narren,
eines Künstlers Leben) 115
12 Madrigals (Es bleibt wohl,
was gesagt wird)................................ 115
12 Madrigals (Frühling) 115
12 Madrigals (Judaskuß) 115
12 Madrigals (Kraft fand zu Form)..... 115
12 Madrigals (Mitwelt) 116
12 Madrigals (Magisches Rezept)....... 116
12 Madrigals (Tauche deine Furcht
in schwarzen Wein) 116
12 Madrigals (Trink aus!).................. 116
Mass 116
Of Household Rule 116
Trooper's Drinking Song 116
True love 116
Vom Hausregiment, Op. 33 116
Wahre Liebe....................................... 116

Holliger, Heinz
Advent 120
Dona Nobis Pacem 120
Die Jahreszeiten 120
Psalm 120

Hosokawa, Toshio
Ave Maria 122
Ave Maris Stella 122

Huber, Klaus
Kanon zum Jahresbeginn.................... 124

Humpert, Hans
Ich bin vergnügt................................. 125

Ichiyanagi, Toshi
Genshiryoku Sensuikan 'Onagazame'
no Seitekina Kokai to Jisatsu no Uta ... 129
Syntax 129

Kaminski, Heinrich
6 Chorales 133
Motet „O Herre Gott".......................... 133
Psalm 130, Op. 1a 133
Der Tag ist hin 133
Vergiß mein nicht,
mein allerliebster Gott 133

Kaufmann, Dieter
Pax 133

Killmayer, Wilhelm
Cantetto.. 137
Canti Amorosi..................................... 137
4 Choruses 137
Geistliche Hymnen und Gesänge 137
3 Kanons 137
Lauda 137
Laudatu 1 & 2..................................... 137
Das Licht auf dem Scheffel................. 137
Lieder, Oden und Szenen 137
Pfannengericht.................................... 137
Sonntagsgeschichten -
Sonntagnachmittagskaffee 137
Sonntagsgeschichten -
Sonntagsausflug 137
Sonntagsgeschichten -
Sonntagsgedanken 137
Speranza... 138
Spucken und Schlucken...................... 138

Kirchner, Volker David
Lamento 139

Křenek, Ernst
Guten Morgen, Amerika 147
Motette zur Opferung 147
Proprium missae 147
Psalmverse zur Kommunion 147

Ligeti, György
Betlehemi Királyok 152
Bujdosó 152
Éjszaka - Reggel 152
3 Fantasies 152
Ha folyóvíz volnék 152
Haj, ifjuság 152
Hortobágy 152
Inaktelki nóták 152
Kállai kettős 152
Lakodalmas... 152
Magány (Solitude) 152
Magas Kősziklának 152
Magyar Etűdök (Hungarian Studies) ... 152
Pápainé (Widow Pápai) 153

Lutyens, Elisabeth
Excerpta Tractatus logico
philosophici, Op. 27 156
The Hymn of Man, Op. 61 156
Magnificat and Nunc Dimitis 156

MacCombie, Bruce
Color and Time 157

Martinů, Bohuslav
Ei, steig auf 160
Gram zernagt mein Herzchen............. 160
Hei! Alle kommt herbei 160
Ja, noch einmal 160
Sag mir, Gott...................................... 160
Unserer Liebe Glück 160
Wandern müssen wir 160
Wie mir ist 160

Martirano, Salvatore
Mass 160

Martland, Steve
Skywalk 161

Marx, Karl
Winterlied, Op. 13/4 161

Maxwell Davies, Sir Peter
Alleluia pro Virgine Maria 162
Carol on St. Steven 162
4 Choruses 162
The Fader of Heven 162
Haylle Comly & Clene 162
Jesus Autem Hodie 162

The Lord's Prayer 162
Nowell 162
O Magnum Mysterium 162

Mohler, Philipp
Es geht wohl anders
als du meinst, Op. 33/1 164
Der Postillion, Op. 33/2 164

Nono, Luigi
Sarà dolce tacere................................ 171

Orff, Carl
Ave Maria 175
Cantus-Firmus-Sätze 175
4 Choruses from Catulli Carmina........ 175
Concento di voci.................................. 175
Lugete o Veneres 175
Odi et amo 175

Paulus, Stephen
A child my choice................................ 179
The Angels and the Shepherds 179
Christmas Eve Carol............................ 179
Come Life, Shaker Life 179
Evensong 179
The First Nowell.................................. 179
Madrigali Di Michelangelo 180
Now is the Gentle Season 180
Peace... 180
Pium Paum 180
4 Preludes on Playthings of the Wind... 180
Shall we gather at the River 180
Wassail Song....................................... 180

Penderecki, Krzysztof
Agnus Dei from the 'Polish Requiem' ... 183
Song of Cherubim 183
Veni Creator....................................... 183

Pepping, Ernst
Bauerngarten....................................... 184
Bei Tag und Nacht 184
Choralsuite Part 1 185
Choralsuite Part 2 185
Choralsuite Part 3 185
Der Wagen 185
3 Evangelien-Motetten 185
German Choral Mass 185
German Mass 185
Das gute Leben 185
Der Herd 185
Herr Walther von der Vogelweide 185
Das Jahr 185
Jahraus - jahrein................................. 185
Das Licht 185
Der Morgen 185
Prediger-Motetten 185
Psalm 90 185
Spandauer Chorbuch 185
Uns ist ein Kind geboren 185
Im Weinland 185

Poos, Heinrich
Der Abt, der reit' 188
Annerle, wo warst du?......................... 188
Chanson 188
3 Choruses 188
Cock a doodle doo 188
Dona nobis pacem 188
Erntedank 188
Gavotte.. 188
Gigue 189
Hochzeit hielt das Mückelein 189
Hypostasis vel Somnium Jacob............ 189
The Keel Row 189
The Keeper 189

Kommt, wir gehn
auf schmalem Wege 189
Magnificat 189
The Miller of Dee 189
Musikanten, warum schweigt ihr 189
Nachklänge - Das Alter 189
Nachklänge - Der Kehraus 189
Nachklänge - Der Soldat (Epilogue) ... 189
Nachklänge - Der traurige Jäger 189
Nachklänge - Klang um Klang 189
Nachklänge - Nachtgruß 189
Nachklänge - Umkehr 189
Nachklänge - Weltlauf 189
The old True Love 190
Pavane 190
Seht es regnen, seht es gießen 190
Sing mir, o Nachtigall 190
Sphragis 190
Suite on English Folksongs 190
Tambourin 190
Tanzlied 190
There's None to soothe 190
Um Jaroschau fließen zwei der Bäche ... 190
Wenn ich durch die Berge
meiner Heimat 190

Rainier, Priaulx
Requiem 193

Regner, Hermann
Choral Studies 194

Reimann, Aribert
Auf verschleierten Schaukeln 198
John III, 16 198

Rein, Walter
Drunten im Unterland 199
Dunkle Wolken 199
Es sungen drei Engel 199
Gegenwart 199
Genialisches Treiben 199
Der Hufschmied 199
Ich wollt, daß ich daheime wäre 199
Komm, Trost der Nacht, o Nachtigall ... 199
O Lamentatione! 200
Schneider Courage 200
Wer sich die Musik erkiest 200
Zum Tanze, da geht ein Mädel 200

Reutter, Hermann
4 Bettellieder, Op. 38b 204
Gleichnis vom
barmherzigen Samariter 204
Gleichnis vom Saemann 204
Gleichnis von den Jungfrauen 204
Hymne an Deutschland 204
Jesu Nachtgespräch mit Nikodemus ... 205
3 Madrigals, Op. 71 205
Tres Laudes - Charon 205
Tres Laudes - Laudes Francisci 205
Tres Laudes - Multas novit amor vias ... 205
Trost der Nacht 205

Ridil, Christian
Nachts 205

Rodrigo, Joaquín
A la chiribirivuela 209
Triste estaba el Rey David 209

Schallehn, Hilger
Das Buch der Weihnachtslieder 214
Herr, dein Wort 214
Ein kleines Lied 214
O lux beata Trinitas 214
Singen ist das Atmen der Seele 214

Sommermorgenlied 214
Steht auf und singt 214

Schidlowsky, Leon
Requiem 215

Schnebel, Dieter
Blasmusik 218
Contrapunctus I 218
Contrapunctus VI 218
Contrapunctus XI 218
Für Stimmen (...missa est) 218
Gesums 218
Harmonik 218
I dt 31,6 218
II amn 218
III :! (madrasha II) 218
In motu proprio 218
Motetus 1 218

Schönberg, Arnold
Dreimal tausend Jahre, Op. 50a 219
Friede auf Erden, Op. 13 219

Schroeder, Hermann
3 Christmas Carols 223
Einst liebt' ich ein Mädchen 223
Mazurka 223
6 Mörike-Chöre 223
Der römische Brunnen 223
Römische Fontäne 223
Spruch 223
Te Deum, Op. 16 223

Searle, Humphrey
Song of the Sun, Op. 42 229

Singleton, Alvin
Epitaph 234

Slavenski, Josip
Herbstnächte - Jesenske noci 235
Hochzeitslied - Svtovska 235
Klagelied des Blinden - Slepacka 235
Liebeslied - Dilberka 235
Scherzlied - Saljivka 235
Spottlied - Rugalica 235

Strohbach, Siegfried
All that Glisters is not gold 244
Come away, Death 244
Hey, Robin, jolly Robin 244
If she be made of white and red 244
It was a Lover and his Lass 244
O Mistress mine 244
Take, o take those Lips away 244

Stürmer, Bruno
Narren überall, Op. 90/3 244

Sutermeister, Heinrich
2 Barocklieder 248
Cantata No.1 - 'Andreas Gryphius' 248
2 Madrigals 248
Mass in Eb 248

Takemitsu, Toru
Songs I 253
Songs II 253
Wind Horse 253

Tippett, Michael
Dance, Clarion Air 257
Lullaby 257
5 Negro Spirituals 257
Plebs Angelica 257
4 Songs from the British Isles 257
The Source 257
The Weeping Babe 257
The Windhover 257

Vasks, Pēteris
Concerto vocale 264
Klusas dziesmas - Silent Songs 264
Liténe 264
Madrigal 264
Mate saule - Mother Sun 264
Pater noster 264
Sava tauta - In his nation 264
Ugunssargs 264
Varonis - The Hero 264
Zemgale 264

Weill, Kurt
Recordare, Op. 11 268

Yuasa, Joji
Projection Onomatopoetic 276

Zehm, Friedrich
Alter Spruch 278
Inserat 278
Spruch 279
Zur Verlobung 279

Zimmermann, Bernd Alois
Bei meines Buhlen Haupte 282

Zoll, Paul
Spanisches Liederspiel 283

Male a cappella

Bresgen, Cesar
Als ich noch ein armer Knecht war 29
Bäckerlied 29
Den Letzten beißt der Hund 29
Dreimal rief die Amsel 29
Drunten in Baranya 29
Finstre Nacht 30
Für fünfzehn Pfennig 30
Hufeisen und Rosen 30
Die Kummermühle 30
Nachtlied 30
Weinschröter, schlag die Trommel 30
Der Weizen muß reifen 30
Wenn sich junge Herzen heben 30
Wer zum Teufel wird sich sorgen 30

Fortner, Wolfgang
Die Entschlafenen 53
Lied der Welt 54

Gál, Hans
3 Portrait Studies, Op. 34 62

Gebhard, Hans
Auf einem Baum ein Kuckuck saß 63
Ein ergötzlich Liedersingen 63
Es saß ein Käfer auf'm Bäumel 63
Froh zu sein bedarf es wenig 63
Lustig, ihr Brüder 63

Genzmer, Harald
An den Flamingo 65
Echo vom Himmel 65
Frühling-Winter 65
2 geistliche Festsprüche 65
Die Gewißheit 65
Hymn 65
In der Nacht gesungen 65
Ein Klagegesang 65
2 Lieder beim Wein 66
Mondaufgang 66
Oft in der stillen Nacht 66
Römische Weinsprüche 66
Rondell 66
Seemannslied 66
Sehnsucht 66
Singe, mein Herz 66

Sonett 66
Stürm, du Winterwind 66
Warnung 67
Der Weinschwelg 67

Gerster, Ottmar
Chor der Bergleute 68
5 Männerchöre 68
Preis des Schöpfers 68
Soldatenlied 68
Vini boni veritas 68

Gotovac, Jakov
Am adriatischen Meer, Op. 71 73
Das gestohlene Mäntelchen, Op. 15/3.... 73

Grainger, Percy Aldridge
Dollar and a Half Day 78
The Running of Shindand 79

Haas, Joseph
Chorfeier-Suite, Op. 98 83
„Die Linien des Lebens
sind verschieden", Op. 79/2 83
Ein Freiheitslied, Op. 78 84
„Mensch, steh still
und fürcht mich", Op. 79/1 85
Morgengloria, Op. 110 85
Morgenlied, Op. 66/2 85
Nur, Op. 110 85
2 Reiterlieder, Op. 67 85
Steh auf, Nordwind!, Op. 66/1 85
Tanzliedsuite, Op. 63 85
Um ein Mägdlein, Op. 83 85
Vom Himmel hoch, da komm ich her... 85
Wachtelschlag, Op. 110 85
Zueignung, Op. 110 85

Helmschrott, Robert M.
Bruder Nacht 92
Leben eines Mannes 92

Herrmann, Hugo
Abendfeier 101
Anruf 101
2 Folk Songs 101

Hessenberg, Kurt
2 Christmas Songs 103
2 Folksongs 103
Lieder und Epigramme, Op. 47 103
Morgenlied, Op. 31 103
3 Poems , Op. 59 103
Wenn die Bettelleute tanzen 103

Hindemith, Paul
Du mußt dir alles geben 115
Erster Schnee 115
Fürst Kraft 115
Galgenritt - The Demon of the Gibbet ... 115
Eine lichte Mitternacht 115
Nun da der Tag des Tages müde wird... 116
Die Stiefmutter 116
Der Tod 116
Über das Frühjahr 116
Variations on an Old Dance Tune 116
Das verfluchte Geld 116
Vision des Mannes 116

Ichiyanagi, Toshi
Requiem 129

Killmayer, Wilhelm
Romantische Chorlieder 137
...was dem Herzen kaum bewußt... 138

Knab, Armin
Ein Brotlaib 141
Den Toten 141
Wir zogen in das Feld 141

Lendvai, Erwin
Glockenlied, Op. 19/2 149
Licht muß wieder werden 149

Ligeti, György
Nonsense Madrigals 153

Miller, Franz R.
Der Winter ist ein rechter Mann 163

Mohler, Philipp
Ach, wie flüchtig,
ach, wie nichtig, Op. 15 164
Das Ewige ist Stille, Op. 42/3 164
Hausspruch, Op. 42/1 164
Singend sei dein Tag, Op. 29/2 164
Der Tod von Flandern, Op. 9/1 164
Ein Traum ist unser Leben 164
Trost, Op. 32/1 165

de la Motte, Diether
2 French Folksongs 165
Ständchen für Don Quixote 165

Orff, Carl
Aufruf - Komm, Sintflut der Seele 175
Concento di voci -
Sunt lacrimae rerum 175
Si puer cum puellula 175
Sonnengesang des
heiligen Franziskus 175

Penderecki, Krzysztof
Benedicamus Domino 183
Ecloga VIII 183

Pepping, Ernst
Christmas Songs 185
Mitten wir im Leben 185

Poos, Heinrich
Abseits 188
An die Freunde 188
Ansprache des Bauern
an seinen Ochsen 188
Ein Jäger längs dem Weiher ging 188
Es kribbelt und wibbelt weiter 188
Frisch auf zum fröhlichen Jagen 188
Gebet 189
Greensleeves 189
Gute Nacht 189
Hat mein Lieb ein Schlehlein 189
Hochzeit hielt das Mückelein 189
In der Frühe 189
Die Linien des Lebens 189
Mir entfloh die Wachtel 189
Musikanten 189
Die Nachtigall 190
O Liebe, Liebe 190
Psalm 126 190
Psalm 23 190
Psalm 77 190
Schneider Courage 190
Singet dem Herrn ein neues Lied 190
Die Sonn' ist untergegangen 190
Spiele mir, Geigerlein 190
Tanzlied 190
Totenklage um Samogonski 190
Über die Heide 190
Das Weltgericht 190
Wie lieblich schallt
durch Busch und Wald 190

Rein, Walter
Ade zur guten Nacht 198
Biergesängel 198
Chor der Bauern 198
Chor der Kaufleute 198
Das Echo 199

Dreimol oms Städele 199
Es schläft in allem Ding 199
Es wollt ein Jägerlein jagen 199
Freiheit, die ich meine 199
Handwerksburschen Abschied 199
Heija, im frischen Mai 199
Hochzeits-Madrigal 199
Jägerlied 199
Junggesellen 199
Komm, Trost der Welt,
du stille Nacht 199
Der liebste Buhle 199
Lob des Herings 199
Ein Mädchen und ein Gläschen Wein... 199
Minnelied 199
Mit Mädchen sich vertragen 199
Muß i denn 200
Nach grüner Farb mein Herz verlangt... 200
O Heiland, reiß die Himmel auf 200
Der Obadrauf 200
Der Sängerwettstreit 200
Sommerdörfchen 200
Stehn zwei Stern am hohen Himmel ... 200
Stundenruf des Wächters 200
Der Tambour 200
Trinklied 200
Tummel dich, guts Weinlein 200
Und in dem Schneegebirge 200
Wach auf, mein Herzens Schöne 200
Der Weinfuhrmann 200
Wunderlichstes Buch der Bücher 200
Zur Ernte 200

Reutter, Hermann
Hymne an Deutschland 204

Sakamoto, Yoshitaka
Kyushu Tanko Bushi -
Kohlengräberlied 213
Sansa Sigure - Tanzlied 213
Shimotzui Bushi -
Der fröhliche Schiffer 213
Soran Bushi-Lied des Fischers 213

Schallehn, Hilger
Altes Marschlied 214
Landser-Frömmigkeit 214
Landsknechts Trinkrunde 214
Singen ist das Atmen der Seele 214

Schroeder, Hermann
Als ich bei meinen Schafen wacht 223
Engel haben Himmelslieder 223
Freu dich, Erd und Sternenzelt 223
Lustig, ihr Brüder 223
Schön ist die Welt 223
Vom Himmel hoch, o Engel kommt.... 223
Zu Bethlehem geboren 223

Seiber, Mátyás
Alle Leut' sind ausgegangen 231

Singleton, Alvin
Fallen Crumbs 234

Slavenski, Josip
Scherzlied 235
Spottlied 235

Strauss, Richard
Lied der Freundschaft, Op. 45/2.......... 240

Stürmer, Bruno
Narren überall, Op. 90/3 244

Sutermeister, Heinrich
Gratias agimus tibi 248
Der Kaiser von China 248
Die Landsknechte 248

3 Lieder................................ 248
Ode auprès des Roseaux.................... 248
Schilflieder................................ 248
Les Soudards 248

Takemitsu, Toru
Grass 253
Handmade Proverbs........................... 253

Vasks, Pēteris
Baltais fragments - White fragment 264
Musu masu vardi -
Our Mothers's Names........................ 264

Yuasa, Joji
Composition on
Ze-Ami's Nine Grades........................ 276

Zoll, Paul
Abendlied................................ 282
Ach, du liebste mein........................ 282
Aus weiter Ferne 282
Im Frühlingsregen 282
Frühmorgens auf der Jagd 282
Das Glöckchen............................. 282
Im Garten die Beere, die rote 282
Ein Jäger wollt zum Jagen gehn......... 282
Jenseits des Tales standen ihre Zelte ... 282
Laridah................................ 283
Lied in den Rosen 283
Lumpenlied................................ 283
Der Marsch der Könige 283
Meine Heimat 283
Nach Süden nun sich lenken 283
Nobody knows................................ 283
Nun ruhen alle Wälder 283
Old Kentucky home........................ 283
Pferde zu vieren traben................. 283
Die Prinzessin und der Trommler........ 283
Rheinisches Fuhrmannslied................. 283
Ringsum leuchten Apfelblüten 283
Sing, kleine Nachtigall 283
Swanee Ribber............................. 283
Swing low, sweet chariot................. 283
Das Waldkonzert............................ 283
Wohlauf, Gesellen,
seid froh und munter 283
Wohlauf, in Gottes schöne Welt 283
Zu Regensburg
auf der Kirchturmspitze.................... 283
Zwei Spielleut................................ 283

Female a cappella

Bresgen, Cesar
Wanderschaft 30

Eben, Petr
Eine Mozartgeschichte 45
Medicamina sempiterna...................... 45

Gebhard, Hans
Auf einem Baum ein Kuckuck saß...... 63
Ein ergötzlich Liedersingen................. 63
Froh zu sein bedarf es wenig............ 63
Lustig, ihr Brüder 63

Genzmer, Harald
Ablösung................................ 65
An die Zikade 65
2 Chorsprüche................................ 65
Christkindleins Wiegenlied 65
Du sendest Schätze 65
Du tanzest leicht 65
Frau Nachtigall 65
Früh, wenn Tal, Gebirg und Garten..... 65
Käuzlein................................ 65

Kinderpredigt........................... 65
Knabe du................................ 65
Das Täubchen 66
Urlicht 66
Der verschwundene Stern.................... 67
Wacht auf, ihr schönen Vögelein 67

Gerster, Ottmar
Festgesang 68
4 Sinngedichte 68

Grainger, Percy Aldridge
There was a Pig went out to Dig......... 79

Haas, Joseph
Der Butzemann 83
Christ und die Kinder, Op. 44 83
Es blühen die Maien 84
Freund Husch, Op. 44 84
Heißa, Kathreinerle........................ 84
Ich bin schon siebenhundert Jahr 84
Der Kiebitz, Op. 44 84
Kleiner Morgenwanderer, Op. 44....... 84
Kommt ein Kindlein 84
Mädel kämm dich, putz dich............. 84
Mailied, Op. 44 84
Still, o Himmel 85
Trauungsgesang 85
Wiegenlied, Op. 44 85

Herrmann, Hugo
Rosmarienbaum 101

Hiller, Wilfried
Das große Lalula 105

Hindemith, Paul
4 Canons 115
Spruch eines Fahrenden.................... 116

Killmayer, Wilhelm
Lazzi 137
7 Rondeaux 137

Knab, Armin
Brot und Wein........................ 141
Drei Laub auf einer Linden 141
Es, es, es & es........................ 141
Geboren ist uns ein Kindelein 141
Mitten wir im Leben sind 141
Der Morgenstern 141
St. Michael am Meer 141

Ligeti, György
Betlehemi Királyok 152
Húsvét........................ 152
Idegen Földön (Far from Home)........ 152
Mátraszentimrei Dalok
(Songs from Mátraszentimre)............. 152
Pletykázó asszonyok........................ 153

Mohler, Philipp
Ein freier Mut 164
Die Gedanken sind frei 164
Im Frühtau zu Berge 164
Zum Abschied 165

Nono, Luigi
'Ha Venido'........................ 171

Orff, Carl
Sonnengesang
des heiligen Franziskus 175

Paulus, Stephen
Cats, Friends & Lovers........................ 179

Pepping, Ernst
Alle Vögel sind schon da 184
Auf einem Baum ein Kuckuck saß...... 184
Christmas Songs 185
Folksongs 185
Schlaf, Kindlein, schlaf 185

Spandauer Chorbuch 185
Wohlan, die Zeit ist kommen 185

Poos, Heinrich
Alalá........................ 188
Ei Baur, was kost dei Heu 188
Es muß geschieden sein 188
Fein sein, beinander bleibn............... 188
Gestern bei Mondenschein 189
Lieder im Rosenhag........................ 189
Musikanten, warum schweigt ihr 189
O Liebe, Liebe 190
Rosen im Tal........................ 190
Stehn zwei Stern am hohen Himmel... 190
Tanzlied........................ 190
Die Tochter der Heide 190
Um Jaroschau fließen zwei der Bäche.... 190
Zu Bethlehem geboren 190

Rein, Walter
Aufregung im Hühnerhof 198
Blüh auf!........................ 198
Es wollt ein Jägerlein jagen............... 199
Frisch auf in Gottes Namen 199
Die Gezeiten 199
Hausspruch 199
Herr, schicke, was du wilt 199
Kein Feuer, keine Kohle................. 199
Nach grüner Farb mein Herz verlangt... 200
Sandmännchen 200
Spaßige Geschichte 200
Streit zwischen Löffel und Gabel........ 200
Tanz Rüber 200
Und in dem Schneegebirge 200
Zum Tanze, da geht ein Mädel 200

Schallehn, Hilger
Abkühlung 214
Down by the Riverside 214
Freundinnen 214
Go down Moses 214
Good News 214
Little David, Play on your Harp......... 214
Rock my Soul 214
Selig sind die Toten 214
Sometimes I Feel
like a Motherless Child 214
Stimmen........................ 214
Das Vespergeläut -
Les cloches des vêpres 214

Schnebel, Dieter
Amazones 218

Schroeder, Hermann
Als ich bei meinen Schafen wacht 223
Ave Maria, gratia plena 223
Engel haben Himmelslieder 223
Freu dich, Erd und Sternenzelt 223
Vom Himmel hoch, o Engel kommt.... 223
Zu Bethlehem geboren 223

Seiber, Mátyás
Alle Leut' sind ausgegangen 231

Singleton, Alvin
Alleluia 234

Toch, Ernst
Der Tierkreis, Op. 52........................ 259

Vasks, Pēteris
Ganu dziesma - Shepherd's Song....... 264
Kekatu dziesma - Carnival Song........ 264
Liepa - The Lime-Tree 264
Mazi silti svetki 264
Musu dziesma - Our Song.................. 264
Ne tikai lirika........................ 264

Skumja mate - Sad Mother 264
Vasara 264
Ziles zina - Message of a Titmouse 264

Wanek, Friedrich K.
Ammenuhr 267

Werdin, Eberhard
Es stund ein frowe alleine 270
Ich will truren varen lan 270
Reigen der verschmähten Mädchen 270

Zoll, Paul
Eia, mein Kindchen 282
Hat zwei Fenster meine Seele 282
Der Kuckuck ruft im grünen Wald 283
Die Lerche 283
Das verlassene Mägdelein 283
Wär ich ein Mädchen
ohne Mann geblieben 283
Wiegenlied 283

Children a cappella

Bresgen, Cesar
Sonne, Sonne, scheine 30

Eben, Petr
Eine Mozartgeschichte 45

Haas, Joseph
Christ und die Kinder, Op. 44 83
6 dreistimmige Kanons 83
Freund Husch, Op. 44 84
Heißa, Kathreinerle 84
Ich bin schon siebenhundert Jahr 84
Der Kiebitz, Op. 44 84
Kleiner Morgenwanderer, Op. 44 84
Mädel kämm dich, putz dich 84
Mailied, Op. 44 85
Still, o Himmel 85
Wiegenlied, Op. 44 85

Hiller, Wilfried
Das große Lalula 105

Hindemith, Paul
Angst vorm Schwimmunterricht 114
Bastellied 115
Lied des Musterknaben 115
Schundromane lesen 116

Hosokawa, Toshio
Tenebrae 122

Ichiyanagi, Toshi
Heso no Uta 129

Ligeti, György
Mátraszentimrei Dalok
(Songs from Mátraszentimre) 152

Pepping, Ernst
Folksongs 185

Rein, Walter
Komm, Trost der Welt,
du stille Nacht 199
Stundenruf des Wächters 200

Schroeder, Hermann
Als ich bei meinen Schafen wacht 223
Engel haben Himmelslieder 223
Freu dich, Erd und Sternenzelt 223
Lustig, ihr Brüder 223
Schön ist die Welt 223
Vom Himmel hoch, o Engel kommt 223
Zu Bethlehem geboren 223

Weill, Kurt
Recordare, Op. 11 268

Werdin, Eberhard
Vier Kinderchöre 270

Yuasa, Joji
Uta Asobi (Play Songs)
on Onomatopoeia 276

Unison/Folk a cappella

Maxwell Davies, Sir Peter
Alma Redemptoris Mater 262

Orff, Carl
3 Choruses 275
2 Sacred Choruses 275

Mixed and Instrument/Ensemble/Orchestra

Ahrens, Joseph
Ave Maria 13
Missa choralis 13
Missa Dorica 13
3 weihnachtliche Liedsätze 13

Bresgen, Cesar
Das dreifache Gloria 29
Es ist ein Ros entsprungen 30
Glockensprüche 30
Ruf und Mahnung 30

Brugk, Hans Melchior
Bläsermesse, Op. 30 31
German Te Deum, Op. 15 31

Bryars, Gavin
On Photography 33

Burkhard, Willy
Psalm 93, Op. 49 33
Te Deum, Op. 33 34

Castiglioni, Niccolò
Anthem 37
Gyro 37
Symphony in C 37

Cowie, Edward
Gesangbuch 39
Kelly Choruses 39
Missa Brevis 39

Eben, Petr
Prager Te Deum 1989 45

Egk, Werner
La Tentation de Saint Antoine 47

Fortner, Wolfgang
The 100th Psalm 53

Foss, Lukas
Geod 54

Fricker, Peter Racine
Musick's Empire, Op. 27 60

Furer, Arthur
Portum Inveni 61

Gebhard, Hans
Es begab sich aber..., Op. 35 63
Missa Gotica, Op. 20 63
Wenn alle Brünnlein fließen, Op. 29 ... 63

Genzmer, Harald
3 antike Gesänge 65
Moosburger Graduale 66
Vom Abenteuer der Freude 67

Goehr, Alexander
Babylon the Great is Fallen, Op. 40 72
„I said, I will take Heed", Op. 56 72
5 Poems and an Epigram
of William Blake, Op. 17 72

Grainger, Percy Aldridge
The Bride's Tragedy 78
Harvest Hymn 78
I'm Seventeen come Sunday 78
The Immovable Do 78
Kipling „Jungle Book" Cycle 78
The Lads of Wamphray 78
The Lost Lady Found 78
Marching Tune 79
Recessional 79
The Sea Wife 79
Shallow Brown 79
Sir Eglamore 79
The Three Ravens 79
We have fed our Seas
for a Thousand Years 79
Ye Banks and Braes O'Bonnie Doon ... 79

Haas, Joseph
Deutsche Chormesse, Op. 108 83
Deutsche Messe 83
Deutsche Vesper, Op. 72 83
4 Elisabeth-Hymns, Op. 84b 84
Lob der Freundschaft, Op. 109 84
Lobpreis der
heiligen Elisabeth, Op. 84a 84
Praeconium, Op. 113 85

Harvey, Jonathan
The Annunciation 90

Henze, Hans Werner
Chor gefangener Trojer 101
Lieder von einer Insel 101
5 Madrigals 101
Musen Siziliens 101

Herrmann, Hugo
Cantata Primavera 101

Hindemith, Paul
Apparebit repentina dies 115
Lügenlied 116
Old Irish Air 116
Sing-und Spielmusiken, Op. 45/1 116
Wer sich die Musik erkiest, Op. 45/2 ... 116

Höffer, Paul
Fröhliche Wanderkantate 117
Weihnachtskantate, Op. 38 117

Holliger, Heinz
Gesänge der Frühe 120
Jisei I 120
Jisei II 120
Jisei III 120

Huber, Klaus
Hiob 19 124
„.... inwendig voller Figur..." 124

Kaminski, Heinrich
Motet „O Herre Gott" 133

Kaufmann, Dieter
Pax 133

Killmayer, Wilhelm
Lauda 137
Laudatu 1 & 2 137

Korngold, Erich Wolfgang
Passover-Psalm, Op. 30 145

Křenek, Ernst
Ich singe wieder, wenn es tagt 147

Lutyens, Elisabeth
Encomion, Op. 54 156

Martirano, Salvatore
O that Shakespeherian Rag 160

Maxwell Davies, Sir Peter
4 Choruses 162
O Magnum Mysterium 162
O Magnum Mysterium 162
Te Lucis Ante Terminum 162

Mohler, Philipp
Festliche Liedkantate, Op. 37.............. 164
Spanische Szenen, Op. 45 164
Wandspruch Kantate, Op. 29.............. 165

de la Motte, Diether
Festliche Kantate 165

Nono, Luigi
Cori di Didone 171
Liebeslied.. 171
La victoire de Guernica 171

Orff, Carl
Cantus-Firmus-Sätze 175
Dithyrambi... 175
Ecce gratum....................................... 175
Fremde sind wir.................................. 175
Der gute Mensch 175
Rota.. 175
Veni creator spiritus........................... 176
Vom Frühjahr, Öltank
und vom Fliegen 176
Von der Freundlichkeit der Welt.......... 176

Paulus, Stephen
An American Medley 179
Angels we have Heard on High 179
Barbara Allen..................................... 179
Bring a Torch, Jeannette Isabella 179
Built on a Rock................................... 179
Canticum Novum................................ 179
Christmas Tidings: 5 Carols 179
Echoes Between the Silent Peaks........ 179
For all Saints...................................... 179
Hallelu! 179
Jesu Carols.. 179
Lately arrived from London 179
Let All Creation Praise 179
Marginalia.. 180
O Little Town of Bethlehem 180
Personals 180
Run, Shepherds, run! 180
Sacred Songs 180
Sing hevin imperial 180
Single Girl 180
Visions from Hildegard (Part 1) 180
Visions from Hildegard (Part 2) 180
We give Thee but Thine Own.............. 180
Whitman's Dream............................... 180

Penderecki, Krzysztof
Canticum Canticorum Salomonis........ 183

Poos, Heinrich
Des Antonius von Padua Fischpredigt ... 188
Ave Maria 188
Erntedank... 188
Gloria Patri 189
Ich will truren fahren lan.................... 189

Regner, Hermann
I Dream a World 194

Rein, Walter
Alles ist Liebe..................................... 198
Heimat 199
Heimat 199
Komm, Trost der Nacht, o Nachtigall ... 199
Laßt uns glauben 199

Reutter, Hermann
Bauernhochzeit 204
Der glückliche Bauer, Op. 44............. 204
Das große Welttheater 204
Hochzeitslieder, Op. 53...................... 204
Hymne an Deutschland 204
Phyllis and Philander 205
Trost der Nacht 205

Rodrigo, Joaquín
Cántico de San Francisco de Asis 209

Roslawez, Nikolaj Andrejevich
Komsomolija 211

Schallehn, Hilger
Das Buch der Weihnachtslieder........... 214

Schnebel, Dieter
Schumann-Moment 218
Das Urteil.. 218

Schönberg, Arnold
Friede auf Erden, Op. 13 219

Schroeder, Hermann
Leben und Bestehen 223
Te Deum, Op. 16 223

Schwantner, Joseph
Evening Land (1992)........................... 227

Seiber, Mátyás
Cantata Secularis 231

Sutermeister, Heinrich
Der Papagei aus Kuba - Cantata No.5.... 248

Tippett, Michael
Magnificat and Nunc Dimittis............. 257
Music 257
Ritual Dances..................................... 257
The Shires Suite................................. 257

Vogel, Wladimir
An die Jugend der Welt 265

Werdin, Eberhard
Verzierte Volksliedsätze...................... 270

Wimberger, Gerhard
Heiratspost Kantate 272

Wyttenbach, Jürg
Sutil and Laar 273

Zoll, Paul
3 Folksongs 282
Spanisches Liederspiel 283

Male and Instrument/ Ensemble/Orchestra

Bloch, Augustyn
Gilgamesh... 23

Bryars, Gavin
Cadman Requiem 33

Genzmer, Harald
Adventsmotette................................... 65
4 Gedichte.. 65
2 geistliche Festsprüche...................... 65

Gotovac, Jakov
Koleda, Op. 11.................................... 73

Grainger, Percy Aldridge
Danny Deever 78
The Hunter in his Career 78
Kipling „Jungle Book" Cycle.............. 78
The Lads of Wamphray 78
The Lads of Wamphray 78
Scotch Strathspey and Reel 79
The Widow's Party 79

Killmayer, Wilhelm
Romantische Chorlieder 137

Mohler, Philipp
Festliche Liedkantate, Op. 37............. 164

Müller-Zürich, Paul
Chor der Toten, Op. 16....................... 167

Orff, Carl
In taberna quando sumus.................... 175
Des Turmes Auferstehung 175

Paulus, Stephen
Too many Waltzes 180

Poos, Heinrich
Zeichen am Weg 190

Rein, Walter
Freiheit, die ich meine........................ 199
Heimat 199
Mörike-Zyklus 199
Musik und Jägerei 200
Türmerlied 200
Weihe der Nacht 200

Reutter, Hermann
Der glückliche Bauer, Op. 44.............. 204
Hymne an Deutschland 204

Schallehn, Hilger
Irische Liebesgeschichten................... 214

Siegl, Otto
Das Gebirge 233

Sutermeister, Heinrich
Sonnenhymne des Echnaton -
Cantata No.7...................................... 248

Weill, Kurt
Divertimento, Op. 5............................ 268

Werdin, Eberhard
2 Trinklieder nach alten Texten 270

Yuasa, Joji
Shin Kiyari Kanda Sanka 276

Zehm, Friedrich
Grasshoffiade..................................... 278

Zoll, Paul
Bei den Klängen des Fandango 282
Lobt den Herrn, ihr Wesen all 283

Female and Instrument/ Ensemble/Orchestra

Bresgen, Cesar
Die alte Lokomotive 29
Das dreifache Gloria.......................... 29
Glockensprüche 30
Der Goldvogel 30
Ruf und Mahnung 30
Der Struwwelpeter 30

Haas, Joseph
Alemannischer
Liederreigen, Op. 89/1........................ 83
Deutsche Kindermesse, Op. 108 83
Deutsche Messe, Op. 83...................... 83
Fränkischer Liederreigen, Op. 89/2..... 84
Kommt, laßt uns allesamt, Op. 73....... 84
Des Lebens Sonnenschein, Op. 73...... 84
Marianische Kantate, Op. 112............ 85
Zum Lob der Arbeit, Op. 81/4............. 85
Zum Lob der Musik, Op. 81/1 85
Zum Lob der Natur, Op. 81/2............. 85

Helfritz, Hans
9 Mexican Folksongs.......................... 91

Hessenberg, Kurt
Struwwelpeter-Kantate, Op. 49 103

Hindemith, Paul
Lied von der Musik -
A Song of Music................................. 115
Wer sich die Musik erkiest 116

Humperdinck, Engelbert
Abendsegen 125

Křenek, Ernst
Cantata for Wartime, Op. 95 147

Ligeti, György
Clocks and Clouds 152
Mohler, Philipp
Vergangen ist die Nacht, Op. 14 165
Paulus, Stephen
Fountain of My Friends 179
In the Moon of Wintertime 179
This is the Month 180
Poos, Heinrich
Es ist ein Gesang
in meinen Sommer gefallen 188
Nacht und Träume 189
Rein, Walter
Es ist Weihnacht 199
Heimat 199
Reutter, Hermann
Hymne an Deutschland 204
Schroeder, Hermann
6 Christmas Carols 223
Leben und Bestehen 223
Singleton, Alvin
The World is here with me 234
Slavenski, Josip
Kolo 235
Sutermeister, Heinrich
3 Choruses 248
Tippett, Michael
Crown of the Year 257
Zoll, Paul
Iberisches Liederspiel 282

Children and Instrument/ Ensemble/Orchestra

Bresgen, Cesar
Die alte Lokomotive 29
Armer kleiner Tanzbär 29
Die Bettlerhochzeit 29
Der Goldvogel 30
Das Riesenspiel 30
Das Schlaraffenland 30
Tiertanzburlesken 30
Von Mäusen, Autos
und anderen Tieren 30
Haas, Joseph
Fränkischer Liederreigen, Op. 89/2 84
Schelmenlieder, Op. 71 85
Helfritz, Hans
9 Mexican Folksongs 91
Henze, Hans Werner
Wiegenlied der Mutter Gottes 101
Hessenberg, Kurt
Struwwelpeter-Kantate, Op. 49 103
Hindemith, Paul
Wir bauen eine Stadt 117
Maasz, Gerhard
Das Hasenspiel 156
Klingende Jahreszeiten 156
Mohler, Philipp
Vergangen ist die Nacht, Op. 14 165
Rein, Walter
Gesellen der Nacht 198
Laßt uns glauben 199
Lied der Sonne 199
Weihe der Nacht 200
Reutter, Hermann
Hymne an Deutschland 204

Rodrigo, Joaquín
A la clavelina 209
Schallehn, Hilger
Hallo Kinder, hört mal her 214
Sutermeister, Heinrich
3 Choruses 248

Unison/Folk and Instrument/ Ensemble/Orchestra

Banks, Don
Benedictus 18
Degen, Helmut
Festliches Vorspiel 41
Egk, Werner
Mein Vaterland 47
Grainger, Percy Aldridge
The Lost Lady Found 78
Shallow Brown 79
Haas, Joseph
Bernhardus-Lied 83
Christ-König-Messe, Op. 88 83
Deutsche Messe 83
Deutsche Messe 83
Deutsche Weihnachtsmesse, Op. 105 ... 83
Ecce Sacerdos Magnus, Op. 80a 83
Münchner Liebfrauen-Messe, Op. 96 ... 85
Speyerer Domfest-Messe, Op. 80 85
Trali Trala, Op. 47 85
Hindemith, Paul
Sing-und Spielmusiken, Op. 45/5 116
Poos, Heinrich
Singen heißt verstehen 190
Tippett, Michael
Bonny at Morn 257
Music 257

Mixed and Solo (Soli)/ Instrument/Ensemble/Orchestra

Beaser, Robert
Psalm 119 20
Beck, Conrad
Der Tod des Oedipus 22
Der Tod zu Basel 22
Biersack, Anton
Passions-Kantate 23
Blake, David
Lumina 23
Blomdahl, Karl-Birger
Anabase 24
In the Hall of Mirrors 24
von Bose, Hans-Jürgen
...im Wind gesprochen 27
Symphonic Fragment 27
Todesfuge 27
Bresgen, Cesar
Christkindl Kumedi 29
Kantate von der
Unruhe des Menschen 30
Uns ist kommen ein liebe Zeit 30
Brouwer, Leo
Cantigas del Tiempo Nuevo 31
Bryars, Gavin
The War in Heaven 33
Castiglioni, Niccolò
Aria 37
3 Miracle Plays 37

Cowie, Edward
Choral Symphony 39
Degen, Helmut
Wenn der Bauer Hochzeit macht 42
Eben, Petr
Heilige Zeichen 45
Egk, Werner
Furchtlosigkeit und Wohlwollen 47
Eisenmann, Will
Die Weise von Liebe und Tod
des Cornetts Christoph Rilke 48
Fortner, Wolfgang
An die Nachgeborenen 53
Chant de Naissance 53
Gladbacher Te Deum 53
Grenzen der Menschheit 54
Herr, bleibe bei uns 54
Nuptiae Catulli 54
Die Pfingstgeschichte 54
Foss, Lukas
The Fragments of Archilochos 54
Françaix, Jean
L' Apocalypse selon St. Jean 59
Fricker, Peter Racine
The Vision of Judgement, Op. 29 61
Frommel, Gerhard
Begegnung in der Eisenbahn 61
Genzmer, Harald
3 Hymns 65
Mass in E 66
Racine-Kantate 66
Goehr, Alexander
The Death of Moses, Op. 53 72
Sutter's Gold, Op. 10 72
Virtutes Nos. 1-9 72
Grainger, Percy Aldridge
Father and Daughter 78
Soldier Soldier 79
Grandis, Renato de
La Commedia Veneziana 79
Haas, Joseph
Christnacht, Op. 85 83
Die heilige Elisabeth, Op. 84 84
Das Jahr im Lied, Op. 103 84
Das Lebensbuch Gottes, Op. 87 84
Das Lied von der Mutter, Op. 91 84
Lieder der Sehnsucht, Op. 77 84
Schiller-Hymne, Op. 107 85
Die Seligen, Op. 106 85
Te Deum, Op. 100 85
Totenmesse, Op. 101 85
Hamilton, Iain
The Bermudas, Op. 33 85
Hartmann, Karl Amadeus
Friede Anno 48 90
Henze, Hans Werner
Cantata della Fiaba Estrema 100
Das Floß der Medusa 101
Jephte 101
Novae de Infinito Laudes 101
Scenes and Arias 101
Vocal Symphony 101
Herrmann, Hugo
Cantata Concertante 101
Triumph der Liebe 101

Hessenberg, Kurt
Christmas Cantata, Op. 27 103
Fiedellieder, Op. 22 103
Psalmen-Triptychon, Op. 36 103
Vom Wesen und Vergehen, Op. 45 103
Die Weihnachtsgeschichte, Op. 54 103

Hiller, Wilfried
Schulamit 105

Hindemith, Paul
Ite, angeli veloces -
Custos quid de nocte 115
Ite, angeli veloces -
Gesang an die Hoffnung 115
Ite, angeli veloces -
Triumphgesang Davids 115
Mainzer Umzug 116
Plöner Musiktag 116
In Praise of Music 116
Das Unaufhörliche 116
When Lilacs Last
in the Door-Yard Bloom'd 116

Holliger, Heinz
Der magische Tänzer 120
Scardanelli Zyklus 120

Hosokawa, Toshio
Hiroshima Requiem 122

Jirásek, Jan
Lukas-Passion 132

Killmayer, Wilhelm
Une leçon de français 137

Kirchner, Volker David
Babel-Requiem 139
Missa (Missa moguntina) 139
Passion 139
Requiem 139

Knab, Armin
Grüß Gott, du schöner Maien 141
Weihnachtskantate 141

Kovách, Andor
Mariennacht 1735, Op. 109 145
Song of Paradise 145

Liebermann, Rolf
Streitlied zwischen Leben und Tod 149

Ligeti, György
Scenes and Interludes 153

Lutyens, Elisabeth
De Amore, Op. 39 156

Maler, Wilhelm
Cantata 158
Der ewige Strom 158

Malipiero, Riccardo
Cantata Sacra 159

Mohler, Philipp
Nachtmusikanten, Op. 24 164

Müller-Siemens, Detlev
Arioso 167

Müller-Zürich, Paul
Te Deum 167

Negri, Gino
Antologia di Spoon River 169

Nono, Luigi
Il canto sospeso 171
Epitaffio No.1 171
Epitaffio No.1, 2 e 3 171
Epitaffio No.3 171
Intolleranza - Concert Suite 171
Der rote Mantel - Concert Suite (A) ... 171
La terra e la compagna 171

Orff, Carl
Carmina Burana 175
Catulli Carmina 175
Trionfo di Afrodite 175

Paulus, Stephen
Canticles: Songs and Rituals
for the Easter and the May 179
I Gave my Love a Cherry 179
Letters for the Times 180
North Shore 180
Silver the River 180
So Hallow'd is the Time 180
Voices 180
The Water is wide 180

Penderecki, Krzysztof
Kosmogonia 183
Lacrimosa from the 'Polish Requiem' ... 183
Magnificat 183
Polish Requiem 183
Prelude, Visions and Finale
from 'Paradise Lost' 183
Sanctus from „Polish Requiem" 183
Die schwarze Maske -
2 Scenes and Finale 183
Te Deum 183
Utrenja I 183
Utrenja II 183

Poos, Heinrich
Magnificat 189
Pater noster 190
Pax et Bonum 190
Singen heißt verstehen 190

Reimann, Aribert
Nunc dimittis (Canticum Simeonis) 198
Requiem 198
Verrà la morte 198

Rein, Walter
Der Winter 200

Reutter, Hermann
Choral Fantasy, Op. 52 204
Christmas Cantilena 204
Gesang des Deutschen, Op. 49 204
Der große Kalender, Op. 43 204
Hamlet Symphony 203
Der neue Hiob, Op. 37 205
Pandora, Op. 72 205
Triptychon 205

Rietz, Johannes
Chorische Tänze 205

Rodrigo, Joaquín
Cantan por Belén Pastores 209

Rudzinski, Zbigniew
Requiem 212

Schilling, Hans Ludwig
Legende vom Weisen und Zöllner 215

Schnebel, Dieter
Missa 218
Totentanz 218

Schönberg, Arnold
Der erste Psalm
'O du mein Gott', Op. 50c 219
Der Tanz um das goldene Kalb 219

Schroeder, Hermann
Carmen mysticum, Op. 30 223

Schulhoff, Erwin
H.M.S. Royal Oaks 223

Schwantner, Joseph
Evening Land 227

Searle, Humphrey
The Shadow of Cain, Op. 22 229

Seiber, Mátyás
3 Fragments from „A Portrait
of the Artist as a Young Man" 231
Ulysses 231

Sgambati, Giovanni
Missa da Requiem, Op. 38 232

Shchedrin, Rodion
The Sealed Angel 232

Singleton, Alvin
Gloria (from Messa) 234
Messa 234

Sutermeister, Heinrich
Dem Allgegenwärtigen -
Cantata No.3 248
Cantata No.2 248
Ecclesia 248
Erkennen und Schaffen -
Cantata No.6 248
Gloria 248
Das Hohelied - Cantata No.4 248
Missa da Requiem 248
Omnia ad unum - Cantata No.8 248
Te Deum 1975 248

Takemitsu, Toru
My Way of Life 253

Tippett, Michael
A Child of Our Time 257
The Mask of Time 257
Ritual Dances 257
The Vision of St. Augustine 257

Toch, Ernst
Das Wasser, Op. 53 259

Turnage, Mark-Anthony
Leaving 260

Weill, Kurt
Ballad of Magna Carta 268
Kiddush 268

Wimberger, Gerhard
Ars Amatoria 272
4 Sätze nach deutschen Volksliedern... 272

Zehm, Friedrich
Nonstop-Songs 279

Zimmermann, Bernd Alois
Die Brünnlein, die da fließen 282
Lob der Torheit 282
Requiem für einen jungen Dichter 282

Zoll, Paul
Lobt den Herrn, ihr Wesen all 283
Requiem 283

Male and Solo (Soli)/ Instrument/Ensemble/Orchestra

Gerster, Ottmar
An die Sonne 68

Grainger, Percy Aldridge
Anchor Song 78
Danny Deever 78

Haas, Joseph
Nachtwandler, Op. 102 85

Hessenberg, Kurt
Weinlein, nun gang ein!, Op. 72 103

Ishii, Kan
Gesang eines welken Baumes
und der Sonne 130

Killmayer, Wilhelm
Antiphone 137
Maasz, Gerhard
Wir sind die Musikanten 156
Mohler, Philipp
Laetare, Op. 43 164
Viva la Musica, Op. 41 165
Viva la Musica, Op. 41a 165
Müller, Karl-Josef
Omnia translata omnia 165
Poos, Heinrich
Ein jegliches hat seine Zeit 189
Rodrigo, Joaquín
Himnos de los Neófitos de Qumran 209
Stravinsky, Igor
Babel 242
Unterschale 242
Stroe, Aurel
Musique pour
'Oedipe à Colone de Sophocle' 244

Female and Solo (Soli)/ Instrument/Ensemble/Orchestra

Beck, Conrad
Lyrische Kantate 22
Bresgen, Cesar
L' Europe curieuse 30
European Folk and
Children's Songs Vols.1 & 2 30
Uns ist kommen ein liebe Zeit 30
Goehr, Alexander
Psalm 4, Op. 38a 72
Hand, Colin
In the Beginning 87
Holliger, Heinz
Siebengesang 120
Knab, Armin
Mariä Geburt 141
Korngold, Erich Wolfgang
Prayer, Op. 32 145
Nono, Luigi
Canciones a Guiomar 171
Paulus, Stephen
Love Letters 180

Speaking Choir

Eisenmann, Will
Die Weise von Liebe und Tod
des Cornetts Christoph Rilke 48
Höller, York
Décollage 118
Orff, Carl
Pieces for Speaking Chorus 175
Sprechstücke 175
Vogel, Wladimir
Arpiade 265

Vocal Music

Voice Solo

Goehr, Alexander
The Mouse metamorphosed
into a Maid, Op. 54 72
Huber, Klaus
Traumgesicht
from „... inwendig voller figur ..." 123
Rainier, Priaulx
Cycle for Declamation 193
Reimann, Aribert
Eingedunkelt 197
Entsorgt 197
Lady Lazarus 197
Parerga 197
Reutter, Hermann
Das zeitgenössische Lied 203
Schnebel, Dieter
Nostalgie 216

Voices Solo

Bryars, Gavin
Glorious Hill 33
Casken, John
Sharp Thorne 35
Cowie, Edward
Ancient Voices 39
Gilbert, Anthony
Canticle II - „Anger" 69
Holliger, Heinz
Variazioni su nulla 119
Martland, Steve
Skywalk 161
Terra Firma 161
Schnebel, Dieter
Amazones 218
Laut - Gesten - Laute 217
lectiones 217
Museumsstücke I, II 216
Übungen mit Klängen 217
Zeichen-Sprache 217
Vasks, Pēteris
3 Poems 264
Yuasa, Joji
Kansoku 276

Voice and Piano

Banks, Don
3 North Country Folk Songs 18
5 North Country Folk Songs 18
Beaser, Robert
The Old Men
admiring themselves in the Water 19
Quicksilver 19
The Seven Deadly Sins 19
Beck, Conrad
3 Herbstgesänge 21
Blomdahl, Karl-Birger
5 Canzone 24
von Bose, Hans-Jürgen
Omega 26
Bryars, Gavin
The Black River 33

Casken, John
Ia Orana, Gauguin 35
Cowie, Edward
Brighella's World 39
Dahl, Ingolf
A Cycle of Sonnets 40
3 Songs 40
Einem, Gottfried von
Japanische Blätter, Op. 15 48
Fortner, Wolfgang
Shakespeare-Songs 53
4 Songs 53
Terzinen 53
Widmung 53
Françaix, Jean
5 Poèmes de Charles d'Orléans 58
Prière du Soir - Chanson 58
Genzmer, Harald
Liederbuch 64
Gerster, Ottmar
5 einfache Lieder 68
5 Lieder 68
5 Lönslieder 68
Goehr, Alexander
Das Gesetz der Quadrille -
The Law of the Quadrille, Op. 41 72
In Theresienstadt 72
4 Songs from the Japanese, Op. 9 72
Warngedichte, Op. 22 72
Grainger, Percy Aldridge
Bold William Taylor 77
British Waterside (The Jolly Sailor) 77
David of the White Rock 77
Dedication 77
Died for Love 77
Love Song of Har Dyal 78
The Men of the Sea 78
The Pretty Maid Milkin' her Cow 78
A Reiver's Neck Verse 78
Shallow Brown 78
Six Dukes went a-fishin' 78
A Song of Autumn 78
The Sprig of Thyme 78
The Twa Corbies 78
Willow Willow 78
Haas, Joseph
Christuslieder, Op. 74 82
Frühling, Op. 59 82
6 Gedichte, Op. 48 82
Gesänge an Gott, Op. 68 82
Heimliche Lieder der Nacht, Op. 54 ... 82
Kuckuckslieder, Op. 37 82
Lieder der Reife und Ernte, Op. 92 83
Lieder der Sehnsucht, Op. 77 83
Lieder des Glücks, Op. 52 83
Lieder vom Baum und Wald, Op. 97 ... 83
Lieder vom Leben, Op. 76 83
Schelmenlieder, Op. 71 83
Trali Trala, Op. 47 83
Unterwegs, Op. 65 83
Hartmann, Karl Amadeus
Lamento 90
Henze, Hans Werner
3 Auden Songs 99
Whispers from Heavenly Death 99
Hessenberg, Kurt
Wenn ich,
O Kindlein, vor Dir stehe, Op. 30 102

Hindemith, Paul
Bal des Pendus 113
9 English Songs 113
3 Hymns, Op. 14 113
Das Kind 113
La Belle Dame sans Merci 113
8 Lieder, Op. 18 113
6 Lieder 113
Lustige Lieder
in Aargauer Mundart, Op. 5 113
Das Marienleben
(New version), Op. 27 113
Das Marienleben
(Original version), Op. 27 113
14 Motets (1. Exit Edictum) 113
14 Motets (10. Vidit Joannes Jesum) ... 114
14 Motets (11. Nuptiae factae sunt) 114
14 Motets
(12. Cum descendisset Jesus) 114
14 Motets
(13. Ascendente Jesu in Naviculam) ... 114
14 Motets (2. Pastores Loquebantur) ... 113
14 Motets
(3. Dicebat Jesus scribis et pharisaeis) ... 113
14 Motets (4. Dixit Jesus Petro) 113
14 Motets
(5. Angelus Domini apparuit) 113
14 Motets (6. Erat Joseph et Maria) 114
14 Motets (7. Defuncto Herode) 114
14 Motets (8. Cum natus esset) 114
14 Motets (9. Cum factus esset Jesus) ... 114
Nähe des Geliebten 114
7 Songs 114
2 Songs
(Else Lasker-Schüler, Guido Gezelle) ... 114
2 Songs (Oscar Cox) 114

Holliger, Heinz
Dörfliche Motive 119
6 Lieder 119
5 Mileva-Lieder 119

Humperdinck, Engelbert
Abendsegen 125
Besenbinderlied 125
Lied des Taumännchens 125

Ichiyanagi, Toshi
Aru Toki 129

Ireland, John
Songs sacred and profane 130

Jarnach, Philipp
Der wunde Ritter, Op. 15/4 132

Killmayer, Wilhelm
Blasons anatomiques
du corps féminin (Cycle II) 136
3 Gesänge nach Hölderlin 136
Heine-Porträt 136
Hölderlin-Lieder (Cycle I) 136
Hölderlin-Lieder (Cycle II) 136
Hölderlin-Lieder (Cycle III) 136
Huit Poésies de Mallarmé 136
9 Lieder 136
8 Lieder 136
3 Lieder nach Texten von Eichendorff ... 136
Salvum me fac 136
Die Zufriedenheit 136

Knab, Armin
12 Lieder 141
Litauische Lieder 141

Korngold, Erich Wolfgang
Einfache Lieder, Op. 9 144
Lied des Pagen 144
3 Lieder, Op. 22 144
5 Lieder, Op. 38 144
Lieder des Abschieds, Op. 14 144
Mariettas Lied 144
4 Shakespearian Songs, Op. 31 144
Sonett für Wien, Op. 41 144
3 Songs, Op. 18 144
Songs of the Clown, Op. 29 144
Unvergänglichkeit -
The Eternal, Op. 27 144

Kreisler, Fritz
Caprice viennois (Cradle song), Op. 2 ... 146

Křenek, Ernst
5 Lieder , Op. 82 147

Ligeti, György
Két dal 152
Mysteries of the Macabre 152

Martirano, Salvatore
Chansons Innocentes 157

MacCombie, Bruce
Leaden Echo, Golden Echo 160

Mihalovici, Marcel
Abendgesang, Op. 75 163

Orff, Carl
Early Songs 175

Paulus, Stephen
All my Pretty Ones 178
Artsongs 178
Bittersuite 178
3 Elizabethan Songs 178
Mad Book, Shadow Book:
Michael Morley's Songs 178
Songs of Love and Longing 178

Pfitzner, Hans
Complete Songs 186

Picker, Tobias
Aussöhnung 187
Half a Year Together 187
Native Trees 187
Remembering 187
To the Insects 187
When we meet again 187

Rainier, Priaulx
3 Greek Epigrams 193

Reimann, Aribert
Drei Sonnette von William 197
Shakespeare 197
Engführung 197
5 Gedichte von Paul Celan 197
Impression IV 197
Kinderlieder 197
Nacht-Räume 197
Nachtstück 197
Nachtstück II 197
Neun Sonnette der Louïze Labé 197
Nightpiece 197
Die Pole sind in uns 197
Shine and Dark 197
Six Poems 197
Tre Poemi di Michelangelo 197
Wir, die wie der Strandhafer Wahren 197

Reutter, Hermann
3 altägyptische Gedichte 202
Bogenschützen 202
Chamber Music 202
Christmas Cantilena 202
Epitaph für einen Dichter 202
5 Fragmente nach Friedrich Hölderlin 202
Ein Füllen ward geboren 202
Hamlet's first and second Monologue ... 203
Hymne an Deutschland 203
Die Jahreszeiten 203
6 Late Poems 203
4 Lieder, Op. 54 203
5 Lieder, Op. 58 203
3 Lieder, Op. 60 203
3 Lieder, Op. 61 203
12 Lieder, Op. 65 203
3 Lieder, Op. 67 203
9 Lieder 203
4 Lieder 203
5 Lieder 203
Lieder der Liebe 203
3 Lieder der Ophelia 203
9 Lieder und Gesänge, Op. 59 203
Meine dunklen Hände 203
Russian Songs, Op. 21 203
Russian Songs, Op. 23 203
3 Songs, Op. 56 203
7 Songs, Op. 64 203
Triptychon 'Sankt Sebastian' 203
Die Weise von Liebe und Tod, Op. 31 ... 203
3 Zigeunerromanzen 203

Rodrigo, Joaquín
Arbol 208
Barcarola 208
Canción del Cucú 208
Canción del Grumete 208
Canciones 208
Canço del Teuladí 208
Canticel 208
Cantiga 208
Coplas del Pastor Enamorado 208
Esta Niña se Lleva la Flor 208
Estribillo 208
Fino Cristal 208
Folias Canarias 208
La Grotte 208
12 Popular Spanish Songs 208
Por qué te llamaré? 208
Romance de la Infanta de Francia 208
Romancillo 208
Serranilla 208
Sobre el Cupey 209
Soneto 209
35 Songs 209
Un Home, San Antonio! 209
Villancicos 209

Roslawez, Nikolaj Andrejevich
Lieder und Romanzen I 211
Lieder und Romanzen II 211
Lieder und Romanzen III 211

Schnebel, Dieter
Kaschnitz-Gedichte 217
Lamento di Guerra 217
Mein Herz ruht müde 217

Schroeder, Hermann
3 Christmas Carols 223

Schulhoff, Erwin
5 Songs 224

Schulthess, Walter
Lieder (Text: Christian Morgenstern) ... 225
Lieder (Text: Karl Stamm) 225
Schwantner, Joseph
2 Poems of Agueda Pizarro 226
Seiber, Mátyás
The Owl and the Pussy-Cat 231
To Poetry.................................... 231
Stephan, Rudi
2 ernste Gesänge.............................. 237
Ich will Dir singen........................... 237
7 Lieder 237
Up de eensame Hallig......................... 237
Stravinsky, Igor
Pastorale 242
Sutermeister, Heinrich
4 Lieder (Swiss Troubadors) 247
4 Lieder (Text: various)...................... 247
The Seventieth and
Eighty Sixth Psalm 247
Tippett, Michael
Boyhood's End 256
The Heart's Assurance........................ 256
Songs for Ariel................................. 256
Toch, Ernst
9 Songs, Op. 41 258
Ullmann, Viktor
Sämtliche Lieder............................... 262
Weill, Kurt
Early Songs..................................... 268
2 Folksongs of the New Palestine 268
Langsamer Fox and Algi-Song............ 268
Ofrah's Lieder.................................. 268
Propaganda Songs 268
Rilkelieder 268
The Unknown Kurt Weill 268
Wellesz, Egon
The Leaden
and the Golden Echo, Op. 61 269
Wimberger, Gerhard
8 Chansons...................................... 272
Kästner Liederbuch 272
Zehm, Friedrich
Ein Bündel Chansons 272
Zimmermann, Bernd Alois
5 Lieder 282
3 Sacred Songs 282

Voices and Piano

Grainger, Percy Aldridge
Colonial Song 74
Shallow Brown 78
Humperdinck, Engelbert
Abendsegen 125
Dance Duet 125
Reutter, Hermann
6 Poems, Op. 73 203
Russian Songs, Op. 68....................... 203
Schnebel, Dieter
Quintessenz..................................... 217
Sutermeister, Heinrich
Max und Moritz................................ 247
Weill, Kurt
Maikaterlied, Abendlied 268

Voice and Guitar

Françaix, Jean
Prière du Soir - Chanson 58
Fricker, Peter Racine
O Mistress Mine 60
Henze, Hans Werner
3 Fragmente nach Hölderlin 99
Hosokawa, Toshio
Renka I... 122
Rainier, Priaulx
Dance of the Rain 193
Ubunzima.. 193
Rodrigo, Joaquín
Coplas del Pastor Enamorado............. 208
Folias Canarias 208
3 Spanish Songs............................... 209
Villancicos 209
Seiber, Mátyás
Quatre chansons populaires françaises... 231
Tippett, Michael
Songs for Achilles 256

Voice and String Instrument

Gerster, Ottmar
4 alte Lieder 68
Gilbert, Anthony
Long White Moonlight........................ 70
Knab, Armin
Rosa Mystica 141
Reutter, Hermann
Kleines geistliches Konzert 203
Schnebel, Dieter
Mit diesen Händen............................. 217

Voice and Wind/Brass Instrument

Bergmann, Walter
Pastorale... 22
Henze, Hans Werner
Heilige Nacht................................... 100
Ichiyanagi, Toshi
Music for Art Kites 129
Subotnick, Morton
2 Life Histories................................ 245
Yuasa, Joji
Observations on Weather Forecasts..... 276

Voice with Several Instruments

Banks, Don
Aria from 'Limbo' 18
Settings from Roget........................... 18
3 Short Songs.................................. 18
Tirade 18
Bausznern, Waldemar von
8 Kammergesänge 19
Beaser, Robert
Silently Spring................................. 19
Songs from „The Occasions" 19
Beck, Conrad
Bicinien.. 21
Die Sonnenfinsternis 21
Bloch, Augustyn
Salmo Gioioso 23

von Bose, Hans-Jürgen
Achalm.. 26
Ein Brudermord 26
Guarda el canto 26
5 Kinderreime................................... 26
Sonet XLII 27
7 Textos de Miguel Angel Bustos 27
Bresgen, Cesar
Kleine Musik
über zwei altdeutsche Volkslieder 29
Bryars, Gavin
The Adnan Songbook 33
Incipit Vita Nova 33
A Man in a Room, Gambling 33
Pico's Flight 33
The White Lodge 33
Burkhard, Willy
Herbst, Op. 36 33
Burton, Stephen Douglas
Ode to a Nightingale 34
Cowie, Edward
Kate Kelly's Road Show 39
The Roof of Heaven 39
Egk, Werner
La Tentation de Saint Antoine............ 47
Fortner, Wolfgang
Berceuse royale 53
Fragment Maria 53
Mitte des Lebens 53
Fricker, Peter Racine
Elegy, Op. 25 60
3 Sonnets of Cecco Angiolieri
da Siena, Op. 7 60
Gilbert, Anthony
Beastly Jingles 69
Inscapes, Op. 26 70
Love Poems 70
Vasanta with Dancing 70
Grainger, Percy Aldridge
Colonial Song 78
Died for Love 78
The Twa Corbies 78
Willow Willow.................................. 78
Hamilton, Iain
Dialogues.. 87
Henze, Hans Werner
Ariosi 100
Being Beauteous 100
El Cimarrón 100
Whispers from Heavenly Death 100
Hessenberg, Kurt
10 Lieder, Op. 32.............................. 102
Der Tag, der ist so freudenreich 102
Hiller, Wilfried
Muspilli.. 105
Traum vom verlorenen Paradies.......... 105
Hindemith, Paul
Die junge Magd, Op. 23/2................... 114
Melancholie, Op. 13 114
Serenades, Op. 35 114
Des Todes Tod, Op. 23a 114
Wie es wär', wenn's anders wär' 114
Holliger, Heinz
„Beiseit"... 120
Erde und Himmel 120
Glühende Rätsel................................ 120
5 Mileva-Lieder 120
4 Miniatures.................................... 120
Schwarzgewobene Trauer.................... 120

Hosokawa, Toshio
Banka 122
Birds Fragments I 122
Renka II 122
Renka III 122

Killmayer, Wilhelm
Altissimu 136
Aussicht 136
Blasons anatomiques
du corps féminin (Cycle I) 136
Merlin-Liederbuch 137
Rêveries 137
Romances 137
Sappho 137
8 Shakespeare Lieder 137

Kirchner, Volker David
3 Lieder 137
Orfeo 137
Riten 137

Paulus, Stephen
Letters from Collette 179
Mad Book, Shadow Book:
Michael Morley's Songs 179

Reimann, Aribert
Epitaph 197
Mignon 198
Sechs Gesänge, Op. 107 198
Unrevealed 198

Reutter, Hermann
5 antike Oden, Op. 57 203
Ein kleines Requiem 203
Missa Brevis, Op. 22 204
3 Nocturnes 204
Prediger Salomo (12,1-9) 204
Solo Cantata, Op. 45 204
3 Songs, Op. 3 204
3 Songs, Op. 3 203

Rodrigo, Joaquín
Despedida y Soledad 209
Espera del Amado 209
San Juan y Pascua 209

Schnebel, Dieter
Fragment 216
Lieder ohne Worte 217

Schulhoff, Erwin
Die Wolkenpumpe, Op. 40 224

Schwantner, Joseph
Sparrows 226

Seiber, Mátyás
The Owl and the Pussy-Cat 231
Quatre chansons populaires françaises ... 231

Singleton, Alvin
A Seasoning 234

Souster, Tim
Poem in Depression Wei Village 236

Strauss, Richard
Alphorn, o.Op. AV 29 238

Stravinsky, Igor
Pastorale 242

Subotnick, Morton
Hungers 245
The Last Dream of the Beast 245
Play! No.4 246

Sutermeister, Heinrich
4 Lieder 247

Tippett, Michael
Songs for Ariel 256

Turnage, Mark-Anthony
Her Anxiety 260
Lament for a Hanging Man 260

Ullmann, Viktor
Herbst - Lied der Tröstung 262

Vasks, Pēteris
Latvija 264

Weill, Kurt
Klops Lied 268

Wellesz, Egon
The Leaden
and the Golden Echo, Op. 61 269

Westergaard, Peter
Cantata No.3 270

Wimberger, Gerhard
Singsang 272

Yuasa, Joji
Mutterings 276

Zimmermann, Bernd Alois
Die fromme Helene 282

Voice with Orchestra

Banks, Don
5 North Country Folk Songs 18

Basi, Daniel, R.
Dos Alusiones 18

Beaser, Robert
The Seven Deadly Sins 19
Symphony 20

Beck, Conrad
Elegie 21
Herbstfeuer 21
Kammer-Kantate 21

Blomdahl, Karl-Birger
Resan i denna nat
(Le Voyage cette Nuit) 24

von Bose, Hans-Jürgen
5 Gesänge 26
4 Lieder 26
Love after Love 26
Sappho-Gesänge 27
Three Songs 27

Brauel, Henning
Ophelia 28

Bryars, Gavin
Doctor Ox's Experiment (Epilogue) 33
Pico's Flight 33
The White Lodge 33

Burkhard, Willy
Das ewige Brausen, Op. 46 33

Casken, John
Firewhirl 35
Still Mine 35

Castiglioni, Niccolò
Canzoni 37
A Solemn Music I 37
A Solemn Music II 37
Sweet 37

Cowie, Edward
Columbine 39

Dallapiccola, Luigi
Tre poemi 41

Egk, Werner
Chanson et Romance 47
Nachgefühl 47
Natur-Liebe-Tod 47
Peer Gynt -
Tango, Zwischenspiel und Arie ... 47

Quattro Canzoni 47
La Tentation de Saint Antoine 47
Variationen über
ein altes Wiener Strophenlied 47

Fortner, Wolfgang
Berceuse royale 53
The Creation 53
Immagini 53
Machaut-Balladen 53
Prelude and Elegy 53

Françaix, Jean
La Cantate de Méphisto 59
Invocation à la Volupté 59

Fricker, Peter Racine
Cantata, Op. 37 60
O longs Désirs, Op. 39 60

Genzmer, Harald
3 Songs 64

Gilbert, Anthony
Certain Lights Reflecting 70

Goehr, Alexander
Behold the Sun, Op. 44a 72
4 Songs from the Japanese, Op. 9 ... 72

Gotovac, Jakov
Lieder der Sehnsucht, Op. 21 73
Riswan Aga, Op. 19 73

Grainger, Percy Aldridge
Bold William Taylor 78
The Lost Lady Found 78
Shallow Brown 78

Haas, Joseph
An die Heimat 83
Tag und Nacht, Op. 58 83

Hamel, Peter Michael
Dharana 86

Hamilton, Iain
5 Love Songs, Op. 36 87
A Testament of War 87

Hartmann, Karl Amadeus
Gesangsszene 90
Symphony No.1 90

Henze, Hans Werner
Apollo et Hyazinthus 99
3 Arias
from 'Elegy for Young Lovers' 99
Ariosi 100
2 Concert Arias
from the opera 'König Hirsch' ... 100
Kammermusik 1958 100
Ein Landarzt - Monodram 100
Nachtstücke und Arien 100
5 Neapolitan Songs 100
El Rey de Harlem 100
Songs and Dances 100
Versuch über Schweine 100
Violin Concerto No.2 100
Wesendonk - Lieder 100

Hessenberg, Kurt
3 Lieder, Op. 32a 102

Hindemith, Paul
Es trägt die Nacht 114
3 Gesänge , Op. 9 114
Mag Sonne leuchten 114
Das Marienleben, Op. 27 114
6 Songs 114
Was gabst du mir 114
Ein Wille treibt mich 114
Die Zeit vergeht 114

Holliger, Heinz
3 Liebeslieder 120
2 Lieder 120
Huber, Klaus
... Ausgespannt... 123
Psalm of Christ 124
Killmayer, Wilhelm
Hölderlin-Lieder (Cycle I) 137
Hölderlin-Lieder (Cycle II) 137
Huit Poésies de Mallarmé................... 137
Le petit Savoyard.............................. 137
Preghiere 137
Tamquam sponsus.............................. 137
Tre canti di Leopardi 137
Kirchner, Volker David
3 Gesänge - „Abgesang" 139
Knab, Armin
Liebesklagen des Mädchens 141
2 Solo Cantatas 141
Korngold, Erich Wolfgang
Einfache Lieder, Op. 9........................ 144
Lieder des Abschieds, Op. 14............. 144
Mariettas Lied
from 'Die tote Stadt', Op. 12 144
Tanzlied des Pierrot,
from 'Die tote Stadt', Op. 12 144
Lehmann, Hans Ulrich
Dis-cantus 2 149
Rondo... 149
Lendvai, Erwin
5 Sonette der Louïze Labé, Op. 33...... 149
Ligeti, György
Mysteries of the Macabre (1991) 152
Mysteries of the Macabre (1992) 152
Lokschin, Alexander
3 Scenes from Goethe's Faust 154
Lutyens, Elisabeth
And Suddenly it's Evening, Op. 66..... 156
Catena, Op. 44 156
MacCombie, Bruce
Leaden Echo, Golden Echo 157
Martland, Steve
Glad Day.. 161
The Perfect Act 161
Müller-Siemens, Detlev
Songs and Pavanes 167
Paulus, Stephen
Night Speech 179
Picker, Tobias
Symphony No.2 187
Reimann, Aribert
Chacun sa Chimère............................. 197
Drei Lieder... 197
Finite Infinity 197
Fragments from 'Lear' 198
Gedichte der Maria Stuart, Op. 135 198
Hölderlin-Fragmente 198
Inane 198
Lines 198
Ein Totentanz - Suite 198
Zyklus 198
Reutter, Hermann
Andalusiana 203
Aus dem Hohelied Salomonis 203
Kleine Ballade von den drei Flüssen... 203
Lyrical Cantata, Op. 70 204
Monolog der Iphigenie, Op. 74 204
3 Monologe des Empedokles 204
3 Songs, Op. 3 204

Szene und Monolog der Marfa............ 204
Weltlicht.. 204
Rodrigo, Joaquín
Cantico de la esposa 209
Cuatre Cançons en llengua catalana.... 209
La Espera 209
Rosaliana 209
Serranilla 209
Triptic de Mosén Cinto 209
Villancicos 209
Villancicos y Canciones de Navidad... 209
Sackman, Nicholas
And the World-A Wonder Waking 213
Schnebel, Dieter
Metamorphosenmusik 217
O Liebe! - süßer Tod 217
Sinfonie X 217
Wagner-Idyll 218
Schüler, Johannes
Die fünf Marienlieder des Kuno Kohn ... 223
Schwantner, Joseph
Dreamcaller 226
Magabunda (Witchnomad) 226
Steinbrenner, Wilfried
Kristall 236
Stephan, Rudi
Abendlied.. 237
Dir 237
Liebeszauber 237
Pantherlied 237
Sternberg, Erich Walter
The Raven... 237
Strauss, Richard
Ganymed, o.Op. AV 187...................... 240
Sutermeister, Heinrich
Consolatio philosophiae 247
7 Liebesbriefe 247
6 Liebesbriefe 247
Romeo and Juliet - Juliet's Aria 247
Tippett, Michael
Byzantium.. 256
The Heart's Assurance 256
Songs for Dov..................................... 256
Sosostris' Aria.................................... 256
Symphony No.3 256
Toch, Ernst
Die Chinesische Flöte, Op. 29............ 258
Music
for Orchestra and Baritone, Op. 60..... 259
Turnage, Mark-Anthony
Some Days... 260
Ullmann, Viktor
6 Songs, Op. 17 262
Wand, Günter
Odi et amo 266
Wanek, Friedrich K.
Due Sonetti 267
Weill, Kurt
5 Songs from Huckleberry Finn 268
4 Walt Whitman Songs 268
Westergaard, Peter
Cantata No.2 270
Wildberger, Jacques
Liebestoto 270
Wimberger, Gerhard
3 Lyrical Chansons 272
Wyttenbach, Jürg
De Metalli 273

Xiaogang, Ye
Purple Fog & White Poppy 274
Zimmermann, Bernd Alois
„Ich wandte mich und sah an alles
Unrecht, das geschah unter der Sonne" ... 282

Voices with Several Instruments

Banks, Don
Limbo.. 18
Bryars, Gavin
Effarene 33
Fortner, Wolfgang
Aria 52
Farewell 53
That Time.. 53
Françaix, Jean
Triade de toujours............................... 59
Goehr, Alexander
The Deluge, Op. 7 72
Sing, Ariel, Op. 51 72
Grainger, Percy Aldridge
Colonial Song 74
Henze, Hans Werner
3 Lieder über den Schnee 100
Das Urteil der Kalliope....................... 100
Hindemith, Paul
Sing-und Spielmusiken, Op. 45/2 116
Holliger, Heinz
Schaufelrad 120
Martland, Steve
El Pueblo Unido Jamas Sera Vencido... 161
Principia 161
Maxwell Davies, Sir Peter
Leopardi Fragments............................ 162
Müller-Siemens, Detlev
Tom-a-Bedlam 166
Rainier, Priaulx
The Bee Oracles 193
Rodrigo, Joaquín
Duérmete, Niño 209
Sackman, Nicholas
A Pair of Wings 213
Schnebel, Dieter
Jowaegerli... 217
Das Urteil... 217
Singleton, Alvin
Necessity is a Mother 234
Tippett, Michael
Suite: The Tempest 256

Voices with Orchestra

Banks, Don
Walkabout... 18
Egk, Werner
Die Verlobung in San Domingo -
3 Pieces.. 47
Joan von Zarissa - Suite 47
Fortner, Wolfgang
2 Exerzitien.. 53
Isaaks Opferung 53
Machaut-Balladen 53
„Versuch eines Agon um...?"............... 53
Goehr, Alexander
Eve Dreams in Paradise, Op. 49......... 72

Grünauer, Ingomar
Besichtigung, Versteigerung
und Beseitigung von 5 Künstlern 80
Sinfonietta... 81

Henze, Hans Werner
Concert-Suite 100
Il Ritorno d'Ulisse in Patria -
Scenes and Arias................................ 100
Voices 100

Hosokawa, Toshio
Super Flumina Babylonis 122

Ichiyanagi, Toshi
Symphony „Berlin Renshi" 129

Kaufmann, Dieter
Semi-Buffa, Op. 23............................. 133

Killmayer, Wilhelm
Französisches Liederbuch 136

Kirchner, Volker David
Golgatha.. 139
Symphony No.2 139

Ligeti, György
Scenes and Interludes 153

Nono, Luigi
Canti di vita e d'amore 170

Reimann, Aribert
Ein apokalyptisches Fragment............ 197
Fragments from 'Melusine' 198
Wolkenloses Christfest 198

Reutter, Hermann
Hamlet Symphony 203
Der himmlische Vagant 203
Der Liebe will ich singen 204
Spanischer Totentanz 204

Schnebel, Dieter
Metamorphosen des Ovid oder
Die Bewegung von den Rändern
zur Mitte hin und umgekehrt 217
St. Jago 217
Thanatos-Eros 217

Subotnick, Morton
The Double Life of Amphibians......... 245

Turnage, Mark-Anthony
Greek - Suite....................................... 260

Weill, Kurt
Die Sieben Todsünden 268

Yuasa, Joji
Suite Fushi Gyo-Un 276

Zimmermann, Bernd Alois
Die Soldaten 282

Speaker with Instrument(s)/ Ensemble/Orchestra

Bamert, Matthias
Circus Parade...................................... 16
Once Upon an Orchestra 17

von Bose, Hans-Jürgen
In hora mortis 26

Eisenmann, Will
Orpheus, Eurydike, Hermes 48

Fortner, Wolfgang
That Time... 53

Gilbert, Anthony
Inscapes, Op. 26 70
Upstream River Rewa 70

Heller, Barbara
Lalai - Schlaflied zum Wachwerden?... 92

Henze, Hans Werner
Orpheus - Concert Version 100
Paraphrasen über Dostojewski 100

Hiller, Wilfried
Der Josa mit der Zauberfiedel 104

Hindemith, Paul
Lustige Sinfonietta, Op. 4 114

Holliger, Heinz
Alb-Chehr 119

Ince, Kamran
Matinees.. 130

Klebe, Giselher
Römische Elegien, Op. 15................... 140

Liebermann, Rolf
Musik 149

Paulus, Stephen
Suite from 'Harmoonia' 179
Voices from the Gallery...................... 179

Picker, Tobias
The Encantadas (1983)....................... 187
The Encantadas (1986)....................... 187

Regner, Hermann
„mit musik" 194

Reimann, Aribert
Denn Bleiben ist nirgends 197
Trovers 198

Reutter, Hermann
Hamlet Symphony 203
Liebeslied
aus dem Chinesischen des Sao Han 204

Schnebel, Dieter
Baumzucht 217
glossolalie 217
Glossolalie 61 217
St. Jago 217

Schoeller, Philippe
Légendes I. Water 219

Schwantner, Joseph
New Morning for the World 226

Searle, Humphrey
The Riverrun, Op. 20........................... 229

Sutermeister, Heinrich
Die Alpen 247

Takemitsu, Toru
Family Tree.. 253

Tippett, Michael
„Words for Music Perhaps"................. 257

Ullmann, Viktor
Die Weise von Liebe und Tod
des Cornet Christoph Rilke 262

Keyboard Instruments

Solo Piano Two Hands

Arnell, Richard
Recitative and Aria, Op. 53 15

Badings, Henk
Arcadia - Vol.1.................................... 15
Arcadia - Vol.2.................................... 15
Arcadia - Vol.3.................................... 15
Piano Sonata No.1 15
Piano Sonata No.2 16
Reihe kleiner Klavierstücke 16
Sonatina 16

Banks, Don
Pezzo Dramatico.................................. 17

Bate, Stanley
7 Piano Pieces 18

Beaser, Robert
Landscape with Bells........................... 19

Beck, Conrad
Piano Pieces Vol.1............................... 21
Piano Pieces Vol.2............................... 21
Sonatina 21
Sonatina No.2 21

Berkeley, Lennox
4 Concert Studies, Op. 14/1 22

von Bose, Hans-Jürgen
Labyrinth II... 26
3 Little Piano Pieces 26

Brehme, Hans
Concert Suite, Op. 37 28

Brouwer, Leo
Sonata 'piano e forte' 31

Ciry, Michel
Ballade No. 1, Op. 42 37

Cowie, Edward
Kelly Variations 38
Piano Variations 39

Dahl, Ingolf
2 Fugues by Anton Reicha 40
Hymn and Toccata............................... 40
Pastorale Montano 40
Preludio e Fuga Burlesca.................... 40
Reflections 40

Degen, Helmut
Capriccio Scherzando 42
30 Concert Studies............................... 42
Concerto in 2 Parts 42

Donatoni, Franco
Composizione in quattro movimenti ... 43
3 Improvvisazioni................................ 43

Eben, Petr
Briefe an Milena 45
Die Welt der Kleinen 45

Egk, Werner
Piano Sonata 47

Elgar, Edward William
Salut d'Amour, Op. 12 49
Salut d'Amour, Op. 12 49

Erding Swiridoff, Susanne
Chillam 49
Maske und Kristall 49

Fairchild, Blair
Some (12) Indian Songs and Dances ... 50

Fortner, Wolfgang
7 Elegies 52
Epigramme... 52
Kammermusik 52
6 Late Pieces 52
Piano Sonatina 52

Françaix, Jean
5 'Bis' 57
Éloge de la Danse 57
Nocturne 57
Piano Sonata 57
5 Portraits de jeunes Filles 57
La Promenade
d'un Musicologue éclectique............... 58
Scherzo 58
10 Stücke
für Kinder zum Spielen und Träumen ... 58
8 Variations
on the name Johannes Gutenberg........ 58

Fricker, Peter Racine
14 Aubades 60
4 Impromptus, Op. 17 60
4 Sonnets 60
12 Studies, Op. 38 60
Variations, Op. 31 60

Fromm-Michaels, Ilse
Langsamer Walzer 61

Frommel, Gerhard
Caprichos, Op. 14 61

Genzmer, Harald
Capriccio 64
Kleines Klavierbuch 64
Piano Sonata No.1 64
Piano Sonata No.2 64
Piano Sonatina No.1 64
Piano Sonatina No.3 64
Suite in C 64

Gerster, Ottmar
Divertimento 68
Introduktion und Perpetuum 68

Gilbert, Anthony
Piano Sonata No.1 69

Goehr, Alexander
Capriccio, Op. 6 71
...in real time , Op. 50 71
Nonomiya, Op. 27 71
Piano Sonata, Op. 2 71
3 Pieces, Op. 18 71

Gould, Glenn
5 Little Pieces 73
2 Pieces 73

Grainger, Percy Aldridge
Après un Rêve (Fauré) 76
Blithe Bells (J.S.Bach) 76
Children's March:
Over the Hills and Far Away 76
Colonial Song 76
Country Gardens 76
Cradle Song (Brahms) 76
Eastern Intermezzo 76
Handel in the Strand 76
Harvest Hymn 76
Hornpipe (Handel) 76
The Hunter in his Career 76
The Immovable Do 76
In a Nutshell Suite 76
Irish Tune from County Derry 76
Jutish Medley 76
Knight and Shepherd's Daughter ... 76
Lullaby from 'Tribute to Foster' ... 77
The Merry King 77
Mock Morris 77
Molly on the Shore 77
My Robin is to the Greenwood Gone... 77
Now, o now, I needs must Part
(John Dowland) 77
One more Day my John 77
Paraphrase
on Tchaikovsky's 'Flower Waltz' ... 77
Scotch Strathspey and Reel 77
Shepherd's Hey 77
Spoon River 77
The Sussex
Mummers' Christmas Carol 77
To a Nordic Princess 77
Walking Tune 77

Gretchaninoff, Alexander Tikhonovich
Flüchtige Gedanken, Op. 115 79
Glasperlen, Op. 123 79
The Gretchaninoff Collection 79
Das Großvaterbuch, Op. 119 79
Im Grünen, Op. 99 79
Das Kinderbuch, Op. 98 80
Sonatina in F, Op. 110 80
Sonatina in G, Op. 110 80
Der Tag des Kindes, Op. 109 80
Tautropfen, Op. 127a 80

Haas, Joseph
Alte, unnennbare Tage, Op. 42 ... 81
Deutsche Reigen
und Romanzen, Op. 51 82
Eulenspiegeleien, Op. 39 82
Fantasie-Bilder, Op. 9 82
Gespenster, Op. 34 82
Hausmärchen, Op. 35 82
Hausmärchen, Op. 43 82
Hausmärchen, Op. 53 82
Klangspiele, Op. 99 82
Piano Sonata No.1
in D major, Op. 61/1 82
Piano Sonata No.2
in A minor, Op. 61/2 82
Schwänke und Idyllen, Op. 55 ... 82
4 Sonatinas, Op. 94 82
Stücke für die Jugend, Op. 69 ... 82
Wichtelmännchen, Op. 27 82

Hamilton, Iain
Nocturnes with Cadenzas 87
3 Piano Pieces, Op. 30 87
Piano Sonata, Op. 13 87

Hartmann, Karl Amadeus
Jazz-Toccata and Fugue 90
Little Suite No.1 90
Little Suite No. 2 90
Piano Sonata No.1 90
Sonata '27 April 1945' 90
Sonatina 90

Heller, Barbara
Anschlüsse 91
Freude und Trauer 91
Für jeden Tag 91
Intervalles 91
Piano Muziek voor Anje 92
Scharlachrote Buchstaben 92

Henze, Hans Werner
Cherubino 98
Lucy Escott Variations 98
La Mano Sinistra 98
Une Petite Phrase 98
Piano Sonata 98
Piano Variations, Op. 13 98
Piece for Peter 99
6 Pieces for Young Pianists 99
Pulcinella Disperato 99
Toccata mistica 99

Hessenberg, Kurt
Kleine Hausmusik, Op. 24 102
7 Little Piano Pieces, Op. 12 102
10 Little Preludes, Op. 35 102

Hiller, Wilfried
2 Miniatures for Children 105
Phantasie
über ein Thema von J.A. Hiller ... 105

Hindemith, Paul
Berceuse 110
In einer Nacht, Op. 15 110
Klaviermusik (2 Vols.), Op. 37 ... 110
Klavierstück 110
Kleine Klaviermusik, Op. 45/4 ... 110
Lied 110
Ludus tonalis 110
Piano Sonata, Op. 17 111
Piano Sonata No.1 in A - 'Der Main' ... 111
Piano Sonata No.2 in G 111
Piano Sonata No.3 in B 111
Sing-und Spielmusiken, Op. 45/4 ... 111
Suite '1922', Op. 26 111
Tanz der Holzpuppen 111
Tanzstücke, Op. 19 113
Variations 113
Wir bauen eine Stadt 113

Höffer, Paul
Tanzvariationen 117

Höller, Karl
2 Piano Sonatinas, Op. 58 117
Tessiner Klavierbuch, Op. 57 ... 117

Holliger, Heinz
Chinderliecht 119
Elis - 3 Nachtstücke 119

Hopkins, Bill
Studies Vol.1 120

Hosokawa, Toshio
Melodia II 122
Nacht Klänge 122

Hummel, Bertold
Notturno, Op. 75b 124

Husa, Karel
Piano Sonata, Op. 11 126

Ichiyanagi, Toshi
Cloud Atlas I, II, III 127
Cloud Brocade - Cloud Atlas VII ... 127
Cloud Current - Cloud Atlas IX ... 127
Cloud Falls - Cloud Atlas VI 127
Cloud in the Distance -
Cloud Atlas VIII 127
Cloud Rainbow - Cloud Atlas V ... 127
Cloud Vein - Cloud Atlas IV 127
Farewell to 127
Imaginary Scenes 128
In Memory of John Cage 128
Inexhaustible Fountain 128
Inter Konzert 128
Music for Piano No.6 128
Piano Nature 128

Ince, Kamran
The Blue Journey 130
My Friend Mozart 130
An Unavoidable Obsession 130

Jarnach, Philipp
Das Amrumer Tagebuch, Op. 30 ... 131
Ballabible, Op. 17/1 131
Burlesca, Op. 17/3 131
10 kleine Klavierstücke 131
Piano Sonata No.1, Op. 18 131
Piano Sonata No.2 131
Sarabande, Op. 17/2 132

Killmayer, Wilhelm
An John Field 135
Douze Études Transcendentales ... 135
5 Neue Klavierstücke 136
3 Piano Pieces 136
Rundgesänge und Morgenlieder ... 136
Trois Études blancs 136

Kirchner, Volker David
Piano Sonata 139
Knab, Armin
Lindegger Ländler 140
Piano Chorale 140
Piano Sonata in E Major................ 140
Komarova, Tatjana
Sonata 141
Korngold, Erich Wolfgang
Don Quixote 142
Geschichten von Strauß, Op. 21 142
Große Fantasie......................... 142
4 kleine fröhliche Walzer.............. 142
4 Little Cartoons for Children, Op. 19 ... 144
7 Märchenbilder, Op. 3................. 144
Piano Sonata No.2 in E Major, Op. 2 ... 144
Piano Sonata No.3 in C, Op. 25 144
3 Pieces 144
Schach Brügge! 144
Tanzlied des Pierrot 144
Violanta-Potpourri (2 parts)........... 144
Zwischenspiel 144
Kosma, Joseph
Autumn Leaves.......................... 145
Kreisler, Fritz
Caprice viennois (Cradle song), Op. 2 ... 146
Liebesfreud 146
Liebesfreud (Sergej Rachmaninoff) 146
Liebesleid 146
Liebesleid (Sergej Rachmaninoff)....... 146
Schön Rosmarin......................... 146
Lehmann, Hans Ulrich
Instants for Piano..................... 148
Ligeti, György
Capriccio No. 1 150
Capriccio No. 2 150
Étude pour Piano No. 14a 150
Étude pour piano No. 15 150
Études pour Piano - Deuxième livre ... 152
Études pour piano - Premier livre ... 150
Invenció 152
Musica Ricercata 152
Lutyens, Elisabeth
5 Bagatelles, Op. 49 155
Symphonics for Solo Piano 155
MacCombie, Bruce
Gerberau Musics........................ 157
Majo, Giulio di
Caprichos 158
Maler, Wilhelm
3 Little Piano Pieces
on Old Christmas Songs................. 158
Martinů, Bohuslav
Esquisses de Danses 159
Les Ritournelles....................... 160
Martland, Steve
Kgakala 161
Maxwell Davies, Sir Peter
5 Piano Pieces, Op. 2 162
Müller-Siemens, Detlev
Under Neonlight 2 167
Under Neonlight 3 167
Nancarrow, Conlon
Studies for Player Piano Vol.1......... 168
Studies for Player Piano Vol.2......... 168
Studies for Player Piano Vol.3......... 168
Studies for Player Piano Vol.4......... 168
Studies for Player Piano Vol.5......... 169
Studies for Player Piano Vol.6......... 169

Naoumoff, Emile
13 Anecdotes 169
Impasse 169
Piano Sonata 169
4 Preludes 169
Rhapsodie 169
Sur le nom de Bach 169
Paulus, Stephen
Dance 178
Preludes, Vol. 1 178
Translucent Landscapes................. 178
Pepping, Ernst
Fugue on B-A-C-H 184
Piano Sonata No.1 184
Piano Sonata No.2 184
Piano Sonata No.3 184
2 Romanzen 184
Sonatina 184
Tanzweisen und Rundgesang 184
Picker, Tobias
The Blue Hula 187
Old and Lost Rivers.................... 187
3 Piano Pieces 187
When Soft Voices die 187
Pütz, Eduard
How about that, Mr. Offenbach! 191
Jazz Sonata 191
Let's swing, Mr. Bach 191
Mr. Clementi goin' on Holidays 191
Nachtstücke 191
Valsette 191
Rainier, Priaulx
Barbaric Dance Suite 192
5 Keyboard Pieces 192
Ravel, Maurice
Jeux d'Eau 193
Miroirs 193
Regner, Hermann
Es war einmal ein König 194
Reimann, Aribert
Auf dem Weg, Vol. 1 195
Spektren 197
Variations for Piano 197
Rein, Walter
Piano Music on Folksongs 198
Reutter, Hermann
Dance Suite, Op. 29.................... 202
Fantasia Apocalyptica, Op. 7.......... 202
Little Piano Pieces, Op. 28 202
Die Passion in 9 Inventionen, Op. 25.... 202
Variations, Op. 15 202
Rodrigo, Joaquín
A L'Ombre de Torre Bermeja............ 206
Bagatela 206
2 Berceuses 206
3 Evocaciones 208
Music 208
5 Piezas del Siglo XVI 208
Preludio al Gallo Mañanero 208
The Rodrigo Collection 208
Serenata Española 208
Sonatas de Castilla 208
3 Spanish Dances 208
Suite para Piano 208
Roslawez, Nikolaj Andrejevich
Piano Pieces 210
Piano Sonata No.1 210
Piano Sonata No.2 210
Piano Sonata No.5 210
5 Pieces 210

Rouse, Christopher
Little Gorgon 211
Sackman, Nicholas
Piano Sonata 213
Schnebel, Dieter
Auguri 216
Bagatellen 216
concert sans orchestre................. 216
espressivo 216
Monotonien No. 1-7 218
Schroeder, Hermann
Minnelieder............................ 222
Piano Sonata No.1 in A Minor 222
Piano Sonata No.2 222
Susani................................. 223
Schulhoff, Erwin
11 Inventions, Op. 36 224
Suite No.3 224
Schwantner, Joseph
Veiled Autumn 226
Scott, Cyril
Arabesque 227
Butterfly Waltz........................ 227
Carillon 227
Cherry Ripe, Old English Air 227
3 Country Dances 227
Danse élegiaque, Op. 74/1 227
Danse langoureuse, Op. 74/3 227
Danse negre, Op. 58/5 227
Danse orientale, Op. 74/2 227
Egypt.................................. 227
Impressions from the Jungle Book...... 227
Indian Suite 228
Lotusland, Op. 47/1 228
Miniatures 228
Miss Rennington (Scherzo) 228
Old China Suite 228
A Pageant 228
Piano Sonata, Op. 66 228
Poems 228
Rainbow Trout 228
Suite No. 2, Op. 75 228
Toy Box 228
Zoo.................................... 228
Searle, Humphrey
Suite, Op. 29.......................... 229
Seiber, Mátyás
Easy Dances............................ 230
Rhythmical Studies..................... 230
Scherzando Capriccioso 230
Senfter, Johanna
Berceuse............................... 231
Fugues, Nos. 4, 5 & 7 231
3 Klavierstücke, Op. 83 231
2 Klavierstücke, Op. 129 231
Klavierstudie 231
6 kleine Stücke für Anfänger........... 231
Mazurka 231
Passacaglia, Nos. 5, 7 & 9 231
Scherzo 231
Vogelweise 231
Sgambati, Giovanni
Piano Etude, Op. 10/2 232
Singleton, Alvin
Argoru 1 234
Changing Faces 234
Cinque................................. 234
Mutations 234
Slavenski, Josip
Jugoslawische Suite, Op. 2 235
Piano Sonata, Op. 4 235

Stravinsky, Igor
Berceuse... 242
Circus Polka.................................... 242
Danse infernale, Berceuse, Finale 242
Ronde des Princesses........................ 242
Tango 242

Stürmer, Bruno
Little Sonata, Op. 103 244

Subotnick, Morton
Liquid Strata 245
Play! No.3 245

Sutermeister, Heinrich
Bergsommer.................................... 247
Hommage à Arthur Honegger 247
Sonatina in Eb 247
Winterferien 247
12 zweistimmige Inventionen 247

Szelényi, István
Musikalisches Bilderbuch 249
Nocturne 249

Tajcevic, Marko
Balkantänze 249

Takemitsu, Toru
Litany... 252
Rain Tree Sketch 252
Rain Tree Sketch II 252
Les yeux clos II 252

Tcherepnin, Alexander Nikolajevich
Concert Studies, Op. 52..................... 253

Tippett, Michael
Piano Sonata No.1 256
Piano Sonata No.2 256
Piano Sonata No.3 256
Piano Sonata No.4 256

Toch, Ernst
5 X 10 Etüden, Op. 55-59 258
Burlesques, Op. 31 258
5 Capriccetti, Op. 36 258
Der Jongleur, Op. 31/3 258
Kleinstadtbilder, Op. 49..................... 258
3 Piano Pieces, Op. 32 258
Piano Sonata, Op. 47 258
Tanz und Spielstücke, Op. 40............. 258

Turina, Joaquín
El Circo, Op. 68............................... 259
En la Zapatería -
Chez le Cordonnier, Op. 71 259
Miniaturas, Op. 52........................... 259
Radio Madrid, Op. 62........................ 259
Tarjetas postales, Op. 58................... 259
The Turina Collection........................ 259
Viaje maritimo 259

Turnage, Mark-Anthony
Entranced 260

Ullmann, Viktor
Piano Sonatas Nos. 1-4...................... 262
Piano Sonatas Nos. 5-7...................... 262
Variations and Doublefugue 262

Vasks, Pēteris
Autumn Music 263
Fantasia - „Izdegusas zemes ainavas" ... 263
A Little Night Music 263
Pavasara Muzika - Spring Music 263
White Scenery 264

Wanek, Friedrich K.
A propos Haydn............................... 266
Nocturnes and Capriccios 266
Ragtime - Fantasy............................ 267
Zyklus 267

Weismann, Julius
Piano Sonata in A Minor, Op. 87 268

Weiss, Harald
My Blue Diary................................. 269

Wyttenbach, Jürg
3 Pieces 273

Xiaogang, Ye
Ballade 274

Yuasa, Joji
Cosmos Haptic II............................. 276
Projection Esemplastic 276
Subliminal Hey J. 276

Zehm, Friedrich
Intermezzo 278
Little Suite 278
Ommagio a Domenico Scarlatti 278
Sonatille 278

Zimmermann, Bernd Alois
Enchiridion 281
Konfigurationen................................ 281

Solo Piano Three or More Hands

Arnell, Richard
Sonatina, Op. 61 15

Badings, Henk
Arcadia - Vol.4............................... 15
Arcadia - Vol.5............................... 15

von Bose, Hans-Jürgen
Origami 26

Elgar, Edward William
Salut d'Amour, Op. 12 49

Fricker, Peter Racine
Nocturne and Scherzo, Op. 23 60

Genzmer, Harald
Spielbuch No.1 64
Spielbuch No.2 64

Gilbert, Anthony
Piano Sonata No.2, Op. 8/2 69

Grainger, Percy Aldridge
Country Gardens.............................. 76
Harvest Hymn 76
Zanzibar Boat Song 77

Gretchaninoff, Alexander Tikhonovich
Album 79
Im Grünen, Op. 99........................... 79

Hessenberg, Kurt
Sonata in C Minor, Op. 34/1 102

Hindemith, Paul
Ragtime... 111
Sonata 111
Symphonische Tänze 111
Symphony „Mathis der Maler" 111
Toccata 113
Walzer, Op. 6 113

Husa, Karel
8 Böhmische Duette 126

Ince, Kamran
Cross Scintillations........................... 130

Killmayer, Wilhelm
Paradies 136

Ligeti, György
Early Pieces 150

Orff, Carl
Carmina Burana............................... 174

Pütz, Eduard
3 Jazz Waltzes................................. 191

Rodrigo, Joaquín
Atardecer 206
Juglares 208

Schroeder, Hermann
5 German Christmas Carols, Op. 18 ... 222

Schulhoff, Erwin
Ironien, Op. 34................................ 224

Seiber, Mátyás
Easy Dances................................... 230

Singleton, Alvin
Inside-Out 234

Stravinsky, Igor
Feu d'artifice 242

Szelényi, István
Colorit.. 248
Piano Sonata 249

Wanek, Friedrich K.
3 Etudes 266
Klangspiegel 266
3 Studies 267

Werdin, Eberhard
Slawische Tanzweisen
mit Variationen 270

Zehm, Friedrich
Wie spät ist es, Signor Haydn?........... 278

Two Pianos

Beck, Conrad
Sonatina 21

Bryars, Gavin
My First Homage............................. 32
Out of Zaleski's Gazebo 32

Casken, John
Salamandra 35

Cowie, Edward
The Falls of Clyde 38

Françaix, Jean
8 Danses exotiques 57
Scuola di Ballo 58

Fricker, Peter Racine
4 Fughettas, Op. 2 60
Sonata for 2 Pianos, Op. 78............... 60

Genzmer, Harald
Sonata for 2 Pianos......................... 64

Grainger, Percy Aldridge
Blithe Bells (J.S.Bach) 76
Children's March:
Over the Hills and Far Away 76
Country Gardens (1932)..................... 76
Country Gardens (1936)..................... 76
Eastern Intermezzo 76
English Dance 76
English Waltz.................................. 76
Green Bushes 76
Handel in the Strand 76
In a Nutshell Suite 76
Jutish Medley 76
Lincolnshire Posy 76
Molly on the Shore 77
Shepherd's Hey................................ 77
Spoon River 77
Two Musical Relics of my Mother...... 77
The Warriors 77

Henze, Hans Werner
Divertimenti................................... 98

Hiller, Wilfried
Pas de deux.................................... 105

Hindemith, Paul
Sonata 111

Ichiyanagi, Toshi
Two Existence.................................. 128

Killmayer, Wilhelm
Paradies 136

Klebe, Giselher
Sonata for 2 Pianos, Op. 4................... 140

Ligeti, György
Monument. Selbstportrait. Bewegung ... 152

Martland, Steve
Dance Works.................................... 161
Drill... 161

Picker, Tobias
Pianorama 187

Rodrigo, Joaquín
5 Piezas Infantiles........................... 208

Schroeder, Hermann
Duplum 222

Scott, Cyril
3 Symphonic Dances........................ 228

Stravinsky, Igor
Circus Polka..................................... 242
Concerto for 2 Pianos 242
Concerto in Eb................................. 242
Danses concertantes........................ 242
Scherzo à la Russe........................... 242
Sonata for 2 Pianos 242
Tango 242

Vasks, Pēteris
In Memoriam.................................... 263
Music 263
Toccata... 264

Wanek, Friedrich K.
Musique pour
Deux à deux Instruments à Clavier 266
Präambel - Passacaglia - Toccata 266

Wyttenbach, Jürg
Nachspiel in 3 Teilen........................ 273

Yuasa, Joji
Projection Esemplastic 276

Zimmermann, Bernd Alois
Monologe... 281
Perspektiven...................................... 281

Solo Organ

Ahrens, Joseph
Cantiones Gregorianae pro organo
(Vol. I).. 13
Cantiones Gregorianae pro organo
(Vol. II) 13
Cantiones Gregorianae pro organo
(Vol. III) 13
Choralpartita 13
Choralpartita „Lobe den Herrn"........ 13
Christus ist erstanden....................... 13
Orgelmesse 13
Toccata eroica and Fugue 13
Triptychon über Bach 13
Veni Creator Spiritus 13
Verwandlungen I 13
Verwandlungen II 13
Verwandlungen III 13

Beck, Conrad
Chorale Sonata.................................. 21
2 Preludes 21
Sonatina 22

Burkhard, Willy
Choralvariationen No.1, Op. 28/1 33
Choralvariationen No.2, Op. 28/2 33
Fantasy, Op. 32................................. 33

Castiglioni, Niccolò
Sinfonie Guerriere et Amorose........... 37

Eben, Petr
Hommage à Dietrich Buxtehude 45
Hommage à Henry Purcell 45

Elgar, Edward William
Salut d'Amour, Op. 12 49

Fortner, Wolfgang
Intermezzi 52
Praeambel and Fugue 52
4 Preludes for Organ........................ 52
Toccata and Fugue 53

Françaix, Jean
Messe de Mariage............................. 57
Suite profane.................................... 58

Fricker, Peter Racine
Choral 60
Pastorale... 60
Ricercare, Op. 40.............................. 60
Wedding Processional....................... 60

Genzmer, Harald
Organ Sonata 64
Tripartita in F................................... 64

Goehr, Alexander
Chaconne for Organ, Op. 34a............. 71

Grainger, Percy Aldridge
Colonial Song 76
The Immovable Do........................... 76

Guilmant, Félix Alexandre
Cantilene 81
Grand Choeur 81
March on a Theme by Handel............ 81
Prière et Berceuse 81

Haas, Joseph
8 Präludien....................................... 82

Hamilton, Iain
Fanfares and Variants 87

Henze, Hans Werner
Toccata senza Fuga........................... 99

Hessenberg, Kurt
Choralpartiten No.1, Op. 43 102
Choralpartiten No.2, Op. 43 102
Fantasia, Op. 115.............................. 102
Trio Sonata in B, Op. 56 102

Hiller, Wilfried
Tarot-Toccatas.................................. 105

Hindemith, Paul
Ludus tonalis 110
Organ Sonata No.1 111
Organ Sonata No.2 111
Organ Sonata No.3 111

Höller, Karl
Choral Passacaglia, Op. 61................ 117
Ciacona, Op. 54 117

Hosokawa, Toshio
Sen IV.. 122

Humpert, Hans
Prelude and Toccata.......................... 125
Prelude, Canzone and Fugue 125

Ichiyanagi, Toshi
Dimensions 127
Fantasy... 127
Multiple Space 128

Jarnach, Philipp
Konzertstück, Op. 21........................ 131

Knab, Armin
7 Organ Chorales 140

Lehmann, Hans Ulrich
Noten 148

Ligeti, György
2 Études for Organ 150
Ricercare... 152

Litaize, Gaston
Diapason 154
Reges Tharsis.................................... 154
Sonata à deux 154

Lutyens, Elisabeth
Sinfonia, Op. 32............................... 155

Maxwell Davies, Sir Peter
Organ Fantasia
on „O Magnum Mysterium" 162

Müller-Zürich, Paul
Prelude and Fugue
in E Minor, Op. 22............................ 167
Toccata in C Major, Op. 12 167
Toccata No.3 in A, Op. 50................. 167

Naoumoff, Emile
Fantasy for Organ 169

Pepping, Ernst
Choralpartita (1932) 184
Choralpartita (1933) 184
4 Fugues in C,D Eb and F 184
2 Fugues in C Sharp 184
3 Fugues on B-A-C-H 184
Great Organ Book 184
Little Organ Book 184
25 Organ Chorales 184
Organ Concerto No.1........................ 184
Organ Concerto No.2........................ 184
Praeludia-Postludia zu 18 Chorälen 184
Toccata and Fugue 184

Rainier, Priaulx
Organ Gloriana 192
Primordial Canticales 192

Reimann, Aribert
Dialog 1 197

Rouse, Christopher
Liber Daemonum............................... 211

Schnebel, Dieter
Toccata mit Fugen 217
Zwischenfugen.................................. 217

Schneider, Norbert
Toccata „Schlafes Bruder" 218

Schroeder, Hermann
Concerto piccolo............................... 222
Kleine Intraden 222
Little Preludes and Intermezzi 222
Die Marianische Antiphone 222
6 Organ Chorales, Op. 11 222
Organ Fantasy, Op. 56...................... 222
Organ Sonata No.1 222
Organ Sonata No.2 222
Organ Sonata No.3 222
Orgel Ordinarium
„Cunctipotens genitor Deus".............. 222
Orgelchoräle im Kirchenjahr............. 222
Partita „Veni Creator Spiritus" 222
Praeambeln und Interludien............... 222
Prelude and Fugue 222
5 Sketches 223
Variations on the 'Tonus Peregrinus' ... 223

Schwantner, Joseph
   In Aeternum 2 226
Searle, Humphrey
   Toccata alla Passacaglia, Op. 31 229
Senfter, Johanna
   2 Choralvorspiele 231
Tippett, Michael
   Preludio al Vespro Di Monteverdi 256
Vasks, Pēteris
   Cantus ad pacem 263
   Musica Seria 263
   Te Deum 264
Widor, Charles-Marie
   Symphonie gothique, Op. 70 270

Solo harpsichord

Bryars, Gavin
   After Handel's „Vesper" 32
Françaix, Jean
   L' Insectarium 57
   2 Pièces 57
Fricker, Peter Racine
   Suite for Harpsichord 60
Henze, Hans Werner
   6 Absences 98
   Euridice 98
   Lucy Escott Variations 98
Huber, Klaus
   La Chace 123
Ligeti, György
   Continuum 150
   Hungarian Rock 152
   Passacaglia Ungherese 152
Pütz, Eduard
   Jazz Sonata 191
   Let's swing, Mr. Bach 191
Rainier, Priaulx
   Quinque 192
Singleton, Alvin
   Le Tombeau du Petit Prince 234
Takemitsu, Toru
   Rain Dreaming 252
Vasks, Pēteris
   Cantata 263

Chamber Music

One Instrument

String Instrument

Violin

Badings, Henk
   Violin Sonata No.3 16
von Bose, Hans-Jürgen
   Edge.....,..................................... 26
   Violin Sonata 26
Françaix, Jean
   Tema con 8 Variazioni 58
Hartmann, Karl Amadeus
   2 Suites for Solo Violin 90
   Violin Sonata No.1 90
   Violin Sonata No.2 90
Heller, Barbara
   Solovioline 92

Henze, Hans Werner
   Étude Philharmonique 98
   Für Manfred 98
   Serenade 99
   Sonata 99
Hindemith, Paul
   Etudes for violinists 110
   Violin Sonata, Op. 31/1 113
   Violin Sonata, Op. 31/2 113
   Violin Sonata, Op. 11/6 113
Holliger, Heinz
   Trema 119
Ichiyanagi, Toshi
   Friends I 127
   Perspectives 128
Knab, Armin
   Volkslied Variationen 140
Kreisler, Fritz
   Recitativo
   und Scherzo-Caprice, Op. 6 146
Martinon, Jean
   Sonatina No.6, Op. 49/2 159
Martinů, Bohuslav
   Rhythmische Etüden 160
Penderecki, Krzysztof
   Cadenza 183
Picker, Tobias
   3 Lullabies 187
Rodrigo, Joaquín
   Capriccio 208
Schnebel, Dieter
   Stück III 217
Scott, Cyril
   Bumble Bees 227
   Idyll 227
Senfter, Johanna
   Violin Sonata G Minor, Op. 61 231
Sitt, Hans
   20 Studies, Op. 62 235
Staeps, Hans-Ulrich
   Virtuose Suite 236
Stravinsky, Igor
   Elegy 242
Takahashi, Yuji
   Sieben Rosen hat ein Strauch 249
Wanek, Friedrich K.
   Violin Sonata 267
Yuasa, Joji
   My Blue Sky, No.3 276
Zimmermann, Bernd Alois
   Violin Sonata 281

Viola

von Bose, Hans-Jürgen
   ... „vom Wege abkommen" 26
Gilbert, Anthony
   Crow Undersongs 69
Grainger, Percy Aldridge
   Arrival Platform Humlet 76
Heller, Barbara
   Nah oder fern 92
Henze, Hans Werner
   An Brenton 98
Hindemith, Paul
   Viola Sonata, Op. 11/5 113
   Viola Sonata, Op. 25/1 113
   Viola Sonata, Op. 31/4 113
   Viola Sonata 113

Holliger, Heinz
   Trema 119
Lehmann, Hans Ulrich
   Viola Studies 148
Ligeti, György
   Viola Sonata 152
Penderecki, Krzysztof
   Cadenza 183
Rainier, Priaulx
   Suite 193
Reutter, Hermann
   Cinco Caprichos sobre Cervantes 202
Singleton, Alvin
   Argoru 4 234
Stravinsky, Igor
   Elegy 242
Subotnick, Morton
   Mandolin 245
Uhl, Alfred
   Suite 261
   30 Viola Studies 261
   20 Viola Studies 261
Yuasa, Joji
   Viola Locus 276
Zimmermann, Bernd Alois
   Viola Sonata 281

Violoncello

Badings, Henk
   Cello Sonata 15
Banks, Don
   Sequence 17
Beck, Conrad
   3 Epigramme 21
von Bose, Hans-Jürgen
   Solo 26
Casken, John
   A Spring Cadenza 35
Fortner, Wolfgang
   Suite 53
   Theme and Variations 53
Haas, Joseph
   Ein Sommermärchen, Op. 30a 82
Henze, Hans Werner
   Capriccio 98
   Serenade 99
Hiller, Wilfried
   Die feindlichen Nachbarn oder
   Die Folgen der Musik 105
Hindemith, Paul
   Cello Sonata, Op. 25/3 110
Holliger, Heinz
   Chaconne 119
   Trema 119
Hosokawa, Toshio
   Sen II 122
Huber, Klaus
   Transpositio ad Infinitum 123
Kirchner, Volker David
   Und Salomo sprach 139
Kovách, Andor
   Cello Sonata 145
Ligeti, György
   Cello Sonata 150

Mainardi, Enrico
Ballata della lontonanza 157
Cello Sonata.. 157
Cello Studies and Pieces 157
7 Preludes 158
Sonata Breve.. 158
7 Studi Brevi.. 158

Penderecki, Krzysztof
Capriccio per Siegfried Palm 183
Divertimento 183
Per Slava.. 183

Rainier, Priaulx
Suite 193

Reimann, Aribert
Solo for Cello 197

Rodrigo, Joaquín
Como una Fantasia 208

Rouse, Christopher
Morpheus.. 211

Schnebel, Dieter
5 Inventions 216

Singleton, Alvin
Argoru 2... 234

Vasks, Pēteris
Gramata cellam - The Book 263

Double Bass

Henze, Hans Werner
S.Biagio 9 Agosto ore 12.07............... 99
Serenade... 99

Hindemith, Paul
Pieces 111

Vasks, Pēteris
Sonata 264

Woodwind Instrument

Recorder

Andriessen, Louis
Sweet 14

Cooke, Arnold
Serial Theme and Variations............... 38

Linde, Hans-Martin
Amarilli mia bella............................... 153
Das Basler Blockflötenbuch................ 153
Blockflöte virtuos 153
Fantasien und Scherzi 153
Märchen... 153
Music for a bird................................... 153
Neuzeitliche Übungsstücke 154
Serenade... 154
Una Follia nouva 154

Regner, Hermann
Meditations 194

Rodgers, Philip
Sight Reading Exercises 205

Staeps, Hans-Ulrich
Virtuose Suite 236

Flute

Françaix, Jean
Suite 58

Genzmer, Harald
Neuzeitliche Etüden - Vol.1................ 64
Neuzeitliche Etüden - Vol.2................ 64

Hiller, Wilfried
Schulamit.. 105

Hindemith, Paul
8 Pieces 111

Holliger, Heinz
Sonate (in)solit(aire), dite
„le Piémontois Jurassien“ 119
„(t)air(e)“ 119

Hosokawa, Toshio
Sen I 122
Vertical Song I..................................... 122

Ichiyanagi, Toshi
Kaze no Iroai 128
Wind Stream 128

Lehmann, Hans Ulrich
Monodie.. 148

Linde, Hans-Martin
Anspielungen.. 153

Schnebel, Dieter
Pan 216

Scott, Cyril
The Extatic Shepherd 227

Singleton, Alvin
Argoru 3.. 234
Argoru 5b.. 234

Takemitsu, Toru
Air 252
Itinerant.. 252

Vasks, Pēteris
Landscape with Birds 263
Sonata 264

Willi, Herbert
Piece.. 271

Yuasa, Joji
Domain 276
Terms of Temporal Detailing............... 276

Zgraja, Krystof
3 virtuose Flamenco-Studien............... 279

Oboe

Castiglioni, Niccolò
Alef 37

Holliger, Heinz
Studie II 119

Ichiyanagi, Toshi
Cloud Figures 127

Rainier, Priaulx
Pastoral Triptych.................................. 192

Vasks, Pēteris
Touchings.. 264

Clarinet/Bass Clarinet

Both, Heinz
Let's play together 27

Cowie, Edward
Kelly-Nolan-Kelly 38

Goehr, Alexander
Paraphrase, Op. 28............................... 71

Penderecki, Krzysztof
Prelude 183

Singleton, Alvin
Argoru 5a.. 234

Sutermeister, Heinrich
Capriccio... 247

Uhl, Alfred
48 Etudes Vols. 1&2 261

Vasks, Pēteris
Moments musicaux............................... 263

Wanek, Friedrich K.
21 Soli.. 267

Yuasa, Joji
Clarinet Solitude.................................. 276

Saxophone

Hindemith, Paul
Sonata 111

Bassoon/Contrabassoon

Hosokawa, Toshio
Sen VII 122

Schulhoff, Erwin
Baßnachtigall.. 224

Uhl, Alfred
15 Bassoon Studies.............................. 261

Brass Instrument

Horn

Hindemith, Paul
Sonata 111

Trumpet

Henze, Hans Werner
Trumpet Sonatina................................. 99

Takemitsu, Toru
Paths... 252

Trombone

Henze, Hans Werner
Trombone Sonatina............................... 99

Tuba

Penderecki, Krzysztof
Capriccio... 183

Subotnick, Morton
The First Dream of Light 245

Plucked Instrument

Guitar/Lute/Zither

Beaser, Robert
Canti Notturni...................................... 19
Notes on a Southern Sky 19

Bresgen, Cesar
Malinconia.. 29

Brouwer, Leo
3 Apuntes 31
Canticum... 31
Danza Caracteristica
para el 'Quitate de la Acera'............... 31
Elogio de la Danza para Guitarra 31
La Espiral eterna para Guitarra 31
Memorias de „El Cimarrón".............. 31

Bryars, Gavin
The Squirrel
and the Ricketty-Racketty Bridge 32

Castelnuovo-Tedesco, Mario
Guitar Sonata in D Major 36
Rondo in E minor, Op. 129 36
Suite in D minor, Op. 133 36
Tonadilla auf den Namen
Andrés Segovia, Op. 170/5 36
Variations à travers les Siècles 36
Cowie, Edward
Commedia Lazzia 38
Eben, Petr
Tabulatora nova 45
Fetler, Paul
4 Movements 50
5 Pieces 50
Françaix, Jean
Serenata 58
Hand, Colin
Guitar Sonatina No.2 87
Henze, Hans Werner
3 Märchenbilder............................... 98
Memorias de El Cimarrón 98
Minette... 98
Royal Winter Music (Sonata No. 1).... 99
Royal Winter Music (Sonata No. 2).... 99
3 Tentos.. 99
Hosokawa, Toshio
Intermezzo 121
Kröll, Georg
Estampida 147
MacCombie, Bruce
Nightshade Rounds........................... 157
Reutter, Hermann
Abendangelus - Bolero - Fandango..... 202
Cinco Caprichos sobre Cervantes........ 202
Fantasiestücke, Op. 28...................... 202
Die Passion in 9 Inventionen, Op. 25 ... 202
Rodgers, Philip
Elisabethan-Melodies (Vol. 1) 205
Elisabethan-Melodies (Vol. 2) 205
Rodrigo, Joaquín
3 Spanish Pieces 208
Triptic for Guitar 208
Un Tiempo fue Italica Famosa 208
Segovia, Andrés
Estudio sin luz 229
Estudios 229
Seiber, Mátyás
8 Dances 230
Smith Brindle, Reginald
El Polifemo de Oro............................ 235
Etruscan Preludes 235
Fuego Fatuo 236
Guitar Sonata No.3 236
Guitar Sonata No.4 236
Guitar Sonata No.5 236
Guitarcosmos Vols.1-3....................... 236
Nocturne 236
Pagan Dance 236
4 Poems of Garcia Lorca.................... 236
Sonatina Fiorentina 236
Vita Senese 236
Takemitsu, Toru
All in Twilight 252
Equinox... 252
In the Woods 252
Tippett, Michael
The Blue Guitar................................ 256
Torrent, Jaume
Secuencias estivales........................... 259
Tableaux.. 259

Turina, Joaquín
Fandanguillo, Op. 36......................... 259
Homenaje a Tárrega, Op. 69 259
Miniaturas 259
Ràfaga, Op. 53 259
Sonata 259
Uhl, Alfred
Sonata Classica................................. 261
Vasks, Pēteris
Vientulibas Sonate 264
Vogel, Wladimir
Musette 265
Wanek, Friedrich K.
10 Essays 266
Yuasa, Joji
Projection for Electric Guitar(s) 276
Zehm, Friedrich
Musica notturna 278
6 Preludes and Fugues....................... 278

Harp
Cowie, Edward
Harlequin 38
Françaix, Jean
Suite 58
Hindemith, Paul
Harp Sonata 110
Holliger, Heinz
Prelude, Arioso and Passacaglia.......... 119
Sequenzen über Johannes I,32............. 119
Ichiyanagi, Toshi
Still Time III 128
Paulus, Stephen
Berceuse.. 178
Schnebel, Dieter
Circe... 216
Silvestri, Constantin
Sonate, Op. 21/1 233

Percussion Instrument

Marimba
Abe, Keiko
Ancient Vase 13
Little Windows 13
Memories of the Seashore 13
Variations
on Japanese Children's Songs 13
Wind in the Bamboo Grove................. 13
Henze, Hans Werner
5 Scenes from the Snow Country........ 99
Ichiyanagi, Toshi
Portrait of Forest.............................. 128
The Source 128
Kirchner, Volker David
Dybuk 139
Schwantner, Joseph
Velocities 226
Singleton, Alvin
Argoru 6.. 234

Vibraphone
Genzmer, Harald
8 Fantasien 64
Hummel, Bertold
Tempo di Valse 124

Singleton, Alvin
Argoru 7.. 234

Carillon
Genzmer, Harald
Variationen....................................... 64
Rouse, Christopher
Trarames 211

Harmonica Instrument

Accordion
Hosokawa, Toshio
Sen V 122
Schnebel, Dieter
Medusa.. 216
Seiber, Mátyás
Easy Dances..................................... 230

Another Instrument
Schnebel, Dieter
Marsyas 216
réactions.. 217
visible music I 217

Two Instruments
Duos for String Instruments

Two Violins
Beck, Conrad
Duo 21
Bryars, Gavin
Die letzten Tage................................ 32
Hindemith, Paul
2 Canonic Duets 110
Canonic Piece 110
14 Easy Pieces 110
Schulwerk, Op. 44/1 111
Ligeti, György
Ballad and Dance.............................. 150
Mori, Kurodo
Difference 165
Pepping, Ernst
Variations and Suite........................... 184
Reutter, Hermann
Pfingstmusik, Op. 41/2 202
Szelényi, István
Duos and Sonatine............................. 249
Takemitsu, Toru
Rocking Mirror Daybreak 252

Violin and Viola
Beck, Conrad
Duo 21
Dahl, Ingolf
Little Canonic Suite........................... 40
Gerster, Ottmar
Divertimento.................................... 68
Toch, Ernst
Divertimento
for Violin and Viola, Op. 37.............. 258

Violin and Violoncello

Fortner, Wolfgang
Duo 52
Holliger, Heinz
Duo 119
Duo II 119
Felicity's Shake-Wag 119
Kirchner, Volker David
Saitenspiel 139
Toch, Ernst
Divertimento No.1
for Violin and Cello, Op. 37 258

Viola and Violoncello

von Bose, Hans-Jürgen
Threnos-Hommage
à Bernd Alois Zimmermann 26
Hindemith, Paul
Duet 110
Sackman, Nicholas
Holism 213

Two Violoncellos

Hiller, Wilfried
Schildkröten-Boogie 105
Hindemith, Paul
Duett 110
Duett 110
Regner, Hermann
15 Easy Duets 194
Wanek, Friedrich K.
7 Aphorismen 266
Zehm, Friedrich
Modern Dances 278

Duos for String and Wind Instrument

Hindemith, Paul
2 Duette 110
6 ganz leichte Stücke 110
Ludus Minor 110
Musikalisches Blumengärtlein
und Leyptziger Allerlei 110
Plöner Musiktag 111
Stücke 111
Schnebel, Dieter
Pan 216

Duos for Wind Instruments

Two Recorders

Genzmer, Harald
11 Duets 64
European Folksongs 64
Tanzstücke - Vol.1 64
Tanzstücke - Vol. 2 64
Roehr, Walter
Im Duett 209
Staeps, Hans-Ulrich
Reihe kleiner Duette 236

Two Flutes

Beck, Conrad
Sonatina 21
Fortner, Wolfgang
9 Inventionen und ein Anhang 52
Françaix, Jean
Le Colloque des deux Perruches 57
Genzmer, Harald
Flute Sonata in F Sharp minor 64
Hindemith, Paul
Canonic Sonata, Op. 31/3 110
Yuasa, Joji
Mai-Bataraki II 276
Zehm, Friedrich
6 Caprices 278
Neue Duettstudien 278
Zgraja, Krystof
Modern Flutist II 279

Two Clarinets

Dahl, Ingolf
5 Duets 40
Wanek, Friedrich K.
4 Dialogues 266
Zehm, Friedrich
Klarinetten im Duett 278

Two Saxophones

Hindemith, Paul
Konzertstück 110

Two Bassoons

Szelényi, István
Suite 249

Two Trumpets

Eben, Petr
Duetti per due Trombe 45

Mixed Wind Duos

Françaix, Jean
7 Impromptus 57
Kalabis, Viktor
Variations, Op. 31 133
Schnebel, Dieter
Sisyphos 217
Wanek, Friedrich K.
3 Burlesque Pieces 266
Wyttenbach, Jürg
Serenade 273

Duos for Plucked Instruments

Two Guitars

Bryars, Gavin
The Squirrel
and the Ricketty-Racketty Bridge ... 32
Henze, Hans Werner
Memorias de El Cimarrón 98
Minette 98

Hindemith, Paul
Rondo 111
Maasz, Gerhard
10 Easy Pieces 156
Smith Brindle, Reginald
Chaconne and Interludes 235
Las Doce Cuerdas 235
The Pillars of Karnak 236
Takemitsu, Toru
Bad Boy 252
Zehm, Friedrich
11 Stücke für den Anfang 278

Mixed Plucked Instruments

Zehm, Friedrich
Sonatina 278

Duos for String and Plucked Instrument

Françaix, Jean
Duo baroque 57
Hosokawa, Toshio
2 Pieces 122
Reimann, Aribert
Nocturnos 197
Rodrigo, Joaquín
Serenata al Alba del Dia 208
Smith Brindle, Reginald
5 Sketches 236
Ten-String Music 236

Duos for Wind and Plucked Instrument

Badings, Henk
Sonata for Flute and Guitar 16
Beaser, Robert
Il est né, le Divin Enfant 19
Mountain Songs 19
Françaix, Jean
5 Piccoli Duetti 57
Sonata 58
Gretchaninoff, Alexander Tikhonovich
Bachkiria, Op. 125 79
Holliger, Heinz
Mobile 119
Linde, Hans-Martin
Music for two 153
Musica da camera 153
Paulus, Stephen
Fantasy in Three Parts 178
Ravel, Maurice
Pavane pour une Infante défunte ... 193
Regner, Hermann
Mondzeit 194
Rodrigo, Joaquín
Serenata al Alba del Dia 208
Smith Brindle, Reginald
Hathor at Philae 236
Takemitsu, Toru
Le Fils des Étoiles 252
Toward the Sea 252
Toward the Sea III 252

Wanek, Friedrich K.
5 Impromptus.................................. 266

Zehm, Friedrich
Serenade... 278

Duos for Other Mixed Instruments

Casken, John
A Belle Pavine 35

Dahl, Ingolf
Variations on an Air by Couperin........ 40

Gilbert, Anthony
Moonfaring 69
Treatment of Silence........................... 69
Ziggurat 69

Haas, Joseph
Church Sonata in D Minor, Op. 62/2 .. 82
Church Sonata in F Major, Op. 62/1 ... 82

Henze, Hans Werner
3 Sacred Concertos 99

Hosokawa, Toshio
Utsurohi 122

Ichiyanagi, Toshi
Before Darkness appears 127
Ten, Zui, Ho, Gyaku........................... 128
Transfiguration of the Moon 128
Troposphere 128
Wind Gradation 129

Kelkel, Manfred
Suite, Op. 10 134

Killmayer, Wilhelm
Tre Dance....................................... 136

Litaize, Gaston
Diptyque 154

Rees, Howard
Doug's New Flute Thing 193

Rouse, Christopher
Lares Hercii 211

Schroeder, Hermann
5 Pieces 222
Prelude, Canzone and Rondo 222
Sonata 223
Sonata 223

Subotnick, Morton
Passages of the Beast........................ 245

Yuasa, Joji
Cosmos Haptic III 276
Mai-Bataraki from Ritual for Delphi.... 276

Three Instruments
Trios for String Instruments

Violin/Viola/Violoncello

Beck, Conrad
String Trio No.1................................ 21
String Trio No.2................................ 21

von Bose, Hans-Jürgen
String Trio...................................... 26

Fortner, Wolfgang
String Trio No.1................................ 52
String Trio No.2................................ 53

Françaix, Jean
Trio 58

Grainger, Percy Aldridge
Colonial Song 76

Hessenberg, Kurt
String Trio, Op. 48............................ 102

Hiller, Wilfried
Der Fiedler...................................... 105

Hindemith, Paul
Des kleinen Elektromusikers
Lieblinge...................................... 110
String Trio No.1, Op. 34..................... 111
String Trio No.2................................ 111

Lutyens, Elisabeth
String Trio, Op. 57............................ 155

Maasz, Gerhard
Miniatrio 156

Maler, Wilhelm
String Terzett 158

Paulus, Stephen
7 Miniatures 178

Penderecki, Krzysztof
String Trio...................................... 183

Rainier, Priaulx
String Trio...................................... 193

Reimann, Aribert
String Trio...................................... 197

Schroeder, Hermann
String Trio in E Minor, Op. 14/1 223

Strauss, Richard
Variationen
über „s'Deandl is harb auf mi"........... 238

Zimmermann, Bernd Alois
String Trio...................................... 281

Other Stringtrios

Badings, Henk
Trio Cosmos (Nos.1-16) 16

Bamert, Matthias
Ations... 16

Fortner, Wolfgang
6 Madrigals 52

Genzmer, Harald
Spielbuch 64

Gerster, Ottmar
Kleine Musik zu festlichem Tag........... 68

Holliger, Heinz
Come and go.................................... 119

Killmayer, Wilhelm
String Trio...................................... 136

Rein, Walter
Spielbuch 198

Schroeder, Hermann
String Trio, Op. 14/2 223

Singleton, Alvin
Be Natural...................................... 234
Intezar 234

Szelényi, István
Sinfonietta a tre per violini................. 249

Trios for String and Wind Instruments

Cooke, Arnold
Qua... 38

Dahl, Ingolf
Concerto a Tre 40

Husa, Karel
Evocations de Slovaquie 126

Lehmann, Hans Ulrich
3 Regions 148

Reimann, Aribert
Canzoni e Ricercari 197

Singleton, Alvin
Et Nunc.. 234

Trios for Wind Instruments
Three Recorders

Fricker, Peter Racine
Suite for Recorders........................... 60

Gál, Hans
Divertimento, Op. 98 62

Genzmer, Harald
Trio 64

Hindemith, Paul
Plöner Musiktag................................ 111
Trio 112

Knab, Armin
Kleine Musik 140

Roehr, Walter
Wir musizieren zu dreien.................... 210

Scherer, Johann
Sonate in B Major, Op. 1/1 214
Sonate in F Major, Op. 1/2 214

Three Flutes

Holliger, Heinz
Come and go.................................... 119

Zgraja, Krystof
Modern Flutist III 279

Zimmermann, Bernd Alois
Tempus Loquendi 281

Three Clarinets

Bamert, Matthias
Trio 16

Goehr, Alexander
Prelude and Fugue, Op. 39 71

Holliger, Heinz
Come and go.................................... 119

Three Trumpets

Tippett, Michael
Fanfare No.3 256

Mixed Wind Trios

Fortner, Wolfgang
Caprices 52
Serenade... 52

Françaix, Jean
Divertissement 57

Hindemith, Paul
Des kleinen Elektromusikers
Lieblinge...................................... 110

Lehmann, Hans Ulrich
Tractus 148

Lutyens, Elisabeth
Wind Trio, Op. 52............................. 155

Schulhoff, Erwin
Divertissement 224
Zehm, Friedrich
Hindemith Variations 278

Trios for Plucked Instruments

Henze, Hans Werner
Carillon, Récitatif, Masque 98
Hindemith, Paul
Rondo 111
Smith Brindle, Reginald
Concerto 'Cum Jubilo' 235
Zehm, Friedrich
11 Stücke für den Anfang 278

Trios for String and Plucked Instruments

Lutyens, Elisabeth
Nocturnes, Op. 30 155

Trios for Wind and Plucked Instruments

Lehmann, Hans Ulrich
Spiele 148

Trios for Other Mixed Instruments

Banks, Don
Trio 18
Françaix, Jean
Suite -
from „L'Apocalypse selon St. Jean" ... 58
Trio 58
Gilbert, Anthony
O'Grady Music 69
Henze, Hans Werner
Selbst-und Zwiegespräche 99
Hiller, Wilfried
Zauberfiedel-Suite 105
Hindemith, Paul
Des kleinen Elektromusikers
Lieblinge 110
Holliger, Heinz
Trio 119
Hosokawa, Toshio
Birds Fragments III 121
Birds Fragments IV 121
Huber, Klaus
Sabeth 123
Kauffmann, Leo Justinus
Divertimento 133
Linde, Hans-Martin
Serenata à tre 154
Lutyens, Elisabeth
Capriccii, Op. 33 155
Scena, Op. 58 155
Schnebel, Dieter
anschläge - ausschläge 216
Handwerke - Blaswerke I 216

Schroeder, Hermann
Concertino 222
Takemitsu, Toru
And then I knew 'twas Wind 252
Wyttenbach, Jürg
3 Sätze 273

Four Instruments
Quartet for String Instruments

Two Violins/Viola/Violoncello

Badings, Henk
String Quartet No.2 16
Banks, Don
4 Pieces for String Quartet 17
Beaser, Robert
String Quartet 19
Beck, Conrad
String Quartet No.3 21
String Quartet No.4 21
String Quartet No.5 21
von Bose, Hans-Jürgen
String Quartet No.1 26
String Quartet No.2 26
String Quartet No.3 26
Brauel, Henning
String Quartet No.2 28
Bryars, Gavin
A Man in a Room, Gambling 33
String Quartet No.1 32
String Quartet No.2 32
Casken, John
String Quartet No.1 35
String Quartet No.2 35
Cowie, Edward
String Quartet No.2 39
String Quartet No.3 39
String Quartet No.4 39
Egk, Werner
Die Nachtigall 46
Fortner, Wolfgang
String Quartet No.1 52
String Quartet No.2 52
String Quartet No.3 52
String Quartet No.4 52
Françaix, Jean
String Quartet 58
Fricker, Peter Racine
String Quartet
in One Movement, Op. 8 60
String Quartet No.2, Op. 20 60
String Quartet No.3, Op. 73 60
Gál, Hans
String Quartet No.2, A Minor , Op. 35 ... 62
Genzmer, Harald
String Quartet No.1 64
Gilbert, Anthony
String Quartet No.2 69
String Quartet No.3 69
Goehr, Alexander
String Quartet No.1, Op. 5 71
String Quartet No.2, Op. 23 71
String Quartet No.3, Op. 37 71
String Quartet No.4, Op. 52 72

Grainger, Percy Aldridge
Molly on the Shore 77
Gretchaninoff, Alexander Tikhonovich
Quatrième Quatuor, Op. 124 80
Haas, Joseph
String Quartet in A Minor, Op. 50 82
Hamilton, Iain
String Quartet No.1, Op. 5 87
String Quartet No.2 87
Hartmann, Karl Amadeus
String Quartet No.1 - Carillon 90
String Quartet No.2 90
Henze, Hans Werner
String Quartet No.1 99
String Quartet No.2 99
String Quartet No.3 99
String Quartet No.4 99
String Quartet No.5 99
Hessenberg, Kurt
String Quartet No.2, Op. 16 102
String Quartet No.3, Op. 33 102
String Quartet No.4, Op. 60 102
String Quartet No.7, Op. 112 102
Hindemith, Paul
Minimax 110
Ouvertüre zum Fliegenden Holländer,
wie sie eine schlechte Kurkapelle
morgens um 7 am Brunnen
vom Blatt spielt 111
String Quartet No. 1 C Major, Op. 2 ... 111
String Quartet No.2
in F Minor, Op. 10 111
String Quartet No.3
in C Major, Op. 16 111
String Quartet No.4, Op. 22 111
String Quartet No.5, Op. 32 111
String Quartet No.6 in Eb 111
String Quartet No.7 111
Holliger, Heinz
String Quartet 119
Hosokawa, Toshio
Landscape I 121
Huber, Klaus
Moteti-Cantiones 123
Humperdinck, Engelbert
String Quartet in C Major 125
Husa, Karel
String Quartet No.1, Op. 8 126
String Quartet No.2 126
Ichiyanagi, Toshi
String Quartet 128
String Quartet No.2 „Interspace" 128
String Quartet No.3 „Inner
Landscape" 128
Killmayer, Wilhelm
String Quartet No.1 136
String Quartet No.2 136
Kirchner, Volker David
String Quartet 139
Knab, Armin
Festlicher Reigen 140
Variationen über ein Kinderlied 140
Korngold, Erich Wolfgang
String Quartet No.1
in A Major, Op. 16 144
String Quartet No.2
in Eb Major, Op. 26 144
String Quartet No.3
in D Major, Op. 34 144

Kreisler, Fritz
String Quartet in A Minor 146
Ligeti, György
Andante - Allegretto 150
String Quartet No.1 152
String Quartet No.2 152
Maler, Wilhelm
String Quartet in G-Major 158
Martinon, Jean
String Quartet, Op. 43 159
Martland, Steve
Crossing the Border 161
Patrol 161
Toccata and Fugue BWV 565 161
Maxwell Davies, Sir Peter
String Quartet No.1 162
Müller-Siemens, Detlev
String Quartet No.1 167
Orff, Carl
Quartettsatz 174
Paulus, Stephen
Music for Contrasts 178
Quartessence 178
String Quartet No.2 178
Penderecki, Krzysztof
String Quartet No.2 183
Der unterbrochene Gedanke 183
Pepping, Ernst
String Quartet 184
Picker, Tobias
String Quartet No.1 187
Rainier, Priaulx
String Quartet 193
Roslawez, Nikolaj Andrejevich
String Quartet No.1 210
String Quartet No.3 210
String Quartet No.5 210
Rouse, Christopher
String Quartet No.1 211
Sackman, Nicholas
String Quartet No.1 213
String Quartet No.2 213
Schidlowsky, Leon
String Quartet 215
Schnebel, Dieter
Stücke 217
Schroeder, Hermann
String Quartet in C Minor, Op. 26 223
String Quartet No.2, Op. 32 223
Schulhoff, Erwin
5 Pieces 224
Seiber, Mátyás
String Quartet No.3 230
Sekles, Bernhard
String Quartet, Op. 31 231
Singleton, Alvin
Secret Desire to be Black 234
String Quartet No.1 234
Subotnick, Morton
A Fluttering of Wings 245
Sutermeister, Heinrich
String Quartet No. 3 247
Takemitsu, Toru
A Way a Lone 252
Tcherepnin, Alexander Nikolajevich
String Quartet No.1, Op. 36 253

Tippett, Michael
String Quartet No.1 256
String Quartet No.2 256
String Quartet No.3 256
String Quartet No.4 256
String Quartet No.5 256
Toch, Ernst
String Quartet No.11, Op. 34 258
Ullmann, Viktor
String Quartet No.3, Op. 46 262
Vasks, Pēteris
String Quartet No.1 264
String Quartet No.2
„Vasaras dziedajumi" 264
String Quartet No.3 264
Wanek, Friedrich K.
5 Epigrammes 266
String Quartet 267
Weill, Kurt
2 Movements for String Quartet 267
String Quartet in B Minor 267
Wellesz, Egon
String Quartet No.5, Op. 60 269
Werdin, Eberhard
Kleine Suite 270
Wyttenbach, Jürg
Execution ajournée 11 273

Four Violins
Rein, Walter
Spielbuch 198
Szelényi, István
Little Suite 249

Four Violoncellos
Pütz, Eduard
Tango Passionato 191

Another Mixed Quartet
Cowie, Edward
Kelly Passacaglia 38

Quartet for String and Wind Instruments

Dessau, Paul
Concertino 42
Françaix, Jean
Quartet 58
Penderecki, Krzysztof
Clarinet Quartet 183
Rainier, Priaulx
Quanta 192
Schroeder, Hermann
Quartet, Op. 38 223
Seiber, Mátyás
Pastorale 230

Quartet for Wind Instruments

Flute/Oboe/Clarinet/Bassoon
Françaix, Jean
Wind Quartet 58
Seiber, Mátyás
Dance Suite 230
Tardos, Béla
Divertimento 253

Four Recorders
Genzmer, Harald
Quartettino 64
Hand, Colin
Fenland Suite 87
Linde, Hans-Martin
Quartett-Übung 154
Suite 154
Lotz, Hans-Georg
Quartet 154
Saux, Gaston
Quartet No.1 in F 214
Quartet No. 2 in G 214
Seiber, Mátyás
Dance Suite Vol.1 230
Dance Suite Vol.2 230
Dance Suite Vol.3 230
Tippett, Michael
4 Inventions 256
Werdin, Eberhard
Kleine Suite 270

Four Clarinets
Both, Heinz
Captain Morgan's March
and other six Pieces 27
Singleton, Alvin
Apple 234
Turnage, Mark-Anthony
A Deviant Fantasy 260
Uhl, Alfred
Divertimento 261

Four Saxophones
Bryars, Gavin
Alaric I or II 32
Françaix, Jean
Petit Quatuor 57
Suite 58
Gilbert, Anthony
Six of the Bestiary 69

Four Horns
Françaix, Jean
Notturno 36
Notturno e Divertimento 36
Hindemith, Paul
Sonata for 4 Horns 111
Rein, Walter
Divertimento 198
Waldmusik 198
Tippett, Michael
Sonata for 4 Horns 256

Four Trumpets

Tippett, Michael
Fanfare No.2 256

Another Mixed Quartet

Casken, John
Music for the Crabbing Sun 35
Fortner, Wolfgang
New-Delhi-Musik 52
Hessenberg, Kurt
Serenade, Op. 89 102
Hindemith, Paul
Plöner Musiktag................................. 111
Sutermeister, Heinrich
Serenade No.1.................................... 247
Szelényi, István
Suite 249
Zehm, Friedrich
Neue Bläserstücke 278

Quartet for Plucked Instruments

Four Guitars

Rodrigo, Joaquín
Dos piezas caballerescas...................... 208
Smith Brindle, Reginald
Concerto de Angelis 235

Quartet for String and Plucked Instruments

Bryars, Gavin
After the Requiem 32
Suite from 'Wonderlawn' 33

Quartet for Other Mixed Instruments

von Bose, Hans-Jürgen
Die Menagerie von Sanssouci 26
Nancarrow, Conlon
Study No. 14...................................... 169
Schnebel, Dieter
Zahlen für (mit) Münzen 217
Westergaard, Peter
Quartet 270

Five Instruments

Quintet for String Instruments

Hosokawa, Toshio
Landscape IV...................................... 122
Lutyens, Elisabeth
String Quintet, Op. 51 151
Picker, Tobias
String Quartet with Bass 187

Quintet for String and Wind Instruments

Françaix, Jean
Quintet (1977) 58
Genzmer, Harald
Quintet 64
Hindemith, Paul
Clarinet Quintet, Op. 30 110
Holliger, Heinz
Quodlibet pour Aurèle 119
Hosokawa, Toshio
Fragments II....................................... 121
Lutyens, Elisabeth
The Fall of the Leafe 155
Seiber, Mátyás
Divertimento...................................... 230
Slavenski, Josip
Aus dem Dorfe, Op. 6 235
Stravinsky, Igor
Pastorale.. 242
Takemitsu, Toru
Entre-temps.. 252
Herbstlied... 252
Werdin, Eberhard
Concertino 270

Quintet for Wind Instruments

Flute/Oboe/Clarinet/Bassoon/Horn

Beaser, Robert
Shadow and Light................................ 19
Egk, Werner
5 Pieces 47
Fortner, Wolfgang
5 Bagatelles 52
Françaix, Jean
Wind Quintet No.1 58
Wind Quintet No.2 58
Fricker, Peter Racine
Wind Quintet, Op. 5 60
Grainger, Percy Aldridge
Lisbon 76
Walking Tune...................................... 77
Hamilton, Iain
Sonata for 5 87
Helm, Everett
Wind Quintet 92
Henze, Hans Werner
Quintet 99
Hindemith, Paul
Kleine Kammermusik, Op. 24/2.......... 110
Holliger, Heinz
„h" for Wind Quintet 119
Hosokawa, Toshio
Fragments III 121
Kelemen, Milko
Etudes Contrapuntiques...................... 234
Kröll, Georg
Invocazioni 147
Lehmann, Hans Ulrich
Episodes... 148

Ligeti, György
6 Bagatelles 150
10 Pieces for Wind Quintet 152
Müller-Siemens, Detlev
Les Sanglots longs
des Violons de l'Automne 167
Rainier, Priaulx
6 Pieces.. 192
Schuller, Gunther
Woodwind Quintet.............................. 225
Seiber, Mátyás
Permutazioni a Cinque 230
Vasks, Pēteris
Quintet - „In Memory of a Friend"..... 263
Quintet - „Music for Fleeting Birds" ... 264

Another Mixed Quintet

Borsheim, David J.
Sonata 25
Casken, John
Clarion Sea 35
Hamilton, Iain
Brass Quintet 87
Hand, Colin
Festival Overture 87
Hartmann, Karl Amadeus
Dance Suite.. 90
Henze, Hans Werner
L' Autunno 98
Fragmente aus einer Show 98
Hindemith, Paul
Plöner Musiktag................................. 111
Sonata for Wind Quintet..................... 111
Martland, Steve
Full Fathom Five 161
Orff, Carl
Carmina Burana.................................. 174
Paulus, Stephen
Concerto for Brass Quintet.................. 178
Landmark Fanfare 178
Ordway Fanfare 178
Sackman, Nicholas
Time-Peace 213
Singleton, Alvin
Woodwind Quintet.............................. 234
Werdin, Eberhard
Serenade.. 270
Suite 270

Quintet for String and Plucked Instruments

Castelnuovo-Tedesco, Mario
Quintet in F Major, Op. 143............... 36
Hosokawa, Toshio
Landscape II 121

Quintet for Other Mixed Instruments

Françaix, Jean
Quintet (1934) 58
Quintet (1988) 58
Quintet No.2 58

Genzmer, Harald
Konzertante Musik 64

Gilbert, Anthony
Calls around Chungmori 69

Hosokawa, Toshio
Landscape V 122

Ince, Kamran
One Last Dance 130

Roslawez, Nikolaj Andrejevich
Nocturne 210

Takemitsu, Toru
Rain Spell 252

Sextets

String Instruments

Henze, Hans Werner
Der junge Törless 98

Hiller, Wilfried
Bestiarium.. 105

Kirchner, Volker David
Gethsemani 139
Orphischer Gesang 139
Stringsextet No. 1 139
Stringsextet No. 2 139

Korngold, Erich Wolfgang
String Sextet in D Major, Op. 10 144

Vasks, Pēteris
Pavasara Sonate 263

Werdin, Eberhard
Suite 270

String and Wind Instruments

Françaix, Jean
Divertissement 57

Müller-Siemens, Detlev
Sextett 167

Werdin, Eberhard
Concertino 270

Wind Instruments

von Bose, Hans-Jürgen
3 Epitaphs 26

Dahl, Ingolf
Fanfare on A and C............................ 40
I.M.C. Fanfare 40

Françaix, Jean
Sixtuor 58

Hand, Colin
Fanfare for a Festival, Op. 64............. 87

Hummel, Bertold
Eine kleine Blasmusik 124

Maxwell Davies, Sir Peter
Alma Redemptoris Mater 162

Sutermeister, Heinrich
Serenade No.2.................................... 247

Szelényi, István
Chamber Music 248

Tippett, Michael
The Wolf Trap Fanfare 256

Werdin, Eberhard
Concertino 270

Another Mixed Sextet

von Bose, Hans-Jürgen
Befragung 26

Fricker, Peter Racine
Serenade No.1, Op. 34........................ 60

Goehr, Alexander
Suite, Op. 11 72

Killmayer, Wilhelm
The Woods so Wilde -
Kammermusik No.1 126

Reznicek, Emil Nikolaus von
Donna Diana 205

Singleton, Alvin
La Flora 234

Toch, Ernst
Dance Suite, Op. 30........................... 258

Septets and Larger Ensembles

String Instruments

Bryars, Gavin
„In Nomine" (after Purcell)................ 32

Fortner, Wolfgang
Madrigal.. 52

Françaix, Jean
Aubade 57
„Noël Nouvelet" et
„Il est né, le Divin Enfant"................ 57
Scuola di Celli 58

Hindemith, Paul
Schulwerk, Op. 44/1 111

Hummel, Bertold
Klangfiguren 124

Kirchner, Volker David
Choralvariationen 139

Rodrigo, Joaquín
Dos piezas caballerescas.................... 208

Schnebel, Dieter
Harmonik 216
In motu proprio.................................. 216

Singleton, Alvin
Again 233

Wind Instruments

Bryars, Gavin
3 Elegies for Nine Clarinets 32

Casken, John
Kagura 35

Françaix, Jean
Cortège burlesque 57
Trois Ecossaises & Variations sur un
Air populaire allemand...................... 57
Le Gay Paris 57
Petite Valse européenne 57
Schön Wetter angesagt....................... 58

Gilbert, Anthony
Canticle I - „Rock Song".................... 69

Hamilton, Iain
Sonatas and Variants.......................... 87

Hartmann, Karl Amadeus
Lied 90

Henze, Hans Werner
Sonata per otto ottoni 99

Hessenberg, Kurt
Sinfonietta, Op. 122............................ 102

Hiller, Wilfried
Notenbüchlein für Tamino................... 105

Hindemith, Paul
Wind Septet 113

Holliger, Heinz
Kreis 119

Hosokawa, Toshio
Variations... 122

Huber, Klaus
2 Movements for 7 Brass Instruments... 123

Kirchner, Volker David
Trifoglietto per undici musicisti di
Kirzehwan - Canonetto....................... 139

Lutschewitz, Martin
2 kleine Festmusiken 155

Orff, Carl
5 Pieces for Brass 174

Regner, Hermann
Bläserübung I..................................... 194
Intrade 194

Schnebel, Dieter
Harmonik 216
In motu proprio.................................. 216

Stein, Egon
Sinfonietta.. 236

Tcherepnin, Iwan
9 Wheelwinds 253

Tippett, Michael
Fanfare No.1 256

Turnage, Mark-Anthony
Set to 260

Wanek, Friedrich K.
Divertimento 266
Finaletto 266
6 Miniatures 266

Werdin, Eberhard
Suite 270

Zádór, Eugen
Divertimento 277

Zehm, Friedrich
Scherzino in Fis.................................. 278

String and Wind Instruments

von Bose, Hans-Jürgen
Nonett 26
Parerga 26

Egk, Werner
Polonaise, Adagio and Finale 47
Sinfonia concertante
in Eb Major, Op. KV. 297b 47

Françaix, Jean
Dixtuor.. 57
Mozart New-Look 57
Octet... 57
11 Variations 58

Fricker, Peter Racine
Octet, Op. 30 60

Goehr, Alexander
Lyric Pieces, Op. 35 71

Grainger, Percy Aldridge
My Robin is to the Greenwood Gone... 77

Henze, Hans Werner
Quattro Fantasie................................. 99

Hindemith, Paul
Octet... 111
Sonata for 10 Instruments, Op. 10a..... 111

Holliger, Heinz
Kreis.. 119
Killmayer, Wilhelm
Per nove strumenti...................... 136
Müller-Siemens, Detlev
Octet.. 167
Variationen
über einen Ländler von Schubert 167
Schnebel, Dieter
Harmonik..................................... 216
Turnage, Mark-Anthony
This Silence 260

Other Mixed Instruments

Banks, Don
Equation I and II.......................... 17
Take Eight................................... 18
Bresgen, Cesar
Morgenmusik................................ 29
Bryars, Gavin
Aus den letzten Tagen 32
Casken, John
Infanta Marina 35
Dallapiccola, Luigi
Piccola Musica Notturna 41
Genzmer, Harald
Septet 64
Goehr, Alexander
Variations on Bach's Sarabande 72
Hiller, Wilfried
Fanfare 105
Ince, Kamran
Sonnet #395 130
Linde, Hans-Martin
Capriccio...................................... 153
Martland, Steve
Big Mac 161
Dance Works................................ 161
Nancarrow, Conlon
Study No. 16................................. 169
Orff, Carl
Einzug und Reigen 174
Penderecki, Krzysztof
Actions... 183
Entrata.. 183
Picker, Tobias
Octet.. 187
Regner, Hermann
Bläserübung II 194
Reimann, Aribert
Reflexionen................................... 197
Schnebel, Dieter
Chorale Prelude I/II 216
Fragment....................................... 216
raum-zeit y................................... 216
Stuhlgewitter................................. 217
Subotnick, Morton
And the Butterflies begin to sing 245
Turnage, Mark-Anthony
Three Farewells 260
Vasks, Pēteris
Drei Blicke 263
Werdin, Eberhard
Concertino 270
Wyttenbach, Jürg
Kunststücke, die Zeit totzuschlagen 273

Chamber Music with Piano

Duos for Piano and String Instrument

Violin

Arnell, Richard
Violin Sonata No. 2, Op. 55 15
Badings, Henk
Capriccio...................................... 15
Violin Sonata No.2 16
Banks, Don
Violin Sonata 18
Beck, Conrad
Sonatina 21
von Bose, Hans-Jürgen
3 Studies 26
Burkhard, Willy
Sonatina, Op. 45 33
Cowie, Edward
Voices of the Land 39
Elgar, Edward William
Salut d'Amour, Op. 12 49
Fairchild, Blair
Mosquitos 50
Fortner, Wolfgang
Violin Sonata 53
Françaix, Jean
Sonatina 58
Fricker, Peter Racine
Violin Sonata, Op. 12 60
Genzmer, Harald
Violin Sonata No.1 64
Violin Sonata No.2 64
Violin Sonatina No. 1 64
Violin Sonatina No. 2 64
Violin Sonatina No. 3 64
Grainger, Percy Aldridge
Harvest Hymn............................... 76
Mock Morris 77
Molly on the Shore 77
The Sussex Mummers' Christmas
Carol 77
Gretchaninoff, Alexander Tikhonovich
In aller Frühe, Op. 126a 79
The Jester..................................... 79
Morning Stroll 80
Haas, Joseph
Grillen, Op. 40............................. 82
Heller, Barbara
Lalai - Schlaflied zum Wachwerden? ... 91
Helm, Everett
Violin Sonata 92
Henze, Hans Werner
5 Nachtstücke 98
Violin Sonata 99
Violin Sonatina 99
Hessenberg, Kurt
Violin Sonata in F Major, Op. 25 102
Hindemith, Paul
Movement..................................... 110
Nobilissima Visione...................... 111
Violin Sonata in C 113
Violin Sonata in D, Op. 11/2 113

Violin Sonata in E.......................... 113
Violin Sonata in Eb, Op. 11/1 113
Holliger, Heinz
4 Lieder ohne Worte 119
Lieder ohne Worte II 119
Hosokawa, Toshio
Manifestation 122
2 Pieces 122
Vertical Time Study III 122
Humpert, Hans
Violin Sonata 125
Ichiyanagi, Toshi
Intercross 127
Scenes IV 128
Scenes V 128
Sonata 128
Ince, Kamran
Köçekçe 130
Killmayer, Wilhelm
Fantasie 135
Humoreske 135
5 Romancen 136
Klebe, Giselher
Violin Sonata, Op. 14 140
Korngold, Erich Wolfgang
Caprice Fantastique 142
Gesang der Heliane 142
Mariettas Lied.............................. 144
4 Pieces 144
Tanzlied des Pierrot 144
Violin Sonata in G Major, Op. 6 144
Kovách, Andor
Obscur Clair................................. 145
Kreisler, Fritz
Album mit ausgewählten Stücken 145
Altdeutsches Schäfermadrigal 146
Aucassin und Nicolette................. 146
Berceuse romantique, Op. 9 146
Caprice viennois, Op. 2 146
Marche Miniature Viennoise 146
Polichinelle 146
Romanze, Op. 4 146
Rondino
über ein Thema von Beethoven.......... 146
Synocopation 146
Tambourin chinois 146
Zigeuner-Cappriccio 146
Lutyens, Elisabeth
3 Duos - No.3, Op. 34 155
Mainardi, Enrico
Violin Sonata 158
Martinon, Jean
Duo, Op. 47 159
Martinů, Bohuslav
Rhythmische Etüden...................... 160
Müller-Siemens, Detlev
Nocturne 167
Paulus, Stephen
Bagatelles..................................... 178
Partita 178
Penderecki, Krzysztof
Violin Sonata 183
Picker, Tobias
Invisible Lilacs 187
Rhapsody 187
Romance 187
Pütz, Eduard
Blues for Benni 191
Twilight Dream............................. 191

Reutter, Hermann
Rhapsody, Op. 51 202
Violin Sonata, Op. 20 202

Rodrigo, Joaquín
7 Cançiones Valencianes 208
2 Esbozos 208

Roslawez, Nikolaj Andrejevich
3 Dances 210
Legende 210
24 Préludes 210
Violin Sonata No.1 210
Violin Sonata No.2 210
Violin Sonata No.4 210
Violin Sonata No.6 210

Schnebel, Dieter
4 Stücke 217

Schroeder, Hermann
Duo, Op. 28 222

Schulhoff, Erwin
Violin Sonata No.2 224

Scott, Cyril
Aubade... 227
Cherry Ripe, Old English Air 227
Tallahassee Suite.............................. 228
Violin Sonata No.1, Op. 59 228

Seiber, Mátyás
Concert Piece.................................... 230
Violin Sonata 230

Senfter, Johanna
Melodie und Elegie, Op. 13 231

Stephan, Rudi
Groteske 237

Stravinsky, Igor
Berceuse... 242
Berceuse... 242
Circus Polka..................................... 242
Prélude et Ronde 242
Scherzo 242

Stürmer, Bruno
Sonatina in C 244

Szelényi, István
Improvisation.................................... 249
Kinderwelt auf vier Saiten................. 249

Takemitsu, Toru
Distance de Féc 252
From far beyond Chrysanthemums
and November Fog 252

Toch, Ernst
Violin Sonata, Op. 44 258

Turina, Joaquín
Sonate Espagnole.............................. 259

Vasks, Pēteris
Masa vasaras muzika -
Little Summer Music........................ 263

Wanek, Friedrich K.
Violin Sonata 267

Zehm, Friedrich
Rhapsodische Sonate 278

Zimmermann, Bernd Alois
Little Suite 281
Violin Sonata 281

Zipp, Friedrich
Sonatine, Op. 23a 282

Viola

Beck, Conrad
Sonatina 21

Bryars, Gavin
The North Shore 32

Gilbert, Anthony
Dawnfaring....................................... 69

Hamilton, Iain
Viola Sonata, Op. 9 87

Hand, Colin
Progressive Pieces 87

Hartmann, Karl Amadeus
Concerto for viola with piano............. 88

Henze, Hans Werner
Viola Sonata..................................... 99

Hessenberg, Kurt
Viola Sonata, Op. 94......................... 102

Hindemith, Paul
Nobilissima Visione 111
Viola Sonata, Op. 25/4 113
Viola Sonata 113
Viola Sonata in F, Op. 11/4 113

Höller, Karl
Viola Sonata in E, Op. 62.................. 117

Kauffmann, Leo Justinus
Little Suite 133

Killmayer, Wilhelm
Die Schönheit des Morgens................ 136

Mohler, Philipp
Konzertante Sonate, Op. 31............... 164

Naoumoff, Emile
Petite Suite...................................... 169

Paulus, Stephen
Seven for the Flowers near the River... 178

Rainier, Priaulx
Viola Sonata..................................... 193

Ravel, Maurice
Pavane pour une Infante défunte........ 193

Reutter, Hermann
Music 202

Roslawez, Nikolaj Andrejevich
Viola Sonata No.1 210
Viola Sonata No.2............................ 210

Takemitsu, Toru
A Bird came down the Walk 252

Zehm, Friedrich
3 Elegies 278

Viola d'amore

Hindemith, Paul
Little Sonata, Op. 25/2 110

Violoncello

Banks, Don
3 Studies 18

Beck, Conrad
Sonata No.2 21

Bryars, Gavin
The South Downs 32

Dahl, Ingolf
Duo 40
Notturno... 40

Dohnányi, Ernst von
Sonata, Op. 8 43

Elgar, Edward William
Dream Children, Op. 43 48
Salut d'Amour, Op. 12 49

Fortner, Wolfgang
Cello Sonata..................................... 52
Zyklus 53

Françaix, Jean
Berceuse... 57
Habañera 57
Mouvement perpétuel......................... 57
Nocturne 57
Rondino-Staccato............................... 58
Sérénade... 58

Fricker, Peter Racine
Cello Sonata, Op. 28 60

Genzmer, Harald
Cello Sonata No.1 64

Goehr, Alexander
Cello Sonata, Op. 45 71

Grainger, Percy Aldridge
La Scandinavie - Scandinavian Suite .. 77
The Sussex Mummers' Christmas
Carol 77
Youthful Rapture 77

Gretchaninoff, Alexander Tikhonovich
In aller Frühe, Op. 126 79
In aller Frühe, Op. 126b 79
Sonata, Op. 113 80
Sonata in G minor, Op. 129............... 80

Haas, Joseph
2 Grotesken, Op. 28......................... 82

Hamilton, Iain
Cello Sonata, Op. 39 87

Heller, Barbara
Lalai - Schlaflied zum Wachwerden?.. 91

Hessenberg, Kurt
Cello Sonata in C Major, Op. 23........ 102

Hindemith, Paul
Cello Sonata, Op. 11/3 110
Cello Sonata (1948).......................... 110
3 Easy Pieces 110
Little Sonata (1942).......................... 110
Nobilissima Visione 110
3 Pieces 111
Variation... 113

Ichiyanagi, Toshi
Interrelation 128

Killmayer, Wilhelm
8 Bagatellen 135
5 Romanzen 136

Kreisler, Fritz
Andantino 146
Liebesfreud 146

Lutyens, Elisabeth
3 Duos - No.2, Op. 34 155

Mainardi, Enrico
Cello Sonata..................................... 157
Cello Sonata quasi Fantasia.............. 157
Cello Sonatina 157
Recitative, Aria and Epilogue............. 158

Paulus, Stephen
Air on Seurat (The Grand Canal)........ 178
American Vignettes 178
Banchetto Musicale 178

Pütz, Eduard
Short Stories 191

Rainier, Priaulx
Grand Duo 192

Ravel, Maurice
Pavane pour une Infante défunte........ 193

Regner, Hermann
Mein Lieblingslied von gestern........... 194

Reimann, Aribert
Cello Sonata..................................... 197

Reutter, Hermann
Sonata Monotematica 202

Rodrigo, Joaquín
Sonata a la Breve 208
Roslawez, Nikolaj Andrejevich
Cello Sonata No.1 210
Cello Sonata No.2 210
Meditation 210
Tanz der weissen Jungfrauen 210
Schulhoff, Erwin
Cello Sonata 224
Scott, Cyril
Concerto 227
Danse from „Deux Préludes" 227
Élégie, Op. 73/1 227
The Gentle Maiden (Irish Air) 227
Pastoral and Reel 228
Pierrot amoureux, Andante 228
Poème Erotique
from „Deux Préludes" 228
Romance, Op. 73/2 228
Sonnet Nos. 1 & 2 228
The Melodist and the Nightingales 228
Seiber, Mátyás
Fantasy 230
Stürmer, Bruno
3 kleine Hausmusiken 244
Takemitsu, Toru
Orion 252
Toch, Ernst
Cello Sonata, Op. 50 258
Turnage, Mark-Anthony
Sleep on 260
Vasks, Pēteris
Partita 263
Weill, Kurt
Cello Sonata 267
Zehm, Friedrich
4 Easy Pieces 278
Zimmermann, Bernd Alois
Intercomunicazione 281

Doublebass

Hindemith, Paul
Double Bass Sonata 110
Wanek, Friedrich K.
Sonata 267

Duos for Piano and Wind Instrument

Recorder

Andriessen, Louis
Melodie 14
Bate, Stanley
Sonatina 18
Sonatina 18
Bender, Wilhelm
Sonate 24
Bergmann, Walter
Sonata (1965) 24
Sonata (1973) 24
Berkeley, Lennox
Sonatina, Op. 13 24
Bresgen, Cesar
Sonatina 29
Casken, John
Thymehaze 35

Cooke, Arnold
Suite 38
Gál, Hans
3 Intermezzi, Op. 103 62
Genzmer, Harald
Recorder Sonata No.1 64
Recorder Sonata No.2 64
Grainger, Percy Aldridge
Shepherd's Hey 77
Shepherd's Hey 77
Shepherd's Hey 77
Hand, Colin
Plaint 87
Sonata Breve 87
Hummel, Bertold
Sonata Brevis, Op. 87b 124
Kelkel, Manfred
Suite, Op. 10 134
Linde, Hans-Martin
Fünf Studien 153
3 Jazzy Tunes 153
Sonate 154
Sonate in d moll 154
Maasz, Gerhard
Little Suite 156
Migot, Georges
Sonatine nr. 2 163
Poos, Heinrich
Greensleeves 188
Reizenstein, Franz
Partita 200
Rodgers, Philip
20 Simple Tunes 205
Roehr, Walter
Sonatina No. 1 in F Major 209
Sonatina No. 2 in F Major 209
Sonatina No. 3 in F Major 209
Sonatina No. 4 B-Dur 210
Schneider, Otto
Theme and Variations 218
Scott, Cyril
Aubade 227
Shchedrin, Rodion
Echos 232
Sollima, Eliodoro
Sonata 236
Stockmeier, Wolfgang
Sonatine 238
Wohlgemut, Gerhard
Sonatine 273
Zipp, Friedrich
Sonatine, Op. 23a 282

Flute/Altoflute

Arnell, Richard
Andante and Allegro, Op. 58/1 15
Banks, Don
3 Episodes 17
Bate, Stanley
Sonatina 18
Beaser, Robert
Minimal Waltz 19
Variations 19
Beck, Conrad
Sonatina 21
Both, Heinz
Dancing Flute 27

Bresgen, Cesar
Flute Sonata 29
Dahl, Ingolf
Variations on a French Folksong 40
Fortner, Wolfgang
Flute Sonata 52
Françaix, Jean
Divertimento 57
Gál, Hans
3 Intermezzi, Op. 103 62
Genzmer, Harald
Flute Sonata No.2 in E minor 64
Gilbert, Anthony
The Incredible Flute Music 69
Goehr, Alexander
Variations, Op. 8 72
Helm, Everett
Flute Sonata 92
Henze, Hans Werner
Flute Sonata 98
Hessenberg, Kurt
Flute Sonata in B, Op. 38 102
Suite, Op. 77 102
Hindemith, Paul
Echo 110
Flute Sonata 110
Höller, Karl
Flute Sonata No.2 in C, Op. 53 117
Mohler, Philipp
Capriccio, Op. 19a 164
Naoumoff, Emile
3 Bilder aus der Kindheit 169
Pütz, Eduard
Blue Waltz 191
Ravel, Maurice
Le Jardin féerique 193
Schwantner, Joseph
Soaring 226
Scott, Cyril
Aubade 227
Seiber, Mátyás
Dance Suite 230
Szelényi, István
Improvisation 249
Takahashi, Yuji
Ji(t) 249
Wanek, Friedrich K.
Flute Sonata 266
Wyttenbach, Jürg
Paraphrase 273
Zbinden, Julien-François
Sonatina, Op. 5 277
Zgraja, Krystof
Modern Flutist I 279
Zipp, Friedrich
Sonatine, Op. 23a 282

Oboe/Cor anglais

Beck, Conrad
Sonatina 21
Haas, Joseph
Ein Kränzlein Bagatellen, Op. 23 82
Hand, Colin
Aria and Giga 87
Hindemith, Paul
Cor Anglais Sonata 110
Oboe Sonata 111

Huber, Klaus
Noctes Intelligibilis Lucis 123
Kelemen, Milko
Oboe Sonata.......................... 134
Schroeder, Hermann
3 Dialogues 122
Searle, Humphrey
Gonderliera, Op. 19 229
Seiber, Mátyás
Improvisation........................ 230
Tippett, Michael
Prelude: Autumn....................... 256

Clarinet/Bassclarinet

Banks, Don
Prologue, Night Pieces
and Blues for Two 17
Both, Heinz
Dancing Clarinet..................... 27
Bryars, Gavin
Allegrasco........................... 32
Gilbert, Anthony
Spell Respell, Op. 14................ 69
Goehr, Alexander
Fantasias, Op. 3 71
Hamilton, Iain
Clarinet Sonata, Op. 22 87
3 Nocturnes, Op. 6. 87
Hindemith, Paul
Clarinet Sonata 110
Lutyens, Elisabeth
5 Little Pieces, Op. 14/1 155
Naoumoff, Emile
3 Pieces............................. 169
Paulus, Stephen
Duo for Clarinet and Piano.......... 178
Rainier, Priaulx
Suite 193
Searle, Humphrey
Suite, Op. 32 229
Seiber, Mátyás
Andantino Pastorale................. 230
Dance Suite......................... 230
Tcherepnin, Alexander Nikolajevich
Clarinet Sonata 253
Uhl, Alfred
Andante semplice 261
Vasks, Pēteris
Tris Skandarbi - Three Pieces....... 264
Zehm, Friedrich
Sonatina giocosa 278

Saxophone

Both, Heinz
Dancing Clarinet.................... 27
Dancing Saxophone.................. 27
Bryars, Gavin
Allegrasco......................... 32
Ciry, Michel
Capriccio, Op. 52.................. 37
Françaix, Jean
5 Danses exotiques 57
Fricker, Peter Racine
Aubade............................ 60
Hummel, Bertold
Invocations, Op. 68b 124

Reutter, Hermann
Pièce concertante 202
Schulhoff, Erwin
Hot-Sonate (Jazz-Sonate) 224
Seiber, Mátyás
Dance Suite....................... 230
Turnage, Mark-Anthony
Sarabande......................... 260
Two Elegies Framing a Shout 260

Bassoon

Françaix, Jean
Bassoon Concerto 57
Gould, Glenn
Sonata 73
Hindemith, Paul
Bassoon Sonata.................... 110
Naoumoff, Emile
3 Elegies 169
Impression 169
Reutter, Hermann
Sonata Monotematica 202
Schneider, Otto
5 Miniaturen 218
Schoff, Manfred
2 Impromptus...................... 219
Zehm, Friedrich
Pentameron 278

Horn

Cooke, Arnold
Rondo in B Major.................. 38
Fricker, Peter Racine
Horn Sonata, Op. 24 60
Haas, Joseph
Horn Sonata, Op. 29 82
Hamilton, Iain
Aria 86
Sonata Notturna 87
Hindemith, Paul
Horn Sonata 110
Hummel, Bertold
Sonatina, Op. 75a 124
Kirchner, Volker David
Lamento d'Orfeo 139
Tre Poemi........................ 139
Litaize, Gaston
Triptyque......................... 154
Lutyens, Elisabeth
3 Duos - No.1, Op. 34 155
Strauss, Richard
Introduktion, Thema
und Variationen, o.Op. AV 52...... 238
Zehm, Friedrich
Ballad........................... 278

Trumpet

Arnell, Richard
Allegro, Op. 58/2................. 15
Beck, Conrad
Facetten.......................... 21
Eben, Petr
Fantasia vespertina 45
Hamilton, Iain
Capriccio......................... 87

Henze, Hans Werner
3 Sacred Concertos................ 99
Hindemith, Paul
Trumpet Sonata.................... 113
Hummel, Bertold
Invocations, Op. 68a.............. 124
Killmayer, Wilhelm
3 Pezzi........................... 136
Ligeti, György
Mysteries of the Macabre.......... 152
Martland, Steve
Duo 161
Maxwell Davies, Sir Peter
Trumpet Sonata, Op. 1............. 162
Seiber, Mátyás
Dance Suite....................... 230
Sutermeister, Heinrich
Gavotte de Concert................ 247
Zehm, Friedrich
Canto e Rondo 278
Sonata Brevis..................... 278

Trombone

Guilmant, Félix Alexandre
Morceau Symphonique, Op. 88....... 81
Hindemith, Paul
Trombone Sonata................... 113
Kalabis, Viktor
Sonata, Op. 32 133
Sackman, Nicholas
Trombone Sonata................... 213

Tuba

Hindemith, Paul
Tuba Sonata 113

Duos for Piano and Plucked Instrument

Castelnuovo-Tedesco, Mario
Fantasia, Op. 145................. 36
Genzmer, Harald
Sonatina for Mandoline and Piano.. 64
Ichiyanagi, Toshi
Flowers Blooming in Summer 127

Trios for Piano and Two String Instruments

Piano/Violin/Violoncello

Andreae, Volkmar
Trio, Op. 1 14
Badings, Henk
Piano Trio 16
Fortner, Wolfgang
Piano Trio 52
Françaix, Jean
Trio 58
Goehr, Alexander
Piano Trio, Op. 20 71
Grainger, Percy Aldridge
My Robin is to the Greenwood Gone.. 71
Hamilton, Iain
Trio, Op. 25 71

Henze, Hans Werner
Adagio, Adagio 98
Chamber Sonata 98
Hosokawa, Toshio
Dan-sô 121
Killmayer, Wilhelm
Brahms-Bildnis 135
Kirchner, Volker David
Trio 139
Knab, Armin
Lindegger Ländler 140
Mainardi, Enrico
Due Tempi Romantici 158
Piano Trio 158
Martinů, Bohuslav
Piano Trio 159
Müller-Siemens, Detlev
Phantasie 167
Paulus, Stephen
Life Motifs 178
Music of the Night 178
Pfitzner, Hans
Piano Trio in B Major 186
Roslawez, Nikolaj Andrejevich
Trio No.2 210
Trio No.3 210
Trio No.4 210
Schroeder, Hermann
Piano Trio, Op. 33 222
Scott, Cyril
Cornish Boat Song 227
Little Folk Dance 228
Trio No. 2 228
Shchedrin, Rodion
Piano Terzetto 232
Strauss, Richard
Trio No.1 A-Dur, Op. AV. 37 238
Trio No.2 D-Dur, Op. AV. 53 238
Takemitsu, Toru
Between Tides 252
Vasks, Pēteris
Episodi e Canto perpetuo 263

Piano/Two Violins

Elgar, Edward William
Salut d'Amour, Op. 12 49
Haas, Joseph
Chamber Trio, Op. 38 81
Ichiyanagi, Toshi
Yami o Irodoru Mono 129

Trios for Piano, String and Wind Instrument

Banks, Don
Horn Trio 17
Beck, Conrad
Alternances 21
Blomdahl, Karl-Birger
Trio in B Flat 24
Françaix, Jean
Trio (1990) 58
Trio (1994) 58
Hindemith, Paul
Trio, Op. 47 113
Hosokawa, Toshio
Vertical Time Study I 122
Huber, Klaus
Ascensus 123
Ligeti, György
Horn Trio 152
Linde, Hans-Martin
Drei Skizzen 153
MacCombie, Bruce
3 Designs for 3 Players 157
Mainardi, Enrico
Trio 158
Schroeder, Hermann
Piano Trio No.2, Op. 40 22
Piano Trio No.3, Op. 43 22
Willi, Herbert
Horn Trio 271

Trios for piano and Two Wind Instruments

Beck, Conrad
Trio 21
Bresgen, Cesar
Sonatine über altdeutsche
Liebeslieder 29
Françaix, Jean
Trio 58
Fricker, Peter Racine
Trio, Op. 35 60
Genzmer, Harald
Sonata 60
Grainger, Percy Aldridge
Country Gardens 76
Linde, Hans-Martin
Trio 154
Tippett, Michael
Prelude, Recitative and Aria 256

Quartets for Piano and Three String Instruments

Piano/Violin/Viola/Violoncello

Casken, John
Piano Quartet 35
Dahl, Ingolf
Piano Quartet 40
Ince, Kamran
Fantasy of a Sudden Turtle 130
Strauss, Richard
Arabischer Tanz, o.Op. AV 182 238
Festmarsch, o.Op. AV 178 238
Liebesliedchen, o.Op. AV 182 238
Ständchen, o.Op. AV 168 238

Piano/Two Violins/Violoncello

Korngold, Erich Wolfgang
Suite, Op. 23 144

Quartets for Piano, String and Wind Instrument

Casken, John
Music for a Tawny-Gold Day 35
Hindemith, Paul
Quartet 111
Kirchner, Volker David
Exil 139
MacCombie, Bruce
Elegy 157
Paulus, Stephen
Courtship Songs 178

Quartets for Piano and Three Wind Instruments

Françaix, Jean
Quatuor 58
Gilbert, Anthony
Quartet of Beasts 69

Quintets for Piano and Four String Instruments

Piano/Two Violins/Viola/Violoncello

Françaix, Jean
8 Bagatelles 57
Gilbert, Anthony
String Quartet
with Piano Pieces, Op. 20 69
Henze, Hans Werner
Piano Quintet 98
Hosokawa, Toshio
Im Tal der Zeit 121
Korngold, Erich Wolfgang
Piano Quintet in E Major, Op. 15 144
Schnebel, Dieter
Quintet in B Major 216
Xiaogang, Ye
Enchanted Bamboo Shoots 274

Piano/Violin/Viola/Violoncello/Doublebass

Hiller, Wilfried
Lilith 105
Picker, Tobias
Nova 187

Quintets for Piano, String and Wind Instruments

Gilbert, Anthony
Nine or Ten Osannas, Op. 10 69
Hamilton, Iain
Sextet 87
Henze, Hans Werner
Amicizia! 98
Hindemith, Paul
3 Anekdoten für Radio 110
3 Pieces for 5 Instruments 111
Ichiyanagi, Toshi
Piano Quintet „Prana" 128
Kirchner, Volker David
Mysterion.................................... 139
MacCombie, Bruce
Greeting 157
Martland, Steve
Principia.................................... 161
Schnebel, Dieter
Kontrapunkt.................................. 216
Quintet in B Major 216
Singleton, Alvin
Such a Nice Lady 234

Quintets for Piano and Four Wind Instruments

Françaix, Jean
Petit Quatuor................................ 57
Holliger, Heinz
Piano Quintet 119
Ravel, Maurice
Pavane pour une Infante défunte 193

Sextets and Larger Ensembles

String and Wind Instruments

Casken, John
Cor d'oeuvre 35
Françaix, Jean
L' Heure du Berger 57
L' Heure du Berger 57
Hommage à l' Ami Papageno 57
Pour remercier l' Auditoire 57
Septet 58
Variations sur un Thème plaisant 58
Müller-Siemens, Detlev
Pavane....................................... 166
Picker, Tobias
Serenade..................................... 187
Schroeder, Hermann
Sextet, Op. 36 223

Other Mixed Instruments

Banks, Don
Sonata da Camera............................. 17
Bryars, Gavin
Allegrasco 32
The Cross-Channel Ferry 32
4 Elements 32
Les Fiançailles 32
The Old Tower of Löbenicht.................. 32
Sub Rosa 32
Viennese Dance No.1 (M.H.) 33
Casken, John
Amarantos 35
Castiglioni, Niccolò
Masques 37
Henze, Hans Werner
Canzona 98
Sonata for 6 players 99
Ince, Kamran
Waves of Talya 130
Killmayer, Wilhelm
Führe mich, Alter, nur immer in Deinen
geschnörkelten Frühlings-Garten!
Noch duftet und taut
frisch und würzig sein Flor.................. 135
Kammermusik 135
Paradies (Paradise) 136
Martland, Steve
Horses of Instruction 161
Principia.................................... 161
Picker, Tobias
The Blue Hula 187
Sextet No.3 187
Regner, Hermann
Klangspiele 194
Rouse, Christopher
Rotae Passionis 211
Sackman, Nicholas
Corranach.................................... 213
Schnebel, Dieter
Übungen mit Klängen 217
Schwantner, Joseph
Consortium 2 226
Distant Runes and Incantations 226
Music of Amber 226
Singleton, Alvin
Akwaaba 234
Subotnick, Morton
Ten 245
Takemitsu, Toru
Rain Spell 252
Turnage, Mark-Anthony
Release 260
Xiaogang, Ye
Nine Horses 274
Yuasa, Joji
Projection for Seven Players 276
Zehm, Friedrich
Alla Danza 277

Chamber Music with Percussion

Brouwer, Leo
Variantes 31
Bryars, Gavin
One Last Bar Then Joe Can Sing 32
Viennese Dance No.1 (M.H.) 33
Casken, John
Amarantos.................................... 35
Cowie, Edward
Cartoon Music 38
Fetler, Paul
Cycles 50
Genzmer, Harald
Percussion Quartet 64
Gilbert, Anthony
Brighton Piece, Op. 9 69
Vasanta with Dancing 69
Hartmann, Karl Amadeus
Burlesque Music 90
Kleines Konzert 90
Scherzo 90
Henze, Hans Werner
Amicizia! 98
Des Kaisers Nachtigall 98
Des Kaisers Nachtigall 98
Prison Song.................................. 99
Hiller, Wilfried
Fanfare 105
Katalog I 105
Katalog II................................... 105
Katalog III 105
Katalog IV 105
Katalog V 105
Scherzo 105
Hosokawa, Toshio
Sen VI 122
Vertical Time Study II 122
Humel, Gerald
Arabesque 124
Hummel, Bertold
„In Memoriam-", Op. 74 124
Ichiyanagi, Toshi
Distance 127
Hikari-nagi.................................. 127
Paganini Personal 128
Recurrence 128
Time in Tree, Time in Water 128
Transstream.................................. 128
Trio „Interlink" 128
Wind Trace................................... 129
Ince, Kamran
Kaç 130
Sonnet #395 130
Waves of Talya 130
Kelkel, Manfred
Suite, Op. 10................................ 134
Killmayer, Wilhelm
Führe mich, Alter, nur immer in Deinen
geschnörkelten Frühlings-Garten!
Noch duftet und taut
frisch und würzig sein Flor.................. 135
Kammermusik 135
Kindertage - Kammermusik No.3 136
Schumann in Endenich -
Kammermusik No.2 136

Lacerda, Osvaldo
Três Miniatures Brasilieras................. 148
Lutyens, Elisabeth
Capriccii, Op. 33 155
Martland, Steve
Remix... 161
Nancarrow, Conlon
Study No. 17.. 169
Study No. 18.. 169
Study No. 19.. 169
Olah, Tiberiu
Espace et Rhytme 172
Orff, Carl
Kleines Konzert 174
Orff-Schulwerk 174
Regner, Hermann
Bläserübung II 194
Changing Patterns.......................... 194
5 Duos 194
6 Easy Percussion Trios.................. 194
50 Etudes 194
Klangspiele 194
8 Miniatures 194
7 Trios 194
Rouse, Christopher
Ku-Ka-Ilimoku 211
Ogoun Badagris 211
Rotae Passionis 211
Rudzinski, Zbigniew
Quartet 212
Sackman, Nicholas
Corranach.................................... 213
Doubles...................................... 213
Schnebel, Dieter
Analysis 216
raum-zeit y 216
raum-zeit y 216
Rhythmen.................................... 217
Schwantner, Joseph
Consortium 2 226
Distant Runes and Incantations 226
In Aeternum 226
Music of Amber............................ 226
Seiber, Mátyás
77 Breaks for Percussion.................... 230
Singleton, Alvin
Akwaaba 234
Extension of a Dream...................... 234
Soler, Josep
Sonidos de la noche - Klänge der
Nacht.. 236
Subotnick, Morton
After the Butterfly 245
Ascent into Air.............................. 245
The Key to Songs 245
Parallel Lines 245
Ten 245
Szelényi, István
Tambourin 249
Takemitsu, Toru
Rain Spell 252
Rain Tree 252
Turnage, Mark-Anthony
Release.. 260
Yuasa, Joji
Interpenetration No.2...................... 276
A Winter Day -Homage to Bashô- 276
Zehm, Friedrich
Divertimento Ritmico...................... 278

Chamber Music for Traditional Japanese Instruments

Hosokawa, Toshio
Birds Fragments II...................... 121
Birds Fragments III 121
Birds Fragments IV 121
Fragments I 121
Nocturne 122
Sen III 122
Utsurohi 122
Ichiyanagi, Toshi
Accumulation............................... 127
Cloud Shore, Wind Roots.................. 127
Distance 127
Enenraku 127
Hikari-nagi.................................. 127
Hoshi no Wa 127
Katachi naki Mugen no Yoha 128
Ogenraku 128
Reigaku Symphony No.2 „Kokai" 128
Reigaku Symphony
„The Shadows Appearing
through Darkness" 128
Rinkaiikiy 128
Sensing the Color in the Wind 128
Still Time I 128
Still Time II 128
Ten, Zui, Ho, Gyaku 128
Transfiguration of the Flower............. 128
Transfiguration of the Moon 128
Voices of Water............................ 128
Wa 128
Water Relativity 129
The Way 129
The Way II 129
Wind Gradation 129
Winter Portrait II 129
Yuasa, Joji
Ishibutai Ko 276
To the Genesis 276

Chamber Music for Jazz Ensemble

Banks, Don
Equation I and II.............................. 17
Killmayer, Wilhelm
Kammermusik 135
Martland, Steve
Beat the Retreat 161
Horses of Instruction 161
Mr. Anderson's Pavane...................... 161
Remembering Lennon 161
Remix 161
Shoulder to Shoulder 161

Electronic Music

Banks, Don
Commentary 17
Bryars, Gavin
The White Lodge 33
Henze, Hans Werner
Prison Song 99
Holliger, Heinz
Cardiophonie 120
Introitus 120
Not I 120
5 Pieces 120
Ichiyanagi, Toshi
Intoxicant Moon 129
Music for Living Space 129
Parallel Music 129
Présage 129
Tokyo 1969 129
Kaufmann, Dieter
Pax 133
Ligeti, György
Artikulation.................................. 153
Glissandi 153
Pièce électronique No.3.................... 153
Poème symphonique........................ 153
Martland, Steve
Crossing the Border.......................... 161
Rees, Howard
Doug's New Flute Thing 193
Schnebel, Dieter
Environments 218
Hörfunk - Radiophonien I-V 218
ki-no.. 218
Languido 218
Maulwerke 218
Monotonien No. 1-7 218
No - ein Hörspiel 218
Subotnick, Morton
After the Butterfly 245
Ascent into Air.............................. 245
The First Dream of Light 245
A Fluttering of Wings 245
The Key to Songs 245
The Last Dream of the Beast.............. 245
2 Life Histories 245
Liquid Strata 245
Mandolin 245
Parallel Lines 245
Play! No.3 245
Trembling 245
Takemitsu, Toru
A Minneapolis Garden...................... 253
The Sea is Still.............................. 253
Sky, Horse and Death 253
Static Relief 253
Wavelength 253
Yuasa, Joji
Aoi no Ue 276
Icon on the Source of White Noise 276
Music for Space Projection 276
My Blue Sky, No.1 276
My Blue Sky, No.2 276
A Study in White 276
Towards 'The Midnight Sun' 276
Voices Coming.............................. 276
Zimmermann, Bernd Alois
Tratto.. 282
Tratto 2 282

Birthdays / Anniversaries

1997

January

10.1.	Moeschinger, Albert (1897-1985)	100th birthday
17.1.	Badings, Henk (1907-1987)	90th birthday
26.1.	Lhotka, Fran (1883-1962)	*35th anniversary*

March

18.3.	Malipiero, Gian Francesco (1882-1973)	115th birthday

April

14.4.	Höller, Karl (1907-1987)	*10th anniversary*

May

4.5.	Lehmann, Hans Ulrich (*1937)	60th birthday
19.5.	Mainardi, Enrico (1897-1976)	100th birthday
23.5.	Françaix, Jean (*1912)	85th birthday
29.5.	Korngold, Erich Wolfgang (1897-1957)	100th birthday

June

2.6.	Elgar, Edward William (1857-1934)	140th birthday
5.6.	Stravinsky, Igor (1882-1971)	115th birthday
6.6.	Hamilton, Iain (*1922)	75th birthday
9.6.	Donatoni, Franco (*1927)	70th birthday
10.6.	Badings, Henk (1907-1987)	*10th anniversary*
21.6.	Maler, Wilhelm (1902-1976)	95th birthday
29.6.	Gerster, Ottmar (1897-1969)	100th birthday

July

8.7.	Grainger, Percy Aldridge 1882-1961)	115th birthday
15.7.	Hamel, Peter Michael (*1947)	50th birthday
17.7.	Castiglioni, Niccolï (*1932)	65th birthday
25.7.	Höller, Karl (1907-1987)	90th birthday
26.7.	Jarnach, Philipp (1892-1982)	105th birthday
26.7.	Dombrowski, Hansmaria (1897-1977)	*20th anniversary*
27.7.	Dohnányi, Ernst von (1877-1960)	120th birthday
29.7.	Stephan, Rudi (1887-1915)	110th birthday
30.7.	Müller-Siemens, Detlev (*1957)	40th birthday
31.7.	Niculescu, Stefan (*1927)	70th birthday

August

5.8.	Gál, Hans (1890-1987)	110th birthday
10.8.	Goehr, Alexander (*1932)	65th birthday
15.8.	Foss, Lukas (*1922)	75th birthday
18.8.	Gebhard, Hans (1897-1974)	100th birthday
18.8.	Schulhoff, Erwin (1894-1942)	*55th anniversary*
20.8.	Dombrowski, Hansmaria (1897-1977)	100th birthday
20.8.	Eisenmann, Will (1906-1992)	*5th anniversary*
21.8.	Killmayer, Wilhelm (*1927)	70th birthday

September

5.9.	Fortner, Wolfgang (1907-1987)	*10th anniversary*
11.9.	Mohler, Philipp (1908-1982)	*15th anniversary*
15.9.	Arnell, Richard (*1917)	80th birthday
25.9.	Gould, Glenn (1932-1982)	65th birthday
29.9.	Tcherepnin, Alexander N. (1899-1977)	*20th anniversary*

October

3.10.	Gál, Hans (1890-1987)	*10th anniversary*
12.10.	Fortner, Wolfgang (1907-1987)	90th birthday
16.10.	Gotovac (1895-1982)	*15th anniversary*
24.10.	Grandis, Reanto de (*1927)	70th birthday
27.10.	Nancarrow, Conlon (*1912)	85th birthday

November

8.11.	Martinet, Jean-Louis (*1912)	85th birthday
10.11.	Brehme, Hans (1904-1957)	*40th anniversary*
11.11.	Zbinden, Julien-François (*1917)	80th birthday
13.11.	Ohana, Maurice (1914-192)	*5th anniversary*
18.11.	Biersack, Anton (1907-1982)	*15th anniversary*
27.11.	Zoll, Paul (1907-1978)	90th birthday
29.11.	Korngold, Erich Wolfgang (1897-1957)	*40th anniversary*
30.11.	Biersack, Anton (1907-1982)	90th birthday

December

7.12.	Toch, Ernst (1887-1964)	110th birthday
9.12.	Turina, Joaquín (1882-1949)	115th birthday
16.12.	Shchedrin, Rodion (*1932)	65th birthday
17.12.	Jarnach, Philipp (1892-1982)	*15th anniversary*
19.12.	Walter, Fried (*1907)	90th birthday

1998

January

1.1.	Ullmann, Viktor (1898-1944)	100th birthday
24.1	Einem, Gottfried von (*1918-1996)	80th birthday
22.1.	Zehm, Friedrich (*1923)	75th birthday

February

| 3.2. | Rainier, Priaulx (1903-1986) | 95th birthday |
| 4.2. | Ichiyanagi, Toshi (*1933) | 65th birthday |

March

16.3.	Lopatnikoff, Nicolai (1903-1976)	95th birthday
1.3.	Pauels, Heinz (1908-1985)	90th birthday
20.3.	Zimmermann, Bernd Alois (1918-1970)	80th birthday

April

| 7.4. | Bresgen, Cesar (1913-1988) | *10th anniversary* |
| 14.4. | Subotnick, Morton (*1933) | 65th birthday |

May

| 28.5. | Ligeti, György (*1923) | 75th birthday |
| 12.5. | Regner, Hermann (*1928) | 70th birthday |

June

| 14.6. | Blomdahl, Karl-Birger (1916-1968) | *30th anniversary* |
| 19.6. | Müller-Zürich, Paul (1898-1993) | 100th birthday |

July

| 10.7. | Egk, Werner (1901-1983) | *15th anniversary* |
| 21.7. | Müller-Zürich, Paul (1898-1993) | *5th anniversary* |

August

1.8.	Malipiero, Gian Francesco (1882-1973)	*25th anniversary*
11.8.	Grünauer, Ingomar (*1938)	60th birthday
17.8.	Hessenberg, Kurt (1908-1994)	90th birthday
30.8.	Wimberger, Gerhard (*1923)	75th birthday

October

16.10.	Bresgen, Cesar (1913-1988)	85th birthday
25.10.	Banks, Don (1923-1980)	75th birthday
22.10.	Mihalovici, Marcel (1898-1985)	100th birthday

November

26.11.	Mohler, Philipp (1908-1982)	90th birthday
23.11.	Penderecki, Krzysztof (*1933)	65th birthday

December

5.12.	Hartmann, Karl Amadeus (1905-1963)	*35th anniversary*
18.12.	Zillig, Winfried (1905-1963)	*35th anniversary*
24.12.	Komma, Karl Michael (*1913)	85th birthday
15.12.	Lhotka, Fran (1883-1962)	115th birthday
25.12.	Poos, Heinrich (*1928)	70th birthday
27.12.	Zoll, Paul (1907-1978)	*20th anniversary*
28.12.	Hindemith, Paul (1895-1963)	*35th anniversary*

1999

January

14.1.	Turina, Joaquín (1882-1949)	*50th anniversary*
15.1.	Kelkel, Manfred (*1929)	70th birthday
21.1.	Tcherepnin, Alexander N. (1899-1977)	100th birthday
22.1.	Eben, Petr (*1929)	70th birthday
29.1.	Nono, Luigi (1924-1990)	75th birthday

February

3.2.	Dallapiccola, Luigi (1904-1975)	95th birthday
5.2.	Ferrari, Luc (*1929)	70th birthday
9.2.	Genzmer, Harald (*1909)	90th birthday
14.2.	Kounadis, Arghyris (*1924)	75th birthday
15.2.	Rouse, Christopher (*1949)	50th birthday
23.2.	Elgar, Edward William (1857-1934)	*65th anniversary*
27.2.	Haubenstock-Ramati, Roman (*1919)	80th birthday

March

1.3.	Brouwer, Leo (*1939)	60th birthday
10.3.	Brehme, Hans (1904-1957)	95th birthday
15.3.	Meier, Jost (*1939)	60th birthday
19.3.	Haas, Joseph (1879-1960)	120th birthday
26.3.	Schroeder, Hermann (1904-1984)	95th birthday
30.3.	Kelemen, Milko (*1924)	75th birthday

May

5.5.	Pfitzner, Hans (1869-1949)	130th birthday
21.5.	Holliger, Heinz (*1939)	60th birthday
22.5.	Pfitzner, Hans (1869-1949)	*50th anniversary*
26.5.	Weiss, Harald (*1949)	50th birthday

June

8.6.	Schulhoff, Erwin (1894-1942)	105th birthday
11.6.	Strauss, Richard (1864-1949)	135th birthday
12.6.	Ohana, Maurice (1914-192)	85th birthday
19.6.	Vogel, Wladimir (1896-1984)	*15th anniversary*
22.6.	Frommel, Gerhard (1906-1984)	*15th anniversary*
28.6.	Dessau, Paul (1894-1979)	*20th anniversary*

July

15.7.	Casken, John (*1949)	50th birthday
24.7.	Malipiero, Riccardo (*1914)	85th birthday
26.7.	Gilbert, Anthony (*1934)	65th birthday

August

7.8.	Kosma, Joseph (1905-1969)	*30th anniversary*
12.8.	Yuasa, Joji (*1929)	70th birthday
13.8.	Bloch, Augustyn (*1929)	70th birthday
23.8.	Roslawez, Nikolaj A. (1881-1944)	*55th anniversary*
28.8.	Martinů, Bohuslav (1890-1959)	*40th anniversary*
31.8.	Gerster, Ottmar (1897-1969)	*30th anniversary*

September

1.9.	Humperdinck, Engelbert (1854-1921)	145th birthday
8.9.	Maxwell Davies, Sir Peter (*1934)	65th birthday
8.9.	Strauss, Richard (1864-1949)	*50th anniversary*
13.9.	Schönberg, Arnold (1874-1951)	125th birthday
27.9.	Scott, Cyril (1879-1970)	120th birthday

October

18.10.	Ullmann, Viktor (1898-1944)	*55th anniversary*
1.10.	Toch, Ernst (1887-1964)	*35th anniversary*
2.10.	Gebhard, Hans (1897-1974)	*25th anniversary*
7.10.	Schroeder, Hermann (1904-1984)	*15th anniversary*
10.10.	Martland, Steve (*1959)	40th birthday
31.10.	Beck, Conrad (1901-1989)	*10th anniversary*

November

8.11.	Wellesz, Egon (1885-1974)	*25th anniversary*
11.11.	Wanek, Friedrich K. (1929-1991)	70th birthday
24.11.	Brugk, Hans Melchior (*1909)	90th birthday
30.11.	Huber, Klaus (*1924)	75th birthday

December

19.12.	Dessau, Paul (1894-1979)	105th birthday
26.12.	Weismann, Julius (1879-1950)	120th birthday

2000

January

1.1.	Reutter, Hermann (1900-1985)	*15th anniversary*
2.1.	Tippett, Sir Michael (*1905)	95th birthday
10.1.	Martinon, Jean (1910-1976)	90th birthday

February

1.2.	Fricker, Peter Racine (1920-1990)	*10th anniversary*
2.2.	Kreisler, Fritz (1875-1962)	125th birthday
9.2.	Dohnányi, Ernst von (1877-1960)	*40th anniversary*
19.2.	Dallapiccola, Luigi (1904-1975)	*25th anniversary*

March

2.3.	Weill, Kurt (1900-1950)	100th birthday
14.3.	Schnebel, Dieter (*1930)	70th birthday
30.3.	Haas, Joseph (1879-1960)	*40th anniversary*

April

1.4.	Zillig, Winfried (1905-1963)	95th birthday
3.4.	Weill, Kurt (1900-1950)	*50th anniversary*
9.4.	Steinbrenner, Wilfried (1943-1975)	*25th anniversary*
12.4.	Sackman, Nicholas (*1950)	50th birthday
13.4.	Dianda, Hilda Fanny (*1925)	75th birthday
17.4.	Burkhard, Willy (1900-1955)	100th birthday

May

4.5.	Seiber, Mátyás (1905-1960)	95th birthday
8.5.	Nono, Luigi (1924-1990)	*10th anniversary*
24.5.	Linde, Hans-Martin (*1930)	70th birthday

June

10.6.	Turnage, Mark.-Anthony (*1960)	40th birthday
17.6.	Reutter, Hermann (1900-1985)	100th birthday
18.6.	Burkhard, Willy (1900-1955)	*45th anniversary*
28.6.	Klebe, Giselher (*1925)	75th birthday

July

8.7.	Antheil, George (1900-1959)	100th birthday
10.7.	Brauel, Henning (*1940)	60th birthday
10.7.	Orff, Carl (1895-1982)	105th birthday

August

2.8.	Hartmann, Karl Amadeus (1905-1963)	105th birthday
10.8.	Zimmermann, Bernd Alois (1918-1970)	*30th anniversary*
12.8.	Mihalovici, Marcel (1898-1985)	*15th anniversary*
12.8.	Sutermeister, Heinrich (1910-1995)	90th birthday
23.8.	Kotonski, Wlodzimierz (*1925)	75th birthday
23.8.	Křenek, Ernst (1900-1991)	100th birthday
26.8.	Searle, Humphrey (1915-1982)	85th birthday

September

5.9.	Fricker, Peter Racine (1920-1990)	80th birthday
12.9.	Banks, Don (1923-1980)	*20th anniversary*
14.9.	Liebermann, Rolf (*1910)	90th birthday
25.9.	Seiber, Mátyás (1905-1960)	*40th anniversary*
27.9.	Moeschinger, Albert (1897-1985)	*15th anniversary*
29.9.	Stephan, Rudi (1887-1915)	*85th anniversary*

October

8.10.	Takemitsu, Toru (1930-1996)	70th birthday
11.10.	Gotovac (1895-1982)	105th birthday
21.10.	Wellesz, Egon (1885-1974)	115th birthday
22.10.	Kosma, Joseph (1905-1969)	95th birthday

November

16.11.	Hindemith, Paul (1895-1963)	105th birthday
22.11.	Schuller, Gunther (*1925)	75th birthday
27.11.	Hummel, Bertold (*1925)	75th birthday

December

2.12.	Wyttenbach, Jürg (*1935)	65th birthday
7.12.	Mieg, Peter (1906-1990)	*10th anniversary*
8.12.	Martinů, Bohuslav (1890-1959)	110th birthday
22.12.	Weismann, Julius (1879-1950)	*50th anniversary*
28.12.	Singleton, Alvin (*1940)	60th birthday
31.12.	Scott, Cyril (1879-1970)	*30th anniversary*

2001

January

4.1.	Roslawez, Nikolaj A. (1881-1944)	110th birthday
14.1.	Degen, Helmut (1911-1995)	90th birthday
22.1.	Dutilleux, Henri (*1916)	85th birthday

February

1.2.	Pepping, Ernst (1901-1981)	*20th anniversary*
9.2.	Benguerel, Xavier (*1931)	70th birthday
9.2.	Maasz, Gerhard (1906-1984)	95th birthday
13.2.	Pütz, Eduard (*1911)	90th birthday
19.2.	Knab, Armin (1881-1951)	110th birthday
20.2.	Grainger, Percy Aldridge 1882-1961)	*40th anniversary*
20.2.	Takemitsu, Toru (1930-1996)	*5th anniversary*
22.2.	Borck, Edmund von (1906-1944)	95th birthday
25.2.	Papandopoulo, Boris (1906-1991)	95th birthday
29.2.	Vogel, Wladimir (1896-1984)	105th birthday

March

1.3.	Martinon, Jean (1910-1976)	*25th anniversary*
3.3.	Eisenmann, Will (1906-1992)	95th birthday
4.3.	Reimann, Aribert (*1936)	65th birthday
7.3.	Ravel, Maurice (1875-1937)	125th birthday
15.3.	Hiller, Wilfried (*1941)	60th birthday

April

6.4.	Stravinsky, Igor (1882-1971)	*30th anniversary*
11.4.	Mainardi, Enrico (1897-1976)	*25th anniversary*
13.4.	Wanek, Friedrich K. (1929-1991)	10th birthday
14.4.	Lutyens, Elisabeth (1906-1983)	*15th anniversary*
23.4.	Petsch, Hans (1891-1978)	110th birthday

May

7.5.	Poot, Marcel (1901-1988)	100th birthday
17.5.	Egk, Werner (1901-1983)	100th birthday
25.5.	Werdin, Eberhard (1911-1991)	*10th anniversary*

June

8.6.	Vieru, Anatol (*1926)	75th birthday
16.6.	Beck, Conrad (1901-1989)	100th birthday
21.6.	Kaminski, Heinrich (1886-1946)	*55th anniversary*
23.6.	Knab, Armin (1881-1951)	*50th anniversary*

July

1.7.	Henze, Hans Werner (*1926)	75th birthday
4.7.	Kaminski, Heinrich (1886-1946)	115th birthday
9.7.	Lutyens, Elisabeth (1906-1983)	95th birthday

August

7.8.	Frommel, Gerhard	95th birthday
7.8.	Husa, Karel (*1921)	80th birthday
21.8.	Ishii, Kan (*1921)	80th birthday

September

5.9.	Mieg, Peter (1906-1990)	95th birthday
12.9.	Pepping, Ernst (1901-1981)	100th birthday
27.9.	Humperdinck, Engelbert (1854-1921)	*80th anniversary*

October

7.10.	Lopatnikoff, Nicolai (1903-1976)	*25th anniversary*
10.10.	Rainier, Priaulx (1903-1986)	*15th anniversary*
19.10.	Blomdahl, Karl-Birger (1916-1968)	85th birthday
19.10.	Werdin, Eberhard (1911-1991)	90th birthday
29.10.	Streul, Eberhard (*1941)	60th birthday

November

6.11.	Heller, Barbara (*1936)	65th birthday
7.11.	Humel, Gerald (*1931)	70th birthday
8.11.	Martinet, Jean-Louis (*1912)	90th birthday
22.11.	Rodrigo, Joaquín (*1901)	100th birthday

Eulenburg Study Scores
Classic Contemporary Composers

A Selection

Ernest Bloch
- *Symphony, C minor*
Order No. ETP 8030

Edward Elgar
- *Introduction and Allegro for strings, Op. 47*
Order No. ETP 885
- *Enigma Variations, Op. 36*
Order No. ETP 884
- *Symphony No. 1, Ab major, Op. 55*
Order No. ETP 8005
- *Symphony No. 2, Eb major, Op. 63*
Order No. ETP 8006
- *Violin Concerto, B minor, Op. 61*
Order No. ETP 1817
- *Cello Concerto, E minor Op. 85*
Order No. ETP 1814

George Gershwin
- *Rhapsody in Blue*
Order No. ETP 8012
- *An American in Paris*
Order No. ETP 1398
- *Piano Concerto in F*
Order No. ETP 1819

Paul Hindemith
- *Symphony 'Mathis der Maler'*
Order No. ETP 573
- *Concerto for Orchestra, Op. 38*
Order No. ETP 8036
- *Symphonic Metamorphosis on Themes of Carl Maria v. Weber*
Order No. ETP 1394
- *Der Schwanendreher. Concerto on old folk song for viola and small orchestra*
Order No. ETP 1816
- *Cardillac, Op. 39 (1926)*
Order No. ETP 8013
- *Septet for flute, oboe, clarinet, bass clarinet, bassoon, horn, trumpet*
Order No. ETP 1407

Gustav Holst
The Planets. Suite for large orchestra, Op. 32
Order No. ETP 8007

Arthur Honegger
- *Symphony No. 3 'Liturgique'*
Order No. ETP 151
- *Symphony No. 5 'die tre re'*
Order No. ETP 1519
- *Pacific 231. Symphonic Movement*
Order No. ETP 1397

Luigi Nono
Il Canto sospeso
Order No. ETP 8029

Carl Orff
- *Carmina Burana*
Order No. ETP 8000
- *Catulli Carmina*
Order No. ETP 8015
- *Trionfo di Afrodite*
Order No. ETP 8016

Hans Pfitzner
- *Symphony, C# minor, Op. 36 a*
Order No. ETP 1521
- *Piano Concerto, Eb major, Op. 31*
Order No. ETP 1820
- *Violin Concerto, H minor, Op. 34*
Order No. ETP 8019

- *Cello Concerto, A minor, Op. post. (1888)*
Order No. ETP 1821

Sergej Prokofjew
Peter and the Wolf
Order No. ETP 1393

Max Reger
- *Variations und Fuge über ein Thema von Beethoven , Op. 86*
Order No. ETP 1400
- *Variationen und Fuge über ein Thema von J. A. Hiller, Op. 100*
Order No. ETP 835
- *Klavier-Konzert, Op. 114*
Order No. ETP 8021
- *Vier Tondichtungen nach Arnold Böcklin, Op. 128*
Order No. ETP 8020

Joaquín Rodrigo
- *Concierto de Aranjuez for guitar and orchestra*
Order No. ETP 1809
- *A la busca del más allá for orchestra*
Order No. ETP 1455
- *Fantasia para un Gentilhombre for guitar and orchestra*
Order No. ETP 1823
- *Concierto Madrigal for 2 guitars and orchestra*
Order No. ETP 1824
- *Concierto Andaluz for 4 guitars and orchestra*
Order No. ETP 8026

Arnold Schönberg
- *Moses und Aron*
Order No. ETP 8004
- *Five Pieces for Orchestra, Op. 16*
Order No. ETP 1328

Dimitri Schostakowitsch
Synphony No. 5, D minor, Op. 47
Order No. ETP 579

Alexander Scriabin
- *Symphony No. 2, C minor, Op. 29*
Order No. ETP 503
- *The Poème of Ecstasy, Op. 54*
Order No. ETP 497
- *Prometheus. The Poem of Fire, Op. 60*
Order No. ETP 8008
- *Piano Concerto, F# minor, Op. 20*
Order No. ETP 1287

Jean Sibelius
- *Symphony No. 3, C major, Op. 52*
Order No. ETP 531
- *Violin Concerto, D minor, Op. 47*
Order No. ETP 770
- *String Quartett, D minor, Op. 56*
Order No. ETP 294

Richard Strauss
- *Burleske, D minor, for piano and orchestra*
Order No. ETP 1253
- *Romanze, F major, for cello and orchestra, Op. AV 75*
Order No. ETP 1399
- *Suite, Bb major, for 13 wind instruments, Op. 4*
Order No. ETP 1410
- *Dance Suite after Couperin, Op. Av. 107*
Order No. ETP 1453
- *Concert Ouverture, C minor, Op. Av. 80*
Order No. ETP 1135

Symhonic Poems
- *Also sprach Zarathustra , Op. 30*
Order No. ETP 444
- *Don Juan, Op. 20*
Order No. ETP 440
- *Don Quixote, Op. 35*
Order No. ETP 445
- *Ein Heldenleben, Op. 40*
Order No. ETP 498
- *Macbeth, Op. 23*
Order No. ETP 441
- *Symphonia Domestica, Op. 53*
Order No. ETP 510.
- *Till Eulenspiegel, Op. 28*
Order No. ETP 443
- *Tod und Verklärung, Op. 24*
Order No. ETP 442

Igor Stravinsky
- *The Firebird. Ballet (1910)*
Order No. ETP 8043
- *The Firebird. Ballet suite (1945)*
Order No. ETP 1389
- *Jeu de Cartes. Ballet*
Order No. ETP 1392
- *Scherzo fantastique for orchestra, Op. 3*
Order No. ETP 8017
- *Fireworks, Fantasie for orchestra, Op. 4*
Order No. ETP 1396
- *Dumbarton Oaks. Concerto in Eb major*
Order No. ETP 1813.
- *Symphony in C*
Order No. ETP 1511
- *Symphony in three movements*
Order No. ETP 574
- *Concerto in D for violin and orchestra*
Order No. ETP 1815

Alexander Tcherepnin
Georgiana. Suite for Orchestra , Op. 92
Order No. ETP 1310

Michael Tippett
Fantasia Concertante on a theme of Corelli for strings
Order No. ETP 1395

Ralph Vaughan Williams
- *Symphony No. 4, F minor*
Order No. ETP 1505
- *Symphony No. 5, D major*
Order No. ETP 1506
- *Symphony No. 6, E minor*
Order No. ETP 1507
- *The Lark Ascending. Romanze for violin and orchestra*
Order No. ETP 1388

Edition Eulenburg

COMPOSERS OF OUR TIME
IN SCHOTT INSTRUMENTAL SERIES

Violin Library
Viola Library
Cello Library

Original Music For Recorder
The Modern Recorder Series

Il Flauto traverso
Oboe Library
Clarinet Library
Bassoon Library

Il Corno
La Tromba

Guitar-Archives

A Battere
Works for Percussion

Concertino
Easy Orchestral Music

A SELECTION

W. Adams · L. Andriessen · D. Aplvor · V. Asencio
S. Bacarisse · H. Badings · J. Z. Bartos · G. Becerra-
Schmidt · C. Beck · W. Bender · H. Benker · F. M. Beyer
C. Bresgen · L. Brouwer · L. Berkeley · J. Casken
M. Castelnuovo-Tedesco · E. Cossetto · E. Doflein
P. Eben · J. Feld · P. Fetler · W. Fortner · J. Françaix
P. R. Fricker · W. Fussan · H. Gál · H. Genzmer
G. Gershwin · F. Geyson · W. Goetze · G. Gould
J. Haas · P. Haletzki · K. A. Hartmann · B. Heller
H. W. Henze · K. Hessenberg · W. Hiller · P. Hindemith
P. Hoch · K. Höller · K. Huber · B. Hummel · K. Husa
K. Johannsen · P. Kadosa · V. Kalabis · M. Kelemen
M. Kelkel · W. Killmayer · E. W. Korngold · B. Kováts
E. Krenek · M. Kymlicka · A. Lauro · W. Leigh · G. Ligeti
H.-M. Linde · G. Maasz · J. Manen · B. Martinu · H. May
P. Mieg · G. Migot · M. Miletic · P. Mohler · F. Moreno
Torroba · E. Naoumoff · K. Penderecki · E. Pepping
M. M. Ponce · F. Reizenstein · H. Reutter · J. Rodrigo
H. K. Schmid · D. Schnebel · O. Schneider · M. Schoof
E. Schulhoff · C. Scott · A. Segovia · M. Shinohara
W. Stockmeier · R. Strauss · I. Strawinsky · R. Suter
H. Sutermeister · A. Tansman · F. Tarrega · A. Tcherepnin
W. Thomas-Mifune · J. Torrent · A. Traeg · J. Turina
A. Uhl · P. Vasks · W. Vogel · F. K. Wanek · S. Weiner
H. Weiss · E. Werdin · H. Willi · B. Williams
G. Wohlgemuth · J. Wyttenbach · N. Yepes · F. Zehm
B. A. Zimmermann · F. Zipp

SCHOTT
**Please find further information
in the special catalogues**

Music of Our Time
STUDY SCORES

A Selection
(Sales Material)

Don Banks
Violin Concerto
Order No. ED 11090

Conrad Beck
Hommages
Two pieces for orchestra
Order No. ED 551

Karl-Birger Blomdahl
Forma Ferritonans
for orchestra
Order No. ED 11017

Hans-Jürgen von Bose
Idyllen
for orchestra (1982/83)
Order No. AVV 122

Henning Brauel
Zweites Streichquartett
Order No. AVV 40

John Casken
Maharal Dreaming
for orchestra from the opera 'Golem'
Order No. ED 12374

Niccolò Castiglioni
Consonate
for flute and chamber orchestra
Order No. AVV 72

Peter Maxwell Davies
Sinfonia
for chamber orchestra
Order No. ED 10820

Henri Dutilleux
L'arbre des songes
Concerto for violin and orchestra
Order No. ED 7627

Werner Egk
• **La Tentation de Saint Antoine**
for alto, string quartet and string orchestra
Order No. ED 4559
• **Spiegelzeit**
for orchestra
Order No. ED 6919

Wolfgang Fortner
• **Aulodie**
Music for oboe and orchestra
Order No. ED 6312
• **Immagin**
Version for large string orchestra and Soprano
Order No. ED 6307
• **Triplum**
for orchestra with 3 obl. pianos
Order No. ED 5513

Jean Françaix
• **Divertissement**
for bassoon and string orchestra
Order No. CON 185
• **Symphonie en sol majeur**
Order No. ED 7708

Peter Racine Fricker
Symphonie Nr. 3, Op. 36
Order No. ED 10748

Harald Genzmer
Divertimento giocoso
for two woodwind instruments and string orchestra
Order No. CON 61

Anthony Gilbert
Towards Asavari
for piano and small orchestra
Order No. ED 12195

Alexander Goehr
• **Violin Concerto, Op. 13**
Order No. ED 10813
• **Little Music, Op. 16**
for string orchestra
Order No. ED 10892
• **Symphony in one movement, Op. 29**
Order No. ED 12101

Iain Hamilton
Symphony No. 2, Op. 10
Order No. ED 10575

Karl Amadeus Hartmann
• **Concerto funebre**
for solo violin and string orchestra
Order No. ED 5002
• **Gesangsszene**

for Baritone and orchestra
Order No. ED 5506
• **1. Sinfonie
(Versuch eines Requiems)**
for alto and orchestra
Order No. ED 4577
• **Symphonische Hymnen**
Order No. ED 6650

Hans Werner Henze
• **Appassionatamente**
Fantasia sopra 'Lo Sdegno del Mare' for large orchestra
Order No. ED 8428
• **Compases para preguntas ensimis-madas**
Music for viola and 22 players
Order No. ED 6321
• **Das Floß der Medusa**
Oratorio volgare et militare
Order No. ED 6326
• **2. Klavier-Konzert**
Order No. ED 6301
• **Requiem**
Nine sacred concertos for concertante trumpet and large chamber orchestra
Order No. ED 8198
• **Sinfonia N. 8**
Order No. ED 8276
• **Tristan**
Preludes for piano, recording tapes and orchestra
Order No. ED 6629
• **2. Violin-Konzert**
Order No. ED 6332

Paul Hindemith
• **Mathis der Maler**
Order No. ED 4575
• **Philharmonisches Konzert**
Variations for orchestra
Order No. ED 3505
• **Symphonie
'Die Harmonie der Welt'**
Order No. ED 4061
• **Violin-Konzert**
Order No. ED 3529
• **Viola-Konzert
(Kammermusik Nr. 5), Op. 36/4**
Order No. ED 3443
• **Trauermusik**
for viola (cello or violin) and string orchestra
Order No. ED 3514

Heinz Holliger
• **Atembogen**
for orchestra
Order No. ED 6848
• **Turm-Musik**
for flute, small orchestra and recording tape
Order No. ED 7680

Toshio Hosokawa
Ferne Landschaft I
for orchestra
Order No. Order No. SJ 1079

Klaus Huber
Tenebrae
for large orchestra
Order No. AVV 304

Toshi Ichiyanagi
• **Interspace**
for string orchestra
Order No. SJ 1047
• **Piano Concerto No. 2
'Winter Portrait'**
Order No. SJ 1060

Wilhelm Killmayer
• **Grande Sarabande**
for string orchestra
Order No. ED 6944
• **Überstehen und Hoffen**
Poème symphonique for orchestra
Order No. ED 6905

Volker David Kirchner
Bildnisse I
for orchestra
Order No. ED 7145

Erich Wolfgang Korngold
String Quartet No. 1 A major, Op. 16
Order No. ED 8122

György Ligeti
• **Kammerkonzert**
for 13 Instrumentalists
Order No. ED 6323
• **Klavier-Konzert**
Order No. ED 7746
• **Lontano**
for large orchestra
Order No. ED 6303
• **Melodien**
for orchestra
Order No. ED 6334
• **Ramifications**
for string orchestra or 12 solo strings
Order No. ED 6305

Alexander Lokschin
Drei Szenen aus Goethes „Faust"
for soprano an orchestra
Order No. KIN 1002

Elisabeth Lutyens
Music for orchestra II, Op. 48
Order No. ED 10878

Bohuslav Martinu
Sinfonia concertante
for two orchestra
Order No. ED 4403

Steve Martland
Babi Yar
for large orchestra in 3 groups
Order No. ED 12356

Alexander Mossolow
5. Symphonie
Order No. KIN 1001

Detlev Müller-Siemens
Under Neonlight I
for chamber orchestra
Order No. AVV 315

Luigi Nono
• Intolleranza
Order No. AVV 75
• Variantii
Music for solo violin, strings and woodwind instruments
Order No. AVV 51

Carl Orff
• Carmina Burana
Order No. ED 4425
• Catulli Carmina
Order No. ED 75
• Der Mond.
Order No. ED 6481
• De temporum fine comoedia.
Order No. ED 7365

Krzysztof Penderecki
• Die Teufel von Loudun
Order No. ED 6225
• 1. Sinfonie
Order No. ED 6614
• Adagio.
4. Symphony for large orchestra
Order No. ED 8064
• Adagietto
from 'Paradise Lost' for orchestra
Order No. ED 6902
• Kanon
for strings and recording tape
Order No. ED 6342
• Viola-Koncert
Order No. ED 7573
• Kosmogonia
for solo, choir and orchestra
Order No. ED 6324

Hans Pfitzner
• Violoncello-Konzert G-Dur, Op. 42
Order No. ED 3512
• Palestrina.
Overtures of the 1st, 2nd and 3rd act
Order No. ED 4557

Aribert Reimann
• Die Gespenstersonate
Chamber opera
Order No. ED 8021
• Rondes
for string orchestra
Order No. AVV 302
• Zyklus
for baritone and orchestra
Order No. AVV 310

Hermann Reutter
Phyllis und Philander
for mixed choir, piano and 6 wind instruments
Order No. ED 147

Joaquín Rodrigo
• Cançoneta A major
for violin and string orchestra
Order No. CON 209
• Concierto como un Divertimento
for violoncello and orchestra
Order No. ED 8370
• Concierto in modo galante
for violoncello and orchestra
Order No. ED 8357
• Preludio para un poema
a la Alhambra
for orchestra
Order No. ED 8356

Nikolaj Andrejewitsch Roslawez
Violin Concerto No. 1
Order No. ED 7823

Nicholas Sackmann
A Pair of Wings
for 3 soprano and ensemble
Order No. ED 11377

Dieter Schnebel
• Sinfonie X
Order No. ED 8326
• Versuche
I Analysis for string instruments and percussion
II Stücke for string instruments (string quartet)
III Fragment for chamber ensemble (and voice)
IV Composition for orchestra
Order No. ED 6336

Erwin Schulhoff
Divertissement
for oboe, clarinet and bassoon
Order No. ED 7736

Mátyás Seiber
Elegie
for viola and small orchestra
Order No. ED 4585

Rodion Shchedrin
Alte Russische Zirkusmusik
3. Concert for symphony orchestra
Order No. ED 8182

Rudi Stephan
Musik für Orchester
in one movement
Order No. ED 3462

Richard Strauss
• Elektra
Order No. AF 5650
• Salome
Order No. AF 5500

Igor Strawinsky
• Circus Polka
Order No. 4274
• Concerto in Es 'Dumbarton Oaks'
Order No. ED 3527
• Danses concertantes
Order No. ED 4275
• Four Norwegian Moods

Order No. ED 6333
• Ode
Triptychon for orchestra
Order No. 5942
• Tango
Order No. ED 4569

Heinrich Sutermeister
• Divertimento Nr. 1
for string orchestra
Order No. ED 5004
• Marche fantasque
for large orchestra
Order No. ED 4406

Toru Takemitsu
• Dreamtime
for orchestra
Order No. SJ 1027
• Far Calls. Coming, far !
for violin and orchestra
Order No. SJ 1005
• Rain Coming
for orchestra
Order No. SJ 1012
• To the edge of dream ...
for solo guitar and orchestra
Order No. SJ 1022
• Twill by Twilight
for orchestra
Order No. SJ 1053

Michael Tippett
• A Child of Our Time
Order No. ED 10899
• The Midsummer Marriage
Order No. ED 11158
• The Rose Lake.
A Song without words for orchestra
Order No. ED 12435
• Symphony No. 4
Order No. ED 11395
• Triple Concerto
for violin, viola, violoncello and orchestra
Order No. ED 11860

Ernst Toch
Violoncello-Konzert, op. 35
Order No. ED 3473

Mark-Anthony Turnage
• Momentum
for orchestra
Order No. ED 12416
• Three Screaming Popes
for large orchestra
Order No. ED 12377

Peteris Vasks
Simfonija stigu orkestrim 'Balsis'
Symphony for strings 'Voices'
Order No. ED 8032

Friedrich K. Wanek
Vier Grotesken
for 4 wind instruments and percussion
Order No. ED 6667

Kurt Weill
• 1. Sinfonie
in one movement
Order No. ED 5937
• 2. Sinfonie
Order No. ED 5512

Herbert Willi
• Für 16
Little chamber concerto for chamber orchestra
Order No. ED 8016
• Konzert
für Orcherster
Order No. ED 8348

Gerhard Wimberger
Stories
for wind instruments and percussion
Order No. ED 7194

Joji Yuasa
• Revealed Time
for viola and orchestra
Order No. SJ 1063
• Time of Orchestral Time
for orchestra
Order No. ED 6820

Friedrich Zehm
Schwierigkeiten & Unfälle
mit 1 Choral
Satire for 1 conductor and 10 wind instruments
Order No. ED 6655

Bernd Alois Zimmermann
• Canto di speranza
Cantate for violoncello and small orchestra
Order No. ED 4588
• 'Ich wandte mich und sah an
alles Unrecht,
das geschah unter der Sonne'
Ecclesastical action for two speakers, bass solo and orchestra
Order No. ED 6330
• Photoptosis
Prélude for large orchestra
Order No. ED 6311
• Die Soldaten
Order No. ED 6343
• Stille und Umkehr
Orchestral sketches
Order No. ED 6319

SCHOTT

CD-ROM

Carl Orff

Leben und Werk · Life and Work

60 Minutes of Sound Examples

More than 400 Pictures and Photographs

20 Minutes of Video Recordings

Comprehensive Index of Subjects and Names

Requirements:
- PC 486/33 MHz (486/66 MHz or Pentium™ recommended)
- Double speed CD-ROM drive
- 8 MB RAM
- Graphics card with 640x480 pts. and 256 colours (32,000 colours recommended)
- 16-bit sound card compatible with Microsoft Windows™
- ca. 3 MB storage capacity available on hard disk
- Microsoft Windows™ 3.1

CD-ROM
English and German
version optional
Order No. MV 0801-0

musicavision
Schott Wergo Music Media

SCHOTT

An international series for symphonic wind bands, wind bands and wind sections.

The outstanding features of this series are excellent readability, the use of the latest music-engraving technique and thorough editing.

All editions for wind band contain parts in the Swiss and Benelux notation unless otherwise indicated.

Sales Material

High and highest levels

Stephan Adam
Mouvement symphonique
for wind band
Score   Order No. SHS 1016
Set of parts   Order No. SHS 1016-50

Hans Gál
Promenadenmusik
for wind band
Score
Order No. SHS 1007
Parts
Order No. SHS 1007-70

Georg Friedrich Händel
Instrumentalsätze aus dem Oratorium „Saul"
für Blasorchester, eingerichtet von Norbert Studnitzky
Dirigierauszug   SHS 1006-10, DM 41,–
Stimmen   SHS 1006-70, DM 180,–

Hans Werner Henze
Ragtimes & Habaneras
Symphony for brass band
• Original version for brass band
arranged by Henning Brauel
Score   Order No. SHS 3002
Set of parts   Order No. SHS 3002-70

• Version for symphonic wind band
by Marcel Wengler
Score   Order No. SHS 1004
Set of parts   Order No. SHS 1004-50

Hans Werner Henze
Die Abenteuer des Don Quixote
Suite from the opera of the same name adapted from Paisiello
for symphonic wind band
arranged by Norbert Studnitzky
Conductor's part   Order No. SHS 1005-10
Set of parts   Order No. SHS 1005-50

Paul Hindemith
**March
from 'Symphonic Metamorphoses'**
on Themes von Carl Maria von Weber for large wind band
arranged by Keth Wilson
Score   Order No. SHS 1012
Set of parts   Order No. SHS 1012-50
(without Swiss and Benelux parts)

Paul Hindemith
Symphony in B flat
for wind band
Score   Order No. SHS 1009
Set of parts   Order No. SHS 1009-50

Bertold Hummel
Symphonische Ouverture, Op. 81d
for large wind band
Score   Order No. SHS 1001
Set of parts   Order No. SHS 1001-50

Carl Orff
Carmina Burana
Suite for large wind band
arranged by John Krance
Score   Order No. SHS 1015
Set of parts   Order No. SHS 1015-50

Ernst Toch
Spiel for wind band, Op. 39
Score   Order No. SHS 1003
Set of parts   Order No. SHS 1003-70

Medium and low levels

Ottmar Gerster
Oberhessische Bauerntänze
for wind band
arranged by Norbert Studnitzky
Conductor's part   Order No. SHS 1002-10
Set of parts   Order No. SHS 1002-70

Franz R. Miller
Fanfare und Entrata
for 4 fanfares or solo trumpets
with wind or brass band
Conductor's part   Order No. SHS 2006-10
Set of parts *   Order No. SHS 2006-70

Kurt Noack
Heinzelmännchens Wachtparade, Op. 5
for wind band
Conductor's part   Order No. SHS 2003-10
Set of parts *   Order No. SHS 2003-70

Willy Schneider
Notzinger Volkstänze, Op. 38
for wind band
Conductor's part   Order No. SHS 2005-10
Set of parts *   Order No. SHS 2005-70
(without Benelux parts)

Leslie Searle
Blue and Gold
Concert and Parade March
for wind band
Conductor's part   Order No. SHS 2004-10
Set of parts *   Order No. SHS 2004-70

Leslie Searle
Chips in a bag
Disco for wind band
Conductor's part   Order No. SHS 2001-10
Small set of parts *   Order No. SHS 2001-70
Large set of parts *   Order No. SHS 2001-50

Leslie Searle
Dis & Co.
Disco for wind band
Conductor's part   Order No. SHS 2002-10
Small set of parts *   Order No. SHS 2002-70
Large set of parts *   Order No. SHS 2002-50

Ensemble Music

Alfred Löchel
Weihnachtliche Turmmusik
Five-part movements for brass band
Score (performing score for trombone chorus)
Order No. SHS 3001
Parts: trp. (flhn) I, II (Bb) / hn (Eb) / thn (tbn) I, II (Bb) /
tbn I, II / tuba (C,B 𝄢)

Carl Orff
Fünf Stücke
for brass band
4 trp (Bb), 2 hn (F), 4 tbn, tuba, timp ad lib.
arranged by Hermann Regner
Score   Order No. SHS 3004
Set of performing scores   Order No. SHS 3004-70

Hermann Regner
Intrade
for 12 horns in three choirs
Score   Order No. SHS 3003
Set of parts   Order No. SHS 3003-70

Richard Zettler
Tanzsätze aus Europa
for three instruments of equal
or unequal temperament
or for combinations of variable
instrumentation
Performing score (C 𝄞)   Order No. SHS 600
Performing score (Bb 𝄞) Order No. SHS 6002
Performing score (Eb 𝄞) Order No. SHS 6003
Performing score (C 𝄢)   Order No. SHS 6004

* with inserted conductor's part

SCHOTT

Books on Music
Life and work of important 20th-century composers
German Editions

Ferenc Bonis
Béla Bartók
His life in pictorial documents
290 pages with numerous illustrations – Hardcover
Order No. ISBN 3-254-00009-9

Schädler / Zimmermann (Ed.)
John Cage
Anarchic Harmony
John Cage 80
A book on the 'Frankfurt Feste '92 / Alte Oper Frankfurt'
316 pages with numerous music examples and illustrations –
Paperback
Order No. ISBN 3-7957-2002-8

Siegfried Mauser (Ed.)
Karl Amadeus Hartmann
und die Musica Viva
Essays. Hitherto unpublished letters to Hartmann.
Exhibition catalogue.
August 1980. Edited by the Bayerische Staatsbibliothek
376 pages – Paperback
Order No. ISBN 3-492-02615-X

Alexander Goehr
The Music of Alexander Goehr
Interviews and Articles (English edition)
Edited by Bayan Northcatt
120 pages – Paperback
Order No. ISBN 0-901938-05-X

Paul Hindemith
Komponist in seiner Welt
Weiten und Grenzen
366 pages – Hardcover
Order No. ISBN 3-254-00191-5

Briner / Rexroth / Schubert
Paul Hindemith
Life and work in pictures and words
290 pages with numerous illustrations and music examples –
Hardcover
Order No. ISBN 3-7957-0204-6

Paul Hindemith
„Das private Logbuch"
Letters to his wife Gertrud
Edited by Friederike Becker and Giselher Schubert
526 pages with numerous illustrations – Paperback
Order No. ISBN 3-7957-8355-0

Giselher Schubert (Ed.)
Paul Hindemith
Aufsätze – Vorträge – Reden
353 pages – Hardcover
Order No. ISBN 3-254-00197-7

Schaal / Schader (Ed.)
Über Hindemith
Essays on the works, aesthtics and interpretation
390 pages with music examples – Hardcover
Order No. ISBN 3-7957-0285-2

Schaal / Storm-Rusche
Paul Hindemith
Der Komponist als Zeichner
199 pages with 206 drawings from the years 1921-1963,
four-colour printing – Paperback
Order No. ISBN 3-254-00200-8

Brigitta Weber
Wolfgang Fortner
und seine Opernkompositionen
287 pages with numerous music examples – Hardcover
Order No. ISBN 3-7957-0308-5

Siegfried Mauser (Ed.)
Der Komponist Wilhelm Killmayer
472 pages with numerous music examples, index of works and
commentaries, 16 b&w photos – Hardcover
Order No. ISBN 3-7957-1856-1

Peter Petersen
Hans Werner Henze
Works of the years 1984 -1993
305 pages with numerous music examples and
prints – Hardcover
Order No. ISBN 3-7957-1794-9

Hans Werner Henze
A catalogue of works 1946-1996
(English · German · Italian)
436 pages with numerous b&w and
four-colour illustrations and facsimiles
Order No. ISBN 3-7957-0322-0

Wolfram Schwinger
Gershwin
A biography
272 pages with numerous illustrations and
music examples – Paperback
Order No. ISBN3-7957-82171

Hans und Rosaleen Moldenhauer
Anton von Webern
History of his life and his works
720 pages with numerous illustrations – Hardcover
Order No. ISBN 3-254-00033-1

Dietrich Kämper
Frank Martin
The compositional work. 13 Studies
210 pages – Hardcover
Order No. ISBN 3-7957-1892-9

Jürg Stenzl (Ed.)
Luigi Nono
Texts, studies on his music
478 pages with numerous music examples – Hardcover
Order No. ISBN 3-254-00035-8

Wolfgang Burde
Strawinsky
Life – Works – Documents
A monograph
485 pages with numerous b&w photographs and music examples
• Hardcover
Order No. ISBN 3-7957-2302-7
• Paperback
Order No. ISBN 3-7957-8283-X

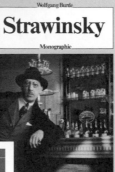

Martina Sichardt
**Die Entstehung der Zwölftonmethode
Arnold Schönbergs**
225 pages with numerous music examples – Hardcover
Order No. ISBN 3-7957-1857-0

Klaus Ebbeke
Sprachfindung
Studies on the late works of Bernd Alois Zimmermann
140 pages – Hardcover
Order No. ISBN 3-7957-1793-0

Hermann Conen
Formel-Komposition
Karlheinz Stockhausen's Music of the Seventies
282 pages – Hardcover
Order No. ISBN 3-7957-1890-2

Beyer / Mauser (Ed.)
Zeitphilosophie und Klanggestalt
Studies on the works of Bernd Alois Zimmermann
146 pages – Paperback
Order No. ISBN 3-7957-1795-7

Chris Walton
Othmar Schoeck
Biography
412 pages with numerous pictorial documents
and a complete index of works – Hardcover
Order No. ISBN 3-254-00168-0

Willi Schuh
Richard Strauss
Reflections and Reminiscences
261 pages with numerous illustrations – Hardcover
Order No. ISBN 3-254-00057-9

Werner Thomas
Carl Orff
Biography (Engl.)
Translated from the German by Verena Maschat
22 pages – Paperback
Order No. ISBN 0-946535-09-4

Franz Willnauer (Ed.)
Carmina Burana von Carl Orff
Origin · Effects · Text
308 pages with noumerous illustrations, facsimiles
and music exemples – Paperback
Order No. ISBN 3-7957-8220-1

Werner Thomas
Das Rad der Fortuna
Selected essays on the work and achievements of Carl Orff
360 pages – Hardcover
Order No. ISBN 3-7957-0209-7

Werner Thomas
Orffs Märchenstücke
Der Mond – Die Kluge
236 pages with numerous music examples and fascimiles –
Hardcover
Order No. ISBN 3-7957-0266-6

Christian Martin Schmidt
Schönebergs Oper „Moses und Aron"
Analysis of the diastematic, formal
and musico-dramatic composition
336 pages – Paperback
Order No. ISBN 3-7957-1796-5

Natalja Pawlowna Sawkina
Sergej Sergejewitsch Prokofjew
Biography
277 pages including 53 b&w picture pages and index of works–
Paperback
Order No. ISBN 3-7957-8281-3

Natalja Walerewna Lukjanowa
Dmitri Dmitrijewitsch Schostakowitsch
Biography
272 pages with 62 b&w pictures and index of works – Paperback
Order No. ISBN 3-7957-8284-8

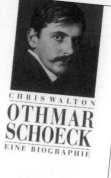

SCHOTT

Schott Catalogues and Brochures

Please ask for our detailed separate and special catalogues:

- ❑ **Piano / Harpsichord**
- ❑ **Organ / Harmonium**
- ❑ **Keyboard / Electronic Organ**
- ❑ **String Instruments**
- ❑ **Wind Instruments**
- ❑ **Recorder / Orff Instruments**
- ❑ **Guitar**
- ❑ **Accordion**
- ❑ **Percussion Instruments**
- ❑ **Chamber Music / Harp**
- ❑ **Ensemble Music**
- ❑ **Concertino**
  Easily playable orchestral music
- ❑ **Wind Orchestra / Wind Band**
- ❑ **Scores**
- ❑ **Eulenburg Study Scores**
- ❑ **Edition Schott – Separate Edition (0-Edition)**
  Editions for Piano, Organ, Strings, Flute and Vocal
- ❑ **Catalogue of Selected Works**
  Selection of the most popular titles from the General Catalogue

- ❑ **Books on Music – Complete Catalogue**
- ❑ **Books on Music – Series Atlantis · Schott**
- ❑ **Books on Music – Musical Education**
- ❑ **Complete Edition**
- ❑ **Christmas Music**
- ❑ **Vocal Music**
- ❑ **Mixed Choir**
- ❑ **Men's Choir**
- ❑ **Children's Choir, Songs, Stage Works**
- ❑ **Women's Choir**
- ❑ **Rock Pop Jazz**
- ❑ **Wergo Music of Our Century**
  CD Catalogue
- ❑ **Catalogue of Stage Works - Opera / Ballet**
- ❑ **Catalogue of Stage Works - Operetta / Musical**
- ❑ **Catalogue of Orchestral Works (hire material)**
- ❑ **Musical Theatre for Children and Young People**

Catalogues of Works of numerous of our composers are available on request.

MUSIC OF OUR CENTURY
MUSIK UNSERER ZEIT

THEODOR W. ADORNO · BÉLA BARTÓK · CATHY BERBERIAN · LUCIANO BERIO · GÜNTER BIALAS · HANS-JÜRGEN VON BOSE · PIERRE BOULEZ · REINER BREDEMEYER · JOHN CAGE · ELLIOTT CARTER · AARON COPLAND · CLAUDE DEBUSSY · SILVANA DELUIGI · PAUL DESSAU · PAUL-HEINZ DITTRICH · MAURICE DURUFLÉ · WERNER EGK · HANNS EISLER · GABRIEL FAURÉ · WOLFGANG FORTNER · JEAN FRANÇAIX · HARALD GENZMER · GEORGE GERSHWIN · LUTZ GLANDIEN · ALEXANDER GOEHR · FRIEDRICH GOLDMANN · SOFIA GUBAIDULINA · G.I. GURDJIEFF · JOSEPH HAAS · PETER MICHAEL HAMEL · KARL AMADEUS HARTMANN · THOMAS DE HARTMANN · HERBERT HENCK · HANS WERNER HENZE · JÖRG HERCHET · LEJAREN HILLER · WILFRIED HILLER · PAUL HINDEMITH · HEINZ HOLLIGER · ADRIANA HÖLSZKY · KLAUS HUBER · KLAUS K. HÜBLER · CHARLES IVES · GEORG KATZER · WILHELM KILLMAYER · VOLKER DAVID KIRCHNER · BABETTE KOBLENZ · CHARLES KOECHLIN · JOACHIM KREBS · CLAUS KÜHNL · GYÖRGY LIGETI · MICHAEL MCNABB · OLIVIER MESSIAEN · DARIUS MILHAUD · MEREDITH MONK · DETLEV MÜLLER-SIEMENS · CONLON NANCARROW · EMILE NAOUMOFF · LUIGI NONO · CARL ORFF · PETER PANNKE · KRZYSZTOF PENDERECKI · WILHELM PETERSEN · ROBERT HP PLATZ · FRANCIS POULENC · SERGEI S. PROKOFIEFF · MAURICE RAVEL · MAX REGER · ARIBERT REIMANN · MICHAEL RIESSLER · WOLFGANG RIHM · JEAN-CLAUDE RISSET · JOAQUIN RODRIGO · NIKOLAJ ROSLAVEC · ERIK SATIE · GIACINTO SCELSI · CHRISTFRIED SCHMIDT · DIETER SCHNEBEL · NORBERT J. SCHNEIDER · ARNOLD SCHÖNBERG · ERWIN SCHULHOFF · KURT SCHWITTERS · JOHANNA SENFTER · ALEXANDER SKRJABIN · KARLHEINZ STOCKHAUSEN · RICHARD STRAUSS · IGOR STRAWINSKY · MORTON SUBOTNICK · WALTER TILGNER · JOAQUIN TURINA · PĒTERIS VASKS · MICHAEL VETTER · HEITOR VILLA-LOBOS · FRIEDRICH K. WANEK · ANTON WEBERN · KURT WEILL · HARALD WEISS · CHARLES-MARIE WIDOR · CHRISTIAN WOLFF · JAMES WOOD · IANNIS XENAKIS · GERD ZACHER · HELMUT ZAPF · RUTH ZECHLIN · ALEXANDER ZEMLINSKY · BERND-ALOIS ZIMMERMANN · and others

schott wergo music media

Fordern Sie unseren CD-Katalog (WERGO) an.
For more details (WERGO CD catalog) please contact:
Schott Wergo Music Media GmbH · Postfach 36 40 · D-55026 Mainz

Catalogues of Works

If you need detailed information on

- biographical data
- works
- instrumentation
- dates of premieres

...of Conrad Beck · Hans-Jürgen von Bose · John Casken · Werner Egk · Wolfgang Fortner · Jean Françaix · Harald Genzmer · Anthony Gilbert · Alexander Goehr · Joseph Haas · Karl Amadeus Hartmann · Hans Werner Henze · Wilfried Hiller · Paul Hindemith · Heinz Holliger · Toshio Hosokawa · Volker David Kirchner · Armin Knab · Wilhelm Killmayer · Erich Wolfgang Korngold · György Ligeti · Steve Martland · Philipp Mohler · Detlev Müller-Siemens · Carl Orff · Krzysztof Penderecki · Heinrich Poos · Aribert Reimann · Hermann Reutter · Nicholas Sackman · Dieter Schnebel · Hermann Schroeder · Igor Strawinsky · Heinrich Sutermeister · Toru Takemitsu · Michael Tippett · Ernst Toch · Mark-Anthony Turnage · Peteris Vasks · Friedrich Zehm · Bernd Alois Zimmermann among others, please ask your dealer or the publisher for our free catalogues of works using the order form attached to this catalogue.

ARIBERT REIMANN

TORU TAKEMITSU

BERND ALOIS ZIMMERMANN

TOSHIO HOSOKAWA

CARL ORFF

WILFRIED HILLER

WILHELM KILLMAYER

Our catalogues are updated regularly!

SCHOTT

OPERA IS ALIVE!

Paul Hindemith: Mathis der Maler (WER 6255-2/3 CDs)

Detlev Müller-Siemens: Die Menschen (WER 6253-2/2 CDs)

Paul Hindemith: Neues vom Tage (WER 6192-2/2 CDs)

Karl Amadeus Hartmann: Simplicius Simplicissimus (WER 6259-2/2 CDs)

Paul Hindemith: Cardillac (WER 60148-50/2 CDs)

Hans Werner Henze: The English Cat (WER 6204-2/2 CDs)

Paul Hindemith: Das Nusch-Nuschi (WER 60146-50/CD)

Wolfgang Rihm: Die Hamletmaschine (WER 6195-2/2 CDs)

György Ligeti: Le Grand Macabre (WER 6170-2/2 CDs)

Paul Hindemith: Mörder, Hoffnung der Frauen (WER 60132-50/CD)

Hans Werner Henze: La Cubana oder Ein Leben für die Kunst (WER 60129-50/2 CDs)

Paul Hindemith: Sancta Susanna (WER 60106-50/CD)

For Experts and Art Lovers

Collections of reproductions

György Ligeti
Notenbilder

Collection of multi-colour facsimiles of music autographs including a Ligeti portrait by Klaus Böttger.

Edition A
• Original etching of the Ligeti portrait by Klaus Böttger, printed on handmade 'Hahnemühle Kupferdruck' paper, paper size 27 x 34 cm, numbered and signed by the artist
• 6 facsimiles of music autographs, printed on handmade 'Vélin Arches' paper, paper size 36 x 46 cm, numbered and signed by the composer,
Imprint, numbered and signed by both artists
Order No. BN 301-80

Edition B
• Reprint of the original etching, printed on handmade 'Vélin Arches' paper, paper size 36 x 46 cm, numbered and signed by the artist
• 6 facsimiles of music autographs, printed on handmade Vélin Arches paper, paper size 36 x 46 cm, numbered and signed by the composer,
Imprint, numbered – no signature
Order No. BN 302-60

Single sheets from Edition A
• Ligeti portrait, original etching by Klaus Böttger
Order No. SKK BN 301-80
• Reprint of the original etching
Order No. SKK 30-01

Facsimiles from Edition B
• Volumina für Orgel (sketch)
Order No. SKK 31
• Etudes pour Piano (sketch of study I)
Order No. SKK 32

• Monument - Selbstporträt - Bewegung
Three pieces for two pianos (fair copy from 'Bewegung')
Order No. SKK 33
• Violinkonzert (sketch of the 2nd movement)
Order No. SKK 43
• Klavierkonzert (sketch of the 3rd movement)
Order No. SKK 35
• Requiem (sketch of part 3)
Order No. SKK 36

Krzysztof Penderecki
Skizzenmappe

A lavish collection of four-colour facsimiles of sketches of the following works was designed on the occasion of the composer's 60th birthday (1993):
• Die schwarze Maske
• Utrenja I/II
• Kosmogonia
Order No. ED 8244

Art Books

Paul Hindemith
Der Komponist als Zeichner

Edited by Susanne Schaal and Angelika Storm-Rusche
This publication is the first comprehensive selection of the composer's drawings preserved by the Paul Hindemith Institute, Frankfurt/Main. Created between 1921 and 1963, the last year of Hindemith's life, all drawings are a testimony to Hindemith's talent as a graphic artist; they all are characterized by comic elements ranging from the innocent or ironic to the subtle.
199 pages with 206 drawings, four-colour reproduction – Paperback
Order No. ISBN 3-254-00200-8

Paul Hindemith
Ludi Leonum

Facsimile edition of a 1950 copy of **Ludus tonalis** coloured by Paul Hindemith. Edited by Giselher Schubert on the occasion of the composer's 100th birthday.

It is the playful and humorous that, almost high-spiritedly and amusingly, brightens this edition created by Hindemith on the occasion of the 50th birthday of his wife Gertrud. Gertrud Hindemith was born under the sign of Leo, and as a «lion» she takes possession of the work, so to speak. All her dresses, plays and positions in the staves match exactly

the character and the structure of the music, telling their own story. Hindemith himself, born under Scorpio, appears at the end of these picture stories.
60 pages facsimile, 4 pages epilogue (G./E./Fr./Sp./Jap.) – Hardcover
Order No. ISBN 3-7957-0289-5

Carl Orff / HAP Grieshaber
Carmina Burana

Music manuscripts of the composer and 12 colour woodcuts by HAP Grieshaber as well as the textbook with German translation by Wolfgang Schadewald. Introduction by Werner Thomas.

Carl Orff and HAP Grieshaber were kindred spirits who were bound to meet each other. Strangely enough, it was almost at the same time – in 1934 – that they came across a treasure of spiritual tradition: the ãCodex BuranusÒ. Grieshaber, the budding woodcutter, found themes and motifs in the coloured miniatures of the codex that had to seem familiar to him. Orff, the musician, was fascinated by the timeless freshness and the antique sound of the Latin texts. On the basis of such an «unsought-for» constellation on the one hand and a kindred spirit on the other hand, a jointly created picture book opened up almost automatically when the time was ripe.
38 pages, Japanese binding, handmade paper used as lining and slipcase cover - cloth binding , printed in colour in a slipcase.
Limited edition of 1,000 copies – only a limited number of copies available
Order No. ISBN 3-7957-0294-1

SCHOTT

BOOKS ON MUSIC
COMPOSERS MONOGRAPHS
GERMAN EDITION

Ulrich Dibelius

LIGETI

EINE MONOGRAPHIE IN ESSAYS

Ulrich Dibelius

LIGETI

A monograph in essays

The compositions of György Ligeti have more than once caused much surprise, even astonishment. By critically examining the varieties of contemporary compositions and adopting different musical traditions, György Ligeti has created a work that encourages the listeners in the freedom of association, the joy of discovery and openness that the composer himself has retained over the changing constellations of this work until today. The essays in this book deal exclusively with the approach to Ligeti's music, follow external and internal causes of its creation, uncover structural and spiritual links, but also refer to the multifarious ideas he has been inspired with by extramusical things or events that are so important to the composer's work. In the final conversation Ligeti talks about stages of his life, aesthetic principles and current projects.

299 pages with illustrations, numerous music examples as well as a biographical survey, index of works, select discography and bibliography.
**Order No.
ISBN 3-7957-0241-0**

Jürgen Schebera

WEILL

EINE BIOGRAPHIE IN TEXTEN, BILDERN UND DOKUMENTEN

SCHOTT

Wolfram Schwinger

PENDERECKI
Life and Work
Encounters, data, commentaries

Penderecki's importance in the musical life of today is undisputed. In the first part of this book, Wolfram Schwinger, a close friend of the composer, shares the life and work of Penderecki with the reader in a very personal way, explains to him the everyday life of an artist who is getting his ideas and creative powers from commitments throughout the world.
In the second part, the author examines thoroughly Penderecki's work. Commentaries on the works give the expert an interesting insight into the workshop of the composer and open up to the interested layman a new access to the composer's work in the field of tension between tradition and innovation. Thus the connection between Penderecki's compositions and musico-historical tradition is made as clearly as are his inclinations in the matters of sound generation and compositional technique.

387 pages with numerous illustrations and music examples, index of works, discography, index - hardcover
Order No. ISBN 3-7957-0265-8

• English Edition
290 pages with numerous illustrations and music examples - paperback
Order No. ISBN 0-946535-11-6

Wolfram Schwinger

PENDERECKI

LEBEN UND WERK

Kurt Pahlen

DE FALLA

UND DIE MUSIK IN SPANIEN

Kurt Pahlen

DE FALLA
and the music in Spain

Though many works of Manuel de Falla (1873-1946) are an integral part of the concert and theatre repertoire, it was impossible to find a German book about the life and music of this great Spanish composer who devoted himself to the opera, ballet, puppet theatre, piano and orchestral music. Kurt Pahlen met the composer in his Argentinian «asylum» in 1943, having many conversations with Manuel de Falla. He combines the memory of this meeting with a description of Manuel de Falla's career and with examinations of his compositional work, referring emphatically and impressively to the tradition of Spanish musical history before and after de Falla.

Looking at the connections of the Spanish way of life and the art of Manuel de Falla does not only convey a vivid picture of the country's musical life but also makes the personality and greatness of this important Spanish musician of the 20th century accessible to the reader.

204 pages with numerous illustrations and music examples
Order No. ISBN 3-7957-0239-9

Jürgen Schebera

WEILL
A biography in texts, pictures and documents

An extraordinary biography of an artist from this century: from the son of a Jewish choirmaster and organist from Dessau to the master-class student of Ferruccio Busoni in Berlin, from the creator of advanced orchestral and chamber music of the early 1920s to the leading reviver of the opera in the Weimar Republic, from the founder of a new song style (together with Brecht) to a successful Broadway composer and representative of the American opera in succession to Gershwin.
This biography, including plenty of historical texts, photographs and documents, follows the stages of the composer's life and, by means of short summaries and analyses respectively, introduces his most important works to the reader.
This is the first time that large extracts from letters of Kurt Weill are published in German.

301 pages with numerous illustrations, chronicle, bibliography, discography and register
Order No. ISBN 3-7957-0208-9

IN PREPARATION:

Jürgen Schebera
EISLER
A biography in texts, pictures and documents
Order No. ISBN 3-7957-2383-3

Wolfgang Burde
REIMANN
Life and work
Order No. ISBN 3-7957-0318-2

Gisela Nauck
SCHNEBEL
Life and work
Order No. ISBN3-7957-0303-4

Rudolf Frisius
STOCKHAUSEN
• I An introduction to the oeuvre
Conversations with Karlheinz Stockhausen
Order No. ISBN 3-7957-0248-8
• II The Works
Order No. ISBN 3-7957-0249-6

SCHOTT